# STEVE McQUEEN

(Courtesy of Star File Photos)

# STEVE McQUEEN

## PORTRAIT OF AN AMERICAN REBEL

## BY MARSHALL TERRILL

Plexus, London

Copyright © 1993 by Marshall Terrill
Published by Plexus Publishing Limited
26 Dafforne Road
London SW17 8TZ
First Printing 1995

British Library Cataloguing in Publication Data

   Terrill, Marshall
   Steve McQueen: Portrait of an American
   Rebel
   I. Title
   791.43028092

ISBN 0 85965 231 9

First Published in the United States by
Donald I. Fine, Inc., 1993

The right of Marshall Terrill to be identified as author of
this work has been asserted by him in accordance with
the Copyright, Designs and Patents Act, 1988

Printed in Great Britain by J W Arrowsmith

10  9  8  7  6  5  4  3  2  1

*For my parents, Mike and Carolyn Terrill,*
*who encouraged me in whatever I did*
*and taught me to never give up on a dream.*

M.T.

# AUTHOR'S NOTE

OVER THE COURSE of the three and a half years I spent researching this book, I was often asked why I chose to write about Steve McQueen. My answer was always simply, "Because his is the most fascinating character study I could have undertaken."

Steve McQueen was many individuals wrapped in one. He was honest, dishonest, loving, hating, caring, devious, simple, complex, intelligent, uneducated, modest, cocky, mature, childish. He was capable of espousing his love for his wife, and truly mean it, then suddenly have an affair. He could be extremely cheap with his friends while being generous to strangers. He would talk of the dangers of drugs, yet he couldn't stop himself from taking them. Paradoxes have always fascinated me, and Steve McQueen was the ultimate paradox.

I was raised on Steve McQueen. Every time my father took me to a movie, it always seemed to be a McQueen film. Not that I minded; I enjoyed them as much as my father did. That was the magic of Steve McQueen: his films were popular with men, women, and children, not only in the United States, but all over the world.

The idea for this project came about in September of 1989. My wife had just left me, I had been fired, and I was in dire financial straits having just finished college. With no wife, no job, no money, and a fresh education, I set out to do this book.

My goal was to write the definitive biography of a man known more for his hell-raising and motorcycle racing than for his acting. Five other biographies of McQueen had been published in the span of six years. However, I felt that they covered only sections of his personality. They left a lot of questions unanswered; more importantly, they neglected Steve McQueen the great film actor.

In preparing this book I interviewed many of the people who worked with McQueen and who were closest to him. I tried to gather everything ever written on him, quite a feat considering he was a major celebrity. I found it interesting that McQueen stopped giving interviews in 1969, at the height of his popularity. He made only one concession, in 1979, that for a high school newspaper. His reason for granting the interview: "I like kids." This was quite typical of McQueen.

Many of McQueen's friends and associates still feel his loss, as if it happened yesterday. His friends were friends for life, and many speak here for the first time. They trusted me to do an accurate and fair portrayal of McQueen as a man and as an artist. I hope I have not let them down.

This book is a result of much good luck and a lot of determination. To my dying day, I owe a debt of gratitude to McQueen's best friend and karate instructor, Pat Johnson. Pat put his faith in me to tell the story of a man who was like a brother to him.

Thanks to Phil Parslow, who made veracity my watchword. Phil pushed me to be the best that I could be and didn't sugarcoat his opinion of me or my work.

My special thanks to Loren Janes, who encouraged me to dream, and dream big.

I also thank David Foster for his invaluable time while I picked his brain for days.

Also to Hilly Elkins, who supported me from the beginning. Thank you for your kindness to a first-time author.

Thanks to Teena Valentino, McQueen's guardian angel at Plaza Santa Maria. Your attention to detail and honesty kept me on the straight and narrow regarding Steve's last days. I hope I did well by you.

Special thanks go to those who participated in this book: Haig Alltounian, John Alonzo, Richard Attenborough, Marty Baum, Tony Bill, Richard Bright, John Calley, Eric Christmas, James Coburn, Gary Combs, Vicki Daly, Mike Dewey, Leslie DeWitt, Doug Dullenkopf, Charles Durning, Von Dutch, Richard Dysart, Bud Ekins, Susan Ekins, Crystal Endicott, Mort Engleberg, Steve Ferry, Claudia Fielding, Freddie Fields, Mike Frankovich, Jr., Tom Gallagher, Don Gordon, John Guillermin, Katy Haber, Kathryn Harrold, Robert Hauser, Walter Hill, Bo Hopkins, Mario Iscovich, Carole James, Kent James, Ben Johnson, Sue Johnson, L. Q. Jones, Marvin Josephson, Lee Katzin, Nikita Knatz, Yaphet Kotto, Rick Penn Kraus, Alan Levine, Carrie Lofton, Mako, Pete Mason, Sammy Mason, Kay McDonell, Leslie Miller, Richard Moore, Edward Morehouse, Harry Northup, Felice Orlandi, Gelina Parslow, Wilma Peele, Felton Perry, Suzanne Pleshette, Martin Ransohoff, Robert Relyea, the late Lee Remick, Jeb Rosebrook, Bob Rosen, George

Schaefer, Perry Schreffler, Elliot Silverstein, Sally Struthers, the late John Sturges, Alan Trustman, Kent Twitchell, Robert Vaughn, Bobby Visciglia, Tracey Walter, David Weddle, Adam West, Haskell Wexler, Robert Wise, and Peter Yates.

For research support and facilities, I would like to acknowledge the staff at the Academy of Motion Picture Arts and Sciences in Los Angeles, the Library of Congress in Washington, D.C., the Museum of Broadcasting in Manhattan, and the Federal Bureau of Investigation in Washington, D.C.

I also wish to thank Chris Rodriguez for her thoughtful review of the entire manuscript.

My gratitude goes to Diane Dolbee, who put me up for free every time I came to visit Los Angeles. You, too, Eric.

My best friend in the world, Brian Taylor, has listened, encouraged, and supported me in this endeavor from the beginning. You'll never know how much your faith in me to finish this project meant.

To my brothers and sisters, Mike and Lorraine, Mischael and Andy, and Mark and Allison.

Thanks also to my good friends Greg Korn, Rick Fisher, and Jan Stookenschnieder.

My work would never have been published without the help and guidance of my agent, Sidney Porcelain, and the people at Donald I. Fine, Inc.: Larry Bernstein, Sarah Gallick, Adam Levinson, Jason Poston, Andrew Hoffer, and Donald Fine. Thanks, guys; you are the best in the business.

Last of all, to my parents, Mike and Carolyn. Their constant love, inspiration, and support helped me to overcome any obstacles in my way. Thanks for being the most wonderful parents in the world.

MARSHALL TERRILL

It matters not how long you live, but how you live.
Only the rocks live forever.

JAMES MICHENER

# INTRODUCTION

It is no exaggeration to say that I am obsessed with Steve McQueen. In my youth, his *Great Escape* screen image of the sympathetic rebel seemed to tap into my generation's collective unconscious. His vulnerability, which I could identify with, was balanced by a toughness I admired. His boyish manner, his fascination with motorcycles and cars, his mischievous expression seemed to show that even as an adult it was possible to get in touch with the kid inside yourself, to allow that kid to "bust out," as McQueen might say. A phrase one of his gifted directors, John Sturges, used to describe him comes to mind: "The tough guy with the grand grin."

Years later I learned enough about technique to look beyond the roles McQueen played and to study how he played them, coming to the conclusion that McQueen knew more about pitching his performance to the camera than any other American film actor. Although he gives the impression of being totally spontaneous on the screen, the truth is that McQueen was an extremely calculating actor, constantly working out sophisticated physical effects, and one measure of his considerable talent is that the calculation never shows. Watch his fine performance in *The Magnificent Seven*. Now ask yourself how he manages to dominate the screen in a supporting role with only about a dozen lines of dialogue. Then rewatch the film, but this time keep your eye on what he does with his hat.

After McQueen's death from cancer in 1980, details emerged about his private life—his temper, his womanizing, his abuse of alcohol and drugs—proving that he was a much better actor than even I imagined. The real Steve McQueen was too often the opposite of the sympathetic characters he portrayed. Further revelations made bittersweet sense out of this tortured actor's character flaws and a life that seemed doomed from the start because of the abuse he suffered as a child, emotional assaults from which he never recovered. His flaws made his talent all the more extraordinary and, for reasons I don't fully understand, increased my fascination with him.

To my great regret, I never met McQueen. For six months in 1975 he committed himself to playing Rambo in the screen adaptation of a 1972 novel that I had written, *First Blood*. But McQueen was 45 and Rambo was in his early twenties. The script couldn't account for the difference in ages, and eventually the actor had to bow out, despite his eagerness to be in the police car-motorcycle chase.

In lieu of meeting him, I've had to rely on reading about him. I've collected every book about this quintessential American film actor, every scrap of information I can get my hands on, and Marshall Terrill's *Steve McQueen: Portrait of an American Rebel* is by far the best, most interesting and most sensitive analysis of this fascinating complex man. No other book contains as much background about McQueen's troubled life and as much insight into his one-of-a-kind talent. I learned something new on every page. Sometimes heartbreaking, other times shocking, always instructive, this is a must-read for McQueen's fans and anyone who cares about the tragedies and triumphs of American popular culture.

DAVID MORRELL, author of *First Blood*

# HUMBLE BEGINNINGS

*I'm out of the Midwest. It was a good place to come from. It gives you a sense of right or wrong and fairness, which I think is lacking in our society.*

STEVE MCQUEEN

STEVE MCQUEEN'S LIFE was predestined. "My life was screwed up before I was born" was how he summarized it.

Terrence Steven McQueen was born on March 24, 1930, in the Indianapolis suburb of Beech Grove. His mother, Jullian Crawford, was a teenage runaway and alcoholic when she gave birth to him. Jullian got caught up in a whirlwind romance with William McQueen, a stunt pilot for a flying circus. "Red," as he was nicknamed, would take off for the friendly skies when young Terrence was only six months old, leaving an irresponsible Jullian to raise the child. The series of events that followed would affect Steve for the rest of his life.

Julia Ann Crawford, known as Jullian, was born to Lillian and Victor Crawford in Slater, Missouri, in 1910. Slater, a small farming community located eighty miles east of Kansas City, was typical of heartland America.

By Slater standards, Jullian was born into a charmed life. As an only child, she was pampered by her mother, Lillian, who did everything possible to provide the best for her. She stitched fine dresses, saved money for a private education, and handpicked all of Jullian's friends. Lillian wanted to raise a quiet, well-mannered, proper little girl. What she got was just the opposite: a spoiled, rebellious, take-it-for-granted brat.

Lillian's devoutness and strict disciplining irritated her daughter. By her teens, Jullian had spent so much time in church and doing volunteer work that she became fed up and started running with the wrong

1

crowd. She became the embodiment of a flapper. It was the Roaring Twenties, and Jullian wanted to roar. A blond-haired, blue-eyed looker, she liked the attention that men showered on her. Small-town life held no interest for her; the hedonistic delights of the big city were what she yearned for. At the age of sixteen, she took off for Indianapolis in search of good times and good men, and what they could provide for her.

"Dashing and romantic" is how Jullian later described Bill McQueen. Bill would fascinate the young farm girl from Slater with stories of daredevil stunts and death-defying feats. In a week's time they became sexually involved. Soon after Jullian became pregnant. Bill did the honorable thing and married her. When Jullian bore a son, it was Bill who chose the name Terrence Steven. "My father named me after a one-armed bookie pal of his, Steve Hall. He must have had a weird sense of humor," Steve would comment years later. It would be the only thing Bill McQueen would give to his son, as he deserted Jullian and young Steve six months after his son was born. Though years later Steve would frantically search for his father, he would never get the chance to meet him face to face.

After Bill left, Jullian found herself jobless, broke, and left with no other alternative than to return home to Slater with her tail between her legs. Lillian and Victor welcomed her back and asked no questions. Besides, Lillian could have a second shot at motherhood. Maybe this child would turn out right. To Lillian, Steve looked just like Jullian as a child—same blond hair, same blue eyes, the bluest she'd ever seen. There was not a prouder grandmother in all of Slater.

Lillian was raised a devout Catholic. She hoped to raise young Steven in the same righteous way. There would be no tolerance for ungodly behavior. Again, Jullian couldn't stand the pious ways of her mother. And again, she left for Indianapolis with Steve in tow, breaking her mother's heart.

After three financially strained years of living on the margin, Jullian came back to Slater. This time she was not going to stay, for she had a purpose: to drop off Steve for good. Though Jullian would visit infrequently, to Steve, both of his parents had deserted him. When Jullian left Slater this time, she also left behind huge emotional scars that would never heal properly.

It was 1933 and the effects of the Great Depression were felt in the Crawford household. Victor, a local businessman, lost everything. With nowhere else to go, he, Lillian, and three-year-old Steve moved in with Lillian's estranged brother, and Steve's great-uncle, Claude Thomson.

Claude W. Thomson was a successful hog farmer whose financial situ-

2

ation was not affected by the horrors of the depression. He owned nearly 320 acres of prime Missouri farmland. Claude had a penchant for the good life. His huge farmhouse was tastefully decorated, for the most part, by himself. Drinking, hell-raising, and partying were constants in his life. In his younger days, he carried a revolver on him wherever he went. Slater legend had it that he shot his brother over a woman.

Claude was by no means unstable. He worked as hard as he played. He rose before dawn every day to do the chores that a farm requires for its upkeep. He was smart with a dollar and invested wisely. He was stern, but generous as well. His word was as good as gold. Said Steve, "He was a very good man. Very strong. Very fair. I learned a lot from him."

All in all, it was hard for Lillian to move in with her brother. Perhaps she was a bit jealous of Claude. Life had dealt her a bad hand. After all, it was she who attended church faithfully every week. It was she who performed volunteer work. It was she who led an exemplary life. Yet it was Claude who was the successful one. She despised everything he stood for. But it was his household that she had to live in, and he was the master. Claude ruled with an iron fist. He would also be the closest thing to a father that Steve would ever know.

Claude would grow to love Steve like a son. Not a physically demonstrative type, Claude would develop an emotional bond with "the boy." Both would ride into town together, with a wide-eyed Steve in the front seat. When Steve became old enough, Claude enlisted his help around the farm. "He had no use for slackers," Steve said of his great-uncle. Steve would learn at an early age that sleeping late would be a luxury. Claude could be counted on to get Steve up on cold, dark mornings. There were chores for Steve to perform. "I milked cows, worked the cornfield, cut wood for the winter. . . . There was always plenty to do. I came to love and understand animals and to feel that in a few ways they are superior to human beings," Steve said. On those mornings Steve was not so eager to earn his keep, Claude would be quick to discipline. "When I'd get lazy and duck my chores, Claude would warm my backside with a hickory switch. I learned a simple fact: you work for what you get."

In return, Steve was rewarded. He was given his own room, a luxury for a kid his age. Claude also treated Steve to Saturday matinees at the Kiva movie house in downtown Slater. Said Steve, "Westerns were my favorite. I used to bring my cap pistol and fire at the villains." For Steve's fourth birthday, he received a red tricycle from Claude. "That started my racing fever," he recalled. "There was a dirt bluff behind the farm, and I'd challenge other kids in the area. We'd race for gumdrops. I usually reached the top first. Got some skinned knees, but I sure won a lot of gumdrops!"

When it came time for Claude to herd hogs into the railroad pens in town, he brought Steve along to learn the trade. Steve would make believe he was a cowboy, handling a wild herd with his trusty stick, urging the hogs into the pens. Farm life suited Steve well, and he would remember those days fondly. It was also the start of a lifelong love he would have for the great outdoors.

Being an only child, Steve had only his imagination to keep him company. An awareness of his mother arose in him. Neile, his first wife, said of this period, "He began to wonder about his mother and where she might be and what she was doing." He also began fantasizing about his father. It was only a matter of time, he thought, before they would both come and get him and they could be a family once again. When other kids talked about their fathers, Steve remained painfully silent. Only his dreams could soothe the pain that consumed him.

At the age of six, Steve began to attend school. To get there, he walked two miles each day. The building was an old-fashioned one-room schoolhouse where each student was taught on a different level. Learning was difficult for Steve. He had great difficulty comprehending the letters on the pages of a book. Years later it was discovered that he suffered from dyslexia, but that did nothing to comfort him in those painfully embarrassing years of schooling. "I wasn't clever in any academic way. School wasn't a big thing for me; I didn't click too well in it. I tried." Steve also suffered from a hearing loss, brought on by a mastoid infection, an inflammation of the temporal bone behind his right ear. Antibiotics could have cured the infection, but in 1936 they were not yet available.

Steve's learning came from nature. Fishing and hunting held his interest. He recalled, "When I was eight, Uncle Claude would let me use the family rifle to shoot game in the woods. But he never gave me more than one shell. I either hit something first shot, or I came back empty-handed. Well, one day I came back carrying two dead pigeons. I said that I'd waited in the woods for them to line up, just right, side by side, and that I'd calculated things like the wind angle and muzzle velocity and that I'd killed 'em both with a single shot. Claude was amazed. Bragged about me to all his huntin' cronies back in town. I never did tell him the truth, which was that I'd gone into a neighbor's silo and shot at some nesting pigeons. The bullet hit one, went right through him, glanced off the side of the silo, and hit another. To his dyin' day,

Uncle Claude remained convinced I was a miracle marksman with a rifle."*

There he was, living a Huckleberry Finn–like existence, having a sense of placement. Then suddenly it was all taken away again: Jullian came back to Slater to get her boy. Her timing couldn't have been worse.

While Jullian had been away in Indianapolis, she married the second of her many husbands. Steve later could not recall how many times his mother had been married, nor would Jullian ever volunteer the information. She came back to Slater now hoping to put her life in order again. That meant getting her nine-year-old boy back. Claude didn't put up a fight, knowing that the wrong thing to do would be to deny a boy his mother, even though she was downright irresponsible. Before they left for Indianapolis, Claude called Steve aside for a private moment together. "Here, I want you to have this to remember me by," he said. Steve reached out and Claude placed in his hands a gold pocket watch. Steve opened the case. Inside he saw an inscription that read: "To Steve—who has been like a son to me." As Steve wiped the tears from his eyes, Jullian hurried him away.

Fatherless, motherless for long periods of time, dyslexic, semi-deaf in one ear, and now, worst of all, uprooted from the only stable home in his young life, Steve felt overwhelmed. He took the move to Indianapolis very hard. With no friends, an unstable, alcoholic mother, and a strange man whom he had to call "Daddy," he began roaming the streets and eventually got involved in a gang. "I feel I was simply in a neighborhood of Indianapolis where one inevitably grew up with gangs," he said. He stayed out all night, slept on the streets, and skipped school. "We would break into lockup shops—that sort of thing," Steve confessed years later. "It wasn't that we did this in terms of money—because we were never short of money [though he was]— but as a relief from boredom." He was on a one-way ticket to reform school.

Steve was out of control and Jullian was desperate. She sent him back to Slater.

Jullian's second marriage dissolved quickly. The men in her life would basically be the same type: charming at first, then turning into alcoholic bullies. Jullian found it easier to cope if she just lived off them. That way she shed more responsibility onto them. In her heart, she wanted to be a good mother, but her drinking affected her judgment. Steve hated nothing more than a woman who was drunk.

---

* Nolan, William, *McQueen* (New York: Congdon & Weed, 1984), 8.

When Steve was twelve, Jullian wrote Claude, again asking for the boy. She was now living in the Silver Lake area of Los Angeles. She married again, this time to a man named Berri. Steve couldn't remember his new stepfather's first name, for he had no need to. Berri was the type of man who had no qualms about hitting women or children. Not too fondly, Steve recalled of Berri, "He was a prime son-of-a-bitch. We locked horns from the first day we met." And, he added, "He used his fists on me." Steve ended up spending more nights on the streets than in the Berri household.

Jullian tried to keep quiet about Steve to Claude, Lillian, and Victor. She knew that her son was the way he was because of her. She didn't want to be looked upon again as a failure. In desperation, she wrote to Claude, telling him how bad Steve was becoming. She was going to send him to reform school, as she had no alternatives. Claude interceded for Steve and told Jullian to send the boy back to Slater and set him on the right track.

When Steve came back to Slater, he found that many things had changed. Victor, his grandfather, had died. Lillian, in turn, had retreated deeper and deeper into her own little world. She began talking and praying to herself for hours on end. The time had come for Claude to have her committed to a mental institution. As her acting legal guardian, he did just that. Years later, while in the sanitarium, Lillian confessed that she had once tried to kill Jullian, then herself. This single act drove Jullian away from Slater. Steve would never know that his grandmother had tried to kill his mother. He just kept blaming his mother for his troubles.

Claude had remarried a younger woman named Eva Mae, one of the many housekeepers that he had bedded. Eva had spunk, and he wanted to make her his wife. Her youth and beauty tantalized the seventy-year-old Claude; she was only thirty-three herself. Eva brought into the marriage an illegitimate child named Jackie. Jackie was introduced as her niece if any of the neighbors asked.

Steve arrived on the front porch dirty and starving. Eva took him in and immediately fed him, then made him take a bath. Claude was glad to have his "son" back. The first thing out of Claude's mouth was, "If you get into trouble, I'm going to send you back to your mother." In Steve's mind, he knew that ultimately meant reform school.

A traveling circus found its way to Slater in 1944, and Steve was anxious to see it. Circuses always fascinated him. Spotting the excited fourteen-year-old in the crowd one day, a man selling pencils told Steve, "Yes, son, you can see the world, make great money selling pen-

6

cils. Oh, I can spot talent a mile away and you have it, kid. What do you say?" Steve said yes. He left Slater without saying good-bye to anyone, including his great-uncle. Claude searched for days on end to find Steve, but he finally gave up. He was heartbroken.

As for Steve, he left behind a town that held extremely painful memories for him. When in 1957, having married Neile Adams, Steve came back to show Claude that he had "got it together," he purposely skirted Slater to get to the Thomson farm. Slater's most famous son wanted nothing to do with it, for there was, in Steve's words, "a lotta pain there."

# MY ALMA MATER

*Boys Republic saved my life.*
Steve McQueen

Steve's stay with the circus was short-lived. It was more of a convenient excuse to escape his past than the start of a new career. He led the life of a young hobo. Sneaking on freight trains, hitchhiking, and eating around campfires were his way of life now. Soon, he found his way back to Jullian and Berri in Los Angeles. His relationship with Berri had not lost any of its hostility. He found that the streets were friendlier than the Berri home. "I learned early on in life not to trust anyone." He bore that mistrust toward everyone, and it carried into his adult life. When Steve became famous, he grew even more mistrusting. Of his time on the streets, he said, "The world didn't seem a very friendly place."

It didn't take long for him to get involved with a gang. To the other gang members, he was known as a "hick off the farm." Steve had to prove that he was just as tough as any city boy. Said Neile, "He had to prove he was the 'baddest ass' of them all. If they said to steal ten hubcaps for the day, he'd bring back twenty." He mastered two fields of expertise: stealing hubcaps and shooting pool.

With his bravado, Steve eventually became the leader of the gang. As the leader, he was known to local authorities. He was brought before a judge one day for being involved in a rumble. The judge was lenient and let him off with a warning: "Next time you appear before me, you will do some time in jail, young man." Each time Steve got in trouble with the authorities, he received a beating from Berri. Once when Steve was spotted stealing hubcaps, he was handed over by a police officer to Berri, who proceeded to give him the beating of his life. Berri ended the fight by throwing Steve down a flight of stairs. With blood running from his mouth, Steve gave Berri a death stare and hissed, "You lay your stinkin' hands on me again, and I swear I'll kill ya."

8

Berri did not like the look in the boy's eyes. It spooked him and he took his words to heart. He did what he felt he had to do to get Steve out of his life: he made Jullian sign a court order stating that her son was incorrigible, and Steve was immediately sent off to reform school. Years later, when Jullian spent time with Steve and his family, she told Neile, "I had lost control of Steve, I had a very hostile husband, and I had to work. I had no other recourse but to sign that court order that sent him to Boys Republic." Then she asked Neile, "Do you think he has forgiven me?" Trying to soothe her mother-in-law, Neile replied, "Oh, of course." But Neile knew better. Steve never would forgive his mother for the pain she brought to him.

"I was looking for a little love, and there wasn't much around. I guess I was difficult. I ran around with a bad crowd and I hated school—the regimentation and everything," McQueen offered.

The California Junior Boys Republic at Chino was founded in 1907 by Margaret Fowler. Its methods and procedures were progressive in practice and in theory. Bars and fences were nonexistent at the site. "Trust is the operative word here," said then principal of Boys Republic Frank Graves.

Steve arrived at Boys Republic on February 6, 1945. He could reel off his assigned number, 3188, years after his stay.

Boys Republic is an honor-based program that stresses hard work, getting along in society, and trying to give boys who are down on their luck a sense of self-worth. They had their hands full the day Steve McQueen arrived.

Graves remembers McQueen as "a quiet kid who stood on his own two feet pretty much. He was active and energetic—you knew he was around, all right—but he was not very articulate."

Steve was not very popular when he arrived at the school. Each boy was assigned to a bungalow with several others, and together they comprised a team. Steve was a loner and didn't help out with his share of the chores. More than once, he was beaten up, which, of course, was mainly brought on by himself. He explained, "Say the boys had a chance once a month to load into a bus and go into town and see a movie. And they lost out because one guy in the bungalow didn't get his work done right. Well, you can pretty well guess they're gonna have something to say about that. Yeah, I paid my dues with the other fellows quite a few times. I got my lumps, no doubt about it. The other guys in the bungalow had ways of paying you back for interfering with their well-being."*

---

* McCoy, Malachy, *Steve McQueen The Unauthorized Biography* (New York: Signet Books, 1975), 32–33.

9

Their slogans seemed corny to Steve. "That stuff seemed so stupid to me. So after three months of doin' classes in the morning and laundry in the afternoon, I got bugged and split. But I didn't get far. I was hidin' out in a stable when the cops grabbed me." The process was to start all over again for Steve, except this time was going to be even harder. "They had me diggin' ditches, uprootin' tree stumps, mixin' cement. They even had me cleanin' out the urinals." The punishment still wasn't getting through to Steve; he was planning another breakout. As luck would have it, his case was brought to the attention of a Mr. Panter, whom Steve would remember fondly. "He reminded me of my Uncle Claude. Stern but just." Panter immediately perceived Steve as an angry young man trying to find himself. He recognized that the rehabilitative measures of punishment were damaging rather than helpful, and he put a stop to it immediately. Panter and Steve began to spend evenings with each other, talking things out. "He was sayin' some straight things—and I began to listen, to soak in what he was tryin' to get across." Panter also told Steve that he saw something in him that was special. "Give life an honest shot," he told the teenager. "You could be somebody special someday." Steve said, "No one in authority ever talked to me like that. No one seemed to give a damn about my future life as an adult—but he did, and it meant a lot to me."

Steve gave Boys Republic another chance and it paid off. Before long, he became a role model for the others and was elected to the coveted Boys Council, who made the rules and standards for the others to follow. Steve also finished his ninth-grade courses before his release. He was forever thankful for his last few months at Boys Republic. His new-found self-confidence and his ability to function in society were a ray of hope. In return, Steve gave back to the Boys Republic a lifetime of gratitude. "It's damn good for boys," he said of the program. "You know, those years from twelve to eighteen are pretty crucial in a boy's life. I mean, he really shapes up in that time, or he doesn't. I think it's a good idea for the boys to run the boys. After all, adults are deadly enemies to the young, especially to kids who have been in some kind of trouble. Believe me, a boy learns to toe the line when he's got the force of twenty other boys seeing to it that he behaves."

When Steve became famous, he would often go back to Boys Republic for sit-down chats with the kids. He knew their language, how to talk to them. He sat right down on the floor with the boys as if to show that he was on the same level as they were. He was then "Mr. McQueen," but to the kids at Boys Republic he was just "Steve." Said McQueen, "I go back when I can. I just sit down and talk to the boys; that's the best way I can function with them. Boy, they're smart and bright. They know the scam. But they have a hard time adjusting to school, just as I did. It's different from the streets. You've got to learn to get along. But they make it. Insecurity is a pretty good motivation." When he was showered with hundreds of fan letters a week, he gave the mail from the Boys Republic special favor. Says a past employee of McQueen's, "Steve would check the mail personally. Any letter from anybody at Boys Republic went into his hip pocket. He answered each of them personally." The Steve McQueen fund was established in 1962, a generous four-year scholarship to the best graduating student. The winner was allowed to pick the college of his choice.

Steve's completion of his term at Boys Republic coincided with the death of Berri. Jullian wrote to Steve, telling him she had moved to New York City, where he could come and live with her. She managed his release at the end of his fourteen-month sentence, and he left there in April of 1946. It was to be a new start, one of the many that left him disappointed.

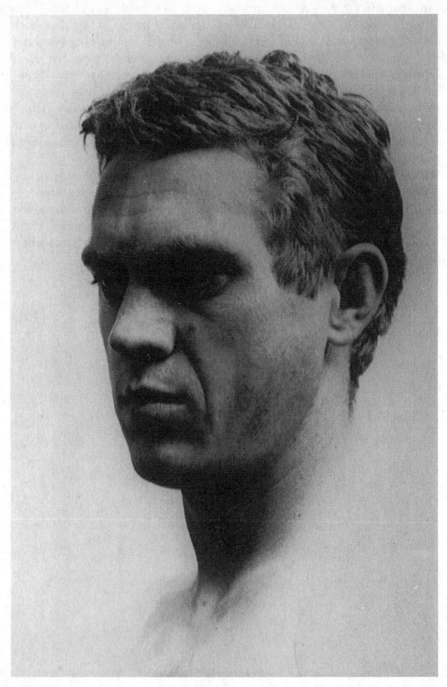

A young Steve McQueen ponders his future. (Photo by Roy Schatt)

# FIVE YEARS IN LIMBO

*I scrounged around for the next couple of years, trying to get the scam on the human race and just where the hell I fitted in—I discovered there were no openings.*

Steve McQueen

"My mother was going to get married again, so she sent me the bread and I went across country. I got off the bus feeling like Lil' Abner. There I was in my big high shoes, Levi's and a Levi's jacket, a California tan and a square-cut haircut. I remember standing on 34th Street, and that was a bad crowd I was seeing," recalled Steve.

Jullian was at the bus depot to greet Steve when he arrived. He could smell the liquor on her breath. She was nervous about their reunion. She never came to visit him while he was in Boys Republic, and she feared that he wouldn't forgive her.

Greenwich Village was to be their new home. When they arrived at the apartment, they were greeted by Jullian's new boyfriend, Victor Lukens. It was Steve's understanding that he and Jullian were to live together in the apartment as mother and son. Jullian explained gingerly that his place was downstairs. "You do understand, honey, don't you?" Jullian asked. "Sure," Steve replied icily. "Um, one other thing, Steve. You have to share the apartment with another man," Jullian added. Steve walked into his new apartment and found his roommate-to-be cradled in another man's arms. Jullian had conveniently forgotten to tell him that his roommate was gay. This was too much to take. Steve stormed back upstairs to tell Jullian he was leaving. "This is a rough city and you're just a kid. You won't last a week," Jullian warned. Then she added, "And if you leave, don't come back." Steve barked, "I won't be coming back." Then and there he wrote Jullian off. She would drift in

13

and out of his life when he made it, but she caused him much pain and suffering.

With no permanent home to go to, Steve wandered the streets of the Big Apple. He found refuge in a bar and struck up a conversation with two friendly sailors. Ford and Tinker were characters out of a classic comedy. They bought the impressionable sixteen-year-old a few drinks and told him of high adventure in the merchant marines. As Steve recalled, "I was underage. They stood me for drinks, told me how great the merchant marines were, shippin' out for new places. Got me hopped up on the idea of going to sea. Next thing I remember is shippin' out of Yonkers on the SS *Alpha*. They probably got a kickback for bringin' me aboard." (Ford later committed suicide by jumping off the Staten Island ferry. As for Tinker, the last McQueen saw of him, he had developed a nasty infection on his leg. He assumed that the leg was later amputated.) The job was anything but an adventure. Steve swabbed the decks under a blazing sun. He was assigned to the garbage detail and had to clean out all the urinals as well. "I smelled so bad that nobody in the crew would come within a hundred feet of me," he recalled.

For his first assignment, the *Alpha* was to pick up a cargo of molasses in the West Indies. The ship was in no condition to go that far. "That ol' tub was in really sad shape. It caught fire not long out of harbor and damn near sank." But the *Alpha* did recover and docked in the Dominican Republic. Steve figured that since he was underage, nothing would happen to him if he left, so he jumped ship and never boarded the *Alpha* again.

From Cuba, he found his way to the Dominican Republic, where he worked in a brothel as a towel boy for eight weeks. With a shortage of blond-haired, blue-eyed boys, the prostitutes found him attractive. "Got to sample some of the wares. Those ladies treated me real, real fine," Steve would say with a wink.

He eventually found his way to Port Arthur, Texas. Steve drifted from job to job, state to state. Oil rigging in Corpus Christi. Back to selling pencils in a traveling carnival until he got fired. "I was sellin' cheezy pen and pencil sets for twenty-five cents, and was charging a buck and pocketing the profit. I figured he was scammin' the public, so I scammed from him." Next, he found himself in Canada as a lumberjack. From there, he drifted to the Carolinas to "check out the southern belles." It didn't take long for Steve to meet someone. "Met a girl down in Myrtle Beach. Her name was Sue Ann. She had big green eyes." He celebrated his seventeenth birthday with her and her family. Looking back over his life, Steve recalled, "I was an old man by the time I was seventeen."

Though he enjoyed the time with Sue Ann, Steve grew restless and got the notion to join the marines. It seemed that a recruitment poster had caught his eye. No doubt he would break Sue Ann's heart, but he promised her he would be back.

In April 1947 Steve became Private First Class McQueen. He was assigned to the tank division. His stint turned out to be less than perfect. "I was busted back down to private about seven times. The only way I could have made corporal was if all the other privates in the marines dropped dead," he joked.

Steve learned the hard way that the Marine Corps didn't play games. After a few months, he had a weekend pass coming to him. He conveniently stretched that weekend into two weeks. The time was spent with Sue Ann, to whom he made good on his promise. The shore patrol caught up with Steve, and he greeted them with fisticuffs. That got him twenty-one days in the brig, with an additional twenty days for fighting. "That session in the brig really didn't tame me down much, but it got one message clear. When you're in the marines, Uncle Sam calls the shots. What you don't do is go runnin' off to see your chick." He drew inspiration from his experience in the brig for his role as the Cooler King in *The Great Escape,* but that would be many years and many setbacks later.

After the forty-one-day session in the brig, McQueen focused his energies on improving himself. He threw himself into his work. "I'd often wondered if a tank could be speed converted. We figured on havin' the fastest tank in the division. What we got was plenty of skinned knuckles. I found out you can't soup up a tank."

Later on in his stint, while on a military exercise in the Arctic, he personally saved the lives of five other marines. He managed to rescue all five from their tank before it plunged through the ice. Soon after that, he received his highest honor in the marines when he was assigned to the honor guard in charge of protecting President Harry Truman's yacht.

Steve discovered that when he put his mind to something, he was very capable of achieving success. He acknowledged that "the marines gave me discipline I could live with. By the time I got out, I was able to cope with things on a more realistic level. All in all, despite my problems, I liked being in the marines." Private McQueen was honorably discharged after three years in April 1950. He then set out for Myrtle Beach and Sue Ann.

Sue Ann was born into wealth. Her family was close-knit, something Steve had never experienced. He recalled, "It was great getting all slicked up, going over to her big fancy house for dinner, meeting her

15

friends, taking her to dances. . . . It was more like a special world I'd heard of. I just fell into it the way you fall into a dream." Sue Ann's father had taken a liking to Steve. One evening he put his arm around Steve and said, "I have special plans for you." He wanted the good-looking, energetic young man to marry his daughter and have his grandchildren. He offered Steve a job with an excellent salary. No doubt Steve would have been set for the rest of his life. But Steve knew himself too well. He knew he could not maintain a facade. He knew that Sue Ann's people were a breed apart from his family and would not be able to understand him or his past. So he left town abruptly after that night. He would comment about his youth, "When you're young, that's the time to sow your wild oats." And he had a lot more oats to sow and more worlds to conquer. He felt life was passing him by, and so he left Sue Ann and her world, never seeing her again.

Steve made his way north to Washington, D.C. There he got a job as a taxi mechanic and drove a cab part time. To him, though, nothing was happening in Washington. "New York seemed to be where the real action was, and that's where I headed."

# THE BIG APPLE

*I really don't like to act. At the beginning, back in '51, I had to force myself to stick with it. I was real uncomfortable, real uncomfortable.*

Steve McQueen

DESPITE HIS RESTLESS ENERGY, Steve yearned for a place he could call home. He took a liking to Greenwich Village. It was there he could do what he pleased and not feel out of place, which is not to say he went unnoticed. "For the first time in my life I was really exposed to music, culture, a little kindness, a little sensitivity."

New York City in the fifties was a gentler place. Explained McQueen, "It was a time when people lived there because they were broke, not because it was fashionable. You could live in a cold water flat for twenty-three bucks a month, no questions asked, and the bathroom was in the hall." The city provided whatever one was looking for and in abundance. Women, friends, and opportunity are what Steve sought. "Things happened in the Village," he noticed. "Good things. Bad things. People expected you to be a little off-center when you lived there. The chicks were wilder and the pace was faster. I dug it." And the chicks dug Steve. He had a certain intensity behind the reserved cool, and women found this trait intriguing. They felt a little bit in danger in his presence. The fact that he could explode at any moment and yet be so boyish at the same time was too much to resist. More often than not they did the pursuing. Steve liked the fact that he didn't spend many nights in his flat, somehow always managing to find shelter in a young woman's apartment. Says an ex-lover at the time, "He liked that women had to pay his way for him."

Actor Yaphet Kotto remembers two things Steve never had: money or cigarettes. When Steve left one apartment building, Kotto moved in. The landlord asked Kotto what he did for a living. "I'm an actor," he said. The landlord then asked, "Do you know some bum named McQueen? He just stiffed me on the rent." Kotto feigned ignorance.

Now that he had a city to call home, he looked for work that would stimulate him. Steve drifted through jobs. He made handcrafted sandals, lugged radiators out of condemned buildings, loaded bags in the post office, recapped tires in a garage, collected bets for a local bookie, sold ballpoint pens and artificial flowers, sold encyclopedias door to door. Of that job, he said, "I felt like a shark going into those poor family homes and talking them into encyclopedias." He even tried his hand at boxing ("after getting knocked flat on my duff, I gave it a quick pass"). In desperation at times, he rolled drunks for their wallets. Steve was haunted by a vision that he would be standing on a street corner at age fifty, begging for spare change.

As luck would have it, he wandered into a drugstore in the Village one day and happened to pick up a shower nozzle. A clerk walked by and asked Steve if he would like to return the item. "Yes," he replied, and was promptly handed $5.30 for a shower nozzle he hadn't purchased. He ate for two days on that giveaway and a scam was born. "It happened by mistake, but I used the idea after that," he admitted. Steve would even pull this trick years after he had made it, just to test its effectiveness.

Tired of minimum wage jobs, he got the idea to lay tile, which was very good money. "I got this crazy notion about going to Spain, where there's a lot of tile, and studyin' over there—but this chick I was with, who was tryin' to break into show business, had an idea that sounded even crazier: she told me I should become an actor." Friend Mark Rydell, who would direct Steve in *The Reivers* in the late sixties, knew McQueen when he was debating his future. He asked Rydell, "What do you think? Do you think I ought to make bathrooms, or do you think I ought to go to the Neighborhood Playhouse?" Rydell commented on McQueen, "I think he got into acting because he didn't want to bust his ass." Other friends observed it was a great way to meet women. His stint with the marines gave Steve the right to use the GI Bill if he so desired to go to school. He applied to Sanford Meisner's Neighborhood Playhouse on June 25, 1951. Steve phoned the legendary teacher, who agreed to interview him. "I walked over to his office, telling myself the odds were maybe a hundred to one against my having any kind of favorable impact on Meisner. I figured he'd take one look and shoo me out the door. But I was wrong." Indeed he was. Said the perceptive

Meisner of that meeting, "He was an original—both tough and childlike like Marilyn Monroe, as if he'd been through everything but had preserved a certain basic innocence. I accepted him at once."

Steve always thought there was something unmanly about acting. "Candy-ass" was a favorite term of his. He didn't find the company of actors very exciting: "Actors; they bore me; they're mostly cornballs." The thought of wearing leotards for dance class did not appeal to him. "I found it damn embarrassing," said McQueen. "Felt like a damn clown in those funky tights." The Playhouse staff thought of McQueen as a goof-off, and with good reason. He let it be known that he found the classes to be a waste of his time and energy, mostly, though, a silly game. Voice teacher Carol Veazie remembers, "His whole attitude was, 'Well, so show me.' He was awfully short-tempered, and he'd cut classes. Just not show. When he did show up he'd often fall asleep. Yet, when Steve chose to put himself into a scene or character, he was absolutely compelling. I kept pushing him because I knew the talent was there, beneath the surface. One day I made him listen to his voice on tape. He didn't like what he heard. 'I can do a helluva lot better,' he told me—and that was the turning point."

Steve was described as a one-man powerhouse. He amazed other students with his drive to succeed. When the class assignment was to bring in five improvisations, he would show up with ten. Susan Oliver, an actress at the Playhouse, found the unrefined McQueen to be "a local character, roaring around the Village on his Harley with his shirt off. . . . Steve had a casual, cool, don't-give-a-damn attitude that a lot of women found very attractive. I rode with him on the back of his cycle. One thing I remember is how hungry he always was. He'd eat with a slab of pie in one hand and a sandwich in the other, as if each meal were the last. Intense. That's what Steve was—very intense. Even in the Village, people noticed him. And I think he liked the attention."

The Neighborhood Playhouse took a toll on Steve. He enjoyed the classes but found that the GI Bill wasn't going to cover his living expenses. He had to find a full-time job to keep from living on the streets. He found work driving a truck, making deliveries from seven in the evening, then grabbing an hour of sleep before classes started in the morning. When summer rolled around, Steve quit his nighttime job and landed his first paying role in a Jewish repertory company stage production on Second Avenue. McQueen had a mere three words of dialogue. He had to come out on stage, looking grim, and say, "Nothing will help," in Yiddish. After the fourth night, he was fired. Years later, he joked, "I guess it was my lousy Yiddish." Meisner assured McQueen, "If you'll stay with it, you can make it."

Steve's luck was to take a turn for the better. Auditions were being held for the prestigious Herbert Bergoff Drama School. His six months at the Neighborhood Playhouse had paid off. McQueen's audition was good enough to land a scholarship with the school in 1952.

It wasn't hard for agent Peter Witt to spot talent. Back in the fifties, Witt would show up for the Neighborhood Playhouse's annual performance of scenes from selected plays. These productions would double as the students' final exams. Always on the watch for new talent, Witt would make it a point to be in attendance for anyone who might catch his eye. In a scene from *Truckline Cafe,* Steve played the Marlon Brando role of a sailor.

When the scene was over, Witt found himself mesmerized by the all-American-looking actor. After the performance, he made his way backstage and gave Steve his business card. Witt asked him if he needed an agent. "Not yet; I'm still a student," said the cautious McQueen.

A few days passed before Witt had the opportunity to talk to Meisner about the annual show. Meisner asked Witt who impressed him. "Sandy," said Witt, "there was only one actor in that whole group." "And who might that be?" asked Meisner. "The kid in the sailor suit." Meisner scoffed. "That's a boy by the name of Steve McQueen. And he's not an actor, he's a bum!"

With the completion of his first year at the Neighborhood Playhouse, Steve treated himself and a drinking buddy named Red to a vacation in Miami, to get out of the dreary cold of New York. McQueen wanted to do some scuba diving. Red asked him if he had any experience. "Nope," said Steve, "but I've been meaning to do it. We could rent us a boat and take off from there. How about it?" Red was all for it.

Steve discovered a whole new world. He was fascinated by the different colors on the ocean floor. He even spotted some sharks. "We kept clear of those babies but carried spearguns just in case." The explorer in Steve got the better of him. With each dive, he went a little deeper; so deep, in fact, that he punctured his left eardrum, the same one that had developed a mastoid infection. Now he had caused permanent damage to it. His hearing would never be the same again.

While in Florida, he received some great news: the Neighborhood Playhouse had accepted him for a second year of its two-year program. For once, McQueen was going to finish something he started. In addition, he would be awarded a half-scholarship of $350, but he would have to come up with the $40 costume fee.

Steve picked up a little extra money by competing in a few motorcycle races each weekend at the Long Island City raceway. By saving up his wages from his truck driving days, he was able to purchase his first motorcycle, a used Harley-Davidson. Being a natural athlete as well as just plain daring, Steve turned into quite a racer. He would win a couple of races every weekend and come home with over a hundred dollars in his pocket. "That, and my poker money, kept me going without having to drive a truck each night." That meant he could spend more time honing his acting skills.

Between acting jobs, Steve would frequent Louis', an Italian restaurant. He met the cook, Sal, and point-blank said that he didn't have a dime to his name. "I'll pay you back the first job I get," he proposed. Sal agreed, and nicknamed the young actor Desperado. He served McQueen veal, spaghetti, and garlic bread. [In addition, he set a limit of twenty dollars, and with each job McQueen landed, he would pay back faithfully.] "Trust is different when you're broke," he explained. "You're on the other end then, and the common commodity is sharing with other guys. We all shared a lot in the old days in New York." A few years later, when Steve visited New York for the premiere of *Never So Few,* he brought along Frank Sinatra and Peter Lawford to Louis' to repay the favor to Sal. As the three stars walked through the door, Sinatra and Lawford were ignored as Sal clasped his hands high in the air and exclaimed, "Ah, Desperado!"

Edward Morehouse was a student at the Herbert-Bergoff school at the same time as Steve. He remembers McQueen as a "real he-man tough guy. He wasn't as sophisticated as he became," says Morehouse.

The two became distant friends, sharing an occasional lunch together. McQueen gave Morehouse his first motorcycle ride one day when Morehouse was running late. Steve asked him if he was going uptown, and Morehouse nodded yes. "He scared the shit out of me," says Morehouse. "Weaving in and out of traffic, and going speeds that were quite dangerous. I couldn't tell you how fast he was going. He was like a hell-raiser, a wild kid.

"He didn't take class that seriously. I don't think he was very disciplined. I don't think he sat around talking about how fabulous he was, as a lot of actors sometimes do. He talked about politics. I was just amazed that he became a star, because he was lazy in class. The people who became famous [surprised me]. There's no way to know."

The two discussed fame one day outside class. Out of the blue, Steve said, "I'll have to work my ass off if I'm going to make it."

After Steve left the school, Morehouse didn't see or hear from him in years. "I heard he was in California after a while. Then I saw him on a movie screen and said to myself, 'By God, he's made it.' "

Morehouse today runs the HB Studio and is still amazed that Mc-Queen became a movie star. "It's like, why did I listen to who I listened to if I don't end up working and he was the one working more than anyone I know? All of the things we were told to do, he didn't seem to want to do. We were all told to work on this or that, and we did and he didn't and he became successful. We weren't successful and we all went into parts of the theater or had to work harder to get what we got, if we got anything. He really became a big star."

When *The Thomas Crown Affair* was released, Morehouse went to see the picture and was astounded. "He really matured so and his personality really developed. I thought he was phenomenal because I saw him and knew him as someone who was rather streetwise. I associated him with motorcycles and blue jeans. He had really done a lot of work on himself."

Before the summer came to an end, Steve snared a minor role opposite star Margaret O'Brien in *Peg O' My Heart,* in Fayetteville, New York. He remembered *Peg O' My Heart* as a turning point in his career. One night he became very nervous and forgot some of his lines. When the curtain fell, a member of the cast walked over and calmly told him, "I want you to know that your performance tonight was just plain embarrassing." "That kinda took the wind out of my sails," he recalled. He figured that he could do one of two things: either quit and not embarrass himself any longer or take the criticism and use it constructively to improve himself. He chose the latter.

In Rochester, New York, he worked with Ethel Waters in *The Member of the Wedding*. Of Waters, Steve said, "She knew how to reach an audience, make them care about what she was doing up there every minute on that stage. And I just soaked it in."

For the first time in his life, McQueen was making money from acting. His paycheck was $175 a week. Unfortunately, he let it get to his head. Just weeks before, he didn't have a dime to his name. Now, he was spending money like it was burning a hole in his pocket. He would order steak every night for dinner. He bought himself the biggest motorcycle available. In addition, he bought a used British MG sports car. He claimed he was fired because of the MG. "The full price of the car was $750, so I told the guy to hang onto the car and I'd send him the rest of the bread from the various cities we were due to play along the road. Which I did. The MG was finally delivered to me by the time we reached Chicago. I was broke, having just made the final payment, so I asked for a raise. They said no, and I was out of the play." The real explanation of why he was fired wasn't that simple.

Peter Witt had been getting daily phone calls of McQueen's cocky behavior. He pleaded with his client to settle down: "Steve, you've got to behave. You can't afford to be fired from your first job. Your name will be mud in the business." McQueen took no heed of Witt's warnings. The veteran actor Melvyn Douglas, a member of the cast, had had enough. Douglas told the producer to fire McQueen. The producer then in turn called Witt to inform him of what was going to happen. Witt pleaded with the producer, "Don't fire him. I'll get him to resign."

Now Steve took Witt's advice and sent a letter of resignation. He returned to New York unemployed and dejected. Even though he officially resigned, the word was out on him. He was unofficially blackballed from the stage and couldn't get another part for three years.

Things began to pick up again in 1955 when Witt sent McQueen to audition for the lead young male in *Two Fingers of Pride*. Recalls Witt, "I don't think he read even one page." Steve landed the prized role.

It took him three years to get back in the good graces of the acting community, and he wasn't going to screw this one up. He managed to get through *Two Fingers of Pride* without any damage to his reputation.

In 1956 Steve was cast in his first film role in Robert Wise's *Somebody Up There Likes Me*, starring Paul Newman. The part was originally written for James Dean, but a few weeks before filming, Dean died in a car accident and Paul Newman replaced him. Somehow, McQueen felt the part belonged to him.

Robert Wise recalls that first meeting with McQueen. "He came in, in a sport jacket, kind of gangly and loose and he had a little cap. A little bill around the top of his head. I guess it was his cocky manner somehow, not fresh, but just nice and cocky and a bit full of himself that just caught my eye and I cast him in this small part. It was the part of some kid on a rooftop fighting back in New York." Steve played Fido, a bit part that paid $19 a day. He looked on the sidelines, green with envy, as Paul Newman was given the star treatment. It was at that point that McQueen began using Newman as a measuring stick for his success, and it would take him nineteen years to catch up. Ten years after *Somebody Up There Likes Me*, Wise would direct McQueen in his only Oscar-nominated role in *The Sand Pebbles*.

A few months later, Steve auditioned for the role of Johnny Pope in *A Hatful of Rain* and beat out some of the biggest names on Broadway. "I'd go to an audition and find that they'd put me on stage right away because so many other actors had talked about me," he said incredulously. Just four years ago, he was unable to get an acting job. *A Hatful of Rain* was a major hit, and McQueen would go on to replace Ben Gazzara in the lead role. His name was going to be in neon lights on Broadway.

# NEILE ADAMS

*Neile was the anchor in that relationship.*

NORMAN JEWISON

STEVE REHEARSED HARD for *A Hatful of Rain*. It meant something to him to be on Broadway. He would work that much harder to keep his new-found status. Of course, it was a feat that Neile Adams had accomplished many times over.

Steve's path crossed Neile's for the first time in June 1956 when she was walking up the street and he stood deliberately in front of her. "Hi, you're pretty," said a cocksure Steve. Not knowing how to respond to such a direct approach, Neile was dumbfounded, but not speechless. "Well, you're pretty, too," was the only reply she could think of. Someone in the distance called for Steve and he was gone. "See ya," he told her.

A few nights later the two caught each other's eye at Downey's, an in spot for actors on an actor's budget. While Steve was gobbling down a plate of spaghetti, in walked Neile. He reconstructed the moment he laid eyes on her: "I looked up, and here was this absolute knockout, with smooth tan skin and neat dancer's legs in a pair of super tight toreador pants with a big, white-toothed smile on her face, laughing up at this guy she was with. I got so shook watching her go by that I dropped a whole forkful of spaghetti in my lap." Neile walked by on cue and said, "Hey—good one, kid." Steve, knowing that Neile had him shaken, could do nothing but laugh at himself, only endearing him even more to her. Neile's friends at her table noticed the starry-eyed looks the two gave each other and were quick to offer advice. "He's cute, but stay away from him. He fucks anything that moves," Neile was told. Curiously, Neile asked, "Who is he?" Again she was warned: "Steven McQueen. He's currently in rehearsal to replace Ben Gazzara

25

in *A Hatful of Rain*. Pass, kid. He's not so hot from what we hear. At least, not as hot as he thinks he is."* Steve did not ask Neile out that night; he wanted to wait until his name was on the marquee. Only then would he approach her for a date.

The competition for *A Hatful of Rain* was fierce. Among those who auditioned for the lead role of a tormented dope addict were George Peppard and John Cassavetes. Steve won the part through hard work and was not going to let this opportunity slip away from him.

The playwright for *A Hatful of Rain* was Mike Gazzo, who encouraged Steve to hang out with some real-life junkies to get the feel for the part. Steve was introduced to them and fell right in. He was still a street person at heart.

One night after rehearsal, Steve, Frank Corsaro, and Ben Gazzara went to Downey's to get a bite to eat and talk about Steve's role. In came Neile Adams with another date on her arm, then actor Mark Rydell. Neile walked by the table where the three men were sitting, flashed Steve her most dazzling smile, and said hello to no one in particular, but that smile was definitely meant for Steve. A few minutes passed when Neile left to go to the rest room. Steve then walked over to Mark Rydell and told him exactly what he planned to do: go after Neile. "Hey, man, all's fair in love in war," he said as he patted Rydell on the back. When Neile returned to her seat, Rydell excused himself. Steve seized the moment and approached Neile. "If any other man had done this, I would have been annoyed. But I thought he was cute," remembered Neile. She expected him to ask her out, but not yet, as he wasn't starring in *A Hatful of Rain*. He was proud of Neile, yet intimidated at the same time.

With *A Hatful of Rain* in its run, Steve wasted no time approaching Neile after one of her shows. His natural cockiness was faltering when he found the words to ask her out. "You're, ah, not going to see Mark tonight, right?" he asked. Neile wondered how he knew and nodded. He then hesitated. "Since you're-ah-well-ah-free tonight, why don't I pick you up after the show and we'll have a bite to eat?" Neile replied, "You can pick me up after the show tonight."

Remembers Neile, "Before Steve arrived, I got all prettied up in my daintiest, frilliest dress, certain he'd take me for a walk through Central Park or maybe to a movie. When he arrived in blue jeans and a black leather jacket, I should have been prepared for a different kind of evening."

Later that night, Steve came roaring up the alley on his motorcycle.

---

* McQueen Toffel, Neile, *My Husband, My Friend* (New York: Atheneum Books, 1986), 45–46.

When he led Neile to the bike, she was stunned. She wondered how on earth she was going to ride gracefully on it. Steve then picked her up, placed her on the back of the seat, and told her to put one arm around his waist. "Hold on to your dress and hold on to your heels!" Steve's commanding manner struck a chord inside her. Although she was very much an independent woman, she liked being told what to do by him. He really took charge, something that never happened with other men. "He was an absolute wild man," she commented.

For that first date, Steve took Neile to Greenwich Village to expose her to his world, the other side of life. He tore up the streets at a reckless speed, and Neile relished the danger of it all. They would stop to talk at a coffee shop, then take off again, going to another coffee shop. They talked about everything—their childhoods, their mothers, their fathers—and realized that they had much in common. They instinctively knew then and there that they would be a part of each other's lives. "We went to the Village and started talking and talking and talking. Out of this marathon conversation we found that we had so many similarities in our backgrounds, and we knew that, somehow, from that moment on, we had only each other," says Neile.

Neile Adams was Steve McQueen's natural-born soul mate. Her accommodating nature and easygoing temperament were a perfect match for Steve's moody and sensitive personality. On the surface, they seemed like an odd pairing. She was a vivacious, pert, outgoing stick of dynamite, quick to laugh at any moment or at herself. Steve, on the other hand, was introverted and withdrawn. She was exotic looking. He looked like a midwesterner. At the same time, they had very similar backgrounds. Both had fathers who left home at an early age, both had mothers who bore a child in her teens, and both had very painful formative years.

Neile Adams was born June 10, 1933, in the Philippines. Her parents divorced when she was an infant, and Neile never saw her father after the divorce. At the height of World War II, the Japanese took control of the Philippines. Neile's mother, Carmen, who worked for the Allied underground, was put in a Japanese concentration camp with nine-year-old Neile, at Santo Thomas. There Neile learned how to speak fluent Japanese and was used as a messenger for the guerrilla movement. To this day, she doesn't like to talk about the experience: "It was hard, painful, and brutal." She also claimed that the soldiers made her and Carmen "do certain things," and left it at that. She was there for four years. At age thirteen, Neile and Carmen were released. She counted it as a blessing that she even survived.

Carmen hooked up with a wealthy man when she was released. Taking advantage of that, she sent Neile to a convent school in Hong Kong. Neile had been through so much at such a young age that Carmen wanted to compensate by giving Neile a privileged education. After a year in Hong Kong, Neile was sent to a boarding school in Connecticut. Movies were her escape, and after seeing *The King and I,* she was moved deeply. She wanted to become a professional dancer, so she not only dreamed of becoming one, she worked hard at making her dream come true. The hard work, combined with a natural talent for dancing, eventually earned her a scholarship with instructor Katherine Dunham. Not long after, she landed a part in the Broadway production of *Kismet.* Neile had what it took to become a star. She studied hard, danced all day until she practically dropped, and had that little extra something that separated her from the rest: the desire to succeed.

Neile's next outing was a nightclub review of her own at the Versailles. She was a constant draw and caught the attention of Broadway director George Abbott. He wanted Neile to replace Gwen Verdon in *Damn Yankees,* but her booking with the Versailles kept her at the club until the contract expired. Abbott waited patiently until she was available and employed her in *The Pajama Game.* It was her second major Broadway show, and already her name was up on the marquee. *Life* magazine devoted a four-page layout on her, and she was on her way to the top—that is, until she met the man at Downey's who spilled spaghetti in his lap when he laid eyes on her.

Steve's intentions at first were purely sexual. He even admitted, "All I wanted to do was make it with Neile. She was a real good-looking chick, and I couldn't see any reason going with her. The last thing I ever wanted to do was fall in love with some broad. But things kept getting deeper for us." Neile was hip to Steve's view of women: "He was used to women giving in to him, and was real upset when I didn't immediately hop into bed." After a week of seeing each other, Steve suggested they move in together. The formalities were skipped when Steve asked only one question: "Your place or mine?" Neile asked, "Where do you live?" Steve told her, "In a five-story cold water flat," then added, "and I don't think you'll like it." The very idea of moving back to a primitive cold water flat made Neile's decision easy. "Mine," she said. Steve arrived at her apartment with three items: a suitcase full of clothes, a beat-up motorcycle helmet, and a bus stop sign that he used for a barbell. Neile dryly commented, "The man was obviously used to traveling light."

Life with Steve was, in Neile's words, "anything but normal." She found him to be given to many mood swings, set off by his use of marijuana, a habit he indulged in daily.

Though Steve loved Neile very much, he never quite gave up his philandering ways. She suspected he wandered, but she wasn't asking him directly and he wasn't offering any information.

Soon Neile was talking of marriage, but her suggestion was shrugged off. "I ain't the marrying kind," he put it. She once asked him, "Don't you like the spring? Don't you like the trees, the air warm and gentle, the sun high in the sky? Doesn't it make you feel good? Doesn't it make you feel life has some promise of love and hope for you, for me—for everyone?" Steve replied, "Nah, that jazz is for women and children." Neile's face registered shock. He then asked, "What do you mean, love and hope? I don't get you."

Tears welled up in her eyes. "I guess it was at that instant that I really understood what made Steve the way he is," said Neile. "Because for the first time I saw innocence in his eyes and heard it in his voice. You see, he really didn't know what love was. And hope was something that he dismissed as a trick by others to soften him up. He was so tough, so ready to tear the world apart at the slightest provocation, so sure that life was one long dogfight. Yet for all the ugliness that smeared his life, he was an innocent man. He had never known the meaning of love and hope. It's what I saw at that instant that made me cry. He didn't know love and hope because no one had ever loved him. No one had ever given him hope."

Neile's run with *The Pajama Game* was ending September 22, 1956, because of an offer she had received to go to Hollywood under MGM to screen-test for director Robert Wise. He was casting for the film *This Could Be the Night*. Steve's run with *A Hatful of Rain* came to an abrupt halt that same weekend: he was being replaced. The crew's consensus was that Steve had become progressively worse in the role of Johnny Pope. He wasn't as fresh as he was at the beginning. Steve also did things to alienate himself from the company and crew. He never participated in any of the poker and crap games, the bull sessions, etc. Actress Shelley Winters was in the play and remembers Steve, even at the start of his understudy, as not being serious. "He was supposed to watch the show and instead he would make funny faces. He would be cross-eyed and he would break us up. I thought it was just sort of a lark, that he must have been a rich kid who was just fooling around." In six short weeks, Steve was given the pink slip. "I'm not sure why, but I think I physically kind of washed out on stage. I'm kind of blond. Ben Gazzara was dark. And I don't think I felt inherently Italian," Steve would admit. (Ironically, seven years later, he would portray a New York Italian in *Love with the Proper Stranger*.) Steve had worked hard and rehearsed like he never did before, yet still he was fired. He didn't know what to do and he had nowhere to go.

At home, Neile claims Steve was not outwardly depressed, but she could tell he was deeply hurt. "Makes no never big mind to me," he stated with no emotion. Neile knew better. It hurt him even more deeply that her career seemed to be soaring as his was on the decline.

The time came for Neile to leave for the screen test in Hollywood. She would be gone for ten days, and since Steve had nothing better to do, she suggested he come along and keep her company. Steve's macho code wouldn't allow him to do that. "I need time to think things over," he told her. He wanted to use this period to sort out his feelings. He didn't like the idea of falling in love at such an early age, yet he could not deny the feelings he had for Neile. Alone and restless, Steve and some buddies took off on a motorcycle trip to Cuba. He calculated it would take two weeks. Neile wanted to get back to New York as soon as possible because she missed Steve. His escapade to Cuba would only delay their reunion. On October 3, 1956, two days before she departed Hollywood for New York, Neile received a cable from Steve in Havana. It read:

I LOVE YOU HONEY. SEND ME MONEY. LET ME KNOW WHAT'S HAPPENING. IN CARE OF WESTERN UNION CON AMOR.

ESTEBAN

The cable also read that the sender was waiting for an immediate reply. Steve recalled that trip to writer Robert F. Jones: "We were quite a group. An actor, a poet, and a guy who was just plain nuts, or maybe we all were. Hurricane Audrey was sloshing around on the East Coast while we zipped down to Florida. Then we ran from Havana to Santiago, about 967 or so kilometers, as I recall. Batista and Castro were shooting it out down there in Sierra Maestra, and there were uniforms everywhere. I was still a little wild in those days, particularly when I was on the juice. So what happens? I get thrown in the calabonzo. I sent a telegraph to Neile so's I could get out." The only problem was, Neile said no to Steve's request. She was plenty pissed at Steve for leaving and sending him money, she decided, would only delay his return. But Steve adjusted to his surroundings. "It wasn't so bad," he recalled. "The guard was a friendly dude, and he'd let me out of the cell so we could have lunch together—cheese and onions and wine—and that hot sun with the smell of the manzanita and the sewers."

He made his way back to New York eventually but had to resort to pawning several bits of his personal belongings, bit by bit, including his motorcycle helmet, to get back to the Big Apple. He came to realize one thing, though: Neile Adams was no pushover.

Neile returned from Hollywood four days before Steve did from Cuba. She was nervous that when he got back he would be mad at her. She opened the apartment door and spotted a dirty-looking Steve slouched in a living room chair. She blurted out quickly, "I'm sorry I didn't send you the money." Steve, never one to forgive so easily, did an about-face that day and said, "It's all right, baby. I admire your spunk," and Neile felt relieved. He added, "I love you, baby. It sure is nice to be home." All was well once more.

Neile's screen test went well, and once again Robert Wise sent for her. Again, Neile pleaded with Steve to go to California with her, but his mind couldn't be changed. He put her off again. "I still need time to think. You go on ahead." Upset and hurt, Neile left for California thinking she'd never see Steve again. Three days later, the phone rang and it was Steve. "I'm coming out there. I'm gonna make an honest woman out of you," he declared. Never hearing that phrase before, Neile vaguely knew what he meant by the comment. She had always dreamed of the day when the love of her life would drop on one knee and ask for her hand in marriage. Not with Steve. He had his own way of doing things.

He had no money to call his own. Neile paid for the food and rent. Says one friend, "Steve was like most men who lived off women, one arm around the girl, one arm on the refrigerator." Steve recalls, "I didn't have the price of a flight to California, so I had to pawn my gold pocket watch, the one Uncle Claude had given to me. I loved that ol' watch, but I loved Neile more." Steve caught up with Neile on the MGM sound stage and, as Neile remembers, "swooped me off the floor and gave me a big kiss." Steve then pulled out a ring, which he had a jeweler he knew in Greenwich Village especially design for Neile. He had put down a $25 deposit and let Neile pay off the balance, which lasted two years.

Not known for his patience, Steve wanted to get married as soon as possible. Neile was confused. Just weeks earlier, he wanted no part of marriage. She loved Steve but didn't know if she wanted to get married to him, right now, and he wasn't the most stable person in the world. She called her manager, Hilly Elkins, in desperation. She explained her predicament to Elkins. She wanted to find a graceful way to say no to the idea of marriage yet still keep Steve. Elkins offered no words of encouragement. "He's marrying you for your money. Don't be a schmuck," he warned. As Elkins saw it, "From the first meeting with him, I thought he was wrong for her. She was friendly, warm, and wonderful and very, very talented. I felt that Steve was a spoiler, a very hardened, tough opportunist. He was competitive with every actor he ever worked with, and he was competitive with Neile. It was that kind of passionate desire to succeed, to get out of the situation he was in, that was a thread that ran through his life, because he realized that if he didn't take care of number one, nobody else would."

That Friday, three days after his arrival, Neile left work early for an extended weekend with Steve. She couldn't fend him off any longer; she decided she would marry him. He rented a Ford Thunderbird and they headed for San Juan Capistrano. Steve learned that the swallows return there every spring. "Romantic, huh?" he asked.

They both were raised Catholic and made the attempt to have a Catholic wedding. Back in the late fifties, it took at least six weeks to have the banns published, and a nun at the church told the young couple there was no getting around that. "Fine," Steve huffed, "then we'll just go live in sin." With that said, he grabbed Neile's hand and headed for the car. Neile felt relieved. Maybe this would buy her some time to think things over. But Steve would have none of it, he wanted to get married today. He drove very fast in search of a justice of the peace. On the way Steve was pulled over by two patrolmen for speeding. Before they had a chance to say, "Where's the fire, buddy?" Steve blurted out, "We just want to get married." The cops were willing to go along with the gag, thinking that Steve was trying to pull a fast one. They didn't write up a ticket and one patrolman repeated, "You want to get married? Okay, follow me." When the officers, with Steve and Neile following them, arrived at the police station, the captain on duty happened to know of a minister who was hosting a party and might still be up. The captain phoned and asked the minister if he would be willing to marry two young adults at 11:30 P.M. The minister agreed and opened the church where the ceremony would take place. The two officers served as witnesses. "It was kind of far out," Steve recollected. "Here we were gettin' hitched and these two big cops with their belted pistols an' all. Felt like a shotgun wedding." The deed was done. On November 2, 1956, Steve and Neile were officially husband and wife, just four months after meeting each other.

On the drive to Mexico for the honeymoon, Neile began to feel serene. She looked over at Steve and noticed his tense expression. He pulled the car over and got out to walk around. He looked down at the ground, kicking the gravel, and finally blurted out, "Jesus, what have I done?"

The following Monday, Neile went back to work on *This Could Be the Night*. The honeymoon was just a short weekend in Ensenada, and the only proof that existed was a picture of Neile in Mexican garb and a sombrero, sitting on a donkey. She had asked Steve to join in the pic-

McQueen strikes a pensive pose with his first wife Neile Adams. She was the mother of his two children and the most patient and understanding of his three wives, 1966.
(COURTESY OF THE NEILE McQUEEN COLLECTION)

ture. "No way," replied the romantic groom. "That picture might come back and haunt me later on."

While Neile had work to do, Steve hung around the set like a puppy dog. Director Robert Wise was so annoyed with Steve that he asked Neile not to bring him anymore. Being out of work, Steve spent Neile's money like water. He gambled with it, treated himself to a new Corvette, and bought himself anything he wanted. He figured whatever was hers was his.

Also in his free time, Steve became obsessed with finding his father again. Now that he was a married man and wanted a family in the future, he began thinking about Bill McQueen. His hatred for his father was just as strong as it was for his mother. Steve was afraid he might "lose it" if he didn't find a way to deal with this hatred; finding Bill McQueen was his way of dealing with it. Steve called Jullian and asked his mother where she had last talked to Bill. "California" was what he was told. Steve dragged Neile during her spare time, which was little, if any, to search for leads to his father's whereabouts. They would drive frantically through neighborhoods in search of any clues. Neile described his behavior as obsessive. "Steve had a very low patience quotient. He would throw himself into a project with an enormously concentrated effort, but when that effort proved fruitless, he would lose interest and drop the project abruptly, almost as if to recharge himself for the time to come when a sudden renewed interest would again spark the flame and then would resume with the same fury that had consumed him in the first place."*

They had not settled in Los Angeles, and New York was still their home. Neile was having Steve flown in every weekend at her expense. Not only did she have to work, but she also had to do the household chores. She was tired after shootings and didn't always have the energy to cook. One night she thought she could trick Steve into believing that she had cooked a homemade meal for him. She prepared a TV dinner, then dished it out on a dinner plate, trying to disguise its appearance. With a nervous smile she presented it to Steve. Steve took one look at it and picked up the dish and threw it against the wall. Neile then promptly called Hilly Elkins. "Hilly, you have to do something about Steve. You have got to work with him. He's driving me nuts," she pleaded. Elkins agreed to have lunch with Steve. Afterwards, he called Neile and told her, "He's rude, crude, and obnoxious. There are too many blond-haired, blue-eyed boys in Hollywood. I can't handle him." As an afterthought, Elkins said, "Besides, he married you for your money. Let's get rid of him." Neile drew the line. "Are you crazy? You're talking about my husband."

In *The Defenders*, a two-part television show presented on February 25 and March 4, 1957, as part of the *Studio One* series, Steve played a young man who murders a psychiatrist's wife. His previous roles hadn't garnered any attention, and Steve couldn't figure out what he could do to make a breakthrough. Says Neile, "Instinctively, I knew that what was showing through wasn't the man that I knew." She told him, "What I see is Brando or Dean and it just isn't working." Steve realized that she was right. He had to make his own mark, not emulate the others. She coached him. "Smile a little bit. I know it's a tough thing to do because you're playing a killer, but when you're talking to your mother or something, you've got to be able to show something of you. So he did and for the first time he got fan mail, and he said, 'Yeah, yeah, that's good.' And for the first time he realized that I was on his team," said Neile.

Elkins happened to catch a few minutes of *The Defenders*, and what he saw hit him like a bolt of lightning: Steve's eyes. "I saw one minute of *The Defenders* and he just broke through the screen. Those eyes just really came out at you." He called up Neile and told her, "I'm very wrong about Steve and I'm sorry. I'd be glad to sign him."

Hilly Elkins got Steve his first movie role since *Somebody Up There Likes*

---

* McQueen Toffel, Neile, *My Husband, My Friend* (New York: Atheneum Books, 1986), 63.

*Me.* Steve wanted to be in films, and Elkins figured that B movies were as good a place to start as any.

Steve was fourth billed in Harold Robbins's *Never Love a Stranger.* He portrayed Martin Cabell, a Jewish district attorney who finds out that his childhood friend is not a Catholic.

Actor Felice Orlandi knew McQueen when Steve was his understudy in the 1952 play *Circle in a Square.* "He was always a little reserved. I think he was shy. He was hustling in New York just like everybody else," remembers Orlandi. "I think he had very close, intimate friends. In New York it's different being an actor than it is in Hollywood. In New York, there's only a half a dozen places where actors go and eventually your paths cross with everybody. In Hollywood, it's so spread out that you can go ten years without seeing someone you know. I could say I was a good acquaintance with Steve, but not a close friend. If he said he was your friend, you could depend on that." When asked if Mc-Queen was an obvious candidate for stardom, Orlandi replied, "In retrospect, I would have to say no to that. He didn't have much luck in New York and when he went to Hollywood, he had major, major things happen to him."

*Never Love a Stranger,* which was filmed in New York, portrayed the Jewish community there in a favorable light. [This was too much for the Ku Klux Klan to swallow when it was shown in the south.] Two years after its filming, the movie was released to lackluster public response. McQueen's only recorded words on the movie: "That turkey wasn't released for two years, and the only notice I got was from a critic who said my face looked like a Botticelli angel had been crossed with a chimp."

It was also on the set of *Never Love a Stranger* that Steve had his first affair. Actress Lita Milan was the first of many costars that Steve would bed in his lifetime. It was said of McQueen, "If it walks, he'll seduce it."

Steve was offered by producer Jack H. Harris a lead role in the independently produced *The Blob.* The film was budgeted at $240,000, with Harris putting up $150,000 of his own money. Steve was offered the choice of either $3,000 up front or 10 percent of the film's gross. He figured the movie was never going to do anything, so he opted to take the money and run.

Jack Harris recalls his first meeting with the young star. "He electrified me. I was sitting in my chair half asleep and I woke up and couldn't get over how Steve McQueen looked and acted over the tube."

McQueen acted and behaved on the set of *The Blob* as if he were a big star. "He had a reputation for being a troublemaker and he earned it sincerely," says Harris. "He was very hard to deal with. Whenever we had a problem, the director would call me and say, 'Well, your star is acting up again.' And I'd run out to the set and sit down with Steve, and once I got past the 'I'm going to call my agent, I'm going to call my manager, I'm going to call my lawyer' routine, we were able to talk out what was wrong. In the end, we came to terms. What he was looking for was not to tell everybody what to do. He wanted approval. He wanted somebody to be Daddy and say, 'You're a nice guy and I like you.' "

Steve played the role of a high schooler, though he was twenty-eight at the time. The film became an instant cult classic—the acting was so bad, it was enjoyable to watch over and over again. The film eventually grossed $12 million and Steve could easily have become a millionaire in his twenties, since his share would have netted him $1.2 million. It was a hard lesson, but a lesson he would not soon forget. "The real money is in the gross profits," he would later preach.

Steve would grow to both hate and love *The Blob*. Once, when daughter Terry was a teenager and living with Neile, he called her up at a late hour to tell her that *The Blob* was on television. Years later, when Steve was a megastar, he was having lunch in the Warner Brothers executive dining room where all of the great stars had framed posters hanging on the walls. Steve suggested, "Wouldn't it be great if they had a photo of me in *The Blob* hanging up there?"

*The Blob* was an embarrassment in later years, but it also showed Steve, and the world, for that matter, just how far he had come.

A few months later, Steve landed his first lead in *The Great St. Louis Bank Robbery*. Filming was to take place in Missouri, and both Steve and Neile claimed that this was the hardest period of their marriage. "It was the one and only terrible part of our marriage," claimed Neile. "We were thousands of miles apart. We didn't know each other very well and the minute we separated, all the insecurities flooded in." Neile had every reason to feel insecure, as Steve began another on-location affair.

While the two were away from each other, the phone bills climbed to $1,500 a month, with Neile taking care of that little expense. The real problem in the marriage was the underlying fact that Neile simply made more money than Steve did. It irked him that Neile was the real breadwinner at $50,000 a year compared to his paltry $4,000. That never stopped him from spending her money, though. Neile's accountant advised her to get separate accounts, but her attitude was that her money was his money, and Steve spent it as fast as she made it. When it came to his own money, he professed, "I throw around money like manhole covers." He thrived on the fact that he was cheap.

In early 1957, Neile signed a contract to appear in Las Vegas at the Tropicana Hotel. It was there that she drove Steve's used Corvette. She was taught the basics of how to operate the car, but she soon wrecked it while going too fast. She told Steve and he blew his top. He yelled, then she yelled, and the two hung up on each other. Steve didn't phone her for two weeks. He then wrote her a two-page note, saying, "I like you, baby. Love is one thing, but I like you very much. You're part lover, part friend, part mother, part sister; above all, we're pals."

Steve's career was at a standstill. He could no longer keep making B movies and sustain any kind of career. He was going nowhere fast. New York was a dead end. His luck was about to change for the better, for it would be only a matter of months before Steve McQueen became a household name.

# WANTED: STEVE MCQUEEN

*He was a fascinating, crazy, irascible, lovable, roguish,
likable, dislikable guy. Yes, he was all of those things."*

DAVID FOSTER

NEILE ADAMS WAS on the brink of stardom when she arrived in California.
Steve McQueen's career was finished in New York, and Hollywood was
his last hope.

McQueen had been in Los Angeles for a few weeks when he was
called by Hilly Elkins to have lunch with him at the famous Polo
Lounge. Elkins had lent McQueen his motorcycle and hadn't seen hide
nor hair of his bike—nor McQueen, for that matter. As Steve gobbled
down his hamburger and mashed potatoes and gravy, Elkins asked,
"Where's my bike?" McQueen sheepishly replied that he had jumped
over a hill and broke it in two pieces. Elkins figured if he were ever to
get his money back, he'd have to find employment for the irresponsible
son-of-a-bitch.

Back in the late fifties Vince Fennelly was the producer of the successful CBS series *Trackdown*. He wanted a companion piece for the show.

Fennelly came up with the idea of a bounty hunter in the Old West
who was paid a reward every time he brought in an outlaw, dead or
alive. He wanted to present the idea as a pilot. If the two-hour made-
for-TV movie was successful, it would then become a weekly half-hour
series.

Hilly Elkins felt that Steve would be well suited for the role of Josh
Randall, the bounty hunter. He sent Steve a copy of the script but did
not receive an immediate response to read for the part. At the time,

Steve wanted desperately to break into the movies. He knew that money and prestige were the rewards of being a movie star. Television would pay the bills, but at this point in his career he could not afford to be so picky. Said Elkins, "It had always been our plan that the road to film was through television, though at the time, no television star had ever made the transition from television to film."

When Steve read the script for the pilot, he wasn't too thrilled, but he sensed he could change, bend, and mold the character into what he thought could be an interesting role.

Josh Randall was a man who could not win. He made his living by bringing in criminals and would kill in an instant if he had to. The criminals didn't like him for obvious reasons, and the lawmen didn't like him because he didn't operate by their rules. It was the first time a heavy would be the lead character in a television series, and that's what appealed to Steve. He knew he would have to walk a fine line to win over the audience.

"You know, a bounty hunter is sort of an underdog," said Fennelly. When Steve read for the part, Fennelly found his underdog. "I picked him because he was a little guy. Everyone's against him except the audience. And McQueen was offbeat. He wasn't the best-looking guy in the world, but he had a nice kind of animal instinct. He could be nice but with some hint of menace underneath."

For the pilot, actor Robert Culp made a special appearance to introduce the Josh Randall character in the *Trackdown* series. The two were friends in New York and raced bikes and competed for the same girls. Culp was more than happy to help out an old friend. Hilly Elkins also handled Culp's career at the time, but instinctively he knew that McQueen would someday be one of the biggest movie stars of all time. "Steve had 'it.' Whatever 'it' is. I know I can't define it, but I know 'it' when I see it," Elkins said. "He had a quality you couldn't mistake if you had any judgment at all. There was never a question in my mind that this was a major star."

CBS picked up the pilot in September 1958 and titled the new series *Wanted: Dead or Alive*.

It was on the set of *Wanted: Dead or Alive* that Steve developed his legendary status in Hollywood as being "difficult." To others who like to put it more bluntly, he was a major pain in the ass.


Today, Loren Janes is a man in his early sixties with a body any eighteen-year-old would be proud to have. His daily workout consists of biking five miles up into the Sand Canyon Mountains, running a five-mile loop back to his bike, then biking back home. When he arrives there, he works out on his high bar, parallel bars, and trampoline and climbs a thirty-foot rope hanging from a tree in his backyard. Says Janes, "Then I go to work."

He is considered to be the greatest stuntman alive. He has been dubbed in Hollywood "One Take" Janes, because he gets most of his stunts on camera in one take, thus saving studios thousands of dollars a day. He has worked with such legendary stars as John Wayne, Kirk Douglas, Yul Brynner, Marlon Brando, Jack Nicholson, Jon Voight, and Paul Newman, as well as Steve McQueen.

Janes is a shockingly intelligent man for the type of job he chose as his profession. He is an expert on the U.S. Constitution and has given several lectures on the subject. He also served two years in the Marine Corps and is fiercely patriotic.

Born the son of a marine in Hollywood, but raised at the foot of Mount Wilson, California, Janes learned to love the outdoors at an early age. "I read at a very young age," he says. "I read everything I could on the Indians. I was impressed with them. All the Zane Grey books, too."

Steve McQueen as Josh Randall in *Wanted: Dead or Alive*.
(COURTESY OF STAR FILE PHOTOS)

But it wasn't until Janes read all of the Tarzan books that he got "really fired up."

Soon Janes spent weeks in the wilderness alone, with only a breech-cloth and a knife. No shoes, no clothes, no comfort of home. "I'd live off the land, leap out of trees on the back of deer, and kill them for meat. I spent all of my time in the mountains doing that."

When Janes was thirteen, his father was killed while on duty overseas. He now had to get a job to help support the family. "I went to school from 8:00 A.M. to 2:00 P.M., then went to work at a dairy from 3:00 P.M. to 12:00 A.M., seven days a week for five straight years." Before school started, the disciplined young man would get up and practice his true love, gymnastics. He was also very good at diving and competed when his schedule allowed.

After high school, he enrolled at California Polytechnical State University. During the summers he was a lifeguard and saved a man's life once by giving him mouth-to-mouth resuscitation after the medical team had pronounced him legally dead. In four years, Janes graduated and earned a degree in biological science.

When Janes left Cal Poly, he was at a crossroads in his life: he wanted to try opera singing. He taught high school trigonometry as a way to pay for his singing lessons. Meanwhile, he also gave diving exhibitions at the high school for his students. At the same time, MGM was looking for divers to perform a stunt off Catalina Island. The stuntmen in Hollywood who could do the work were elsewhere on location. Some of the students whose parents were in the business told them, "Our trigonometry teacher is a diver." A representative of the studio called the school and a meeting was set up with Janes. But first, Janes had to tell the principal that he needed time off. The principal thought, "A teacher working in the movies. That's neat."

It was 1954 and *Jupiter's Darling* was the film, starring Esther Williams and Howard Keel. Janes performed an eighty-foot dive and some underwater sequences and was thrilled by the physical challenges of stunt work.

A month later MGM called Janes again. Nine months had passed since *Jupiter's Darling*. Over the course of the picture the principal had changed his tune and was getting fed up with Janes's absence from school. "You either teach or work in pictures," was the ultimatum. "See you later," Janes told the principal.

Janes knew that Hollywood was not all glamour and stardom. He knew about the actors and stuntmen in Hollywood standing in the unemployment lines. He then set a goal for himself: at the end of three

41

years, if he hadn't doubled his teaching salary, he would quit and walk away from it all.

The first and second years proved to be hard. When not working, Janes bused tables to pay the bills. "It takes time in this business to build your reputation and for people to trust you," he says.

As Janes entered his third year, he wasn't even close to his teaching salary. The deadline was closing in. Janes had one week left and he kept true to his word. He said to himself, "Okay, at the end of this week I'll walk away and that's it." Later that week, Universal called and wanted Janes to compete with forty-five other stuntmen for a job. Janes didn't know what the picture was or who was directing.

The recruits were asked to line up in formation, and in came director Stanley Kubrick and actor Kirk Douglas. Douglas eyed each one as he walked slowly along the line. He spotted Janes, put his thumb on him, and said to Kubrick, "Him." The picture was *Spartacus* and Janes went on salary for the next eighteen months. "Needless to say, I doubled my salary. The day I started was the day I was going to quit. That was thirty-five years ago."

Steve began the very first day of *Wanted: Dead or Alive* by firing three stuntmen. The first two didn't have the right look. The third one, actor Richard Farnsworth, teased Steve a little too hard.

Farnsworth at the time was one of the top stuntmen in Hollywood. Born and raised on a ranch, he later entered the rodeo circuit and did stunt work on the side. Farnsworth was a real cowboy.

McQueen was fresh from New York when he landed the lead role in *Wanted: Dead or Alive*. On the set, Farnsworth noticed Steve sitting down, rolling the back of his cowboy hat. That didn't make sense to Farnsworth; real cowboys didn't do that. "You're making that hat look like a tortilla," he teased. Steve took the comment seriously and had Farnsworth fired immediately. Stuntman number three had come and gone.

Loren Janes had just gotten off a job when the phone rang. It was Four Star Studios. They had an actor by the name of Steve McQueen who was being very difficult and wanted to know if Janes could handle him. "I'll handle him," assured the confident stuntman. "Well, come over quickly," pleaded the executive.

When Janes arrived at Four Star, he was promptly handed western attire, the same exact gear that McQueen would be wearing. Janes came onto the set and headed for the director to check in with him first. He felt the heavy look that Steve gave him.

After talking to the director, Janes headed for a table with coffee, tea, and soft drinks. As Janes walked by McQueen, he heard him snap his fingers and demand, "Coffee . . . black." Thinking fast, Janes spun around to face McQueen. "Coffee—black?" asked Janes. "Let me explain something to you. I guess you must be new around here. Are you Mr. McQueen?" McQueen shot Janes a look as if to ask, "Who else would I be?" Janes continued with the charade. "I'll have you know that I'm your stuntman and I'm here to make you look good, to make you look better than you can make yourself look, and I've got a hell of a reputation. I don't want you blowing my close-ups. I'm not a servant to anybody. I don't go get coffee or anything else. Nobody orders me to do anything." And with that, Janes left McQueen thinking, "Blowing his close-ups?"

McQueen then scurried over to the director, waving his arms and pointing over at Janes. "He's a tough guy, Steve," said the director. "Don't mess with him." McQueen inquired, "Really?" The director went on, "Oh yeah, he's as hard as nails and he's tough and doesn't put up with anybody. He's the best stuntman around." Steve became intrigued. "Really? Oh . . ." The director then ended any thoughts of Steve getting into a fight with Janes. "Besides, he's an ex-marine." McQueen looked over at Janes. "He is?"

Janes was fixing his drink when he caught Steve staring at him in admiration. He decided to give McQueen another chance. He said aloud, "Oh, Steve, while I'm over here, can I bring you some coffee? Actually, the iced tea is better for you." Steve replied politely, "Yeah, would you bring me one, please."

When Janes brought McQueen the tea, he sat down for a few minutes for a polite chat. "Well, we're getting ready to do the first stunt, so I've got to check it out. See ya."

For the first stunt, Janes had to come around a corner and jump on a horse and perform a Pony Express mount. His gymnastics experience gave him an edge over most other stuntmen in Hollywood, and the scene was done in one take. "Boy, did Steve like that," says Janes.

In the next stunt, Janes had to dive through a narrow window five feet high. He dove right through, turned a somersault, landed on his feet, and kept right on going. Picture perfect, and again in one take. "That impressed him," Janes comments.

For Janes's next feat, the scene called for Josh Randall to get in a fight and take a tumble down a cliff. Remembers Janes, "This was a real steep ugly-looking cliff and it had a little spot that kind of came out four feet, then dropped off again. I'm looking at this and thinking it's about sixty feet." The director turned to Janes and said, "I want you to go as far as you can go and really make this work. Where are you going to stop?" Janes marked his spot mentally and said, "That yellow brush. I'll end up there. Do you want me on my back or face?" The director commented, "Sixty feet, Loren! If you stop there, you'll be lucky."

Meanwhile, Steve was taking all of this in on the sidelines. With his hand on his chin, he walked over to Janes and asked in a whisper, "You're really going to hit that spot?" McQueen shook his head and walked away to watch the stunt behind the camera.

The time came for Janes to take the tumble. He took his cue and kicked off, did a one-and-a-half somersault, hit the ground on his back, and lay there on the spot where he promised he would land. In one take.

The crew broke into applause, while Steve came bounding down the hill like a cat. He leaned over and asked the stuntman, who was still on his back, if he was all right. Janes turned over and confidently said, "Yeah, I'm fine." Steve held out his hand and Janes took it. As McQueen lifted Janes to his feet, he said, "You're all right, kid!" Jokingly, Janes said, "Kid? Well, how old are you?" McQueen told him. "Well, I'm only two years younger than you are," Janes informed him. Having to have the last word, Steve replied, "Oh well, you're still a kid."

"He slapped me on the back and we walked up the hill, tugging each other up. I was with him for twenty-two years until he died," says Janes.

Steve got along better with stuntmen on the set than with the executives. Explains Janes, "I think one of the reasons he liked me was that I put him in his place. He didn't like for people to kowtow to him and brownnose him. They didn't last long at all."

Steve's push for realism drove the executives at Four Star nuts. His behavior made some people feel as if he had lost control of his faculties. "He drove the directors and producers crazy. He drove them nuts. If he didn't like a script, he literally threw it out. The result was a killer series," says Hilly Elkins.

Westerns in the late fifties were a dime a dozen, and Steve instinctively knew that if this show were to be a success, it would have to be different. Says Elkins, "Steve was a perfectionist, but if he felt something was important, it didn't matter if it was important or not to anyone else, it was important to him. Most of his energies were focused on things that made a difference. His instinct about himself was unerring. Steve made that character in that show his own. It was his contribution that made it something other than another television show.

"Josh Randall was a reactor; that was Steve's greatest talent. It was body language, it was the face, it was the raised eyebrow, it was the look across the camera, and the camera loved Steve. This man with no literary, artistic background had this incredible animal instinct about himself and about what worked," says Elkins.

Steve not only wanted to act, he wanted to learn how to make himself better as an actor. He commented, "Any actor who works on a TV show and just takes home the money every week is crazy. I mean, this is a great opportunity to learn your craft. Emotionally, it's important for me to be a good actor. I don't want to be second best."

For his wardrobe, Steve was handed shiny new clothes, a hat, and saddle. He promptly handed them back. "I fell out with the interpretation of Randall," said Steve. "One row was over my cowboy hat. They thought all cowboys had shiny new saddles and that their hats were never crumpled. What real cowboy has a shiny new hat, I ask you?"

David Foster was a publicist for Jim Mahoney & Associates in the fifties and was assigned to work with Dick Powell at Four Star Television. Powell, in turn, had to work with Steve McQueen. Powell felt that Foster would be the guy to handle McQueen. They were both contemporaries whose wives were family oriented. "We kinda grew up together in this business," says Foster. "He had this rebel image and we just connected. We were the same age and our wives were the same age. We had kids that were the same age. Our kids would go to his kids' birthday parties and vice versa.

"We got along very well, even though he was a difficult person to get along with. A psychologist would have had a field day trying to figure him out. One day he would be your best friend, the next day your enemy. Let's just say he was moody.

"Quite truthfully, he would fire me three times a year, I would fire him a couple of times a year, then our wives would say, 'You guys are assholes,' and they would always get us back together. This went on throughout our relationship. It was definitely a love/hate thing."

Before the three stuntmen were fired on the first day of shooting *Wanted: Dead or Alive*, Steve's first casualty was actually a horse. Steve told reporter Henry Gris, "They gave me this real old horse they had put on roller skates and pushed on the sound stage. I went to Dick Powell and said, 'Listen, let me pick out my own horse. We're going to be doing this series for a while; I'd kind of like a horse I got something going with, you know?'

"So I went to a friend of mine, a cowboy I knew, and I asked him if he had any good quarter horses. He said, yeah, and we looked at a sorrel, and a dapple gray, and they had a white palomino. They also had this black horse that the cowboy was working. I said, this one, and I pointed to the black horse. I got on him and he bucked me off right away. So this decided me. I wouldn't have any other horse."

The horse would be named Ringo and though he would be remembered with much affection by Steve, there wasn't much love lost between the two of them at the time.

"The first week of shooting, the horse kicked out four or five lights and was biting and kicking other horses. He broke my big toe stamping up and down and bit me in the back four times," said Steve. Publicist David Foster was present when McQueen retaliated and punched Ringo square in the nose. "It was wild," remembers Foster. "This horse was getting pretty nervous under the lights and all, so the dumb beast balked and stepped on Steve's foot. So Steve balled up his fist and punched the fucker right in the snoot."

McQueen explained his relationship with Ringo. "For three long years that horse and I fought like fanatics, both of us bent on winning. He'd step on me. On purpose, again and again. And I'd punch him each time for stepping on me, but he would do it again. We never did compromise, and I sort of liked the idea that he would never compromise. The son-of-a-bitch, no matter how much he was paid back in kind, he stood his place. And we really loved each other, but he never surrendered and this is how he taught me a lesson. He proved better than me, and smarter."

As for the weapon that Josh Randall would use, Steve brought a shotgun to friend Von Dutch. The end result was a sawed-off shotgun called the "Maire's Laig." Before the shotgun could be altered, the producer had to pay a then handsome fee of $1,100 to the federal government for a manufacturer's permit, plus $200 licensing fees for each of the three rifles used on the show. The gun proved to be much more powerful than anyone imagined.

Steve recalled the first time he fired the Maire's Laig. "I fired my first full-power blank. The gun was pointed at the camera. The blast nearly knocked me down, blew the hat off the cameraman's head, and knocked all of the pages out of the script girl's hands." A plastic shield would have to be put over the camera for future scenes.

To Steve, Josh Randall was real, and he was going to portray the character in a way he thought he himself would react in a situation. For one particular scene, the script called for Randall to fight several men at once. Steve took the director aside and explained the situation. "Look, I'm not going to fight a guy who's eight feet tall or shoot it out with Billy the Kid. If somebody pushes me too far so that I don't have anywhere to go, I'm going to fight with him, and I'll get him any way I can. If I rip his ear off or put his eye out, that's the ball game. I don't play around. I want to win."

For an example, Steve would refer to an incident in the Marines. "I remember once there were these two guys who always stuck together.

One kept provoking me. One day we had a real argument, but his friend was standing there, so I bowed out. But I got him alone the next day. I waited for him in the toilet, and I said, 'Hey, you,' and he turned around and I punched him and kicked the hell out of him. And the other guy never bothered me. I made my point."

Steve's quest for realism made him many enemies on the set. Friend and actor Don Gordon noticed that Steve was not too well liked and told him so. Steve replied, "I'm here to do a job. All the nice guys are in the unemployment line."

The scriptwriters in particular bore the brunt of Steve's wrath, none more so than writer Ed Adamson. "Steve isn't argumentative arbitrarily. Nobody would know more about Josh Randall than Steve. He knows exactly what Randall would do and what he wouldn't do. That doesn't mean I like it any better, but I do have respect for Steve. And when I look at the finished product, I love him. Many times I think he's wonderful, and that's hard for me to say some days," Adamson said at the time.

Stuntman Loren Janes acknowledges that Steve's behavior on the set wasn't perfect. "He obviously got a bad reputation. A lot of the guys didn't like him. He was so definite about what he wanted and what his character needed. He argued with writers, directors, and producers. He argued with everybody. He had a good sense, a good feeling, an intuitiveness. Plus, he'd been around. He knew life, he knew the bad part of life and the sad part. He knew all of these little things they didn't. Here's a guy from New York, never been around horses, doesn't know anything about it, and he's going to play a bounty hunter. He has a short haircut and carries a sawed-off shotgun instead of a pistol. He does everything you're not supposed to do. But he worked at his acting. He worked at cowboy moves and how they thought. He wanted to make it different because the series was different. He had that charisma that just jumped out at you on the screen. Gals would come up to him on location and say excitedly, 'You're Steve McQueen!' And then he would turn around to look at them. Then they'd say, 'Oh God, you're ugly.' And they'd be stunned because he had the cracks in his face. He'd just look at them and smile. And the girls would die a thousand deaths. They just told their hero he was ugly. Then he'd just start talking to them, and they'd be charmed to death. I could hear them walk off saying, 'That's the handsomest guy I've ever seen.' I saw that happen many times," says Janes.

Steve's only promotional appearance for *Wanted: Dead or Alive* took place at a rodeo in Texas. "In some godforsaken little town," remembers Hilly Elkins. Elkins asked McQueen on the plane what he was going to do. "I don't know," came the response. The two quickly put their heads together and decided that a coin would be tossed in the air while Steve rode around on a horse in the ring, but Elkins would throw the houselights just as Steve took aim and fired at the coin. Elkins remembers the execution. "We did it exactly according to plan. Threw the coin, put the lights out, shot at the coin, ran out, got in the car, and drove home. To this day, I don't know if he hit or missed the coin. That was his only appearance. We decided that for five grand, it wasn't worth it. He was just going to stick to acting."

Elkins was still managing Neile's career at the time, but she wasn't doing much except concentrating on having their first child. "Steve had the avant-garde view of women that their place was in the kitchen, if they were lucky. That's what he wanted Neile to do, raise a family," says Elkins. McQueen's final thoughts on the matter were, "All I can say is that so far as I'm concerned, a woman should be a woman. By day she should be busy making and keeping a home for the man she loves." He added, "At night she should be sleeping with him." Luckily, this comment slipped past the feminists of the day.

At the end of the first year on *Wanted: Dead or Alive,* Steve and Neile's first child, a girl, Terry Leslie, was born on June 5, 1959.

At first, Steve was disappointed that it was a girl, but soon he thought the idea of having a daughter was not so bad. "I was a little hacked when the old lady bore me a daughter, but this kid is really gonna be a gas." Steve even changed his tune. "I wanted a boy, but now I want another girl."

Eighteen months later, on December 28, 1960, Neile delivered a boy, Chadwick Steven McQueen.

Steve brought cigars to the set to pass out to the crew. He also brought with him some pictures for bragging rights. Says Loren Janes, "He was thrilled to death. Very proud papa. He was no different than anyone else. He loved the kids. He loved his wife. We always kidded him when he had Chad if he got him a motorcycle yet."

Steve and Neile wanted to raise their kids in the right type of atmosphere. Steve realized that being actors' kids could be a detriment later in life. "I want them to have their own identification and not grow up in the shadow of some movie star image."

McQueen went on to say, "The kids are off limits. They can't fight for themselves—I have to do that for them. If anybody hurts my family, I'm gonna put them down in a little black book."

Though Steve may have been the proud papa, his schedule didn't leave him much time to spend with the kids. "On a scale of one to ten, I'd say he was a five and a half," says Hilly Elkins. "He dearly loved his kids, but that's only half the battle. Raising them is the other part of the responsibility." Neile agreed. "When the children were little, when they were first born, he couldn't relate to them. He just sort of dismissed them until they were able to become little persons. As soon as their personalities started evolving, then Steve could relate to them."

With parenthood came a desire to find his own long-lost father. Steve would spend any spare time he had combing neighborhoods, tracking down leads, anything to find the father who had left him.

The search for Bill McQueen started when Steve was a teenager and on the road. "I was sixteen and getting in all sorts of trouble. I didn't have much to go on. When I was in the Marines, I tried the Navy files, but nothing happened."

Steve and Neile acted on a tip one day in 1959 and went to a little town outside Los Angeles. An older woman answered the door. Steve stated his name and his business. He was looking for Bill McQueen. The woman, who happened to be Bill's lady friend, invited the couple in. She politely told Steve that his father had passed away three months earlier. Then she told him that Bill spent every week faithfully in front of the television watching *Wanted: Dead or Alive*. And almost faithfully Bill would wonder aloud, "I wonder if that's my boy?"

Bill McQueen's lady friend then excused herself and went into a bedroom. When she came back, she handed Steve a picture of Bill and a Zippo lighter engraved "Red."

When Neile looked at the photo, she was convinced right away that Steve had finally found his father. Steve said years later, "All I know is [my parents] didn't get along. The way I figure it, it's their business.

"Did I resent him leaving us? I really don't know what to feel about him. I just wanted to meet him. I just wanted to stand and talk to him, no more or less. Although I never met him, I felt a real sense of loss when I found out he died."

When Steve and Neile left the house, Steve later told his friend Bud Ekins, he "flung the lighter down the road and that was the end of that."

Pat Johnson, another of Steve's friends, revealed that the situation with his father bothered him more than he let on. Johnson says, "He really wanted to meet his father, wanted to talk to him. This was a source of great frustration for him, because there were so many things left undone, unsaid, that were never resolved, even to the time of his death. He always felt this emptiness. He often mentioned to me that he wished he had a chance. One of his great regrets in life was that he wanted to be able to go up to his father and say, 'Look what I've done with my life, and I didn't need you.' He told me that his father was a no-good bum. A drunken bum. Period."

In later years, his anger toward his father did arise when critic Tom Hutchinson talked to McQueen in London in 1969. Hutchinson asked him, "What if you could meet your father right now?" The involuntary response had been, "I'd probably kill him." Hutchinson was taken aback. McQueen rethought the question and took back his first response. "No, that's the wrong thing to say. I wouldn't kill him—I'd feel sorry for him because he missed out on me, on me growing up, as much as I missed out on him. He was foolish in what he did."

McQueen resolved that his children would never have to endure the loneliness he had felt as a child. He vowed, "I believe in a lot of love, security, and discipline. I'll never be able to see my father in this world, but at least I can be a good father to my own kids."

It was also around this time that Steve met longtime friend and companion Bud Ekins. Ekins was a motorcycle enthusiast and owner of a bike shop on Ventura Boulevard.

Ekins would know Steve for a longer period of time than any of McQueen's other friends. His friendship with Steve lasted over twenty-two years. McQueen coveted his relationship with Ekins. "Now, Bud is my friend in the fullest meaning of the word. He's got two kids and I've got two kids. The old ladies hang around together. We're pitching our kids off to get married when they grow up."

Steve at the time was in his first year on *Wanted: Dead or Alive* when he rode into Ekins' shop one day on a motorcycle with a younger man on the back.

Dick Powell, the president of Four Star Studios, had just purchased a bike from Ekins. Powell's wife didn't like the idea of her husband owning such a dangerous machine, so he in turn sold it to Steve.

When *Wanted: Dead or Alive* became a hit, Powell decided that McQueen had to sell the motorcycle. When McQueen arrived at Bud Ekins' shop, it was to sell the bike to the younger man. Steve wanted to show Ekins the warranty before he sold it. Who did he sell the bike to? Dick Powell's son Norman, the other passenger.

Steve then began to frequent Ekins' shop. Remembers Ekins, "I recognized him from the show. He was a nuisance. He was just picky about everything, picky about things he didn't even know about. I think I had something he wanted. That was the key with Steve; if you had something he wanted, then he was around."

The two men started attending cross-country races and got together every weekend. They liked each other enormously, but Ekins couldn't help but notice McQueen's paranoia. Says Ekins, "There's an old joke that there was this guy who wouldn't go to a football game, because when the team got in the huddle, the guy thought they were talking about him. Yeah, he was paranoid."

For the most part, Steve enjoyed being around motorcycles and the men who enjoyed the sport. They didn't care if he was an actor or not, and Steve was always drawn to people who didn't need or want anything from him. "They're clean-cut people who work hard for their dough, and they don't compromise. I'm the only movie guy, and they don't hold it against me except when something happens, like that fashion layout [*Harper's Bazaar,* a women's magazine, had done a photo layout with Steve and a group of fashion models]. You should have heard them then: 'Hey, McQueen, we sure like those bracelets on your arms!' Man, they sure put me on!

"It's pretty involved—what makes people friends. There's something almost chemical to start with, some interests and experiences to share together. In any activity, someone comes across, and you come across, and the relationship progresses. But these buddies of mine are the ones you can count on when you get right down to the real nitty-gritty. If I'm right, they're with me. If I'm wrong, someone nails me—quick!"

Steve was attracted to other men at the top of their profession because he realized what it took to get there. He respected Bud Ekins because he proved to be one of the best in the sport. "Steve admired the motorcycle guys. Again, if he could learn from you, that's where he was heading," says Ekins.

Steve's quest for learning all about motorcycles amazed Ekins. "Steve was something. One night he called up and said he wanted to know something about old bikes. I told him I had a whole library of books, probably the largest collection around. He said, 'Where's that?' I said, 'Right here at the house.' He said, 'I'll be right up.' He came over about eight o'clock at night. He said, 'When I get tired, I'll just spend the night.' I went to bed, but he stayed up all night. He just set his mind on something and he'd want it now. When he got on a motorcycle, he wanted to know the complete history of the bike. From the beginning. Why did this company do this? Why did this company do that? Of course, I gave him thirty years' knowledge in a year. He pretty well knew it, too. He was a good student."

Steve Ferry and his wife, April, became part of the McQueens' world as two of the few people they associated with. Ferry had worked with Neile on Broadway in *Kismet.* He was soon settled in Los Angeles as a props manager. The Ferrys were doing well for a young couple and were living in a small house in Laurel Canyon.

The McQueens were still New York residents when Steve came out to

Los Angeles looking for television work. The Ferrys were the only people the McQueens knew, and Steve slept on their floor for nearly a month while Neile was in Las Vegas working.

Ferry and McQueen found a mutual interest in cars. At the time, McQueen was driving a beat-up Jaguar. Ferry owned a Porsche. Steve then asked Ferry if he could drive the Porsche. "Coming over the hills of Laurel Canyon, I managed to hang on to the back end of the car," says Ferry. "He realized he could go around corners much faster in a Porsche, so he got rid of his Jaguar and got a Porsche." With Neile's money, of course.

Ferry noticed that McQueen could not sit still for very long. "He had to stay busy doing something every minute. He very rarely sat for any amount of time before he was up to something else. It was as though he had a surplus of energy and didn't need to sit and rest and was troubled by nonmovement."

Another McQueen trait that caught Ferry's attention was the fact that Steve never carried any money on him, often leaving Ferry stuck with the bill. "It was a quirk that I never fully understood and certainly became irritated at. If he had any money in his pocket, he scored it from a producer or agent or me or any of his friends." On the other hand, Steve's generosity would spill over and he would pay back the money in spades. Says Ferry, "He was just as quick to pay back in strange ways. He would arrange a weekend that didn't cost you anything. It all came out in the wash."


*Wanted: Dead or Alive* ended up in the top ten in its first season. The show drew much attention for its violence. Steve defended it to *The Hollywood Reporter,* explaining, "The fans don't care if there is violence in their TV western fare—what they want most is action, and the action must be sustained or there is a quick twist of the dial."

The November 12, 1959, *Hollywood Reporter* article drew the attention of the FBI, which started a dossier on McQueen. The article, along with a handwritten comment by an FBI agent, "Gangster Glorification Movies," is the earliest dated piece on McQueen. Throughout his life, the agency kept a distant tab on him. Even someone as patriotic as McQueen was not above suspicion.

Before Steve agreed to star in *Wanted: Dead or Alive,* he had envisioned himself as a movie star, not as a TV celebrity. Just a few years later, when McQueen was indeed a star, he, James Garner, and James Coburn were invited to actor Jimmy Cagney's home. Publicist David Foster's partner, Rick Ingersoll, was a dear friend of Cagney's, and

Foster had prevailed on Ingersoll to set up the meeting. Garner, Coburn, and McQueen were in awe of Cagney, especially McQueen, since Cagney was his idol. After dinner, they went to the living room to talk. The three young stars sat at Cagney's feet while he relaxed in a chair. Cagney took a special liking to McQueen. In his inimitable style, he said to Steve, "Yeah, yeah, kid. I see you on TV. I catch you on that western." That's just what McQueen didn't want to hear. He said to Cagney apologetically, "Uh, Mr. Cagney, I'm into movies now. Yeah, movies."

In Steve's best interest, Hilly Elkins made a verbal agreement with Dick Powell that if a movie role came along, every possible attempt would be made to work out a schedule to allow him to make the film. Powell, an actor himself, sympathetically lent an ear. He said to Elkins, "Hey, I used to be an actor. I know what he's going through; we'll work it out."

Such an opportunity arose during the first summer break in the series.

*Never So Few,* an epic World War II movie, was the story of a few good men who waged a battle against thousands of Japanese soldiers on the Burma-Chinese border. It starred Frank Sinatra as Captain Reynolds, the leader of the renegade soldiers.

Sinatra didn't like to make films. One of the most powerful men in Hollywood, he didn't necessarily like the art of filmmaking; he just wanted the experience to be tolerable. This was done by placing his friends in costarring roles. Sinatra loyalist Peter Lawford was handed one such part, but the prize role of Corporal Ringa went to Sammy Davis, Jr. The job was to pay a handsome $75,000 and Davis needed the bread, since he spent money just as fast as he made it.

Then in a moment of either serenity or stupidity, Davis was mysteriously off the picture.

In his book *Hollywood in a Suitcase,* Davis merely stated that he was "busy" with his career at the time. Hilly Elkins, who represented both McQueen and Davis, knew better. A radio broadcast from the Chez Paree in Chicago revealed that Davis had bit the hand that fed him. The emcee had asked Davis, "You're a big star now, Sammy. Who do you think is number one, you or Frank?" Sammy replied, "Well, to tell you the truth, I think I'm number one now." Astonished, the emcee asked again. "You think you're bigger than Frank?" Davis put it bluntly, "I love Frank, but I think I'm bigger than he is."*

* Spiegel, Penina, *McQueen: The Untold Story of A Bad Boy in Hollywood* (New York: Doubleday Books, 1986), 105.

A man of Sinatra's power and ego could not let the dismissal go without some sort of retribution. Davis was off the picture, and the role of Corporal Ringa was up for grabs.

Defending Davis, Hilly Elkins said, "The comment just came off wrong. I mean, Sammy adored Frank. He just adored him. But, as the last concert tour they did together will tell anyone, Frank was Frank, and you didn't fuck with him."

Hearing about the new vacancy, Hilly Elkins brought in McQueen to meet with director John Sturges. Sturges took one look at the star and gave the okay. "I've always had good luck seeing people in person, and he just looked right to me. He didn't particularly impress me on *Wanted: Dead or Alive.* He looked good in person," said Sturges.

Hilly Elkins managed to sign McQueen to a three-picture deal starting with *Never So Few.* His salary for the movie was a paltry $25,000 compared to what Sammy Davis, Jr., was going to get. Nevertheless, Elkins was just glad to get Steve started. "My theory was to get Steve in three pictures and let's see what happens. The career started with *Never So Few.*"

Frank Sinatra took a liking to Steve immediately. Steve recognized and acknowledged Sinatra's position in Hollywood. He shyly looked on from the sidelines at first, trying to figure out how to behave toward Sinatra. Sinatra tested Steve. Once while on location, between setups, McQueen was studiously reading the script when Sinatra snuck up behind him and put a lit firecracker in the loop of his gun belt. When it went off, "I jumped about three feet in the air. Which naturally delighted Frank," said Steve.

Not one to back down, McQueen quickly grabbed one of the prop tommy guns, jammed in a clip of blanks, and yelled at Sinatra as he was walking away, "Hey, Frank!" Sinatra turned around and McQueen squeezed the trigger. Bullets came spewing out, hitting the ground around Sinatra. The crew thought McQueen must have been crazy for giving it back to Sinatra like that. The two men stared at each other, neither blinking. It was an Old West standoff. McQueen observed, "The whole set just went dead still. Everybody was watching Frank to see what he'd do. He had a real bad temper, and I guess they all figured we were gonna end in a punchout. I wasn't sure myself, as we stared at each other. Then he just started laughing, and it was all over. After that, we got along just fine. In fact, we tossed firecrackers at each other all through the picture. Off camera, that is. I'd done the right thing. Once you back down to a guy like Sinatra, he never respects you. When I first met Frank, we sort of found each other on the same wavelength—we dug one another. We're like minds; we're both children emotionally."

For the picture, Loren Janes doubled for Sinatra, McQueen, and Charles Bronson and was constantly on the set. He remembers the trio as "the three devils." He comments, "They had so much fun. When they got together it was, 'What trick can we pull? Who's bed can we short-sheet?' That type of thing."

Throughout filming, the firecrackers and cherry bombs were a constant source of entertainment. One time Steve opened the door to Sinatra's dressing room, threw in a powerful cherry bomb, shut the door, and waited for the explosion. The burst was so powerful that it knocked out the wardrobe man's hearing aid, Sinatra later told McQueen. Outwardly, Sinatra feigned sympathy for the poor man, but inside he was convulsed with laughter.

One other incident involved Loren Janes and almost took his life. Janes remembers, "They were all trying to outdo each other, with firecrackers and little bombs going off everywhere. They would light one, walk away, and pop! and the guy would jump. They'd laugh and go on and on. When this paled, they tried to figure out the one thing that would be the coup de grâce. Turned out the one person they wanted to nail was the stuntman who was doubling all three—me!"

Some of the filming took place at night, so whenever he could manage it, Janes would try to get some sleep. He was assigned a small teardrop trailer in which the only thing to do was sleep. "I'm the type of guy who can sleep when all the normal noise is going on. The moment it gets suddenly quiet and someone's sneaking around, I can hear it. I'm alert to it. All of the normal things were going on this one day, and then all of a sudden it got quiet. Too quiet. And I woke up. Then I hear this whispering and giggling. I pull my curtain open and there's all three of them hanging outside my door. They've got strings of firecrackers and cherry bombs and they're wrapping them all together, and I hear them say they're going to open my door, light the firecrackers, and shut the door. I just thought, 'I don't trust these guys,' and I snuck out through a small panel door. I barely squeeze  through and I'm off in the distance looking at these guys. They're laughing and giggling and carrying on. They twist the fuses together and light them and shut the door. All of a sudden there's this big BOOM! It blew a hole in the ceiling. Then the trailer caught on fire. It sounded like a machine gun going off in there, the biggest noise you ever heard in your life. Just blew the hell out of this little teardrop trailer. They're all still laughing when they open the door and now they see the mattress with big gaping holes in it, the roof is torn off, and the place is on fire. Now it dawns on them that I'm in there. 'My God! Loren . . .' They start ripping the place apart looking for me. Meanwhile, I'm standing with my arms folded, just watching them. They're thinking, 'Poor Loren's in pieces.' Finally, I just burst out laughing and they spot me and chase after me. After a while, each one of them took me aside and apologized for almost blowing me up."

Sinatra recognized the rebel in Steve that he himself was just a few years earlier. Laughs Hilly Elkins, "He recognized a kindred soul."

Robert Relyea, the first assistant director at the time, felt that Sinatra was the older brother. "He thought Steve was funny, in the sense of his energy level. I have a hunch Frank said to himself, 'I remember when I had that much drive and desire to get everybody's attention.' In turn, Sinatra gave Steve the camera."

Adds Relyea, "Frank would never say, 'What's the deal with me?' As a matter of fact, Frank would say, 'Why don't you focus on McQueen and I'll go home.'"

"Frank Sinatra was terribly generous to Steve, and John Sturges took advantage of that generosity and focused the camera on Steve," says Neile.

Sturges offers, "Obviously, he was a personable fellow. You could see that on the screen, and when you meet an actor, you look for that quality. Steve looked like a movie star, which he turned out to be."

Sinatra asked the McQueens to attend the New York premiere of *Never So Few* with him. He liked Steve's company, and soon it looked as if the "Rat Pack" were going to have a new member.

The firecrackers once again were brought out in New York, and Steve began throwing them out his hotel window. The police were soon at his door, and he had to do some pretty fast talking. Comments friend Steve Ferry, "Steve had a gift for talking the police out of arresting him. In California, he got in a lot of trouble because he didn't carry anything in his pockets and he didn't carry his driver's license. He always talked himself out of it, though. He charmed the people."

Columnist Hedda Hopper heard about the incident with the police, and when Steve got back to Los Angeles, she called him into her office.

In the 1950s, Hedda Hopper and Louella Parsons, rival gossip queens, wielded a power never before seen in Hollywood and never seen since. If one of the two liked you, you had a great chance of being a star. Ever since seeing Steve on *Wanted: Dead or Alive*, Hopper had taken a liking to the "feisty little bastard."

When McQueen arrived at her office, Hopper sat him down for a stern lecture. She had heard through the grapevine that he was considering starring in *Ocean's Eleven*, a Rat Pack film with Dean Martin and Sammy Davis, Jr. (who was back in Sinatra's good graces). She posed this question to Steve: "Do you want to be a movie star or a Frank Sinatra flunky?"

Steve thought it over and realized that Hopper was on his side. Not many people were on Steve's side early in his career, and he appreciated her sound advice.

Steve never forgot her kindness. Years later, when he was in Taiwan filming *The Sand Pebbles,* the news of Hopper's death affected him greatly. Shortly afterward, the back pages of both the *Hollywood Reporter* and *Variety* magazines featured an unsigned tribute to a "great lady— Hedda Hopper." Ever so curious, Hopper's staff checked on the anonymous donor of the ads and were convinced that it was none other than Steve McQueen.

While *Never So Few* didn't make Steve a star, his performance did show that he was on the right path. Says Neile, "We knew after that that he had a very good chance." Paul Beckley of the *New York Herald Tribune* wrote, "Steve McQueen looks good as a brash, casual GI. He possesses that combination of smooth-rough charm that suggests star possibilities."

Steve returned to *Wanted: Dead or Alive* for a second season a reluctant man. The pleasant atmosphere during the film's shooting and the chance to be in the big leagues made him want out of the series more than ever. Actor James Coburn played the part of a heavy that second season and noticed that Steve was bored with the show. To relax, the two would indulge in a puff of marijuana in Steve's trailer. "We had a good time," laughs Coburn. "It would take fifteen minutes to set up a shot, and Steve was off on his motorcycle for thirty minutes. He was causing the producers a lot of anxiety because those spare fifteen minutes cost them money. On a couple of those trips, he would take me to the dressing room, smoke a joint, and come back. Authority figures and machines he always wanted to dominate."

Besides being bored, Steve had to work twice as hard on the series as he did on a film. He commented on the daily monotony: "You don't have any idea what a rough grind it is, doing a TV series. I had to be up at 5:00 A.M., to the studio by 6:30 A.M. . . . Then worked all day on the set and usually didn't get home till 9:00 P.M. Sometimes, under deadline pressure, we'd film a whole episode in a single day!"

Then came another call from John Sturges, who was planning to do a remake of *The Seven Samurai,* the Japanese film classic by director Akira Kurosawa. He wanted to make this one into his own classic, a western called *The Magnificent Seven.*

The plot was simple but effective. A small Mexican village is the constant target of outlaw bandits, who come to the town whenever they want and take whatever they want. In desperation, the villagers turn to a hired gunslinger, Yul Brynner. Brynner seeks out a handful of other gunmen, the "Magnificent Seven," and they in turn deal with the bandits in their own type of justice. Steve's role, Vin, would be Brynner's counterpart, the second costarring position.

There was only one problem with the role: it had only seven lines of dialogue. Hilly Elkins was negotiating with Four Star to get Steve into the movie. How was he going to get Steve out of his contract for a part with only seven lines? He called Sturges. "John, there's only seven lines of dialogue here." Sturges replied, "I know, Hilly, but I promise I'll give him the camera." Comments Elkins, "John Sturges was one of the few men in this town whose word was as good as gold." Steve agreed to do the part, but Four Star Productions did not.

Rather than working with their star, Four Star feared that if they let McQueen out of his contract, he would be lost forever, and *Wanted: Dead or Alive* would be lost as well.

Shooting would run into the beginning of the series, and Four Star would not give Steve the necessary time off for the movie. Hilly Elkins sought out Dick Powell. "Hey, remember when you told Steve when he needs to do a film, you would let him? I've got a real chance to make him a star on this film." Powell put his hand up and cut off Elkins. "Don't talk to me about this, because the company's grown and I don't deal with that aspect any longer." Elkins was steered to Tom McDermott.

"Tom McDermott, may he rest in peace," says Elkins politely, "was out of New York and was a tough guy, a tough Irishman, and knew what I was coming in his office for." McDermott said sternly, "Steve's got a series commitment." Elkins tried to appeal to the business side of McDermott. "I know. He's got a real opportunity and it'll bring attention to the series. Give him a couple of weeks' compensation leave. I know that in the spirit of Dick Powell, you're going to help us out." Said McDermott, "Fuck you. He's got a commitment. He's going to do the series." Fearing that he might have to play hardball, Elkins offhandedly commented, "Geez, it's so terrible you say that because Steve's so emotionally set on this, he might get really upset." Perceiving this as a threat, and rightly so, McDermott was set off. "Don't try that Mafia bullshit with me. I'll take you and Steve on and kick both of your asses. Okay?"

Elkins went back to his office. Steve and Neile happened to be in Boston at the time. When Elkins got Steve on the phone, he calmly said, "Have an accident."

"McQueen being McQueen drove into the side of Boston's main banks, narrowly missing a police officer, with Neile in the car. And he came back to Los Angeles with a neck brace on," laughs Hilly Elkins. Not exactly what he had in mind, but it worked nonetheless.

The neck brace had the desired effect, and Steve began receiving flowers from Dick Powell. Soon after that came the inevitable phone call from Tom McDermott.

"Okay, you win," McDermott conceded to Elkins. "You can do a picture." Elkins knew the phone call was hard enough for McDermott, but to make it sting a little more, to show who was in charge, to rub salt in the wound, he replied, "Wrong. You double his salary. You double his points in Four Star." He heard McDermott scream on the other end of the line, "You motherfucker!"

No matter how many obscenities Elkins heard that day, he got Steve the part. "Steve went on to do *The Magnificent Seven* and the rest is history," he says.

*The Magnificent Seven* was Steve's first real shot at stardom. The movie centered on its star, Yul Brynner, and funding was based solely on his appearance in the film. Director John Sturges was to handpick Brynner's costars, to make sure that all of them would complement Brynner, not upstage him. Steve would make sure that somehow, someway, he stood out from the rest.

Besides Brynner and McQueen, the cast of *The Magnificent Seven* included James Coburn, Eli Wallach, Robert Vaughn, Charles Bronson, Brad Dexter and Horst Buchholz.

The movie would be filmed entirely on location in Cuernavaca, Mexico. The first scene slated was a shot of the seven crossing a stream. Throughout the movie, Yul Brynner was always to come in first, the others would merely fill out the landscape. The rest of the cast, though, had their own agenda.

As soon as shooting began, the camera would focus in on Brynner, with the others simply riding along. Steve, making the first move, chose to scoop up some water into his hat. Charles Bronson began to unbutton his shirt, and the rest of the actors followed suit. Each one was scene stealing and was perceived as a threat by Brynner. Each was determined to stand out, but none had the street smarts to compete with Steve McQueen.

Steve was nicknamed "Tricky Dick," because of his underhanded way of getting what he wanted. Brynner already had what he wanted— stardom—and Steve was determined to steal the movie out from under him.

Recalls James Coburn, "Steve's main aim was to promote Steve McQueen. Steve was prepared in all of his roles. He had a great reputation for his draw. Very quick. It really worked for him. I remember Yul

McQueen, Robert Vaughn, and James Coburn all competed to top each other on the set of *The Magnificent Seven*. It was McQueen, not Yul Brynner, who eventually stole the movie.

saying, 'I don't know what to do with my gun.' And Steve gave him an ordinary move to draw the pistol and put it back in the holster. It's been done a thousand times over and Yul used it. So Steve was very proud that he conned Yul into a simple move, while he did this fancy thing with his pistol." Brynner knew Steve's moves with a pistol would draw the attention of the audience and tried to talk him into using a rifle instead. Yul could be just as conniving as Steve, but Steve didn't take the bait. "He wanted me to use a rifle in the film so that I wouldn't outdraw him, but I wouldn't have that," recounted Steve. "We were shootin' the first battle sequences. I got three shots out before he even had his gun out of his holster."

Manager Hilly Elkins was present for a scene between the two stars and saw why "Tricky Dick" earned his nickname. Remembers Elkins, "Steve and Yul Brynner weren't that tall. In one of their scenes, Brynner built himself a little mound of dirt to stand on to appear taller. Steve is circling him and saying his lines. Every time he passes Yul, he kicks away at the dirt pile Yul is standing on, so throughout the scene, you see Yul getting smaller and smaller. By the end of the scene, Yul is in a hole!" Steve commented, "When you work in a scene with Yul, you're

McQueen and Robert Vaughn share a quiet moment on the set of *The Magnificent Seven*, 1960. (Courtesy of United Artists)

supposed to stand perfectly still ten feet away. I don't work that way. So I protected myself."

For the ultimate humiliation, Steve saved his best con for Brynner's biggest action scene. He knew that Brynner was out of his element when it came to handling horses. Though Steve may not have liked horses, he at least knew a thing or two about them. He also knew that Brynner was watching his every move. When Steve whacked his horse *gently* across the neck to get the horse to take off, Brynner did the same thing, except he whacked his horse *hard*. The horse went cross-eyed and his legs went straight out from under him, doing a split. Brynner couldn't figure out what he did wrong.

The tension between the two stars crackled. Steve was very jealous of Brynner's stardom. "He was the king," says James Coburn of Yul Brynner. "He had this whole entourage, but he didn't like anyone walking within ten feet of him. He had this ambience around him. He liked to have his cigarette lit for him at the snap of a finger. Movie star treatment.

"John Sturges was from the old school. For instance, Yul Brynner got whatever he wanted; Steve got almost everything he wanted, and so on down the line. That's the way Sturges worked."

John Alonzo, then an actor (and later director of photography on *Tom Horn*), noticed Steve's envy for Brynner's star position. "It was kind of fun to watch the two of them, because Steve was the hottest thing on television, so he expected to be treated like a star; but in Mexico, they didn't know who he was. Yul Brynner was an international star and was treated much better by the Mexican people, because they knew who Yul Brynner was and had no idea who Steve McQueen was. It was amusing because they set up a dressing room, a motor home for Yul right in the middle of the set, and Steve had to go off the set to get to his trailer."

As for most of their scenes together, Steve did his best to upstage the star in his most subtle manner. One scene required Brynner to give a speech to the group, with his back to McQueen. Steve began flipping a coin. Once again, he was scene stealing. Word got back to Brynner about McQueen's exploits and for their next scene together, Brynner took off his cowboy hat. With his big shiny bald head on the screen, no amount of scene stealing could keep the audience's eyes off Brynner.

Steve showed the way, and soon the others began to pick up on his lead. One scene called for a stagecoach ride with all the "Seven" on board. As the stagecoach rolled forward, Steve began to imitate a pig and threw his voice like a ventriloquist, "Oink, oink, oink." Brynner began looking around to see where the noise was coming from. Robert Vaughn, thinking Brynner looked like a pig with his bald head and pointed ears, began to carry on where Steve left off and all throughout the movie oinked out loud whenever Brynner wasn't looking.

"There wouldn't have been a rivalry if Steve hadn't pushed it," notes James Coburn. "Steve wasn't what you would call a giving guy. He had a lot of power and presence. He loved to play. It was in his nature. An abandoned child always tests everything. And he tested Yul."

Director John Sturges noticed there was "friction" between the two stars. "Naturally, there were some clashes. They're dissimilar characters; Yul was like a rock, while Steve was volatile. Steve probably figured that Yul was being a big star and that he wasn't willing for anyone to catch flies. Yul probably thought Steve was being an undisciplined smart aleck, always trying to catch a fly."

Hilly Elkins explains: "Yul was precise and demanding; Steve was an American phenomenon. Steve wasn't going to take any shit from the bald fellow. And the bald fellow wasn't going to take any shit from Steve."

Robert Relyea agrees. "Steve and Yul were such different personalities that there was never a chance theirs was going to be a 'warm relationship.' It reverted to 'I'll be there, and I'll work with you.' By their natures, they were not people who would get close to each other. If they made ten pictures together, they would have never been close."

To add fuel to the fire, United Artists dreamed up an idea to keep the picture in the papers. In the story, it claimed that Brynner and McQueen were fighting on the set daily. Brynner saw the story and hit the roof. He grabbed McQueen by the shoulders and stated, "There's a story in the paper about us having a feud. I'm an established star and I don't feud with supporting actors. I want you to call the paper and tell them the story is completely false!" McQueen responded, "Take your hands off me! You know what you can do with your orders. Shove 'em." Steve later said of that encounter, "I don't like people pawin' me. What had I got to lose? I've got a busted nose and teeth missing and stitches in my lips and I'm deaf in the right ear. What could I lose from a little fight? Yul Brynner was one uptight dude. I think I represented a threat to him. He doesn't ride very well, and he doesn't know anything about quick draws and all of that stuff. I know horses. I know guns. I was in my element and he wasn't."

Years later, Steve was in France for *Le Mans* when a stranger beckoned him outside his hotel. "Hey, Steve, don't you remember me?" Steve had no idea who the man was. The stranger continued, "I was the company publicist for United Artists on *The Magnificent Seven*. I did a hell of a job, you know. I'm the guy who wrote those things about you and Brynner. I created it all." McQueen cocked his head back and laughed heartily. He later confided to friend Phil Parslow, "I couldn't be mad at the guy. He made me a star. By putting me in the paper on the same level with Brynner, the guy made me a star!"

And it was Steve McQueen, not Yul Brynner, who emerged as the star of *The Magnificent Seven*. His performance was singled out, which did not endear him to his costars. Years later, at the Beverly Wilshire Hotel, Steve and James Coburn met for a friendly lunch. Coburn revealed to McQueen that he, Charles Bronson, and Robert Vaughn hated McQueen at the time. He told Steve, "We were so busy hating you that you stole the movie. You were the smart guy. We were dumb." The three noticed how Steve would quietly walk up to Sturges and say, "Can I make this line change? Can I do this to my character?" They could only mutter, "Look at that kissass." But Coburn laughed it all off. Years had passed and he, Bronson, and Vaughn became stars in their own right, but they never reached the level of stardom that Steve did. Says Phil Parslow, "That movie made Steve a star because Steve kissed ass, talked to Sturges, did things his way. He didn't want to be Josh Randall the rest of his life. And Steve became bigger than all of them. They never made it as big as Steve. Steve became even bigger than Yul Brynner because Yul could do only one thing. Steve could just about do anything and get away with it. He went on to become a megastar."

Steve's quest for movie stardom had not been fully realized. He was still tied to *Wanted: Dead or Alive*. He now commanded a salary of $100,000 per season. In his mind, he knew he was not a bona fide movie star unless he could rid himself of the series. One particular review of *The Magnificent Seven* incensed him: "If he can ever get sprung from television, McQueen's going to be a big star."

In March 1961 Steve's prayers were answered when the series was canceled. "We wanted out very badly," explains Hilly Elkins. "The market was going in a different direction. This was the early Four Star days when you had *Zane Grey Theater* and *Trackdown* and *Wanted: Dead or Alive* and a whole slew of westerns on television. The mood of the American public started going away from that type of show, and it just got more expensive to produce, so after so many years, you went on to a new situation." Says David Foster, "There's two ways to get what you want. One, is to kill them with kindness, and that was never Steve's style. Two, is to be angry and bully. That's why the show didn't stay on the air, because it was just too painful for all of those people to work under

Steve McQueen in *The Magnificent Seven*, 1960.     (COURTESY OF STAR FILE PHOTOS)

those circumstances. On a film, if someone is unhappy, you only have to work with them that one time and they're gone after three months. On a series, where it's a continuing relationship, week after week, it's a killer. I don't care how popular that show might have been, it just couldn't go on."

When Steve was told on the set that the series was canceled, he reportedly did a pirouette and whooped with delight. After 117 episodes, *Wanted: Dead or Alive* was history.

A reporter asked the newly out-of-work star if he was upset over the network's decision not to renew the series. "Hell, no! I was delighted. That series was murder on me. Still, I'm grateful to ol' Josh Randall. I'll always owe him one for giving me a running start in this business. Right now, I've got a real chance to grab that brass ring, and, man, you better believe I'm ready to do some grabbin'."

And as one career came to a close, another was to begin.

# THE BIG PICTURE

*Stardom equals financial success, and financial success equals security. I've spent too much of my life feeling insecure. I still have nightmares about being poor, of everything I own just vanishing away. Stardom means that can't happen.*

STEVE MCQUEEN

WHEN STEVE WASN'T WORKING, he found a much-needed release in riding motorcycles and driving fast cars. His fascination with wheels started early in life. "The first time I saw a wheelbarrow, I think it was," said Steve, "I liked the way it moved."

When stardom came with *Wanted: Dead or Alive,* Steve entered his first race in a sports car, a Porsche, at Santa Barbara in 1959. He joked, "The worst possible thing happened: I won. That *really* got me hooked."

Racing was real to McQueen. The racing world didn't give a damn who he was. When he pushed his bike up to the start line, he was the enemy, and Steve liked that mind-set. "You see," he said, "around the studios everybody waits on me. They powder my nose and tell me what they think I want to hear. And after a while you're convinced you are superhuman.

"But when you're racing a motorcycle, the guy on the next bike doesn't care who you are. And if he beats you in the race, well, it means he's a better man than you are. And he's not afraid to tell you that you're lousy.

"Racing keeps my equilibrium intact. It makes it difficult to believe I'm God's gift to humanity."

Simply put, racing is what made Steve happy. "When I'm humming along on that bike I say to myself, 'Man, this is where I want to be. This is what I want to be doing.'"

One person McQueen didn't make happy was neighbor Edmund W. George. Several times George complained to local police about McQueen's wild driving. In addition, George complained to police that McQueen's dog, Mike, had been running loose. Steve decided that the two of them should shake hands and start over.

The incident made the papers, and each man had his own version to tell. McQueen stated, "I went over there to tell him we should be friends and ask him to stop calling the police about me. I even took my little girl along, and was carrying her in my arms.

"George and his wife began screaming and calling me a coward. George yelled, 'Get off my land,' and rushed at me, hitting me in the chest. I dropped my daughter."

George's version was somewhat different. "He came over looking for a fight. He dared me to come out in the street and then he hit me.

"He said, 'I came here to make friends, but if you want trouble, I'll give you trouble.'

"I asked if that was a threat or a promise. He said it was a threat."

Each party signed a battery complaint against the other, but no arrests were made and the fracas never went to court.

A writer who knew Steve on a personal level wrote, "To Steve, life is black and white. He believes in an eye for an eye and a tooth for a tooth and will fight for his friends with the same vigor as he does for himself."

"Do these look like the hands of an actor?" Steve would proudly show them to anyone who cared to look. To Steve, racing had dignity, and he wasn't sure that acting could compare. But he did compare the two worlds to a reporter. "Each field takes total concentration to become successful. In order to be proficient in racing, you must eat, sleep, and think about it all the time, and you must devote every minute practicing to keep a winning edge at peak."

Friend and fellow motorcycle enthusiast Bud Ekins observed, "He got interested in dirt bike riding and he had me build him a bike, so I built him one. We went racing together. He would have been put into the expert class except that he would go off and make a film and that would keep him down to the amateur rating. Steve was competitive with anyone, be it lagging coins or playing hopscotch or what have you."

Fellow actor Don Gordon firmly believed that McQueen raced because "it was him and a car against somebody else in a car. He wanted to see what kind of human being he was, what kind of person he was, what kind of man he was. He was on the edge. He was always on the edge. How far could you go? It was machines, it was mechanics who could make it purr and hum. It was a purist kind of thing."

Steve's son, Chad, noticed, "With his old motorcycles and his motorcycle buddies he could be himself. Nobody could give a damn if he was a movie star. He was just one of the boys."

Motorcycles, cars, and speed would forever be linked with Steve Mc-Queen.


With Four Star Studios and *Wanted: Dead or Alive* out of his hair, Mc-Queen set out to make himself a movie star.

Steve was under a nonexclusive contract to MGM when the studio offered (after Cary Grant had turned it down) *The Golden Fleecing*. The plot was about a navy lieutenant who schemes to use the ship's electronic computer to break the roulette table at a Venice casino. Later retitled *The Honeymoon Machine*, it was McQueen's first starring role at a major Hollywood studio.

Manager Hilly Elkins was given the task of babysitting Steve's costar, actress Brigid Bazlen, the daughter of *Chicago Sun Times* writer Maggie Daly. Bazlen, then only twenty-one, was a pretty, if not moody, match for McQueen. Daly called Elkins and asked him to watch over her daughter during filming. As Elkins recalls, it was quite an experience. "My job was to keep the two from killing each other, either with fisticuffs, verbal attacks, or fucking. It was a choice, depending upon the moods of the two kids."

*The Honeymoon Machine* was Steve's first attempt at comedy, and it

Steve McQueen in a publicity photo, 1960.

went over as badly as the script. "I will take full credit for that one," Elkins boldly laughs decades later. "It was a dumb move. It was a dumb move for both Steve and me. We were looking the other way and we should have passed."

*The Honeymoon Machine* was both a box office and a critical failure. The *New York Herald Tribune* declared, "There is little to laugh at. Even though the basic premise may be potentially funny—and this must still be demonstrated—its cause is hardly clumsy slapstick and the cavorting of an actor, Steve McQueen, who confuses posturing with entertaining." *Variety* complained, "*The Honeymoon Machine* is in need of a little lubrication on some of its running parts, and could have done with a few hasty repairs in the performance department." *The Saturday Review* suggested that McQueen "go back to TV westerns and selling cigarettes."

McQueen still found himself in demand, as he told the *Los Angeles Times*. "Just think, five years ago I couldn't even get through the door of the *U.S. Steel Hour* office. Now, I've just turned down a good script and good money. No time."

For McQueen's next film, he decided that he should get back to what he did best: action.

*Hell Is for Heroes* was Steve's next film, taken from the Robert Pirosh script *Separation Hill*. The film is an ensemble piece starring Steve as Reese, a renegade and openly rebellious soldier. The rest of the cast included James Coburn, Bobby Darin, Fess Parker, Nick Adams, Bob Newhart, and Harry Guardino. Reese, very much like McQueen, is a loner and alienates himself from his unit.

The World War II film is actually based on the true incident of seven men who are ordered to hold their position until their replacements arrived a few days later. In order to accomplish the task, the seven use various tactics to convince the Germans that they are a much larger force.

From the get-go, McQueen pushed, bullied, and fought for everything he could. The script's author, Robert Pirosh, was set to direct as well. Pirosh wrote the Oscar-winning screenplay for *Battleground* and had one other World War II film to his credit, *Go for Broke,* starring Van Johnson. *Separation Hill* was a project dear to his heart, since he had waited seven years for the U.S. Army to declassify material for his script.

McQueen felt the character of Reese perfectly suited him, and, amazingly, he and Pirosh hit it off. Says Pirosh, "As I see it, Reese in *Hell Is for Heroes* was just a guy who probably couldn't make it on the outside and away from the army and who had terrible feelings about going back to civilian life.

"He was an off-center guy, a misfit, a killer, but not a psychopath."

Steve receives birthday greetings via telephone on the set of Metro-Goldwyn-Mayer's *The Honeymoon Machine*. (COURTESY OF CINEMOBILIA FILM BOOK SHOP & GALLERY, INC.)

Recalls Pirosh, "Steve was very stimulating to work with during the script stage. He was fun, and he had some terrific ideas that helped me develop the Reese character. He came up with little bits of dialogue. I thought the guy was great. He was going to give a great performance, and I was going to get some credit for it."*

A week into the shooting, Steve felt that he had not been singled out as the star. Now he wanted the script changed to his benefit. Pirosh balked and refused to change a word. He felt the story was about a group of brave soldiers, not a starring role for any one actor. The two men locked horns, and Pirosh was fired by Paramount. The picture was shut down for a week while the studio searched for a new director. Says costar James Coburn, "Steve had an incredible instinct of knowing what was right for him. He knew that Pirosh was not well suited as the director. He wanted to be totally alone as the star. He said to me, 'Why can't they just do the picture about one guy—me!" It was really an outrageous statement. I didn't say anything, but I couldn't believe it. He didn't want to have anybody else around. Steve wanted the film to be about him, and he got as close as he could get."

---

* Rubin, Steven Jay, *Combat Films* (Jefferson, N.C.: McFarland & Company, Inc., 1981), 180.

A new person was brought in to spruce up the part. Writer Richard Carr was given the task of appeasing McQueen. Says Carr, "McQueen felt, and I think rightfully so, that his character wasn't clearly defined and that there was no empathy for him."

Upon McQueen's approval, director Don Siegel was hired. Together, he and McQueen put the final touches on the script. Remembers Siegel, *Hell Is for Heroes* is a film I inherited. It's an honest movie that has something to say. At the beginning I refused to shoot certain scenes that seemed to me too anodyne, too delicate for a war film. It would have turned out more like a brass band regiment. But I do think war's a sordid thing. I tried to get to the heart of it, and my film is, I think, extremely realistic."*

"Don Siegel was putting Steve on," says Coburn. "He would say to Steve, 'Sure, go ahead and do that. You want to shoot when? Sure, we can accommodate that.' When Steve wasn't around, he'd shoot something else. He was very, very easy. There was no opposition. If there's no opposition, there's no conflict."

Siegel won McQueen's respect early on in the picture. Remembers Siegel, "He walked around with the attitude that the burden of preserving the integrity of the picture was on his shoulders, and all the rest of us were company men ready to sell out to the studio bosses. One day, when we were sitting together on the set, I told him that his attitude bored me, that I was as interested in the picture being good as he was, and that when this fact sunk through his thick head we would get along. I could see he was angry. But I decided that if he stood up and came for me, I would hit him first as hard as I could and hope for the best. Fortunately, for me, he didn't stand up."

Costar L. Q. Jones offers, "Don Siegel was the kind of guy who got along well with everyone. He had a very insidious way, which was very clever, of getting you to do what he wanted done by example and observation. Steve seemed to get along quite well with Don.

"Steve knew what he could do best, but I think he understood what he could do well and he tended to take a scene and work it so that he could bend it to work for him. If you came at him with not wanting to change the dialogue to his liking, then yes, he could be difficult, but he was a pro. Siegel sort of provided an outlet for Steve in letting Steve do what he felt was best for the picture and it paid off," says Jones.

Later, Siegel revealed his tactic in turning McQueen into a pussycat. "In making the film as realistic as possible, I found one way was to play Steve as a professional, a real pro who was surrounded by amateurs.

---

* Kass, Judith, *Don Siegel* (New York: Tantivy Press, 1975), 180.

Certainly, with our cast, which came from all walks of life in the entertainment world, there was hardly a professional aura, and that made Steve stand out all the more."

The shooting took place in the woods of Redding, California. Says Siegel, "I really felt the picture began when we got up on the ridge. I thought the setting in the studio was pretty obviously studio stuff, which was unfortunate. I think we'd have been much better and much less Hollywood if I'd just started the picture on the ridge, really right with it. But I wasn't equal to it, and there was great pressure of time and quite a rewrite."

It was so hot outside in the woods (with the temperature sometimes reaching 117 degrees) that most of the filming had to take place at night. That left Steve with a lot of time on his hands during the day, and he tended to find trouble. McQueen's contract stipulated that he could have a rental car to drive. He wrecked three rental cars, the last one being a Mercedes convertible 300 SL. James Coburn recalls, "Steve was coming to work one morning up over these winding roads and drove the car through thick brush, through bushes, the whole bit. As he was driving 100 mph through the woods, he came to a fork in the road where he came face to face with these two tractors with spirals in the front of them. He swerved the car off through the trees until he smashed head on into a big tree. The car was destroyed. Steve was really shaken. He had these little scratches on his head, and that was all that happened to him. This happened right in front of the crew as we were waiting for him so we could shoot the scene." Paramount executives fired off a memo to McQueen stating that if he wrecked another rental car, the cost would come out of his pocket. Steve didn't wreck a fourth car.

The first shutdown, script rewrites, production delays, McQueen's wrecked cars, and the limited budget ($2.5 million) had threatened to shut down the picture once again, but this time for good. As Paramount executives arrived on the scene, Steve knew what their mission was. He knew that if the picture were shut down, it would be his name that would be tarnished. His reputation in the business was on the line, and he knew what he had to do. As they approached him, he calmly pulled a branch from a tree and drew a line in the dirt with it. He announced, "Anyone who steps over that line gets the shit knocked out of him." The executives backed off and let the movie finish filming.

Writer Robert Carr revealed the magic of McQueen's acting. "Originally, we had planned this scene where Reese's true character would be revealed. Pike Fess Parker] would come over and ask him, 'Were you right?' and Reese would respond with an illuminating speech.

"Unfortunately, it came out stilted. McQueen and I worked on the speech and we tried to cut it down. Finally, it was Steve's idea that there would be no explanation, just a simple, 'How do I know!' And that carried a lot more impact than a bunch of words or phony Freudian explanations."*

*Hell Is for Heroes* wrapped in late summer of 1961, almost four months after principal photography. Siegel was pleased with the end result. "I'm particularly pleased with the last shot and, in fact, with the entire ending in which Steve McQueen is killed and the battle goes on as the picture ends. That wasn't the end of the picture as we had written it. The end was more affirmative, and we had shot it that way. But when I was editing the picture I realized that at the peak of battle I had nothing else I wanted to say, no feeling of possible affirmation. I wanted to show that my hero was blown up, which was horrifying, and that the rest were still going forward, that he would be forgotten, that the action of war is futile. I hadn't designed anything for an ending like that, so I optically zoomed in on the pillbox. It didn't bother me a bit that it was grainy. It had an authentic quality and it made me feel right about the picture."

The film opened to enthusiastic reviews, especially for Steve, as the critics raved about his performance. *Variety* wrote, "McQueen plays the central role with hard-bitten businesslike reserve and an almost animal intensity, permitting just the right degree of humanity to project through a war-weary-and-wise veneer." The *New York Times* agreed, as it assessed, "An arresting performance by Steve McQueen, a young actor with presence and a keen sense of timing, is the outstanding feature in *Hell Is for Heroes*." And, the *Times* boasted, "Steve McQueen is extraordinarily good."

Despite the good reviews, Paramount was disappointed with the film and released it as a double feature with *Escape from Zahrain*. The picture sank into oblivion.

In the years since its release, *Hell Is for Heroes* has become a minor World War II classic. Director Stanley Kubrick said of McQueen's performance, "It is the best portrayal of a solitary soldier I have ever seen."

Steve followed *Hell Is for Heroes* with a British World War II film called *The War Lover*. Upon the disappointing box office failure of *Hell Is for Heroes*, Steve decided to take matters into his own hands. "I'd made eight films up to then, and only one, *The Magnificent Seven*, was any good. I just wasn't making the right connections—so I tried doing a film in Europe."

---

* Rubin, Steven Jay, *Combat Films* (Jefferson, N.C.: McFarland & Company, Inc., 1981), 190.

McQueen as pilot "Buzz" Rickson, a hard-fighting, hard-loving hellion in *The War Lover*, 1962. (COURTESY OF COLUMBIA PICTURES)

On the surface, Steve's character in *The War Lover*, Captain Buzz Rickson, was a continuation of the Reese character in *Hell Is for Heroes*. Whereas Reese was silent, angry, and cold, Rickson was all that and more. It was McQueen's first role that allowed him to go over the top.

McQueen also had another reason to go to England: racing. "Acting is all right, but it's car racing I love," he told an English reporter. "Speed is incredible and beautiful. Slipstreaming around a turn in the middle of a pack is what separates the men from the boys. If you can't cut in you may have to back out. It's as simple as that."

While in England, Steve met up again with Sterling Moss, then the greatest race car driver in the world. McQueen had first met Moss in 1959 in California. Moss recalls this meeting: "Steve and his wife were living in a funny little house at the back of Hollywood when I first met him. He was then riding a motorcycle. When I next met him, he had hit the high spots. He had a D-type Jag, among other things, and a fantastic house. I considered him a cool type of guy. He didn't waste words— he believed in actions rather than words. Very keen to learn, very keen on things, interested to get advice and take it—which I consider very intelligent. I can remember that night we had together in London around that time; I think Sammy Davis came into it at some stage. If you ask me the kinds of things we talked about, that's fairly simple—girls and cars. Yes, in that order."

McQueen rarely had any idols, but Sterling Moss was an exception. The two had taken to each other and Moss encouraged Steve to race a Formula Cooper at Brands Hatch, a racecourse in Sussex, some fifty miles from London. "I learned a lot by racing in Europe," said McQueen.

"I would follow Sterling around the course. He'd signal with one hand, indicating with his fingers which gear to use. He was driving with one hand and there I was hanging on for dear life.

"Following Moss is like taking your first drink of sake!" McQueen said in amazement.

Columbia Pictures, the studio financing *The War Lover,* as well as McQueen's $75,000 salary, had caught wind of McQueen's racing activities and quickly sought to prevent McQueen from indulging in his latest passion. Columbia reminded McQueen of the $2.5 million policy, which in effect meant that McQueen could be sued for that amount if his racing antics caused the movie to shut down. Laughed Steve, "They couldn't stop me, but they did threaten to sue."

While in London, Steve stayed in a plush suite at the world-famous Savoy. Manager Hilly Elkins was put up in an adjoining room, with a living room connecting the two bedrooms. "Steve liked his room very hot and I liked mine cold. It was about ninety degrees in his bedroom and fifty degrees in mine. We had this neutral living room in which we met to work on the script," laughs Elkins.

Their stay at the Savoy didn't last long after McQueen hosted a wild night with his racing buddies. Wanting to entertain his friends with cheese toast, he had bought a plug-in electric hot plate. As he was serving his guests, happy as the congenial host, he heard a shriek. The curtains above the hot plate had caught fire. Clad only in his boxer shorts, Steve rushed into the hallway in search of an extinguisher. Other guests, on hearing the ruckus, peered out and saw the blond-haired, blue-eyed Yankee parading around in his undershorts. They hurriedly closed their doors and put in a call to management. McQueen quickly extinguished the fire to the laughter of his British friends.

The next morning the hotel management terminated McQueen's stay, as several guests had complained the previous night that a "wild man is running loose in the hotel."

Amazingly, McQueen managed to finagle Columbia into renting a three-story mansion from Lord John Russell at $300 a week.

Mike Frankovich, Jr., son of Columbia Pictures president Mike Frankovich, was in charge of publicity on *The War Lover*. He had arranged for a *Life* magazine cover story, a stroke of luck on McQueen's part, considering that this could launch him as a movie star.

Frankovich and *Life* writer George Barris were to meet with McQueen at the Carlton Towers in London at a specified time. After waiting for over an hour, Frankovich called Neile. "He's meeting with George Barris at the Carlton Towers," he was told. Baffled, Frankovich apologized to Barris and the cover story was scrapped.

A day later, Frankovich, who happened to race as well, was chitchatting with one of his racing buddies. "Oh, you know that movie star you're working with?" said the friend. "Yeah?" Frankovich asked. The friend continued, "Yeah, he was down at John Cooper's racing school yesterday." "Son-of-a-bitch," thought Frankovich. To add insult to injury, McQueen hadn't liked the fact that the publicity man had called Neile. He put in a call to Frankovich's boss at Columbia and said that Frankovich had been rude to his wife. Was there any way he could be fired? "I was very close to getting fired," says Frankovich. "George Barris went to my boss and told him how the story had transpired and saved my job.

"I don't think Steve McQueen understood the value of publicity, not at that time anyhow. Later on, most of the publicity he got was because he was a bad boy. His antics gave him that bad-boy image, which was part of his success."

It was only because Frankovich loved wheels as much as McQueen did that their relationship recovered. Frankovich had a specially tuned station wagon, and McQueen said, "Oh, I want to drive that." Frankovich quickly dismissed the notion. McQueen then jumped in a jeep and took it out behind the runway at Shepperton Studios, eventually burying the jeep upside down in a lake. "He was kind of a nutsy guy," remarks Frankovich. "Nice enough guy, but he was really hell on wheels."

*The War Lover* is the story of Captain Buzz Rickson (McQueen), a hell-raising, cocky, competitive fighter pilot. He and copilot Robert Wagner find themselves competing for the same girl, played by British actress Shirley Anne Field. When Rickson's hell-bent attempts to woo Field into bed fail, he alienates himself from Wagner and Field. In the end, it is Rickson's personality that eventually does him in.

It was McQueen's most ambitious part yet, and to prepare himself for the role, he went all out like never before. "I have to stay in character," said Steve. "I always try to immerse myself in the role I'm playing, and Buzz Rickson is no shrinking violet.

"He's a complex guy. Not just another flying wise guy. He's selfish and selfless. He has the respect of the crew that pretty much generally hates him. He's not really the kind of guy that anybody really likes. He's a helluva flier and can make a B-17 stand up on its tail and dance. But he's filled with repressions and deep complexes. All of that makes him an interesting guy to portray. Maybe next time I'll play a nice Madison Avenue soft-sell guy or a comedy cutup. And that's what I'll be, on stage and off. It goes with the part."

Mike Frankovich noticed that McQueen was rude and brash to costar Field. He was "bullying Shirley Anne and playing a little bit of the ugly American. She developed an intense dislike of Steve, and quite frankly, that was fostered by McQueen." McQueen would goad Field: "We Americans, we're real movie actors. Here, you don't know how to act in movies." Says Frankovich, "The attitude of a lot of Americans in those days was, 'We're above you Brits.'"

As for McQueen and costar Robert Wagner, the two got along famously. Much of the credit goes to Wagner, since his ego wasn't a problem. McQueen always made sure that if he and Wagner had a scene together, that Wagner was on the set waiting for him, an old Hollywood put-down. Wagner was above this kind of testing, and this put McQueen at ease. Says Hilly Elkins, "Bob Wagner is a very sweet man. He went out of his way for Steve, and Steve adored him. That was a good relationship."

McQueen also got along well with director Philip Leacock. Leacock's style of direction was much like that of Don Siegel's in that he let it be known that Steve was the star. Comments Frankovich, "Phil Leacock used to get along with everybody. There was a testing early on with McQueen, but Leacock was one of those guys who could almost command any actor to the way he was thinking. He would tell his actors, 'You may want to do it this way, but this is not what I want, and the overall importance is the picture.' He was able to convey that to Steve somehow."

Toward the end of filming, Leacock managed to save the picture when McQueen crashed his car on a rainy day at Brands Hatch raceway. Luckily, McQueen suffered only a few cuts and a fat lip. A British reporter who witnessed the incident wrote in full detail about the almost fatal crash: "As he hurtled downhill, off the road, McQueen did a superb job of propelling the Cooper between a series of poles and metal signs that could have demolished it. He controlled his slide until the final instant, looped, and slammed the car at an angle into a dirt embankment. The Cooper snapped around like a top, whirling around and bouncing, but miraculously did not turn over."

For the last scene of the film, shot in the cockpit of an airplane, Leacock let McQueen, complete with fat bottom lip and scratches, wear an oxygen mask to hide any bruises that might show up on the screen.

When *The War Lover* was released in October 1962, it was met with mixed reactions. In Britain, the film was an instant success and propelled Steve to movie stardom. In the U.S., it was a different story. The film didn't do quite as well, as one critic called the film "a curious mixture of authentic and phony." The *Washington Post* felt the picture "goes to remarkable trouble to avoid what it is talking about." Manager Hilly Elkins agreed. "It was a good idea that went amok. We agreed to do it because it was an interesting role, though the picture was flawed. The picture had no cohesiveness."

Even though the picture was flawed, McQueen's performance was not. *The War Lover* proved that Steve McQueen was not just a reactor, but an actor as well. His portrayal of Buzz Rickson is seriously underrated as one of the best in his early career. Mike Frankovich observes, "He could turn his character on and off. At certain moments, he became the little boy with that side grin of his—then, boom, he's back in the driver's seat again as an actor, totally immersed in what he's doing. That suit of clothing that he could put on once the cameras were rolling was amazing, so he did have that ability. If I were to make a judgment, I think he was having a little fun at people's expense. People expected him to be the consummate Method actor in the mold of Marlon Brando. I think he fooled a lot of people. It made him a better actor because of it.

"He lived life like there was no tomorrow. He lived life all out. Damn the torpedoes, full speed ahead."

Safely back in California, Steve kept up his Formula racing and was genuinely flattered when John Cooper asked him to become a team member of the British Motor Corporation (BMC) and race professionally in Europe. Steve faced the most difficult decision of his professional career. He told William Nolan, "They gave me a weekend to make up my mind. I spent two full days in a sweat, trying to decide whether I wanted to go into pro racing, earning my money on the track, or whether I wanted to continue being an actor. It was a very tough decision for me to reach, because I didn't know if I was an actor who raced or a racer who acted. But I had Neile and our two children to consider, and that made a difference. I turned down the BMC offer. But I came very close to chucking my film career. I hadn't done anything really important or outstanding on the screen, and I was tired of waiting for the 'big picture,' the one that hopefully would break me through."*

Hilly Elkins had tired of the Hollywood scene. He felt unfulfilled in the management area and wanted to try his hand at producing Broadway plays. Then the vice president at General Artists Corporation, Elkins left his position to work with Sammy Davis, Jr., in *Golden Boy*. But before leaving Hollywood, he perhaps made the best career move for McQueen, by placing him in the very capable hands of agent Stan Kamen at the William Morris Agency.

McQueen and Elkins had been together for over five years when the two parted ways. "There was always a testing in that relationship," Elkins notes. "How big am I really? How much shit can I get away with? He wanted to get my opinion on a project before he got his opinion out on the table, threatening in a benign way to do something that was off the wall. When push came to shove, he backed down. We were very close. We spent a lot of time together and I enjoyed it.

"Steve was very quixotic and had very wide mood swings, capable of having enormous fun. We were two juveniles fucking with the system and having it work. We would spend a week on location and mostly had laughs until someone fucked up, a self-contained, nonverbal kind of fury.

"He knew he was a good actor, and he was able to communicate that on the screen. But there was a streak of paranoia that kept him from totally enjoying his life."

For one year the two men did not communicate, but eventually McQueen did call. They stayed in touch throughout Steve's life and remained friends.

*The Great Escape* was a film Steve entered into with great trepidation. When the call came from John Sturges for the part of Captain Virgil Hilts, Steve told the director, "I dunno, Johnny. I just did two World War II flicks, and they both died in the stretch."

McQueen felt that the part of Hilts had "no juice." The script itself

---

* Nolan, William, *McQueen* (New York: Congdon & Weed, 1984), 47.

McQueen starred as Captain Virgil Hilts, also known as "Cooler King," in
*The Great Escape*. McQueen listens intently as director John Sturges makes a
suggestion.                                              (COURTESY OF UNITED ARTISTS)

was not finished, and what Steve saw of it, he wasn't that impressed. He
was not alone.

*The Great Escape* was taken from Paul Brickhill's 1950 novel (though
actually based on a true story) recounting a breakout from a World War
II German prisoner of war camp.

In March 1943 Brickhill was shot down over the Tunisian desert in
North Africa. He was then captured by Rommel's notorious Afrika
Korps and taken, along with 700 American and British officers, to a
newly constructed compound in Sagan, Germany, just ninety miles
southeast of Berlin.

The compound featured the latest in security measures, surrounded
by nine-foot-high barbed wire fences complete with machine-gun towers and fully armed soldiers on foot. The camp, called Stalag Luft III,
was considered inescapable.

Brickhill, along with 250 other prisoners, had planned to make "The
Great Escape." The night of the breakout, however, only seventy-six
men actually managed to escape via an underground tunnel. Of those

seventy-six men, only three made their way to England. The others were recaptured and executed by the German gestapo or returned to high-security prisons. Brickhill was one of the three survivors.

Four years after his escape, Paul Brickhill completed his account.

Director John Sturges read the book in 1950 and firmly believed that it would make an incredible movie. For thirteen years, he tried to get the project off the ground. "It was the perfect embodiment of why our side won! Here was the German military machine, the sparkling uniforms and the absolute obedience to orders. On the other side of the wire, there were men from every country, every background, makeup, and language, doing everything they pleased. With no arbitrary rules, they voluntarily formulated an organization that eventually clobbered the German machine."*

Though Sturges had several hit films under his belt, he still had to pitch his idea to Louis B. Mayer, head of MGM. In a private meeting, he gave Mayer and the other executives a quick synopsis of the story. Dismayed by the execution of the prisoners at the end of the story, they put Sturges through the wringer. "What the hell kind of a great escape is this? Only three people get away," Mayer grumbled. In the end, it was decided, the film would cost MGM $10 million. Sturges was shown the door.

Says associate producer Robert Relyea, "You ever see a bulldog with lockjaw? That was John Sturges." Sturges continued to make successful films, and eventually, in 1959, he broke away from MGM and made *The Magnificent Seven* for United Artists and The Mirisch Corporation. *The Magnificent Seven* was such a success that Sturges could now write his own ticket. "You always have problems getting a movie off the ground," said Sturges. "I waited till I had enough prestige as a director. If you make successful movies, big hits, and you come up with something they may not like, they may hate it, but if you want to do it, they start to think, 'If we don't let him do what he wants, he'll go to another studio that will let him and we'll lose him.' That was the case with *The Great Escape*. The only reason why United Artists agreed to do it was that it was a multiple-character story, and I had done *The Magnificent Seven* for them and it was a success. You can't argue with the guy who just made a big hit. He's liable to say, 'I'll see you around.' "

United Artists gave the project the green light and a tight budget of $4 million. With the film to be shot totally on location in Germany, Sturges would have to make do with a lot of nothing.

Sturges then wrote a letter to Brickhill, espousing his love for the

---

* Rubin, Steven Jay, *Combat Films* (Jefferson, N.C.: McFarland & Company, Inc., 1981), 85.

book and describing his thirteen-year journey to getting it made as a movie.

For years, Brickhill had had generous film offers from Hollywood, some downright crazy, but he had visions of his book being turned into an unfactual account of his stay in prison. He agreed to meet with Sturges in Hollywood and was struck by Sturges' sincerity. Under no terms would the story be changed, Brickhill was assured. The two men shook hands and a deal was struck.

A first draft, only sixty-four pages long, was written by William Roberts. Then a second draft was assigned to writer Walter Newman. Newman never finished his version, as he complained that Sturges was too busy working on other projects at the time.

Veteran scriptwriter W. R. Burnett was brought in to add American characters to the British-dominated storyline. McQueen's character, American Captain Virgil Hilts, "the Cooler King," was based on the life of George Harsh, a British soldier who led the attempted breakout. Harsh himself didn't escape, but he did survive the war. (He died of natural causes in 1978 in Toronto, Canada.)

A hardly presentable draft was completed when McQueen was asked to play Hilts. James Garner was already signed as "the Scrounger," and Steve felt that Garner's role was much more defined than his. Sturges told McQueen, "The loner's the part you want." McQueen trusted Sturges in the past and figured that he had nothing to lose by trusting him again. He had one stipulation, though: that he escape by motorcycle at the end of the film. Sturges agreed, but he had his own stipulation: Steve could not do any riding off the set of the movie. McQueen later commented, "I figure I came out a winner, but Sturges thought he also won with the exciting scenes he got of the bikes being driven pell-mell over the countryside."

With the motorcycle scenes in mind, Steve paid a visit to Bud Ekins's motorcycle shop. Remembers Ekins, "I had known him about two years and one day in '62 he says, 'Gonna make a movie in Germany. Gonna have a motorcycle in it. Called *The Great Escape*. I steal a motorcycle and we have a big chase sequence. Wanna come to Germany and double me?' Ekins thought, "Bullshit. Never happen." To be obliging, but without much sincerity, Ekins said, "Yeah, sure."

A week later Ekins received a phone call from the actor. "Gotta suit?" Ekins was asked. "Yeah, why?" he asked. McQueen continued, "Well, put it on. I want you to come down and meet the director. I'll pick you up." Laughs Ekins, "So I've got on this stupid suit and McQueen pulls up in his Jag and he's wearing blue jeans and a T-shirt. We drive down to the studio and Sturges is wearing the same thing. He'd do weird things like that, just to put me on. Nothing harmful; he'd just twist things around, I don't know why. Anyway, I get there and Sturges opens the door and Steve says, 'This is Bud.' He looks at Steve and me and nods his head. Hell, in a few weeks, I was in Germany."

For his part, McQueen was paid a hefty $100,000 to secure his name to the picture, while the rest of the cast was assembled. Eventually, the cast was rounded out by James Garner, Charles Bronson, James Coburn, James Donald, Richard Attenborough, David McCallum, and Donald Pleasance.

The British actors, Richard Attenborough, James Donald, and Donald Pleasance, arrived later on location, with McQueen, Coburn, Bronson, and Garner waiting for them. The wait only seemed to make McQueen more nervous. Remembers Bud Ekins, "I can tell you that some of those heavy-duty English actors on *The Great Escape* really scared the shit out of Steve. All those English guys were stage people, and they had a different presence than McQueen." Just a year earlier, McQueen had been boasting to Shirley Anne Field on *The War Lover* that the Americans were far superior actors on the screen than the British. In his heart, he may have felt that was true, but his actions did not back up his boast. "In my country, actors are looked down on," he now said. "Not in Britain . . . because there you have the background of the theatrical dignity."

Costar Richard Attenborough disputes McQueen's claim. "It was a unique situation. The American actors arrived first, then the British actors arrived. The Americans expected the British actors to be a bit snobbish, because the British actors back then were held in such high regard. It's funny because ever since Brando came on the scene, the Americans were way ahead of the British cinema. The British cinema was a bit "talky," whereas the American films relied primarily on expressions and emotions. It was just more realistic. Little did the American actors realize that we were just as much in awe of them as they were of us."

A fourth writer, James Clavell of *King Rat, Shōgun,* and *Tai-Pan* fame, was brought in to put the final touches on the script (dubbed by Sturges now "The Great Headache"). By June 4, 1962, John Sturges's dream project was under way.

After Steve's thrilling opening sequence in the film, he is not seen again until thirty minutes into the movie. McQueen pleaded with Sturges to add extra scenes to his role to keep his character alive. Sturges had made an oversight, he admitted, and would try to make amends. He asked McQueen to stay on hand until he worked something out. "Nothing doing," Sturges was told, and Steve temporarily walked off the picture.

Steve made a phone call to agent Stan Kamen, and Kamen was on the next plane to Germany to try and patch things up.

"Garner's controlling the picture," Steve complained to Kamen. "He's going to come out of this a star, not me!"

Kamen held a meeting with Sturges and told the director of McQueen's fears. "He has nothing to worry about," said Sturges. A writer was assigned to Steve, and new parts were eventually added to placate the insecure actor. Said on-location screenwriter W. R. Burnett, "McQueen was an impossible bastard. A third of the way through the picture he took charge. I had to rewrite scenes and rearrange them. Ohhh, he drove you crazy."

Costar James Coburn says, "Steve made people on *The Great Escape* uptight. In fact, I don't think he cared if he made people uptight. He demanded things, and he got them. If he didn't get them, he didn't go to work. I can remember Richard Attenborough and me waiting around on the set for Steve, and then he asked me, 'What's the matter with Steve? Why does he act that way?' And I couldn't answer him. It was just his nature to be who he was. It seemed that everybody else was in control and had an awareness of who he was and what he was doing. Steve was always worried about this or that, like bad things were going to come after him. Paranoia. Imaginary fear of being dominated, of somehow being put in a compromising position.

"Steve liked to watch the scene being rehearsed and watch how the others would act so he would know all of the boundaries to watch out for. The British would always base their character on what the character would do, whereas Steve would base his character on what Steve McQueen would do. And, strangely enough, it worked for him. That personality, that theme is what he created and everybody in the theater wanted to see it," says Coburn.

"It didn't cause other people happiness, but it did cause him to be a star, so you can't fault that. He was a very complicated, complex guy, yet he was very simple. Very simple and straightforward. He was selfish, but I don't think he thought he was being selfish. I thought he was doing everything for the good of him. That's not selfish, but self-protective. I think that stems from being an abandoned child. It was all a test. A psychological thing.

"The role in *The Great Escape* wasn't originally built around him. He had to develop it. He wanted that separation from the other men. He was in the cell and always had to be brought in as a separate prisoner.

Making booze on the set of *The Great Escape*, 1963. Director John Sturges talking to James Garner and Steve McQueen. (COURTESY OF UNITED ARTISTS)

He was always an individual, which was very clever of him," Coburn notes.

Richard Attenborough remembers a different side of McQueen on *The Great Escape*. "Steve was very professional," says Attenborough. "If the script was bad, which it was in the first draft of *The Great Escape*, then yes, he put up a fuss. He was a perfectionist in every sense of the word. All those rumors about his being hard to get along with are scandalously untrue. I can remember rehearsing with him for weeks, because we had a lot of scenes together. Not one incident of ugly behavior sticks out in my mind. I admired his integrity.

"He had that aura of mystique that at any time he was going to blow up into a thousand pieces. He was available emotionally. There were no pretenses. He gave you that feeling that if you were to meet him on the street, he would be totally approachable. He also had that slight wickedness that came across on the screen," says Attenborough.

As McQueen did in real life, his character in *The Great Escape* tested the bounds of authority. The brash, cocky dialogue Steve injected into

Steve McQueen with James Garner on the set of *The Great Escape*, 1963.

Hilts defined the McQueen code. Hilts is first introduced in the film rolling a baseball against the barbed wire fence, a test to find out if the guards can see him at a certain angle. Hilts is caught by the guards and brought before the commandant, Von Luger.

> VON LUGER: You are the first American officer I have met. Hilts, isn't it?
>
> HILTS: Captain Hilts, actually.
>
> VON LUGER: Seventeen escape attempts.
>
> HILTS: Eighteen.
>
> VON LUGER: Tunnel man, engineer?
>
> HILTS: Flier.
>
> VON LUGER: I suppose you're called in the American Army "a hotshot pilot."
>
> HILTS: Mmmhmm.
>
> VON LUGER: Unfortunately, you were shot down anyway. So we are both grounded for the duration of the war.
>
> HILTS: Well, you speak for yourself, Colonel.
>
> VON LUGER: You have other plans?

HILTS: I haven't seen Berlin yet from the ground or from the or the air, and I plan on seeing both, before the end of the war is over.

VON LUGER: Are all American officers so ill-mannered?

HILTS: About 99 percent.

VON LUGER: Then perhaps when you are with us, you'll have a chance to learn something. Ten days isolation, Hilts.

HILTS: (Grabs his lapel) Captain Hilts.

VON LUGER: Twenty days.

HILTS: Right. Oh, uh, you'll still be here when I get out?

VON LUGER: Cooler.

HILTS: (Smiles)

As Hilts heads for the cooler, he takes his baseball and glove with him. There he sits on the floor, throwing the baseball against the wall and catching it, thinking of his next escape.

If Steve was selfish as an actor, he was just as generous when not in front of the camera. Bud Ekins was brought along as McQueen's stunt double. One day on the set, while he and Steve were talking, Ekins got up to get some coffee. "You want any?" he asked McQueen. "Yeah. Hang on. You sit down. I'll get it." Ekins objected. "I can get the damn coffee." Steve made it clear that he was going to go. Ekins said, "Okay, go get the damn coffee." McQueen came back and handed Ekins a cup, but not before telling him, "Lesson number one in the movie business: everybody knows you're a friend of mine. That's why you're here. If you get my coffee, that also means you're my fuckin' flunky. You ain't my fuckin' flunky, so I'll get the coffee from now on." In retrospect, says Ekins, "It goes to show you Steve's personality as far as dealing with people. He was very astute. He knew how people thought. Pretty intelligent for a guy with no education."

With renewed vigor in his growing role, Steve was a happy man. The movie's finale, the motorcycle chase, was ready to be filmed. Steve's character, Hilts, breaks out of the prison compound and manages to steal a motorcycle from a German soldier by stretching piano wire across a road and knocking the soldier off his bike. Sturges read that the French Underground had actually done this. "What they would do was wait until nightfall along the forest roads where the dispatch cars ran," said Sturges. "No one knew who rode in them, high brass or couriers, but they would often travel like a bat out of hell with motorcycle guards front and rear. The French quickly got the notion of stretching piano wire across the road at a forty-five-degree angle terminating in a gully.

McQueen tells director John Sturges how he perceives a particular scene on the set of *The Great Escape*, 1963.          (COURTESY OF UNITED ARTISTS)

They would let all these fellows pass by and then lift the wire on the last rider, who was immediately clobbered."

Hilts then undresses the German soldier and takes his motorcycle. Soon thereafter, he is asked for identification by another soldier. Hilts kicks the soldier, takes off his uniform, and is off again with a whole slew of Germans chasing him.

For that particular scene, McQueen kept outrunning the German stunt riders. As Sturges tried to figure out what to do, he felt someone tapping on his shoulder. He turned around and saw McQueen dressed as a German soldier, donning a pair of granny glasses. "Now you know they wouldn't recognize me," said Steve. "By God, they wouldn't," replied the director.

In effect, Steve McQueen was in pursuit of Steve McQueen. Through clever editing, you could never tell it was Steve. Said Sturges, "The

Germans had a lot of guts, but they weren't really stuntmen. Curiously enough, if you're a real motorcyclist, you're not necessarily a good stuntman, because a stuntman knows how to fall off a bike, whereas a real professional bike rider's whole purpose is to try and stay on the bike. We were lucky to have Steve stay with us. With exceptional cutting he could have played the entire German motorcycle corps."

McQueen's most exciting moment in *The Great Escape* is the climactic motorcycle jump over a six-foot-high barbed wire fence. This was why Bud Ekins was brought to Germany. The fence was in the middle of the German countryside, and a ramp could not be used to make the jump.

A natural wallow was located near the barbed wire. Ekins recalls, "John Sturges came to me one day and said, 'Bud, can you jump a motorcycle over a fence?' I said, 'Yeah.' He asked, 'How high?' I said about five feet. He goes, 'Yeah, okay.' So that was that. And he accepted that. Later on Sturges showed us the wallow we were to jump over the fence with."

The first jump made by Ekins only got up two feet in the air and ten feet in length. Ekins discovered that if they dug a ramp out of the dirt, he could increase the height and the distance of the jump. McQueen, Ekins, and Australian stunt rider Tim Gibbs spent the rest of the day digging. Pretty soon the jumps got up to four feet, then six feet, then ten feet. Says Ekins, "The ramp was shaped like a spoon. You come and you drop, which drops your suspension, then you come around and you lift up. The way we designed it was that you would land uphill, taking off downhill. We maxed out at fourteen feet high and sixty-five feet long."

The scene was to take place the next day, and the three men were so excited that they made a vow to keep it a secret. The next day, a Monday, at two o'clock, Ekins already had on his makeup, his wardrobe, and was ready to make the jump. "That barbed wire was the real damn thing," he says.

Sturges and crew were ready to film. McQueen was on the sidelines holding his breath as Ekins revved the souped-up Triumph. Ekins was given the signal, and he accelerated toward the wallow. He hit the ramp and sailed over the six-foot-high fence with ease. "Nothing like that had ever been done before," claims Ekins.

As the crew cheered and whistled, Ekins was the hero of the day. McQueen offered his hand and exclaimed, "That was bitchin'!"

Movie audiences around the world couldn't believe what they saw. Kent Twitchell, a U.S. Air Force serviceman stationed in England, remembered, "When *The Great Escape* first came out in movie theaters, every Saturday night the Mods and the Rockers would pack the theaters

Steve takes a break on the set of *The Great Escape*, 1963.

just to see the jump. As McQueen soared over that fence, these British kids would go bananas and stand up and cheer wildly, even though they had seen the movie several times."

In the Soviet Union, McQueen was voted Best Actor in the Moscow International Film Festival, the first time an American had taken the honor.

Steve's instinct to separate himself from the other actors in the film proved correct, as he was singled out as the star of the film. Judith Crist of the *New York Herald* wrote, "A first-rate adventure film, fascinating in its detail, suspenseful in its plot, stirring in its climax and excellent in performance. Steve McQueen plays a familiar American war-movie type —brash, self-interested, super-brave emoter. For sheer bravura, whether he's pounding a baseball in his catcher's mitt in solitary or stumping cross-country on a motorcycle with scores of Germans in pursuit, Steve McQueen takes the honors."

*Variety* observed, "The most provocative single impression is made by Steve McQueen. He has a style, an individuality, that is rare in the contemporary scene."

*Life* magazine declared him "the next big movie star."

John Sturges commented on the McQueen appeal, "When you find somebody with that kind of talent, you use him. Steve is unique. The way Cary Grant is unique, or Spencer Tracy or Marlon Brando. There's something bubbling inside of him; he's got a quality of excitement that he brings to everything he does. Like most good actors, he likes an 'attitude'—he likes to know where he stands in relation to the action of a scene, rather than just come on and act—then he goes from there. Steve has a great interest in people. Watch him as he sits there and listens, hunching himself up. That's why you can't take your eyes off him on screen. He's alive!"

*The Great Escape* went on to become part of cinematic history. The film grossed $16 million at the box office. Suddenly Steve McQueen was the hottest name in Hollywood. "Actually, Steve was a star after *The Magnificent Seven*," commented John Sturges. "It just took *The Great Escape* to get it through the producers' heads that Steve was a star."

Movie producers put in the trade papers that they were looking for a "Steve McQueen"–type actor. Steve laughed. "What does this mean? I don't even know how to classify myself."

Just as Bud Ekins made the jump over the famed barbed wire fence, so Steve McQueen made the jump from television celebrity to international movie star, the first actor ever to do so successfully.

Publicity photo for *The Great Escape*, 1963. This film would prove to be McQueen's breakthrough as a star.

(Courtesy of United Artists)

# MILK AND HONEY

*I just want the brass ring and the pine trees and my kids and the green grass. I want to get rich and fat and watch my kids grow.*

STEVE MCQUEEN

STEVE REVELED in his newfound celebrity status. Stardom ensured him happiness, or so he thought. With the smashing success of *The Great Escape*, he could now write his own ticket. "Then he got very demanding," says James Coburn. "He went for the moon and got as much as he could."

The McQueens were moving up in the world. Steve and Neile purchased a $300,000 estate in the exclusive Brentwood neighborhood, dubbed by the McQueens "the Castle." The Spanish-style house came complete with an imposing front gate that stood fifteen feet high and thirty feet wide. A winding driveway went up to the red-tiled house set on three and a half acres. The property featured a large swimming pool, a yard filled with trees, and a grand view of the Pacific.

Now that Steve's salary had climbed to $300,000 a film, he and Neile spent money with a vengeance. Most of it went into classic cars Steve had always dreamed of owning. His collection included a D-type mint condition Jaguar, a Triumph, a Mini-Cooper, a Lincoln, a Porsche, a Ferrari, a Volkswagen, a dune buggy, and most curiously, a U.S. Army half-track Land Rover. Once while in Palm Springs, Steve took Don Gordon to the drive-in movies in the half-track. Says Gordon, "One day McQueen says to me, 'Hey, man, let's go to the drive-in movies.' Neile bought him this half-track for his birthday. The front of the truck has wheels like a regular truck and the back of it is like a tank. It is a tank. It has an area for a fifty-caliber machine gun. So, we go to the drive-in in this half-track. And where does he go? Over the sands and over dunes.

That's how we went to the movies. How can you not have fun with a guy like that?"

To his close friends, stardom didn't change Steve a bit. He was the same as he was when he was a struggling actor. "When an actor's riding the crest, it's hard to keep his balance. People at the studio fetch and carry for you, running errands, assuming responsibilities. A star doesn't have to look around when he sits down. Somebody's always there to do it for him. But away from the studio—that's when you have to remember it's all wrong. That's when you have to watch for the phonies. You've got to remember who you really are. Because, man, you may not be up there very long," Steve took note. "When you start believing everything that is written about you, there is a tendency to get too big for your britches." McQueen pointed out that it was Neile and his close friends who kept him centered. "When I start thinking I'm the cat's behind, my old lady says to me, 'What's your story, McQueen?' And I'm back to normal. My friends treat me no differently than they treat anybody else. As far as how important I am, that doesn't mean beans to them or to me. The people I'm concerned about are ordinary guys. I don't care what a guy does for a living, whether he's a statesman or a farmer." It was only the studio executives who felt the wrath of the mighty McQueen.

Neile purchased furnishings for their new home: antiques, chandeliers, paintings, and rugs. Steve commented at the time, "Neile never buys things just to buy them. Every piece of furniture, every picture has to be just right—what she thinks I am. They've become part of our lives, every chunk. Part of my blood, too."

McQueen no longer had to rely on Hedda Hopper or Louella Parsons to keep his name in the papers. *Life* magazine had wanted to do a story on Steve since *The War Lover,* but he had put them off. He now felt that he was a bona fide movie star and obliged them. David Foster set up the article and *Life* sent photographer John Dominis to Los Angeles. The two men agreed that because McQueen was such a physical person with cars, motorcycles, and such, a feature with him camping in the great outdoors would be a good idea for part of the layout. Steve agreed to it and decided to enlist the help of James Coburn, Bud Ekins, Don Gordon, and David Foster. Recalls Coburn, "Steve called me up and asked me to go camping with him. 'Gotta make me look good, Coburn. Gotta make me look good.' "

The men decided to go to the Ojai mountains, just an hour outside Los Angeles. Says David Foster, "John Dominis is really an outdoorsman. He's like the Marlboro man, and Steve brings along this nice fancy tent and spiffy utensils. He's cooking beans and they're exploding all over the place. Dominis pulls me aside and asks, 'Does he know what he's doing?' and I say, 'Yeah, as far as I know, he does.' "

James Coburn remembers, "It was funny. None of us knew how to camp. It was an awful routine. We sent out for hamburgers. Everything was a pretense. Pretending to be something that we weren't. Every chance we got, we'd go out in Steve's Land Rover and smoke a joint, then head back to the campsite. We just wanted a change of consciousness because we were so bored. It was all a put-on for *Life*."

Dominis realized after a while that they really didn't know what the hell they were doing, but he continued to play it straight. McQueen was miserable but felt that the layout would be great for his image, so he stayed. The next morning Dominis started taking pictures. Steve pulled out a hunting knife and began shaving with cold water minus the shaving cream. Sensing the boredom, Dominis told McQueen he'd taken enough shots. McQueen announced, "Great, let's go!" They were packed within minutes and were home within an hour. Laughs David Foster, "McQueen didn't want to be in the woods. He wanted to be home in his million-dollar mansion and kick back."

The week before the story was to come out, John Dominis was sent to the Vatican to cover President Kennedy's meeting with the pope. Dominis was chosen as one of the proof photographers—one of only three covering the event. *Time, Newsweek,* and *Look* magazines were all going to use the Dominis photos of the papal meeting for their cover story. *Life* decided to go with the Steve McQueen cover, and it outsold all of them.

The *Life* magazine story caught the attention of the FBI. The text accompanying the pictures, quotes from Steve, raised some eyebrows over at the FBI office in New York. A memo regarding the interview read:

Report of: (deleted)              Office: NEW YORK, NY
    Date: August 1, 1963
    Title: <u>STEVE McQUEEN</u> subject of "Life" Magazine article.

On the cover of the July 12, 1963, issue of "Life" Magazine appears a photograph of <u>STEVE McQUEEN</u> and his wife bearing the notation, "<u>Steve McQueen</u> Moves in on the Movies and Becomes Its Hottest New Star," sub-captioned "The Bad Boy's Breakout." On page 68, in part, appears the following:

"Man, if I hadn't made my own scene," says <u>STEVE McQUEEN</u>, "I could have wound up a hood instead of an actor." He talks the lingo of the rough world that spawned him, a world of hipsters, racing car drivers, beach boys, drifters and carnival barkers. STEVE has been all of these. He has also tended bar, sold encyclopedias, made sandals and been a runner in a Port Arthur, Texas, brothel—going from one job to the next, trying to run from his dreary, dreadful past.

STEVE has been running that way ever since he was a kid. His father began it by running out on the family while STEVE was still a baby. Mrs. McQUEEN farmed STEVE out to an uncle in Missouri. At 12 STEVE fled to New York. He later lived with his mother and new stepfather in California, but that was no improvement. He spent so much time in the streets and so little time in school that his mother sent him away for rehabilitation. He promptly ran away and wound up in jail. Even in the marines, STEVE wouldn't stay put. He spent 41 days in the brig for going AWOL.

(deleted) was acquainted with STEVE McQUEEN. (deleted) stated that STEVE left home of his own accord.

(deleted) described STEVE McQUEEN as a "tough kid" who was very aggressive, moved around with the beatnik crowd, and was always interested in motorcycles." STEVE worked at acting, which was the only thing in his life.

Fame can be a double-edged sword, glamorous and intoxicating, yet dangerous. As Steve was becoming more famous, he was being watched more closely by Big Brother, only he didn't know it.

On August 28, 1963, a group of sixty to ninety Hollywood personalities were to march in Washington, D.C., in support of Dr. Martin Luther King, Jr., and the civil rights movement. Steve was rumored to be participating in the march, and again his name was put in the FBI's little black book. One memo read:

### MARCH ON WASHINGTON (MOW)
8/23/63

(deleted) advised August 12, 1963, that a group of about 60 to 90 movie personalities (deleted) plan to take part in the March on Washington, August 28, 1963. He furnished a list of the following individuals, who he stated have confirmed their intention to be in the above-mentioned group:

| | | |
|---|---|---|
| Charlton Heston | Harry Karl | Blake Edwards |
| Tony Franciosa | Debbie Reynolds | James Garner |
| Marlon Brando | Harry Belafonte | Fred Zinneman |
| Tony Curtis | Edward Lewis | Mrs. Ivan Tors |
| Billy Wilder | Sidney Poitier | Curtis Harrington |

| | | |
|---|---|---|
| Burt Lancaster | Diahann Carroll | Lou Garfunkel |
| Dean Martin | James Baldwin | Dennis Harper |
| Peter Brown | Lena Horne | Brooke Hayward |
| Virgil Frye | Nat Cole | Eartha Kitt |
| David Susskind | Joanne Woodward | John Houseman |
| Steve McQueen | Paul Newman | Alan King |
| Gene Kelly | Sammy Davis, Jr. | Martin Ritt |
| Jack Paar | Ossie Davis | Pearl Bailey |
| Gregory Peck | Ruby Dee | Eugene Franke |
| Doug McClure | Lorraine Hansberry | Richard Rust |
| George Jessel | Robert Goulet | Sandra Lynn |
| Stanley Shapiro | Carol Lawrence | Fred Rousse |
| Robert Wise | John Oliver Killens | Toni Kimmell |
| Charles Lederer | Rita Moreno | Aram Kantarian |
| Judy Garland | Dick Gregory | Kirk Douglas |
| Mel Ferrer | | |

(deleted) stated that this group agreed that they did not desire a group name, but that they plan to charter a Lockheed Electra airplane with a 92-person seating capacity for $14,000 through the American Fliers, Inc., Burbank, California.

He stated this plane is scheduled to leave Los Angeles International Airport the evening of August 27, 1963, that the group will participate in the March on Washington on August 28, 1963, and on this same date will return to Los Angeles in the evening.

(deleted) stated that funds for the chartered plane will be raised from *this above described group of participants* only and that *this group* is not coordinating any other Los Angeles group intending to participate in the March on Washington.

This document contains neither recommendations nor conclusions of the FBI. It is the property of the FBI and is loaned to your agency; it and its contents are not to be distributed outside your agency.

For whatever reasons, Steve did not participate on the March in Washington. He did, however, express his opinions on politics and race to *Variety:* "Though actors who mix into politics want to do good, they must be sure that the stand they are taking is valid. We have a lot of kitchen cleaning to do in Hollywood, and I think we're doing it. As for the problems of employing Negroes, I think you should use a Negro actor because he is good at his craft and not simply because he is a Negro."

Steve followed *The Great Escape* with the comedy-farce *Soldier in the Rain.* "I hadn't done any comedy since *The Honeymoon Machine,*" Steve said. "I felt it was time to do something different. But the picture just didn't come together. I really don't know why, because all the right elements were there."

Indeed they were, with the script provided by Blake Edwards, later director of *The Pink Panther* films. Ralph Nelson was enlisted to direct it. Hot off the success of *Lilies of the Field,* Nelson was highly sought after. Jackie Gleason, one of the most talented and funniest comedians of the day, was to play opposite Steve. The Gleason/McQueen marquee was a "can't miss."

McQueen played Sergeant Eustis Clay, a bumbling but lovable southern character. His friend, Sergeant Maxwell Slaughter (Gleason), plays the straight man to McQueen's idiot. Clay tries to persuade Slaughter to leave the service and become his business partner. Slaughter is not so eager to leave the army, as he is content with his air conditioner and free soda pop machine. In time, Slaughter reveals his dream of retiring to a Pacific island, holding a girl with one hand, a soda with the other. The ending is bittersweet, with Slaughter dying in a hospital bed. With the death of Slaughter, Clay's dreams end and he reenlists, raising a glass to toast his best friend.

*Soldier in the Rain* was to be done by Solar Productions, a company Steve had formed in 1961. Now that he was a genuine movie star, he decided to put it to use. Though not yet a full-scale production company, Solar was a nice tax shelter for the now in-demand McQueen. His salary was a staggering $300,000 plus any profits the film might show after the break-even point.

Adam West, later television's Batman, had a small part in the film. He remembers having a drink with some friends at the hotel where the cast and crew were staying on location in Northern California. Recalls West, "I was having a beer and in walked McQueen. He looked around, seemed kind of shy, and walked away."

Tony Bill, then an actor and later the coproducer of *The Sting* and director of *My Bodyguard,* was a relative newcomer. Says Bill, "It was Steve McQueen who everybody was in fear of. Ralph Nelson, the director, was an extremely gentle and kind man, but it was very clear that he was not in charge of decision-making on the set. It became very clear that that was going to be Steve McQueen's call. It was my second movie and I was pretty naive. I just treated him like a normal guy and we got along great."

As for McQueen's costar, Jackie Gleason, the relationship was anything but buddy-buddy. Testing Gleason, as he had Robert Wagner on the set of *The War Lover,* McQueen decided that since he was the star, he should arrive only after Gleason. "McQueen had just become a big star off of *The Great Escape,"* says Tony Bill, "so he was really having that heady feeling of stardom at the time and was prone to showing up late on the set. Jackie Gleason found himself in the position of being on the set, waiting for the arrival of young Mr. McQueen. Gleason, being a consummate professional and an extremely experienced performer, started getting annoyed with this. Shortly after we started filming, I guess he let it be known that he would no longer show up at the set before McQueen. Steve got wind of this and there was a short-lived stalemate between the two of them. Neither one would show up until the other was there. That was worked out as the movie progressed."

Steve then turned his arrogance on the director. He asked Nelson if he planned to do the obligatory master shots. "Yes, of course," Nelson replied. The new movie star said, "Well, I don't do master shots." McQueen's legendary status reached an all-time high or low, depending on how you looked at it.

In the film, Gleason rides around in a souped-up golf cart. He was riding around the lot one day when he almost ran over his crass young costar. Steve told Bud Ekins, "He's fucking dangerous! He's going to roll over somebody."

Whatever grievances the two stars had with each other during filming, it was forgotten when *Soldier in the Rain* was released. Gleason told the press, "He's a conscientious kid, and he works hard. There's very little horseplay when you're working with him. He wants to get the job done and go on to something else. Steve put all he had into the role, being well aware that comedy is very serious business." McQueen returned the favor by saying, "Gleason is a much better actor than people give him credit for."

*Soldier in the Rain* was savaged by the critics, as everything about the picture was a disaster. Judith Christ of the *New York Herald* wrote that "McQueen, one of the more exciting actors around, is totally suppressed as a mush-mouthed stupid devoted to dawg and buddy to the point of tears." Bosley Crowther of the *New York Times* pointed out, "The principal character in this flim-flam is a simpleton soldier who Steve McQueen succeeds in making just about as unattractive as any poor bumbling simpleton could be." *Variety* observed, "McQueen will not please his fans with the characterization he has created—a kind of

Southern-fried boob who reminds one of Clem Kadiddlehopper." And Archer Winston of the *New York Post* predicted that *Soldier in the Rain* "should set back [McQueen's] blossoming career one giant step."

The film was released November 27, 1963, just five days after the assassination of John F. Kennedy. (McQueen had actually met Kennedy in 1960 in Santa Monica. He was then invited to the White House but didn't go because he was racing in Europe at the time.) The country, much less the critics, was in no mood to laugh. The film proved to be one of Steve McQueen's biggest bombs.

McQueen quickly followed *Soldier in the Rain* with his first romantic lead in *Love with the Proper Stranger*. Paul Newman was originally sought for the part by director Robert Mulligan. Mulligan, just off the recent success of *To Kill a Mockingbird*, was convinced that McQueen could just as easily do the role as Newman (after Newman had turned it down, of course). This moody, often funny picture was way ahead of its time, with its main theme dealing with abortion. Steve played Rocky, a free-wheeling, bed-hopping musician who spends one night with Angie (Natalie Wood) and quickly forgets her. That is, until she reenters his life to inform him that she is pregnant. Thinking quickly, he replies, "Congratulations!" hoping to slough off any fatherly responsibilities. Deeply despaired, she leaves and Rocky follows after her. The two then decide to raise money for her abortion. But Rocky cannot stand the back alley conditions that Angie must endure. He takes a gallant stand and decides to do the decent thing and marry her. She balks at first, but Rocky shows up where she works and pickets outside, his sign reading "Better Wed than Dead."

Director Robert Mulligan explained, "It has lots of humor, but it is not a comedy in the sense that a Stanley Shapiro movie is a comedy. We are trying for realism. Under such conditions humor can come even from misfortune. It all depends on how well we capture the authenticity of the people."

Throughout the filming, Natalie Wood tried desperately to woo McQueen, as it was well known she took pride in bedding all of her costars. Against his nature, Steve dismissed her openly flagrant come-ons. He liked her ex-husband, Robert Wagner, and felt it would be against his code of ethics. Wood was so desperate, in fact, that she would dangle one leg out her dressing room door as Steve walked by. When Steve arrived home to Neile, he would laugh as he recalled the daily seducement. Neile didn't think it a bit funny, and Steve surprisingly didn't cave in throughout filming, though years later, he made up for what he missed on the set of *Love with the Proper Stranger*.

*The Great Escape* made Steve a movie star, but it was *Love with the*

*Proper Stranger* that established him as a sex symbol. Men wanted to be like him, and women wanted to be with him. Neile believes, *"Love with the Proper Stranger was really the first movie where you saw a three-dimensional Steve. It showed all the aspects that made him really appeal to women so much, because it showed this macho man who dared to be vulnerable."*

The critics applauded McQueen's efforts. The *New York Herald* lauded, "McQueen is first rate as the musician." The *New Republic* noted, "Steve McQueen is probably a better performer than we are allowed to appreciate." And *The Saturday Review* praised, "Mr. McQueen, who has developed lately, is just about the best actor Hollywood has on hand. He always seems to believe in what he's doing and saying, manages humor and emotion without evidence of perceptible strain, and for modesty, offhandedness, and all-around ability, could probably offer Marlon Brando a few lessons. Attention, as they say, should be paid to Mr. McQueen." But it wasn't. The film was nominated for five Academy Awards, including Best Actress for Natalie Wood. McQueen's performance was totally overlooked. It would not be the last time he would be snubbed.

Steve enjoyed the commercial success of *Love with the Proper Stranger* and he decided to work again with Robert Mulligan on *Baby, The Rain Must Fall.* Based on Horton Foote's 1954 play *The Traveling Lady,* it would be McQueen's last black-and-white film.

In the film, Steve portrayed Henry Thomas, an ex-con just released from prison. Henry returns to his wife, played by Lee Remick, and their daughter. The three try to start over again as Henry takes on a singing career. The movie is sensitive and downbeat, a trait in most of Mulligan's films. As Mulligan relates, "It has the violence that rests under Foote's characters—and the terror; bold Gothic strokes. These are people who cannot be destroyed. They will always move toward life. We have deepened the characters and this is what opens up the movie. It was not just that we did a lot of filming outdoors in Texas. The purpose of that was to have infinite horizons. It makes the people look really finite, lost and lonely."

For his part as a country singer, Steve decided to learn to play the guitar. He cautiously admitted, "I'm sure going to give it a try. But if I don't cut it, we'll have to get somebody to dub it." Guitarist Billy Strange was brought in as technical adviser, and he noted of McQueen, "He expels so much energy it's wild. He's got the bile going in this part. He falls into a category of 20,000 hillbillies that I have known. He is aggressive in a part, but not aggressive to work with. He'll try anything you suggest. He's not worried about his image."

Director Robert Mulligan raved. "McQueen has great vitality. He's not afraid to be himself or to use himself when he acts. He has a kind of daring theatricality, the same kind of daring as in racing his car. He does not leave that behind when he comes on stage."

Costar Lee Remick believed that Steve didn't necessarily enjoy his work on *Baby, The Rain Must Fall*. She said, "I was curious what he was like. He was friendly and nice and funny and odd. He wasn't just your ordinary run-of-the-mill actor. I don't think he liked acting very much, that's the feeling I got. I didn't feel his heart was in this movie. He liked action movies better. This was a little too delicate and soft and tender for his taste. He did it very well, however."

McQueen himself said, "Acting is a very exciting thing. In a way it is like racing. You need the same absolute concentration. You have to reach inside of you and bring forth a lot of broken glass. That's painful."

In Neile's book, she claims the two stars had become lovers during the filming. "Steve and Lee Remick had been on location in Texas for *Baby, The Rain Must Fall*, possibly feeling isolated from family and friends. Steve said he wound up in bed with Lee."

Remick had a chance to respond to the charges a few months before her untimely death. "Oh no. Really, now," Remick replied. "Those are [Neile's] words, not mine, so I can't comment on that except to say that it's not true."

*Baby, The Rain Must Fall* was released to lackluster reviews and dismal box office. The *New York Times* declared, "There is a major and totally neglected weakness in this film that troubles one's mind throughout the picture and leaves one sadly let down at the end." *Variety* assessed, "It's somber, downbeat story meanders and has plot holes that leave viewers confused and depressed." *The Saturday Review* wrote, "Steve McQueen, ordinarily a vital performer, seems rather cast down at having to play someone who fails at becoming Elvis Presley, and neither he nor Horton Foote ever makes clear what has instilled in him such a sorry ambition."

With *Baby, The Rain Must Fall* wrapping in May 1963, Steve took the rest of the year off and would not film again until December 1964. Steve had made an astonishing thirteen films and a television series in seven years, three feature films in just the last year. "I became an actor because it was the softest job with the best pay," he admitted. "Now I get up at 5:30 in the morning to be at the studio by 6:30. I come home at 9:00 dog tired. Somewhere along the line, I got caught." Steve decided to relax, race a bit, and take it easy for a year. "We hadn't had enough time together for a couple of years, so I took off and me and my wife had a ball," he said.

Steve found relaxation behind the walls of the Castle. "I have a very tight-knit family, but you've got to build a wall around them to keep people out because the world is full of phonies. It's important for people like me to have sanctuary and privacy. That's why we have this house," he said.

On the subject of phonies, Steve explained, "I mean it's hard to know sometimes. They come on so strong, some of them. You wouldn't believe it, man. Some guy starts up and brings his whole soul into it, like he really bares his soul and you just gotta believe it, because he's way out there, way, way out there telling you things he wouldn't tell his own mother. Then it later turns out the guy is a son-of-a-bitch. It makes you feel terrible. You feel sick inside."

Even people in the business had tried to take advantage of him. "Suddenly, you've got a lot of juice going for you, and in this town [Hollywood] there are a whole lot of guys hitting on you."

McQueen was beginning to show signs of burnout from the public as well. Strange people would accost him. "I'll be walking down the street and some guy spots me and flips out. You can see it happen. He goes temporarily crazy just from looking at me. I know what's going on inside of his head: He's got to make his move. He's got to do it because there's a movie star right in front of him and it may be the only chance in his whole life. After a while, they all turn into the same person: some guy flipping out, trying to get you, trying to eat you, man, because he just can't let you get away!"

In May 1964, a prowler by the name of Alfred Thomas Pucci rang the doorbell of the Castle at 3:00 A.M. on a Saturday. Pucci was met at the door by McQueen, armed with a 9mm Mauser. He was then marched to a tree in the yard while Neile called the police. Pucci was taken to a West Los Angeles police station, where he was promptly booked on a prowling charge. He told the officers, "All I wanted was refuge and peace of mind. I am a good judge of character and thought this guy would understand me, as I have seen many of his movies." The fact that some members of the public could not distinguish reality from fiction drove Steve into a deeper paranoia about his fans. It would not be the last time his life would be threatened. Stardom, he found, was not all that it was cracked up to be.

Later in the year, Steve used his position as a star to express his opinion on the land use controversy in Santa Monica. He pleaded with councilman Karl Rundberg, "Don't close the door in my face. I'm representing juvenile delinquents here, and I want to see that children have an opportunity to play in the mountains. This plan will kill that opportunity. New York corporations will buy up land in the mountain area, build apartments and tract homes with nobody to govern them. They have no interest in the people or the state, they are only interested in making money." His words had the desired effect, and the zoning hearing was pushed back one week. Steve realized that his star status could help in given situations, but where he could help the most, he felt, was in giving back to the Boys Republic.

"When you take a little out," he explained, "you gotta put a little back in." McQueen would often make visits to the Boys Republic for morale boosters. There he didn't preach, he just offered hope. Steve even admitted, "I get kinda nervous when I head back to this place." Once inside the doors, the young men could relate to the prodigal son. "I dig you guys," he would tell them. "I was a hardnosed tough guy—just like most of you—but I shaped up, and this place helped set me straight. The world is as good as you are. You've got to like yourself first. I'm a little screwed up, but I'm beautiful."

Betty Rollin, then with *Look* magazine, accompanied Steve on one of these trips and wrote, "There are a dozen boys waiting when we get there. They all look about fifteen—with old men's eyes. They're leaning on the wall of the main building, looking awkward and shy and pale, like unwatered plants. Steve is good with them. Very good."

"Thing is to find some chicks," said the mentor. "Ya get pretty horny in here. I remember." The group of kids laughed, now feeling more comfortable with the star. "Where didya usta live?" Steve was asked. "Over there," Steve motioned with his thumb. "Worked in the laundry. Man, it sure got hot in there."

When McQueen finished his lunch, he was served a dish of ice cream. He had picked up the habit of eating his ice cream with a fork at Boys Republic as a kid. "Look," one of the kids observed, "he eats ice cream with a fork, just like us!" And indeed he was still one of them. Inside, Steve sometimes felt he was still a troubled kid. He just happened to get lucky.

Years later, he read an article in the newspaper about two Florida teenagers who were caught breaking and entering with intent to commit a misdemeanor. For their crime, they were sentenced to three years in a maximum security prison. The article incensed him. "Those kids don't belong in that lousy place!" he argued.

Steve phoned officials in Florida. He was given the runaround and was told there was nothing he could do. The boys would have to wait for an appeal, and that could take several months.

He then contacted James Bax, Florida's state health secretary. Bax told him the boys were already moved to the Lake Butler adult prison, and there was no way they could be reached. Bax suggested that he call Governor Claude Kirk. McQueen pleaded with Kirk, personally taking responsibility for them if they could be transferred to Boys Republic in Chino.

Kirk carefully thought over his proposal and broke precedent by moving the teenagers to a Florida juvenile rehabilitation home, similar to Boys Republic. McQueen had won out over an injustice for some wayward teenagers.

Steve wondered in amazement. "Sometimes being a superstar does pay off," he said. "As John Doe, I couldn't have done a damn thing about those two, no matter how hard I tried. But they listened to Steve McQueen."

On August 8, 1964, President Lyndon Johnson asked Steve McQueen and costar Natalie Wood, the year's hottest Hollywood screen couple, to cohost a cocktail party in Beverly Hills for Johnson's reelection campaign. Steve danced the night away with the president's daughter, Luci Baines Johnson, and made the front page of the *Los Angeles Times* and the evening news around the country.

In September 1964, Steve was accepted as a member of the American team for the international six-day trials in East Germany. For a motorcyclist, it was the highest honor he could achieve. Steve, along with Bud Ekins, Bud's brother Dave, John Steen, and Cliff Coleman comprised the team that was to compete against others from England, Sweden, Poland, Finland, the Soviet Union, Austria, Scotland, Czechoslovakia, the Netherlands, and the hosting country, East Germany.

The race, first run in Great Britain in 1913, was considered the ultimate test, a grueling 1,200-mile romp through mountainous terrain and woods, along narrow paths and trails. Each member would ride 200 miles a day. It was a race against time, with each individual member of a team going for a gold medal. The team with the most points was given the honor of hosting the event the following year. East Germany had won the 1963 trials and was hosting the event for 1964.

McQueen and company arrived in London and were provided a team van, with the American flag proudly painted on the side. The group drove all night to Germany and were stopped the next morning at the border. There, they were delayed for four hours as the East Germans haggled over their interest in western money. Once inside, they made their way to their final destination at Erfurt. McQueen described his experience: "It was kind of weird, being there behind the Iron Curtain, with everybody watching us.

"The night before the race they had this parade of nations in a big hall the size of a football stadium. The guys from each team marched for their country. I stood up there, holding the American flag, right there between the Russians and the East Germans. It was a great moment for me. I was proud to be there."

The morning of the race, all of the racers were served black coffee, a slice of green tomato, gelatin, and a cold slab of eel. Certainly not a breakfast of champions, thought Steve.

The second day of the race, the Americans were tied with England, who were figured to be the favorite going into the competition. The tide changed for the American team when Bud Ekins broke his leg on the third day. When it was Steve's turn to ride, he did fine until he crashed into a spectator who happened to be riding his motorcycle backwards, sideswiping Steve and causing his bike to slam into a tree. As for Steve, he sailed through the air until he slammed face first into a rock. In addition to gashing his face, he ripped off the skin from his kneecaps. He was out of the race.

The American team was a battered lot, but they were determined to finish. Both Dave Ekins and Cliff Coleman took home gold medals, and John Steen won a silver. For Steve, just competing in the race was good enough. "A lot of people think actors can't do anything but get paid lots of money for performing," he said. "I had to beat that actor's image to prove my capabilities in a sport that's always intrigued me.

"After a broken shoulder, some smashed toes, a few stitches and a broken arm, these boys knew I was in there for real. They saw how thick my mud was and dropped the actor label." For McQueen, that was a sweet victory in itself.

As the six-day trials ended, the American team drove to Frankfurt, where Steve would meet up with Neile. From there, they would take the train to Paris for the premiere of *Love with the Proper Stranger*.

For years now *Wanted: Dead or Alive* had been very popular on French television. The McQueen image of grace under pressure, always maintaining an essence of cool, no matter what the circumstances were, intrigued the French. When Steve became a movie star, he became something of a megastar in France. He was voted France's favorite foreign star, dethroning Marlon Brando, who had held that distinction. (With McQueen's death, actor Mickey Rourke would take the title.)

The premiere of *Love with the Proper Stranger* was a gala event, complete with a celebrity auction (the "Maire's Laig" from *Wanted: Dead or Alive* was auctioned off, bringing in $50,000 for charity) followed by a party at the world-famous restaurant Maxim's. *Paris Match*, France's equivalent of *Life*, agreed to underwrite the cost of McQueen's trip in exchange for an exclusive cover story. The only stipulation McQueen had for them was "to be cool." That meant if they saw him with another woman, or discovered him lighting up a joint, they would look the other way.

The McQueen party was staying at the Creole Hotel on the Place de la Concorde. Waiting outside for him was a screaming mob of fans. "It was like the Beatles all over again," recalls an eyewitness. "It was total mayhem."

In order for him to leave the hotel, a makeup man had to be called to the McQueen suite to disguise the movie star in a mustache and French beret.

After the party at Maxim's, a crowd of teenage fans awaited Steve. Bud Ekins, Dave Ekins, Cliff Coleman, John Steen, Sandy MacPeak, and Tommy Donovan acted as his bodyguards. Recalls Bud Ekins, "There were about eight or nine of us in his party and we were all going back to the hotel. People recognized him and started crowding around him, and Steve did something real stupid. He started running. He was about half a block from the hotel. He started running and the crowd started chasing him. They ran over Tommy Donovan and he got hurt. Steve couldn't go out of the hotel after that. The French really loved him for some reason."

Back safely in his suite, looking out the window at the crowd gathered outside the hotel and shaking his head in astonishment, Steve said aloud, "Can you believe this is happening to a kid from reform school?"

When they returned to the states, Steve found that *The Blob* had been rereleased on November 4, to capitalize on his newfound fame. Though he had more money than he knew what to do with, he was still kicking himself for turning down the gross profit deal offered by producer Jack Harris.

Steve spent a lot of his nights prowling the Sunset Strip, more specifically, the Whiskey A Go-Go. The Whiskey was owned by Steve's friend Elmer Valentine, an ex-cop. It was the day's most popular club and was being investigated by the FBI for racketeering. Again, Steve McQueen's name was brought up. One memo, dated November 13, 1964, read:

WHISKEY A GO-GO
Sunset and Clark
<u>Hollywood, California</u>

This unique entertainment phenomenon continues to draw capacity crowds and features live and recorded watusi music and dancing.

Among its clientele are well known legitimate people, as well as entertainment celebrities and in addition, pimps, prostitutes and other notorious characters. It is probably the most popular spot on the Sunset Strip.

The club was McQueen's favorite nightspot, and he had his pick of any woman there. In her book, *Playing the Field,* Mamie Van Doren, a B-movie starlet, detailed her affair with McQueen after meeting him at the famous nightclub. "Steve turned out to be a good dancer. Dancing several fast songs, we worked up a sweat in the smoky, hot confines of the Whiskey."

After a few minutes of polite conversation, McQueen suggested the two go to her place. As they reached Van Doren's house, they went outside on the balcony to see the lights of the city. "There was the faint smell of sweat from our bodies," she writes, "the result of our exertions on the dance floor. From the rate of Steve's breathing, I could tell he was looking forward to some further exertions in bed."

Two days later, the two agreed to meet at the Whiskey, followed by a party at hairdresser Jay Sebring's mansion. The party was in full swing when Steve summoned Van Doren into a bathroom. "I've got some of the finest Sandoz sunshine acid here. Let's drop a tab or two," he suggested. Van Doren hesitated. "I don't know, Steve. I've always been afraid of that stuff. I don't know what might happen to me." Steve prodded, "No bad trips on this shit. It's made by a pharmaceutical company. It's the best. It makes sex a totally new experience.'"

The two swallowed the LSD tablets at the same time and proceeded to Sebring's master bedroom. As they embraced to kiss, the acid began to take effect on Van Doren. "There was a flash of red light, like a skyrocket across the room. Following that, there was another, and another. Soon the room was crisscrossed by tracings of colored lines of light." Scared of the unknown, she told McQueen, "I can see all these colors. What is it?" Reassuring her, Steve said, "It's the acid. Don't worry. Just let yourself go."

As Steve and Van Doren were about to make love, she noticed that the drug magnified her perception of everything around her. "I could feel the crinkle and crush of the bedspread beneath us as we lay in a tangle of arms and legs, creating our special tempo, our own frantic rhythms. From the haze of our lovemaking I could hear music in the house, guitars mimicking the beat of our bodies. My own voice, as I cried out, sounded as though it was someone else's.

"We encouraged each other to longer, more desperate fulfillments after the tidal wave of our first climax. The moments were too short, too long. We were all time, all beginning, quick thrusting, widening, our bodies each other's receptacle, and death and life were at our side. We kept on and on through the psychedelic night."

McQueen and Van Doren continued to see each other over the next few months. She admitted, "The attraction between Steve and me was purely sexual. He was a man of great energy and imagination who was unabashedly wonderful in bed."

The affair continued, and Steve constantly sought to introduce new highs to his lover. "I refused to take any more LSD," wrote Van Doren, "but Steve used it frequently. He became fond of using amyl nitrate, a prescription drug for heart patients that opens the blood vessels in the head and chest and causes a brief rush. As we were about to reach a climax, Steve would crack open one of the glass vials of amyl nitrate and inhale the vapors deeply."

The relationship came to an end when Van Doren realized that Steve wasn't going to leave his wife and kids. "It was a physical relationship I missed when it was over, but one I could no longer countenance. I have never been one to remain in a love affair with a married man who is unwilling to leave his wife. That sort of doomed-from-the-beginning affair can only cause heartache for all concerned."*

Despite the sexual pleasure he derived from women, Steve didn't care that much for the opposite sex. His distrust of them, stemming from his mother, made it hard for him to open up. "Basically, women were broads, and they were also notches on the belt," says Hilly Elkins. "Like anything else, he had to prove his masculinity and the fact that whatever he wanted, he could get."

In the public eye, he was the rebellious movie star who happened to be a loving husband and father. "When I'm not making a picture, I spend all of my time fixing my car; my wife doesn't have to worry about other women, she knows where to find me," Steve bragged to a reporter. But that was altogether not true. Many nights Steve would find himself in another woman's bed. As long as he came home, Neile would continue to let Steve roam the hills of Hollywood. "To Steve, the world was just a giant sexual supermarket," said Bud Ekins. "He constantly had women chasing after him and he couldn't say no. Steve just couldn't control himself. When he saw something he wanted—a woman, a motorcycle, a car—he'd go for it. Everything he did was extreme. He liked an extreme amount of sex, an extreme amount of marijuana, and an extreme amount of cocaine."

Neile and Steve's close friends understood that he was still the man-

---

* Van Doren, Mamie, *Playing The Field* (New York: Berkley Books, 1987).

child of the streets and that it was his background that made him want to take everything he could get his hands on.

Success, it seemed, had thrown him for a loop. Steve revealed, "That's the hardest part about this business. Once you've established yourself as a professional, you suddenly wake up and say, 'I'm a success, now what?' Then you realize that you were so busy trying to be successful that you haven't had time to grow up, inside, to your new position in life. The only education I had was in survival—and they don't pay any extra goodies for that. I used to be the guy who always banged his head against a stone wall. You know, if there was one guy bucking traffic, it was McQueen. Now everything's turning up green lights. For a guy who's been getting stop signs all his life, green lights can be a problem, too."

Underneath that explanation, though, was a darker, more revealing side. A premonition of an early death is what was his driving force. Steve revealed to Neile, "I'm gonna die young, so I gotta take a big piece out of life."

# THE BRASS RING

*Right now I've got a real chance to grab that big brass ring, and, man, you better believe I'm ready to do some grabbin'. I got me a house on a hill, an ol' lady who digs me, two healthy kids, and plenty of fruit and nuts on the table. The lean days are over—and the ride from here on leads straight to Candyland!*

STEVE MCQUEEN

THE BRASS RING was representative of everything the movie industry was to Steve. It meant choice film roles. It meant staying power at the box office. And it meant financial success as long as he stayed on top of the heap. "I have nightmares about being poor, of everything I own just vanishing away. Stardom means that can't happen," he revealed. Steve's hold on the ring was firm and tight. He made damn sure that no one loosened his grip. He would remain a movie star for the rest of his life.

After a year's rest from the movie business, Steve chose *The Cincinnati Kid* for his return. The screenplay was taken from the Richard Jessup novel about an up-and-coming stud poker player who gets a chance to play Lancey Howard, "The Man," an old and weary card champ who wants to maintain his title one last time.

Steve played the title role of Eric Stoner, the Cincinnati Kid. He could relate to Stoner on many levels. Both were loners, seeking respect, and both were aggressive and wanted to compete with the best. Steve had resorted to playing poker in his New York days to supplement his income. The role was tailor-made for him, yet the filming of *The Cincinnati Kid* soon came to resemble a sinking ship.

Martin Ransohoff, the producer, had the go-ahead from MGM. He signed Paddy Chayefsky to do the screenplay. McQueen knew of Chayefsky's reputation as a wordy screenwriter, and over dinner one night he turned to Ransohoff and said, "Tell Paddy when he's writing that I'm much better walking than I am talking."

111

Ransohoff envisioned *The Cincinnati Kid* as "a gunfight with a deck of cards." Chayefsky's screenplay explored the mystique of the Mississippi and the golden, glorious days of New Orleans. "What is this, Paddy?" Ransohoff asked. He felt that Chayefsky had written the screenplay more as a character piece than as an action movie, which Ransohoff felt was essential to make it entertaining. Chayefsky suggested, "Let's do something else," meaning another project. Ransohoff was adamant about his vision of *The Cincinnati Kid* and parted amicably with Chayefsky. He then turned over the screenplay to Ring Lardner, Jr. Lardner's version was acceptable to Ransohoff, who now had one less worry. Terry Southern was brought in to do the final draft.

Ransohoff already had Steve's commitment, and he now needed an actor to play the role of Lancey Howard. For years, Spencer Tracy had been one of McQueen's idols, and the two men held tremendous respect for each other. McQueen had even written to Tracy, begging him to take the part. He would even allow Tracy to take top billing, a move that was totally out of character for Steve. In a letter dated October 20, 1964, Tracy wrote back to McQueen, stating why he wouldn't be participating in *The Cincinnati Kid:*

Dear Steve,

I'm sorry, too, that it didn't work out. I had felt from the book that it could develop into a very interesting part and a wonderful situation between them, but somehow the old man never came to life for me, and when you're my age, you just cannot play someone you don't comprehend. I think you are very wise to go ahead, for while it's not the book, it's a damn good part. Many thanks for your notes. In another time I hope. Good luck.

Sincerely yours,
Spencer Tracy

Next came the hiring of legendary director Sam Peckinpah. In the late fifties, Peckinpah had directed television before he got his first break in 1961 with his first feature film, *The Deadly Companions.* A year later, he directed *Ride the High Country,* which was well received. *The Cincinnati Kid* would be a breakthrough of sorts as Peckinpah's first nonwestern.

Peckinpah had a reputation as being wild, reckless, egotistical, and stubborn. Ransohoff bent backward to try and please the maverick director.

For reasons unknown, Peckinpah insisted that *The Cincinnati Kid* be filmed in black and white. Ransohoff disagreed, but remained silent. He felt the card scene at the end of the movie demanded that the audience could read the color of the cards, thus having a more dramatic, emotional effect. In addition, a movie that was shot in color was at least guaranteed to break even after the sale of television rights. Black-and-white movies simply did not have the box office pull of color films. Ransohoff relented, however, and let Peckinpah have his way.

Another point of contention was the hiring of actress Sharon Tate for the lead female role of Christian. Tate at the time was Ransohoff's protégée and was being groomed for stardom. Recalls Ransohoff, "Sharon screen-tested for the picture and did very well. Steve and I liked her very much." Peckinpah wasn't as impressed and offered no explanation. Ransohoff didn't question Peckinpah's decision and left it at that. Actress Tuesday Weld later won the role of Christian. She had worked with Steve previously on *Soldier in the Rain*. Even after its box office failure, Steve felt that Weld was "the best actress I've worked with up to that point."

Filming began in the first week of November 1964 and came to a complete halt after only four days. Ransohoff heard that on a Friday night, Peckinpah had sent the featured cast home while he proceeded to shoot a nude scene with an unknown black actress. Peckinpah was also filming a riot scene, involving over 300 extras, a scene not scripted in the screenplay. Ransohoff accused Peckinpah of adding needless sex to a scene not written for that purpose. Peckinpah claimed, "Totally untrue. I did a damn good riot scene and a love scene between Rip Torn and a Negro prostitute in bed." Ransohoff didn't feel the bedroom scene with the black prostitute was an accurate depiction of the era. "I'm not saying that white gentlemen didn't sleep with black women in those days," defends Ransohoff, "but the scene was in a so-called classy hotel and there was not a lot of open fraternization of whites and blacks in the thirties." There was also the question of nudity. An X rating would have affected the box office draw. Peckinpah did not care. He was there to make his movie. Friend and actor L. Q. Jones tried to talk some sense into the director. "Sam, they have millions of dollars invested in this movie; don't you think they have some say in the matter?" asked Jones. Jones also points out, "Sam Peckinpah was a genius when it came to making a movie, but when it came to the business end of it, he was just plain stubborn. And it cost him."

Steve's friend Bud Ekins was to play the part of Rip Torn's bodyguard. Peckinpah liked Ekins and decided he looked right for the part. Word leaked of Peckinpah's impending firing and Ekins was surprised when Steve came up to him while filming the riot scene and said, "Peckinpah's history." Ekins couldn't believe it. Steve said, "As of tomorrow, Sam's off the picture." Ekins replied, "Why are we shooting this scene?"

After Peckinpah was fired, he claimed that he was blackballed from Hollywood and could not find employment for three years. "Forced inactivity would be the appropriate term," he quipped (a false claim, according to Peckinpah intimates; it was his erratic behavior that forced him to become unhirable, they noted).

Years later, Peckinpah said his intention with *The Cincinnati Kid* was to "give a fairly honest look at life in the thirties, in the Depression era, and what happens to a man who plays stud poker for a living, how it affects his life and those around him. I had a feeling I would never do the picture, but I really didn't expect to be fired after I got started. I found out later that no matter what I'd shot—and I thought it was some astonishingly good footage—I was going to be fired, or shall we say sandbagged."*

John Calley, then Ransohoff's partner and later on to become the head of Warner Brothers, states, "Peckinpah was extremely unprofessional. He was drinking and he had problems at home with his wife and he was bringing it to work. That's why McQueen didn't object to his firing. Steve's attitude was, 'I'm the actor, you guys are the producers. If you think this is best for the picture, I won't interfere.' Steve was a professional."

Peckinpah kept the week's worth of black-and-white footage of *The Cincinnati Kid* for his own personal use. When asked if the nude footage was for a "European version," Peckinpah replied flippantly, "It's for my own version."

Firing Sam Peckinpah caused production on *The Cincinnati Kid* to come to a screeching halt. The search was on for a new director, and Ransohoff had his hands full with McQueen. A solution was reached when MGM gave Steve $25,000 in cash to spend in Las Vegas playing poker. A working vacation of sorts.

While Steve was in Las Vegas, his agent, Stan Kamen, approached Ransohoff with another of his clients, director Norman Jewison. Jewison at that time had worked heavily in television and had two feature films to his credit, *The Thrill of It All* and *Send Me No Flowers*, two lighthearted comedies starring Doris Day. He was unproven in serious drama and Ransohoff was gambling. "We were scrambling. His agent sold him to me. I was glad that Jewison was interested in the entertainment value and the color," says Ransohoff. The movie was back on.

---

* Seydor, Paul, *Peckinpah: The Western Films* (The University of Illinois Press, 1980), 71.

The total cost of stopping production of *The Cincinnati Kid* was ultimately $700,000, pushing the budget from $2.6 million to $3.3 million.

When Steve returned from Las Vegas, he met Norman Jewison for the first time. He didn't know what to make of him, but he sure was going to put him to the test. Costar Karl Malden recalls, "The feeling was that the killer instinct in Steve McQueen would take over and really make it miserable for this new director."

Steve's insecurities were heightened when he found out that Edward G. Robinson was hired to play Lancey Howard. Not having worked in over a year only compounded the problem. He lost several hours of sleep trying to regain his composure. "For the first three days on the set I felt like I never acted before in my life!" Steve recalled. Karl Malden assesses, "Steve McQueen realized that he had a big challenge when he did *The Cincinnati Kid*. From my point of view, I have a feeling that he got into the big leagues."

MGM was paying Steve big league money, $350,000, and he was surrounded by a name cast: Ann-Margret, Tuesday Weld, Karl Malden, Rip Torn, Joan Blondell, Cab Calloway, and Spencer Tracy's replacement, Edward G. Robinson. Robinson brought the fear of God out in Steve. "I've got to be ready for him," Steve told a friend, "otherwise the guy will run the picture." Norman Jewison also confirmed the fact that Steve was "a little nervous about Eddie Robinson. Eddie was a star. A sign of insecurity is when another actor looks away. And Steve always used to look down at his feet. Then look up at you. Then he'd look away again." At the time, Robinson realized that art sometimes does imitate life. He said, "Once, back at the start of my career, I had been another McQueen. I'd played the same kind of parts, cocky and tough, ready to take on the old timers and beat them at their own game. I identified strongly with McQueen, and I had a lot of respect for his talent." That did not mean that Robinson was above being jealous. The role was a change for him. Known for his gangster bits, he was now called on to be a suave, debonair, big-time gambler who could afford a freewheeling lifestyle. (In actuality, Robinson was just as sophisticated, as his art collection was legendary in Hollywood.) Robinson was facing just as big a challenge as McQueen. The two privately were in fear of each other's screen presence. Robinson openly questioned Jewison about the rewrites and about cuts in his role. As for Steve, he asked Jewison for a look at the dailies. Jewison asked, "What do you want to see them for?" Steve shrugged and said, "I don't know why, I'd just like to see the dailies." Jewison knew why. Steve was afraid that Robinson was running the picture. The director gave some fatherly advice: "I don't know if that's such a good idea. You know, we've got a lot of important actors in this film." Jewison then proceeded to explain, in detail, why he wouldn't permit Steve to see the dailies. Steve exploded, "You're twistin' my melon, man, you're twistin' my melon. You're gettin' me all mixed up." Jewison had never heard the expression before. "He used to talk so hip, that I didn't know what he was saying half the time," laughs Jewison. He did recognize Steve's anger and tried to soothe the insecure actor. But under no circumstances would he allow Steve to view the dailies. Jewison won that battle, but there were many more to come.

Deep down, though, McQueen liked Jewison. The two came from different worlds. Says visual designer Nikita Knatz, "Remember, McQueen embraced Sam Peckinpah. He was a desert rat like him. Peckinpah drank coffee out of a paper cup. Norman Jewison had his served in a cup and saucer with a spoon. The relationship was hardly father/son. It was more like Mr. Wilson and Dennis the Menace. Jewison tolerated McQueen. It was like a brain surgeon working with a blacksmith."

Steve may have been loved by the world, but Jewison understood the man behind the mask. "I felt he had been hurt badly when he was a child," said Jewison. "He had difficulty in relationships, and yet he had such believability. When I looked through that camera, I would believe him."

McQueen's relationships with his costars were not as friendly. He was taken by Ann-Margret's beauty. "She was a lady," said Steve, "everybody's wet dream." Though he may have lusted after her, he certainly didn't impress her with his behavior. Jewison observed, "I don't think he and Ann-Margret got along that well. As a matter of fact, outside of Neile, I don't know if he treated women that well. I think he was afraid of women. Afraid to trust them."

Steve did earn the admiration of Karl Malden. Malden's self-effacing personality made it easy for McQueen to get along with the veteran actor, but privately he referred to Malden as "potato nose." Malden recalls a scene he did with McQueen and explains, "I was playing the part of Shooter, a professional card dealer, dealing in favor of the kid, so that he would win the game. He has to take some time off to go to his room and rest, and he asks me to come up to his room. He confronts me with the question 'Are you cheating?' McQueen sprung at me like a tiger. There are a number of actors who have that quality that any minute on screen, you're going to see them explode. They're so tense, so high, that you feel, 'I'm gonna be here when he blows his top.' "

For the movie's finale, a card game is set up. Earlier in the film, the Kid awaits a much anticipated match with Lancy Howard. The Kid boldly proclaims, "After the game, I'll be the Man. I'll be the best there is. People will sit down at the table with ya, just so that they could say they played with the Man. And that's what I'm going to be."

The last scene, Ransohoff's vision of a gunfight with a deck of cards, is set up. The original six card players are whittled down to just two, McQueen and Robinson. The Kid has been winning all night and is getting ready to dethrone the Man. It's all down to one hand. The Kid lays down his cards and asks to see Robinson's hand. Coolly, McQueen says, "Okay, let's see it." The Man lays his cards on the table, a royal flush. A million-to-one long shot. The Kid has lost. Says Robinson, "Gets down to what it's all about. Making the wrong move at the right time." Robinson strikes a match, lights up a cigar, and tells McQueen, "You're good, kid, but as long as I'm around, you're second best. You might as well learn to live with it."

Both McQueen and Robinson give strong performances, but Robinson clearly stands out as the Man. It is a credit to McQueen's bravado as an actor that he is willing to lose the card game, lose his girlfriend, and even lose a game of pitching pennies at the end of the movie to a shoeshine boy. (MGM revised the overseas version. Instead of the downbeat ending, the foreign version shows McQueen and Tuesday Weld riding happily off into the sunset.)

Edward G. Robinson paid McQueen the ultimate compliment when he told the press, "He comes out of the tradition of Gable, Bogie, Cagney, and even me. He's a stunner."

When filming ended that summer, Jewison assembled a version for Steve to view. Steve's verdict: He liked the finished product. Jewison won his respect and trust with a perfectly guided performance.

At a prescreening release for MGM, it was more difficult for Steve to enjoy watching himself than the first time around. For Steve, this was a gut-wrenching experience. "I get suicidal when I have to watch my films," he revealed. "When I see myself up there, twenty-four feet high on that screen, I'm into a cold sweat. Each time I think, 'Man, this is gonna bomb at the box office!' In this case, I was wrong." McQueen's performance in the picture has been sadly underrated. The picture has gone on to become the definitive film on poker, and Steve's performance in it remains one of the best of his career.

*The Cincinnati Kid* went on to become a box office hit, bringing in over $6 million domestically and reaching close to $10 million worldwide. For Norman Jewison, it was the start of a long list of hit films in a distinguished career. Just two years later, he won five Academy Awards for *In the Heat of the Night* and went on to direct such memorable films as *Fiddler on the Roof, Jesus Christ Superstar, . . . And Justice for All,* and

*Moonstruck.* Says screenwriter Alan Trustman, *"The Cincinnati Kid* saved Norman Jewison's career."

As for Steve, *The Cincinnati Kid* was the first of five back-to-back worldwide hits, a feat no movie star before or since has equaled. From that point, he was on the top ten ten list of favorite box office stars for ten years in a row.

He was on a roll.

Once *The Cincinnati Kid* was finished, Steve jumped right into filming *Nevada Smith* in July 1965. *Nevada Smith* is the prequel to Harold Robbins' *The Carpetbaggers.* It tells the story of an Indian boy, Max Sand, who tracks down the three vicious killers of his parents. It was to be Steve's first western since *The Magnificent Seven.*

Henry Hathaway believed that directing was a dictatorship, not a democracy. He sat Steve down for a meeting before he began filming *Nevada Smith.* The two shook hands, and Steve took a seat across from Hathaway's desk. Steve was on his best behavior. Hathaway knew of Steve's reputation for giving directors a hard time. Without warning, he proceeded to read McQueen the riot act. "Now, Mr. McQueen, I want you to know something. I'm the boss. Nobody argues with me. I'm not putting up with any shit from you, and if I do get any shit from you, I won't hesitate to deck you." Hathaway shook his fist, showing it to Mc-Queen. "I don't want any of this star complex bullshit," warned Hathaway. "We're a family out there. We're making a movie. Going to put in long hours. The crew's working just as hard as you are. If you've got some ideas, I'll listen. But don't you get bullheaded and scream and holler at me, because I'll holler and scream back. I'm the meanest son-of-a-bitch that ever was!" Steve sat there quietly. No one had ever talked to him that way. Ever. Steve respected the fact that Hathaway spelled out the conditions. After much silence, he smiled, sat up, and offered his hand to Hathaway. "All right, Mr. Hathaway. You've got a deal. That's it, Dad." The two men had an understanding. They then loosened up and began to chitchat. Before Steve left, he made one comment: "I've got a guy who doubles me, and he's going to double me on this film." Hathaway, keeping his temper, told Steve, "That's nice, but I have my favorite stuntman, and he doubles my leads in all my movies. He's the right height for you and there's a great resemblance." Steve adamantly told Hathaway no. "Listen, you little son-of-a-bitch," Hathaway fumed, "nobody's doubling you but Loren and that's that!" and with that, he pounded his fist on the desk and bit through the cigar in his mouth. "What?" Steve asked. Hathaway screamed, "Loren Janes. That's who's going to double you." Steve said, "That's who I'm talking about." Hathaway, laughing, replied, "For God's sake." The two roared with laughter and never had a problem throughout the filming of *Nevada Smith*.

Steve's leading lady, actress Suzanne Pleshette, had known Steve in New York in the late fifties and was the sister that Steve never had. Pleshette was only fourteen years old when she and Steve McQueen happened to meet at an actors' party. Pleshette was with an older man, an actor that Steve had known. Though Steve did not know the young teenager, he pulled Pleshette aside and offered her a ride home. "He just thought we were an inappropriate couple," recalls Pleshette. Steve took Pleshette outside and offered her a ride on his motorcycle. Pleshette spotted a bullwhip on the bike and decided that she had better forgo the ride. "From that day until the day Steve died, he always treated me like I was a baby sister, and he was always very protective and loving toward me. I was just crazy about him. I don't know for what reasons he decided to become my protector, maybe I reminded him of someone and it lasted our mutual lifetime," says Pleshette.

It was Pleshette who was Steve and Neile's first guest in their first apartment in New York. A few years later, it was Pleshette who cooked dinner for the two on the night daughter Terry was born. Simply, Pleshette was family. "I'm finding out that I'm the only leading lady in all of his movies that he didn't go to bed with. I don't know whether to be flattered or pissed off," laughs Pleshette.

McQueen and Pleshette happened to be at the same party in Hollywood when the actress came up to Steve and asked, "Do you know who your leading lady for *Nevada Smith* is?" McQueen asked, "Who?" Pleshette told him, "Me!" Steve slapped his hand on his forehead and exclaimed, "God, no. You've got to be kidding!" Steve immediately thought of the love scene the script called for and realized he was going to be kissing his sister on the screen.

"It's the strangest thing," says Pleshette. "When it came down to it, Steve never thought of me as an actress. He always thought of me as a kid, in spite of the fact that at the time, I really had some outstanding credentials. I think he was shocked to be pulled back into the thought that I was a working actress. He just thought of me as 'Suzy.' I think he needed to readjust his thinking."

The first portion of *Nevada Smith* was filmed in Port Vincent, Louisiana, on the banks of the Amite River. The conditions were hot and muggy, and the river was infested with leeches, water moccasins, cottonmouths, and mosquitoes. A cast member noted, "I walk out of my motel every morning and my glasses steam up. It's like walking into a Chinese laundry."

On the set, director Henry Hathaway, as promised, ruled with an iron fist. It was stuntman Gary Combs's first time on a Hathaway picture. Combs's father had been a close friend of Hathaway's and gave him some simple advice: "Don't go out on the set unless you have something to do."

The day before shooting started, Combs and a few other stuntmen went to dinner near the hotel where the crew was staying. They were laughing it up, having a good time, when someone at the table announced, "Oh shit, here comes the old man." Surprisingly to Combs, Hathaway proved to be charming, telling old war stories and swapping dirty jokes. He even paid for the dinner. As soon as Hathaway left, Combs turned to a crew member who had worked with the director before and said, "Well, he's not so bad." The response came back, "Wait till you see him on the set tomorrow." Combs had a taste of the Hathaway school of directing and later admitted the other crew members were right. "He was Dr. Jekyll and Mr. Hyde. That first day on the set, he was a cranky, nasty, cigar-smoking, vindictive guy. That was the way he made pictures. As long as you understood that, you were okay," says Combs.

Combs made it a point to stand a good distance behind Hathaway to see how the director worked. Hathaway had started in the industry in props and had worked his way up. He knew where everybody was supposed to be and what their jobs were. Hathaway always stood a good twenty feet from the set so he could watch everyone. Combs says, "If you were out there with the actors, you'd better belong there, because if you weren't, you'd get your ass chewed out by Hathaway."

McQueen's hyperkinetic energy drove Hathaway nuts. As soon as a scene would finish, Steve would hop on his motorcycle, rev up the engine, and take off. The noise would scare the horses on the set and would cause Hathaway to yell, "Get that idiot off that bike!" The first thought that came to Gary Combs was, "McQueen's just a spoiled little kid." As Combs got to know him better later on, it didn't make sense to the stuntman that the star of the picture was putting the whole movie at risk. "He took off with no shirt, no helmet, we're in the woods, and he's doing wheelies through the trees and brush. He was a good rider, but I don't care how good you are. If he gets hurt, we all go home for a week or two until he heals up. That's the logic you've got to have on a motion picture. That's why you have stunt people. I knew Henry wanted to kill him when he got on that motorcycle," says Combs.

When it came time for scenes in the swamp, Hathaway knew McQueen couldn't be confined to sitting along the banks of the river all day. He arranged it so that Steve could have a motorboat to putter around in.

Says Suzanne Pleshette, "Henry Hathaway was difficult, but he was a great psychologist and a wonderful filmmaker. He really knew how to handle Steve, knew how to make him comfortable. What every good professional director should know. He knew that Steve had a lot of energy. That was the wonderful thing about Steve when he was on the screen; you had this sense of energy, always going, a wonderful sense of physical ability to react quickly, which is very appealing about him as an actor. When we were out in the swamp, Henry knew there was no way that Steve could just sit still on this raft with the rest of us. He kept Steve's energy up and didn't make him feel he was trapped, which was always so dreadful for Steve."

One scene in particular was very hard for Steve. His character purposely locks himself in a bank vault to give the appearance that he is robbing the bank. He knows that he will be sent to prison, where he will meet up with one of the inmates that helped participate in the killing of his parents a few months back. The prison in which the men are kept reminded Steve of the Boys Republic. He shared his intimate feelings with Pleshette. "I suspected he had a prison experience through our conversations," she says. "It seemed difficult for him, that sequence. He was sharing some feelings with me that night that led me to believe he was incarcerated at some time in his life. That was difficult for him to be in a similar situation, even as an actor, knowing that he could leave."

Another point that proved hard for Steve was a kissing scene with Suzanne Pleshette. Says Pleshette, "It was the hardest thing for us. It was so awkward, we didn't know where to put our lips. We never thought of each other that way, and we were just terrible at it." Pleshette knew of Steve's reputation as a ladies' man. Kidding after the scene was finished, she told him, "You are the absolute worst kisser in the world." Coming from anyone else, Steve would have taken offense.

For *Nevada Smith,* Steve was paid $500,000 from Paramount Pictures. (The film's budget was $4.5 million.) In addition, Hathaway made sure Steve was given a motor home (compliments of Paramount) to make sure that Steve was comfortable. It amazed and amused Pleshette at the time that Steve could be so cheap. While Steve's meals were prepared by a cook and served hot, the crew, along with Pleshette, were being served bagged lunches, perhaps a cold sandwich, an apple, or a muffin. Notes Pleshette, "Steve was being served chicken and all the fixings." Faithfully every day Steve would come out of his trailer and ask Pleshette for an apple or a cookie. She would give it to him without even thinking. Hathaway began to catch on, and one day he intervened. "Wait a minute. I'm going to negotiate this for you, Suzy." He then asked Steve, "Now, what are you going to give up for this cookie?"

Notes Pleshette, "Steve didn't want to give up anything. I think that was the psychology of a very, very poor boy who had little to begin with. To me, he was very giving and loving, but he was notorious for not picking up a check."

After the day's shoot, Steve and Suzy often went to dinner together in the city. Steve would order a steak, then summon a waitress back and order another steak before the first one had arrived. Disturbed, Pleshette would tell him, "Why don't you eat just one, and then if you're still hungry, order a second?" Steve asked, "What if there isn't a second one?" When the steak arrived, Steve would shovel it down as if in a race for time.

When the check arrived, Steve conveniently would tell Pleshette, "Oh, I don't have any money," and Pleshette would dutifully pay the bill. After picking up the check one too many times, she told Steve, "Next time I do a picture with you, if I ever do, I'm getting double per diem!" Pleshette laughs today, but adds, "That was all a part of Steve, and we all knew it. I guess that was what made him so adorable."

McQueen, in turn, not only got to know Pleshette better, but he came to respect her as an actress. It was not an easy shooting. Pleshette was the only woman on location with thirty-six men, but she roughed it out with the best of them and didn't complain. Steve respected her sense of humor and "roll-with-the-punches" attitude. Says Pleshette, "They were awful conditions for a woman to work under. If you had to go to the bathroom, you had to go excuse yourself and swim upstream. I think what Steve always loved about me was that I behaved well under those circumstances."

Pleshette was struck by Steve's kindness. His big brother attitude genuinely touched her. He handled her with kid gloves. In one particular scene, Steve was to pull Pleshette from a canoe and place her on the ground. During the filming, as he put her down, Pleshette sat up and started screaming. There were dry leaves with pointed stems poking into her skin. Steve then grabbed a blanket to cover her, but the blanket had accumulated even more leaves and as Steve covered her, the dry stems poked into her even more, feeling like a million bee bites. Pleshette got up and ran away, leaving Steve feeling awful. "He was horrified that I was in pain, even more so when he discovered he had inflicted it on me. He had a great kindness regarding me," says Pleshette.

The location of *Nevada Smith* moved to Lone Pine, California, where Steve had to work with animals for the first time since *Wanted: Dead or Alive*. He didn't trust animals, and one particular incident with a herd of cattle didn't do anything to change his mind. In the movie, his character, Max, finds one of his parents' killers and corners him in a corral of longhorn cattle, where the two have a knife fight. Max finally outsmarts his would-be killer when he opens the gate and the animals stampede.

For the scene, stuntman Loren Janes doubled for Steve in the corral. Before the scene was actually shot, the F/X department placed air hoses three inches below ground to get the cattle to move when the gate opened. When the air hoses were turned on, the herd went berserk. It was an unexpected reaction, as they began to trample the fences and anything that got in their way. Loren Janes was knocked down three times. He knew he was in serious trouble. Steve and second unit director Richard Talmadge waded through the herd to try and get Janes out. Says Janes, "Both Steve and Richard risked their lives to get me." It was that dangerous. Janes had gotten back on his feet when suddenly he was hit square in the middle of the stomach by a steer. Luckily, he wasn't gored, and instead latched onto the horns of the steer with his arms. It carried him, unbeknownst to McQueen and Talmadge, and along with the rest of the herd he rode out into the pasture a few hundred yards out of view before he pitched himself off the steer.

Janes could see the bright lights of the set and began walking back, thanking his lucky stars that he hadn't been hurt seriously. As he approached, he saw high school buses from the area, stopping to watch the filming. Then he saw McQueen and the crew holding up bits of clothing and saying, "Loren's dead!" He walked into the middle of the set, asking casually, "What's going on?" Someone from the set yelled out, "There he is!" Steve turned around and gasped. He began laughing until he couldn't breathe any longer, and fell to the ground holding his sides. The cast and crew followed Steve's cue and began laughing wildly at the sight of Janes. Then the local high schoolers on the bus began clapping and chanting. Janes didn't get the joke. Steve mustered enough energy to point at Janes's crotch. Janes looked down and discovered that he was stark naked, except for his gun belt and moccasins. He looked like a naked Jesse James. "The cattle had torn off every single shred of clothing. I then placed my hands over my parts and slowly crept back into the dark, with the high school kids laughing in the background. One thing about Steve, he could get the giggles, laughing so hard till he cried. At times he was very childlike. He was a very innocent little child, desperately wanting to love and be loved," Janes remembers fondly.

In October 1965, Steve got a call from Neile. His mother, Jullian, had suffered a cerebral hemorrhage. She had been admitted to Mount Zion hospital, in San Francisco, and was in a coma. Steve and Neile had planned to attend the premiere of *The Cincinnati Kid* in New Orleans. It was to be a benefit for the survivors of Hurricane Betsy, and the South's biggest opening since *Gone with the Wind*. They had looked forward to the premiere, but had to cancel their plans so that Steve could be at his mother's bedside.

For years, Steve had shown disdain for his mother, but when he became a star, she appeared on the scene again. Slowly, he let his mother back into his life because of his kids, although he kept her at arm's length. He would arrange for monthly checks to be dispatched to her, but that was through his business manager. Pictures of the children were sent by Neile every so often, but not a word was written by Steve. It had been at least eight months since they had spoken, but Jullian had grown very proud of her son. Her apartment was filled with magazine articles on him, and anytime one of his movies came out, she made it a point to see the film at least twice. Jullian had grown fat and content in her last days. She no longer seemed to have an interest in men. Her days were filled with having friends over her apartment, sewing new clothes for her grandchildren, and running her own boutique, which Steve had bought her. He had also gotten her a used Volkswagen Beetle so she could get around. Jullian visited occasionally, but it was only for short intervals, as Steve could bear his mother for only so long. Says David Foster, "He took care of his mother, but every time he mentioned her it was with great hostility and anger: 'That bitch! That drunk! She fucked up my life. She never gave a shit about me—here's another check.' It was a very complicated relationship."

Jullian even made one last attempt at a reconciliation, but too much damage had been done, and Steve couldn't bring himself to forgive her.

Jullian was still comatose when Steve arrived at her bedside. Putting aside the hostilities he felt for his mother, Steve kept vigil, never leaving her side. "I have so much energy," he said. "I wish I could give her my energy, so that she can live." Recalls Neile, "Steve kept hoping that she would recover. He had so much to say to her, but now she was dying and slipping away. Unfortunately, she never recovered and, at that point, he just sat down and sobbed." Friend Pat Johnson elaborates, "Steve had this love/hate relationship with his mother. He felt that she deserted him, that she had turned her back on him, and yet she loved him and did the best that she could. She just was not maternal. There were a lot of things he wanted to say to her that were never resolved. He regretted the fact that he had never opened up to her, just as later in his life he regretted that he had never opened up to the public in general. In fact, his relationship with all the women in his life was probably influenced by his mother." On October 15, 1965, Jullian Berri died peacefully in her sleep.

When Steve and Neile went to Jullian's apartment to gather her belongings, they found a dress Jullian was making for Terry still on the sewing machine.

After Jullian's death, Steve didn't have the strength to make arrangements for her funeral, so it was left up to Neile. Steve's fans felt his loss and sent flowers in her honor. His only request was that donations be sent to Boys Republic. Jullian was buried in Gardens of Ascension, Forest Lawn Memorial Park, in Glendale, California, on October 20. Steve bought a plot under a tree. The only attendants were Neile, Stan Kamen, Terry, Chad, David Foster, and his wife, Jackie. There was no priest, no minister, no clergyman; only Steve talked. "Jullian liked shade," said Steve. He fumbled for words. "She would have liked this spot. Shady with no sun." He began to cry. Says David Foster, "Steve may have been a bastard, literally, but he cried at the funeral. He was a lost soul."

As Jullian was laid to rest, so was Steve's past. There was no looking back.


*Nevada Smith* resumed filming when Steve returned from San Francisco. Loren Janes knew Jullian had died, but Steve didn't mention a word to his friend. "Nothing, not a word," remembers Janes. "When he came back, he was kind of quiet and remorseful, and I knew something was bothering him. I thought I'd let him bring it up. He never did mention it or talk about it to me. Ever."

Steve and Henry Hathaway did clash at times. Steve liked to improvise, while Hathaway wanted to stick to the script.

Actor L. Q. Jones, a Hathaway alumni, offered, "Steve knew what he could do best. I think he knew what he could do well and tended to take a given scene and work it so that he could bend and put it to work for him. If you came at him with not wanting to change the dialogue to his liking, then he could be difficult, but he was a professional about it. Sometimes you get a guy like Hathaway who wants to go by the letter, then the shit's going to hit the fan and somebody's going to prevail. In most of Hathaway's pictures, he is the one that prevailed. In *Nevada Smith*, it was sort of a standoff with Steve.

"Henry Hathaway and Sam Peckinpah were cut from the same piece of cloth. In many instances, they had little or no respect for an actor and were determined to get things done their way. Hathaway was a director who nailed an actor's boots to the floor. I can remember a scene with Steve and Strother Martin. Hathaway said, 'Mr. Jones, Mr. Martin, Mr.

McQueen, would you get your asses over here please.' That's how Hathaway approached a scene," observed Jones.

Of all of Steve's starring roles, it was *Nevada Smith* that he liked least. Years later he assessed that he would have approached the role differently. "There were things about the picture that he didn't like, things he wanted to change but wasn't able to," says Loren Janes. The critics weren't enthusiastic about Steve's performance or the movie. Wanda Hale of the *New York Daily News* called it "a tedious Western with too little suspense." *Variety* wrote, "Although excess footage is a prime heavy in film's impact, McQueen's erratic performance also detracts." *Time* magazine observed, "Steve McQueen, unmistakably modern, looks as if he would be more at home in the saddle of a Harley-Davidson than on a horse."

Suzanne Pleshette didn't side with the critics' verdict on Steve's acting in *Nevada Smith*. She believes that "some people have this innate quality that attracts people. Steve had something extra about him and the camera loves him. To think that they don't know how to act or they're not professional is a mistake. Steve was very professional. He worked very hard. He knew exactly what he was doing. He was always very well prepared, and none of this was an accident. He took great pride in acting, and doing it well."

Nevertheless, *Nevada Smith* was another hit, grossing $12 million in the United States alone. Overseas it fared even better, establishing McQueen as the modern-day American hero. In Japan, audiences were quite taken with the revenge story, as the hero, Max Sand, hunts down his parents' killers. Steve told a reporter at the time, "I figure when a guy does something to you, the best thing you can do is hurt him as much as possible," leaving no doubt in the public's mind that he would have done the same thing. In Trinidad, mounted police were called four times in one day to quell the crowds outside a theater who were ready to break down the doors to see the film, proving that McQueen was the biggest international movie star of the day.

The premiere of *Nevada Smith* was held on the Paramount lot, where producer Joe Levine gave a big western theme party for over 1,500 guests. The party ended early when a huge fire broke out at the Paramount and Desilu studios. Steve was the first guest to help firefighters battle the flames. Notes Suzanne Pleshette, "Steve was acting as a fireman. He was there in the thick of things. By nature, he was just heroic."

*Nevada Smith* was Steve's second worldwide smash. Studios were offering up to 50 percent of the box office gross if he would sign his name on the dotted line. "Real stars, like Steve McQueen and John Wayne, are worth their weight in gold," said one producer.

Quite simply, Steve had the world at his feet, though he insisted on staying hungry, to keep looking for projects that would enhance his career. "I've got to keep growing," he said. His life was in a whirlwind, and he liked it. He admitted, "I did everything in a hurry. I got married in a hurry; and I've spent every free moment from films hurrying around race tracks both in the U.S. and abroad, on motorcycles and then the fastest cars I could find. I have a million plans—movies to make, movies to direct and produce with my own company. I want to go to places and I want to go fast. I've hurried all my life. It's a way of life with me."

Neile knew it was something else, something that bothered him at the core of his being. "He's deeply concerned about being poor again," Neile revealed. "He's got the brass ring right now, but he's afraid it might be snatched away. When things are going too well, he worries. It's the fear of being poor and lonely again, of everything good vanishing. I leave him alone or tell him to take a ride in the car. If he wants me to go with him, I go along; if not, he goes alone. I don't press him—I must let him do what he wants to get over this feeling."

Everything in his life at the moment was perfect. It was a feeling he did not trust.

Street scene from *The Sand Pebbles*          (Courtesy of Twentieth Century-Fox)

# AN OSCAR AND A
# GENTLEMAN

*I don't know why it [stardom] happened—but it's kinda nice.
Maybe it's because I'm someone off the streets. Maybe people
relate to me. Every role, I chip off a chunk of myself.*

Steve McQueen

In 1962, Richard McKenna's first novel, *The Sand Pebbles,* spent twenty-eight weeks on the *New York Times* best-seller list. The book was based on his experience as an enlisted navy man in war-torn China in 1926.

Director Robert Wise read the novel and wanted to do the film as soon as possible. The movie rights for the novel had been sold for $300,000 to United Artists. Soon thereafter, a budget dispute evolved and 20th Century-Fox wound up with the rights.

It was early 1963 when Steve McQueen was first mentioned as a possible lead, but Paul Newman had the first right of refusal in Wise's eyes. *The Great Escape* had not yet been released, and McQueen wasn't as big a star as Newman.

Wise knew the kind of effort that had to be put into *The Sand Pebbles,* an epic film. Fox suggested that San Francisco would be an ideal location for filming. Wise nixed that idea. "We could have built cities on the Sacramento River, but no one had a quick answer to obtaining up to twenty river junks, several hundred sampans, and authentic Chinese extras," says Wise. "For some scenes, I needed a thousand people, and I doubt San Francisco could guarantee that on any given day."

No, Wise thought, it would have to be shot on location in the Orient, and it would take time for all the locations to be scouted, the sets to be

The *San Pablo,* then the most expensive prop ever in the movies at a cost of $250,000. 1966. (COURTESY OF TWENTIETH CENTURY-FOX)

built, and the proper permits to be taken care of. It would take eighteen months for *The Sand Pebbles* to get under way. Meanwhile, director William Wyler had left the set of *The Sound of Music* at 20th Century-Fox. Wise was asked to take over the musical, and the rest is history. The picture went on to win the Academy Award for Best Picture, and Wise for Best Director.

Paul Newman had turned down *The Sand Pebbles* and in the last eighteen months of preparation, Steve McQueen had become the number one box office attraction in the world. When Newman dropped out of the race, McQueen was the natural choice for the lead role of Jake Holman.

Wise was invited to the Castle to discuss the film with Steve. As he entered the palatial grounds, he thought to himself, "In a single decade, McQueen had gone from being broke and hungry to living in a mansion on a hill." The last time Wise saw McQueen was when Steve was unemployed and pestering Neile on the set of *This Could Be the Night*. Several times during the filming, Wise had to shoo McQueen away. How times had changed.

When Wise left the Castle, Steve had been offered his most challenging role to date. In addition, he was to be paid most handsomely, a $650,000 salary and a percentage of the profits. Not knowing what was to come, McQueen earned every penny.

"He was the perfect choice for Jake Holman," said Wise. "I've never seen an actor work with mechanical things the way he does. He learned everything about operating that ship's engine, just as Jake Holman did in the script. Jake Holman is a very strong individual who doesn't bend under pressure, a guy desperately determined to maintain his own personal identity and pride. Very much like Steve.

"He's marvelous in the picture, because he has the attitude and looks to carry the dialogue. He's not only an emotional and instinctive actor, but a thinking actor."

Following *The Sound of Music*, 20th Century-Fox gave Wise the red carpet treatment; its success practically bankrolled *The Sand Pebbles'* $8 million budget. Wise could have anything he wanted, and he took advantage of Fox's generosity.

Then the most expensive prop ever for a film, a $250,000 re-creation of a gunboat used in the 1920s, was built for the film, the *San Pablo*.

*The Sand Pebbles* would be the first major American film shot entirely in Taiwan. It had four locations: Keelung, Tamsui, Taipei, and Hong Kong. Wise would bring with him a 111-man crew, with forty-seven speaking parts and thirty-two interpreters. A thousand extras would be required for several scenes. To get the Taiwanese government to agree to this, a $100,000 building was erected near the river for the film's town station, which would be turned over to the local government when the crew left. For all of this to go as planned, eighty days were originally slated for filming. Unforeseen problems turned that into seven grueling months.

Taiwan at the time was still technically at war with China. Just ten days prior to the production startup, a defecting Communist pilot had crash-landed a Russian-built 1L-28 jet bomber near Taipei. A week before, nationalist Chinese gunboats had fought a pitched battle in the

Steve McQueen in *The Sand Pebbles*

(COURTESY OF TWENTIETH CENTURY-FOX)

Formosa Strait, then limped into Keelung victoriously. *The Sand Pebbles* began filming on November 22, 1965.

Between projects, Steve always let himself go a bit. An extra ten or fifteen pounds might be gained when he wasn't on a picture. On *The Sand Pebbles*, Steve never appeared to be more fit. He had his home gym shipped to Taiwan to keep him in shape when he wasn't working. "Lawyers sharpen up with law books, and astronauts in pressure chambers, but an actor has to do it the way a prizefighter does," McQueen reasoned.

Many things contributed to the constant delays that plagued *The Sand Pebbles*. The first major delay occurred when the Keelung River, where the *San Pablo* was supposed to dock, was at low tide, and the crew had to wait two weeks for high tide. When the *San Pablo* finally arrived, the rainy season began. Steve Ferry, an extra on the film, remembers, "For three weeks, the rain put us out of business, but we still got paid." McQueen and crew did the best they could to beat the boredom. "We spent a lot of time together. We were all trapped on a little boat, and we amused ourselves as best we could: playing, diving, swimming, all those warm water things," says Ferry.

Steve found Taiwan to be a whole new world. He watched the people

McQueen never worked harder for any other role then that of Jake Holman
in *The Sand Pebbles*.                    ( Courtesy of Twentieth Century-Fox)

and observed their ways. "The thing is," he insisted, "everything is
different over there. I mean all of life from top to bottom. It was wild.
Like they say that's a nice shirt you've got on, and what they mean is
there's a spot on it." On their work ethic, "They were building a house
near where we lived out in the country, and I used to watch the guys
working. You'd see this cat going over to pick up a beam. A big 8-by-10
beam and this skinny guy gets one end up, see, and he squats down and
lays it on a pad on his shoulder and he works his way in the center and
lifts up the whole damn thing. He's got this huge beam balanced there,
you know, and he runs a couple of steps forward and a couple of steps
backward and leans into it and takes off across the field. I mean one
guy!" Steve added, "And those studs on bicycles. Everything tied on
somehow. You know, boxes and baskets and old suitcases and God
knows what—all piled up ten feet high. Rickety-rackety down the street.
You couldn't believe they'd make it, but they always did."

While in Taiwan, Steve and Neile discovered an orphanage for young
girls, mainly prostitutes, run by Edward Wojniak, a Catholic priest. In

McQueen lets off a little steam.    (COURTESY OF TWENTIETH CENTURY-FOX)

Taiwan, a boy was often the preferred child, as he could help lend a hand and support the family as he got older. A girl's only asset to her family was earning money through prostitution, and Steve found this way of life disheartening. He donated $25,000 to Wojniak's mission and continually supported Wojniak until the priest's death in the late seventies. Says a friend, "Steve supported that mission even after Father Wojniak's death. He sent them money; he sent them clothes; he sent them autographed pictures, and remember, he didn't sign autographs. He never wanted anyone to know about this. He just reached out to help. Steve was a very generous man. He would give the shirt off his back to anyone who needed it."

When the cameras finally did start rolling, Wise found himself at his wit's end with Steve. McQueen insisted that a scene be shot totally opposite the way Wise wanted it. Finally, Wise came up with a solution. A scene would be shot both ways, a Wise version and a McQueen version. If Steve liked his version better when the film was being edited, then Wise would accommodate him. This procedure would prolong filming and eventually add to the film's budget. (Incidentally, none of the scenes that Steve insisted on made it to the final version of the film.) Says Wise, "The thing with him was that you never quite knew what the mood was going to be. I was trying to line up a dolly shot. It was a difficult thing, and then all of a sudden, I felt a tap on my shoulder and it was Steve. He said, 'Now, Bob, about this wardrobe,' and I blew up. I said, 'Steve, for heaven's sake.' I used a little stronger language, frankly. 'Please don't bring that up now, I'm in the midst of something difficult right now. Let's talk about it tonight. That's it.' Well, he was really hurt, and he didn't speak to me for three days. Here I was directing the star of the film and he took directions and he was in the scenes and he would listen to me, but he did not speak one word to me for three days." Steve's agent, Stan Kamen, happened to visit McQueen that weekend. Kamen and Wise got together to decide what to do to get Steve to talk to the director again. It was decided that Wise would let Steve watch his dailies, something that Wise never allowed. "When Steve saw the dailies and saw how good he looked, he decided to talk to me again. As a matter of fact, Steve never gave me a hard time again."

The respect between costar Candice Bergen and Steve wasn't as mutual. Bergen, then all of nineteen years old, played the role of Shirley Eckert, a gentle missionary in China. In the film, a romantic relationship between the two never occurs, and the same relationship was at hand in Taiwan. In her book, *Knock Wood*, Bergen expressed her opinion of McQueen: "Steve was friendly during the shooting, inviting me to dinner with his wife Neile and the kids, advising me—in a well-meant attempt to get me to 'loosen up'—that what I really needed was to 'get it on' with some of his buddies.

"His buddies were hardly my idea of heaven: He'd arrive in Taiwan with a commando unit of six stuntmen, none under six feet and all ex-marines. They were like his personal honor guard and when he moved, they jumped.

"Coiled, combustible, Steve was like a caged animal. Daring, reckless, charming, compelling: It was difficult to relax around him—and probably unwise—for like a big wildcat, he was handsome and hypnotic, powerful and unpredictable, and he could turn on you in a flash. . . . He seemed to live by the laws of the jungle and to have contempt for those laid down by man. He reminded me of one of the great outlaws, a romantic renegade, an outcast uneasy in his skin . . . he tried to find truth and comfort in a world where he knew he didn't belong.

"Hard-drinking, hard-fighting—as time on the island ticked by, McQueen and his gang grew increasingly restless and often spent nights

Co-star Richard Attenborough became a lifelong friend of McQueen's.
(COURTESY OF TWENTIETH CENTURY-FOX)

on the prowl, roaming the little city, drinking, heckling, picking fights and pummeling."*

Steve Ferry, a friend of both McQueen and Bergen, refutes her charges of fighting with the locals. "In all the time I knew Steve, he got in one fight. That was in Hong Kong. He was in a club and some guy gave him the movie star routine and followed Steve into the john. McQueen punched him out and left him there. He panicked because it had just hit him that he was with a publicity guy. He disappeared and left the publicity guy looking for him. He went home immediately."

Loren Janes, Steve's stunt double on the film, actually dated Bergen during the movie. He doesn't remember McQueen getting in fights either. "He'd go out with the boys for a drink every now and then, but he didn't go out and beat people up. I don't think Candice liked him too much."

---

* Bergen, Candice, *Knock Wood* (New York: The Linden Press/Simon and Schuster, 1984), 161–162.

McQueen viewed co-star Candice Bergen with suspicion. He thought she was a snob, she in turn thought he was a "caged animal." 1966.

(COURTESY OF TWENTIETH CENTURY-FOX)

Janes asked Bergen how she felt the picture was going and she responded, "It's going okay under the circumstances." Janes pressed her for a more detailed answer. "What do you mean?" he asked. "Well," responded Bergen, "the director, the actors. How can I work with these people? There's no talent there." Janes couldn't believe his ears. Robert Wise, Steve McQueen, Richard Attenborough, Richard Crenna. How could she work with these people? "In my opinion," says Janes, "the guys with the little parts in the movie had more talent in their little finger than she did in her whole body. I think she was just young, impressionable, and thought there was more to her than there was."

McQueen's other costar, character actor Mako, saw another side of the movie star. The two men first met on the lot of 20th Century-Fox. "He seemed like a quiet, unassuming type of fellow," recalls Mako. "He was wearing blue jeans and a blue polo shirt and sweat socks and sneakers. He did possess confidence and charisma, but he was very quiet."

McQueen and Candice Bergen share a rare laugh. Probably no two stars were more dissimilar. (COURTESY OF TWENTIETH CENTURY-FOX)

Mako was a newcomer to feature films and was portraying Po-Han, a friendly local who befriends Jake Holman on the ship. Mako was pretty much left to do his own acting without much direction from Wise. Mc-Queen, however, liked his scenes acted out before him. During a scene in the engine room, Mako scratched his head during a rehearsal. "Are you going to scratch your head in the scene?" McQueen asked him. Unaware that he was doing anything out of the ordinary, Mako responded, "I don't know." McQueen thought Mako might steal the scene with the very act of scratching his head, something he certainly did with Yul Brynner on *The Magnificent Seven*. Now that Steve was a movie star, no actor, big or small, was ever going to steal a scene from him.

Mako learned later on when seeing the film for the first time that McQueen "really impressed me. Not so much when you're working with him in person, but when you see his work on screen. There is little wasted emotion. He came to know the camera so well. His work was so subtle and right on the money. I think that he was unique in the fact

Steve McQueen as Jake
Holman in his only
Oscar-nominated role
in *The Sand Pebbles*.
(COURTESY OF STAR FILE
PHOTOS)

that he chose to do less on the screen. By doing less, he brought simplicity on the screen, and at the same time he was very much the image of the American man."

On almost every location, Steve had Neile bring Terry and Chad to visit him. His family was his number one priority. "Our family was important to him, and he'd bring us on location to be together," says Terry. The McQueens would stay in a rented villa outside Taipei. For Steve and Neile, it was the best time of their marriage. *"The Sand Pebbles* was our happiest period ever. Steve was having a terrible time, but we were totally together. No temptations."

*Day of the Champion* was a project that Steve and John Sturges had wanted to do ever since *The Magnificent Seven.* Now that McQueen was a force to be reckoned with, the project was set to go at Warner Brothers when *The Sand Pebbles* was finished shooting. At first, Sturges's Alpha Productions would produce, but now it was to be slated as a Solar production, with Warner Brothers to distribute.

*Grand Prix,* another racing picture to be done by MGM starring James Garner, was also going to be made at the same time as *Day of the Champion.* If *Day of the Champion* could get started before *Grand Prix,* then Jack Warner would allow it to be done. The constant delays with *The Sand Pebbles* kept pushing back the start date of *Day of the Champion,* and, eventually, *Grand Prix* won out. What miffed Steve the most, though, was that he only learned about it in a newspaper in Taiwan. Garner was, in fact, one of Steve's friends. He lived just below the McQueen estate in Brentwood. Steve liked Garner's laid-back manner and at times would have fun at his expense. "I could see that Jim was very neat around his place," said Steve. "Grass always cut. Flowers trimmed. No papers in the yard—that sort of thing. So, just to piss him, I started lobbing empty beer cans down the hill into his driveway. At first, he just couldn't figure out where in hell they were comin' from. He'd have the drive all spic 'n' span when he left the house, then go home to find all these empty cans. Took him a long time to figure out it was me . . . we had ourselves some good chuckles over how pissed he got."*

Friend or no friend, in McQueen's eyes, Garner was invading his turf, and Steve felt that he was the only actor in Hollywood who had really earned the respect of professional race car drivers. While McQueen raced and competed with the best, Steve felt that Garner was only "play acting." The good man that he was, Garner called McQueen in Taiwan to tell him the news that Steve already knew. Though Steve remained polite over the phone, inside he was seething. He hung up the phone and didn't speak to Garner for another year. Says Steve Ferry, "When Steve found out that Garner was going to do *Grand Prix* first, it made him go even harder for *Le Mans*." Steve was deeply disappointed, but he managed to say, "I've been rarin' to make an honest, down-to-earth movie with lots of action behind the wheel of a racing car, but an actor's life is full of gambles and unexpected twists of fate. So let's just say that I hope to make that movie someday."

Times got even tougher in Taiwan when Steve became sick with the flu for three days. He had never missed a day on the set, and it was a blow to his ego when he couldn't come to work.

One day, while Steve was out, Wise began shooting the fireball scene in which the extras were throwing torches at the *San Pablo*. Camera operator Paul Hill took a flaming torch in the chest. No one had it easy on *The Sand Pebbles*.

To this day, director Robert Wise claims *The Sand Pebbles* was the most difficult picture he's ever made. "I must say that the cast and crew came through a very difficult situation admirably. It's not easy for Americans to be dropped into a country that is completely foreign, and then be subjected to lengthy delays." (Ten years later, when Francis Ford Cop-

---

* Nolan, William, *McQueen* (New York: Congdon & Weed, 1984), 56.

pola was experiencing the same problems on *Apocalypse Now,* he requested a copy of *The Sand Pebbles* from Wise. He wanted to show the crew what the end result could be in spite of any problems.)

In May 1966, after six months abroad, three months of delays, and $3 million over budget, *The Sand Pebbles* was completed. Said Neile, "I never saw him work so hard or get so bored as he was after those six months in Taiwan. By the time we got to Hong Kong, he'd really had it. He couldn't wait to get home." When the McQueen family safely landed on U.S. soil, Steve got out and literally kissed the ground.

"Anything I ever did wrong," Steve confessed, "I paid for in Taiwan. I just hope something good comes out of it." What came out of it, for Steve McQueen, was an Academy Award nomination for Best Actor.

McQueen took the rest of the year off from filming in pursuit of other projects not related to the movie industry. The July 6, 1966, edition of the *Hollywood Reporter* noted that Steve and his friend Elmer Valentine "are opening up a Spanish restaurant on the Sunset Strip, La Rebellion de Los Adolescents" (The Rebellion of the Adolescents). Nothing ever came of this idea.

Steve had always considered himself a conservationist and, though he was apolitical, in his own way he would contribute to the cause. He narrated *The Coming of the Roads,* a half-hour commentary against destruction of natural beauty, which aired on September 17, 1966.

In early December, according to *The Citizen News,* the McQueens threw the "Moddest wingding of the season." The casual party had Steve dressed in black leather huggers, with Neile in "the briefest 'A' mini-tunic you'll ever see." The list of guests included Joan Collins, Jane Fonda, Anthony Newley, Eva Gabor, Polly Bergen, Elke Sommer, the Milton Berles, the Pat Boones, the James Coburns, the David Janssens, the Peter Falks, John Wayne, Ben Gazzara, Robert Culp, Adam West, the Robert Mitchums, Lee Marvin, Inger Stevens, and the Robert Wises. Lee Marvin commented, "If a bomb dropped on here tonight, half of Hollywood would be gone."

Hollywood embraced the McQueens.

McQueen grew to dislike publicity and didn't trust reporters. Explains Loren Janes, "For one thing, he was hard of hearing and it looked like he didn't understand what they were saying. He was very sensitive about his lack of education and was afraid he might not understand them." McQueen always felt that reporters, in his words, "might cap me up."

For *The Sand Pebbles,* he embarked on an unprecedented publicity tour. David Foster was called by the president of 20th Century-Fox, Richard Zanuck, to accompany Steve to New York for a media blitz. "In those days, publicity in New York helped a picture tremendously," says Foster.

Foster lined up all of the shows on which McQueen was to appear. He first went on *The Ed Sullivan Show*. It was tradition at the beginning of the show for Sullivan to announce a celebrity in the audience. And so, Sullivan said, "Now, tonight in our audience is Mr. Steve McQueen. Steve, would you please take a bow." And Steve took a bow. Next was *What's My Line?*, on which he appeared as a mystery guest. He then did *The Tonight Show* with Johnny Carson. "He was excited about all of these things. It meant that he had arrived," says Foster. "He didn't enjoy doing them, but he also realized that these things made him a star. He was uncomfortable in one sense, but he realized the value of what it did for him. Certain things he did for great pleasure because it elevated him."

Zanuck hired a limousine for McQueen and Foster as they made the rounds. Each day in New York, a full schedule of interviews with reporters was slated. By the second day, Steve had had enough. He told Foster, "You call Fox and dump the limo. I can't stand it. Have them deliver a Volkswagen and I'll drive us around to the interviews." Foster complied with Steve's wishes, and they finished their interviews with McQueen driving them around the Big Apple.

Foster also remembers a night at the Metropolitan Opera when he, his wife Jackie, Steve, and Neile had been given choice seats. Five minutes into the show, Steve got up and left. "He didn't say to us, 'Hey, I'm bored, let's go do something else.' He didn't even bother to tell Neile he was leaving. He just got up and left," laughs Foster.

Three months later, Foster got a phone call from Zanuck. "Remember when you guys were in New York for *The Sand Pebbles*?" Cautiously, Foster answered, "Yeah?" Zanuck continued, "What the hell happened to that Volkswagen?" Foster remembered that he and McQueen had taken a limo back to the airport. He quickly put in a phone call to Steve. "Steve, where did you leave the rental car in New York?" Steve thought about it for a second and remembered, "In the parking lot of the hotel." Foster says incredulously now, "It had been in a parking lot of some hotel for three months and the clock was ticking, and Dick Zanuck was breathing down my neck." It all came down to movie star behavior. Now that the studios were picking up the tab, Steve could act like one.

*The Sand Pebbles* premiered at the Rivoli in New York on December 20, 1966, to rave reviews. Arthur Knight of *The Saturday Review* wrote, "Richard Crenna is outstanding, Candice Bergen attractive, Richard Attenborough effective—and all of them dominated by Steve McQueen, who is nothing short of wonderful in the pivotal role of Holman." The

*New York Times* raved, "Performed by Steve McQueen with the most restrained, honest, heartfelt acting he has ever done, . . . we see the ultimate reward for the kind of service he ruefully performs." *Variety* announced, "Steve McQueen delivers an outstanding performance and looks the part he plays so well. Wise's otherwise expert direction is matched by meticulous production."

*The Sand Pebbles* was nominated for eight Academy Awards, including Best Actor for McQueen, the first and only Oscar nomination of his career. The others nominees were Paul Scofield for *A Man for All Seasons*, Richard Burton for *Who's Afraid of Virginia Woolf,* and Michael Caine for *Alfie*. It was a British sweep for the Oscars that year and Paul Scofield took the Academy Award home, though it is McQueen's portrayal of Jake Holman that is much better remembered today than Scofield's Sir Thomas More.

Neile believed it was fate, as Steve would have been impossible to live with if he had won the Oscar. As to some consolation, Steve won the World Film Favorite award for favorite actor by the Hollywood Foreign Press Association and received the Photoplay Gold Medal Award. In Japan, he was named the most popular foreign star for the second consecutive year.

Life kept throwing Steve curveballs. On January 12, 1967, he was asked by movie critic and teacher Arthur Knight to address the USC cinema department at 20th Century-Fox studios. "Me," thought McQueen, "at the university, answering questions? Me, who stopped at ninth grade? Can you believe that?"

The crowd of young college students loved Steve. He was on their wavelength. One student asked him, "How do you go about picking your movies?" Steve answered, "I do it by instinct. But I have to be careful because I'm a limited actor. I mean, my range isn't very great. There's a whole lot of stuff I can't do, so I have to find characters and situations that feel right. Even then, when I've got something that fits, it's a hell of a lot of work."

As the lecture ended and Steve was making his way out the door, Knight thanked him. "Any time," said Steve. "I got good vibrations in there."

*Variety* reported on March 16, 1967, that "Steve McQueen and Montgomery Ward are talking a $10 million partnership regarding the McQueen motorcycle." Said McQueen, "It will revolutionize the motorcycle industry." (Nothing ever came of that idea, either.)

On March 21, 1967, Steve immortalized his place in Hollywood history by becoming the 153d star to put his footprints and signature in cement at Grauman's Chinese Theater. Steve and Neile pulled up in his burgundy Ferrari before 2,000 fans, who witnessed the event. Life didn't get any sweeter than this. (In a mysterious coincidence, Steve McQueen and Ali MacGraw's cement blocks are the only two on the grounds that are upside down.)

With *Day of the Champion* blown out of the water, McQueen and director Arthur Hiller had a project set for the summer of 1967. However, Hiller's film fell through. Restless, Steve had his heart set on working. He told friend Steve Ferry that he was out of work for the summer. Ferry, just coming off Norman Jewison's *The Russians Are Coming,* mentioned to Steve a new script Jewison had in his possession, then called *The Crown Caper.* Says Ferry, "Norman Jewison hasn't talked to me since."

*The Crown Caper,* later retitled *The Thomas Crown Affair,* was written by Boston lawyer Alan R. Trustman. Trustman recalls, "One Sunday afternoon in 1966, I got bored watching television, it was too early in the season to go skiing, and suddenly for no apparent reason I thought it would be fun to write a screen story. I worked on Sundays and a few nights during the week. In two months *The Crown Caper* was done."

Trustman sent in his screenplay to the William Morris Agency and was soon being courted by a Hollywood agent. Norman Jewison had just come back from Moscow after a screening of *The Russians Are Coming.* "The William Morris Agency, in a brilliant piece of agency work, sold it to Jewison with a stunt," says Trustman. "His plane stopped at JFK on the way back to Los Angeles; they had a messenger meet him at the plane who told Jewison he had exactly five minutes from the landing time to Los Angeles to say no. So, with that sort of background, he was convinced he had the hottest script in years. He went for it."

Jewison boasted of the script, "It was a knockout story with original characters. You have never seen a pair like Thomas Crown and his nemesis, Vicky Anderson, on the screen."

The story involved the distinguished Thomas Crown, an investment banker who has had it all and has done it all. Life has run out of challenges for Crown, so he devises a plan to make things interesting again. He meticulously masterminds a bank robbery with the help of five men, who have never met each other or have ever seen Crown. It is considered the "perfect" crime. Enter Vicky Anderson (Faye Dunaway), a glamorous, but sharp investigator who works for the insurance company that has to reimburse the banks for the $2.5 million heist. Anderson assists the FBI when their efforts lead nowhere. She is given some photos and a list of men who have flown to Geneva in recent months (for deposits in Swiss bank accounts, presumably). She is convinced Thomas Crown is her man, and she always gets her man. The two fall in love, and Crown tests her loyalty when he announces that he intends to rob another bank. She must decide if she can overcome her emotions and maintain her professional integrity.

A request was submitted to the FBI, along with a script, seeking permission to film the FBI headquarters in Boston. The agency was outraged by the film's portrayal of them as bumbling, incompetent idiots. It refused Walter Mirisch and United Artists' wishes. An FBI memorandum dated March 17, 1967, read:

> To: Mr. Wick
> From: M. A. Jones
> Subject: REQUEST FOR BUREAU COOPERATION
> IN FILMING SCENES FOR PROPOSED
> MOTION PICTURE "THE CROWN CAPER"

Mr. Deloach has received a letter dated 3/17/67 from (deleted) of the Motion Picture Association of America, Inc., requesting permission to photograph the Boston office in connection with proposed captioned motion picture being produced by Walter Mirisch. It is noted that on 2/24/67 the Boston Office was contacted in this regard by a Mirisch representative who was told his request would have to be referred to the Bureau. Steve McQueen will star in this film, which is written by Alan R. Trustman.

McQueen indicated he planned to participate in the March on Washington in 1963.

This screenplay has been reviewed in the Crime Research Section. It involves a bank robbery in Boston conceived and directed by Thomas Crown, who employs five others to commit the robbery and then secretes the remaining proceeds in a Swiss bank. The investigation by the Boston FBI Office, headed by Edward Rock, makes no progress until the bank's insurer assigns a beautiful young investigator, Vicky, to work with the FBI. Vicky completely dominates the investigation and entirely through her efforts identifies the subjects and furnishes this information to the FBI. Sex is both explicit and implied throughout the story and is especially apparent in the romantic relationship between Vicky and Crown. Rock is fully aware of the methods being used by Vicky to extract admissions from Crown. The story ends when Vicky and the FBI are outwitted by Crown, who flies to Brazil, leaving a final invitation to Vicky to join him in the country.

OBSERVATIONS:

This is an outrageous portrayal of the FBI, which depicts a Bureau bank robbery investigation being taken over completely by a young girl who uses her physical charms to conduct her mission. No doubt the producer foresees this film as a great money-maker at the box office as a result of its great emphasis on sex and the use of the FBI's good name.

RECOMMENDATION:

That we have absolutely nothing to do with the proposed film and that (deleted) be so advised.

*The Thomas Crown Affair* was the only film that Steve ever had to fight for. Writer Alan Trustman had created the role of Crown with Sean Connery in mind. If he didn't work out, then maybe Rock Hudson or Jean Paul Belmondo could play Thomas Crown. "Jewison didn't want him. Walter Mirisch didn't want him. United Artists did not want him. I clearly did not want him," says Alan Trustman.

McQueen was blue jeans and a T-shirt, gulping can after can of beer. Thomas Crown was tailored three-piece suits, stirring and sniffing a glass of brandy before he tasted it. McQueen raced motorcycles in the desert. Thomas Crown played the sport of the bluebloods, polo. Steve would have to abandon everything that was known to him in order to portray Thomas Crown.

Norman Jewison did actually offer the part to Sean Connery first, but, according to Alan Trustman, "he diddled them." Trustman continues, "He diddled them all the way up to a month before principal photography. Connery made Norman and Walter Mirisch sit there for three days at the Sherry Netherland while he sat there at the Plaza next door and didn't say yes, but he didn't say no. That's the way they behave in this business. You're not required to say no. Now after three days you're supposed to figure out that the answer is no." Connery later conceded to Walter Mirisch that he should have done *The Thomas Crown Affair,* as his James Bond roles typecast him for many years afterward in Hollywood. The movie could have opened up all kinds of doors for him at the time.

It was a strange situation. Norman Jewison held in his hand the hottest script in town, and no one was available to do it; that is, except for Steve McQueen, who wanted to do it very badly. Finally, exasperated, Jewison gave in and awarded the part to Steve. McQueen's signature on the dotted line meant guaranteed ticket sales and actually, Jewison needed McQueen just as much as McQueen needed Jewison. Years later McQueen felt that Jewison "used him" for *The Thomas Crown Affair*.

When Alan Trustman found out that McQueen had been hired, he hit the roof. "At the time, he was a decent character actor with a limited range, beautiful moves, and a reputation for being difficult," remembers Trustman. "There was no way he could play my distinguished Bostonian, but they cast him and that was it." Grumbling, Trustman insisted that United Artists assemble every piece of television and movie footage available on McQueen. For three days, ten hours a day, he viewed every piece of footage on Steve and made a checklist of what the actor could and could not do. "I discovered that if he was comfortable and stayed within a certain range of characterization, he was terrific. The moment he became uncomfortable, you could squirm watching him," notes Trustman.

Based on his checklist, Trustman did the rewrite and McQueen liked what he saw. When Trustman met McQueen, he sat him down to explain the character of Thomas Crown. "You could be the new Humphrey Bogart," explained Trustman. "You are shy, you don't talk too much. You are a loner, but a person with integrity. You're quiet, you're gutsy as hell. You like girls, but are basically shy with women. You have a tight smile, you don't show your teeth, but it's a small smile around your mouth and you never deliver a sentence with more than five or ten words long, because paragraphs make you lose interest or something goes wrong with your delivery. As long as you can stay with that, you can be number one." Adds Trustman, "The reason why my movies made money, I'm convinced, is not that my scripts were brilliant, but that they were good. A movie is made by force of personality that dominates the movie, and if he has a clear idea of what he wants and he gets it on film, you've got a strong central character and a terrific picture. I went over this with McQueen and he dominated *The Thomas Crown Affair*."

Steve had known about the script for some time, and he chose to do nothing about it. Says Neile, "He didn't want it, but he didn't want anybody else to have it either." That is, until one morning, while Neile was fixing his French toast, she casually mentioned to Steve that Norman Jewison didn't want him for *The Crown Caper*. Steve stopped eating his breakfast and shot Neile a quizzical look. "What are you talking about?" Continuing with the charade, Neile pointed out, "Well, you know Norman wants either Sean Connery or Rock Hudson for this part, and I just think it's unfortunate, because I think you could really be terrific in it." Steve looked at her and asked, "What do you mean, Norman doesn't want me for the part?" Neile went on, "He doesn't

want you. He's given the script to everyone in Hollywood BUT YOU."
That did it. His pride was on the line, and when Steve finished his
breakfast, he put in a phone call to Norman Jewison.

"If you're calling about Thomas Crown, you can forget it, Steve," said
the brutally honest Jewison. "How about I come over for a visit?" Steve
asked. Fine by Jewison, but however cunning Steve was going to be,
thought the director, McQueen was simply not Thomas Crown.

Wasting no time when he got there, Steve expressed his desire to play
Thomas Crown. "You're not right for it, Steve," Jewison said. "My God,
this man wears a shirt and tie, he's a Phi Beta Kappa, graduate of
Dartmouth." Steve said, "That's why I want to do it." Jewison says now
that "I think he wanted to grow up; he wanted to play a part that he
had never played before, and maybe, in a secret desire deep within him,
he wanted to be Thomas Crown—you know, who was so bright and
erudite and cultured and sophisticated and chic and smart and a Bostonian from an old family. All of the things that Steve wasn't." McQueen
even admitted, "I hate having to dress up in a tux and black tie. I'm
more myself in a T-shirt and jeans."

Steve was convinced that he could play Thomas Crown. "I thought of
changing my image for more than a year. I felt it was time to get past
those tough, uptight types. This dude [Thomas Crown] wants to show
he can beat the establishment at its own game," said Steve. "He's essen-
tially a rebel, like me. Sure, a high society rebel, but he's my kind of cat.
It was just that his outer fur was different—so I got me some fur."

McQueen totally threw himself into the part. He had to learn polo, a
sport that was foreign to him. His athletic ability and his determination
paid off, and in three weeks he had the sport down cold. Says Norman
Jewison, "He was so competitive that he got out on the polo field and
played until his hands bled. The blood was literally running off his
hands, because he had to prove to those guys out there, those other
professional polo players, that he could play."

For the polo scene, Norman Jewison used the multiple-image design
he first saw in Canada in the short film *A Place to Stand*. The multiple
image was one of many innovative pieces in *The Thomas Crown Affair*.

Before principal photography took place in Boston, Jewison hired
Nikita Knatz for two reasons: to work as a sketch artist and to help keep
an eye on McQueen. Jewison didn't accept prima donnas. That's where
Knatz came in. "McQueen was sitting on top of the screenwriters and
directors and would abuse them every day," says Knatz.

Knatz first met McQueen at the Mirisch Corporation offices. Jewison
invited Knatz in and the two began talking, ignoring McQueen, who
was sitting in the corner, bouncing off the walls, chain-smoking ciga-

rettes. Finally, McQueen stood up and offered his hand to Knatz. "How would you like to shake hands with a movie star?" Steve asked. Knatz was not impressed. "The man was a perpetual motion machine," he observed. "I was not that crazy about him as a human being. He didn't impress me that much, except as a very spoiled brat. He got everything he wanted, whereas I had to work for everything I got."

Soon McQueen became intrigued by Knatz. Knatz, a Russian immigrant from Saint Petersburg, was a child when the Soviets invaded. He lost four brothers, a sister, and his father in the conflict. Knatz and his mother were sent to various prison camps for five years, until a family sponsored him in the United States. Before dying, his father had written his mother a letter stating, "Find Nikita a judo school."

Knatz was a Russian in the fifties, growing up smack dab in the middle of the McCarthy era. "You've got to understand, the kids at that time had a moral right to beat the shit out of you if you were Russian." Knatz partially lost his hearing, like Steve, from one of the many beatings he received. He quickly enrolled in judo and within two years was awarded a black belt. A high school All-American his sophomore, junior, and senior years, he was given a scholarship to any college of his choice. After being named a college All-American in his sophomore year, he was drafted in the fourteenth round by the New York Titans. He lasted nine games before his knee and jaw were broken. Knatz saw the writing on the wall and joined the service, the 101st Airborne division, special security forces. He went on 1,017 jumps, served three years, and earned three Purple Hearts, a Bronze Star, and clusters. After he got out of the service, he saw an ad in the newspaper looking for Russians who could speak English for Norman Jewison's *The Russians Are Coming*. Knatz won a speaking part in the film, but it was his sketching between setups that caught Jewison's eye. "Hey, you're pretty good," Jewison encouraged. Says Knatz, "Norman sponsored me since then."

During the filming of the graveyard scene, in which Thomas Crown picks up his money, McQueen noticed Knatz out of the corner of his eye. Knatz, an accomplished martial artist in many forms, was practicing the handling of a sword. Knatz caught McQueen spying on him. Finally, Steve came over and said, "Show me some moves." Knatz was offended. "That's the time when you shut up and sit down and read the newspaper. What he did was a put-down," he says. McQueen constantly pestered Knatz about martial arts. Knatz couldn't care less if he was a movie star or not. McQueen then asked Walter Mirisch to talk to Knatz about training with Steve on Sundays only. Knatz gave in, and the two began training together. Recalls Knatz, "I had been hanging around

Bruce Lee at the time, and Bruce had more of an ego than McQueen. He couldn't stand to be second banana, so he would do tricks in front of Steve to impress him. Steve started training with both of us, and both Bruce and I were getting sick of Steve."

Steve would constantly invite Knatz to his Palm Springs home, and Knatz would turn him down. McQueen would then show up on his doorstep. "I would just tolerate him. He even followed me where I taught, and one time he almost seriously got hurt. He pulled a Mc-Queen macho thing with Don Anger, a small guy, but a real martial artist. McQueen got on his case a little bit and tested him a bit too much. Don was half of McQueen's size and just threw him across the room, the length of the twenty-four-mat dojo. It was then that McQueen learned his lesson."

However pushy Steve may have been, Knatz felt that he was like a little child, and Knatz felt in some ways his mentor. While jogging on the beach on location one day, Steve spotted bubbles in the sand at low tide. "What are those?" he asked Knatz. "They could be air traps or clams," he was told. McQueen didn't believe Knatz, so he knelt down on the sand and a clam squirted him in the face. "Son-of-a-bitch, the thing crapped on me!" Knatz began laughing. "All it was was salt water. He was a little kid with nature. If McQueen didn't understand a word, he'd make you repeat it seven or eight times and then he'd go look it up in the dictionary. He was embarrassed by his education," says Knatz.

Knatz also remembers a lobster and clambake for the cast and crew. McQueen had never eaten a lobster before and announced, "It looks like a big bug to me" (a line he later parodied in *Tom Horn*). Knatz recalls, "They bring in these lobsters in crates and McQueen picks one up the wrong way and it snaps at him and he tries to shake it off and can't. He starts laughing at the stupidity of it because he knew better than to stick his finger in there. Then he hits himself in the head with this lobster and Chad [McQueen's son] just roars with laughter."


Steve felt more pressure on *Thomas Crown* than ever before. He was never comfortable in a suit and tie, but for the film, he wore one in almost every scene. "Don't forget," says Nikita Knatz, "this role was a hump for him to get over. Out of the blue jeans and into the jackets, so to speak."

Shooting began in June 1967, and the very first scene was the actual bank robbery. Using concealed cameras known only to the crew, bank guards, and tellers, the staged holdup caught the emotions of the customers on film. Says Jewison, "Our actors scared a lot of customers and pedestrians who thought they were seeing a real robbery." He laughs. "But oddly, no one tried to interfere. I think they were afraid to get involved."

Everything about Steve's character had to be perfect, down to the watch he wore. Before shooting one of the first scenes, Steve tried on watch after watch, looking for the right one. "That's not me," he bitched, and tried on another. Five minutes passed, then ten, then twenty. Finally, after twenty-five minutes, with 150 people on the set waiting, Steve said, "Why, my watch is better than any of these!" McQueen approached a film role differently than most actors. "I believe in lots of preparation. I want to look the part of the character I'm playing. It takes time. It takes study. It takes a deep understanding of the character involved."

For *The Thomas Crown Affair,* McQueen was being paid a $750,000 base salary. He was given a dune buggy by the producers and was allowed to keep his tailor-made suits after filming. Yet the day after the watch incident, agent Stan Kamen delivered an envelope to Mirisch. Inside was a bill made up by McQueen reading, "Use of a watch— $250.00." Hollywood lore tells you to act up when you're on top. Steve McQueen more than fully complied.

Steve was given a Phi Beta Kappa key to attach to his vest. "I couldn't get used to the key," he admitted. "My fraternity should be a couple of hub caps on a tire chain."

"He was very nervous about the role," says director of photography Haskell Wexler. "I never really talked to Steve about anything but cars. We went tearing away from the set in a dune buggy one day and the engine literally blew up. I spent about forty minutes with him just stranded. It felt like in those forty minutes, that's when I got to know the real Steve McQueen. I think he just wished that he didn't have to go back to the set and be Thomas Crown for that day."

Nikita Knatz offers, "He was incredibly nervous because he was playing an intellect. Steve redefined that character.

"In the scene after the first bank robbery, he comes home and his butler pours him a drink and he sits backs, drinks the martini, lights the cigar, and Steve starts cackling at his success because the whole reason he does it is to rob the bank. He didn't need the money. He wanted to prove how smart he was, to thumb his nose at society. McQueen's playing himself. It was a metaphor for his whole life. For the people who snubbed him his whole life, first with the industry, then with his childhood. Even after all of his successes, he was never really fully accepted or invited to the A parties in Hollywood."

Not only did Steve's role bring out his insecurity, but his costar, Faye

Dunaway, put him into a downright funk. Dunaway's New York stage presence threw him off completely. In addition, she had all of her lines memorized. Steve confided to Neile, "She threw everything at me but the kitchen sink!"

Nikita Knatz saw them rehearse and feels that eventually McQueen came to regard Dunaway, not as a costar, but as a substar. "She was not at all camera conscious and did not understand the camera. McQueen was extremely camera conscious and knew how to get the shot. It was the money shot each time, and it was always the shot that was better for the project, not just him. He cared about certain projects, certainly that one," explains Knatz.

As for "The Kiss," the sex-with-chess scene that was the trademark of *The Thomas Crown Affair*, McQueen and Dunaway, according to Haskell Wexler, "really went at it." The one-minute shot took eight hours to film and days to set up just right. The shot had to be lined up in silhouette, just as the sun was coming down. With conditions just right, everyone was set to film the scene—except Steve, who was out doing wheelies in the sand with his dune buggy. He came in and said apologetically, "Gee, I'm sorry, I didn't know you were ready." Disappointed, Jewison put his head down and said, "No, we missed it, Steve, so we're not going to shoot it."

Finally, with the shot set up and ready to go, Jewison yelled "Action," and the two stars began to kiss. "McQueen and Dunaway seemed oblivious to everything around them. They were really into it," claims Wexler.

"The Kiss" led to many rumors that the two stars were carrying on an affair. Not that Steve wouldn't have warmed to the idea, but Dunaway kept him at arm's length. She responded to the question directly, "Steve McQueen—he was married and everything. I didn't date him. I thought [married men] would all be trouble, so I didn't want any part of them!"

Norman Jewison adds, "Faye Dunaway gave him a tough time, because I don't think she fell for his charm. I think he always tried to seduce women with this kind of charming, not caring, macho relationship, but she kind of held him off, I think. Maybe that's why they're so good together in that film. It's the love story between two shits."

For all of the many headaches McQueen caused Jewison, the director couldn't help but like his insecure star. "He was very competitive, very tough, but there was something about him I liked. He was like a kid brother, the brother who never went to school, like the brother who'd been hurt. He worked very hard on that film. I think he enjoyed it, but I think he was enormously insecure about doing it, in spite of the fact that he talked me into the part. Maybe that was it, maybe that's why he did it, because I had turned him down," says Jewison.

Faye Dunaway said of him, "I can't say enough good about Steve. I've seen him help young actors to an extreme degree, and he works very hard. There's a feeling of control in him that a woman responds to. It's difficult to try to analyze his appeal. He stimulates that cuddly feeling. He's the misunderstood bad boy you're sure you can cure with a little warmth and some home cooking. There was a time when I couldn't take my eyes off him when he was on the screen. He seems to have the quality of bothering the audience, like Bogart did, and the other greats of the past. They made the audience care when you watched them."*

The $4 million production brought back $14 million at the box office. *The Thomas Crown Affair* was McQueen's fourth hit in a row, and critics agreed it was a new Steve McQueen. Kathleen Carroll of the *New York Daily News* wrote, "A polished McQueen, minus his motorcyclist's mumble, shows a whole new facet of his active personality. He is cast most successfully." The *New York Post* pointed out, "McQueen, dashing with verve, unlimited energy and bright, inquiring eyes, makes you wonder if he's hatching something akin to a turkey." *The Saturday Review* claimed, "Steve McQueen is no underworld hoodlum with dreams of glory, but is himself a member of the Establishment—an impressively successful investment banker."

Steve's tailor-made suits, blond hair, and penetrating blue eyes transformed him into a matinee idol. When the picture was released, the "Belles of Memphis," a group of southern college women, voted Mc-Queen "the sexiest man in America."

*The Thomas Crown Affair* would become Steve's favorite work, as Norman Jewison guided a perfect performance out of him. Nikita Knatz explains, "*Thomas Crown* has no McQueen signatures in it at all. Jewison had McQueen doing what he wanted to do all along. The chess game— it looks like McQueen ad-libbed it. It was all predesigned by Jewison. He took Steve out of his element: high-fashion suits, Phi Beta Kappa key. Jewison really directed the man."

The movie had its world premiere on June 18, 1968, at Boston's Sack Music Hall. A black-tie affair, Steve looked as dapper as he ever had before. He was one of the last to show up, and a mob rushed him as he entered the hall. A few of the police officers assigned to the event had to lift McQueen onto their shoulders to get him past the adoring crowd. He laughed at the absurdity of it all, looking every bit the movie star who was sitting on top of the world.

---

* Hunter, Alan, *Faye Dunaway* (New York: St. Martin's Press, 1986).

McQueen in his most memorable screen role as Lt. Frank Bullitt in the thriller "Bullitt." 1968.　　　　COURTESY OF WARNER BROTHERS/SEVEN ARTS.

# SOLAR POWER

*When I did* **Bullitt,** *I stole some of my best stuff from some of these students at USC. I'd go over there and look at their films, man, and I stole every thing I could.*

STEVE MCQUEEN

STEVE HAD TOYED for years with the idea of a full-scale production company. Solar Productions, Steve's company, was initially formed in 1961 as a tax shelter. Wanting to test his power and fueled by his creativity, he sought to turn Solar into a bona fide force in the industry, appointing himself the boss, buying scripts, choosing material, and making the kind of films that he wanted. He was not content to just act. "I don't mind failing," he said, but "to do safe things doesn't interest me. An actor's profession is the worst sort of profession for ups and downs. It's all chance. For failure there's also tremendous satisfaction of scoring a triumph in something you believe. I go for broke."

Now that he was the president of his own company, Steve saw the world through different eyes. "History has cartwheeled," he said. "Proprietors are not the heavies anymore. The unions are. Here's one example: I do my thinking behind a wheel of a car. I like to drive myself to the location, but the producers association has signed a contract with the Teamsters that says film workers, the star, director, everybody has to be driven to the set. So, if I'm filming in Malibu, I have to get up an hour and a half earlier in Brentwood, drive to Warner's, then get driven all the way west again to Malibu to location. It's ridiculous. It's one area that can be negotiated." Steve admitted, "I'm getting my education as we go along, using my power as an actor."

Robert Relyea had not seen Steve since the making of *The Great Escape.* Five years had passed when Relyea got a call from the William

155

Morris Agency wanting to set up a business deal with him as Solar's vice president and executive producer.

Steve also signed Jack Reddish as the staff production manager. All three would become the lifeblood of Solar, with Steve as the force behind it all.

On August 23, 1967, *The Hollywood Reporter* announced a six-picture deal between Warner Brothers and Solar Productions. Solar was to produce six pictures a year for Warner, two to star McQueen, the other four without him. Those with McQueen were budgeted at $6 million to $7 million apiece, those without him no less than $3 million per picture. The original six pictures Solar was slated to deliver to Warner Brothers were *Bullitt, The Man on a Nylon String, The Cold War Swap, Day of the Champion,* and *Adam at 6:00 A.M.,* and *Suddenly Single,* featuring a young actor by the name of Michael Douglas. Solar Productions had read over 500 properties "to get the stories we want."

"We at Solar think of our company as a family, and when it comes to production, we encourage everyone to contribute ideas," McQueen said. As an example, he pointed out, "Often a grip or juicer will come to us with an idea, and all of us will sit down and discuss it. This is not a normal attitude in the film industry." He added, "We fly by the seat of our pants here, and if we crash, we have no one to blame but ourselves." In Solar's offices, a sign read: TODAY HOLLYWOOD, TOMORROW . . . THE WORLD!

Steve was now a businessman. He took pride in the fact that a kid from the streets was now the president of his own company. His usual blue jeans and T-shirt look had been cast aside for a suit and a tie. He looked forward to going to work every morning. Life was sweet.

On an early morning in January 1968, Steve received a phone call from an anonymous source. The person told him, "There's a new book out now that lists all of the celebrities in Hollywood who are homosexuals. I thought you'd like to know your name is on the list." Then the caller hung up. As Steve placed the phone on the receiver, Neile watched his good mood turn into seething anger.

"What's wrong?" she asked. Steve told her of the caller's message. Most other men would have shrugged it off after a few minutes, but not Steve. The caller caused irreparable damage to his ego.

Neile suggested that they call a friend in the FBI to trace the publication of the book, but after a few weeks, nothing was found. She dropped the subject after a while, but Steve found the insinuation much too damaging to let go of.

Simply put, Steve was repulsed by homosexuals. Often in his days in New York, he wore Bermuda shorts, and many men approached him. "They take me for a damn fag!" he exclaimed. No one had the courage to tell him it was his shorts.

On the set of *The Towering Inferno,* Paul Newman expressed interest in playing the role of a homosexual track coach having an affair with a world-class runner. Steve told Newman point-blank, "Well, Paul, you've got more balls than I do. I could never play a fag." Now, he was being called one and he went out to disprove it. It was the beginning of the end of his marriage to Neile.

*Bullitt* was one picture that Steve did not want to do. It was taken from Robert Pike's novel *Mute Witness,* a story about a New York police detective. The property had been owned by Bill Nantony, who had sold the rights to *Mute Witness* five times, each time at a successively higher price. McQueen and Solar Productions were the fifth purchaser.

The thought of playing a police detective at first appalled him. Once, while Jay Sebring was cutting Steve's hair, Neile brought up the subject of *Bullitt.* Steve's response was, "No way am I playin' a cop. Those kids call 'em pigs, man. What are you trying to do to me?" he asked Neile. He balked: "Why, those kids would turn on me so fast it'd make your head spin!"

Over time he had changed his mind, however, and he decided that an honest portrayal of a cop might help recast the image of police officers. His past run-ins helped him form an opinion at an early age, but recently he was reconsidering. One day he and a reporter took a spin in Steve's Ferrari through the hills of Brentwood, when Steve noticed the speedometer at 70 mph while taking a blind curve in the road. A patrolman on motorcycle was on duty when the car roared by. The officer promptly caught up to the Ferrari and wrote up a ticket. He approached and noticed it was McQueen. Handing over the ticket, he said apologetically, "Steve, if I'd known it was you . . . ." Steve wouldn't hear of it. Cheerfully, he said, "If you play, you pay." The officer chatted with the two for a few minutes before telling Steve, "Wait till I get out of here before you open that thing up again, will you?" After he left, McQueen turned to the reporter and said, "Those guys aren't so bad, you know. Some of them are okay."

Steve also asked his friend Steve Ferry about the idea of playing a cop. Ferry's response was, "It's time that somebody did this and you're up right now. Your time has come."

Solar enlisted the help of Alan Trustman, who had done the screenplay for *The Thomas Crown Affair*. Trustman wrote the first treatment for *Bullitt,* but when he handed over the finished product, McQueen still wasn't terribly excited about the script. Its muddled plot didn't make sense to him, but Neile was totally convinced that the film title alone would bring in business. Trustman defends his treatment of *Bullitt:* "Do you know what a hook is? A hook is a device you use to keep the audience in their seat. If you go out to buy the popcorn during the picture, you're going to miss one line and you won't understand the movie and the confusion is deliberate. There is an inherent plot and you don't put all of it on the screen. It's the opposite of television. A television audience gets infuriated if they don't understand what's going on every five minutes. A movie audience is locked into it by the confusion."

Director Peter Yates was in England when he was sent a script via a Pan Am hostess. He read it and thought it was "awful."

Steve and Robert Relyea saw Peter Yates's *Robbery,* a suspenseful crime drama about the complex heist of the British Royal Mail. They noticed nice little touches in the film, plus a chase scene that left Steve mesmerized. Relyea comments, "Yates had a chase scene in that movie that involved cars moving along very fast, then cutting to these children at a crosswalk. It made you so nervous you couldn't see straight." McQueen wanted Yates to direct *Bullitt* from that very moment.

Agent Marty Baum of the William Morris Agency had been after Yates for some time to come to Hollywood. Yates had done three British films but had never been to America. Baum had arranged for him to reread the script for *Bullitt,* but Yates balked: "I'm not coming to America to make that kind of film!"

Baum did manage to fly Yates to Los Angeles to give his opinion of the script. It was a well-managed attempt to hire him for director of *Bullitt* and within hours later Yates was signed. "I was just happy enough being a director in Hollywood. Who was I to say no?" he laughs.

Yates, who did not know of Steve's reputation for being hard on directors, found McQueen a "delight." He believes, "I was at a great advantage because I had an English accent and Steve took that as a sign that I was much more clever than I actually was. I must say, I found him incredibly supportive at all times." Robert Relyea differs in his opinion. "Steve was difficult on directors," he says. "He knew what he wanted to do, but he put pressure on everybody to try and know what they were doing. He would say to Yates, 'Now, we've talked about this scene a hundred times and I still don't think it's working right.' He would get a little snippy and say, 'I'm doing my job and I want you to do yours'—not to tell the director what to do, but demand he improve it."

Yates realized that the script would have to be rewritten, and *Bullitt* went through another treatment. While it was being worked on, the hiring process went on. Steve was involved in all aspects of *Bullitt*, including the hiring of the cast.

It was all coming together. One by one, the cast was handpicked, and one by one, they all agreed to do *Bullitt*. Steve was so elated that he commented, "Can you believe we got Robert Vaughn? Can you believe we got Simon Oakland?"

Actor Robert Vaughn had tossed the script aside the first time he read it. It didn't make sense to him. Vaughn turned it down three times before he was persuaded to do the film. "I was convinced to do it through a combination of my agent, the fact that Steve was in the film, and Steve's agent [Stan Kamen] calling me, then Peter Yates calling me. I reluctantly did *Bullitt*," says Vaughn. The move turned out to be quite a good one, giving Vaughn his first role of authority. "All of the roles I was doing were romantic, tongue-in-cheek, semi-humorous characters. The role of Chalmers in *Bullitt* set the pattern, which kept me employed for the next twenty years in terms of motion pictures and television."

McQueen's love interest in the film was British actress Jacqueline Bisset. For Bisset, a relative newcomer to films, *Bullitt* was a huge role for her. Of all of his costars, McQueen found Bissett by far the most beautiful. Neile was told that her presence on location in San Francisco would not be needed, with Steve tied up being president of Solar and star. "It's gonna be a heavy location, baby," he told her. Most likely, it was an excuse for McQueen and Bisset to conduct their affair, which went on throughout the filming of *Bullitt*, though on the set, Bissett found McQueen harder to understand. She told Rona Barrett, "It was confusing to me because he spoke in American slang, and I could hardly understand him. He's a nervous man when he's working. He'd repeatedly come over to me and say, 'We've got to discuss this scene,' and then someone would call him away and we'd never get around to it."

McQueen in return said of Bisset, "She catches good. She can throw it back to you with a great depth for a girl of that age."

For Steve's sidekick in the film, he enlisted the help of old friend and actor Don Gordon. Gordon had known McQueen since the late fifties. Steve would drive past Gordon's house on his motorcycle on his way to work on *Wanted: Dead or Alive*. McQueen recognized the actor from his work on television and the two became friendly. The process was very slow though, remembers Gordon: "First, it was drive by and nothing.

Not even an acknowledgment. Then it was drive by and wave. Then it was drive by slow and wave. Then he would drive by really slow, almost stopping at a 'Hi.' Then it was drive by, stop, and a 'Hey, how ya doing?' I knew the son-of-a-bitch a year before he knew my name." Even then, McQueen couldn't remember Gordon's first name. Steve called him every name in the book: "Ed, Fred, Dan." Gordon got fed up. "For chrissakes," Gordon told him, "it's Don. Think of Donald Duck. Something!"

The two eventually got together and agreed to meet the wives. "To me, he was just another actor. Who knew that years later he'd become the megastar that he was? We were friends, just like you'd make in school. He was just a guy," says Gordon.

Steve appreciated Gordon's talent and the fact that Gordon never sought out any special favors from him. Steve always asked Gordon to work for him, not the other way around. Their friendship was based on mutual respect. "We liked each other. We never intruded on each other's personal lives, Gordon says. "Very important with McQueen. We were friends and had a lot of fun together."

It had been nearly ten years when Steve asked Gordon to work with him again on *Bullitt*. In those years, when Steve had gone from a television celebrity to a movie star, to Gordon, Steve remained the same person. "He was always the same. Never changed, at least, not to me. He started like here on a line, and the line just went straight."

Gordon got a call from his agent to meet Peter Yates at Warner Brothers. He didn't know who Yates was or what the movie was about. It would be his first role in a motion picture and a big lift in his career. Yates introduced himself and said, "Steve thinks you would be very good in this role." Throughout the conversation, Gordon kept thinking, "Steve who?" When Gordon left the Warner Brothers lot and got in his car, it hit him: "McQueen, of course." Gordon did not know Steve was starring in a picture called *Bullitt*. Later, at a party on location in San Francisco, Gordon came up to Steve and thanked him for getting him the part. Steve became visibly upset. He told Gordon, "I had nothing to do with it!" Says Gordon, "That kind of tells you about the kind of man he was. He didn't want me to feel that I was beholden to him in this role. He wanted me to be a little arrogant. That doesn't mean nasty or anything. He wanted me to have courage. He wanted me to have a little chutzpah. He wanted me to be able to do the part bravely, and also because he was embarrassed that he got the tough guy here a part."

Yates thought it a good idea that both McQueen and Gordon do some background for their respective roles. Both men went on ride-alongs with the San Francisco police. Though Steve was always well prepared for his roles, the "homework" gave him new insight to the role. Comments Yates, "Steve and Don Gordon really had down their procedures. I thought it would be more exciting, and it was. The basis of that film was to find reality."

Steve was assigned to two officers who assumed that he was just another candy-ass actor who wanted to play cops and robbers. They decided the first place he should be taken to was the morgue. McQueen always liked a good test. He did it quite often to many people, but this time the tables were turned. The detectives wanted to see what McQueen was made of. Steve showed up at the morgue with an apple, casually biting into it as he was shown cadavers. He passed their first test.

For Steve's next trip, he was taken to the hospital to see crime victims firsthand. One person in intensive care had been in a motorcycle accident and was knocked out by McQueen's visit. As Steve left, the patient, knowing he was a biking enthusiast, warned, "Take it slow, Steve" (a line McQueen would use in the film). Says Peter Yates, "Steve was really moved by that visit. He loved anything that he felt helped him get closer to people. He was referred to as 'real people.'"

What touched Steve the most were the police officers themselves. In promoting *Bullitt*, he told reporters, "We're trying to show what a cop could be like. Everybody dislikes cops till they need one."

Don Gordon was taken out on a real drug bust. He was even given a police identification card that read "Delgetti," and carried a badge and a prop gun. He looked like a cop, except to a woman busted for drugs. "I know you," she said, as she got into the patrol car. The fast-thinking Gordon replied, "Yeah, that's because I busted you before." The woman replied, "No, no. Are you sure?" Gordon pulled out his badge and police ID and said, "I made you. I busted you a couple of times." The woman was taken away, but not before she said, "I don't believe it."

Steve's ride-alongs were just as exciting. He saw firsthand how the police handled a riot situation. He was also involved in a drug bust and got to see the "real side of the law." The two detectives that Steve was assigned to were tracking the killer of a young Hispanic woman, who had been brutally murdered on the way to a wedding. The killing sent a shock wave through the community. After months of legwork, a break in the case came about: a credit card charge in the victim's name showed up in Seattle. The killer was tracked down and brought back to San Francisco. The detectives wanted the electric chair and were determined that justice would be served. That first night in custody, however, the killer hanged himself in his cell. Says Robert Relyea, "The detectives were obsessed with this guy coming to justice and felt they were robbed of it. The officers went into a strange state of mind. I think Steve got very bothered. He felt he got a hook on what they were like. He knew them well enough to know what they were going through. The months of paperwork, computer work, and then they caught the guy and he still cheated them. I think that Steve got a real fix on what police work was like. He really understood those two detectives."

When Steve had made his six-picture deal with Warner Brothers, it was with Jack Warner. However, when *Bullitt* was ready to begin shooting, Warner sold his share of stock and retired. Kenneth Hyman replaced Warner and sparks soon began to fly. Warner had grown up in the movie industry and understood what it took to make great films. He was Steve's kind of executive; he made films from a distance, giving the okay and trusting others' judgment. When Steve pitched the idea of *Bullitt* to Warner, the conversation lasted but a few minutes. "You want to make a picture about the cop? Why do you want to do that?" he asked McQueen. "I have a good feeling about how to make a cop very interesting," Steve replied. "Okay, if you feel that strongly about it, you make the movie and be responsible," Warner told him. That was the end of the meeting.

When Kenneth Hyman and Seven Arts took over Warner Brothers, Steve was told, "We will be your partners—creatively, production wise, and in every other way." Says Robert Relyea, "We [Solar] came in with one understanding and then found ourselves in another; it led to misunderstandings on both sides. I don't think Solar was equipped to make that adjustment. We didn't act well to the management change. The management did what they should do if they weren't happy. They said, 'Let's make the six-picture deal a one-picture deal. Good-bye.' They had the right to do that."

*Bullitt* began filming in February 1968. On the first day of shooting, Steve gathered the crew around and announced, "Let's put this behind us. We won't worry about it. We'll find a new home. Let's just execute this picture as well as we can."

Outwardly, Steve was the personification of cool. In his thinking, he had to be confident as company president. Privately, his close friends could tell he was not the same Steve. "On *Bullitt,* he didn't seem to be in as good humor as he was on other films," admits Bud Ekins. "He was bitchy, let's put it that way. He cared more." When stunt coordinator Carrie Lofton played a practical joke on McQueen, it almost cost Lofton his job. A crowd had gathered on the streets where the famed car chase scene was taking place. Lofton decided to pose as a fan and donned a pair of sunglasses. He got behind McQueen and asked, "Would you please give me your autograph?" McQueen obliged and signed the piece of paper given to him, never making eye contact with the fan. Lofton looked at the autograph and said, "Oh shit, I thought you were James Garner." Steve exploded and reached for the autograph. "Let me have that," he demanded, and promptly tore the paper into bits. Lofton took off the sunglasses and Steve realized he'd been had. Says Lofton, "I thought I was going to be out of a job. I thought I had it." Steve's partner, Robert Relyea, noticed Steve's mood as well. "I think Steve saw the responsibility of being, if you will, a principal on a film."

McQueen's good friend Steve Ferry was hired on in charge of props. Ferry was late two days in a row, and Peter Yates wanted him fired. Says Ferry, "I had a very bad attitude at that time." Steve got Ferry the job and could have easily saved him from being fired, but he didn't feel he should abuse his power. "He didn't meddle," says Bud Ekins. "Steve could have stepped in and stopped it, but he wouldn't have because then he would have been doing Jack Reddish's job."

Steve used his street smarts to get the best out of everyone on the set. Says Relyea, "He was terribly loyal to those who were loyal to him. He had a lot of good qualities that I liked that have to do with respect. He wasn't a show-off, not a Hollywood type. He saw and heard what was going on around him. Peripheral thinking. He had what I would call street smarts. He understood people, and he was terribly conscious of himself so that he would think about what he was saying and whether it was offending someone or not. More so than most people, who just open their mouths and think about it later."

Actor Felice Orlandi, who played Albert Rennick in the movie, remembers a special screening of Peter Yates's *Robbery* for the cast of *Bullitt*. Orlandi was the last to arrive and was on his guard. Steve held out his hand and said, "Welcome aboard, Felice." Says Orlandi, "That was so simple, but that was a big thing for him to do. Simple, but important to me. When we had our deal signed with Warner's, me and Jack Reddish and Steve walked into the room and the media was there to take pictures of Steve. He said, 'No, no. I don't have my pictures taken without my partners.' I know he was so smart that I knew what he was doing, but whether he knows it or not, you respect that."

"Steve was always polite to his coworkers," says Robert Relyea. "He was on time, and knew his lines, and had the right wardrobe, and never misplaced his property. He was doing the best he could and he was never shy about asking the same of his coworkers. He would ask, 'Are we all doing the best we can?'"

If McQueen was demanding of others, he was certainly more demanding of himself. "I could have done better. I wasn't very good in that," he would say aloud to anyone around to get their opinion. When he was assured he was fine, he retorted, "Well, they don't photograph you, they photograph me." There was a lot of self-torture on Steve's part to do better. Relyea believes that Steve was "extremely aware of his background, which was not exactly silver spoon. I think that people who come from the other side of the tracks tend to think they'll go broke again and not be able to feed the family the next day. I believe that's a common disease, and Steve had it badly." Director Peter Yates believes Steve used his insecurity as a testing device. Steve would announce something as awful and Yates would tell him it was fine. "Quite often he felt if he said he was worried, he would make other people look at it and examine it. This is something a lot of big stars do. He was always right on the edge of everything," says Yates.

*Bullitt* was a film that was on the edge as well. Said Steve at the time, "I think the film should be of a more impressionistic nature, that you shouldn't have to dot all the *I*s and cross all the *T*s. We want a feeling of realism that the audience can participate in the action."

McQueen insisted the film be shot totally on location in San Francisco. Warner Brothers insisted that it be shot on the lot. Says Peter Yates, "Even then, Los Angeles had the hell shot out of it by the movie industry. My biggest concern was that if we were to make a picture totally on the lot, that it would look like a television series. The only movies at that time that were not shot on the lot were westerns." Steve pleaded, "The theater is in the streets, where the people are. You can't stage it. You have to be there." Helping McQueen's cause was the mayor of San Francisco, Joseph L. Alioto, who rolled out the red carpet for Solar. "We went in and laid our cards out on the table and the city and the movie company grooved together," said McQueen. Reluctantly, Warner Brothers agreed. *Bullitt* was the very first movie to be shot on location with an all-Hollywood crew, the first major film to break free of a studio's grasp.

In return for opening the city of San Francisco to Solar Productions, Steve returned the favor in kind. Solar hired 350 teenagers (many of whom were gang leaders) from the area and paid them at a generous local Screen Extras Guild scale. In addition, Solar donated a community swimming pool in Hunter's Point, an all-black neighborhood.

Yates envisioned *Bullitt* as a French film. It would approach reality and push the limits of filmmaking, only no one else knew it at the time. Yates encouraged his actors to ad-lib and let them become their characters. Frank Bullitt would not just be another cop. "He was a maverick cop," says Nikita Knatz. "McQueen kind of set the standard for all the cops who couldn't afford certain things."

When a scene didn't work, it was abandoned for another. An example was a scene in which McQueen meets with Bisset for dinner. The dialogue wasn't quite right, and Steve became uncomfortable. Yates left the couple inside and told them to act as if they were having a real dinner date and he would film them from the outside. The scene was then shot through the window. A waiter accidentally struck Steve in the eye, and that was used in the film. The new scene took just seconds to relate to the viewer that the couple were having dinner. No dialogue was needed.

Don Gordon remembers the scene in which Delgetti and Bullitt discover a trunk that will help uncover the mystery of a murder. "Both Steve and I didn't know what was going to be in that trunk, so we just ad-libbed the whole scene. What you saw in the film was the first and only take of that scene," says Gordon.

*Bullitt* was the first Steve McQueen movie to use the word "bullshit." In a scene at the airport, in which McQueen as Bullitt and Robert Vaughn as Chalmers meet up for the last confrontation, Chalmers explains that at some time or another, all parties have to compromise. McQueen explodes, "Bullshit." Loren Janes points out, "That's the first time he allowed a swear word in one of his movies. If he got a script and they told him they wanted to put in a nude scene of either him or the girl or a lot of swearing, he'd say, 'Not in a Steve McQueen movie. If my acting isn't good enough to where we have to put that stuff in there to make it worthwhile, no thank you.' It's amazing that he had certain morals and ideals about what he'd do and not do in a movie, and he stuck to that no matter what. Totally separate from his private life."

In another scene with Robert Vaughn, Steve objected to the use of the word "nomenclature." The line read, "In your nomenclature, you blew it." Steve didn't understand the word. His reasoning was, "If Steve McQueen doesn't understand it, you can bet your ass the people going to see my movies aren't going to understand it either." Vaughn suggested "parlance," and the word was substituted for "nomenclature." Says Robert Vaughn, "He did object to language that he felt didn't communicate directly to an audience. He was communicating to the masses and he thought 'parlance' was easier to understand, so that's what we used."

The studio executives at Warner Brothers had been riding Steve hard throughout the filming. There were hard feelings on both sides and whenever an executive appeared on location in San Francisco, he was promptly kicked off the lot by McQueen himself. Notes Nikita Knatz, "He loved to bust executives, and he kicked the Warners people out right and left. He hated authority. He was getting more and more powerful." Peter Yates, a first-time director in Hollywood, looked on from the sidelines in amazement. "I never had heard of McQueen's reputation at all, coming from England. I found him quite extraordinary. I later found out he always liked to fight the establishment, luckily, because he had the studio to fight. He protected us like mad from the studio." When Steve wanted a pool table on location, a window had to be smashed and a crane used to get the table into his apartment. "He maybe played on that pool table twice," laughs Knatz. This display of power left the director in amazement, but the biggest display of power in Yates's mind was the fact that Steve could get Chinese food delivered to his apartment. "That took power," he says.

Warner Brothers main beef with Steve was over money. The studio claimed the film was over budget by a million dollars. In actuality, the film had no real projected budget. "The studio said that because they were trying to get rid of Steve," says Yates. "They had a contract with Steve and apparently he spent a lot of money preparing the script. There was never a good relationship between Kenneth Hyman and Steve. The actual budget went from four million to five million, not to six million, as claimed by Warner Brothers." Robert Relyea warned Yates, "It won't do your reputation any good if the movie goes over budget."

One night after a day of shooting, visual consultant Nikita Knatz took Steve to Chinatown for a karate match; only this was no ordinary match —it was a death duel. McQueen and Knatz were picked up at the San Francisco Airport by one of the local gangs, the White Changs. A limousine then drove them to Chinatown. They were not blindfolded, but they were driven around until they were confused as to their location. Adds Knatz, "We were lost. It's impossible to get lost in Chinatown, because it's only an eight-block-square area, but they only let you see what they want you to see. There's a whole other world to it." As soon as they arrived at a warehouse, the two were escorted down a flight of stairs and into an underground room filled with crates. Knatz describes the event: "These old gentlemen come in and they look like bums, but they're the dons. No words are spoken. They sit down on folding chairs around what looks like a big crate, bigger than the size of a room. Two people enter the crate, one with a raincoat on and the other wearing sunglasses. They go inside the crate and it's nailed shut with a four-by-four piece of wood. Then we hear in Chinese, 'Do it.' With that, one of them comes running toward the other guy and takes him out with one kick. A doctor is there and checks the guy's pulse. He says in Chinese, 'He's dead.' They bring the body out of the crate, put it in a body bag, wrap it up, shove it in a fifty-gallon drum, and take it away. When the winner comes out of the crate, it's a dame. A woman! A one-punch fight.

Handshakes with the elders. Prizes awarded, elegantly wrapped. She bows to the elders and we're asked to leave."

When they arrived safely back at the airport, Knatz asked McQueen for his response to the ritual. "It was staged," McQueen said. A few days later, Steve came across a newspaper article saying that the body of a Chinese man had been found in an oil drum. McQueen rushed to Knatz on the set, the newspaper in one hand. He circled the article with a pen and handed the paper to Knatz. He asked, "Does this have anything to do with the fight we saw the other night?" Knatz remained silent. "He got scared because he didn't want to have any part of it. He thought he might be subpoenaed as a murder witness. He was very nervous," says Knatz.

Loren Janes was called in for the most dangerous stunt of his career. In the movie, Detective Bullitt chases killer Johnny Ross on the airport grounds. Bullitt is forced to duck under a Boeing 707 passenger jet. The stunt involved 240-degree heat blasts from the engines and unpredictable crosswinds. Janes had to talk to the FAA and interview pilots who would not even consider participating in the stunt. He was told that it couldn't be done. After much persuading, he managed to talk a pilot into being part of it. In one take, Janes ran in front of the plane, weaved around the front wheels, fell down to the ground, and positioned himself between two wheels as they rolled over him. He was paid $5,000 for his bravery.

Looking back on the stunt, Janes says, "I did it and walked away, and I don't ever want to do that again!"

The picture's most famous stunt was saved for the last part of filming. The infamous hill-jumping car chase scene in *Bullitt* is now part of cinematic history. It came very close to never appearing on the screen at all.

It is said that success has many parents, and many people claim to have been at the inception of the car chase in *Bullitt*. Writer Alan Trustman says that it was an incident in the summer of 1954, when he and a group of friends were drag racing in the streets of San Francisco, that was the inspiration for the hill-jumping sequence. "I was looking for something for McQueen to do to keep him busy. I had actually driven most of the locations in the movie, though I did not lay out the chase scene. The car chase was in the first post-McQueen script, right down to the hub caps falling off and keeping the camera a foot off the ground. I even wrote in a Mustang. To this day, I claim it as the best automobile advertisement ever," says Trustman.

Peter Yates disputes Trustman's claim, giving the credit to producer Phil D'Antoni. "The person who really pushed the car chase scene was Phil," he says. "I had just done a car chase in *Robbery* and I wasn't up for another chase. McQueen was getting ready for *Le Mans* and he didn't want to do a car chase. In fact, it was only about halfway through filming that we put it in the script at all. Warner Brothers held it like a carrot over our heads, saying, 'If you go over budget any more, you're not going to be able to do the car chase.' It was strategically scheduled to shoot the last two weeks of the film."

A good amount of the credit has to go to Carrie Lofton, who was brought in to coordinate the stunt. Lofton had known McQueen since the late fifties and was always giving the actor a hard time. Lofton first met him at Bud Ekins motorcycle shop. Steve had just taken a spill on his bike, and his face was red and swollen. Lofton spotted Steve at the shop and asked, "Mr. McQueen, is that you?" Insulted, Steve responded, "Yeah, why?" Lofton continued, "You must have one hell of an agent. You mean, you get the same amount of money no matter what you look like? Have you looked in the mirror lately?" Steve walked away, knowing that if he laughed, it would hurt his swollen face. Says Lofton, "I kept needling him so hard that he was about to crack. He was laughing. I intended it both ways, though."

Lofton was considered the best in the business at handling cars. Says Lofton, "McQueen was determined to have the best car chase ever done. I told him I knew a lot about camera angles and speeds to make it look fast. You can underground the camera so you can control everything in the scene. Then when it's run, it'll look like high speed and the car will appear to handle real well. I told him it would be expensive. He told me, 'Money is no object here.' "

Steve took pride in his driving prowess and was determined to perform all of the stunts in the chase sequence. "Steve was a good driver," notes Lofton, "but there's a difference between a good driver and a stunt driver."

It took Lofton four days to get Steve out from behind the wheel. The first day, Steve took a spin, pitched it to the side, and crashed into another car. He tried it a second time and again crashed. He tried a third time with the same results. Lofton called in McQueen's friend Bud Ekins to double Steve. "Get him out of the fucking car. He's going to kill somebody," Lofton told Ekins.

"He was wild," confirms Ekins. "He took corners too fast and he overshot them and crashed into cars."

Director Peter Yates accompanied McQueen on one of the scenes to keep an eye on him. After completing a hill-jumping stunt, Yates told McQueen, "Okay, Steve, you can slow down now. We're out of film." Steve replied, "That's nothing. We're out of brakes." McQueen managed to slow the Mustang down by switching down the gears and turn-

Steve preparing for
the famous hill-
jumping sequence in
*Bullitt*, 1968.
(COURTESY OF WARNER
BROTHERS/7 ARTS)

ing the car up a street that inclined upward. When the car came to a full stop, both men roared with nervous laughter.

Neile had been extremely nervous about the dangerous driving and secretly asked Yates to curtail Steve's involvement. Yates arranged it so that Steve would receive a late wake-up call on the morning of the most dangerous sequence. Bud Ekins came into work at 6:00 A.M. "It was the first time that anyone was using real speeds in movies. We were going well over 100 miles an hour," says Ekins. When Steve arrived on the set hours later, Ekins was already jumping the hills in the green 390 GT Mustang. When the stunt was finished, McQueen ran to the car as Ekins opened the door. "Where'd you learn how to drive like that?" he demanded. "I don't know, Steve," Ekins responded. McQueen continued, "You fucker. You're doing it to me again."

McQueen was referring to the time right after *The Great Escape* when Steve was on the Johnny Carson show. Carson congratulated Steve on the excellent motorcycle jump over the fence. McQueen squirmed a bit, but actually let Carson know that it was his friend and motorcycle stunt rider, Bud Ekins, who had done it.

Ekins asked, "I'm doing what to you again, Steve?" Steve replied, "*The Great Escape*, right? I had to go up in front of the whole world and tell them I didn't make that jump over the fence, and the same thing's gonna happen all over again. I'm going to have to go on the Johnny Carson show and tell him I didn't do it again."

The chase ends with a climactic explosion at a gas station. The stunt had to be done in one shot and was the most costly portion of the film. It had to be perfect. The scene was shot on the last day of filming, and the movie was now on the line. "The car overshot the gas pumps, but by clever editing on the part of Frank Keller, no one's ever known that the car overshot the mark," says Peter Yates.

*Bullitt* finished filming in May 1968, but much uncertainty hung over it. During the shooting, Steve had told writer Ray Lond, "We've got a good one. I know it." However, in private, he didn't know what to make of the film.

Warner Brothers executives had thought the film was going to be such a big bomb that they didn't even bother to attend prescreenings. The studio actually hoped that *Bullitt* would flop and were amazed that Radio City Music Hall had requested the film in advance for an October premiere, the first time an action-adventure would be played there. The request meant that *Bullitt*'s post-production time would have to be cut by a third. Solar's thinking was that if the film were a success, the terms and conditions for distribution would be that much more favorable, which ultimately meant more money in Solar's pocket.

Quincy Jones was the first composer scheduled to score the film. Peter Yates was with Jones at that first screening and when the film was over, Jones sat there in amazement. "That's a motherfucker!" he said. Yates thought he might be on to something. (Jones burst an appendix two weeks prior to scoring the film and was replaced by Lalo Schriffrin.)

At another screening, Alan Trustman was present with several executives from Warner Brothers. Trustman and Yates did not get along with each other, as Trustman had berated Yates in front of the crew early on in the filming over what he felt were deliberate changes on Yates's part to the Jacqueline Bisset character. The two hadn't seen each other since that incident. At the end of the screening, however, Trustman stood up and announced, "I want to thank you for making my good-plus screenplay into a superb piece of film. This film is going to do an incredible amount of business." The Seven Arts executives thought Trustman was pulling their chains. Claims Trustman, "I never pull anybody's chain in this business." He then went over to shake Yates's hand and apologize for his previous behavior. Yates didn't know what to say.

When Yates showed the film to his agent, Marty Baum, Baum told him, "I don't think you quite realize what you've got here. This film is going to guarantee you another nine years in the business."

Post-production was finished and *Bullitt* premiered on October 17, 1968, at Radio City Music Hall. The picture was an instant smash with the audience, and that night was reflective of the movie's unexpected success.

During its run at Radio City, a young, attractive model by the name of Ali MacGraw caught a showing of *Bullitt*. The star of the movie left her breathless and her knees knocking.

*Bullitt*'s success had exceeded anyone's wildest dreams. The gross figures, to this day, remain foggy. Most point to $18 million domestically and $35 million worldwide, but writer Alan Trustman, who had points in the film, contends that *Bullitt* in the first year of release alone had grossed a then amazing $80 million. Trustman says, "It was re-released in the sixth week of its first general release, packaged as a double feature with *Bonnie and Clyde,* which the studio owned 100 percent of, since they bought out Warren Beatty and everyone else. Warner's attributed half the revenues to each picture for all of the costs of *Bullitt,* because they didn't have to advertise for *Bonnie and Clyde;* everyone was already familiar with that picture. To this day, nobody knows what the picture really grossed." Warner Brothers quietly bought out Trustman as he was preparing to take them to court. Years later, he wrote an article for the *Atlantic Monthly* on the box office gross of *Bullitt*. Because the *Atlantic Monthly* did not have libel insurance, Trustman had to fictionalize his account. He labeled executive Sidney KeWitt, though he didn't use his name in the article, "Warner Brothers vice president in charge of fucking talent out of their percentages." The article hit the streets at six o'clock on a Thursday morning and by 8:30 that same day Trustman got a call from Sidney KeWitt himself. KeWitt was irate and Trustman thought he was going to be slapped with a lawsuit. "I finally realize what this guy was saying," says Trustman. "He was outraged that I didn't use his real name. That it was him and everybody knew it was him. He was proud of what he did. He did it better than anybody else. Why couldn't I have used his real name? He just did it masterfully, that's all. They [studio executives] treat it all as a game, and you have to accept it as a game or you walk around in an irrational manner."

Critical reaction matched the box office intake. Archer Winsten of the *New York Post* wrote, "McQueen keeps his cool as only he can, now that Bogart's long gone. The best, most exciting car chase the movies have ever put on film. McQueen, motorcycle and auto racer, knew what he was doing and what had to be done." *Variety* called the film "an extremely well-made crime melodrama, highlighted by one of the most exciting auto chase sequences in years." And Tom Milne of *The Sunday Observer* wrote, "A curiously exhilarating mixture of reality and fantasy, so actual that at times one could almost swear that the fictional adventures must have been shot with concealed cameras."

The chase scene was singled out by both critics and the public as the star of the movie. Twenty-five years have passed since its release, and no film has yet to surpass the overall excitement and originality of the chase. Loren Janes offers this explanation of why the stunt was so successful: "It was wild, reckless driving, but it was planned and coordinated. There was class to the *Bullitt* chase, there was a reason for it, and that's one of the key things people forget: the greatest stunt in the world is worthless if there isn't a reason or a story to it, and *Bullitt* had a story point all the way through."

The public's perception that McQueen had done all of the stunt driving was a main reason for its success, and in an unfamiliar move, Steve took credit for the chase sequence. Carrie Lofton remembers one screening for the press when Steve had casually walked over to Lofton and said, "These people back here are reporters," motioning with his thumb. "I'm going to tell them I did all of my own driving. How does that grab you?" Lofton had joked, "As long as all of your checks clear, it doesn't make a bit of difference to me what you tell them. I'll back you up."

The film's success had swept up everyone involved in it. Lofton, who coordinated the chase sequence, admits, *"Bullitt* did wonders for my career. I would get hired for a job and be told, 'We want a chase scene like in *Bullitt*.' I'd tell them, 'If you got the money, I got the time.' "

Several actors, such as Vic Tayback, Norman Fell, Robert Duvall, and Georg Stanford Brown, went on to become television and movie stars. Steve's friend Don Gordon went on to become one of the leading character actors of the day. Actress Jacqueline Bisset went on to become one of Hollywood's biggest leading ladies of the seventies.

As for debut director Peter Yates, he went on to do such diversified films as *Mother, Jugs and Speed, Breaking Away, The Deep, The Dresser,* and *Suspect*. His career has spanned twenty-five years, almost unheard of by Hollywood standards. "That was my first film in America and without it, I wouldn't be here now," Yates assesses. "If I had to do it all over again, I'd behave much worse," he laughs. The shadow of *Bullitt* has sometimes been a detriment to Yates in a personal sense. "It's annoying at times, because people talk more about *Bullitt* than any other of my films. I've had two films nominated for an Academy Award [*Breaking Away* and *The Dresser*] and they still want to talk about that damned car chase. That's Hollywood for you."

No one benefited more than Steve. The success of the film gave him all the power and glory and money he could ask for. When *Bullitt* wrapped in May 1968, Warner Brothers quickly released Solar Productions from its six-picture deal. "A lot of blood flowed on *Bullitt*," said

McQueen. "If it hadn't worked, we'd be hanging by our thumbs today by the gate at Warner's."

When *Bullitt* became the unexpected smash that it was, Solar became the most sought after production company in Hollywood. Says Robert Relyea, "Steve never gloated about its success to Warner Brothers. He never even said to me, 'Well, see, we showed them.' Never."

Success brought everything to Steve that he had ever wanted, but this time around, it also brought him newfound respect. "I'm a filmmaker," he announced. "I want the respect of the industry. Actors have a bad handle in the world. I'll tell ya, in my own mind, I'm not sure acting is a thing for a grown man to be doing."

*Bullitt* was Steve's fifth hit film in a row, and his biggest success to date. It would be the most memorable movie of his career. He was no longer Steve McQueen movie star, but Steve McQueen superstar.

# THE DAWNING OF
# AQUARIUS

*In '67 or '68 is when the flower children came to be. The
drug culture was upon us. The sexual revolution was upon
us, and now his mid-life crisis was upon us too. Had Steve
not been the age he was, he would have been one of the
flower children. He then adopted their life-style, which, of
course, helped to undermine our marriage.*

NEILE McQUEEN

IT WAS THE TIME of the hippies: flower power; free love; Haight-Ashbury;
tune in, drop out. Steve McQueen, closing in on forty, wanted to try it
all.

Steve was of the streets and never forgot what it was like to come from
there. No matter how rich or famous he got, he always stayed on the
other side. He was smoking marijuana in his teens, dropping acid five
years before the Beatles ever admitted to it. He inhaled amyl nitrate
way before it became fashionable in Hollywood. Though never confirmed, it was also rumored that he shot heroin just for the experience.
In short, he admitted to friends, "I've done it all." Says Nikita Knatz,
"He didn't think he was harming his body, but expanding his mind."

What Steve did in private was entirely different from what was covered by the media. In the newspapers, he was the fiercely patriotic all-
American golden boy. "If Vietnam falls," he was quoted as saying, "the
gateway to Asia falls." Steve also talked of civil rights. "I think in this
country, the white man should start making concessions to the Negro,
and the Negro should to the white man because this is our country, too.
I'm not a politician. I'm only a layman, but as an American, I think very
strongly about my country. It's a wonderful country, and I don't want
to see it go down the drain."

On the hippies, Steve both defended and criticized them in the press.

"Cops shouldn't make trouble for the hippies. They've contributed so much that's groovy. It takes a brave man to walk down Sunset in his bare feet and long hair. They need people like that in the police departments.

"Provincetown, Greenwich Village, Carnaby Street, Haight-Ashbury —their scene has gone now. This taking of methedrine, speed, LSD by the bushel—that's stupid, dumb. The hippies are what I like to call the 'oblique' people, and their obliqueness to the rest of society has helped it.

"But now they should be doing something rather than copping out. I say we need them to get this country away from the Sam Brownes. Man, we've been lied to for a long, long, time. We need to revert to a hip kind of conservatism," said Steve.

And Steve openly criticized the use of drugs: "Although I really dig young people, there are many things that I cannot regard as a healthy sign. For example, I'd never support drug taking, and I'm very unhappy that many youngsters think it's the thing to do."

Not that Steve wasn't telling the truth; it was just one side of him. The other side very few people knew about.

Steve was very careful which side to show and to whom. In front of Bud Ekins and Steve Ferry, he might puff on a joint. In front of family men like Loren Janes and Robert Relyea, he would never dare. The revelation years later took them totally by surprise.

"I never once saw Steve take a drug," says Robert Relyea. "Isn't it peculiar for that many years we were together that I never saw one? I'm not saying he didn't take one. I'm just saying that for someone who spent years with him, and there were long periods of time that I spent day and night with him, that I never saw one."

Loren Janes adds, "If he took drugs, I was totally unaware of it. I never saw him with cocaine, never smelled the pot. I never talked to anybody who did it with him. There were times on location when we were together for long periods. When all this stuff came out about him using drugs, I started looking for it. Never saw it. I never smelled it, and you can smell marijuana a mile away. I don't know whether to believe it or not."

Two known friends of Steve's were linked to hard drugs: Sid Kaiser and Jay Sebring.

Kaiser and McQueen annually took clothes, food, and medical supplies to the Navajo Indians in the desert. Said Steve, "I really dig those Navajos. They have a saying they live by: 'A land where there is time enough and room enough.' I really want that, too." Bud Ekins suspects that Steve had an ulterior motive for going to see the Navajos. "I used to have my suspicions about that," says Ekins. "I think that was an

The aging hippie. McQueen grew his hair longer, took harder drugs and chased more women as the sixties came to a close.

(Courtesy of Star File Photos)

excuse to go out into the desert and use peyote. Sid Kaiser was a druggie. He died of an overdose." A few years later, Steve admitted to *Sports Illustrated* that he did try the drug once: "I was interested in the Indians, and they had given me some peyote. This was way back before the drug culture got started, and people were still serious about the philosophical aspect of the hallucinogens rather than just kicks. Anyway, the peyote really hit me. I took off into the desert on my bike, bound and determined to whip it. I ran flat out, straight into the desert—I was all ego, challenging every bump and every gulch. I don't know how many endos I turned, plenty of them. The cactus ripped me up, the rocks chewed on my hide, I had sand in my nose and kangaroo rats in my ears. I rode until the bike ran out of gas, and after that I just lay there."

Jay Sebring was a different story altogether. Most of the people who took drugs with Steve were nothing more than mere hangers-on. Steve had no use for them once the drugs were gone. Says Loren Janes, "Steve didn't trust leeches. These are people that live off of other people. They want to be seen with a famous person because it makes them feel good. Steve knew the phonies. He made friends with people and then they'd want to go grocery shopping with him and change his tires for him. Pretty soon, they'd be out of his life." Jay Sebring was the exception to the rule. Most of Steve's closest friends were in other fields, but always at the top of their profession. Bud Ekins was the top motorcycle rider of the day. Loren Janes was the best and most respected stunt man in Hollywood. Later, Pat Johnson was the top martial artist in the country. Sebring, the top hairdresser of the day in Hollywood, also got very close to McQueen.

"Sebring was a starfucker," says Nikita Knatz. "McQueen was just one in the stable. Sebring was a nothing, a skinny little haircutter with nothing to offer. I would not buy a used car from him. I did not dislike him, he just didn't impress me. Sebring was a bloodsucker, a leech. He knew how to party, how to leech. He was a drunk and was made out to be a hero."

Like McQueen, Sebring was self-made. It was Sebring who gave Steve the haircut and lightened his hair for *Love with the Proper Stranger*. By doing that, Sebring had a big hand in turning McQueen into a sex symbol.

The two men enjoyed their wealth and the spoils of stardom. Sebring was around the house when a reporter from *Family Weekly* had dropped by for an interview. The reporter asked Sebring what he and McQueen did when they were together. Sebring responded, "Nothing special. We play a little pool or we sit around and gab. Once in a while, if Steve needs a haircut, I give him one right in his living room or on the porch. Most of all, we share a common appreciation for mechanical things." What Sebring neglected to tell the reporter was the common appreciation they shared for drugs and women.

Neile especially did not like Sebring's presence around the house. Every time he opened his briefcase to get his scissors to cut Steve's hair, she spotted neat little packets of cocaine.

The two also shared women with each other. Both men were extremely attractive and wealthy, a combination that women found hard to resist. They shared one particular starlet: the lovely Sharon Tate.

"Sharon Tate was my girlfriend," Steve admitted years later. He had first met her sometime before the filming of *The Cincinnati Kid*. Tate had actually taken a screen test for the movie, but Sam Peckinpah was convinced she wasn't right for the part. Even with Steve's prodding, Peckinpah stood his ground. The part went to Tuesday Weld instead. McQueen had remained friends with Tate over the years and, like many others, had been taken by her beauty.

The sixties became a decade-long party, and Steve was right there in the thick of things. The sexual revolution taught that it was all right to sleep around. "If it feels good—do it!" was the slogan of the day. He didn't bother to hide it from Neile any longer. "I have to be free," he told her matter-of-factly. Not to be mean to her, but as Neile put it, "He would tell me these things out of guilt, to cleanse his soul."

It didn't take long for Solar Productions to find a new home when CBS's Cinema Center Films struck a $20 million production deal in April 1969. "When I think of the $20 million invested in my company, I don't sleep very well," McQueen admitted. "I even have a notebook and pencil by my bed in case I wake up thinking of something." Even *Bullitt's* success had not eased his anxiety.

Cinema Center executives were ecstatic. Said Bob Rosen, "Cinema Center just got into the film business right when Solar was available. We were pleased to have the number one box office attraction in the world."

The irony of the situation was that Rosen had been an assistant to the production manager on the set of *This Could Be the Night* back in 1956. Rosen's first recollection of McQueen was that he was the husband of a starlet, Neile Adams, the next Debbie Reynolds at MGM. "She had all of the publicity people to deal with, the hairdresser, wardrobe, and all of the people fussing over her," remembered Rosen. "Steve told me he was up for a new pilot [*Wanted: Dead or Alive*], but I didn't believe him. He didn't strike me as the next superstar."

In November 1969, Steve McQueen was voted, along with actress Joanne Woodward, "Star of the Year" by the National Association of Theater Owners. The award is presented to the star who packs audiences into the theaters. In 1969, Steve McQueen made the theater owners a lot of money.

The presentation was to take place in Washington, D.C. Steve wouldn't go unless his partner, Robert Relyea, accompanied him. Once up in the air, Steve brought up his latest nagging concern. His follow-up to *Bullitt*, he decided, would be William Faulkner's *The Reivers*. It would be Steve's first attempt at comedy since *Soldier in the Rain*, a complete bomb. Steve felt that he had spent the past six years defining the McQueen image on screen. The brash, cool, moody loner/antihero was his trademark. *The Reivers* was going to be totally different. Steve casually mentioned to Relyea, seated next to him, "After *The Reivers*, I'll probably never be hired again." Relyea, not believing he had heard correctly, asked Steve to repeat himself. "After *The Reivers*, I'll probably never be hired again." McQueen then added, "It's going to be a disaster and no audience will ever want to want to see me again." Relyea tried to talk some sense into him. "Steve, we're going for *you* to receive the award for the most popular actor in the world." McQueen went on the defensive: "You're missing the point. They don't photograph you, they photograph me. And this film will do me in." Says Relyea, "He took insecurity to a new level. He was totally convinced that he was betraying the public by doing a comedy." That insecurity spilled over on the set of *The Reivers,* and Steve took his frustrations out on director Mark Rydell.

Mark Rydell is one of Hollywood's few A-list directors left from the sixties. His screen credits include *The Cowboys, Cinderella Liberty, On Golden Pond, The River,* and most recently, *For the Boys.* He has worked with the biggest actors in Hollywood and has a reputation for going toe to toe with them if things get out of hand. Over the years, Rydell has worked with John Wayne, Katharine Hepburn, James Caan, Henry Fonda, Bette Midler, Michael Caine, Diane Keaton, and Jane Fonda, among others. Says Rydell, "Crews, for the most part, respect and like me. Actors do the same."

When asked who was the most difficult actor he's ever worked with, without hesitation, Rydell responds, "Steve McQueen."

Rydell and McQueen had known each other in the fifties in New York. It was Rydell who had encouraged Steve to pursue a career in acting rather than tile setting. It was also Rydell who had dated Neile until Steve came on the scene (a fact that probably made Steve a bit jealous on the set). A few years later, Steve had gotten Rydell a guest spot on *Wanted: Dead or Alive.*

Rydell had been an actor for several years before he realized that directing was where he wanted to be. He managed to work his way into episodic television (*Gunsmoke* and *I Spy*) and a small feature film, *The Fox,* before getting a shot at directing *The Reivers.* William Wyler was first set to direct, but dropped out. John Huston, who for years had wanted to work with Steve, also dropped out. Steve then thought of Rydell. "McQueen liked to have directors who were making their bones. That way, he had control," says Nikita Knatz. *The Reivers,* Rydell's second feature film, was also his toughest.

*The Reivers* is based on William Faulkner's Pulitzer Prize–winning novel about a group of four people, a man-child, a black man, a prostitute, and an eleven-year-old boy, on a journey to Memphis, Tennessee, in the early 1900s.

While Faulkner's book is clearly focused on the eleven-year-old, Rufus, the script was tailored more for Steve's character, Boon Hogganbeck. Steve employed the husband-and-wife team of Irving and Harriet Ravetch, the Oscar-winning screenwriters of *The Long Hot Summer, The Sound and the Fury,* and *Hud.* "Once he made the decision to make *The Reivers,* based on the script, and Steve really understood the script, like most great actors do, he recognized that he could shift the focus from Rufus to Boon," says Robert Relyea.

In the movie, the part of the black man, played brilliantly by Rupert Crosse, is distant "blood-kin" to Boon. They are the film's main antagonists. It was Crosse's first major role and a breakthrough in his career. Crosse was tall and skinny, and at six foot five, he towered over Steve.

McQueen was very concerned the audience might keep their eyes focused on Crosse. Says director Mark Rydell, "I had to con Steve into it. They had read well together and had kind of gotten along, and we finally cast Rupert. That took a lot of pushing, because Steve didn't want him. He wanted some little guy."

Rydell suggested that McQueen throw Crosse a small party at the Castle to welcome the actor to the company. McQueen thought about it and said, "Yeah, I'll invite him to the house."

Rydell remembers, "I arrived with Rupert, who was looking around. He had never seen anything like it. There were only eight of us; we were talking and having drinks. Steve was very big on *jeet kune do,* a form of martial arts. His friend, Bruce Lee, was with us all during the picture. Bruce used to work out with him every day; this was before Bruce became a star.

"Rupert's sitting there and says, 'You're off balance. You could be knocked down.' Well, to embarrass Steve in front of a group was, first of all, wrong. I'm trying to get that through to Rupert. I'm pulling at his pants. I say, 'That's all right. It's not so off balance.' Rupert says, 'He could be knocked down.' Steve says, 'Oh? Why don't you show me?' I'm thinking, 'Here goes the picture.' I feel it's out the window. Then Rupert unwinds like a praying mantis and stands up to his full height—skinny, maybe 160 pounds. Steve goes pah-toong and drops down three steps, under a pool table. It turned out that Rupert had a black belt in karate. Steve comes up, red with embarrassment. He walks over to Rupert and shakes his hand. They start to shake and suddenly they're almost arm wrestling. We used it throughout the film—every time they'd shake hands."

For reasons unknown, Steve was jealous of Mark Rydell. A comely man himself, Rydell starred on the soap *As the World Turns* for six years. The fact that Rydell had dated Neile in the fifties no doubt left McQueen wondering if Rydell might still have eyes for her. When McQueen, Relyea, and Rydell arrived for the shoot in Carrollton, Mississippi, the women of the area chased after Rydell, not movie star Steve McQueen. The fans recognized Rydell from the soap opera and while they were crowding around Rydell for an autograph, they pushed McQueen out of the way. Richard Moore, the director of photography on *The Reivers,* says, "Everyone was falling over themselves to get to Mark Rydell and when McQueen arrived, they didn't seem to care much. Steve was a competitor, especially around women; he was the center of attraction. It might have tweaked him a little bit that Mark was getting all of this attention."

When Steve hired Rydell, he made it clear that he was the one who signed Rydell's checks for the next few months. "He was the main guy in charge," says Moore. "I frankly sensed that he felt competitive with Mark. Steve may have thought he was bigger than Mark, looking down his nose to a certain degree."

Moore relates, "Mark and I would prep the night before and Steve would drop by and ask, 'Are you guys going over the shot list for tomorrow?' We told him yes. He said one night, "Okay, what we've got to do here is get together and homogulate." The two men looked at each other puzzled. "Homogulate?" With a nod of his head, Steve affirmed, "That's what we've got to do." And with that, he was off. When the door slammed behind him, Rydell and Moore burst out laughing, saying, "What does homogulate mean?" Adds Moore, "I thought it was amusing that Steve was trying to use a big word that he didn't even know the meaning of."

Steve liked to bring a friend or companion along with him on almost every movie he made. For *The Reivers,* he brought along martial artist Bruce Lee. Lee fell into the companion department, as he was most certainly not a close friend. "Both men had what the other wanted. McQueen was impressed with Lee's physical artistry and wanted it," says James Coburn. "It was two giant egos vying for something: stardom for Lee and street-fighting technique for Steve." Jealous as McQueen may have been, Lee was by far the more jealous of the two. Says Coburn, "Bruce wanted to be a star in the worst way."

Lee at the time was the world's most famous martial artist. His list of clients read like a Who's Who in Hollywood, and he charged up to $200 a lesson. McQueen was introduced to Lee through Nikita Knatz, who tired of McQueen's relentless pursuit of him to teach him martial arts. After Lee's canceled television series, *The Green Hornet,* had given him a taste of stardom, he desperately wanted to become a movie star, so much so that he set his sights on McQueen as the person to measure up to. He intended to learn as many tricks from Steve as Steve wanted to learn from him. On the set of *The Reivers,* however, Lee felt like second banana and vowed someday to catch up to McQueen.

Just the next year, Lee was invited to Hong Kong to make a movie. He predicted, "I'll become a star over there, and then the Hollywood producers will want me." Lee's prediction came true, and he called himself the "Oriental Steve McQueen."

Cocky and full of pride, Lee wrote McQueen a letter, stating, "I am now more popular to a wider spread audience than you are now." It was a barb letter. Steve sent back an eight-by-ten glossy photo and signed it, "To Bruce, my favorite fan." Lee received it and called McQueen immediately. In his broken English, he said, "McQueen, you muddafucker, I'm going to kill you. I rip up this picture of you." The photo had the desired effect: it brought Lee down a notch. Knatz says ruefully, "That was McQueen. He loved the expression 'mind-fuck.' He loved psyching people out because it didn't require an education. It required being nimble of mind, and Steve was that."

Steve always did his best work with a strong director at the helm. John Sturges and Norman Jewison certainly proved that when guiding Steve in his performances. Now that Solar Productions was Steve's own company, he simply felt that even though a director might be formally in charge, for all intents and purposes, he was still the head honcho. Rydell wasn't a yes-man in any sense of the word. Though a newcomer to feature films, he was no pushover. It caused friction throughout shooting. "McQueen made it very, very difficult for me," says Rydell.

Rydell couldn't figure out why the two old friends from New York weren't getting along. Finally, someone on the set had to whisper it in Rydell's ear. "A very attractive girl who was going to be in the picture came down to the location and flirted with me, and I responded," says Rydell. "The next day, McQueen was impossible—vocal and negative, challenging every decision I made. I couldn't figure out why. Finally, someone told me that this actress was Steve's girlfriend and I said, 'I'm sorry. I had no idea.' But that was no excuse."

While in Carrollton, McQueen and Rydell attended the stock car races and at intermission, with the crowd egging him on, McQueen agreed to test-drive one of the cars. The delighted crowd of 4,000 cheered the unscheduled exhibition of McQueen's car handling as Rydell watched from the stands in horrified silence.

Rupert Crosse's stay in Mississippi was no picnic, either. Carrollton was still years behind in terms of civil rights, and Crosse had to watch himself. When having dinner with the company in a restaurant, he had to be snuck through the back door into a private dining room.

As for Crosse and McQueen on the set, the two men differed in their acting styles. Whereas McQueen would get most of his scenes on the first take, Crosse would need eight to ten takes until he was comfortable. Says Richard Moore, "Rupert didn't have the same amount of talent that Steve did, and it might have taken him longer to get into the feel of his part. Here's a guy thrust into a pretty big picture with a big-name star. I'm sure he was a little nervous." The perfect solution was found. A stand-in for Steve would interact with Crosse until he was comfortable with the scene. It was then that McQueen would be called in for the scene. The snags with Crosse had been worked out, but there was still one snag left with the director: Who was in charge?

Rydell had been quietly seething throughout the filming of *The Reiv-*

*ers.* He chose to bite his tongue rather than face the wrath of the powerful McQueen. One scene required McQueen and Crosse to push the specially made 1905 Winton Flyer out of the mud. Mud was everywhere, and the two stars were sliding and falling, not having much success at moving the car. McQueen yelled at the director, who was sitting high atop a crane, "Ryyyyyyydellllll, get over here." As Rydell was climbing down from the crane, he recalls, "My heart stopped. The crew stood still. McQueen was a physical presence given to brutality. He'd demonstrated to me many times he was a first-class tae kwon do kicker." When Rydell reached the ground, he stood eye to eye with McQueen. Steve announced loud enough for the crew to hear, "You know, there's only room for one boss on this picture." But before he could continue, Rydell cut him off: "Yeah, that's me." Steve recognized Rydell's courage and backed off. "Inside I was trembling," recalls Rydell, "but he walked away because he saw that if he wanted a fight, I was ready."

Toward the end of filming, Mitch Vogel, who portrayed young Rufus, was involved in a freak accident. When a sprinkler accidentally went off while Vogel was on a horse, he was thrown from the horse and broke his wrist. Filming was shut down for a month. Steve thought it was the perfect time to see the dailies. What he saw horrified him, unjustifiably so.

With an insecurity stemming from his belief that he was betraying the audience that had made him the number one box office attraction in the world, Steve took his frustrations to the head of CBS films, Bill Paley. Steve tried to get Rydell fired from the film. Paley saw the dailies and realized that McQueen was out of line. He told Steve, "Rydell's the director. Shut up and get back to the set."

His pride wounded, Steve then tried to get the director of photography, Richard Moore, fired. Says Moore, "When things are going bad on feature films, very many times the person that gets sacrificed is the DP. It happens all the time." Moore was called in by Rydell during the shutdown. Rydell told him, "I hate to tell you this, but Steve wants to fire you." *The Reivers* was Moore's second feature film. He had been replaced on his first film, *The Scalphunters,* which starred Burt Lancaster, by his camera operator, who just happened to marry Lancaster's executive secretary that same week. He wasn't about to be dismissed again. He pleaded his case to Bill Paley, and again, Paley made the final decision. Moore stayed.

By the time shooting was completed, Rydell had been through the wringer. He later admitted, "Steve was difficult. I've dealt with some major, tough actors. Nobody's had me on the ropes. Steve had me on the ropes. But I hung in there. I told him I was going to outlast him. I said, 'When you're furious with me, I'm still going to be here trying. I'm not going to fold. And I'm not going to give in to you, because you're wrong.' It just drove him crazy, but he did finally surrender."

During the last part of filming in California, the FBI office in Los Angeles received a curious phone call. A memo dated April 4, 1969, to the director of the FBI in Washington, D.C., read:

TO: DIRECTOR, FBI
  FROM: SAC, LOS ANGELES (94-1948) (C)
SUBJECT: STEVE McQUEEN
          INFORMATION CONCERNING

On 3/24/69, (deleted) telephonically contacted the Los Angeles Division from Fort Saskatchewan, Alberta, Canada, telephone (deleted) and advised he formerly was with the Royal Canadian Mounted Police and had been associated with the FBI National Academy, Washington, D.C. (deleted) said the purpose of his call was to determine if this office could relay a message to the actor STEVE McQUEEN for him. (deleted) said McQUEEN was scheduled to travel to Canada to hunt with him on 3/25/69, but that he had injured himself in a hunting mishap and would be unable to join McQUEEN. (deleted) said he did not have McQUEEN's telephone number. He asked that McQUEEN be furnished his telephone number so that McQUEEN could call him in Fort Saskatchewan.

On 3/25/69, (deleted) Solar Productions, Cinema Center Films, Studio City, California, advised that McQUEEN owns this company. He said McQUEEN is currently on location at the Disney Ranch, San Fernando Valley, California, in connection with the motion picture "The Reivers," which this company is producing and in which McQueen is acting. The information furnished by (deleted) was made available to (deleted) who said he would pass the information on to Mr. McQUEEN. (deleted) thanked the FBI for its assistance in this matter.

(deleted) noted, however, that McQUEEN is fully occupied with the making of this motion picture and that McQUEEN has no plans to go hunting in Canada. He noted that (deleted) name is not familiar to him although he is not acquainted with all of McQUEEN's associates. He suggested that (deleted) story about the hunting date with McQUEEN was so much in error that it sounded irrational.

When the ad campaign for *The Reivers* was being drawn up, Steve was concerned that Cinema Center might capitalize on the McQueen image to sell the film. "Steve was extremely articulate with the studio and was possessed with 'Don't ever try to tell an audience this is a McQueen shoot 'em up,' " says Robert Relyea. One of the very first ads in preliminary form showed a picture of McQueen, Crosse, and Vogel in the Winton Flyer. The ad read, "McQueen comes rolling at you again." Steve sternly told the publicity department, "You will not go out and tell the public that this is *Bullitt II—Turn of the Century*. However you want to do it, I'll go along with it and I'll do the ad work and I'll push the picture, but don't try and say that this is a 'Steve McQueen action film.' " Steve knew that the ad campaign would have sold a lot more tickets, but he was more dedicated to the public than he was to selling tickets. "He probably made himself unhappy by doing it. He knew that he made this commitment to something he believed in, in the sense that he loved the script and was worried about his love of the script and what it might do to him as a character," says Relyea.

The final ad showed Steve, clad in overalls, a piece of straw hanging from his mouth and one eye closed, as if he were squinting at the sun. The ad read: "You'll LOVE him as Boon!" Steve also disliked that campaign, citing, "I looked like a village idiot in that shot. But you can't control everything."

*The Reivers* opened Christmas Day 1969 to receptive critical reviews. Kathleen Carroll of the *New York Daily News* wrote, "It's fortunate that McQueen is one of those rare modern actors whose presence carries the right kind of familiarity; he's ingratiating, and that's enough here." *Variety* assessed, "McQueen gives a lively, ribald characterization that suggests he will have a long career as a character actor after his sexy allure thins."

*The Reivers* qualified for the 1969 Oscars, and Rupert Crosse was nominated for Best Supporting Actor. Steve's performance was ignored entirely. Says Relyea, "Everybody loved Rupert and said Steve was fine, which I don't think is very fair. Steve worked very hard on that picture. When he found out Rupert was nominated, he didn't sulk. He called Rupert and said, 'Congratulations. What can I do to help? I think you've got a real shot at the Oscar.' He didn't mope around like, 'What about me?' He was proud of the picture, because he thought he was playing Russian roulette and didn't get shot."

So proud, in fact, that he decided he liked the finished product. "To his credit," says Mark Rydell, "he came up to me after the picture opened and said how proud he was of it." The two men then shook hands, but Rydell vowed he would never work with McQueen again, and he kept his promise.

*The Reivers* fared well domestically ($20 million in the U.S. alone, but it was nowhere near the success of *Bullitt*) but bombed everywhere else in the world. Robert Relyea offers, "It would be considered a moderate success, but it was just so Americana that it didn't do any business overseas."

When *The Reivers* finished filming, Steve retreated to his Palm Springs home for a few days of relaxation. Steve was fond of taking walks in the desert. One night, as he walked alone, he noticed a campfire. As he got closer to the fire, he noticed a couple of young women sitting Indian-style, chanting, with satanic paraphernalia littered about the ground. Steve told friend Pat Johnson, "After this encounter, every Friday night, I would get these intolerable migraine headaches. My head would hurt so bad, and all the while there would be this image of the devil in my mind, and I would get very frightened."

Steve consulted a psychic in Los Angeles and was told, "Every Friday night, all of the witches in England get together and circle and they are praying for your death. They are concentrating that you should die at your own hand. It is only the fact that you have such a strong presence that you are able to resist to this point. They would like you to get further into drugs. They would like for you to begin racing cars. Whatever you do, don't get into any cars that are a combination of red and black. That combination is satanic. Start praying to God and ask for his help."

Solar Productions was the Apple Records of its day. It openly sought fresh new talent and with the success of *Bullitt,* scripts and offers from young hopefuls trying to get a break in Hollywood flooded the office. The scripts were stacked to the ceiling and many had to be overlooked. One script was sent in by Charles Manson, who at the time was trying to achieve fame by any means possible. Manson hung out with Beach Boy Dennis Wilson and tried to convince Wilson that he could sing as well. Anything to make it in Hollywood. Manson would also direct and film home movies, complete with script. When Solar sent back the script with a polite 'Not interested,' Manson would seek his own revenge.

Jay Sebring was a man of mystery. After making it big in Hollywood as the leading hairstylist of the day, he purchased an expensive house in the hills of Benedict Canyon. In the 1930s, agent Paul Bern, who was married to actress Jean Harlow at the time, committed suicide there after a night of sexual violence with her. The Bern-Harlow scandal somehow made the house appeal more to Sebring, and he bought it after only one visit.

The ghost of Paul Bern was said to be roaming the halls of the mansion. Sebring's girlfriend at the time, actress Sharon Tate, stayed a night in the mansion and later told writer Dick Kleiner, "I saw this creepy little man. He looked like all the descriptions I had ever read of Paul Bern." Still in bed, Tate threw on her robe and ran downstairs. As she was heading toward the staircase, she saw a vision of someone faintly familiar she thought might be Sebring or herself, with their throat cut open, and blood spilling freely from the mortal wound. While she made her way to Sebring's room to tell him of her vision, the two could hear the little man bumping around upstairs.

Not only did Sebring enjoy such supernatural tales, but it was said that he hosted several satanic parties. (Steve never attended, though he suspected that Sebring was into such things. "I was always against that," he said.) Sebring supplied McQueen with women and drugs. Said one insider of the Sebring clan, "The beginning of the party could be just like the normal-type party given anywhere in Hollywood, but then, around 1:00 A.M.—or whenever the 'straights' went home—Jay would bring out his goodies. That's when the real party would begin."

Steve would often stay until the straights went home.*

On the night of August 8, 1969, Charles Manson would achieve the fame that he coveted so dearly. When cleaning lady Winifred Chapman arrived at the Roman Polanski–Sharon Tate household on the morning of August 9, she stumbled upon the biggest blood bath of the decade. Four lifeless bodies were littered about the residence of 1005 Cielo Drive. The four found dead were Abigail Folger, Voytek Frykowski, Sharon Tate, and Jay Sebring.

Not only did Sebring's murder give McQueen a good jolt of reality, but it later revealed that death came knocking on Steve's front door.

The night before the murders, August 7, Jay Sebring had come to the Castle to give Steve a haircut. The two men had agreed to have dinner with Sharon Tate, because her husband, director Roman Polanski, was out of town. Sebring would look after her when Polanski wasn't there. Steve was set to have dinner at the Polanski household when he ran into another woman who caught his interest. He decided to forgo the dinner and spent the night with his latest conquest. Her identity may never be known, but one thing's for sure: it may have been that Steve's cheating saved his life.

In the following weeks, Steve grew increasingly paranoid. He now kept a loaded handgun on him at all times. Back at the Castle, he had a television monitor put up on the gate so that he could keep a watchful eye on any intruders. Remembers Bud Ekins, "He got paranoid as hell. The whole place was locked up tight. Sharon Tate and Jay Sebring were

---

* Brad Steiger and Sherry Hansen, *Hollywood And The Supernatural* (St. Martin's Press, 1990), 134.

friends. It hit too close to home. He could have easily been there that night. He hung out with them. It would have scared the shit out of me, too."

During the LAPD's investigation of the murders, it was publicized that Jay Sebring had left behind a legacy of sex, drugs, and decadence. The theory of a drug deal gone bad was looked into. When Steve found out about the murders, he asked some friends to go into Sebring's house and "clean it up." The friends did exactly that but overlooked Sebring's car, where the police found cocaine, hashish, marijuana, and MDA in the glove compartment. Rumors of orgies and bondage sex followed Sebring to his grave.

Sebring also left behind a telephone book listing many of his friends and clients, many Hollywood stars. The LAPD had to question everyone in the book, including Steve McQueen. Says Nikita Knatz, "McQueen washed his hands of that so fast that it was like it never happened."

The murderers were apprehended two months later, on October 3, 1969. They called themselves the Manson family, a hippie cult from Death Valley, California.

Found on the Manson family was a celebrity shopping list of the people they wanted to murder. Since Charles Manson's scripts were being turned down and his singing career was going nowhere, he decided that the only means to achieve fame was through murder.

The list was carefully picked in unison by the family as to who best represented Hollywood at that time. Frank Sinatra, Elizabeth Taylor, Richard Burton, Tom Jones, and Steve McQueen happened to be at the top of the list.

Each celebrity was to be killed in a unique and gruesome way. Sinatra was to be seduced by a young female member of the family and castrated while having sex with her. The Burtons, it was decided, would be boiled alive. And Steve was to "die at his own hand." Just as the psychic had told Steve. It was common knowledge that the Mansons practiced the occult. Now it was clear to Steve who the devil worshipers in the desert of Palm Springs were and who was praying for his death: the Manson family.

Steve didn't know who he could trust anymore. At first, he believed in the hippies. They offered peace, love, and happiness, truly things he wanted. The hippies seemed harmless enough. The Manson family turned that thinking around in one night. The hippie movement left Steve disillusioned as the sixties came to an end. In his disillusionment, he continued to sink further into drugs and adultery. Friend Von Dutch, seeing a self-destructive pattern in Steve's behavior, asked him why he was pissing it all away. Steve's reply was prophetic: "Hey, my mother died when she was fifty, my father died when he was fifty, and I'm going to die when I'm fifty. That means I have ten years left to live it up."

# RUNNING OUT OF LUCK

*I've got a feeling I'm leaving stardom behind, you know. I'm gradually becoming more of a filmmaker, acquiring a different kind of dignity from that which you achieve in acting. After all, I'm no matinee idol, and I'm getting older. I don't think I can be doing my kind of thing in the seventies; I want to be on more of the creative side of business.*

STEVE McQUEEN

STEVE'S DREAM of the definitive racing picture was coming to fruition. He was finally going to get the chance to make the film he'd wanted since the ill-timed *Day of the Champion*. He would pull out all the stops. There were to be no compromises. Attention to accuracy and detail were to be the movie's signature. This one was to be, in Steve's terms, "pure."

"It had always been in Steve's mind that if you are going to make a racing picture, you make it about one race, Le Mans," says Robert Relyea.

When Steve was on location in Taiwan for *The Sand Pebbles*, the decision was made by Jack Warner to forgo *Day of the Champion*. It was no secret that MGM's *Grand Prix* was ready to begin shooting. Two racing pictures in one year didn't excite Warner, but when the constant delays for *The Sand Pebbles* made it clear to Warner that it was to be the second and not the first racing movie of the year, Relyea was given the bad news, "Cancel the picture."

Months later, when Steve returned from Taiwan and Solar Productions struck a six-picture deal with Warner Brothers, McQueen, Robert Relyea, and Jack Reddish threw a little celebration party for themselves. As they lifted their glasses for a toast, in reference to *Day of the Champion*, Relyea announced, "You know, one day, because we're all bad losers, we will have to face up and make a racing picture, because we'll never get over what happened. One day we'll make that picture, and when we do, it'll destroy us all and half the industry." Relyea notes today, "It was supposed to be a joke."

CBS's film arm at the time, Cinema Center, gladly agreed to fund the next Steve McQueen project for $6 million. It was a return to action-adventure for Steve, and any movie with McQueen behind the wheel of a car seemed a good idea. *Le Mans* would be the end all of racing films. Steve said, "We're going to cap it up, so no one will want to do a racing film again. I just hope CBS has the balls to ride with us."

Just as with *Day of the Champion,* John Sturges was set to direct *Le Mans.* If there was one man responsible for Steve's rise to stardom, it was Sturges. He had pulled McQueen out of B-movie purgatory with *Never So Few,* had given him his first taste of movie success with *The Magnificent Seven,* and had directed *The Great Escape,* which made Steve a bona fide star.

In the six years that passed since *The Great Escape,* Steve's star had streaked across the stratosphere. Sturges would be paid by Solar. In short, that meant Steve paid his salary. Sturges was a hired hand at best, and he couldn't have known what lay ahead of him.

The green light was given to *Le Mans* before a final script had been readied. Though not an uncommon practice in the movie business, an unfinished script certainly is a gamble for a studio, but Steve was very optimistic. "I enjoy the fact that we're playing for big marbles. I'm a filmmaker; I feel very strongly about not compromising the film for a business reason. I enjoy the spooky feeling of having it all on my back, but I don't like anyone fucking with my head while I'm doing it," he said.

The unfinished script would be the focal point of the film later on. But for now, the actual race of the 1969 Le Mans had to be filmed. That meant Sturges had to leave immediately without consulting McQueen on the script. The practice was not new to Sturges. *The Great Escape* was an example of an unfinished script that turned into a piece of cinematic history. Adds Sturges, "Very rarely do you get a perfect script. I've only had two. If you want to make movies, that's the name of the game. If you sit around waiting for perfect scripts, you're not going to be a very active film director."

Sturges was hired to convince McQueen that *Le Mans* needed a story. "I thought I could, but I didn't. If I would have known that before, I wouldn't have taken the damn job," he says.

Sturges felt that the movie should be a love story, with *Le Mans* as a background. McQueen wanted to shoot a pseudo-documentary on the sport of racing. Notes Relyea, "We probably never found the direction for the picture to go."

The story line for *Le Mans* is even more enigmatic than *Bullitt*. Steve portrays Porsche driver Michael Delaney in France's annual Le Mans auto race. The year before, in the same race, Delaney had survived a serious accident that killed his nemesis. His competitor's wife, Lisa Belgetti, played by Elga Andersen, appears at the race one year after her husband's death. Again, Delaney is injured and is rushed to the hospital, only to be released after being treated for minor injuries. He then returns to the race, where he encounters Belgetti. It is there that he espouses the thrill of racing and why he can't quit. A rivalry develops with another driver, and the two men cancel each other out during the race. The film ends with McQueen looking on as the crowd converges on the new champion.

Principal photography began on June 7, 1970, and the hardware for *Le Mans* was shipped to location. That included 20,000 props and 26 race cars. Also involved were 52 world-class racers to drive the cars, American and French film crews, and crowd extras, sometimes exceeding more than 350,000 people. *Le Mans* was to be the highest-budgeted film of Steve's career up to that point.

Steve also brought over Porsche mechanic Haig Alltounian to personally maintain the Porsche 917 being used in the film. Alltounian, who was a McQueen fan back in the days of *Wanted: Dead or Alive*, hardly recognized the star when they first met. "When Steve wasn't working," remembers Alltounian, "he let himself go physically. He looked like a bum, hair real long, full beard. He looked like a transient. It was comical." The two men hit it off, and Alltounian was soon calling him "Josh." Regarding Steve's racing skills, Alltounian notes, "What Steve lacked in polish or talent in motor racing, he made up for in courage. He had a full deck when it came to courage."

Alltounian assembled a team for test sessions and groomed McQueen for the filming sequences. After seven club races, McQueen suggested they enter at Sebring, a twelve-hour race that uses the same cars as Le Mans. "Steve was feeling confident and talked the film company into underwriting the expense of entering the club races and Sebring. Let's face it, Steve was going to get as much of this for himself as he could. He was having a ball," says Alltounian.

Peter Revson, a ranked Formula One racer at the time, was contacted by McQueen and consented to race with the star at Sebring. The race was divided into two categories: five-liter and three-liter engines.

Alltounian and his ragtag crew shocked a lot of people. At the end of the race, the Revson-McQueen pairing found themselves in the lead.

Mario Andretti was leading until his car broke down. He went back in the race and caught Revson in the last lap, beating him by just 23.6 seconds. Andretti's car, a five-liter engine, had just barely beaten the three-liter engine commanded by Revson and McQueen. In addition, the crowd believed it was McQueen behind the wheel of that last lap and proceeded to go wild.

At the end of Sebring, the winning cars are driven up to the start/finish line. A presentation is held and trophies, pictures, and champagne are customary. Revson and McQueen won in their class and second overall. Andretti's car was pulled up to the start/finish line first and received warm applause. When the Revson-McQueen car was pulled up, though, the crowd became ecstatic. Most of the crowd was comprised of high school and college kids. Notes Haig Alltounian, "Steve was like a god to people that age. For the number one box office attraction in the world to win a race, it was just like a rock concert." Security could not hold the mob back as they began to surround the car. Alltounian and his crew tried to head them off, but it was no use. The crowd then began to rip off pieces of the car for souvenirs. Steve, seeing a possible riot on his hands, made his way from the pits, worked

One of the brief, happier moments on the set of *Le Mans*, 1971
(COURTESY OF NATIONAL GENERAL)

his way through the crowd, got on top of the car, stood up, and gave the peace sign. "For a second, everything just stopped," says Alltounian. "It was like God had pronounced, 'Halt!' and then the crowd cheered him. Then all of a sudden, they became very docile. For a while I was worried the car was going to be destroyed and the crew was going to get pulverized. We're talking tens of thousands of people, all young teenagers, and they all wanted Steve. It was pretty scary. Steve was in complete control. He wasn't scared of anything. It was the first time I saw him in public where he kind of ate it up.

"We pulled off something there that even Hollywood writers couldn't have done if they tried. It was like somebody had written a script there on the spot. It was a storybook ending. It took Mario Andretti, who was at the top of his profession at the time, to beat us. It was a happy time for us."

The most amazing fact was that Steve had entered the race with a broken foot, set in a cast. Robert Relyea recalls, "He had broken his foot in a motorcycle race down near San Diego, yet he went ahead and raced in Sebring. When he got out of the car, the cast had melted; it was just a bunch of white gauze." The cast had melted during the middle of the race, no doubt, causing Steve excruciating pain, but Steve was too worried that he might compromise his position in the racing world, a fact that caused him to put on his blinders during the making of Le Mans.

Steve didn't want the professional drivers on the set of Le Mans to think of him as an actor. He wanted and needed their respect. So much so, that it totally blinded his judgment. "Steve was extremely sensitive about how he was seen by his peers in the racing world," says Relyea. "He did not want to be looked at as some actor who was a powder puff."

Cinema Center executive Bob Rosen recalls McQueen practicing privately in a garage late at night, getting in and out of the Porsche for six hours straight. "He really worked hard as an actor," Rosen points out. "He wanted it to look normal to him. He felt that if he looked awkward getting into the racing car, the audience would somehow know. He had tremendous vulnerability."

Steve explained his behavior: "People say that all racers are beckoning death, but it's not that way. I don't enjoy sheer speed over which you have no control. That frightens me. The challenge of racing is knowledge that your equipment is best, that you are in command.

"You have to love what you're doing. All the fame or glory that can come your way either as an actor or a racer means nothing if you don't believe in what you're doing. The racers I know aren't in it for the money. They race because it's something that's inside them. They're not courting death. They're courting being alive." When Steve found out that a Belgian driver had told a French reporter that he was doubling for Steve, McQueen fired him on the spot.

The screenplay still needed serious attention, as three different versions had been written since filming began. Visual consultant Nikita Knatz observes, "The writers on *Le Mans* were never together. They were put in three separate caravans. It became a competition as opposed to a team effort. They would each be given the same problem. That's no way to make a movie."

The first major snag the film ran into was that the footage John Sturges had shot during the 1969 Le Mans couldn't be used because the Gulf-Porsche team been been eliminated. In the film, McQueen would be a part of the team and the scenes would be tailored to the race. The problem was, the Gulf-Porsche team had crashed their car early in the race and there would be no way of getting around it; Sturges would have to set up a mock race, adding millions to the budget. Says Rosen, "The problem with *Le Mans* was that the filming process wasn't like any ordinary picture. Our focus was on the race. The picture started when the flag dropped, so we had to be ready. The problem was, we weren't ready and we should have taken that as an omen. It was a big blow financially."

Director John Sturges was having problems in directing Steve. Though the two were friends on a personal level, their professional relationship was becoming strained. "When Steve wasn't a star, he listened to me and took direction," Sturges says, "but when he got so big and had to do it his way, it went right back in his face. On *Le Mans*, I wasn't in a position to tell Steve what to do. When he did *The Magnificent Seven* and *The Great Escape,* he did what I told him to do. For *Le Mans,* he was in a power position, so if he didn't like a line, he didn't read it. If he didn't want to say anything, he didn't. And you could argue with him and he would say, 'Oh, I can get through by not saying anything.' It happens over and over with stars. Lots of stars get into producing and then get lost. It's actors like Spencer Tracy that go on forever. If you gave Tracy a part, he'd play the part and you could direct him." (Steve managed to get by with less than a dozen lines of dialogue in *Le Mans*.)

The conflict with Steve was getting to Sturges. He told Relyea, "If this continues, I'm going home." The first version of the script had been started over seventeen months ago and was still nowhere near completed.

The costs for *Le Mans* were escalating. The drivers, some of the best in the world, included Derek Bell, Jacky Ickx, Mike Parkes, Vic Elford, Richard Attwood, John Miles, Jonathan Wild, and David Piper, all of whom had to be paid handsomely to retain their services. In addition, the new script had called for six of the cars to be involved in a crash, a cost of $45,000 per car. Plus, no suitable female lead had been cast as of yet.

On a particularly bad day, Robert Relyea threw a fit in his office. An old friend, who happened to be employed by Cinema Center, was sitting in Relyea's office, sipping some hot coffee, when Relyea burst into the office, slamming the door behind him, and said, "This damn picture is out of control!" After witnessing Relyea's temper tantrum, the friend quietly finished his cup of coffee and reported back to Cinema Center what had transpired in front of him. "Guess what Relyea just said?" the friend told the executives. Cinema Center had had it. "If they're fighting among themselves, then let's go take this picture over and get tough," they decided. McQueen felt Relyea had blown the whistle on him, and the filming took a downward spiral.

The Cinema Center executives descended on the grounds of the racetrack. Steve resented their presence and fought with them until they had had enough. He personally greeted Cinema Center executive Gordon Stulberg and offered to give him a ride to "Solar Village," as the crew location was called. Stulberg was in for the ride of his life. McQueen revved up his Porsche to speeds well over 100 miles an hour and raced up and down the countryside. It was clearly an intimidation tactic that worked. Bob Rosen laughs, "Gordon's eyes were as big as saucers. Yeah, sure it was Steve's way of intimidating him. Steve was that mischievous child both on and off the camera, but even then, it was endearing."

The picture was shut down for two weeks. Cinema Center had even given Robert Redford a call behind Steve's back, though Redford most likely thought to himself that a battle with McQueen would not have been in his best interest. Solar Productions was faced with two options, the first being to shut down the picture and cut their losses—something Steve would avoid at any cost.

Bob Rosen was a part of the brutal meetings between McQueen and Cinema Center. Recalls Rosen, "Steve was a basket case. Every part of his life was falling apart at the same time. He told me years later he wasn't the same person. He was under a lot of stress. He didn't help his case any when he told the Cinema Center executives, 'The script's in my head.' He would say and react to things that didn't help his cause."

A second option was presented to Steve. He would forfeit his $750,000 salary, plus any points he had coming in the gross profits. Furthermore, Cinema Center would have complete creative control. Not wanting to lose his dream, Steve forfeited everything to keep *Le*

*Mans* afloat. Cinema Center executives told Steve, "Make the movie. Pick out whatever script you want, but for God's sake, make the movie."

Sturges had wanted to work on the script with Steve, but Steve announced that he was taking Neile to Monaco. Sturges was appalled. Steve told the director, "I'll be back when you're ready to resume shooting." Sturges asked, "You won't be here to work on the script?" In deference, Steve said, "No, I'll do whatever you want me to do when I get back." Sturges didn't take the snub kindly. He felt that Steve had put everyone in this predicament with his behavior and now was leaving the set for others to take care of the situation. He found it highly unprofessional of McQueen.

Robert Relyea happened to be on the phone when Sturges walked in after his exchange with Steve. "I'll be off in just a second," he told Sturges. Sturges said quietly, "No, no. Don't bother. I just wanted to tell you I'm going home." Relyea thought Sturges meant the hotel. "Okay, good night," he said. Sturges meant Los Angeles. He had Nikita Knatz drive him to Paris and took the next available flight out. Once back home, he told Relyea, "You know, the business is changing so much, that I can't adjust to it, so I'll be the one to leave." True to his word, Sturges did eventually leave the movie industry.

While Steve was in Monaco trying to salvage his marriage to Neile, it was left for Relyea and Reddish to find another director. Sturges's departure dealt an enormous blow to the crew and everyone involved with *Le Mans*. If a suitable director wasn't found soon, Cinema Center would shut down the movie for good.

Lee Katzin was ready to begin shooting a television movie for Cinema Center when he was called in by his boss, Jim Henshaw. Henshaw asked Katzin, "How would you like to go to Paris?" Two years earlier, Jack Reddish had been an assistant director on *The Rat Patrol*, the television series that Katzin directed. Now Reddish was returning the favor in requesting Katzin's services.

Katzin came to California in 1957 and made films at the University of Southern California after his undergraduate degree at Harvard in clinical psychology. He then worked as an assistant director from 1959 to 1964. From there, he began directing episodic television, including *Mission Impossible* and *The Mod Squad,* as well as *The Rat Patrol*. His first feature film, *The Phynx,* a campy, frolicking farce, was never released. *Le Mans* would be his shot at directing in the big leagues.

Three days after receiving the phone call, Katzin was in France. Katzin had actually met McQueen once when Solar was going to produce *The Cold War Swap*. Though McQueen was not going to star in it, he attended any meetings concerning Solar projects. Katzin remembers

McQueen as an "interesting man." Says Katzin, "He was aware of his situation and aware of who he was. He was a star."

When Katzin was brought into the picture, he realized that he sided with Cinema Center in their assessment that a story line was needed, instantly becoming an enemy in McQueen's eyes.

Haig Alltounian notes, "I don't know if Steve respected Katzin or not. I do know that it was a big chance for Lee. He was a good TV director. It was kind of a joke among the crew: 'We've got a TV director. Let's see what he can do.'"

McQueen put Katzin to the test as well. Remembers Katzin, "Steve would have a blowup and would leave, and we'd have to shoot without him until he came back. It was a difficult set of circumstances for the first six weeks." Early one morning, while he was trying to figure out what he was going to shoot that day, Katzin noticed McQueen staring at him from his motor home on the set. The only two up at that early hour, McQueen walked up to Katzin and told him, "Lee, I am no longer going to be against you. I see what you're trying to do and I'm going to work for you and not against you." The words had taken Katzin completely by surprise. "I had no idea where this came from," says Katzin. "From that time on, we hit it off. I was as surprised as anyone."

The search was on for a leading actress. Steve had opted for Diana Rigg of the television series *The Avengers,* but she had previous commitments. Maud Adams was then flown in. She was seated in Bob Rosen's office when she was first introduced to Steve. As she stood up to shake his hand, Steve noticed that Adams towered over him. Adams was shown the door after Steve told Rosen she wasn't right for the part.

The part was finally awarded to German-born actress Elga Andersen, a blonde, blue-eyed beauty. Most important, she was a few inches shorter than Steve.

Death loomed over the set of *Le Mans* from day one. Professional racers realize the risks involved in their sport; they consider them the hazards of the game. The game highly appealed to McQueen. "Very few people understand about motor racing. If you go to John Public, he says a racing driver is a guy with big balls who puts his foot in it and goes around a corner and hopes he makes it, and he's got a death wish and all this bullshit," reasoned Steve. "I think . . . it's one of the great highs of all time, it has great dignity. It's just a shame when you get killed doing it."

Two unusual accidents occurred during the shooting of *Le Mans.* On the way back from a rehearsal, driver Derek Bell's Porsche caught on fire. Though Bell managed to escape the torched Porsche, his face and hands had to be treated for minor burns.

Driver David Piper was not so lucky. During a second unit shot, Piper hit a guardrail at 200 miles an hour, which sent the Porsche flying down the track. The car broke into several pieces, and Piper was hospitalized with a triple compound fracture. A few weeks later, his right leg had to be amputated below the knee. (The film is dedicated to Piper.)

Haig Alltounian explains, "Race cars have to be warmed up. The tires have to warm up, too. The film was in such a rush to be finished that sometimes I would have to halt the shoot before I let the cars out. I would sometimes have to say no. With race cars, you don't pull that shit."

At the end of shooting one day, Steve himself was almost killed. A Solar truck had accidentally pulled out on the track when Steve attempted to pass a car at 200 miles an hour. Luckily, he maintained total control and remained unharmed.

The shoot for *Le Mans*, scheduled to end in September 1970, looked as if it were slowly edging toward November. Director of photography Robert Hauser remembers Bob Rosen telling him, "Shoot until you run out of light, because we really have to finish the film." Hauser told Rosen, "I can't see the drivers anymore." Rosen responded, "I'll tell you when you can't see them."

Hauser also found the circumstances surrounding the filming ridiculous. For *Le Mans*, part of the agreement Solar reached with the French government was to employ French film crews as well as the Solar crew. He found the imposition costly and clearly a nuisance. Remembers Hauser, "I had a French electrical crew, French grips, and an interpreter. I'd break for lunch for thirty minutes and hustle back to the set. The French crew would straggle back after two hours. I told the interpreter, 'If they pulled that in Hollywood, they'd be fired.'" It would also take Hauser twice the time to give the interpreter instructions for the crew to carry out. "God almighty, what a pain in the ass," he says.

Steve's marriage struggled as well. It was no secret that he was carrying on an affair with actress Louise Edlind, as well as other women who would float in and out of his trailer. "I knew of affairs that were going on right from the start," says Haig Alltounian. Steve confided to Alltounian that his home life was in trouble. "He talked about his personal relationship with his wife and his kids and how much he cared about his kids, what direction his marriage was going. He seemed to be confused. He spoke highly of Neile, too. They had a lot of years together. He abused that privilege, though."

Neile traveled to France as a last-ditch effort to save the marriage. She arrived with the kids in tow, and Steve was sincerely glad to see his family. He rented an actual castle for them to stay in. He told Neile, "Listen, baby, I want you to know that there will be ladies coming from all over the world to visit me." Suspicious, Neile asked, "What type of houseguests?" Stammering, Steve muttered, "Umm, ladyfriends. Look, baby, I wanna fly." Neile didn't know what to say or do. She described the pain she was going through: "My heart began to pound. I felt like someone had my head in a vise. I ran into the courtyard and found an unlocked car and drove, sobbing, around the French countryside until I was exhausted. Steve was hit by the 40-year-old syndrome, and there was no stopping him from taking what he wanted. Steve once boasted of his conquests in Hollywood, " 'I took this town like Grant took Richmond.' "

Mario Iscovich was a teenager at the time he was employed by Solar Productions in the late sixties. He first worked at Solar while Steve was filming *The Reivers*. Iscovich was a likable young man, and Steve took him under his wing, even though Mario got along better with Neile. As a gofer, Iscovich proved to be quite an asset to Steve, and his presence was requested when Neile and the kids flew to France. There, on the set of *Le Mans*, he discovered another side of Steve.

As a test, Steve flagrantly revealed his affairs with other women to Iscovich to see if he would report this to Neile. He warned the teenager, "She may be your friend, but your loyalty is to me, kid." Iscovich painfully kept silent while Steve fooled around on Neile.

One night after filming, McQueen and Iscovich took a ride together. Summing up the courage, Iscovich asked him, "Why are you carrying on like this? You have a wonderful wife, wonderful kids, and you're going to blow it." Steve, eyes glazed, turned to Iscovich and said, "Hey, man, look at me. I'm the world's number one movie star. All those women out there wanna fuck me. I WANT IT ALL!" Iscovich could only shake his head.*

The worst was about to happen. That night, as Steve crawled into bed with Neile, he apologized for his behavior, but not entirely. "I'm sorry, baby. I didn't mean to hurt you. I have to do what I have to do," he stated.

Neile recalls the next series of events. "I took a sleeping pill, but suddenly [I] couldn't stop talking. I told him I'd had an affair with a well-known actor who won an Academy Award! That did it. Steve hit the ceiling."

---

* McQueen Toffel, Neile, *My Husband, My Friend* (New York: Atheneum Books, 1986), 141–142.

What Steve did next, Neile claims, was to pull a gun on her and put it next to her temple. He demanded to know who the actor was. She didn't tell him. McQueen then cocked the hammer of the gun. This frightened her. Again, he wanted the name. Neile cried out, "Maximilian Schell," and collapsed on the bed.

A year earlier Neile had flown to New York to get away from Steve for a few days. She had found out about his Palm Springs philandering and needed to be anywhere but California. On the trip back from New York, she happened to be seated next to Schell. Schell, known as one of Hollywood's premiere pickup artists, turned on the charm, and soon the two agreed to meet at a Beverly Hills hotel.

Neile drove up to the hotel in her Excalibur, dropped off the car to the valet, and proceeded to Schell's room. The two fulfilled each other's needs: Schell, having sex with another actor's wife; and Neile, getting even in her own way with Steve for his affairs. (Years later, ex-wife Ali MacGraw appeared in the movie *Players* as Schell's wife, which must have galled Steve.)

Says Neile, "Steve was a first-class male chauvinist, and I say that with affection. He couldn't stand a wife having an affair, even though she might be justified. From then on, he wouldn't even let me out of his sight. We announced a separation, but it was strange because I had to be in the bedroom every night.

"I was hurt, but I loved Steve so much and I knew what our marriage meant to him. Maybe that sounds crazy, but our marriage was his religion. He wanted to sleep around and still have a tight little family unit."

The filming of *Le Mans* was beginning to rack up casualties. After director John Sturges left, agent Stan Kamen was fired. It was Kamen who first brought McQueen to Sturges. Kamen had nothing to do with *Le Mans,* but was fired out of sheer frustration on Steve's part. Robert Relyea was the next casualty.

Ever since the Cinema Center takeover, Steve had felt the blame rested with Relyea. Though Relyea had accidentally exploded in front of a Cinema Center executive, he clearly had not expected the person to breach his trust. McQueen turned his anger toward him. "Steve felt I had blown the whistle on him," says Relyea, "and that I had betrayed him."

A few days later, they had a talk about the takeover and what led to it. "He talked about his feelings and I talked about my feelings, which left us in the same hostile position," recalls Relyea. "That was the last time we discussed anything. The rest of the picture was done very business-like with a minimum amount of personal remarks to each other. We both just did our jobs."

Mario Iscovich was practically driven off the set of *Le Mans* when one night he, Steve, and actress Louise Edlind took a spin through the French countryside. Iscovich was often used as a beard so that if Steve were with another woman, it didn't look quite so suspicious. Driving at breakneck speed and under the influence of cocaine, Steve took a corner too fast and rammed the car head-on into a tree. He and Edlind crashed through the windshield and landed on top of the hood, while Iscovich suffered a broken arm. Steve stirred first and awakened to a frightening thought: a lawsuit. "Oh shit, man. What have I done?" he said. Edlind remained unconscious, and Steve and Iscovich went to look for help. All three were admitted to a local hospital, and the accident was hushed.

Iscovich spent a few days alone in the hospital. Steve never visited him once. When he arrived back on the set, his arm in a cast, Steve whisked him into his trailer. Iscovich was sworn to secrecy. "Okay then, get back to work," Steve said, without an ounce of regret.

Soon after, Iscovich encountered McQueen's wrath. Steve felt that Iscovich was coming on to one of his groupies, an absurd thought, but very real to him. Mario told McQueen he was crazy. "You'll never work in this business again," Steve warned. Iscovich had one foot out the door when Steve tried a different approach: "Mario, I don't want you to go." Iscovich had seen enough. His idol was tarnished before his eyes. He slammed the door to the trailer and walked out of Steve's life.

As for Neile, she suffered the same fate as the others. Their open-ended marriage was too much for her to take, so she gathered up the kids and headed back to California. Steve didn't stop her. Says a close friend, "If I could read between the lines, he seemed to tire of her."

*Le Mans* wrapped in late November 1970, two months past schedule and $1.5 million over budget. The final day of shooting, Robert Hauser and his wife were involved in a serious car accident, an ironic ending to *Le Mans*.

The ordeal was over and in Steve's mind, he had achieved what he set out to do: to win the respect of professional race car drivers. Says Haig Alltounian, "I think he got that, too. I honestly believe that had Steve pursued a career in racing rather than show business, he probably could have made a living at it."

Andy Ferguson, the former Lotus team manager, said of Steve's ability, "The drivers rate Steve very highly. He's a bright lad." Masten Gregory, a driver at Sebring, commented, "I had an opportunity to do some dicing with Steve, and I thought he was driving bloody well. He's a competitor, and that's very important. He's got the professional attitude." Added driver Mike Parkes, "I wouldn't say he's a natural, but he's certainly high up."

Not only had Steve's obsession with winning the professional racers' respect clouded his judgment regarding the story for *Le Mans*, but others believe that it had affected his marriage. Comments Robert Relyea, "The strain was getting so enormous. It wasn't just a motion picture, it had to do with his credibility with the racing world. I certainly didn't anticipate when we were shooting the script that it would wreak so much havoc with everything. It was a big issue, and you constantly saw small signs of it. It must have rubbed off on the marriage. You can't be possessed with something without it affecting the rest of your life."

Editing *Le Mans* proved to be just as difficult as the filming itself. There were 450,000 feet of film to be edited into a presentable motion picture. (All of the Sturges work was nixed in favor of the new footage.) It eventually took over six months to cut and piece *Le Mans* into a story. Cinema Center had cut Steve from the entire post-production process and left it to the editors to sort out the story. Except, there was never any story to edit. Says Sturges, *"Le Mans* never had a story. Nobody could tell anything that was going on except a lot of racing. In its final release, I challenge anyone to tell you the story of *Le Mans*. There isn't any." Mechanic Haig Alltounian observes, "A lot of the good stuff that was filmed wound up on the cutting room floor. It was like it was because there was no script, so they cut a script into it. With what they had to work with, it probably couldn't have been any better."

Director Lee Katzin still believes *Le Mans* could have been improved. "We knew how the story was going to start. We knew how it was going to end. What we didn't know was what the relationship was between McQueen and this woman whose husband had died in the race the year before, if in fact that was going to be the story, if in fact he was going to meet this woman, and if they were going to have a relationship."

Comments Nikita Knatz, "McQueen, unfortunately, had seen *Easy Rider,* and it had broken through as the new way of making a film. So *Le Mans* became Steve's *Easy Rider* with four wheels."

The time had come for Steve to view the final cut, and everyone at Cinema Center was not anxious for his reaction. "It was a frightening experience putting the film together," said Bob Rosen. "McQueen had nothing to do with the post-production and when we showed him the final version, he liked it. I was dumbstruck." Steve did concede that Sturges had been correct and that the film needed a story line. He made a phone call to Sturges, who says, "He did back off on *Le Mans* and admitted to me he was a jerk. This was before it was released. You didn't have to know before it was released that it wasn't going to be anything.

On *Le Mans,* we were friends. He always had respect for me. I think he thought he knew how to make a film as good as I did, and he certainly didn't. Nonsense."

The premiere for *Le Mans,* in June 1971, was, appropriately enough, in the racing capital of the United States, Indianapolis. The movie was lambasted by the critics for its weak story line, though revered for its photography. *New York Times* reviewer Howard Thompson wrote, "Racing buffs will probably flip over it, but mostly it's a bore. McQueen's exchange of monosyllabic utterances and long, meaningful stares with other drivers simply added up to tepid, monotonous drama." Kathleen Carroll of *New York Daily News* lamented, "There was no attempt at characterization. *Le Mans* is an excuse for Steve McQueen to indulge his passion for auto racing and to show off his skills as a racing driver. An auto race, even a 24-hour endurance test like *Le Mans,* does not make a movie in itself. . . . A script is needed." Jay Cocks of *Time* wrote, "McQueen is potentially a good movie actor, but he needs someone to loosen him up, make him play a part, not pose for it. *Le Mans* may be the most famous auto race in the world, but from a theater seat it just looks like a big drag." In comparison to John Frankenheimer's *Grand Prix,* Cocks called *Le Mans* "Petit Prix."

Perhaps the most stinging review came from the film's technical adviser and Steve's personal hero, driver Sterling Moss. "I thought it was a ghastly film," said Moss. "To me, it was a great letdown. I'm surprised it ever got past him. Absolutely abortive. It had neither passion nor emotion—utterly unrealistic. A very bad film in my opinion. One takes part in the sport because of the passion and humor. Racing drivers are a special lot—great fun. But none of this comes across in the film at all."

Says Bob Rosen, *"Le Mans* had so much hype before the picture was released, that when it came out, it was a major disappointment. The film made money, but it should have been one of the greatest movies of all time. If I went over my résumé of films and I saw *Le Mans,* I would say to myself, 'There was a picture that should have been great!' "

The box office take for *Le Mans* was $19 million worldwide, but Steve didn't get to see a penny of it. In order to save the film from being scrapped, he had given up his salary and points in the picture. On top of that, he was slapped with a $2 million back tax from the IRS.

Robert Relyea and Jack Reddish left Solar Productions shortly after returning from France. Solar Plastics went belly up, as well, and Steve's baby, Solar Productions, went into a holding company. Solar Productions was abandoned and the rest of the staff was fired. The offices were vacated and Solar was restructured as it was in its original inception, a tax shelter. It ceased being an active production company. Any profits from Solar had to be turned over to the government in order to pay the tax bill.

McQueen's empire had crumbled to the ground.

*Le Mans* severed everything important to Steve. His marriage, his company, his wealth, and the movie dearest to his heart, had all been dealt a death blow. "[*Le Mans*] was really a blow to his ego," said Neile. "Something he had wanted so much that had been a part of him suddenly was squashed. The burden of stardom really is very heavy. It's a very difficult thing to handle, especially if you were as macho and chauvinistic as Steve was."

Steve's behavior at this time is best summed up by Haig Alltounian: "I can understand how people in the business go awry. Everything about the business is bizarre: the amount of money it takes to do things, how much money is made. I can understand how stars behave the way they do. It's just a direct reflection of their industry. It takes a very disciplined, moral person to live in that environment and come out normal."

With one final word on *Le Mans,* Steve told a reporter, "It was a blood bath, that picture. It was the most dangerous thing I've ever done. I'm lucky I'm still alive. But unfortunately, we didn't have a script. I think I was wrong about a great deal. But it's difficult to be right all the time."

His best friend, Pat Johnson, said of McQueen at this time, "Steve was probably the most paranoid person that I've ever known. He . . . never wanted to be 'had' by anybody. When he went bankrupt after *Le Mans,* a lot of people deserted him, and he resented that very much. He was even more paranoid after that."

"I believe in a lot of love, security, and discipline. I'll never be able to see my father in this world, but at least I can be a good father to my kids." McQueen with Terry and Chad. (FROM PHOTOPLAY MAGAZINE)

# TO PART IS TO DIE
# A LITTLE

*The one thing that was extraordinary, is that [his] attitude never changed toward our children. He was wonderful with them and he was wonderful with children in general, because he saw the world through the eyes of a child.*

NEILE MCQUEEN

*I always got the impression that he tried to be a good father to his kids.*

CHARLES BRONSON

*McQueen was really wonderful with his children.*

ELI WALLACH

STEVE WAS RETURNING to a simpler life. He got rid of all the lawyers. All of the accountants. All of the managers. All of the public relations people. He gave no more interviews. The suits and ties that he so proudly wore to the office went back into the closet. Solar Productions and Solar Plastics were completely shut down, and Steve was getting back to basics. He painfully recalled, "I put up a suite of offices, a lot of secretaries, accountants, lotsa people on the payroll. I was producing my own films. Just terrific. But I wasn't making any money and I was working sixteen hours a day and I was the president of three corporations. And I was not very happy."

He grew paranoid about his taxes and would simply pay them from any earnings up front; that way, he could never be slapped with back taxes again. "Did you guys pay my taxes?" he would ask his business manager every week. Said an intimate, "Steve did not want to get in trouble with the IRS. I think he read about how they used to get mobsters through tax evasion. He didn't want to get nailed. There were a lot of actors in Hollywood who got in trouble for not paying their taxes. A lot of old-time actors went broke just paying their taxes, and Steve was obsessed about this not happening to him."

Steve would apply this life of simplicity to his acting roles in the future. "I've started cutting everything out," he insisted. "Now I think of Laurence Olivier when he goes to work. He's got a little black bag with a couple of fake noses, his wig, or whatever he's got in there. And that's all I need—a pencil, a script, and a briefcase."

Separated from Neile, on his own for the first time in over fifteen years, and cash poor: it was not a good time in Steve's life.

One bright spot in 1971 was the release of *On Any Sunday,* a motorcycle documentary that showed a different side to the sport. "Most bike flicks in the past concentrated on the outlaw crap," said McQueen. "Hell's Angels and all of that stuff, which is about as far away from the real world of motorcycle racing as I am from Lionel Barrymore. Brando's movie *The Wild One* in the early 1950s set motorcycle racing back about 200 years."

The project actually started in 1969 with director, writer, and producer Bruce Brown, who had successfully made *Endless Summer,* the definitive documentary on surfing. Brown was constantly competing against Steve in motorcycle races, so Steve approached him about making a documentary on the sport. They reached an agreement that Solar would invest the $300,000 needed to make the film. Brown told McQueen, "The only way I make films is to go out and do it myself. I don't do it like Hollywood does. I don't fly first class and sit in the box seats. I sneak in and climb over the fence. I'd cover every little spectrum of the sport from little kids to motorcross in Europe." He was McQueen's kind of guy.

Brown, a self-professed beach bum, called Relyea a week before the premiere. "I don't own any shoes. All I own are sandals and thongs." The thought amused Relyea, as *Endless Summer* had made Brown a multimillionaire. Relyea offered, "I don't think you have to wear a tie, but I think you should buy some shoes."

Steve appeared in the film several times, but only as a motorcycle racer. (He raced under the pseudonym of "Harvey Mushman.") His one line in the movie, "Every time I start thinking of the world as all bad, then I start seeing some people out here having a good time on motorcycles—it makes me take another look," revealed his passion for racing.

*Variety* hailed *On Any Sunday* as "an exciting documentary of one of the most dangerous of all sports. McQueen's prowess as a racer is demonstrated time and again and his name should spark interest in a film that alone stands as a spectacular piece of filmmaking." Gary Arnold of the *Washington Post* wrote, "The last time an actor's athletic feat thrilled audiences for a sustained length of time was probably McQueen's motorcycle ride in *The Great Escape.*"

*On Any Sunday* exceeded anyone's hope of box office intake, with the film grossing $10 million domestically and an astounding $24 million worldwide. Much to Steve's dismay, he didn't see a penny of the profits, since Solar Productions was now a holding company.

In desperate need of some cash, he agreed to film a Honda commercial for a record-breaking fee of $1 million, with the provision that it be shown only in Japan; that way, his movie star image in the U.S. wouldn't be tarnished. (Movie stars didn't do commercials back then.)

Writer William Nolan once pressured Steve for an answer on women and infidelity. In his heart, his words may have been true, but by his actions, McQueen was a hypocrite. Steve told Nolan, "It's very hard to say no to these women sometimes. Some are beautiful, and I'm no saint. Marriage is really difficult when you're in the public eye. You're exposed to so many rumors about other women. You're always under the gun. Lots of pressure. Most marriages in the industry crack up fast, mainly due to this kind of pressure. But me, I'm no party stud. I'm with one woman at a time, and she's my lady and that's it until the ball game's over and we decide to walk in different directions." McQueen insisted, "No matter what you've read in the gossip rags, I'm not a cat who sleeps around when I'm into a heavy relationship. That's just not my style."* But it was his style. He was a party stud. He wasn't a one-man woman. Steve was like a kid in a candy store; he took what he wanted and he wanted it all.

When the shoe was on the other foot, and Steve saw other married men sleeping around, he didn't like it. To him, right was right, and wrong was wrong, but he didn't feel the need to judge himself by that same standard.

Steve no longer felt the need to be discreet. He could be seen in public with actress Lauren Hutton, singer Mary Wilson, and a famous Playboy bunny. "His fooling around wasn't exactly a military secret," says Hilly Elkins. "Neile tried to look the other way, but it was impossible to go anywhere and not bump into him with another woman. It was

---

* Nolan, William, *McQueen* (New York: Congdon & Weed, 1984), 141–142.

obvious enough so that the word would get back in two or three passes in an irreparable manner. That can poison a little after a while.

"I think that that was part of the measure of his attractiveness, his potency, his desirability, how easy, how quick, how many."

Bud Ekins comments, "I would attribute the breakup to his womanizing. I knew he was chasing women around all the time. He was with a different broad every night. It was kind of like, how long was Neile going to put up with it? The older he got, the worse he got. She was Mrs. McQueen and that's who she wanted to be, and she tried to keep being Mrs. McQueen as long as she could with him fucking around, making a fool out of her. She put up with it for years. It didn't matter what Steve did as long as he came home. Christ, he'd walk into a grocery store and walk out with some housewife and get laid that afternoon. Women were always chasing him. He didn't need to chase them, they did the chasing. Good lookers, too."

Around this time, Steve called David Foster and invited him to Palm Springs. "Come on down for the weekend," Steve told him. "We'll ride bikes, fool around, grab some Mexican food." Foster comments, "I'll never forget that weekend."

Foster arrived and the day was wonderful: enjoying the sunny weather, riding motorcycles, and relaxing. At night, Steve, Neile, and Foster went to a tacky little Mexican restaurant they liked to frequent. They ate a hearty meal and washed it down with beer. Steve was not a big drinker in those days and had a little bit more beer than usual. "He loads up on beer this particular night," remembers Foster, "and then he starts in. Oh God, what a horrible night." McQueen said to Foster, in front of Neile, slurring his words, "Do you know she did?" He continued, "She had an affair with Maximilian Schell." Over and over, he kept saying, "Can you believe she had an affair with Maximilian Schell?" Foster was stunned. He knew there was a problem in the marriage, but it hadn't yet gone public. Now it was all coming out. "Neile reached the point where she said, 'Screw him, he's going off and screwing everybody.' And she was simply evening the score in her own way." Neile sat there in stony silence as Steve repeatedly berated his wife. "He, of course, never said he had been doing the same thing," Foster points out. "It's like the old cliché, 'Two wrongs don't make a right.' "

When the three arrived back at the McQueens' Palm Springs home, Foster quietly went to the guest bedroom while Steve and Neile went to their upstairs bedroom. He waited a half hour before packing his things and leaving in the middle of the night. "I was not about to go through that the next day. That was probably the most depressing, emotional experience I've ever had in my life. It was horrific, just horrific," recalls Foster.

The two decided that a separation would be best. Steve told *Sports Illustrated* reporter Robert F. Jones, "We've got our problems and we're trying to work them out." He headed to Prescott, Arizona, to make *Junior Bonner*, while Neile stayed home with the kids.

After Solar Productions folded, Steve's new agent, Freddie Fields, had put together an impressive cast of stars to form the production company First Artists. The company was formed while Steve was making *Le Mans*, and Fields had rounded up friendly rival Paul Newman, Sidney Poitier, and Barbra Streisand. When *Le Mans* went bust and Solar went under, McQueen was encouraged by Fields to join. (A year later, Dustin Hoffman came on board.) Steve admitted, "I just had to take my lumps and move in a new direction. I could no longer depend on Solar alone. I needed more production muscle behind me."

First Artists guaranteed each star almost complete creative control. All they had to do was simply pick the movie they wanted to make and bring the budget of the picture under $3 million. The star would receive no upfront salary, but would be entitled to 10 percent of the gross. It was a make-or-break deal. If a picture did moderately well, the chances of making more money at the back end would bring the salary up to the one they would have made anyway. If the picture were a smash, then the star had the potential of making much bigger dollars than the regular upfront salary. In any case, it was a very attractive deal for everyone involved.

*Junior Bonner* is the story of an aging rodeo champ who wants to win the contest in his hometown just one last time. A New West is on the horizon, and Junior is trying to cope with the inevitable change.

The film was a departure for Steve and would eventually become his favorite. Notes David Weddle, author of *If They Move, Kill 'em: The Life and Films of Sam Peckinpah*, "McQueen had just finished *Le Mans* and was looking for a quiet film. A more character-oriented role. Steve really believed in what it said about the changing of American values."

The concept for the film and the ultimate packaging came together at a whirlwind pace. Writer Jeb Rosebrook came up with the idea for *Junior Bonner* when he attended the 1970 Prescott Rodeo in Arizona for the first time in fifteen years. He noticed how the city had changed. "I saw this old western town turn into a real estate boom and how it was paving the way for the future," said Rosebrook. "When I watched the rodeo, I paid close attention to the cowboys, and I always thought with character, and out of that came a character I named Bonner. It was a contemporary western using rodeo as a metaphor."

At the time, Rosebrook, a former Los Angeles advertising executive, had published his first novel and, for nearly three years, was attempting to gain a career as a screenwriter. The word around town was that Robert Redford was looking for a rodeo picture. An outline was sent to Redford, who turned it down. Producer Joe Wizan thought it better suited for Steve McQueen. McQueen loved the script. "He related to that character," said Rosebrook. "Both men's home life was erratic. Both men never had a real relationship with their fathers. In fact, Steve insisted that [Bonner] call his father 'Ace' instead of 'Dad.'"

Steve agreed to do *Junior Bonner* in April 1971, and by May, Sam Peckinpah had been enlisted to direct. The Prescott Annual Rodeo was the July 4th weekend, and everyone involved jumped into the project headfirst.

Filming began on June 30. Before heading to Prescott, Steve predicted, "Sam Peckinpah, boy, will he and I be some combination. ABC has bought a lot of aspirin."

It was to be the first film since *The Thomas Crown Affair* that he didn't have any administrative input. "I'm tired of being the chief. I just want to be an Indian. I'm going to concentrate for a while on being an actor. I know I've been a pain in the ass to a lot of the studios. I've always been a perfectionist and that's a pain in the ass. As an actor, I have to keep in control, too. I have to find the level on which to relate to the director so I can give him what he needs. He has many things to worry about besides the actors—lights, electricians, prop men, camera angles, the story line. Movie-making can be a snarl of confusion," Steve said.

*Junior Bonner* was a rodeo film and Steve was not anticipating an easy time in his riding scenes: "You look at those big bulls and they really are *big*. I don't want to do it. I'm a born coward. I want to take a glass of iced tea and sit under a tree. I don't know all that much about horses either, except they like you till they kill you. You can't trust animals."

It was the first time that Steve and Sam Peckinpah worked together since Peckinpah was fired from *The Cincinnati Kid*. Deep down, Peckinpah felt that somehow Steve had not stuck up for him when he was let go. During the first part of the picture, McQueen and Peckinpah, in the words of actor Ben Johnson, "fought like cats and dogs." Adds Johnson, "They didn't hit it off too good. They were more or less jealous of each other."

Prop master Bobby Visciglia remembers a phone call from Mc-

McQueen's only film to lose money, *Junior Bonner*, in which he plays an over-the-hill rodeo star who finds it hard to cope with the modern day world, 1972.

(COURTESY OF ABC-CINERAMA)

Queen's business manager, Bill Maher. Maher was concerned about the two men and how were they going to make the film if there were any hard feelings. Both Maher and Visciglia met for lunch, and Maher was skirting around the issue. Visciglia broke the ice: "Bob, let's cut the bullshit. What is your concern?" Maher, on behalf of McQueen, wanted to know how Peckinpah felt about him. Visciglia, on behalf of Peckinpah, informed Maher that there were no hard feelings and that the two could work together and finish the film. "Steve was very respectful of Sam during the making of *Junior Bonner*," Visciglia says. "He called him, 'Mr. Peckinpah.' Somehow, though, I always felt there was a shield throughout the movie between the two."

In the first scene of *Junior Bonner*, McQueen is seen driving a convertible to the next rodeo. Before shooting, he requested that Visciglia hold his wallet. As the cameras began to roll, and Peckinpah yelled for action, McQueen stopped the scene. He wanted to know from Peckinpah where his wallet was. Peckinpah turned to Visciglia and asked about the wallet. Visciglia told him, "The son-of-a-bitch just gave it to me before you yelled for action." Visciglia believes McQueen was testing Peckinpah from the get-go. "What McQueen was saying in so many words to the director was, 'You're ready, I'm not.' McQueen was a little kid some-times. All you had to do was give him a lollipop!"

During their trial separation, Neile stayed away from the filming of *Junior Bonner*. With his personal life in turmoil, Steve told everyone involved on the film, "The press should stay away." Never one to be without a woman for long, he began an affair with actress Barbara Leigh, a natural beauty with long straight brown hair. The affair would continue right to the end of filming.

From the beginning, Steve wanted to perform all of his stunts. Peck-inpah allowed him to perform some, but not all. During the course of the stunt work, Steve managed to sprain a wrist and received a deep cut across his nose. For his close-ups, Peckinpah decided he would have to ride a mechanical bull, a fact that pissed Steve off. Offers Ben Johnson, "When it gets too dangerous or hazardous, I don't think it's too smart for an actor to do his own stunts. If you get halfway through the film and your actor gets hurt, you have to shut down the company. Time is money in this business."

*Junior Bonner* had an exceptional cast surrounding McQueen that included film veterans Robert Preston, Ida Lupino, and Ben Johnson. "That was Marty Baum's doing," added Jeb Rosebrook. "He always felt that a good film had a great cast in it. He wanted to surround McQueen with a cast that would make McQueen stretch his character, and he achieved that."

The idea was brought up of Gene Hackman as Curly Bonner, Mc-Queen's younger brother. McQueen dismissed it rather quickly during a script meeting: "I think Gene Hackman's a good actor, there's no question about that. He'd be good, but he sure wants a lot of money." Newcomer Joe Don Baker was eventually decided on to portray Curly, though on the set, the two film brothers acted liked total strangers. "Joe Don Baker was a pompous ass who tried to kiss up to Steve," notes Bobby Visciglia. "The scene where the two have a fight on the porch could have been for real. Whenever McQueen and Baker had a scene together, Steve would always show up last out of disrespect. Peckinpah didn't like Baker that much either."

Robert Preston was very much respected by McQueen, but Steve had only one question regarding the veteran actor: "How tall is he?" he asked Peckinpah. About six foot, he was told. "Get him some sandals," McQueen replied.

A sequence at the railroad station is the film's most heartfelt. Preston portrays McQueen's father, and the scene is a reconciliation between the two men. Reveals Katy Haber, Peckinpah's personal assistant at the time, "That particular scene at the train station is really a moment that

Sam took from his own father." The scene also proved to be the hardest to film, as Steve couldn't grasp the concept of revealing his feelings to another man. "Steve found it difficult to do a sensitive scene with another man," says Haber. "That's why he was so good in the film. He was breaking new ground."

McQueen referred to Ida Lupino as "Miss Ida." Lupino was from the old school of acting. She was a stickler for details and the consummate professional. Steve's brand of acting was a cause for Lupino to openly scold him for their first scene together. Jeb Rosebrook recalled, "Steve was always changing his lines the night before filming, and on this particular night before his first scene with Ida in the kitchen, eating pie, there wasn't anybody around to consult with on the script, so he didn't learn his lines. That next day, McQueen began to ad-lib the scene, throwing off Ida because he was saying things that weren't in the script. Ida blew up and told him, 'Tomorrow you either know your lines or you're going to be eating a helluva lot of apple pie!' She was a terrific lady."

Filming took seven weeks to complete and when it was over, Steve admitted that the stunts on *Junior Bonner* were the hardest he'd ever performed. Asked if he'd consider making a documentary on rodeos, Steve quipped, "That I'll leave to John Wayne. The great thing about bikes and cars, however dangerous they may be, is that they don't kick and they never bite."

Katy Haber, who was Sam Peckinpah's longtime companion, recalls a funny incident, but harrowing at the time, involving a mean rodeo bull. "Sam was setting up a shot in the center of the ring with the sound and camera crew. Steve thought it would be funny to let open the bullpen. You've never seen so many people scatter so fast. I had grown men climb over me to get out of the way." The bucking bull demolished an expensive 35-millimeter camera. That, Peckinpah didn't think, was too funny. When the bull was finally contained and the crew gathered again for the first time, Haber was moved to ask aloud, "What ever happened to women and children first?"

"Steve was basically a child at heart, a kid from the orphanage who was reliving his youth now that he was a movie star," says Haber.

The last scene of *Junior Bonner* has McQueen buying a first-class ticket to Australia in order for his father to live out his dream of becoming a gold miner. The scene involved an exchange of real money and when it was finished, McQueen handed the bills back to prop master Bobby Visciglia. In a re-creation of his carnival days as a teenager, McQueen pulled a switch on Visciglia, who wound up being out a few hundred bucks. "Damn McQueen," thought Visciglia, "son-of-a-bitch shorted me."

When *Junior Bonner* was released, Steve received some of the best critical reviews of his career. The *Los Angeles Times* boasted, "Steve McQueen is explosive and forceful in one of his finest performances." Kathleen Carroll of the *New York Daily News* wrote, "A nice, loose, easygoing rodeo picture. McQueen has met with a role that fits him like a glove."

Most of the critics were surprised to find *Junior Bonner* a pleasantly nonviolent film, as they came to expect any movie from Peckinpah, dubbed "The Master of Violence," anything but pleasant. John Russell Taylor of the *London Times* summed up what the critics were anticipating: "For those of us who have come to expect (or fear) that each new Sam Peckinpah film will be a new bloodbath, this comes as a pleasant surprise, a reminder of milder, gentler films."

Unfortunately, in the summer of 1972, Hollywood had pumped out its share of rodeo films. *J. W. Coop, The Honkers,* and *When Legends Die,* in addition to *Junior Bonner,* were all unleashed to the public within a three-month time frame.

When ABC Pictures was ready to release the film, Steve suggested a different marketing strategy. "In distributing the picture, I was dealing with a man named Joe Sugar who wanted to release it big—Grauman's Chinese and the whole bit," said Steve. "I told him that it should be released as an art picture starting in more select, smaller theaters and letting the picture catch on. He continued to disagree, and, of course, the picture was released his way and fell flat. But I think it's a picture that'll do well over the long haul. Not today, not tomorrow. But give it time, and people will recognize it for what it's worth." McQueen was correct in that *Junior Bonner* has been proven a succès d'estime.

As for Steve's professional career, *Junior Bonner* became his third flop in a row. The film grossed a mere $2 million worldwide, and ABC Pictures lost $4 million in the process. It remains Steve's only film ever to have lost money. Steve reflected on his feelings about it: "I liked *Junior Bonner* very much. It was the first time I'd worked with Sam, and we got it together. I thought the script was tremendous—one of the best properties I've come across. But I think the film is a failure, at least financially, and in this business, that's what counts." Commented director of photography Lucien Ballard, "Steve is a difficult actor to work with in some ways. For one thing, he equates money with success, which makes him very difficult to reason with unless you've made more money than he has."

* * *

When Steve got back from Arizona, he soon learned he wouldn't have much money left to his name. On March 14, 1972, Neile was awarded a $1 million settlement in addition to a $500,000 per year alimony and child support for the next ten years.

Steve said of the settlement, and of his first wife, "She deserves every penny of it—for without my old lady, there wouldn't have been any in the first place."

The thought that they were no longer married hit Steve harder than it hit Neile. "He was stunned when I filed for divorce," says Neile. "He couldn't understand that I needed to have an orderly life . . . be my own person. I had children to care for. He was furious when I filed."

Both children had been placed in the custody of Neile, but, she claimed, "that was just a technicality. The children are as much Steve's as mine. And I've told both Terry and Chad that I know the time might come when they'd rather live with their father than me. If that happens, they'll go with my blessings."

Both Neile and Steve acted with maturity in the face of divorce, neither one saying negative things in front of the children. "Because he and I have never exhibited any bitterness, our youngsters have been spared the pain of our divorce," said Neile. "It's terrible to make children the pawns of your grief.

"It took four years for us to become friends again. We were in touch, of course, even under the strain. It's an incredible agony you go through with divorce: more traumatic than death because you do it yourself. The wounds were still raw, but we talked about the kids. He was in and out of the house checking on us, though we both had someone else."

No doubt, Steve was in shock. The one constant relationship in his life was over. His relationship with his children, on the other hand, was forever binding. "My biggest concern in life is my children," he said. "And nothing will come between us. I know things are different now, but it's going to work out, because they know I love them and want their happiness most of all. I am prepared to face the incidents that all divorced fathers experience."

Neile said years later, "He loved those kids, no matter how bad our relationship became in the end. That was always constant."

In time, the two became friends. She said at the time: "Just because I'm no longer Mrs. Steve McQueen, or just because Steve and I now realize it's impossible to love one person for your entire life—that doesn't mean we still can't be friends.

"And it most definitely doesn't mean that our children should suffer. We've remained a close family unit in spite of the divorce and we do so many fun things together. When I have a date, it's often Steve who comes over to take care of the children so I can go out."

The two were still making love, and often it was Neile who initiated it. McQueen told a friend, "I feel like a damn secretary who's being chased by the boss around the desk when I go over to her house."

Neile knew that Steve would be a hard act to follow and continued to brag about him in the face of divorce: "Any other man would be so dull after Steve; he's the only one I have ever met who doesn't bore me." Soon after that comment, it was Neile, not Steve, who had the first serious relationship. Steve was not prepared for this new situation and had to bite the bullet. He drove Neile to this point, and he would have to live with it. Neile's steady boyfriend was surgeon David Ross, and Ross was soon a permanent houseguest. McQueen was livid with jealousy.

That was all about to change, as Ali MacGraw was soon to enter his life.

Years before, when they couldn't bear the thought of not being together, Neile had given Steve a gold Saint Christopher's medal. She had it inscribed "To part is to die a little." Now their parting was to be permanent.

# ALI MacGRAW

*I remember seeing him across the swimming pool and my knees were knocking. He radiated such macho energy. Men wanted to be like him. Uptight society ladies and biker molls died to be with him.*

ALI MacGRAW

IT HAD BEEN NEARLY FOUR YEARS and three pictures since Steve had a hit movie, his last one, *Junior Bonner,* being the biggest failure of his career. "Out of all of my movies, *Junior Bonner* did not make one cent. In fact, it lost money," Steve told a friend. It had been nearly all downhill since *Bullitt.*

It had also been a full year since Neile filed for divorce. By the end of 1971, Steve was a broken man, but his luck was about to change.

For years he had been encouraging his publicist, David Foster, to become a producer. "Man, you're so smart, Foster. You really ought to produce," McQueen told his friend.

Foster had tried to find a project suitable for his client to star in and for him to produce. A few mishaps came along the way.

The first project to fall along the wayside was *Butch Cassidy and the Sundance Kid.* "A great friend of mine, Bob Sherman, and I were the first ones to bid on it. With Steve backing us, we thought it would be our ticket to producing," says Foster. The script, written by William Goldman, was perfectly suited for Steve as the Sundance Kid.

Not only did McQueen agree to star in it, but he also recommended that his friend Paul Newman be his costar. A call was immediately placed to Newman by Sherman. Says Foster, "As I understand it, Newman got upset by this phone call, because he was doing *Harper,* which was also written by William Goldman. The writer told Newman about *Butch Cassidy and the Sundance Kid.* They even had a few meetings about it. Newman felt his early participation in the development of the script ensured that he would get first crack at the finished screenplay. But he got it from McQueen via a third party, not from Goldman himself. This upset Newman, I was told."

When the bidding escalated to a record-breaking (at the time) $400,000 for the script, 20th Century-Fox came away the winner. With McQueen came the stipulation that Foster and Sherman would produce the movie, but Fox president Richard Zanuck couldn't accept that part of the deal.

Zanuck's good friend Paul Monash, producer of Fox's hit television series *Peyton Place*, wanted to produce the movie. He was an important profit earner for the studio, and Zanuck had to appease him, which meant Foster and Sherman were out.

Next came the rumor that Newman wanted McQueen out of the picture and Marlon Brando to replace him. The word was that McQueen went crazy. They were acing him out. McQueen was incredulous: "Screw you guys. How dare you! I'm the guy who got it first. I gave it to Newman, and now you want me out?"

Steve interpreted this as a betrayal. A former business associate for both men observed, "For some reason, Newman found Steve a little intimidating. Steve was a bit wilder than Paul. I think maybe Paul feared that Steve's presence on the screen might be stronger than his, as he later proved in *The Towering Inferno*."

When Foster later produced *McCabe and Mrs. Miller*, starring Warren Beatty, McQueen was offended that Foster hadn't asked for his services first. "Oh, so you think Beatty's a fucking better actor than me?" he asked.

Though McQueen may have been offended, they remained friends and business associates. Foster would continue to look for a project that was suitable for the two.

While Steve was in France filming *Le Mans*, Foster was busy acquiring the rights to Jim Thompson's crime novel *The Getaway*. Though Thompson posthumously achieved cult status in the late eighties and early nineties, at the time he was a struggling author looking for a big break. McQueen, too, was looking for a big break, something that could bring him back to the top at the box office. Foster sent McQueen a copy of the novel and was sent back a telegram urging him to "lock it up."

Steve had always wanted to play a good/bad guy role, much in the same vein as Humphrey Bogart. Says David Foster, "For years, I'd been bugging Steve to play an out-and-out gangster—you know, a ruthless, cold, but ultimately redeeming baddie." McQueen found what he had been looking for in the role of Doc McCoy in *The Getaway*.

Commented McQueen, "It's going to be difficult for me. I usually play the Peter Perfect man." The role of Doc McCoy would come with relative ease for McQueen. "He had such a strong fix on that character," says Foster. McQueen tailored much of his character from Bogart in *High Sierra.* "I first saw Bogart on the screen when I was a kid. He nailed me pronto, and I've admired him ever since. He was the master and always will be," said McQueen.

Foster on McQueen, "He would sit in script meetings and say, 'I want my cuffs to be tattered at the bottom, because this guy doesn't have a tailor.' He was a nut for realism, which was really smart of him."

*The Getaway* is the story of a husband-and-wife bank-robbing team, Doc and Carol McCoy. After serving four years for armed robbery, Doc McCoy realizes that if he doesn't get out of prison soon, he may never come back to reality.

Doc has Carol arrange a deal with a corrupt politician, Jack Benyon, who happens to be on the parole board and can greatly influence Doc's chances for an early release.

A deal is struck between the McCoys and Benyon. Benyon will arrange Doc's release in return for the robbery of a small Texas bank loaded with cash. Doc will mastermind the heist and then split the money with Benyon. What follows is a series of double-crosses, exchanged gunfire, car chases, and a race to the Mexican border for the McCoys' ultimate freedom.

Having secured McQueen as the star of the film, Foster now had to find a director. Agent Jeff Berg came to Foster with the idea that his client, director Peter Bogdanovich, should be considered. Berg arranged a special screening of the as-yet-to-be-released *The Last Picture Show.* McQueen and Foster were blown away by what they saw. "We flipped," said Foster. "It was great. After the screening, we said to Berg, 'Yeah, we'd like to meet with Bogdanovich.'" When the director met with the two, a deal was immediately set up. However, Foster inserted a clause into the contract that stated if McQueen and Foster were ready to make the picture and Bogdanovich was unavailable to direct, then the contract with Bogdanovich would be voided.

Berg also had interested screenwriter Walter Hill, now a hugely successful director of such films as *48 Hours, Red Heat,* and *The Long Riders.* Foster and McQueen met with Hill, and he was set to adapt the novel to a screenplay.

Around the same time, Warner Brothers came to Bogdanovich and asked him to direct *What's Up, Doc?* with Barbra Streisand and Ryan O'Neal. The only catch was that he would have to start immediately. It was a go picture.

Steve McQueen in *The Getaway*, 1972. (COURTESY OF NATIONAL GENERAL PICTURES)

"He came up with this idea that he would shoot *What's Up, Doc?* and put it on the shelf for six months, then shoot *The Getaway;* then he'd go back and edit *What's Up, Doc?* and then go back and edit *The Getaway*. With bank interest running for six months, Warner Brothers was not going to let that happen," says Foster.

Finally, McQueen called Bogdanovich in for a meeting. McQueen's ego was on the line. He put it to the director point-blank, "Oh, so Streisand's more important to you than I am, right? Fuck it then, we'll get another director." Bogdanovich pleaded, "Oh, no, no. Don't do that." McQueen turned to Foster and said, "Let's get someone who is ready to go to work."

McQueen and Foster sat around thinking of directors who might be right for *The Getaway*. Steve was the one who brought up Sam Peckinpah. He had just finished *Junior Bonner* with Peckinpah and had enjoyed the experience, regardless of the many times their egos clashed.

Recalls David Foster, "I went to Peckinpah on the idea with my heart in my throat, prepared to hype him till kingdom come, if necessary. Right away, he said, 'I know the story cold, for Christ's sake. I'll do it.' "

As it turned out, Peckinpah had read *The Getaway* when it was first published in 1958 and had even talked to Jim Thompson about the possibility of filming it when he was a fledgling director.

Peckinpah's last five out of six films had all been westerns, and he was ready for a change of pace. "They've finally allowed me to work with cars and trains instead of horse and buggies," joked Peckinpah. *The Getaway* would provide the perfect commercial vehicle for him.

But along with Peckinpah came his reputation as a wild man. Said director Walter Hill, "He was an awfully big drinker, and he pushed the envelope as far as you could. I liked him quite well. He was very encouraging to me when I became a director. I mourn his passing and I think that the saddest thing about Sam was that he didn't make enough films, and the candle burned out much too soon. But, I think because of the way he lived, that that was inevitable."

Declared Foster, "I know Sam had this reputation for giving producers a hard time, but basically Sam was a pussycat. Let me give you an example that really helped me understand the guy before the picture started shooting.

"Sam and I both happened to have gone to the University of Southern California, and we both were football nuts. So this was the football season of '71, while we were still preparing to shoot *The Getaway*. I called and asked Sam if he would like to go with my wife and me to the USC-Illinois football game. He loved the idea.

"So we went, and it was just like Sam was back in school again. Here's this tough guy, right? Well, before the kickoff, the USC band played their fight song, which is a version of 'Conquest.' And what usually happens is that all the Joe Colleges stand up and give this crazy *V* for victory and sing the song. Now, I'm corny up to a point, but I just can't stand up at age forty-five and start singing the fight song. But as the band started to play, I turned to Sam, and he's all choked up. Then he suddenly started singing along with the kids. It was terrific. I've never seen such spontaneous emotion.

"From then on, I realized that Sam relied almost entirely on his emotional responses. If you took him dead serious every single moment, he'd drive you crazy. But if you kept it in perspective, and allowed him to apply those instincts to the picture, there was no problem. And he got some terrific things on film."*

When Peckinpah came on board, he wanted to see the Walter Hill script. "It was kind of a funny thing," recalls Hill. "I was hired by Foster to work with Bogdanovich, but he left, and Peckinpah came in. I just assumed I would immediately get bounced. He was a guy very famous for wanting his own team and only hiring his inner circle of friends. We

---

* Simmons, Garner, *Peckinpah: A Portrait In Montage* (Austin: The University of Texas Press, 1982), 157.

met, he liked the script and didn't change it that much. We cut down a couple of sections. We made it nonperiod and we added a little more action."

With McQueen as the star and Peckinpah set to direct, the production was moving along. The search was on for a starring actress. Peckinpah had enjoyed working with Stella Stevens a few years before on *The Ballad of Cable Hogue* and wanted her for the part of Carol McCoy. If she wasn't available, then Angie Dickinson, Dyan Cannon, Mariette Hartley, or Farrah Fawcett might do. Then David Foster came up with an idea. "Wouldn't it be great if we could get Ali MacGraw? I can see it now on the marquee, 'McQueen and MacGraw.'"

Back in the early seventies, Ali MacGraw was the hottest actress in Hollywood. Her role in *Love Story*, the highest-grossing picture of 1971, put her name on the A list.

Her rise to fame came instantly and without warning. *Love Story* had brought overnight success to the actress, who had two previous film credits to her name. Her second film, *Goodbye, Columbus,* was also a big hit, and it was enough to get the attention of Paramount's production chief, Robert Evans, who was interested in getting to know her again.

Evans and MacGraw had met ten years before when he noticed her modeling work in a magazine. Evans called MacGraw's agent, Eileen Ford, and made arrangements to meet with the dark-haired model. MacGraw and Evans met for lunch, but the conversation kept getting interrupted when Evans's two phones at the table kept ringing. When lunch was finished, Evans took a taxi back with MacGraw to drop her off. As she got out of the cab, he remarked, "Those are the ugliest shoes I have ever seen." Ali never heard from or saw Evans until she landed the role of Brenda in *Goodbye, Columbus*. It wasn't until a year later, when MacGraw won the role of Jennifer Cavilleri in *Love Story*, that the two consummated their relationship.

They were married in July 1969 before the filming of *Love Story* began. Ali became pregnant six months later, and things began to happen at a whirlwind pace.

*Love Story* opened in December 1970 and broke all previous box office records for Paramount. The movie turned MacGraw into an overnight success.

In March 1971, Steve was asked to present the prestigious Oscar for Best Picture. Ali MacGraw was nominated that night for Best Actress. Though the two did not meet backstage that night, they later met at a party after the ceremony. Says actor Ben Johnson, "I guess I had a little bit to do with that. I kinda got them together for the first time. She came over to me and asked me to introduce them, since I knew him from *Junior Bonner*. She was real gung-ho for Steve, so I arranged for them to meet." The two stars did not go home together that night, but their paths would soon cross again.

Robert Evans, representing Paramount Pictures, approached David Foster about Ali's chances for the role of Carol McCoy. He felt that her first two screen roles were similar college, preppy types and wanted her to expand to adult parts. Would they consider her?

The idea of playing a gangster's moll didn't appeal to Ali at all. She had her heart set on one role, Daisy, in F. Scott Fitzgerald's *Great Gatsby*. Paramount had just bought the rights to the book, but production would take at least a year. Evans wanted MacGraw to make a smooth image transition before he would let her star as Daisy. *The Getaway* was the perfect choice for her, he decided.

Evans set up a meeting with Foster, McQueen, and Peckinpah to meet with his wife to discuss the possibility of her starring in *The Getaway*. Her mind was made up from the get-go; she didn't want to have anything to do with McQueen or Peckinpah. "She was terrified of both guys," offered David Foster. "They were wild, two-fisted, beer-guzzlers. Sam would give himself shots of B-12 complex in the butt, right in front of you. These were the guys her husband was pushing her to work with?"

Foster, Peckinpah, and McQueen arrived at the Evans mansion. When Steve and Ali locked eyes, the sparks began to fly. McQueen told longtime friend Pat Johnson, "She had the nicest ass I've ever seen on a woman." Ali was transfixed by Steve. "I had to leave the room to compose myself," she told Johnson years later. "He walked into my life as Mr. Humble, no ego, one of the guys. Steve was this very original, principled guy who didn't seem to be part of the system, and I loved that. He was clever, demure, exciting, and had all the answers. I bought that act in the first second. We had this electrifying, obsessive attraction."

Both McQueen and MacGraw were on a mission. Steve was there to talk Ali into doing *The Getaway*. She, on the other hand, was there to talk Steve into the part of Jay in *The Great Gatsby*. Ali was still hesitant. She didn't have a definite answer. One thing was for sure: when Steve left the Evans mansion, he knew that he and Ali would be lovers.

Though she may have tried with all of the energy she could muster to talk Bob Evans out of letting her go to Texas for the filming of *The Getaway*, her underlying reason had yet to come out. "The real reason I had hesitated was that I knew I was going to get in some serious trouble with Steve. There would be no avoiding it. He was recently separated, and free, and I was scared of my overwhelming attraction to him," she said.

McQueen teaches Ali MacGraw the finer points on how to fire a gun for her role as Carol McCoy in "The Getaway." Propmaster Bobby Visciglia is loading her weapon. (COURTESY OF NATIONAL GENERAL)

Complications began to arise with Paramount and the film's budget, and soon it was left to Steve's agent, Freddie Fields, to come up with a solution. Fields had thirty days to set up a deal with another studio or Paramount would own the rights to the property. Fields had signed McQueen a year earlier to the brand-new First Artists group and suggested they fulfill one of the three pictures he was obligated to give them. "It was like a stampede, all of the studios wanted us. We studied the best offers, and we decided to go with First Artists," says Foster.

The way First Artists was set up, the star would receive no upfront salary, but 10 percent of the gross for the first dollar taken in on the picture. Depending on how well the picture did, it could be a boom or bust.

The other stipulation was that the film's budget, financed by National General, could not exceed $3 million. Now that Paramount was out of the picture, everyone assumed that Ali MacGraw was also out. Then Bob Evans called Sam Peckinpah, asking that Ali should still be considered regardless of the politics of the situation. Peckinpah was delighted.

Says Walter Hill, "I think it's fair to say that Sam became her greatest champion."

With MacGraw's name came the price tag of $300,000. That pushed the budget for the film over its contractual agreement. A compromise was reached when agent Freddie Fields came up with the idea of giving MacGraw all the profits on *The Getaway* from Germany. She cheerfully agreed. Says Fields, "She made a lot more money from Germany than she had ever anticipated." Now, with everything in place, the cameras were set to roll.

*The Getaway* was a movie that, by appearance, was out of control, but as in any Peckinpah movie, that was quite the norm. Says stuntman Gary Combs, "It was probably the dope-smokingest crew I've ever been with in my life." Combs remembers one night he and his wife joined the cast and crew for an Elton John concert. "My wife and I are members of the LDS [Latter-Day Saints] church, so I don't smoke or drink or go out with girls on the side. The producers hired a bus to take us to the college where the concert was being held. Knowing that my wife was coming with me, the crew didn't want to embarrass me by smoking, but they did want to smoke. I get on the bus and there's a pan of brownies in the driver's seat. I've got a bit of a sweet tooth, so I scooped up about three brownies, and I walked to the back of the bus and sat near my friend Kathy Blondell. I got to the seat and said to Kathy, 'How nice. They've prepared brownies.' Kathy says, 'Don't eat the brownies.' I said, 'Why?' She kept repeating, 'Don't eat the brownies.' 'Why, I like brownies, Kathy.' To show you how naive I was, I thought that they might have put Ex-Lax in the brownies and I threw them on the floor. The people in the bus picked them up off the floor and started to eat them. Then it dawned on me that they put the marijuana in the brownies. I'd have been goofier than a billy goat if I had eaten those things. It was a heavy dope- and alcohol-oriented crew, but they could still function."

Sally Struthers, famous for her portrayal of Gloria Bunker in the series *All in the Family*, had a respectable-size role in *The Getaway*. She remembers, "Peckinpah had a severe drinking problem. He and actor Al Lettieri started drinking tequila at 8:00 A.M. and by 11:00 A.M., there was no talking to either one of them."

Shooting began on February 7, 1972, in Huntsville, Texas. The first few scenes were shot at the local penitentiary showing Doc McCoy incarcerated for a previous bank robbery. The opening scene called for McQueen, in actual prison garb, to perform the obligatory functions of a prisoner. The others in the scene were real-life convicts at the prison.

Recalled McQueen, "On our first afternoon there, when the scene was wrapped and Sam yelled 'Cut!' I took off toward my dressing room for some coffee. Well, here I was, in prison duds, splitting away from the other cons. Suddenly, I'm running like hell, because this pack of hounds are snappin' at my ass. They'd been trained to go after any con who broke ranks, and nobody had bothered to tell them this was a movie. I barely made it out of that yard in one piece. I almost got my ass chewed off."

One particular scene had McQueen taking a shower with the other prisoners. Steve knew at the time that they were real prisoners, but what he didn't know was that they were all homosexuals. "When he learned that it was the faggot section of the cellblock, he became unglued," laughs Bobby Visciglia. "It bruised his ego to think that he couldn't handle himself with the real hardcore convicts, but they would have loved to get their hands on Steve McQueen and possibly use him as a hostage. Sam wasn't going to let that happen."

For Ali's part, when she arrived at the prison, she asked the warden to show her the electric chair. "She was an actress doing her homework," says David Foster. "She wanted to know what it felt like to be the wife of a convict."

Ali MacGraw arrived the day after Steve for a scene at the prison. She recalls in her book, *Moving Pictures,* "When I arrived in Texas for that first day of location work, I was met by Steve and Sam Peckinpah and driven back to the rented condominiums where the crew would stay. What a drive! Steve was showing off, and the first thing this ex-formula-one-race-car-driver did was to spin the rented car in a dizzying loop across the four lanes of the freeway. It was a prophetic start to our relationship."*

Says an observer, "The chronology was she arrived on the set on Saturday at 5:00 A.M. and by 6:00 P.M. was bedded down by McQueen."

Prop master Bobby Visciglia disputes the fact the two fell in love right away: "Ali couldn't stand him for the first six weeks." After McQueen and MacGraw had their first scene together, Ali turned to Visciglia and remark, "Keep that son-of-a-bitch away from me!"

According to crew members, McQueen was bossy and overbearing, almost taking on the role of the director.

Visciglia claims it was after McQueen and MacGraw's first love scene that the two fell in love, proving that life does imitate art.

MacGraw said in her defense, "I thought, 'Here's fresh air. He doesn't do any of that charm thing. He's just there!' That was what I wanted in myself, and I went after it in him.

"I was so attracted to my invention of Steve McQueen that I thought

---

* MacGraw, Ali, *Moving Pictures* (New York: Bantam Books, 1991), 95.

Steve McQueen and Ali MacGraw in *The Getaway*.

I could go off with him and be real again. I didn't think about my family life back in Beverly Hills. Selfishly, I just went on my way, rationalizing that I was saving my own life. It was as though I was operating outside of my own sanity and consciousness. I didn't feel complete unless I had a partner. Being in love was like a drug high."

Katy Haber felt the odd pairing was a classic case of opposites attract. "Steve was the ultimate male. He was a stunning-looking guy. He was Superman, and women fell prey to the movie star allure. Ali, on the other hand, has a mind that needs to be constantly working. Steve preferred the company of simple folk rather than intellectuals, but Ali excited him."

David Foster was the last to know about their relationship, while the entire crew was well aware of what was going on with the two stars. Said one crew member at the time to a reporter, "I'm not . . . ah, you know . . . absolutely certain what's going down between him and Ali Mac-Graw, but I bet I could guess. Pick up on the vibe for yourself, my man —it's heavy."

It took Foster three weeks to pick up on the vibe. "I'm not a naive guy," says Foster. "They could have gone to bed that first night for all I know. I wasn't aware of it until three weeks after we began shooting. I would see them snuggling. They got to be very hot and heavy."

Foster had a picture to produce, and this was his worst nightmare being realized. "I was thinking, 'How is all this going to impact my picture? Is Bob Evans going to come down here with a shotgun? Is it going to become a scandal and the picture won't be taken seriously? Are the press going to descend here like they did with Richard Burton and Elizabeth Taylor on *Cleopatra*? If you have half a brain, this goes through your mind as a producer."

The gossip columnists were having a field day as they suspected that an on-location romance was very likely.

Ali told columnist Liz Smith, who visited the set, "There are beautiful things I can tell you about Steve McQueen, but you can't print them. I just adore him. We're having a terrific time. He's wonderful."

She went on to say, "Mostly he's a big surprise to me. I guess Steve is one of the two or three movie actors in the world I think are always fabulous to watch. He's the greatest at what he does. People told me he was difficult, and movie-starrish, which is something I can't stand. I wasn't prepared for his intelligence. It's the first time I have ever worked with a legend."

In a moment of tranquility, someone asked Ali why she was doing this to Evans. "If I wanted to make some scrambled eggs for myself," said Ali, "Bob would say, 'No, no, no. The cook does that.' If I wanted to walk naked in my own house and go into the kitchen and get something out of the refrigerator, I couldn't. There was always somebody there. It wasn't real. It drove me crazy."

Foster offers, "Steve was the total opposite. He went to bed bare-assed and behaved like the average Joe. That appealed to her."

Before filming began, Evans was warned by Peckinpah not to drop in on the set as he might disrupt the filming. Evans, ever the true gentleman, obliged the director. That left it wide open for the love affair to blossom fully. Steve and Ali wouldn't hide their feelings for each other, even when Evans's nanny and son Joshua came to visit.

Foster exploded at McQueen. He gave it to his star with both guns: "You're crazy. You better screw your head back on right." McQueen quickly soothed the irate producer. "Everything's cool. Everything's cool."

Costar Sally Struthers was supportive. "I thought it was sweet. I love to watch people fall in love." Even though MacGraw was still married to Evans, Struthers staunchly defended her fellow actors. "A lot of people are married, and it doesn't always mean they're happy. It doesn't mean

Sensual interplay between McQueen and Ali MacGraw. McQueen holds the world by a string. This pose is representative of the amazingly taut nature of *The Getaway*. (COURTESY OF NATIONAL GENERAL PICTURES)

it's going to last, and it doesn't mean that they married the right person. It happens, and unfortunately it gets glorified in show business. But it happens every day in regular neighborhoods all over. It's just that those people don't wind up in the newspapers."

With all of the attention, Steve brought on even more with his behavior. The company was headquartered in San Marcos, just across from Aquarena Springs. The whole crew was staying at the LBJ condominiums just across from the springs. McQueen had been toying with the idea of driving his rental car into one of the springs. When Ali happened to be in the car with him, showing off, he decided to take the plunge. Academy Award–winning actor and costar Ben Johnson happened to witness the event. "Steve was a bit of a wild character," says Johnson with a sly smile and a shake of his head. "He rented a station wagon, and he and Ali were in the parking lot driving around. All of a sudden, he drives right off the parking lot and into this big hole of water, this big spring. It submerged all but the back end. Here we are, starting the movie, and he's pulling this stunt. I'm watching all of this, and just a little of the back end of the car is sticking out of the water. I ran down there to help them, and they're both sticking their faces out the back window to breathe. I got down there and helped them out. I'll never know why he did that. Maybe he was drinking or something."

When stuntman Gary Combs arrived on the set and needed a car, he was awarded the freshly dunked station wagon to get around town.

Combs was brought into the picture because Peckinpah had taken a liking to him on the set of *The Wild Bunch*. Peckinpah was set to fire Combs one day when he wasn't ready for wardrobe. "I was all ready, but I didn't have my beard on," recalls Combs. "I was sitting around for three whole days in the blazing sun doing nothing. The glue they used to stick the beard to my face was giving me a rash. I decided that when we were ready to shoot, I would go to wardrobe and then apply it. Peckinpah was hollering and waving his arms and throwing a fit when I wasn't ready. I threatened to punch the son-of-a-bitch and then he did a turnaround on me. I found that if you stood up to him, he respected you. He kept me on for the rest of the movie and then afterward he came up to me and put his arm around me and said, 'I'm going to have you in all of my movies.' True to his word, he asked me to do every single movie after that."

It had been seven years since Combs had worked with McQueen on *Nevada Smith*. Now he was asked by Steve and Peckinpah to come in for a meeting regarding the driving scenes. "For years, I had always had this problem with my ears sticking out. I had to tape them down when I did my stunts. It looked like two car doors open. In time, I had them fixed. I go into this meeting and I sit down to discuss this scene. McQueen is across the room, and he looks at me and pulls at his earlobes and flicks his ears," laughs Combs.

For the driving sequence, McQueen wanted a chase scene bigger and better than *Bullitt*. He described a scenario in which a car would be coming down the road, do three 360s, go through a residential area, then get back on the street and drive away. Combs replied, "It sounds like you need a lot of speed to do that. You can't do that here. It's flatter than a tortilla." The scene was never brought up again.

Combs took a liking to the quirky McQueen. Before taking on the job as stunt double, he rang up Loren Janes and asked him for some advice. Combs was told by Janes, "He always makes me wear a trenchcoat over my wardrobe. He doesn't want the public to think he has a stunt double." Combs laughed and quickly forgot the anecdote. When he arrived on the set in San Marcos, Combs quickly got a call to get to the set. He went to wardrobe and was issued an outfit that matched Steve's. He noticed later that McQueen would quietly dismiss himself from the set and go into his trailer to change. Says Combs, "All of a sudden what Loren told me is flashing in my brain. I then decide to experiment on my own. When I put my wardrobe on, Steve would go take his off. When I went to go take mine off, he'd go put his on. I did this a few times to make sure I wasn't going nuts. You see, there was always a lot of people on the streets of San Marcos watching us film." Combs decided to have a laugh. He pulled David Foster over and explained the situation. "Watch this," Combs announced. "Sure enough, Steve went inside his trailer and changed his clothes." Foster doubled over with laughter. Combs offered, "Steve McQueen never had a double as far as he was concerned."

Ali MacGraw noticed that Steve had a penchant for playing up to the public in general. "Steve performs inadvertently at times," she claimed. "He especially performs in front of women. . . . For instance, if there is a street full of drum majorettes, he's on for them. All charm and sex and kind of dirt kicking. But he's different for them than he will be for you today or again tomorrow, or for me talking at dinner, or with his kids, or for the guys of the crew. He responds to everyone differently, and if they don't want to see what he wants them to see, they don't see anything. Young, dumb girls see the best sex symbol in the world. Motorcycle freaks see the best motorcyclist, and so on."

Steve's changing in and out of his clothes was a constant source of irritation for the wardrobe department. After every take, McQueen felt the need to take off his shirt and drop it to the ground. Jimmy George was in charge of the wardrobe on *The Getaway*, but Steve ran George into the ground. By the end of the first two weeks, George was ready for a straitjacket. Bobby Visciglia recalls, "Steve ran circles around Jimmy George. Steve would say, 'Jimmy, there's one cuff that's not even,' and poor Jimmy would be biting his nails." That's where Kent James came in. Kent and Carole James are a successful husband-and-wife team of motion picture costumers. Today they are proud grandparents, but they are actually ageless hippies at heart. Laughter permeates the air whenever they walk into a room.

Kent James recalls the first time he had to tangle with the mighty McQueen. "Steve pulled his stunt where he took off his shirt and dropped it on the ground. I saw this and went straight to David Foster. I told him to get me an airplane ticket home right away. 'I'm not a valet.'" Steve had heard of James's request and went to see him about the problem. James informed him of his shirt-dropping habit. "I'm sorry, Kent, I wasn't even aware of it." James was taken aback by McQueen's sincerity, but nevertheless stood his ground. The two shook hands and remained friends for life. "Kent could make Steve laugh," points out Katy Haber. "Steve would be bitching about something and Kent would say out loud in front of the crew, 'Oh, what is it now, Steve? Do you have another run in your pantyhose?' And Steve would crack up. Kent knew exactly how to treat Steve."

In the movie, Doc McCoy is released from prison when he agrees to rob a bank for a parole board member, Jack Benyon, played by actor Ben Johnson. Benyon provides the backup men for Doc on the job. Doc protests. Benyon states, "You're in charge of the job, but I run the show." Benyon has arranged it so that the backup men will double-cross Doc. One of the men, Rudy Butler, played by Al Lettieri, was originally to star Richard Bright, who eventually was cast in a smaller part in the movie.

Walter Hill brought Bright's name to the attention of director Sam Peckinpah. Hill was astonished by Bright's performance in *Panic in Needle Park*. A meeting was arranged between Peckinpah and Bright. Peckinpah put up Bright for two weeks until McQueen and Foster could meet with him. Peckinpah and Bright sparked each other immediately. "I called him my adopted father," Bright says fondly. Bright became part of the inner circle of actors that Peckinpah liked to use in his films.

When Bright met McQueen on the set of *Never Love a Stranger*, he didn't understand how Steve had gotten the role in the first place. "It was just his whole demeanor. He was wimpy. He didn't seem to be a knock-around kind of guy. I guess that ruggedness came later with the bikes. I didn't see any spark at all."

Now it was fourteen years later, and the transformation in McQueen was apparent to Bright. "I was very taken by the change in him, how drastically he had gone through some metamorphosis. He developed a very strong technique in his craft and got in touch with himself. He found a formula that worked for him and became hugely successful with it."

The formula also was what knocked Bright out of the Rudy Butler role. Bright was a few inches shorter and many pounds lighter than McQueen when the two met again. McQueen knew Bright could act, but he just didn't have the physique that Steve had in mind for Rudy Butler.

Peckinpah had to be the bearer of the bad news. When the two met for lunch, Bright noticed Sam's long face. "What's up, pard?" asked Bright. "It's not going to work," said Peckinpah. Again, Bright asked, "What's not going to work?" Sam replied, "Sorry, Hoss. You're not big enough. Steve thinks you're a fabulous actor and wants to work with you, but doesn't feel that the character that he runs from should be a little guy. I want you, but he can't see himself, for his image, for his fans, being chased by a smaller man. He has it in his mind that running from the little guy is cowardice." Bright allowed himself one parting shot: "But, Sam, it's the little guys you have to watch out for. It's the little guys who will climb up your leg to cut your fuckin' throat."

With First Artists, Steve had complete control of the movie, including the final word on casting. Richard Bright was not the man he wanted for Rudy Butler, and no one was going to change his mind.

The original choice for Rudy Butler had been Jack Palance, but because of the First Artists' budget, it only allowed $50,000 for the part. Peckinpah felt he was so right for the part that he talked Foster and McQueen into upping the salary to $65,000 plus 3 percent of the film's gross. Palance turned it down flat.

While the negotiations between Palance and First Artists were going on, Peckinpah ran into producer Al Ruddy, who was in the middle of post-production on *The Godfather*. He happened to mention that he had some footage of an actor, Al Lettieri, who almost stole the movie in a bit part when he tried to kill the Godfather. When Peckinpah saw Lettieri on film, he immediately wanted him for Rudy Butler.

Lettieri, who had been a writer before turning actor, had worked with Richard Bright on *The Godfather*. When Bright learned that Lettieri had landed the Rudy Butler role, he was pleased: "I thought Al was wonderful as Rudy. I'm glad it was Al and not someone that I didn't know who might not have done justice to the character."

If Lettieri seemed "too real" for audiences, it was because his lifestyle poured over onto the screen. Lettieri's brother was a well-known mafioso in New York, and Lettieri himself was known to have strong-armed a few people in his time. His heavy drinking also seemed to bring out the dark side of him. Says Sally Struthers, "Al had a lot of problems. He had a terrible drinking problem and a personality problem that came with the drinking. He was so nice and sweet when he was sober, and he became so evil when he was drunk. He was really scary."

McQueen found out how scary Lettieri could be when he inadvertently crossed the hot-tempered Italian. Lettieri and Struthers had been dating during the filming. Unbeknownst to McQueen and MacGraw, the two invited Struthers for dinner one night, as Steve had a single friend coming to town and wanted to play matchmaker. When Lettieri found out, he had words with McQueen. Later, when Struthers dumped him altogether, Lettieri showed up on the set with a rather large gun, looking for Steve. For the rest of the filming, Steve hired two big bodyguards to watch Lettieri in case they came to blows. "Steve could take care of himself," says Bobby Visciglia, "but he looked over his shoulder more than once when Al was on the set."

Peckinpah liked to pit the two against each other. If McQueen was watching rushes and Lettieri was in the scene, Peckinpah would play devil's advocate. "Hey, Steve, wasn't Al just terrific in that scene?" he would say.

If the set of the movie seemed out of control, it was because Sam Peckinpah set the pace with his consumption of hard liquor, though he always functioned in a capable manner. Says Richard Bright, "Sam could drink all day, but he wasn't drunk. I watched Sam. He ran a tight crew and a loose company. With the actors, he was loose. With his crew, he cracked a whip. He was drinking, but he wasn't out of control."

In fact, Peckinpah was very much in control of everyone, including Steve. Stuntman Gary Combs remembers one such incident. "We were getting ready to do the car chase with the bombs and Steve kept saying to me, 'Maybe I'll do this stunt.' I said to him, 'I don't care, just as long as I'm getting paid.' This went on for a couple of weeks until the time came for the stunt. Steve and I both have on the same clothes, and Sam knows what Steve's up to. Sam came right up to Steve and said, 'You just sit down and Gary will drive the car.' This is what it all came down to: when Sam said something, you did it and that was it." Adds Katy Haber, "*The Getaway* was a fun film. Sam surrounded himself with his friends, and everyone on the set seemed to be seeing each other socially. It was one of the most pleasant experiences I've ever had."

Carrie Lofton, who had done *Bullitt*, was brought in to choreograph the main car chase. Combs was to drive through a series of bombs that were timed as distractions. The bombs were set to go off the same time as the heist to scatter the local police in different directions. The explosions were set up with live mortar in the ground. Peckinpah used five helicopters and coordinated the camera work over walkie-talkies. On the very first take, Combs's car caught on fire. Although the blaze was minor, Steve ran toward the car to help Combs. Combs looked at him in mild curiosity and asked, "What are you doing?" McQueen yelled back, "The car's gonna blow. The car's gonna blow." Combs revealed, "The car was assembled so that the gas tank was in the back and the fire was in the front, so I knew it wasn't going to blow. I had this oily drum underneath the engine and it was burning. No big deal. I then got back in the car and backed it up to the fire hose. McQueen was just doing his routine, his heroic thing. Anytime there were a lot of people around, you could pretty well imagine he was going to do something to please the crowd."

There was a shortage of stunt drivers on the set when actor James Garner showed up on location. He was delivering an RV to a friend on the set when Lofton recruited Garner for his driving skills. In the film, when Doc makes his escape from the bank heist, it is Garner who is driving an orange Volkswagen Beetle that is the last car to pass Doc on the way out of town. (Garner was paid $25 for his services.)

The McQueen-Peckinpah relationship was rocky at times, though the two admired each other tremendously. Peckinpah would always tell people, "If you really want to learn about acting for the screen, watch McQueen's eyes."

Peckinpah recalled an incident on the first day of rehearsal in San Marcos when the two got into an argument, "Steve and I had been discussing some point on which we disagreed, so he picked up this bottle of champagne and threw it at me. I saw it coming and ducked. And Steve just laughed.

"Then, when we were doing the shoot-out between him and Rudy at that old farm, Steve walked right to where I was sitting carrying a .45 loaded with blanks and shot it off right next to my boot. He really pissed me off.

"He laughed because he had me. He's always in terrific shape, and he outweighs me in muscle by a long shot. Well, that pissed me off even more. So there was this hole that Al [Lettieri] fell into after Steve shot him. I was really mad, so I shoved Steve. Then after I shoved him again, he stepped backwards into that hole, still laughing.

"I figured that was all the shoving I was going to do for a while because he was going to come out of that hole and shove both my arms down my throat so I'd have to scratch my asshole from the inside. But instead, he came up laughing again only harder because now he really had me. He had nothing to prove. He could have taken me apart and put me back together again. He knew it, and I knew it. I had taken my best shot, and it hadn't even fazed him. So we went ahead and made the picture together. I like him. He wants to make a good picture, and he always has a lot to offer. Not many people like him, but I do."*

Notes Gary Combs, "They were alike in many ways. About a brick and a half shy of a load, in some respects. They were both very flamboyant in their own way."

The biggest disagreement the two men had was over the love scene between Doc and Carol. The two are alone together in the bedroom for the first time after Doc's release. For the scene, Steve felt that the character was a hungry animal, not having had sex all the years he had been locked up. He wanted to take Ali's character right to bed. Surprisingly, Peckinpah disagreed. He wanted Doc to be intimidated by the act of

---

* Simmons, Garner, *Peckinpah: A Portrait In Montage* (Austin: The University of Texas Press, 1982).

making love. The scene played perfectly when Doc explains, "It [prison] does something to you . . . It does something to you."

For the following scene, the morning after, Doc is glowing and is cooking breakfast for Carol. Steve had written several pages of dialogue for it. Said director of photography Lucien Ballard, "Sam got him into that cooking thing where he's got eggs and catsup and all of this stuff in a frying pan on the stove. And Steve was really in his element. He loved it. He's very good with props. Then when Ali came down, they embraced. I think they maybe had a couple of dozen words between them total, and that was it."

When McQueen and Peckinpah viewed the dailies that night, Sam said to Steve, "And that was what you wrote seven pages of dialogue to explain?" Laughing, McQueen said, "Well, you know better than to listen to me, Sam."

When it came to props, McQueen was regarded as a genius. Says screenwriter Walter Hill, "He was wonderful at finding a physical piece of business that would extend his character."

Regarding guns, Hill states, "I don't think anybody ever handled guns as well in movies. You can see Steve's military training in his films. He was so brisk and confident in the way he handled the guns. It was a very fresh approach in its time."

It was Steve's idea in the movie to hold two police officers at bay when he catches them off guard. Steve suggested to Sam that Doc shoot up their squad cars with a pump-action shotgun loaded with twenty-aught buckshot. When the officers threw their pistols down and lay in the street, McQueen blasted the cars to where they couldn't chase Doc and Carol. Said Peckinpah, "That shot was entirely Steve's idea, and I thought it was sensational. Steve was extraordinary with props. He made them his—like he had known them all his life. On the screen he really made you believe in his character."

Believability and realism were Steve's driving forces. "God is in the details," was his motto. He knew that the more realistic a scene or character was, the better. "Steve was totally careful about realism," says David Foster. "I couldn't believe the weeks he put in wardrobe and the weapons. He had a very strong fix on what he wanted Doc to look like. Back in the early seventies, prisoners' heads were shaved. He wanted to have a bowl cut so that the rest of the film, he wouldn't have to get his hair cut. On screen, his hair kept growing and growing. It started one way and filled in later on. It was a small touch, but it was his idea. Take a look at the cars on *The Getaway*. They were beat up, the kind a criminal would drive. When reading the script, he would flip right through it

McQueen as "Doc" McCoy in *The Getaway* in which he portrays a gun-wielding, bank-robbing mastermind. (COURTESY OF NATIONAL GENERAL PICTURES)

and say, 'Too many words, too many words. I'll give you a close-up that'll say a thousand words.' That was him. He would give you one big smile and save you three pages of dialogue. He didn't think a convict would be very erudite or have long speeches, and he was correct. The whole film was like that."

McQueen struck costar Sally Struthers as quite original in their only scene together. Remembers Struthers, "Steve did a scene with me where he hit me right smack in the face and knocked me cold in the hallway at the hotel. I didn't want a stunt girl—you can always tell when there's a stand-in. Steve went straight for my face. He didn't do a side-swipe like in the westerns, where the other actor snaps his head to the side and pretends to be hit. Steve did a shot that hasn't been seen in the movies in a long time."

Actor Richard Bright recalls their scene at the Southern Pacific train station in San Antonio, Texas. When Bright first arrived at the set, he noticed a pin with the initials SP on Steve's lapel. Bright asked, "Hey, Steve, what's the SP stand for?" Came back the answer, "Sam Peckinpah." Peckinpah had taken the liberty of handing out the Southern Pacific pins himself. "Here, pardner," Peckinpah would say, "have a Sam Peckinpah pin."

For the scene, Bright plays a con man who helps Ali lift a suitcase filled with the stolen bank money into a locker. He then switches the locker key with her and steals the money when she walks away. When Steve joins her and together they discover the money is missing, Doc deduces that it was the con man who had helped her with the bag. "Find him!" he orders.

Bright hops on the next train, not knowing Doc is already on it. When Doc finds him, Bright gets several vicious blows to the head. "Steve didn't hold anything back," Bright says, "but he had perfect control. A lot of the new actors try to be more realistic, but they don't have control. Steve was a guy who mastered his power and knew how to use it. He would go all out, always putting safety first. I think mentally he would let go to find out everything he could possibly do, and in that sense, he was totally free. Physically, he was a very principled guy. He could throw a slap with an eighteenth of an inch space between his hand and your face. He was extremely careful that it looked good and forceful. I had no sense of him harming me physically. It was wonderful working with Steve."

While Steve was getting kudos from his costars, Ali MacGraw struggled. The part was a stretch for her, and an action-adventure film was new territory for the relatively inexperienced actress. Actor Richard Bright offers, "You have to remember that Ali came from the modeling world, where you have to turn on that face once the camera is on. She is such a wonderfully expressive person, a rainbow of happiness. I'd notice, though, when Sam said, 'An hour till you shoot, Ali,' she would go from fifth to fourth gear. When it was a half hour before she shot, she would go into third gear. She would get a little bit more serious, more tense. By the time it came to shoot the scene, it was like there was a lock on her. That wonderful, fluid human being was choked off and this kind of mask came on. It was always working against her. You could feel her driving inside to be a human being and let herself out. It got in her way and it shows in her other films."

Another aspect was the fact that Ali tried so hard to please not only Steve but Sam Peckinpah, as well. Says David Foster, "I think, for the first time, Sam worked with a lady. Ali MacGraw is really a cultured lady —well educated, well traveled. But she'd been in only two other films. And suddenly she had to deal with this two-fisted, knife-throwing, hard-drinking director. I'm sure she entered the arrangement with a great deal of trepidation.

"But Sam and Ali got along great. Sam was wonderful with her. He loved to holler and scream. It was his way of letting go of the things that had been building up inside him. But Sam also had this tremendously gentle side, and that's the side he showed to Ali."

Steve even commented, "There are some things that Ali has done that are embarrassing on the screen and there are some things she has done on the screen that are brilliant. Her ability is predicated by her ability to relax." In *The Getaway,* she couldn't find the middle ground.

Of her own performance, Ali was very harsh on herself. She later commented, "After we had completed *The Getaway* and I looked at what I had done in it, I hated my own performance. I liked the picture, but I despised my own work. I really couldn't look at it."

One particular scene that Bobby Visciglia will never forget is when Doc and Carol McCoy are in bed together in El Paso and cover themselves with the stolen loot. Visciglia was told by Peckinpah to come up with $35,000 in real money. Visciglia was burned by Steve before in the last scene of *Junior Bonner* and was determined not to let McQueen steal one dollar. The crafty prop master drilled several peepholes in the hotel room and assigned a person to each peephole. "That asshole was making a million dollars a picture and it was going to be taken out of my paycheck if Steve took any money," he says now. When the scene was over, Visciglia played the role of a temporary cop, shaking down a suspect. "I found $250 dollars on him. He hid the money in his mouth, his armpits, behind his legs. I was shaking him down while Ali was laughing her head off over this cheap movie star who was trying to steal money."

For the last scene of the picture, the McCoys manage to fight off Rudy Butler and Benyon's henchmen. They escape on foot until they come across an old-timer, played by Slim Pickens, standing by his truck. Doc orders Pickens to drive them to the Mexican border.

Peckinpah told Pickens to ad-lib the scene. "Throw some dialogue at McQueen and find out if he can act. Turn these kids on. See what they can do," said Peckinpah.

Pickens obliged the director when in the film, as they cross the border, he asks, "Are you kids married?" McQueen's face registered shock, while Ali managed a smile and answered, "Yes."

Recalling the scene, Peckinpah commented, "I said to Slim, 'I want you to talk about marriage and love and morality.' And I gave him about three lines that weren't in the script and let him play it the way he felt. And when Slim asked them if they were married, it really threw them badly. But they stayed with it, and it worked."

It was the last week of filming. Ali's husband, Robert Evans, was coming to El Paso. He had quietly stayed away from the set as Peckinpah had asked him to do. Now he was coming to get his wife.

Producer David Foster suddenly found himself in the middle of the love triangle. He vividly recalls, "I was sitting in Steve's hotel suite in El Paso, and he and Ali are both saying, 'Our lives are such a mess now.' She's married to Evans but loves McQueen, and she's not feeling very good about anything. Now, I adore Ali, but the chink in her armor is the men in her life. So Ali, Steve, and I are sitting in his suite and suddenly Steve says aloud, "Okay, here's the game plan.' He takes over, right? He points at me and says, 'Foster, Ali and I are going to drive back to L.A. It's going to take about three days to get there and we can unwind and take it easy.' He then asks me, 'You're going to fly back tonight, right? I say, 'Right.' He says, 'When you get back, I want you to have a meeting with Bob Evans and tell him that Ali is going to marry me.' I'm sitting there listening to this and I say, 'Are you crazy?' How can a person even think like that? Can you imagine?"

Foster told McQueen outright, "I've got news for you. I'm not going to do your dirty work for you. No way!" Suddenly, all three began laughing aloud. "Steve realized how stupid his idea was and then we all cracked up. When you think about it, it was a totally outrageous situation," says Foster.

MacGraw had been putting off the inevitable for three months. Now it was time to tell Evans that she and Steve were in love. She admitted her affair to Evans, and he quickly called in Sam Peckinpah for a meeting. Evans told Peckinpah he was not going to be made out the fool in this situation. Peckinpah was to assign a person to escort Ali to Los Angeles, where a limousine would promptly pick her up and drive her to Murrieta Springs for two weeks so she could collect her thoughts. Peckinpah assigned Bobby Visciglia the task of escorting MacGraw back to Los Angeles. Peckinpah's only demand: "Steve McQueen is not to be on that plane. You got it?"

Visciglia and MacGraw were settled in the plane, sipping wine in first class. Twenty minutes into the flight, Visciglia felt a tap on his shoulder. A man with a hat and sunglasses who sounded vaguely familiar to Visciglia told him that his services were no longer needed. "It was McQueen in disguise," laughed Visciglia. "He found out what flight Ali was on and bought a coach ticket in disguise so that he could fly with Ali. The biggest pisser was that he sent me back to coach for the rest of the flight so that he could sit with Ali." When the flight landed, McQueen put on the hat and sunglasses and disappeared into the crowd while a limo was awaiting for Ali.

While Ali was resting, Steve was in earnest. He never had to fight over a woman before. Ali was caught in the middle of a tug-of-war between two powerful men.

McQueen invited Katy Haber for a weekend in Palm Springs while Ali was staying at Evans's Palm Springs home. Haber and MacGraw had become friendly, and Steve needed someone to play messenger. Haber pretended to have been in the neighborhood and dropped by to see Ali. When Evans was out of earshot, she whispered, "Steve wants you to call him." Haber recalls, "Both Steve and Ali were in Palm Springs and yet Steve couldn't get a hold of her. They were so close, yet so far. Steve was such a solitary figure. He had very few friends he could talk to. He never knew what it was like to be so passionate, he was so overcome with Ali. He said that he was never in so much pain." It is said that when two deer are not mating, the male deer's neck swells. McQueen told Haber, "My neck is swollen like a deer!"

At the end of her two-week stay at Murrieta Springs, still feeling miserable, Ali moved back into the Evans mansion to give their marriage one last try. While there, she couldn't think of anything but Steve. She had become obsessed with him. She left Robert Evans shortly thereafter.

Ever since his divorce from Neile, Steve had rented a small guest house in Coldwater Canyon. After Ali left Bob Evans, she rented a house within walking distance of Steve's place. In her book, Ali remembered, "Our houses were separated only by a big field. Many were the nights that we would have some terrible row over nothing, and one of us would go out of the house to go home. A half hour later, we would find each other, inching across the field, each of us checking up on the other. It wouldn't be long before we would be laughing at the melodrama of it all."*

They were a glamourous couple filled with passion. There were fights, but there were also reconciliations. Ali commented on their relationship at the time: "He's impossible . . . absolutely flat-out, 100 percent impossible . . . and terrific! We are both born Aries, so should I say we clash a lot at times? Consistently—about a couple of things; but we also understand each other. After the fact, of course. Being an Aries, I'm a fairly opinionated lady, which is not generally the kind Steve likes or is too thrilled to be around. He has very strong male attitudes. And I don't buy them all. If Steve and I ever lock horns, it's because I've said no when he wants me to automatically say yes. I find it funny. He doesn't like the women in his family to have balls."

While the McQueen-MacGraw relationship was under way again in Los Angeles, Steve found himself testing the usefulness of the First Artists contract in regard to *The Getaway*. His contract stated that he had

---

* MacGraw, Ali. *Moving Pictures*. Bantam Books, 1991.

final cut on any film made under the First Artists banner. Control was Steve's ultimate weapon. That meant that Peckinpah could shoot anything he wanted, but it all came back for McQueen's approval. There would be a Steve McQueen version and a Sam Peckinpah version. Under First Artists, McQueen's version made it to the theaters. Peckinpah was incensed.

Actor Richard Bright remembers, "In our scene together at the train station, there were some things that Steve wanted to control and he was getting frustrated when he realized he couldn't control it. He had to accept the fact that he could not control everything. He had to let that go but ultimately got the final cut to the film. He couldn't control it in one way, so he controlled it in another. Steve chose takes that made him look good. Then there were scenes where the other person is talking, but you have Steve's face on the screen reacting to it."

Peckinpah was moved to say, "McQueen's playing it safe, and that's going to be his downfall. He chose all these Playboy shots of himself. He's playing it safe with these pretty-boy shots."

McQueen went so far as to replace Jerry Fielding's finished score with one by Quincy Jones. Fielding, who has since died, commented at the time, "Sam was delighted with the scoring on *The Getaway*. Everybody was [delighted] until Sam and Steve started having a war of some sort. And McQueen simply came in after I had finished the picture and rescored it."

In order to save Fielding any sort of embarrassment, Peckinpah took out a full-page ad in the *Daily Variety*, November 17, 1972, stating:

Dear Jerry,
I know you will be pleased that the second preview of "Getaway" was as great as the first. In fact, it was even more enthusiastically received. Which is surprising, since it was attended mostly by industry people. I want to thank you for the beautiful job you did with the music. I have heard many marvelous comments, particularly on the second showing. Possibly because no one there had impaired hearing, and we had no problem with malfunctioning equipment.
   Once again, congratulations. I am looking forward to the next one.

Best regards,
Sam Peckinpah

McQueen got the last laugh, though, when *The Getaway* won the Golden Microphone Award for best sound effects.

244

The Fieldings had taken their own subtle jab at Steve when Ali gave two kittens to their two young daughters, Claudia and Elizabeth, during *The Getaway*. A year later, when Claudia saw Steve and Ali at Sam Peckinpah's fiftieth birthday party, Ali asked Claudia what she had named the kittens. "Ali, after you, and Gringo." Steve inquired as to why she didn't name the other cat after him. Replied the child, "My mother wouldn't allow me to name the cat after you, so I named it Gringo." Fielding's wife, Camille, was still reeling from the fact that Steve had replaced her husband's sound track.

When Peckinpah saw McQueen's final cut at his home in Mexico, he stood up in his living room, moved forward, and pissed on the screen, loudly announcing, "This is not my film!"

"Steve had a deep mistrust of Sam's commercial and storytelling instincts," says Walter Hill. "Steve wanted his movies to be liked by millions of people. He didn't want them to go over the top and he was very wary of that tendency in Sam. That was a source of friction."

The preview would be the true litmus test. There were actually two. McQueen, MacGraw, Foster, and Hill were all present for the first premiere on Chestnut Street in San Francisco. The response that night from the audience was tepid at best, and Steve became nervous.

The second premiere was held in San Jose and was attended by the whole cast. Remembers Walter Hill, "The San Jose premiere went through the roof, so everyone forgot about the San Francisco premiere and concentrated on San Jose."

Al Lettieri hit the roof for a special screening at the Warner Brothers lot when he declared that several of his scenes with Sally Struthers had been left on the cutting room floor. Lettieri, hoping that this role would lead to bigger parts, was livid. Says David Foster, "Both Al Lettieri and Sally Struthers were incredible on *The Getaway*. Al used to be a writer and was a very funny guy. He had a very quick mind. And Sally is also pretty inventive. Well, they'd come up with some really great bits. Then when Steve recut the picture, some of those things were cut out, and Al really got upset at Sam, because he thought Sam had done it. At the preview of Steve's cut, I thought he was going to kill Sam, and I mean literally. I've never seen anyone so angry, except maybe Sam. But it was Steve's picture, and his instincts were right."

Actress Sally Struthers believes that Lettieri's drinking may have blinded his memory. "I do not remember thinking when I saw the film that I was angry about any scenes missing. I'm not sure what he was thinking except that he was as inebriated as Mr. Peckinpah on the set. I think that in his alcoholic fantasy life, Al believed that we did more than wound up on the screen."

For his part, Steve finally commented on his version of the film: *"The Getaway* meant more to me in a financial and professional way than *Junior Bonner*. I take full responsibility for it. Not full credit, but full responsibility. It's made money for everyone connected with it. That says all there is to say. I know Sam wasn't happy with some of the changes, but I had my reasons. Sam and I are still friends. And, of course, personally, *The Getaway* was a film that I met my lady on. Ali and I had a chance to meet and get to know each other, so it has a sentimental value for me as well.

"I feel that Sam Peckinpah is an exceptional filmmaker. He is a little bit hard on himself sometimes, and I worry about him for that. But I have great respect for anyone as committed as Sam is to his work. He surrounds himself with people who are honest and who are personally committed to what he does. Sam has made a personal commitment to his work, and I feel that a man isn't worth a shit unless he has."

*The Getaway* was not well received by the press when it opened for the Christmas season of 1972.

*The New Yorker*'s Pauline Kael wrote, "The picture's bewildering con is that it makes the pair such lovely, decent gangsters that they can stroll off into the sunset with their satchel stuffed with money as if they'd just met over a malt at the corner drugstore. As for McQueen and Mac-Graw, they strike no sparks on the screen. (They don't even look right together; her head is bigger than his.) His low-key professionalism is turning into minimal acting, and is indistinguishable from the blahs, while she is certainly the primmest, smuggest gangster's moll of all time. Last time I saw Candice Bergen, I thought she was a worse actress than MacGraw; now I think I slandered Bergen."

Kathleen Carroll of the *New York Daily News* wrote, "Too vulgar and violent. At one point in their travels, McQueen and MacGraw wind up in a garbage dump, the very place for this film."

And Jay Cocks of *Time* magazine wrote, "If 'The Getaway' had just rolled off the studio assembly line, the work of a competent craftsman, it could easily have been passed over and forgotten. It is, however, the work of a major American film artist. Peckinpah is pushing his privileges too far."

The movie-going public must not have read the reviews, as they flocked to see it. *The Getaway* recorded a then whopping $18 million domestically, $35 million worldwide, making it the second highest grossing film of the year.

McQueen's take was 10 percent of the gross, netting him $3.5 million and making him the highest paid movie star in the world at the time.

Just as *Le Mans* had taken everything away from Steve that he so dearly loved, *The Getaway* brought it all back. He was passionately in love again with the most desirable actress in the world, he had money in the bank, and he was the world's biggest movie star, again.

Steve McQueen was back.

McQueen in *Papillon*, a film in which he should have won
the Academy Award. 1973.     (Courtesy of Allied Artists)

# TO THE TOP . . .

*A lot of folks got the wrong idea about how I got my breaks.*
*I'm sure they think I tough-guyed my way up to the studio*
*boss and bullied myself into a part. No way. I worked hard,*
*and if you work hard you get the goodies.*

STEVE MCQUEEN

PAT JOHNSON'S HOUSE in Canoga Park, California, very easily could have
been the inspiration for the home of Ralph Papa Thorson, whom Steve
portrayed in *The Hunter.*

Johnson's place is the only one on the street that constantly has its
front door open. If it were a revolving door, you'd swear it was a hotel.
Johnson has taken in more than his share of kids who were on the
wrong path of life. He is both a father and a friend to his kids and his
kids' friends. He can easily swing from one conversation to another
without missing a beat, making each person feel at ease. He is salt of the
earth yet possesses a heroic quality. He is quiet and unassuming, but if
one has the quality of loyalty, that person could be a friend for life.

Johnson is always optimistic. Negativity has no place in his life. Loren
Janes on Pat Johnson, "Pat is the kind of guy when you call him up on
the phone and say, 'How ya doing?' he just peppers up and says, 'I'm
doing wonderful,' not in a phony kind of obligatory way, but he really
means it."

Johnson lives the kind of life others seek to have. He has been married to his lovely wife, Sue, for over twenty years. He has four wonderful, respectful, and well-mannered boys. Hugging and kissing his wife,
kids, and friends comes easily to him. His house is so full of love, even
the cats and dogs get along. You'd swear a man like this had to have
been raised in the same type of environment.

Niagara Falls, New York, in the forties was a tough industrial city, with lots of thick black smoke billowing from the tall smokestacks of the many factories. "I grew up in Hyde Park Village, a black project. There were maybe fifty white-trash families and two thousand black families in this neighborhood. It was pretty rough," remembers Johnson.

Johnson's father, Thomas, was an alcoholic who left his family when Pat was only twenty-eight months old. His mother, Alice, was left to raise eleven kids all by herself. "My mother was an angel on earth," says Johnson. Though they were poor, they by no means knew any different.

When Thomas Johnson up and left, the government deemed Alice Johnson an unfit mother and decided she could not properly care for her children. Alice had the equivalence of a fourth-grade education and never made more than $1.50 an hour in her whole life. Five of the eleven Johnson kids were put in an orphanage (some of Johnson's brothers and sisters were old enough not to be taken away), and Alice vowed that she would get them back one day. "I remember the car ride on the way to the orphanage. I just ate a Hershey's chocolate bar and got sick and threw up all over the backseat. When I first arrived at the orphanage, the first word I remember is 'quarantine.' My first meal was spaghetti with sauce. I was clinging to my older sister Cynthia. I remember that day vividly," adds Johnson.

The orphanage was run by the local Catholic church, and Johnson and his four siblings were raised by nuns.

Johnson thought of his mother daily. He and the others missed her terribly. In the seven years he was there, however, she could only afford to visit three times. The visits were special for him, as Alice would hold him as only a mother could.

One woman who came to visit the orphanage weekly had her eye on Pat. She could not have children of her own and came in search of a child she could mother. "She would visit with me and tell me she wanted me," Johnson recalls. "Coincidentally, she came to visit on the same day my mother did. The office asked who I would like to see. Of course I said my real mother and after that, I never saw that lady again."

Seven long years later, Alice Johnson finally found a job at the local paper mill as a sorter. Now she was eligible to get her kids back, and she made good on her vow. Pat was nine years old when he was released to his mother's custody, but much older inside.

In 1967, Johnson was working in an auto parts store in Cleveland, Ohio. One weekend, while the Grand National Karate Tournament was in town, he met Chuck Norris. The two hit it off and Norris told Johnson that if he were ever in Los Angeles to look him up. Tired of the mundane nine-to-five life, two months later Johnson called Norris from the bus depot in Los Angeles, where Norris swiftly picked him up. Norris then put up Johnson for a few months and, eventually, Johnson became an instructor for Norris' Sherman Oaks school. There, Johnson became Steve McQueen's karate instructor.

Today Pat Johnson is the highest-paid karate instructor in the world. He is instructor to the rich and famous, and his list of clients reads like a Who's Who in Hollywood. Over the years, his students have included director William Friedkin, head of International Creative Management Marvin Josephson, actor Freddie Prinze, singing family the Osmonds, television game show host Bob Barker, and actress Priscilla Presley.

In addition to being a karate instructor, Johnson is one of Hollywood's top fight coordinators for the movies. He is the man behind all of the moves in *The Karate Kid* and *Teenage Mutant Ninja Turtle* films. Johnson also wrote the screenplay for the Chuck Norris movie *A Force of One*.

He is a living legend in the karate world. When he walks onto a mat, whispers of "there's Pat Johnson" can be heard throughout the room. He holds a ninth-degree black belt and is deadly with his hands and feet.

In 1962, Johnson was drafted into the army and was shipped to Korea for duty. The troop ship to Korea was playing *Hell Is for Heroes*, and Johnson took a liking to the star of the movie.

Johnson served as a chaplain's assistant and became quite friendly with the base interpreter. "There wasn't much to do in Korea when you got off duty. As a fertilizer, the Koreans use human excrement all over the land, so there was this putrid smell every time you went outside. As a result, I didn't go outside much." College extension courses were available, but that didn't appeal to the restless young man. That left karate as the last option. The Korean interpreter, an elderly man, asked Johnson if he would give karate a try. Johnson obliged and has stuck with it ever since.

Every year on the first weekend of August, the International Karate Championships are held. The site of the 1968 championships was the Long Beach Arena in California. It was the first time Pat Johnson ever met Steve McQueen. Johnson recalls, "Steve came in with Bruce Lee and sat down in the front row. He had a hat and sunglasses on and slouched down in his seat. He kept looking around to make sure no one recognized him. Then, of course, a lot of people did recognize him. Just before the final bell of the last fight, he and Bruce literally got up and ran from the place. After they started running, people from the stands jumped up and started running after them. Of course, they got away before anyone got to them because they had a head start. Steve was extremely popular at that time."

Back in the sixties, karate did not have the following that it enjoys today. At the highest levels, it was a very small sport. Everyone who fought each other also knew each other on a personal level. Bruce Lee, Chuck Norris, Bob Wall, and Pat Johnson were considered the best.

It was at the Long Beach Arena that Bruce Lee introduced McQueen to Johnson. McQueen struck Johnson as aloof, very courteous but not warm at all. Says Johnson, "There was nothing in his body language to indicate that he was receptive or happy to meet me. He let it be known that he had no desire to carry on that relationship, not just with me, but with everyone he met. Any further than, 'Hi, how are you? I'm Steve McQueen and you are?' That was my impression, that he was a very private and closed individual." It would be four years before their paths would cross again.

Chuck Norris remembers going to see *On Any Sunday* and watching Steve McQueen on the big screen, racing competitively, not caring about his million-dollar face being destroyed if he smashed it on the next turn. Norris remembers thinking, "If there's any actor in the world I'd like to meet, it would be him."

When *The Getaway* was completed, Steve rented a place in Coldwater Canyon. It was there that he learned his twelve-year-old son, Chad, had been involved in a fight at school. Steve wanted Chad to learn how to defend himself. Bruce Lee once told McQueen, "If you ever want to take karate lessons, Norris is the best."

In 1972, Norris and partner Bob Wall owned a studio in Sherman Oaks. It was there that Norris's secretary calmly buzzed him in his office: "Steve McQueen on line one." Norris replied, "You're kidding, right?" Norris picked up the phone, thinking it was one of his friends pulling a fast one. He heard the voice on the other line say, "Chuck, this is Steve McQueen. I'd like to bring in my son Chad for lessons." Norris hung up, not knowing for sure if it was the real Steve McQueen.

The next day, Steve and Chad arrived at the scheduled time. In his book, *The Secret of Inner Strength—My Story*, Norris recalls that meeting: "I was especially impressed with Steve, who lived up to my expectations. He was a no-nonsense type of man who got directly to the point."

Though Norris taught McQueen his first few private lessons over a ten-week period, their training was constantly being interrupted when Norris's career in movies began to take off. Norris recommended to McQueen that his senior instructor, Pat Johnson, take his place when he was away on business.

Chuck Norris can count his best friends on one hand. Pat Johnson is one of them. In his book, Norris says of Johnson, "Pat is a unique person. He is a born leader. He is also one of the best karate instructors in the world."

McQueen was reluctant to go with Johnson at first. "He wanted to train with only Chuck," says Johnson. With people that he was going to associate with, McQueen didn't like it when people fawned all over him. Says friend Nikita Knatz, "In order to retain his respect, you had to distance yourself from him socially." Even though Johnson was a fan of McQueen's, on the karate mat things were different. He wouldn't allow anything but a 100 percent effort. Star or no star, Johnson treated everyone as equals on the mat. It was just what Steve needed and, most importantly, wanted. "C'mon, Steve. You've got to get with it. You're not concentrating hard enough. You're going to get your ass kicked if you keep this up," Johnson would taunt.

The turning point in their relationship came three months into their training. Johnson had no reason to think he meant anything to Steve other than a good workout. A week before Norris was to come back and resume his lessons with Steve, Johnson told Steve, "Chuck is going to be back next week and you can start training with him again." Johnson was startled and amused when McQueen replied, "I'd rather keep training with you." Says Johnson, "That was the very first indication that perhaps I was something other than a karate teacher to him, that we had some kind of relationship."

Their relationship would blossom into a friendship that would remain throughout Steve's lifetime. Other than Ali MacGraw and Barbara Minty, no one person would see Steve more in his last eight years. He would become McQueen's mentor. Says Loren Janes, "Pat Johnson was more of a father figure to Steve. He was really in awe of Pat. He would have given anything to have the qualities that Pat has. I think Steve confided more in Pat than in anyone else."

Their friendship was a slow process. Initially, Steve would come in for his karate lesson and leave, going about his business. After a few months, he would ask Johnson out for breakfast. "He very slowly began to tell me about his personal life, his feelings about things," says Johnson. "I never tried to ask questions of him, because I never wanted him to think I was prying. I kind of had a feeling where he was coming from. I came from the same place. I'm sort of paranoid, but not nearly as paranoid as he was." Johnson then began to open up to McQueen about his past. Steve realized that Johnson may have had it even worse than he. Johnson was of the streets, as well. "Having grown up on the streets, having always been conscious of someone being nice and friendly to me, I always ask, 'What does he want from me?' That's my

253

first reaction. 'What's his con? What's his game?' I understood that instantly with Steve, so I never put him in a position where he could even have thought that about me, that I was trying to con him in some way. The less I tried to open him up, the more he opened up to me."

Steve began to rely on Johnson's opinion more and more. He knew whatever question he had, he would be given an honest answer. With stardom, Steve became increasingly paranoid, so he relied on Johnson's opinion more than ever. Says Johnson, "If a person is going to be a karate student, I look at that person and I give them a character analysis. I listen to what they say. I watch what they do. I watch how they treat other people, how they talk to other people. As time goes on, I develop a profile of this person. I ask myself, 'What can I expect of this person in a given set of circumstances? Would this person watch my back in an alley fight? Can I trust his word? Is he a person that I can put my wallet on the table and know it's going to be there when I return? Could I trust him with my wife?' It doesn't make anybody bad if they have any flaws, but the main thing is to never put that person in a position where his flaw is going to make you vulnerable. I told Steve, 'You can never be disappointed in a person for doing something that their character dictates they do in those circumstances. You have to anticipate it. You have to expect it.' He appreciated that advice and followed it."

The two men developed a system. When Steve was to meet with an associate and Johnson was with him, after they left, McQueen would turn to Johnson and ask, "Well, what do you think?" The highly perceptive Johnson would size up the person in that time and give Steve his opinion. Once, when Steve was thinking of investing in a professional soccer team, he was told by Johnson, "Steve, soccer will never be big in America." He followed Johnson's advice.

They enjoyed a real friendship, not just a teacher-pupil relationship. McQueen put it to Johnson, "Pat, I don't want you to ever think that you are with me as my bodyguard. You're not part of an entourage. You are my friend. When we're together, don't feel like you have to push people away from me; I can take care of myself." McQueen didn't even like to be away from Johnson while he was on location. Johnson accompanied him on *The Towering Inferno, Tom Horn,* and *The Hunter.* Steve even turned down the lead for *Apocalypse Now* because Johnson didn't like the idea of being away from his kids for a long period of time. Remembers Johnson, "Steve said to me one day, 'Pat, how do you feel about going to the Philippines for six months?' I said, 'I don't think much of it at all.' At the time, two of my boys were very young, and I had turned down a number of shows that were out of town. I would only coordinate shows in town so that I could be with my boys in their real formative years. Steve said, 'Well, Coppola has come to me with this script about the Vietnam War, but I'm not even going to consider it if you're not going with me.' I said, 'Steve, if you go, I'm going to be with you. If you want me to be with you, I'll be there, but it's not something that I would look forward to.' " Also, McQueen hated the thought of all the vaccination shots he would need for going overseas. *Apocalypse Now* would have to be done without him.

McQueen took to his karate lessons like a fish to water. Chuck Norris noticed early on that "Steve had excellent reflexes and natural athletic ability. He trained hard and was a born fighter. He was not afraid to mix it up with anybody. Once he made up his mind to do something, he went all out." Pat Johnson notes that McQueen's concentration level was the most intense he'd ever seen in a student: "He was incredible. In all of the hundreds, thousands of rounds that we fought each other, I never saw him have a lapse of concentration. He was an absolute pleasure to work with."

Steve found that karate was the perfect release when he wasn't acting. Observes Pat Johnson, "Steve was really alive when he was acting. It forced him to focus. In the course of a twelve-hour day, you might actually spend a total of four or five hours a day doing your craft. By the time the lights are set up, you take the time to rehearse, and the camera actually starts rolling, you're only making contact with another actor for a short amount of time. Karate required that same focus and concentration, and Steve could do that every day and get that same high."

In time, McQueen became quite effective with his hands and feet. He got up to the rank of red belt, one level below black belt. McQueen trained long enough to become a third-degree black belt but never tested for it. "He never tested because he felt that if he ever went to court for punching somebody, the fact that he was a black belt could be used against him. So he kept that part of his life very low key," says Johnson.

McQueen had had a few scuffles in his lifetime.

Marvin Josephson, who was not only Steve's last agent, but also a student of Pat Johnson, remembers Steve's short temper. "Steve could attract trouble. He was always challenging and had a very aggressive attitude. He didn't have a lot of stamina; he ran out of gas fairly early. Later, I would realize it was because of his lung condition. In a fight, he had to win early on. He had vicious and lethal opening moves. He wasn't scared to hurt you, so he would just go at it."

One such scuffle, mentioned in Neile McQueen's book, was the time Steve almost knocked out actor John Gavin. Gavin had dated Neile a few times after she and Steve were divorced. Even though they were no longer married, Steve still did not like the thought of another man being with his wife. In the early days of their pending divorce, Steve went to the house to collect some of things he felt were rightly his. One item in particular, a pool table, was what Steve really came for. To get his goat, Neile announced, "You really don't want that pool table, do you?" Curious, Steve replied, "Well, why not?" Neile said casually, "Well, John Gavin and I made love on it the other night and you wouldn't want to think of that every time you play pool on it, would you, honey?" Steve gave her an icy stare for what seemed the longest time. Suddenly, he burst out, "You're right. I don't want it," then quickly left. Years later, at the Beverly Wilshire Hotel, Steve was on the pay phone a little bit too long. Two men were waiting to use it. One was big, like a football player; the other was small. The big one said impatiently to McQueen, "Hurry up, man." Steve replied nicely, "I'll be finished in just a minute." Then the big guy turned abusive: "Hey, man, I gotta use the phone. Hurry it up, will ya?" Steve quietly seethed inside, hung up, and walked up to him and said, "You know, you're a real asshole." The big guy then shoved Steve. McQueen took his karate stance and knocked the guy out in a matter of seconds. He then turned to the other man to take him on. "Hey, I didn't start anything," said the smaller man. The big guy got back up and Steve was coming toward him when John Gavin, who had been watching the fracas on the side, approached Steve and got in between the two. "Steve," said Gavin, "don't do this. Think of who you are and where you are." Gavin was the last person McQueen needed to see. He grabbed Gavin by the lapels and cocked his fist back. He hissed to Gavin, "You! You son-of-a-bitch. You fucked my old lady on my pool table!" Gasping, Gavin pleaded, "Wait, wait, wait. What's going on?" Neile goes on to say in her book that Steve decked Gavin. McQueen told Pat Johnson the same story with the exception that he did not punch Gavin. "No, he never decked Gavin, but he did deck the big guy," says Johnson. "He did grab Gavin and cock his fist back. He did not and would not hit John Gavin." Needless to say, Neile wouldn't be receiving any phone calls in the near future from John Gavin asking her out for a date.

Johnson acknowledged that McQueen had a short fuse. He believes that karate is not only a sport, but an art form that will eventually let your true personality come out. "Steve was the most competitive individual I ever knew, very, very aggressive. For example, I'm not an aggressive person by nature so I'm very much of a counterfighter. I generally let my opponents make all of the moves, and I take advantage of their mistakes. In my life, I have an imaginary circle around me, and

I never will bother anyone if they don't cross that line. I would never go out after anybody, but if they step into my perimeter, my safety zone, then I react. Steve was just the opposite. He was such an aggressive individual by nature. In karate, you bow to each other before you begin to actually fight. Once we bowed, he would come across the ring at me, I mean both feet, arms, swinging and punching and kicking as hard as he could. Now, I know he loved me like his brother, but that was his nature, this aggressiveness, this competitiveness. But I never knew it to be anything negative."

The karate lessons proved to be paying off for Chad. Not only did he not have to worry about the kids in school, but he could take on adults, as well. A year later, when Steve and Ali moved to Trancas Beach, their neighbor was none other than Keith Moon, drummer for the rock group The Who. Moon, known as "Moon the Loon," had earned his reputation for his passion of driving automobiles in backyard swimming pools. The last time he counted, he had drowned twenty-two cars. He was a known alcoholic, and his behavior was erratic at best. Steve would get up early in the morning and spot Moon in a Nazi SS uniform, yelling, "Heil, Hitler!" at the ocean. Sometimes, he even came over to the McQueen household looking for Steve. McQueen thought Moon harmless and always ignored him. While Steve and Ali were gone one day, Chad answered a knock on the door. It was Moon, asking for Steve. "He's not here," Chad replied. Moon got aggressive. "Look, I know he's here and you're not telling me," Moon slurred. He then pushed Chad out of the way and entered the house. Chad delivered a roundhouse punch to the chin that put Moon to sleep. When Steve found out Chad had knocked Moon out, he became a beaming father. He was proud of Chad for "holding down the fort."

Sometime after that incident, Moon had installed bright floodlights on his front porch. They were so bright at night, that they would light up McQueen's bedroom so he couldn't get to sleep. Steve politely asked Moon to turn them off before he went to bed. Moon ignored the request, so McQueen remedied the situation by grabbing his shotgun and blowing out the lights with a few live rounds. That settled that. Says Pat Johnson, "Steve thought Keith Moon was an asshole and a total nutcase."

*Papillon* is hands down the best performance of Steve McQueen's twenty-eight-film career. The film is an adaptation of the worldwide bestseller by author Henri Charrière, "the butterfly." It tells the story of Charrière's stay on Devil's Island, a French Guiana prison from which no man had ever escaped. Papillon's quest for freedom is quelled by several mishaps and double-crosses.

Known as a ladies' man and an excellent safecracker, Papillon is framed for the murder of a pimp. Though Charrière claims his innocence, he is sentenced to Devil's Island for life. His story tells of the atrocities he endured while incarcerated and his quest for personal freedom. After nine escape attempts, Papillon became a free man. By 1969, Charrière had written a book and become an instant celebrity and folk hero in France. Charrière viewed himself as a modern-day Robin Hood and took pride in the fact that the only safes he cracked were those that belonged to state agencies, not to private enterprises or people.

McQueen, the ultimate movie escape hero, would be matched with the ultimate escape story.

Recognizing *Papillon*'s potential screen success, publisher Robert Laffont guarded the rights to the book very closely. Smelling a potential hit film, European producer Robert Dorfman bought the rights from Laffont for a whopping $600,000. Dorfman thought *Papillon* would do excellent business in France and throughout Europe if Jean-Paul Belmondo were lured as its star. Belmondo was Europe's biggest star and would attract only European dollars. Dorfman could attract much more business if he could break into the U.S. market with a big-name American star who also had a wide following in the European and Asian film markets. Only one person fit those requirements: Steve McQueen. (McQueen was France's biggest foreign star to boot.)

If McQueen could be obtained, financing could easily be set up. Franklin Schaffner, the director of *Papillon,* offered, "The only people who make international movies are the Americans. That is why they came first to McQueen and myself."

The first chore of any film is to convert the book into a filmable script, not an easy task. "Licking the script involved the problem of selectivity, of deciding what to use from a book of 434 pages. We also had to flesh out character relationships, which the book lacked," said the director. Dorfman hired writers Robert Benton and David Newton to whip the first draft into shape, at the cost of an additional $500,000. When the first draft was completed, Dorfman read then scrapped it completely. Franklin Schaffner then took it to reliable American writer William Goldman of *Butch Cassidy and the Sundance Kid* fame. [This time, Schaffner's vision of the Goldman script was not what he envisioned *Papillon* to be.] Stated Schaffner, "Revenge is the motivating theme of Charrière's book, and that's not dramatic." Schaffner wanted the script to deal with the inhumanities of prison and man's eternal quest for freedom.

Before Goldman left the project, he had heard that Dustin Hoffman was eager to participate in *Papillon*. "Hoffman is really hot to do it," was the word in Hollywood. Hoffman was only interested in doing the film if it were a legitimate piece. "I knew that I wouldn't be interested in doing the film if it was going to be one of those buddy prison pictures, where McQueen and I would be required to play charismatic head to head," said Hoffman. The trouble was that there was literally no role for Hoffman to play. One had to be created. The role of Dega, eventually played by Hoffman in the movie, was nowhere near the magnitude of that in the original book. That meant another whole new rewrite of the script in order to expand the Dega character, which, in turn, meant more money. McQueen was going to get $1.75 million for his services and Hoffman was to receive $1.25 million. As Schaffner put it, "Dustin was bought—not brought—into the film."

Hoffman's character, Dega, would eventually be worked out with screenwriter Dalton Trumbo. "Actually," said Hoffman, "the character I play in the film is composed of several characters in the book—the result of many long discussions with Dalton Trumbo.

"Trumbo's sophistication overlays a dynamic strength and integrity, which I felt was applicable to Dega."

Hoffman studied for weeks in a New York library reading everything concerning French penal colonies. "I studied about ten or twelve books on prison life there. One of the books was by a former inmate, an art forger whose life had great similarities with what I thought about Dega, who was a counterfeiter. I drew from this many real-life experiences as a frame of reference for filling out my concept of Dega."

Steve first became aware of Dustin Hoffman when he and Neile had heard rave reviews about the 1967 Mike Nichols film, *The Graduate*. Both enjoyed the movie, but Neile noticed that Steve was very quiet on the car ride home. Once back at the Castle, Steve wondered aloud, "What's going to happen to us, do you suppose?" Neile asked, "Us? What do you mean? Why should anything happen to us?" Steve corrected himself, "No, no. I mean 'us'—like Newman and me—you know?" Neile still didn't know what he was getting at. "No, I don't know, Steve. Tell me." Finally, he let it out: "God, baby, I can't believe this guy's going to be a movie star, can you? I mean, he is one ugly cat. Good actor, yeah, but he sure is homely!" Steve then took off his shirt and stood in front of the mirror to show off his body. "Look at that, baby, take a look at that face and that body and tell me the truth. Who would you pick, him or me?" Steve asked. Neile started to laugh and then Steve joined in, though she knew deep down he was dead serious.*

Six years later, Hoffman was to be McQueen's next costar. Steve had never worked with an actor of Hoffman's talent and ability. Hoffman was all of the things that McQueen was not. Dustin worked hard on his stage skills in New York for years; Steve was fired from his first and only major Broadway play and left New York before honing his acting technique. Hoffman came into a scene with a hundred different ideas; McQueen liked to keep it simple. Hoffman got better with more takes; Steve was most effective on the first take. Hoffman was a thinking man's actor; McQueen worked from the gut level.

The costs for *Papillon* were escalating. In addition to McQueen's and Hoffman's salaries, Schaffner was to receive $750,000 to direct. Not one, but two film crews had to be paid. Since the film was to be shot partly in Spain, the government there wanted its piece of the pie. The budget skyrocketed from $4 million to $14 million, making it the highest-budgeted film of 1973.

Money would be a constant problem during the filming of *Papillon*. The film was to be distributed by Allied Artists, which at the time was virtually out of the production and distribution business. *Papillon*'s $14 million budget was six times the total net worth of Allied Artists. Allied, in return, sought financial help from other backers.

Allied Artists struck a deal with Corona and Walter E. Heller Factors. Heller would provide Allied Artists with $7 million, plus an additional $2.5 million to cover any budget overruns, with an additional 20 percent interest rate. This meant that *Papillon* would have to gross $14 million before Allied Artists could recover the $7 million loan from Heller. With the loan came certain stipulations. First and foremost, McQueen had to star in the film. Knowing the background of the project, McQueen had many misgivings about the packaging. Says Franklin Schaffner, "He was in and out, in and out, in and out; or if he wasn't in and out, he was threatening." Allied added another $250,000 to McQueen's salary to make it an even $2 million to ensure his name on the picture, making Steve McQueen the first movie star ever to make $2 million upfront for one film.

The other stipulation was that *Papillon* had to be ready for a December 1973 release to capitalize on the Christmas season. It was now February 1973. That meant the film had nine months to be scouted for locations, shot, scored, and edited. Filming would have to begin right away even if the script wasn't ready, a dangerous situation to be in in

---

* McQueen Toffel, Neile, *My Husband, My Friend* (New York: Atheneum Books, 1986), 172.

the film industry. Schaffner later acknowledged this was not a normal procedure in shooting a film: "We started shooting late February 1973 with about sixty pages of script. That, on the surface of it, would appear to be madness. But either we proceeded or the financing would be jeopardized. Morale among the crew was hitting a questionable plateau, and after all the months I had been on the project, it seemed the wisest course of action to sink or swim."*

The first step, scouting for locations, proved to be as difficult as the financing. The French Guiana prison that Papillon was locked up in had deteriorated to the point where it was in ruins and would prove useless. In addition to a prison, Schaffner needed a jungle for certain scenes, plus a livable area to put up the crew. He needed a country that was politically as well as economically sound. After considering Honduras, Guatemala, and the Cayman Islands, Schaffner decided on Spain and Jamaica.

Next, was a feasible script. Schaffner could not use anything from the two previous versions. He enlisted the help of legendary screenwriter Dalton Trumbo. Trumbo, during the McCarthy hearings in the 1950s, was one of the Hollywood Ten who did not name names during the blacklisting of suspected Communists in the industry. In order to write the new screenplay, Trumbo had to be kept on location throughout the entire filming. Only ten pages ahead of schedule, *Papillon* had to be shot like a play, in sequence. This made the film much more expensive, because the actors had to be retained for their services. For Don Gordon, it was a paid working vacation: "You don't see my character anymore after my body is in the jungle. That was two months later. In other words, I was sitting around Jamaica doing diddly. I was visiting the set and having a good time, because they were going to shoot in sequence. When I got off the ship, they normally would have told me to go home, but they kept me there for the shot in the jungle. Two whole months for one scene." Not only did Schaffner have to shoot the film during the twelve-hour workday, but then he had to collaborate with Trumbo a few hours every night to ensure the script was ahead of production.

Shooting had begun and there were still problems with the incoming money, or lack thereof. The crew had been in Spain for over a month and hadn't been paid a dime. Says director of photography Fred Koenekamp, "I went five weeks without a paycheck, which is very unusual for a movie." Remembers Don Gordon, "We weren't getting our per diems. McQueen wasn't getting his. Hoffman wasn't getting his.

---

* Kim, Erwin, *Franklin J. Schaffner* (The Scarecrow Press, Inc., 1985), 292.

The crew wasn't getting paid. McQueen already had his salary upfront, but he went to the producer and said, 'If the crew isn't paid, I don't work.' " McQueen was true to his word. Allied Artists had to learn it the hard way when the shoot came to a halt for five days. Until everyone got paid, only then would McQueen begin to work again. Allied's costly mistake was to the tune of $50,000 a day for five days, a whopping $250,000 budget overrun that could have easily been avoided.

Don Gordon kept hearing nasty rumors about how the producers were raising money. "From what I understand," says Gordon, "the producer would take a couple of reels of film, get on an airplane, go back to France, show them reels of film, get money, get back on an airplane, and bring it back on a lease." It was catch as catch can.

Regardless of any other hassles the film encountered, Schaffner thought his biggest headache throughout filming would be the egos of his two stars. "Obviously, Steve McQueen was the superstar in films. Dustin Hoffman was a star as an actor, if I can make that distinction. And they both looked forward to performing with one another."

Schaffner later revealed his technique in handling them: "I would always shoot on McQueen first to make him commit and then turn around and shoot on Hoffman. It seemed to work better that way, because if I covered Hoffman first, Steve would become restless about what he was doing. The quicker you got him comfortable, the better the scene would play. Hoffman, on the other hand, is a totally electric performer. He comes in with ninety-nine different ideas of how to approach a scene."

Though Hoffman may have been the more critically acclaimed actor of the two, it was McQueen who had more experience on film. Hoffman couldn't quite get a fix on his character. He seemed to be babbling incoherently. Veteran character actor Charles Durning remembers talking with Hoffman on the set of *Tootsie* some ten years later after he did *Papillon*. Hoffman told Durning that McQueen offered some simple advice, "Less, Dusty. Do less. Just throw that out, you don't need it. Keep it simple." Durning asked Hoffman what he did. Says Hoffman, "I took his advice. It turned out he was right." So there it was: Steve McQueen was giving Dustin Hoffman acting tips for the big screen.

Costar Don Gordon relates, "Steve worked very hard on *Papillon*. He worked very hard as an actor. A lot of people think he didn't, but he did. He was a working actor. Plus the fact that Dustin Hoffman kept McQueen on his toes, kept him honest. One day Dustin showed up with his teeth all colored and wearing Coke bottle glasses. McQueen had to be aware, he had to work even harder than he normally did. He really came into maturation on *Papillon*."

The McQueen-Hoffman relationship at first was strained. Both were wary men and suspect of each other. They didn't talk to one another until filming began. Gordon offers, "Okay, you've got two guys who are talented. McQueen was older, he looks around, and here comes this youngster, because Dustin at that time was young. On the set, Dustin would be sitting with a stand-in. I'd sit with McQueen. In all of the time that I knew McQueen, he never talked about other actors. There wasn't any time for that. If anybody's looking for gossip, they're going to have to make it up because so what if they didn't talk to each other. I don't think Steve cared what Dustin thought of him. The important thing was the movie, people tend to forget that. When you're doing a movie, what takes precedent over anything is the film. Personalities don't mean shit."

In the middle of the filming, the real-life Papillon, Henri Charrière, visited the set in Spain, where a replica of the prison he was sent to was built. He found it an eerie sight, bringing him back to the horrors he had endured nearly forty years before. Ali MacGraw refers to Charrière in her book as "quite a charming character, but with a huge ego." Pat Johnson recalls that Steve was quite taken with Charrière. Steve himself said, "I kept being driven by this restless feeling. I seemed always to be looking for something—never knowing what it was—but always there was the sense that I couldn't be confined. And that's exactly what I felt in common with Charrière's Papillon. This man, who had been restless and moving, suddenly found himself imprisoned, and his natural behavior and involuntary reaction was, 'I must get out of this damned place.' Of course, the kind of inhuman, brutalizing treatment practiced in the French penal colonies in those days added to his desire to be free. My name could easily have been Papillon, too."

Director Franklin Schaffner saw the similarities. He was moved to say, "Success as an actor, and the wealth that has come with it, has never changed the underlying nature of Steve. He's still basically the same youngster whose resistance to any restraints led him to minor encounters with the law and then Boys Republic."

Don Gordon remembers hearing that Schaffner was not as taken with Charrière. "Schaffner told me that he never believed half the things he said in the book, that Charrière was a lying son-of-a-bitch." Nonetheless, Charrière died before filming was completed and never did get to see a final screening of *Papillon*.

Back on the set, McQueen and Hoffman were in for some backbreaking work. One scene called for the two men to tackle a crocodile. In the movie, actor Vic Tayback, who plays a prison guard, spots a crocodile swimming in the swamps where the prisoners have cleanup detail. The crocodile skin can fetch a pretty penny on the black market, so Tayback shoots the crocodile and orders McQueen and Hoffman to round it up. Though the animal is shot, it is still clearly moving when both men have to approach it. The scene is one of *Papillon*'s few bright comedic spots. For it, the crocodile was temporarily drugged and had its mouth wired shut, but McQueen and Hoffman still had to tackle the beast. They walk around the wounded twenty-two-foot crocodile, circling clumsily, waiting for the right moment. Finally, it is McQueen who musters the courage to jump on the razor-toothed reptile first, with Hoffman faithfully leaping on right behind McQueen. Kent James laughs: "Steve jumped on it first, so Dustin had to jump on it to prove he wasn't chickenshit." James recalls McQueen asking him to bring a towel to him near the crocodile. "I ain't getting any closer than right where I am and if you think I'm a chickenshit, you're damn right I am!" said James.

Another scene called for Steve to be chained with his hands behind his back while lying on his stomach and attempt to eat bread and water out of a plate. Don Gordon recalls that as the most physically and emotionally demanding scene in the movie: "All of that work for him was very tough. He just busted his ass. He worked. That's what he did. Forget about him being a star, he was an actor. He did his part better than any other actor in the world who could have done *Papillon*. He brought to it another dimension."

For his role in *Papillon*, Steve did not apply Method techniques. While Dustin Hoffman starved himself on a coconut a day, Steve drank Red Stripe beer with a vengeance. "He really had a weight problem on that film. He actually had quite a gut on him and it kept getting bigger," said Kent James. For his solitary confinement scene, McQueen is put on rations and is supposed to appear gaunt and starving. Kent James had to find bigger and baggier clothes to give McQueen an emaciated look.

Steve's best moment came in the middle of the movie when the inmates escape from the prison but not from the island. They stumble upon a leper colony, which consists mainly of outlaws and bootleggers. They contemplate killing the lepers so as to not draw attention to themselves. Papillon is invited into a den. In the book, Henri Charrière describes the harrowing details of their appearance:

> I sat down on a stool. Three lamps were lit, and they placed one of them on a table directly in front of me. Five of them stood, so that I couldn't make out their faces. Then one of them sat near me. That's when I saw my first leper. I had to make an effort not to look away or otherwise show my feelings. His nose was completely eaten away, flesh and bone; there was only a hole in the middle of his face. I mean what

I say: not two holes, but a single hole as big as a silver dollar. The right side of the lower lip was also eaten away and exposed three long yellow teeth that jutted out of the bone of the upper jaw. He had only one ear. Only his left eye had an eyelid; the lid of his right eye was gone and a deep scar stretched from the top of his forehead, where it disappeared into his shaggy gray hair.*

The scene called for Steve to talk to the head leper, played by actor Anthony Zerbe. Papillon's show of integrity is put to the test by the leper when he enters the room. He smells the air and takes in a big breath of the cigar smoke permeating the area. The leper, noticing his face light up when he smells the smoke, asks, "Do you like cigars?" Papillon obliges, "Whenever I can get 'em." The leper offers his cigar: "Well, try mine." Not knowing if the leprosy is dry or contagious, Papillon takes the cigar and puffs in horror. Not a word of dialogue, just a few puffs and a look of uncertainty. "How did you know I had dry leprosy?" asks the leper. "I didn't," is the reply. It was classic McQueen.

McQueen and Hoffman's respect for each other was growing. Both men admired each other's ability and professionalism. Steve was very astute, however, and noticed something wasn't right about Hoffman. He was taking drugs. Being a movie star isn't all glamorous. A very small percentage of the job is glitzy. Don Gordon offers, "People don't understand what it's like to be a movie star. I only understand because I've been around a lot of them. I was there on *Papillon*. I watched what was going on. It's tough being a movie star because you're carrying the movie. The whole film depends on you, the power to attract people to come to the theater to see you. When somebody is coughing up twenty, forty, sixty million dollars, they're saying to this guy, 'We think you can draw these people to the movie theater.' That's a load. So, sometimes you can forgive the temperamental star because it's a bitch. It's tough."

Because of his relationship with Ali, Steve had sworn off drinking and drugs. Says Pat Johnson, "It was at that time that Steve was coming out, because it was in the late sixties that he was very heavy into drugs. Now Ali was in his life and it was a whole new awakening for him. He was coming out of that late-sixties phase."

For Hoffman, it was just the opposite. He had only been a leading man for a few years and was beginning to hit his stride. Naturally, Hoffman had a lot of nervous energy. The trappings of stardom had affected his judgment. McQueen spotted this and advised Hoffman of the pitfalls of drugs. Hoffman told McQueen, "It's none of your busi-

---

* Charrière, Henri, *Papillon* (New York: William Morrow & Company, Inc., 1970).

ness." Hoffman took no heed of McQueen's friendly advice, as Steve was drinking Red Stripe beer and smoking Jamaica's finest ganja like a fiend. "Steve was never clean of drugs," revealed a friend. "From the time he got to Hollywood to the day he died, he always had something in his blood. Steve made the transition from hard drugs to pot and beer, and it wasn't a fast transition, either. It took many years. Maybe Dustin felt like it was the pot calling the kettle black." Steve backed off.

"The fact that they had a falling out was over an enormously petty issue," says Franklin Schaffner. That petty issue turned out to be Hoffman's invitation to a couple of guests to visit the set. The guests brought their cameras with them, and when McQueen spotted them, he had them thrown off the set. "That should have been run through me first!" he exclaimed. Hoffman and McQueen's relationship never recovered, and for the rest of the shooting they exchanged no words before or after their scenes together. Kent James acted as their go-between. Years later, Hoffman recalled to James, "Can you believe that son-of-a-bitch had my guests thrown off the set?" There were hard feelings on Dustin's part, but Steve had nothing but kind words to say about Dustin Hoffman. There were many times Steve wanted to call Hoffman. "I should call Dusty, just to talk," said Steve. "I know I could help him get his shit together." Says a friend of Steve's, "Steve always thought highly of Dustin, and he had wished their relationship had been smoother. He liked him very much. He respected him as an actor, but more so as a person, and could see the self-destructive behavior in the drugs, the drugs that Steve already had been through. The two men had an immense respect for each other; what you saw on the screen was genuine."

At the end of the film, McQueen's and Hoffman's characters, Papillon and Dega, have aged considerably. It is the only time Steve appears on film as an elderly person. In the scene, after Papillon has served a five-year sentence in solitary confinement for his attempted escape, he emerges from the dimly lit cell to the sunlight, walking with a limp. Friend Phil Parslow thought the limp was a nice touch. When Parslow asked him how he came up with the idea, McQueen offered, "I felt Charrière should have some kind of physical handicap when he is finally released after five years of solitary confinement. I kept looking for some type of inspiration. Then I watched Franklin Schaffner walk. He walked with a limp. I just copied him and that's how Papillon developed his limp." From solitary confinement, Papillon is transported back to Devil's Island, where the older prisoners can spend their last years roaming and living freely in a place from which they cannot escape. The ocean surrounding the island serves as its prison walls. On the island, Papillon meets up with Dega again. Dega's spirit has been broken through years of disappointment and heartache. The yearning for freedom, however, still swells inside Papillon.

Papillon is clearly restless on Devil's Island, as he sits on a bench and studies the waves. "Coconuts," he mutters to himself. "What if you tied a bag of coconuts together like a raft and floated out on the waves." Every seventh wave, he notices, heads back out to sea.

The last scene of the movie is the most heartfelt. Papillon is preparing to jump over a cliff into the roaring ocean and float away on a bed of coconuts to freedom. Warns Dega, "You'll be killed, you know." Papillon replies, "Does it matter?" Then the two embrace in a brotherly hug, for they know they will never see one another again. "Seventh wave," Papillon announces. Without warning, he leaps off the cliff into the rough waters below. He catches the seventh wave that takes him out to sea on the path to freedom. "Hey, you bastards, I'm still here," Papillon yells toward the sky.

*Papillon* miraculously wrapped a week ahead of schedule.

The reviews for *Papillon* when it was released in December 1973 were severely harsh, but that didn't stop the public from flocking to the theaters to see it. The film eventually grossed $25 million in the U.S. and almost $50 million worldwide and became Allied Artists' most successful film ever. Years later, *Papillon* was revered as a classic, yet at the time the critics' main complaint was the somber mood of the film. "Emotionally draining," observed Stuart Byron. Andrew Sarris wrote, "Schaffner has really made an exhilarating movie out of the most dangerously depressing material." And Pauline Kael observed that *Papillon* was "a monument to the eternal desire of movie-makers to impress people and win awards. To put McQueen in a role that requires intense audience identification with the hero's humanity is madness. If there ever was a wrong actor for a man of great spirit, it's McQueen." Time has outlasted the critics' initial blasting of the film, for *Papillon* remains McQueen's acting tour de force.

Epic films like *Papillon* are expected to take home the Oscar and Golden Globe awards. It looked like it would be a shoe-in. Despite all of the negative reviews, *Box Office* magazine predicted, "McQueen has never done finer work and will doubtless be remembered come Oscar time." In early 1974, Steve received a phone call from the Golden Globe committee for his work in *Papillon*. He was told that he had been chosen for the Best Actor category. "That's wonderful. I'm very honored," he told the representative. "You can send the award to me at my address." The representative said, "Oh no, you have to be present at the awards ceremony to receive it." Says Pat Johnson, "Steve did not like all the peripheral stuff that went with acting, the awards and the glamour."

The glamorous couple—McQueen and Ali MacGraw attend the premiere of *Papillon*, 1973. She, according to many of McQueen's friends, was the love of his life. (COURTESY OF THE NAISTHINE WALSH COLLECTIONS)

McQueen adamantly refused. "No, I can't be there. If I won the award, and you think I deserve it, then please, you may mail it to me. You may mention my name. I'll issue a statement to the press on behalf of the Golden Globes, but I won't be there in person to pick it up." Steve was told on the other end, "Well, Mr. McQueen, we're very sorry you can't make it." The award was given to Robert Redford for *The Sting*. Redford was present when he picked it up at the ceremony.

The Golden Globes are the forerunner to the Academy Awards, and whoever wins an award builds momentum for the Oscar. Perhaps Steve's insistence of not playing the Hollywood game cost him the Academy Award. Jack Lemmon took home the Oscar that year for *Save the Tiger*. *Papillon* won only one award, that for Best Score. Steve's costar, Dustin Hoffman, was nominated for Best Supporting Actor. He was outraged that Steve hadn't even been nominated and told the press after the ceremony, "Not only should Steve McQueen have been nominated for *Papillon*, he should have won!" Friend Phil Parslow says, "It was no secret that Steve was not well liked by his fellow actors." The nominations come from the category that you work in, so McQueen had to be nominated by other actors. Says Phil Parslow, "I firmly believe that the reason why Steve was nominated only once in his whole life was that his fellow actors did not like him. Not necessarily the ones who worked with him, but the actors as a whole did not like him because he was a competitor. He stole movies deliberately. Deliberately. He would intentionally set out to steal a movie. He climbed over a lot of bodies. He was with a lot of actors' wives. He had everything they didn't. They were simply jealous of his stature. For Steve not to have won for *Papillon* is simply ridiculous."

To Steve, it was a double slap in the face.

# STEVE McQUEEN

\* \* \*

When *Papillon* wrapped in May 1973, Steve and Ali wanted a place they could call home. With Steve came Chad and with Ali came Joshua. They settled in Trancas Beach, just beyond Malibu. Steve wanted to get away from it all, and Trancas was perfect. It was a hidden little town just off the Pacific Coast Highway. Ali MacGraw describes in her book life in Trancas: "Steve and I had the best of it: our children educated in the local public school, our dog free to roam the beach from one friend's house to another. Life was wonderful—tuna fish sandwiches and surfboards and bicycles, each child with a little core of friends, whose parents we also enjoyed."\*

Steve made his intentions clear from the start: he wanted a wife, not an actress. MacGraw was only too happy to comply. With the constant hounding of the press, she had turned inward. She told a Los Angeles reporter, "I'm the scarlet lady. It's the opposite of the Golden Girl syndrome, and I was the Golden Girl for a time. They [the critics] suddenly find out you're not the greatest actress in the world, which they should have known anyway. The legend of *Love Story* carried me along with it. My nervous system wasn't cut out for doing this for years and years. I am starting to realize that personal peace is more important. I have a child—and an immensely complicated private life. I've had all the glitter and all the best-dressed lists. I've had the dessert, but I've never dealt with the business of living. I can get the laundry done and cook dinner, but reality is dealing with your child and the man in your life and the few friends who matter and not getting sidetracked by spending all your emotional energy on being a big movie star." She added, "I loathe studio politics and all that. Bob [Evans] worked so hard that he and I didn't see too much of each other. That sort of life has nothing to do with where my head is. I am much more interested in living and being a mother. I am not wildly ambitious or very social. I am really quite private. Right now, with Steve, I've virtually gone into hiding."

Steve asked Neile what she thought about Ali giving up her career to be a housewife. Neile thought it was a bad move. Ali was on top of the world, and it would be a crime to take that away from her. It was exactly what Steve didn't want to hear.

Not much talk of marriage came up in their conversations. When they did, a fight erupted. Then, without warning, out of nowhere, Steve delivered the ultimatum, "Okay, baby—if you want to get married, it's

---

\* MacGraw, Ali, *Moving Pictures* (New York: Bantam Books, 1991), 105.

tomorrow or never. That's it." MacGraw later commented, "Not exactly moonlight and roses, but pretty much in character."

There was still the business of the prenuptial agreement to be taken care of. Paranoid that Ali would take him to the cleaners if they ever divorced, Steve held out the papers for Ali to sign before they took a trip to the altar. "Before we were married," says Ali, "he made me sign a prenuptial agreement that there would never be any alimony. I was scared to death of his disapproval, and his rage was gigantic. You never knew what his mood would be."

The wedding was to take place in Cheyenne, Wyoming. Steve wanted no press, so he took the pains to make it as hard as possible for the paparazzi to find the glamorous couple. Terry, Chad, and Joshua were rounded up to be a part of the ceremony. The plan was to fly halfway to Cheyenne, then rent a truck, drive into town unannounced, and be married by a justice of the peace. MacGraw described the unromantic setting of the night before the wedding: "We checked into one of those basic avocado-and-orange, shag-carpeted Holiday Inns. Steve and Chad shared one hard little bed, while Steve's daughter, Terry, and I were in another. Josh was in a rented crib under the coat rack, a rather hyper two-year-old surveying us with a baby bottle half-full of celebratory champagne."*

Justice of the Peace Arthur Garfield received a phone call on July 13, 1973, while playing a round of golf. "Hi, this is Steve McQueen. I'm in town and I'd like you to marry me and Ali MacGraw today, if that's possible," said the famous movie star. Garfield was not convinced it was McQueen, but he did sound awfully convincing. "Yes, sir, it is me," said Steve. Garfield instructed McQueen to meet him at the courthouse. "Well, sir, I'd kind of like to be married under a big shade tree with lots of green grass around." Garfield complied.

Garfield instantly recognized the famous couple and married them right away, with the children as witnesses. The groom wore a short-sleeved plaid cowboy shirt with snap buttons and blue jeans. The bride and bridesmaid wore matching white shirts and plaid shorts. It would be representative of their lifestyle back in Malibu.

On July 20, 1973, actor Bruce Lee died of a severe brain hemorrhage. (Many rumors floating around Hollywood contradict the official reason for his death.) Lee and McQueen had become rivals after Lee got into the movie business. McQueen had been the highest-paid movie star in

---

* MacGraw, Ali, *Moving Pictures* (New York: Bantam Books, 1991), 105.

the world when he received $2 million upfront to star in *Papillon*. Lee then topped that when he was paid $3 million to star in *Enter the Dragon*. Lee bragged to James Coburn, "I did it! I made more money than McQueen!" Coburn added, "Well, then McQueen came back in *The Towering Inferno* and blew him away."

The last time the two men saw each other, Lee had conquered Hong Kong triumphantly and was now a bona fide star. With money rolling in, he was thinking of buying a brand-new Porsche. "I'm finally gonna get my dream caw," Lee boasted in his broken English. McQueen told Lee, "Before you buy one, why don't I take you for a ride in mine and then you can see how it handles? It's not a toy, and you've really got to know what you're doing. Why don't I come by and give you a test drive?"

McQueen picked up Lee and proceeded to winding Mulholland Drive. He told Lee, "Hold on, I'm going to take it through its paces." Then he revved up the Porsche to nearly 150 miles an hour around the curves. Steve acted as if this were a normal speed. Lee, however, was a white-knuckled passenger, a man not in control of an out-of-control situation. All he could think about was the impending doom. "Watch how I can slide it through these tight curves," said McQueen. Lee was cringing. Steve announced, "Now, watch how this baby can do a beautiful 180." And Steve downshifted, slammed on the brakes, spun the car around, and did a 180 in the middle of the road. He then went full speed back in the other direction. "Well, Bruce, what do you think?" McQueen looked over and Lee was not in his seat. "Where the hell did he go?" said a mystified McQueen. He pulled the car over and came to a stop. Lee came up from the floor screaming, "McQueen! You crazy muddafucker! I kill you!" McQueen roared with laughter until he looked into Lee's eyes. The karate expert was livid. McQueen began to accelerate the car again. He told Lee, "Bruce, I'm going to drive as fast as I can until you calm down." Lee put his hands up and conceded, "Okay, okay. I'm calm, Steve." Surprisingly, Lee went out and bought a Porsche anyway.

Despite any jealousy between the two men, Steve was asked to be a pallbearer at the funeral, along with James Coburn and Chuck Norris. They flew to Seattle, the site of Lee's American funeral. (Lee also had a funeral in Hong Kong.) Coburn delivered a beautiful eulogy and everyone who attended was in tears. That is, everyone but Steve McQueen. "We were all saddened by his death," says Coburn. "I think that I felt more saddened than Steve. Steve didn't feel that much because he wasn't that emotional of a guy. He wasn't sentimental about anything. He would hold it all inside."

* * *

Steve was growing weary of the movie industry. His success meant he had the luxury of shooting one picture a year. Even at that pace, it was getting to be too much. He admitted, "Sometimes I wish I was Jack Warner's son and didn't have to work."

Back in the fifties, when Steve was having difficulty getting out of his contract with Four Star to do *The Magnificent Seven,* he threatened to leave Hollywood and go to Australia to become a sheep farmer. The shoot from *Papillon* had left him exhausted. He wanted to get on with his life with Ali. Freddie Fields was instructed to come up with a "sweetheart of a deal." Steve also added, "No out-of-state locations for the next one. Gotta be right here in California. And I want some fat percentages. That's where the heavy bread is. Get me one!" One thing Steve always was was a quick study. He learned early on that "they can kill you on net, but on gross you make out like a bandit!"

For his next film, *The Towering Inferno,* Steve not only made out like a bandit, but made enough money from its gross profits that he could have never worked again if he chose to do so. He would eventually earn a staggering $12 million just from the one film.

Steve had always admired Fields's tenacity. "I need someone who isn't afraid to play dirty," he said. Fields came to Steve with the biggest movie deal of the year: $1 million up front with 7.5 percent of the box office gross.

Producer Irwin Allen spawned a fad in the early seventies with the release of *The Poseidon Adventure.* Heavy-duty special effects and stunts were the key to its success. It was the first of many disaster movies that would follow.

Allen held a simple theory of why so many moviegoers enjoyed such movies: "Survival is the key. The brave and the weak all in it together, fighting for their lives. I believe there is a bit of Walter Mitty in everyone. People get a delight out of escaping into movies. They watch the actors face enormous obstacles and conquer them. When they come out of the theater, they tell themselves, 'I could have done that, too.'" *The Towering Inferno* would be the biggest, grandest, and best disaster movie of all.

It is not uncommon in Hollywood for different studios to be working on the same type of picture and release them at the same time to a less than enthusiastic reception. It had happened just two years earlier with *Junior Bonner.* Two other films on the subject of the modern-day rodeo were released in the same month, and all had died a quick death. The same was about to happen with *Day of the Champion* and *Grand Prix*, until Jack Warner pulled the plug on *Day of the Champion*.

Twentieth Century-Fox was interested in the rights to a book titled *The Tower*, written by Richard Martin Stern. *The Tower* was the story of a fire in a tall skyscraper. Fox, hoping to repeat the success of *The Poseidon Adventure*, was bidding for it, with Allen contracted to produce and John Guillermin set to direct.

The other big studio in town, Warner Brothers, outbid Fox, finally shelling out $390,000 for the rights to the book. It looked as if Fox were "outfoxed."

That is, until just three weeks later, when Allen received a proof of the novel *The Glass Inferno*, written by Frank Robinson and Tom Scortia. Fox immediately snapped up the rights to it, paying $300,000 for the privilege. It was then that Irwin Allen came up with an idea that would make history in the motion picture industry.

Allen suggested that the two studios join forces rather than compete with one another. Both studios could see money being thrown out the window if they released two separate movies. "Actually, it was the amazing similarity of the two novels that brought about the marriage of the two studios to cosponsor the film," said Allen.

"Both were concerned with high-rise fires in unusually identical circumstances. We all felt it would have been foolhardy to compete in a race to beat each other to the box office with the same movie, so we formed an amalgamation to create a single blockbuster script from the two books and to share the costs and rewards."

In October 1973 a deal was hammered out between the two monster studios, both agreeing that Irwin Allen would produce and direct. Warner Brothers and Twentieth Century-Fox issued a statement on their temporary and historical partnership:

> It's as though General Motors and Chrysler combined their respective brainpower and manpower and went Dutch treat on the bill to produce a new model automobile.
>
> For the first time in motion picture history, two major studios have effected a union to make a single movie. The movie is Irwin Allen's production of *The Towering Inferno* and the cooperative companies are Warner Brothers and Twentieth Century-Fox.
>
> It all came about because each studio had purchased a different literary property dealing with the identical subject: to wit, a modern-day skyscraper wrapped in flames with a lot of big and little people trapped in the sky.
>
> With more than three-quarters of a million dollars invested in the

books, it only made sense that the two companies should join hands and pocketbooks and make a big thing out of what might have been two lesser ones.

Warners and Fox not only put a lot of money, excitement and "movie magic" into *The Towering Inferno,* but they amassed a collection of star actors as dazzling as their salaries.

Fox and Warner Brothers were to split the production costs right down the middle. The latter would release the picture abroad, and Fox would be entitled to the U.S. release, splitting all profits evenly.

A record-breaking fifty-seven sets had to be built, only to be burned down by the end of the shoot. One hundred stuntmen had to be hired and were to be paid five times the normal fee for performing some spectacular and oftentimes dangerous stunts.

Four different camera crews worked simultaneously over a spread of five different locations. Actual shooting of the film took only seventy days to complete.

Holding true to his new policy of not granting interviews to the press, McQueen told both studios he would not give the movie any type of publicity. Under no uncertain terms would he promote the movie. "I don't need the publicity and I don't want it," he told them.

The film got more promotion out of Steve's real-life heroism than any interview he could have given. On May 6, 1974, Steve and Ali had been going over some preliminary instruction with Los Angeles Battalion Chief Peter Lucarelli, who had been hired for *The Towering Inferno* as the technical adviser. While the three were talking, an alarm sounded and a call was taken by Lucarelli, informing him to report to a fire nearby at the Goldwyn Studios. Two stages were engulfed in flames. Lucarelli offered to take Steve along, saying, "I'll show you what it's really like to fight a fire. Maybe you can learn something."

Never one to back down from any danger, Steve took the battalion chief up on his offer. The blaze, it was learned, had started out as a freak accident. The entire cast and crew of a new children's show, *Sigmund and the Sea Monsters,* were assembled on the soundstage when suddenly a large spotlight burned and shattered. Sparks fell everywhere along the set. The fire started when it hit highly flammable polyfoam that was being used as a prop cave in the show. Suddenly, without notice, the soundstage had become covered in flames. The people on the set headed toward the exit doors. One door wouldn't open, which left only one door through which to exit. By the time all the members of the cast and crew were out, a list of casualties arrived at the hospital, the most serious one being a man in critical condition with 75 percent of his

274

body burned. Others suffered from smoke inhalation. The heat from the fire was so intense that twenty-five cars parked in the studio lot were reduced to a pile of ashes.

Next in line were the production offices. The hope was to save them from the fire.

When Lucarelli, McQueen, and MacGraw arrived at the lot, they found 200 firefighters attacking the blaze. Lucarelli immediately began gearing up in a helmet, jacket, and boots, and Steve followed suit. He gave Ali a quick kiss on the cheek and headed toward the fire. Ali warned him, "Be very careful in there."

As Lucarelli and Steve entered the building through a lower floor window, they grabbed onto a hose and began dousing the fire. A firefighter on the hose across the way glanced over at the newcomers, did a double take, and announced, "Holy shit! Steve McQueen! My wife will never believe this!" Without missing a beat, Steve said, "Neither will mine."

While Steve was inside battling the fire, outside Ali was wringing her hands. Ever the supportive wife, she said to a reporter on the scene, "He has to do his thing, I know. But, this fire! I'm really afraid for him."

An hour later, he emerged from the ruins. Red-eyed from the smoke, and a few pounds lighter from the heavy protective gear, a sweaty Steve spotted Ali. She rushed up to him and whispered, "Thank God you're all right." He grabbed her by the hand and led her to the car, where they departed the studio lot.

The estimated damage from the fire was $80 million. The publicity Steve "didn't want or need" made headlines across the country.

Not only did Steve emerge from the fire unharmed, but he came out with a newfound respect for firefighters, as only McQueen could put it: "These guys [firefighters] really hold their mud. The difference between me and them is that I'm paid millions of dollars. This poor firefighter is doing it for a few hundred and he's putting his life on the line every day."

*The Towering Inferno* gave Steve the opportunity to surpass his friendly rival, Paul Newman, in terms of stardom. It had all started in 1956 on the set of *Somebody Up There Likes Me,* when McQueen looked on from the sidelines as Newman got the star treatment. It went on from there. It was Newman who was originally sought out for the lead in *Love with the Proper Stranger.* [That next year, Newman was on top of the list for *King Rat.*] McQueen was offered the part only after Newman had turned it down. Then in 1966, it was Newman who was approached first by Robert Wise for the Jake Holman role in *The Sand Pebbles*. In McQueen's mind, he was second fiddle to Paul Newman.

When David Foster showed the *Butch Cassidy and the Sundance Kid* script to Steve, McQueen thought it would be the perfect opportunity to show the world who was the bigger star. But then Newman balked at the idea of working with Steve, possibly fearing that McQueen would be the more dominant of the two on screen.

The tide turned for Steve on *Bullitt*. With its smashing success, McQueen was more sought after than Paul Newman. McQueen held the juice. Now it was Steve whom the producers came to first. Says James Coburn, "Steve was the reason the bankers came up with the bread to fund *The Towering Inferno*. They said, 'We need that guy,' and they got him."

McQueen was originally offered the role of the architect, the one later played by Newman. Steve read the script and sensed the role of the fire chief had more of a possibility for heroic proportions. John Guillermin, director of *The Towering Inferno*, recalled, "Ernest Borgnine was originally asked to play the fire chief and McQueen was going to be the architect. The fire chief had ten pages in the first draft, but Steve had tremendous instinct for the heart of the picture. He felt the role of the architect was pasted together. Steve said, 'If somebody of my caliber can play the architect, I'll play the fire chief.' That's where the idea to cast Paul Newman came in." Once again, Steve used his old sounding board, Neile, for advice. "I'm more intrigued with the fire chief, but it's a smaller role." Neile asked him, "Is it a cameo role?" Steve answered, "No, no. But he doesn't come in till halfway through the film. What do you think about that?" Neile assured him that he'd be fine. He had always dominated the screen with his presence and, as long as his role continued to the end of the movie, the audiences would remember that.

The two separate scripts still had to be combined into one, and that task was left to veteran screenwriter Sterling Silliphant, considered by many to be the best in the business. He found out early in the production that working with McQueen wasn't going to be easy.

The original script had the architect, Newman's role, with more lines of dialogue. When McQueen decided on the role of the fire chief and knew Newman was going to play the architect, he decided to test his power. He counted up the lines for both of the characters, that of the architect and the fire chief, and noticed that Newman would have twelve more lines of dialogue than he did. Steve wanted to surpass Newman on equal terms, both having the same amount of dialogue, both having an equal amount of screen time. He put in a call to Silliphant.

McQueen found out that Silliphant was on holiday, out at sea. Steve's determination was that of a bull. He couldn't wait until Silliphant got back. He made Fox executives call the writer back to shore to write twelve additional lines of dialogue for McQueen's character to make sure both stars had the same amount of lines. No more, no less. "Sterling was very pissed about that one," chuckled an executive for Fox.

McQueen was very cautious about the words he used on film. He liked to keep it simple. He felt he had an obligation to use words like the everyday man. He knew his appeal lay in that image. Sterling Silliphant described a scene with McQueen over the use of his dialogue:* "Steve wouldn't tell me what he didn't like about certain parts of the dialogue. He just said, 'I don't like that shit.' I kept confronting him about it. I said, 'That's not shit, it happens to be very brilliant. Tell me what you don't like.' Finally, he took me out in the hall and said, 'Look, I'm not an educated guy. I was a street kid. I did time. Okay, I can't say certain things . . . certain words I can't say. I have trouble with Zs and Ss . . . honestly, the dialogue is okay. I just can't say it.' " McQueen also had a problem saying the line "There are Ping-Pong balls in the back room that are combustible." Silliphant also offered, "Steve has the nagging instinct of what is right for him based on his ability. He doesn't like long speeches. He likes them to be terse, sharp, almost proverbial."

Director John Guillermin found McQueen a "pussycat" to work with. On their first meeting, McQueen came to Guillermin with an all-consuming problem. The helmet he was to wear in the film, he felt, made him look like an English bobby. "I look like an idiot!" he told the director. The night before filming, Guillermin had dinner with a fireman who was serving as a technical adviser. He spotted an old-style fire helmet sitting on the mantle and thought it perfect for Steve. "May I borrow this helmet for the movie?" he asked. Said Guillermin, "I brought it back to Steve and he put it on and liked the look. That was the biggest thing I ever did for him and he trusted me from that point on. Filming was a piece of cake."

The problem of billing still had to be dealt with. In recent years, ever since *The Great Escape,* it was Steve who had brought in the bigger box office dollars, but Newman had been around a little bit longer. The problem was solved when Freddie Fields brought up the idea of both names on the marquee. One would be on the left, one on the right, a little higher than the name on the left. Knowing that people read from left to right, McQueen opted for the name on the left. When the movie was released, it indeed appeared that Steve McQueen was its star.

---

* Litwak, Mark, *Reel Power* (New York: William Morrow and Company, 1986), 192.

In addition to McQueen and Newman, *The Towering Inferno* cast was to include William Holden, Faye Dunaway, Fred Astaire, Susan Blakely, Richard Chamberlain, Jennifer Jones, O. J. Simpson, Robert Wagner, and Robert Vaughn.

Though not billed, actor Felton Perry, a relative newcomer to films, had a moderate-size role as a firefighter. Perry remembers being starstruck on the set: "Here were all of these stars I used to watch when I was growing up and now I'm acting with them. Jennifer Jones, William Holden, Fred Astaire, Paul Newman, and Steve McQueen, who was my idol ever since *The Great Escape.*" Perry would get a special kick whenever he passed his idol, who would greet him with a "Hiya, kid."

William Holden was particularly upset. He felt he should get top billing since he had been a star much longer than McQueen or Newman.

While on the set of *The Towering Inferno,* Holden repeatedly complained to his agent, "It's a lousy script. McQueen and Newman have all the action. I spend all of the time talking on the telephone."

Holden was also further miffed when actress Faye Dunaway made him wait two hours for a scene between the two of them. When Dunaway finally arrived, Holden took her by the shoulders and slammed her against the soundstage wall. "You do that to me once more and I'll push you through that wall."

Many wondered how McQueen and Newman would get along. "They acted like two old college buddies," notes costar Robert Vaughn. McQueen would often call Newman "Ol' Blue Eyes." He ribbed Newman: "You know, two Paul Newman autographs will get you one Steve McQueen autograph."

A constant theme in Neile's book was that Steve was in awe of Paul Newman. "That is not true," says Pat Johnson. "Steve wasn't in awe of anyone. It was Paul who was always coming over to Steve's trailer on the set. Not once did Steve go to see him." Says costar and friend Don Gordon, "I never knew Steve was in awe of Paul Newman. I think Steve liked him and admired him as an actor, as I do." Says an intimate of McQueen's, "Steve liked to give Paul a hard time. He would rag on Newman's wife [actress Joanne Woodward] because she was a real ballbuster. When Newman got in a motorcycle accident, she made him sell the bike. It was 'Paul fell off his bike and now he can't play anymore.' Steve had a good laugh over that one. McQueen did whatever, whenever he wanted."

Of all the actors he knew, McQueen was probably closest to Newman. When Paul Newman's son, Scott, overdosed on drugs a few years later, McQueen wanted to console Newman. "Something like that I can relate to, and yet the best thing I can do for Paul is just to stay away, not even mention it." Pat Johnson interjected, "Well, Steve, there are probably not too many people he can talk to about it." Steve concluded, "Yeah, well, he knows that if he ever needs me to talk about it, I'm here."

Of the rest of the cast, McQueen said of Faye Dunaway, "The best actress I've ever worked with." On Richard Chamberlain, "He was a snob." McQueen didn't dislike Chamberlain, but was always a bit put off by the rumors that surrounded Chamberlain that he was gay. On Robert Vaughn, "Ever since *Bullitt,* he was always a bit distant. I'm not sure if he's putting on airs now or what. He's not as friendly as he used to be." On Robert Wagner, "A good guy. A very good friend." On Fred Astaire, "The guy is one of the best athletes in the world."

For years, Steve had been performing a lot of his own stunts. His respect for Newman deepened even more when he discovered that Paul also performed a majority of his own stunts. Naturally, for *The Towering Inferno,* they both requested that there be no doubling for them. Producer Irwin Allen expressed his mixed emotions: "Both Steve and Paul insisted on being personally involved in scenes that placed them in the middle of the fire and the man-made flood we created in a desperate effort to put out the flames. As the action director, I was pleased by their willing cooperation. But as the producer, I was aware of the great risk and the fact that a single misstep could cause injury and shut down production if Steve or Paul became unavailable. I was very nervous until those scenes were completed."

One scene required that the fire chief, Steve, be dropped onto the roof of the skyscraper and into the middle of a lake of fire. The shot was going to be a close-up, so Steve insisted that he do the stunt. "Can't fake this one, Irwin," he said. Steve put on a flame-resistant suit and jumped fifteen feet out of a helicopter into the rooftop fire. But that was not to be his most dangerous stunt.

The climactic flood scene in the Promenade Room at the end of the picture proved to be the most dangerous. In the movie, in order to stop the blazing fire that has taken over a majority of the skyscraper, it is decided to completely deluge the building. Plastic explosives would be placed on the rooftop water storage tanks. A timer on the explosives would be triggered, causing the tanks to explode and sending the water down below to put out the fire.

Commented Irwin Allen, "Fire and water are the most unpredictable elements to work with in danger scenes. Once you let them go, they can't be recalled. And they're harder to control, too. We fired almost a million gallons of water at our performers, some of it shot from extreme heights, some of it shot from water cannons, some hurled through high-pressure fire hoses."

Adds stunt coordinator Paul Stader, "When we flooded the nightclub, we faced the problem of nobody knowing just where the water would hit. The stars in the scene would have to take the full force of the tanks themselves. Most of the stuntmen and women had to find tables or other objects to hang onto in order to keep afloat." Stader admits that *The Towering Inferno* was the toughest assignment of his career.

Felton Perry remembers getting ready for the big scene. He looked over at McQueen. "He had this certain look on his face, like he's ready for anything. He looks over at me and says, 'Let's get to it.' And then the flood was turned loose."

"Our stars did their own stunts because the cameras were directly aimed at each one. McQueen, Newman, Holden, Astaire, Felton Perry, all of them. We built our set twenty-five feet off the ground so water would have some place to go after it hit. Otherwise, they all would have faced the possibility of drowning," said Allen. "There was no chance for a second shot because the set was destroyed by the deluge. In all my years of making movies, that was the most terrifying moment I have ever faced."

No stuntmen or women were hurt or burned throughout the whole movie.

The last scene of the film finds Paul Newman and Faye Dunaway reunited as lovers on the steps of the skyscraper that had claimed so many lives. McQueen slowly walks past the hallway where his brave firefighters are lined up in body bags. He makes his way to his car, but not before spotting Newman and Dunaway. The fire chief warns the architect, "You know, they'll keep building them higher and higher. And I'll keep eatin' smoke until one of you guys asks us how to build 'em." Looking over his shoulder, viewing the smoking ruins, Newman says, "Okay, I'm asking." McQueen responds, "You know where to find me. So long, architect." McQueen gets the last word.

*The Towering Inferno* took in $55 million dollars in the U.S. alone, and over $100 million worldwide, making it then the largest grossing film of all time.

*The Towering Inferno* has only three scenes in which McQueen and Newman interact. In those scenes, never has McQueen dominated the screen with such ease. Film historian Derek Elley noted, "McQueen dominates every scene. His performance is one of the most authoritative of his career. Once again, amid a starry cast, McQueen emerges as the outsider, existing within his own set of principles and beliefs."

Newman's fears dating back to *Butch Cassidy and the Sundance Kid* had

McQueen managed to dominate every scene with friendly rival Paul Newman in *The Towering Inferno*, 1974. McQueen earned a staggering $12 million for this film, making him the world's highest paid movie star. (COURTESY OF TWENTIETH CENTURY-FOX/WARNER BROTHERS)

finally been realized. "It was strange," says James Coburn. "Newman was fearful of Steve in some way. The role of the architect was originally offered to Steve. Steve said, 'No, no. He's too vulnerable.' If you notice in the movie, it's the architect who makes the mistake and the fire chief who has the more dynamic role. He could put Newman down, which he probably loved." Said John Guillermin, "McQueen was inspired. I remember one scene in particular, where his character was talking to the fire chief and he just flopped in the corner. He said, 'My character has been fighting this fire all night and he's really tired by now.' So for that scene, he just sat in the corner and chose not to move, which gave the scene an unusual power. He had a sharp mind, he had the ability to put his finger on the very nerve of the scene—exhaustion." Newman may have had more range as an actor, but it is McQueen who emerges as the star of *The Towering Inferno*. And it is McQueen who became the undisputed king of Hollywood. He had no more worlds to conquer.

In October 1974, a fund-raiser was put together for actor James Stacy. Stacy was driving his motorcycle on Mulholland Drive when he crashed into another car. As a result of the accident, he lost an arm and a leg. He was to have been the next big movie star.

A benefit was arranged by Frank Sinatra, Sammy Davis, Jr., Liza Minnelli, and Stacy's ex-wife, actress Connie Stevens, to help pay for his medical expenses. McQueen was asked to attend the black-tie affair.

Not one to socialize with the Hollywood crowd, Steve asked Pat Johnson and his wife, along with a then unknown Chuck Norris and his wife, to attend the event with him and Ali. "Everybody who was anybody in Hollywood was there," remembers Johnson. It was a black-tie affair, but McQueen showed up in a plaid Benetton lumberjack shirt, blue jeans, boots, and a long beard.

Not once during the event did McQueen get up. Instead, everybody in the room came over to greet him like he was royalty. Says Pat Johnson, "The cream of the crop from Hollywood came over to Steve to shake his hand. Clint Eastwood, John Lennon, Burt Reynolds, Carol Burnett, all came over to the table. It was like they were paying homage to him. They were all in awe of him. He was not in awe of anybody."

And in his mind, Steve McQueen had finally made it to the top.

# . . . AND OVER THE EDGE

*People in Hollywood will hem and haw playin' all kinds of cute little games, and then you'll finally realize they want something from you. And eventually you'll have to ask, "You want something from me, don't you?"*

STEVE MCQUEEN

*My dad reached a point in his life where he asked, "Is this all there is?"*

CHAD MCQUEEN

*After* The Towering Inferno, *it was as if the effort to catch up to Paul Newman had tired him out.*

NEILE MCQUEEN

HE HAD SCALED THE HEIGHTS of superstardom and had remained there for over fifteen years. With each passing year, his popularity grew. At the age of forty-five, his star was brighter than ever. Then Steve McQueen took everyone by surprise—he dropped out of the race.

He appeared to have everything. He was Hollywood's biggest star. His wife was a beautiful and desirable woman. He had two great kids, and he was on friendly terms with his ex-wife.

Lurking behind the image of the celebrity who had everything, however, was a man in trouble. Steve had grown disillusioned—disillusioned with the movie industry, with his marriage to Ali, and with what the future held for him.

For years he had threatened to pack it all up and go far, far away. Right after *The Getaway,* he told a reporter, "I sometimes hate to go back to work. I want my life as simple as possible. I'm at an age where I'm not as ambitious as I used to be. I've been surrounded by a whirl of activity for a long time. I just want to be happy. I don't really care that

283

much. If I feel a film will have something to say, I'll do it. But now, it seems so fruitless to keep banging away."

And he made good on his promise. For two whole years, he did absolutely nothing but ride dirt bikes and drink beer. "The thing is, I've had it all; and I find that best is nothing," he said. "In the simplest form, jeans and a shirt. I can ride only one motorcycle at a time. That's my mentality. I don't get moon-sick about acting."

Chad noticed that people in general ate away at his father. "Everybody's hustling for this and that. When you reach the stardom that my dad did, everybody wants a piece of you," he pointed out. Says Phil Parslow, "More people said they were friends of Steve than you can fucking believe. Just because Steve said hello to somebody or was not rude to them, people would say, 'Yeah, my buddy Steve.' " Adds James Coburn, "Steve was pretty put off by people."

Steve withdrew from the public and retreated with Ali to their secret hiding place, Trancas Beach in Malibu. He would not be seen again on the screen for another five years.

He was a changed man. Gone was the fire in his eyes. The motivation for making movies was nonexistent. He would begin his days by gulping down a few beers and increasingly turned to marijuana. Slowly, he began to put on weight.

Years before, Steve had stated, "If they see John Milquetoast up there on the screen, John Public says 'good-bye.' "

The *National Enquirer* ran an article claiming that he had ballooned up to 240 pounds, and accompanied it with an unflattering picture. Pat Johnson maintains, "Steve never weighed over 185 pounds. I was his karate instructor. I should know. He had bad posture. He hunched over when he sat down, plus twenty extra pounds on Steve looked like a lot on him. He had a wiry frame, but he was never that fat." Friend and producer Phil Parslow agrees: "He may have been a little chunky. People had this thing where they said he was fat. Forget that. He dressed in baggy, loose clothes. The beard gave the appearance that he was heavier than he actually was."

Besides the beard, Steve grew his hair long. He systematically became unrecognizable and reveled in his newfound anonymity.

As a lark, Steve visited Bud Ekins on the set of *Dixie Dynamite*, a drive-in movie starring Christopher George. Ekins was the stunt coordinator on the film and said he could use a hand with some motorcycle stunts. Steve obliged him. When McQueen's name showed up on the pay roster (McQueen was paid $175 a week for his services), the assistant director asked Ekins, "Is this *the* Steve McQueen?" Ekins nonchalantly replied, "Yeah, he sometimes works for me."

One morning, as Steve was driving on the freeway, he noticed a Porsche broken down on the shoulder. He decided to help out and pulled over. Quickly, he got under the Porsche and went to work for over an hour. He got the car started, and the owner handed him a hundred dollar bill, but McQueen refused. The Porsche owner never realized that the man who had gotten underneath his car was multimillionaire box office champ Steve McQueen.

Close friends of the past now didn't even recognize the hermitic star. Norman Jewison recalled an incident on the MGM lot when he walked by McQueen without recognizing him. From behind him, Jewison heard someone say, "Hey, stranger, don't you say hello to your old friends anymore?" Jewison recalls looking at McQueen's face that day: "I saw these piercing blue eyes that really looked hot. Then I realized it was McQueen."

The everyday struggle of being a movie star was wearing thin on Steve. He confided to Bud Ekins, "I've had it with exercise. Why should I kill myself liftin' weights . . . screw that jazz. If I get fat, that's my business. I'm not planning on entering any beauty contests."

His health was not the only thing deteriorating. His marriage to Ali was falling apart also.

Theirs was a clash of wills. The two constantly told friends, "We're both under the sign of Aries, so we butt heads a lot."

He possessed a legendary stubbornness, while Ali had an ever-present independent streak. Steve wanted Ali to be totally submissive to his needs. "I couldn't even go to art class because Steve expected his 'old lady' to be there every night with dinner on the table," says Ali.

First wife Neile commented, "He wanted Ali there because his mother hadn't been there when he needed her."

The fights were becoming more commonplace. Ali was known to throw dishes, glasses, anything she could get her hands on at the moment. Steve was known to throw Ali.

Chad recalls an incident when he and Terry were watching television and heard Steve and Ali arguing. "Ali, you need to cool off, damn it!" they heard Steve yell. As they looked toward the window, they saw a large object fall from above and splash into the pool below. Both McQueen kids looked at each other in amazement. "What was that?" Chad asked. "I think that was Ali. Dad just threw her off the terrace!" said Terry.*

The daily struggle in living together was getting to Ali. Steve's consumption of beer and marijuana frightened her. In desperation, she

---

* McQueen Toffel, Neile, *My Husband, My Friend* (New York: Atheneum Books, 1986), 282.

turned to Pat Johnson. "Would you talk to him for me, Pat?" she asked him. "He's blowing the pot and he's drunk all the time. I don't know what to do."

Johnson obliged Ali and called Steve. "Steve, Ali is very concerned about you and what you've been doing. Look, this isn't good for you at all." McQueen was apologetic. "I know, Pat. What you're saying is right. I know what I'm doing is wrong."

To ease her torment, Ali decided to see a psychiatrist. It helped so much, in fact, that she started making daily appointments.

A friend of Ali's couldn't help but notice her demeanor. While she was out, she would now stare straight down at the sidewalk, purposely not making eye contact with anyone and hoping not to be noticed. The woman once described as "a rainbow of happiness" was now miserable.

Ryan O'Neal, Ali's famous costar in *Love Story*, noticed her once at a stoplight in Beverly Hills. He saw how angry she looked, how she gripped the steering wheel very tightly. He smiled at her and waved from the inside of his car. She looked over at him, but her attention was elsewhere. He got out of his car and walked over, tapping lightly on her window. She stared. Then it hit her. Ryan O'Neal. She pushed the button to bring down the electric window. "Hey, remember me? Ryan? We made a movie together," he teased. "Ryan, how are you?" Ali asked politely. Then she added, "I was just thinking about you. Didn't I just read something about you in *Women's Wear*?" O'Neal began to answer her when the light turned green. Ali cut him off before he could finish. "Gee, Ryan, I've got to go. It's been super seeing you again." And off she went. As her car faded from view, Ryan O'Neal was left scratching his head.

One public charade almost brought Ali to the point of leaving Steve. For her thirty-seventh birthday, Ali and a group of friends decided to celebrate at the expensive Le Bistro in Beverly Hills. All of the guests were present except for her husband. Suddenly, there was the faint roar of a motorcycle that kept getting louder and louder. Then, weaving magnificently in and around the tables, in came Steve, holding a birthday cake. "Happy birthday, baby," he said with a shit-eating grin on his face and liquor on his breath. Apparently, Ali didn't like her birthday telegram "McQueen-style" and told him then and there in front of the guests to get his act together. She said point-blank, "Either straighten up, or I'm taking Josh and we're leaving. I'm tired of living with a drunken beach bum." Steve sobered quickly and shifted gears: "I found a project I want to do. It would be the biggest risk of my life." He now had Ali's attention. "I want to do Ibsen," he went on. In bewilderment, Ali asked, "You mean you want to do a classic play by Ibsen?"

"Yeah, but not for the stage. And not just act in it, I also want to produce and direct. The whole bag. That's why I've been growing this beard—for the role." It was news to Ali.

Though Steve had considered himself retired from the movie business since *The Towering Inferno,* he still had to fulfill the First Artists contract he had signed in 1971. According to the contract, he was to deliver three pictures in five years. It was now 1976 and he had delivered only one, *The Getaway.*

Steve turned his anger toward the man who had gotten him into the First Artists deal, Freddie Fields.

McQueen conveniently forgot that it was Fields who had made Steve's comeback possible with three powerhouse movies in a row: *The Getaway, Papillon,* and *The Towering Inferno.* Says a business associate of McQueen's, "When Steve started a film, he was always negative about them. If you add up all of Steve's films that he would kill to do, there weren't many. He was always talked into something, and then he made it better. Steve's first reaction was always 'No' or 'I don't want to do it' or 'It's too much trouble.' Then a guy like Freddie Fields has to beg him and if it works, then Steve takes the credit, and if it doesn't work, then he's got somebody to blame. He always went into a movie that way."

Now that Steve had dropped out completely, he was wanted more than ever. Scripts flooded his home, so much so, that he removed the mailbox at the Trancas house and arranged for a local gas station to handle his mail.

"You've got to remember that every major script that came out of Hollywood went into Steve's hands first," says Pat Johnson. Among the scripts were *One Flew over the Cuckoo's Nest, First Blood, The Gauntlet,* and *Close Encounters of the Third Kind.*

In January 1976, Steve turned down the most ambitious piece of work to come his way in years, the lead in Francis Ford Coppola's *Apocalypse Now.* Coppola had set up a meeting with McQueen to offer him the role of Willard. McQueen liked the script but didn't like the idea of spending sixteen weeks in the Philippines shooting the movie. "I've had it with the Far East ever since Taiwan. No damn [vaccination] shots for me."

Steve came up with a plan. He simply was going to outbid himself for the role. McQueen told Coppola that he would take the $1.5 million that was offered up front. Coppola agreed. Then Steve added, "And I'll take $1.5 million deferred." Coppola countered: "There's a role that'll take three weeks of shooting, the role of Colonel Kurtz." McQueen agreed. He felt that the role of Kurtz was better suited for him, anyway. "Okay," Steve said, "but my price still stands." Coppola balked.

"What?" Steve coolly stated, "Three million for three weeks of shooting. Take it or leave it."

"I thought about that for a very long time," Coppola recalls. "On the one hand, he [McQueen] makes a valid point that his appearance in the picture has a solid commercial value regardless of the number of weeks he works. On the other hand, they all weigh how many weeks are involved and compare how much other stars are getting per week. I began to see if this kept up the industry would some day be paying three million for eight hours, plus overtime, and have to shoot at the actor's house." As an afterthought, Coppola contends, "I can't blame him for asking."

Freddie Fields had tired of being an agent and wanted to become a producer. McQueen encouraged him in this endeavor and on that note, Fields sold his company, CMA, to Marvin Josephson's International Creative Management.

In the meantime, Fields had struck a deal with Paramount Pictures, and parted amicably with McQueen. He has since gone on to produce movies for Paramount, including such classic films as *Victory* and the award-winning *Glory*.

When Josephson was handed over the business, he didn't inherit McQueen as a client; he had to earn that privilege.

Marvin Josephson is a rarity in the industry. His reputation precedes him. He is honest, straightforward, and very well read.

His clients at the time were mostly political figures, including then-President Jimmy Carter, Henry Kissinger, and Barbara Walters. Says Josephson, "Steve McQueen's name would add the top of Hollywood to my list, whereas I already had the top of New York and Washington. His name looked good for the company."

Josephson had to sell himself and his company to McQueen. He had one advantage: Bill Maher, who was McQueen's personal business manager and friend, was now working for Josephson. "As Pat Johnson was Steve's best blue-collar friend, so Bill Maher was Steve's best white-collar friend," said a close associate. Maher was single and would become Steve's drinking buddy. Though Josephson was technically Steve's agent, it was Maher who did most of the legwork in that relationship. While Josephson remained in New York, it was Maher who headed up the Los Angeles office and was the second man in charge of ICM.

A meeting was set up in Palm Springs for McQueen and Josephson. Josephson came with ammunition. Under his arm was the script of the century. At the time, ICM was representing Margaret Mitchell's estate and had agreed to allow a movie sequel to *Gone with the Wind* called *Tara:*

*The Continuation of Gone with the Wind.* Steve would be awarded the lead role, that of Rhett Butler. Adds Josephson, "I brought a nice piece of bait with me."

When Josephson met with McQueen, he was struck by many things about the actor. "For one thing," says Josephson, "you knew you were dealing with a star. He had a certain quality both on and off the screen."

McQueen tested Josephson as he had done with many others. "He tried to intimidate me several times," says Josephson. "If Steve thought he could find your weakness, you were dead with him. You couldn't have a relationship with Steve, because if he thought you were weak with him, then you were weak with other people. Steve would say to himself, 'Wait a second, this fella's going to be weak with me when he deals for me, too.'"

Maher introduced McQueen to Josephson on a busy street in Palm Springs. The three were walking down the street when McQueen announced, "Hey, I've got to take a pee." Josephson relates, "He then took his penis out and began urinating. I'm sure he was waiting for me to be shocked, but I just ignored him. That was his problem, not mine. My instinctive reaction was just to ignore him. I realized over time that this was one of his tests. Steve had a very good mind and he used that on you.

"The other thing I learned about Steve was his method of reacting to things. I came from a background where being a lawyer had trained my instincts to be part of an intellectual thinking process. One thing I learned from Steve was that there was a whole other way to react to things that was also effective to get to your objective."

In Hollywood, the industry rule is that an agent gets 10 percent from the client. In order to get McQueen, Freddie Fields broke that rule.

Fields set up a deal with McQueen that would allow Fields to collect 10 percent on the first million and 5 percent on the next. It wound up that CMA would collect 7.5 percent on Steve McQueen. Steve was accustomed to this arrangement and felt that Josephson should carry on the tradition.

Josephson told Steve sternly, "If you're going to sign with us, you must pay 10 percent." In disbelief, Steve said with a chuckle, "You must be kidding." Josephson held his ground. "No, Steve. I'm the head of the company, and I have to set an example." Says Josephson, "He did end up signing, but he didn't like it." It would be a source of friction later on when Josephson landed Steve a record-breaking $10 million for one film.

After McQueen and Josephson had finalized the deal, Steve asked him to abolish the First Artists deal.

Back in late 1971, when Steve had first joined the production company, he envisioned more control over the projects he would choose. He tested his power with *The Getaway* and was very pleased with the results, except now there was a twist.

The budget for *The Getaway* had been $3 million. Even in 1972, that was considered skimpy. Four years earlier, *Bullitt* had cost twice that amount, at $6 million.

Now it was 1976 and the budget for First Artists films was still the same, $3 million. Any film that was budgeted at that price was considered a joke, or at least a B movie, and Steve McQueen didn't make B movies.

Steve was now being pressured by the president of First Artists, Phil Feldman. Feldman told McQueen to fulfill his obligations or face a possible lawsuit.

Josephson sighs with disbelief when he remembers the scripts that passed his desk. "You wouldn't believe all the scripts that I read that are now classics. Every film that was great could have had a Steve McQueen role."

When Josephson went to meet with Feldman to persuade him to agree to let Steve film one movie outside First Artists, Feldman adamantly refused. Comments Josephson, "He was rigid. From his point of view, he was the head of a public company. Steve's commitments were very valuable commitments. It became impossible to even talk to him about allowing Steve to do some other film."

At that point, Steve took matters into his own hands. In an uncharacteristic move, he offered a compromise to Feldman. "Look, Phil, I really can't do a great picture today for three million," said Steve. "Why don't you give me the budget for two movies and I'll deliver to you a great western." Feldman agreed; two Steve McQueen pictures were better than one. But, he threatened, "If you don't deliver two pictures, there's going to be legal action."

"This is when Steve ballooned up to 185 pounds," said Pat Johnson. "It was a very low period in his life."

Steve found himself in a predicament: he was the world's number one box office attraction, yet, because of his contract with First Artists to complete two more films, he was being paid scale wages.

Josephson urged Steve to forget everything else and get on with the two films for First Artists. "Let's just get it done," he urged. But Steve McQueen was not a good loser.

A feather in McQueen's cap was that First Artists allowed him to pick any project he wanted to do as long as the other board members okayed it and he could bring it in under $3 million. There weren't too many projects like that around, and Steve realized he was in a no-win situation. But he could also be cunning. He knew that if he picked a subject so uncommercial, it would also bring down First Artists with him. So he chose Henrik Ibsen's play *An Enemy of the People,* and it was done directly out of spite.

McQueen told Pat Johnson, "I've chosen *An Enemy of the People.* It's a wonderful play, it's a great actor's part, and it's not going to make a bit of money!"

Warner Brothers head John Calley said, "McQueen was just trying to get out of his First Artists contract. For McQueen to do Ibsen was a harebrained idea. In fact, the whole deal with First Artists was not a good idea because all of the actors involved wanted to pick projects that weren't mainstream and it went against everything that made them popular."

Says Marvin Josephson, "It got to the point where this was what Steve was going to do and it just became a dare." As usual, Steve didn't back down from a fight.

*An Enemy of the People,* written in 1882, told about a poisoned spring in a small Scandinavian resort town. The spring is the town's main attraction and the main source of income for the townspeople.

Steve's character, Doctor Thomas Stockman, discovers that the spring is polluted and discloses his findings in a well-documented report to his brother. His brother, who happens to be the mayor of the town, chooses to sit on the report in order to keep the town economically sound.

Stockman then takes his report to the local newspaper, which agrees to publish it until the mayor quashes his efforts. The local townspeople learn of Stockman's plan and try to drive him and his family out of town.

As with most Ibsen plays, the story ends with a question: Should Stockman and his family quietly leave town or fight the injustices of the system and do what is right?

What started out as a slap in the face to Phil Feldman turned into a labor of love for Steve. Steve checked into several directors' backgrounds and found that one name kept coming up: George Schaefer.

Schaefer had garnered twelve Emmy Awards over the years for his *Hallmark Hall of Fame* productions. He admits to having been quite surprised by the phone call from McQueen. A meeting was agreed upon between the unlikely pair. "We met on a Sunday afternoon over at the Hamburger Hamlet in West Hollywood," recalls Schaefer. McQueen had just come back from a swap meet in Pasadena and proudly showed Schaefer a few antique auto lamps that happened to fit one of his many

George Schaefer gives direction while Steve and Phil Parslow listen.
(PHOTO BY MEL TRAXEL; COURTESY OF THE PHIL PARSLOW COLLECTION)

cars. "More importantly, he had not been recognized at the swap meet," laughs Schaefer.

The director had never been a fan of McQueen's. "I had seen him in *Junior Bonner* and a few other films and had always liked him tremendously, but he had never been particularly an actor that I wanted to work with." At the same time, Schaefer found the idea of McQueen wanting to do Ibsen intriguing. "I think Ibsen would have liked the idea," says Schaefer. "Ibsen was a very interesting man. He was an ornery cuss. He wrote *An Enemy of the People* because he was angry with the critics who had criticized his play *Ghosts*. He dealt with subjects that were simply not done on the stage. Ibsen was a loner who didn't go along with the majority. He and Steve in another time would have hit it off."

In the booth at the Hamburger Hamlet, Steve began to pitch his idea of bringing *An Enemy of the People* to the screen. "He was serious about it as a movie, not a play," says Schaefer. McQueen told Schaefer, "I really wanna do this. It's something I've gotta get out of my system and if we do it, I want you to hire the best cast in the world. I don't want you to protect me by gettin' people that I'm gonna not look so good against. It's my funeral if I can't act." It was McQueen's bravado that won over Schaefer, and it was at that moment that *An Enemy of the People* went forward.

The first thing that Schaefer did was to put in a phone call to his friend Phil Parslow.

Parslow had been an assistant director under Schaefer for the feature film *Doctors' Wives,* in 1971. He carried with him the reputation of being able to keep a tough actor in line and was fearless in his dealings with them.

Schaefer told him, "I'm going to be doing *An Enemy of the People* with Steve McQueen and I want you to be the associate producer." Parslow asked, "Where's he been for the past few years?" Schaefer answered, "Hanging out at the beach, I guess." Schaefer then said, "I want you to come in to meet him and when you do meet him, don't let him scare you. He scares the hell out of me. Come on over and see what happens."

Parslow recalls that first meeting in vivid detail. "We met at George Schaefer's office in Century City. I came in the room and saw him. I was surprised because he had this full beard, a T-shirt and blue jeans on. He was a little chunky, but not fat. I meet Steve and he's just staring at me. He then takes me over in the corner and whispers, 'I'm crazy. I'm crazy. I think we'll get along great, but just remember what I'm telling you, I'm crazy.' He used the word 'vibe' a lot. That was one of his favorite words."

McQueen and Schaefer spent the next six months preparing the script. They decided that playwright Arthur Miller should update the script and inject a more modern tone. The two also debated whether to shoot the film on location in Scandinavia or to build the sets in the studios. Eventually they decided it would be cheaper and more comfortable for everyone to use the studios. The casting of the film proved the most lengthy task.

Schaefer drew up a list of people who he felt might mesh well with McQueen personally, as well as act as a cohesive unit. All three went back and forth from Los Angeles to New York so that Steve could see each of them personally. "Finally, we got it all together," says Schaefer, "though we did run into some snags."

Veteran character actor Charles Durning won the role of Peter Stockman, the antagonist of Thomas Stockman, to be played by Steve.

The role was originally set aside for Nicol Williamson, who, Schaefer insists, "was a nightmare."

"He was going through one of his mental problems, I guess. He had

Phil Parslow and Steve McQueen on the set of *An Enemy of the People*, 1976. Autograph reads: "To quarterback Phil . . . You're almost perfect like me . . . Without a nose job. With love and respect . . . Steve."

<small>(PHOTO BY MEL TRAXEL; COURTESY OF THE PHIL PARSLOW COLLECTION)</small>

many at the time," remembers Schaefer. McQueen liked Williamson because of his more obvious heavy looks. Schaefer kept pushing Durning. "I had worked with Charlie a lot and he was a little bit more offbeat, which is what the role required," says Schaefer.

Other members of the cast were hired on after a simple meeting with Steve. A handshake, a few words, and a vibe were all that were necessary for him.

Richard Dysart, who later played Leland in *L.A. Law,* recalls his meeting with McQueen. "My getting the role all hinged on my meeting with McQueen. His acceptance. I wasn't aware of that until much later.

"I went to George Schaefer's office to talk about the part. I didn't know McQueen was going to be there. I got out of the elevator and was walking toward George's office. This guy walked right by me. He looked like a lion—very heavily bearded, jeans and an open shirt. He looked at me and nodded. I nodded back. And I kept on going to where I was supposed to go. I was talking to George and in walks this hippie that I'd seen in the hall. He comes in and sits down on George's couch and listens in on our conversation. When I get up to leave, he gets up and comes over to shake my hand. He's smiling and has this gleam in his eye because he knows that I don't recognize him. He seemed to take a great deal of pride in that. And I think I got the role because I was nice to the hippie in the hallway, not Steve McQueen the movie star."

With the casting ready to go, three weeks of rehearsals were set aside in the month of September. The first day of rehearsals, Schaefer received some bad news: Nicol Williamson was nowhere to be found. Says Schaefer, "Nicol, Steve, and I were going to discuss costume, makeup, and technique. He didn't show up and I thought maybe his plane was late. I called his agent and they started scouting around town for him. Apparently, he had some other kind of battle. He was fighting with his wife or girlfriend at the time. He arrived in town dead drunk. That afternoon, Steve was at my house and we were working and the phone rang. It was Nicol Williamson. Steve got on the other end to listen in on the conversation. Williamson began mumbling incoherently into the receiver. I got off the phone with him, made notes, and found out he was in Honolulu, where he had spent a drunken week. Steve and I gave him the heave-ho immediately."

Schaefer then put in a phone call to Charles Durning. Durning had originally been offered the part of the sea captain, but had turned it down. His eye was on the mayor, Peter Stockman. When the phone call from Schaefer came, Durning jumped at the chance to work with Steve. "He gave thrilling performances, and I admired his work and still do," says Durning.

Surprisingly, McQueen found in Durning an actor he respected tremendously as well as a new friend. Durning remembers McQueen with much admiration and affection. "I had expected something else from him," admits Durning upon meeting McQueen for the first time. "People told me he was short-tempered and had no regard for anyone. I found him to be the total opposite. I found him to be loyal to the people that he worked with, even defending them."

Durning remembers an incident when one of the actors unknowingly parked his car in a reserved spot for an MGM studio executive. The guard came into the stage area and began to berate the actor: "If you ever park there again, we'll kick you out and you'll never park on this lot." Noticing the ruckus, Steve interrupted the guard, pulled him aside, and asked, "Do you know what you're doing to this man? He's got to go inside and act. Do you know what an actor has to do to prepare himself for a role? All he brings to his job are his emotions, and you have just destroyed this man's potential to make a living today." The belligerent guard, not recognizing Steve under the beard, angrily asked, "Well, who the hell are you?" McQueen pointed to the administrative office and announced, "You go over there and ask them who I am, and if you don't know then, you're fired!"

With that, McQueen stormed off, leaving the guard in bewilderment. The guard then asked Charles Durning, "So, who was that guy?" Durning replied, "Try Steve McQueen." The guard said, "Oh my God," then asked Durning, "What can I say to him to keep my job?" Durning offered, "Look, just go up to him and say, 'Mr. McQueen, I'm sorry. I'm an asshole.'"

The guard ended up saving his job, but not without one last lashing by McQueen: "If you ever talk that way to an actor, I will personally see to it that you are walking the streets." Durning sums up, "McQueen defending the other actor showed me what kind of man he was."

A friendship blossomed between the two men. "He was really child-like in a lot of ways," Durning recalls. "He liked to have me come up and watch him perform karate. He'd say excitedly, 'Come upstairs and see this.'" Durning was invited to several outings with Steve and Ali. "We went to jazz concerts at the Hollywood Bowl. I was really surprised he was into such things."

Durning saw in McQueen a unique movie star, someone who was really down to earth. Says Durning, "I felt no competition around him whatsoever. We rehearsed for three weeks before shooting. At the beginning of the first week, he was asking, 'Do we really have to rehearse this? Let's just do it.' After the second week he asked, 'Are we only gonna have one more week of rehearsal?'"

Before the rehearsals began, Steve issued a statement to the press: "We don't have an auto chase to sell in this one. What we do have is dignity and truth. If the people who see it leave the theater enriched, they're going to tell their friends and an audience will be created." It was wishful thinking on Steve's part, but George Schaefer was more realistic. "I think that Steve thought the movie would do business on his name alone, though I knew full well this movie was never going to do anything. I would joke to my cinematographer, 'This is the most expensive educational film of all time.'"

The first day of rehearsals, Steve gathered the cast around him and told them, "This is your world, not mine. I'm a little out of my depth here, but I can promise you I'll give the best I have in me. If I fail, I won't blame anybody. The fault will be mine." The cast couldn't help but be endeared to him.

Acting in the past few years had failed to interest him. Now, *An Enemy of the People* had excited him again. He was so moved one day that he said to Charles Durning, "For the first time in my life, I really feel like

I'm acting." Steve told George Schaefer, "You know, this really is the most exciting business in the world."

As the third week of rehearsals ended, McQueen felt that he identified more than ever with Stockman. Both men tried to take on the establishment and change it, too. He also felt that the play's message was timely. *"An Enemy of the People* has meaning to me," he said. "It reads like it was written yesterday. I've seen a change in our society over the years. People aren't straight—very rarely are they straight in business. I wanted to do something that was pure."

When Steve accepted a role, he transformed himself into that character. "Steve really did believe he was Doctor Stockman," says George Schaefer. "Both men were naive in a sense and bullheaded as can be." For the role, McQueen not only grew the beard, but donned a pair of granny-style glasses to give himself a more scholarly look. He even wanted to wear a pillow around his midsection to add extra weight. Schaefer discouraged him, since the camera would add ten pounds to his appearance.

By the time rehearsals ended, the cast could run through the entire play nonstop. "We could have put it on the stage if we had really wanted to," says Schaefer.

Before actual shooting began, Steve decided he wanted to commit himself totally to *An Enemy of the People.* Coincidentally, his Trancas beach house was in dire need of remodeling, and he decided he would stay at the Beverly Wilshire Hotel during the week and spend the weekends with Ali in Malibu.

In Ali's book, she states, "After we divorced, I was told by more than one friend who stayed at the hotel that Steve's room, right next to the pool, was the scene of a constant parade of models and starlets. Sensing that, I never set foot in that hotel apartment."*

Responds Phil Parslow, "That's not true. Warren Beatty had a suite down the hall from Steve, so that's where all the models and starlets could have come from. You have to understand that at the time, the Beverly Wilshire was a hangout for starlets, models, and anybody else looking for Steve McQueen, Warren Beatty, or whomever. The El Padrino room was the 'in place' to table hop. A lot of business was conducted there and it was the showbiz place to be.

"Steve was a morning person. He ran out of gas early at night and would go to bed around 8 P.M. He wanted a place in town to get away from everybody. He really was a loner. He wasn't as intimate as people would have you believe," says Parslow.

---

* MacGraw, Ali, *Moving Pictures* (New York: Bantam Books, 1991), 112.

When shooting began on September 7, 1976, Steve told Schaefer and Parslow, "George, Phil, get me in the morning or you're dead with me after lunch."

McQueen's takes were scheduled in the morning, when he was at his best. "Come the afternoon, though," says Parslow, "he couldn't remember his head." Marijuana was the major reason.

"If I were ever to do a movie with Steve again, I would schedule another week to compensate for Steve's work habits," says Schaefer. "I got irritated with him late in the day because he would smoke pot, which everybody knew, and then he would be on the telephone. Sam Peckinpah would be calling him from Paris, and we'd be raring to work on the set and end up waiting twenty minutes for him. He would sneak in and never apologize; but what the hell, it was his own money and his own company."

The first week of shooting, McQueen put Schaefer to the test. Steve was worried about a complicated scene and wanted to discuss the day's shooting schedule with Schaefer and the cinematographer, a breach of etiquette. Schaefer adamantly refused McQueen's request. Says Schaefer, "Steve was worried that I didn't know what I was doing, which is actually pretty silly. I had done two hundred odd shows at that point, and I knew exactly what I was doing."

Steve pouted for a few hours before coming back to Schaefer. He finally said to the director, "Well, you know, you don't know how to deal with a big star." Schaefer replied, "Oh, Steve, come off it now. I usually deal with real big stars." Schaefer then began to name thirty of the world's best actors. "And they're not petty." That ended the conversation, and Schaefer was never bothered again for the rest of the filming.

Steve was a stranger in a strange world. He was out of place and was terrified. But the rest of the cast admired his courage. Noticed actor Eric Christmas, "Mind you, he had done some stage work early in his career. Now, all of a sudden, he was surrounded by people whose experience had been on the stage. Ninety-five percent of that cast came from a stage background. 'Respectful' is the word I'm looking for. He was quiet at first, but he was respectful of the kind of people he was around and of the material itself."

"Actors in general were his kind of people," says Pat Johnson. "As long as they were the type of people that he thought that actors should be, someone who respected his craft, who really worked hard at it. He was very conscious of the work of his peers." McQueen in particular liked the work of Clint Eastwood. "Now, here's a guy who knows how to make a good movie," he said. He also liked Burt Reynolds, who, he

298

thought, "really has fun at his craft." Pat Johnson also remembers that *New York, New York* was filming right next door at the same time as *An Enemy of the People*. McQueen summoned Johnson over to his trailer. "C'mon next door with me," he said to Johnson. "I want you to meet somebody who is going to be a really terrific actor someday." Steve introduced Johnson to actor Robert De Niro. "That was the only time Steve ever went to somebody else's trailer," Johnson remembers. "Steve was encouraging him and said a lot of nice things to him and it was like the old star saying nice things to the new star. Steve really liked him."

McQueen may have been in the theatrical world, in a sense, but since this was a film, the two worlds met at times. McQueen's ability to catch the audience's eye was half technique. Actor Richard Dysart remembers, "There was a reaction scene where the two of us were supposed to stand and talk. He watched the setup of the scene and the rehearsal. He was not in the reaction scene. He asked George to hold on a minute for his shot and he disappeared for a few minutes. He came up to me with this handkerchief and he said, 'Here, take this. You've got to put some movement in this scene. Make believe you've got a cold.' He gave me something to do so that each time the film was edited, there would be something there for the audience to watch. There would be some movement in the scene instead of two people just talking. That was very helpful because it taught me a bit of film technique. To this day, I still have the handkerchief."

Dysart also remembers having a beer with McQueen in his trailer. Says Dysart, "I was in my hippie phase then, with long hair and a beard, and I'd wear sandals." McQueen joked, "You know, Richard, there's only one thing wrong with your image. You drive a Volvo. You'd look good in a truck." Laughs Dysart, "He didn't think I looked proper in a family station wagon."

Charles Durning found working with McQueen an exhilarating experience. "The better you were, the more he applauded you," says Durning. McQueen would stand on the sidelines as Durning would say his lines. McQueen would encourage, "Give it more, Charlie. Give it more. Do more there, Charlie, go ahead." After the scene, Steve pulled Durning aside to say, "I don't know when you're going to do it or how you're going to do it, but someday you're going to break through." McQueen's prediction came true eventually. Charles Durning has become one of Hollywood's great character actors, costarring in such films as *Tootsie, The Best Little Whorehouse in Texas,* and *The Sting*.

Acting in films itself is a selfish profession. On the stage, the goal of the production company is the play itself. There is only one star, and that is the play.

In theory, the film is the star, but that is not always the case. It is usually the person who gets the most camera time, the most lines, who ends up the star. That results in millions of dollars if the right person ends up the star.

Steve was fed up with that system. He found that working on *An Enemy of the People,* the cast, the crew, the company, all were a total pleasure. He confided to Durning, "I thought about giving up on acting for good, because I'm tired of so-called actors trying to steal the scene all the time when it didn't belong to them. I'm so happy to be working with real actors. From now on, those are the types of projects I'm going to be working on." And Steve kept true to his word, as his last two films, *Tom Horn* and *The Hunter,* were "companylike" films.

If Steve's experience on the set of *An Enemy of the People* was happy, his personal life was just the opposite. He truly loved Ali MacGraw, yet he could not bring himself to stop being unfaithful to her. He confessed to George Schaefer, "For one year, I didn't look at another woman, one whole year." Says Schaefer, "He was crazy about Ali. I think he played around a lot. Ali couldn't take that."

Actor Yaphet Kotto remembers bumping into Steve at the Broad Beach market in Trancas. Steve did not like Kotto for some reason. He had snubbed him in New York in the fifties and on the set of *The Thomas Crown Affair,* in which Kotto had a bit part. Kotto decided to let bygones be bygones. "Hey, Steve, how ya doing?" he called out. McQueen walked past him as if he weren't there. "That does it," thought Kotto. Once and for all, he was going to tell McQueen what he thought of him. He followed McQueen outside to the parking lot. "Hey, McQueen, what happened to all of that money your mama gave you for charm school lessons?" Kotto taunted. McQueen kept his eyes to the ground, jumped on his motorcycle, and got the hell out of Dodge. "There was a lady on the back of the motorcycle with him," revealed Kotto. "And it wasn't Ali."

"There were too many women available to him," says Phil Parslow. "I would be talking to him and he's telling me of his devotion for Ali and I believed it. He really meant it, how terrific a wife she was. Then all of a sudden, any good-looking female would walk by, probably for a reading, and he says, 'Whoa, did you see that gal that just walked by?' Then he'd leave the room, chase the girl down, put his arm around her, and I wouldn't see him for the next two or three hours. That was him. It didn't mean that he didn't love Ali. It didn't mean that he was terrible to her. The other brain clicked in. He never flaunted to anyone who he was. He had the natural charisma, charming as hell, and treated women very well. He was like a snake, but he would never push himself on anybody."

Pat Johnson explains, "Up until the day he died, Ali MacGraw was the love of his life. He took that love for her to the grave. What you have to understand is that Steve was the most virile man on earth. Every time you looked around, there was another lady throwing her body at him. In all of the years that I knew him, he never went out specifically with the idea of 'I'm gonna go find me a woman tonight.' He loved Ali very much. She was all the woman he needed."

MacGraw didn't necessarily think so. "Steve's idea of hot was not me," she claimed years later. "He liked blonde bimbos, and they were always around."

McQueen was smart enough to realize that it was the image of a movie star they wanted, not Steve McQueen the human being. "It's not me they're doing this to," said Steve. "I could have scabs all over my face and be filthy dirty, but because I'm Steve McQueen they want to jump all over me."

Says Phil Parslow, "Steve had this ability to walk into a room and light it up. Women loved him. They dangerously loved to cuddle. People talk about how Steve went after women. What about the women who went after Steve? He would come into an office and a secretary would be sitting there and say, 'Can I fix you some coffee, Mr. McQueen?' and he'd say, 'No, I'll get it and what would you like in yours?' He'd fix her coffee and then sit on her desk and she would just eat it up."

Pat Johnson remembers an incident during this time when he, Steve, and one of Johnson's karate students, Larry Spira, had lunch after a karate session. Spira was a doctor and Johnson felt that he and McQueen were the right sparring partners since they had been involved in the sport the same amount of time. "There was this gorgeous, gorgeous young lady sitting at this counter eating. She was a knockout. This gal was a ten!" says Johnson. "So Larry is checking her out and says, 'Man, McQueen, if I were you, I would be all over her in an instant.' Steve says, 'Okay, Larry, since you like her so much, I'll fix her up with you.' Steve then calls the waitress over and says, 'Would you please send that young lady over there a drink and tell her it's from this table.' The waitress did that and the girl turned around and looked at the table. She recognized Steve and was immediately overwhelmed. It turns out that she was also an aspiring actress. Larry and I were sitting on one side of the booth and Steve was sitting alone on the other. She saddled up right next to Steve. She turned her back to Larry and me and started talking to Steve. Steve says to her, 'I would like you to meet my friends, Larry and Pat.' She looked over her shoulder real quick and said, 'Hi,' and continued talking to Steve, totally ignoring both of us. Then Steve started talking about Ali. He said, 'You know, Ali and I have been having such a good time together. We're going to do a film together.' He kept talking about Ali to let her know that he didn't want anything to do with her, that he had called her over for Larry. Now Larry took a hundred dollar bill out of his pocket and licked it and stuck it to his forehead. This gal never even looked at Larry or the hundred dollar bill or anything else for that matter. She was totally transfixed on Steve.

"So, women were always available to him whenever he wanted them. It was inevitable that at some point along the way, there was going to be a night when Ali was away or they would have an argument. A woman's going to take a shot at Steve, and he's going to be in the right frame of mind and that's it. It was always understated, but rather overtly understated."

Robert Relyea remembers a phone call one night during Steve's stay at the Beverly Wilshire. The two had not spoken to each other since *Le Mans*. "He called me up and acted as if no time had passed whatsoever," says Relyea. McQueen told Relyea, "I'm staying over at the Beverly Wilshire. Why don't you drop by for a visit." As an afterthought, he added, "I'm not havin' any trouble with my old lady." Relyea thought it odd that Steve would say that since he had thought nothing of it.

When Steve greeted Relyea at the door, Relyea thought he looked like Smokey the Bear. McQueen wanted to talk about the past. "We kept walking around the block, just talking about the people we had worked with. It was probably a bad time in his life, and he thought he'd call to reminisce about 'the good ol' days.' It was kind of like a high school reunion. You're nice to the guy you used to play ball with, but not too close.

"I would say that he was lonely. It was a desire to get some identity with those days. He was so happy at the height of Solar. He had a funny habit; he'd rub his hands together and stick his tongue out. He did that the first thing in the morning and you'd better be on your skates, because he was so full of piss and vinegar, going ninety miles an hour. He had a lot of those days back then. If I had to guess, he was missing those extremely happy days. He was so happy back then he couldn't see straight.

"I hear that his relationship with First Artists wasn't to his liking. Knowing him, he'd make a picture just to make a point," said Relyea. "Whatever possessed him to do Ibsen I don't know. He wouldn't have done it unless he thought he could make a good picture out of it, but at the same time, I could tell he was unhappy." That was the last time Robert Relyea would see his old friend and one-time business partner.

Nikita Knatz also paid McQueen a visit. "He was a very bitter man then. He realized that he had made a mistake. Neile was truly his backbone. Remember, she brought him to Hollywood. She brought him to William Morris. She got him the series. Neile was the most instrumental factor in his life. He admitted his suffering to me. He was crushed. He was depressed. He was destroyed. He was drinking, eating, overindulging in everything. He was not a happy camper," remembers Knatz.

A flare-up did occur toward the end of filming. Steve had been out the night before and had come in to work without having memorized his lines. He had a lot of dialogue to remember and had even hired a script supervisor to help out. "I've never seen George Schaefer get that mad with anyone," says Phil Parslow. "But George was redder than a beet." Schaefer exploded at McQueen, "Damn it, Steve, learn your lines. Come prepared." Steve had never had any director talk to him that way, not even the crusty Sam Peckinpah. Says Parslow, "George's yelling at Steve shocked him. Steve asked me, 'What's wrong with George? What did I do?' I said, 'He wants you to learn your lines, Steve.'"

The time had come for Steve to perform his big speech. Steve never liked a lot of dialogue. He was a reactor, and his reactions on screen could cancel out pages of dialogue. When Chuck Norris brought Steve to a screening of his first film, McQueen gave him some friendly advice: "You are verbally acting out what we have seen visually on the screen. Let your character actors fill in the plot, and when you have something pertinent to say, then you say it. Audiences will remember what you say. Memorable lines are what you need."

Now Steve was doing just the opposite. His monologue was more than three pages long. It was to be his longest in film, and it was to be shot in the afternoon. Phil Parslow was worried. Then Steve delivered the speech perfectly, line for line. Says Parslow, "He came through with bells on and he was terrific. He did a fantastic job. I know how hard that was, because when he had more than three lines to remember, it was just tough."

The cast of *An Enemy of the People* felt a great sadness when the time came to part ways. McQueen felt such a tremendous bond that he and Ali hosted a wrap party in a posh restaurant in Malibu.

Charles Durning remembers that it was the last time he saw Steve. "Steve said to me, 'Keep in touch, because we'd really like to see you again.'" Durning didn't know how to take Steve's comment. Says Durning, "What happens in Hollywood is that everyone says that, and, unfortunately, you don't know when they mean it or don't mean it."

Phil Parslow remembers a sad moment at that wrap party. Everyone in the cast was dressed to the hilt, with the exception of Steve. McQueen wore a corduroy jacket with patches on the elbows and black denim pants. As he hunched forward to talk to someone across the table, Ali leaned back to speak to Phil Parslow. What Ali said threw him: "Can you believe I gave up a mansion to ride on the back of a motorcycle with this guy?" Parslow offered, "You must really love him, Ali." She replied gently, "Yeah, I do."

One bright spot for Steve during this period came when stuntman Loren Janes headed up a campaign to make McQueen an honorary member of the Stuntmen's Association of Motion Pictures in recognition of Steve's desire to perform his own stunts. "It's a special honor given to an actor who supports stuntmen, and Steve loved stuntmen," says Janes. "On the whole," says Phil Parslow, "stunt guys were really fond of Steve. Steve liked to hang out with physical people."

McQueen was so taken by the gesture that he showed up in person to receive the award. At the ceremony, he said, "Thanks. This means more to me than any Academy Award."

There was still much post-production work to be done to make *An Enemy of the People* presentable. Parslow recalls that the editing process was a nightmare. "We had to put in a whole different shade of background color," he says. "Some of Steve's scenes had to be reedited because he would warble when he talked."

When the final version was ready to be screened, Arthur Miller wanted to see how his adaptation had been interpreted. "George Schaefer was out of town and Steve was scared to death to see Miller's reaction, so it was left to me to screen it for him," says Parslow.

Miller brought his son with him to the Warner Brothers screening room and was quiet throughout the whole movie. When it was over, he stood up, turned to Parslow, and announced, "That was done as well as it could have been done."

When post-production was finished, the studio faced an even bigger problem: how to market the film. It eventually spent more than $400,000 alone in the ad campaign.

Eighteen months after principal photography, Warner Brothers began to test the film on college campuses, hoping to draw a more liberal-thinking audience who were also McQueen fans. Parslow tested the film in an art house in San Francisco. "Warner Brothers made more of an effort to market the film than they would like you to believe. The chairman of the board, Frank Wells, and several top executives flew in for

304

the showing. That should tell you something. I don't know of any chairman of the board who ever went to a sneak preview before." Of the audience reaction, Parslow says, "People didn't know what to make of it. Warner Brothers spent hours in campaign testing. How do you tell people that Steve McQueen is not in an action-adventure film? The perception of the title is that Steve McQueen is playing a gangster. People go in with that perception and there's a riot."

The studio then tried another approach. The new ad had a photo of a bearded McQueen, surrounded by shots of him taken from classic films of the past. The copy read:

In a time when people say there are no more heroes—there is still STEVE McQUEEN. You cheered for him in *The Great Escape,* prayed for him in *Cincinnati Kid* and held your breath with him in *Bullitt . . .*

Now Steve McQueen portrays the most striking hero of them all— the man they called . . . *AN ENEMY OF THE PEOPLE.*

That didn't work either.

McQueen realized that he would have to go out there and sell the picture to the public. On October 13, 1978, he made a rare live appearance with film critic Charles Champlin at the film school at Loyola Marymount and presented a lecture on "The Genius of Ibsen."

Steve told the students, "McQueen doing *Ibsen* is like making a purse out of a sow's ear, let's face it. There's all sorts of courage, I suppose. I spent a great deal of my life being a coward and spent a lot of that time trying to overcome that influence. *Ibsen* showed the courage in the common man; that's why I did the film.

"I thought people in white-collar positions would come and see this film. I counted on the educational system here, but I was surprised; hardly anyone knew who Ibsen was. The average man comes down and wants to see Archie Bunker. We want our own American heroes."

The critics savaged the film, based mostly on the bad prepublicity created by Warner Brothers. Phil Feldman refused to talk about the project, citing, "I'm not going to say anything. I won't talk about *An Enemy of the People.*"

Another Warner Brothers executive was even harsher. "It's an embarrassment, a piece of junk," he was quoted as saying. "Who wants to see McQueen running around with a beard and weighing 210 pounds?"

Michael Sragow of the *Los Angeles Herald-Examiner* wrote, "Think of Clark Gable as the tragic 'Parnell,' or Gregory Peck playing Ahab as if he were Abraham Lincoln. Recall Elizabeth Taylor as the Cleopatra of

Great Neck. Then add to this list of big-star follies the typically lean, tight-lipped action hero Steve McQueen. Here he's plump, bearded, and avuncular, a bit like Kris Kringle. For McQueen to play Ibsen's volatile, idealistic intellectual Dr. Stockman is as unusual as it would be for Dr. Carl Sagan to try and play Darth Vader."

Arthur Knight of *The Hollywood Reporter* wrote, "It's a handsomely photographed, solid-looking movie, but it has no juice to it, no life to it at all. There's no way for that picture to make contact with a modern audience. McQueen has no understanding of the play, and it took me twenty minutes to recognize him under all those whiskers."

One lone voice in the wilderness who praised Steve's courage was wife Ali MacGraw, who said, "Steve's brilliant in it. He made me cry. The truth is that behind his tough-guy image he's the most sensitive man I know. I'm very proud of him. But I've tried to tell him that the garage mechanics and electricians won't go to see the movie. And I've also tried to tell him it won't matter, that they'll all go to see the next Steve McQueen spear or gun picture."

Actor Clint Eastwood was so impressed by McQueen's courage that he told Steve, "You have the guts and the courage that I don't. I would love to be able to leave a classic behind, but I can't."

The other cast members of *An Enemy of the People* were not surprised by the reaction of the press. Actor Eric Christmas offers, "The thing you have to realize is that one of the big differences between theater and the movies is that you go to the theater to listen to something. You go to a movie to be visually entertained. The movie public is out of practice in listening. This was the challenge to the audience. When you get a fine piece of theater, that's far more important than a performance. That's what McQueen realized: that the play and the questions raised by the play were far more important than any reviews."

Scared of the harsh reviews, Warner Brothers decided the film could not make any money. They pulled the film from distribution. It was the only McQueen film to never be officially released. *An Enemy of the People* was the most notoriously shelved film of the decade.

Steve's initial reason for making the film was to spite Phil Feldman. Nevertheless, he became more involved in this one film than in any other of his movies. He told writer William Nolan, "Funny, the things that can hurt you the most. When I talk about hurt, I don't mean broken bones. What happened with *An Enemy of the People* hurt me more than almost anything I can remember. I put my heart and guts into that film. When it got the reaction it did, I was wiped out. I never expected it to be a blockbuster hit, that's for sure. But when most of the critics dumped on it, and Warners refused to put up the distribution money . . . well, that was just hard to take."*

Years later, actor Richard Dysart remembers a phone call from a friend who told him that *An Enemy of the People* was showing at a nearby second-rate movie house at an odd hour. Dysart remembers, "The theater was packed, and that was rather odd, because it was showing at a strange time. The quality of the print was terrible, it was just filthy. The audience response to the film was very receptive."

A few months after Steve died, the Ibsen Society requested a print of the film from George Schaefer. Schaefer found the "snooty crowd in New York" very receptive to the film. Remembers Schaefer, "I was trembling, because I thought they might light into it. On the contrary, they were impressed with the performances, and the look and the wardrobe and the whole flavor of it. I think we did all we could with it, considering the budget we had. I think Steve accomplished what he wanted to. It got some nice reactions, and I think it's right for cable and it's right for study."

Thus ended the McQueen-Schaefer relationship. Schaefer's thoughts about Steve remain happy: "Steve could make really good jokes. He had a good deadpan sense of humor. He would love to go to a restaurant and say to me, 'I wonder how long it will take for them to recognize me?' He had a lovely laugh and a playful attitude. He enjoyed life and lived it fully."

With *An Enemy of the People* out of the way, Steve still had one more picture to deliver to First Artists to fulfill his contract. That was the last of his worries, as his marriage to Ali MacGraw was eroding quickly.

Steve still kept his Beverly Wilshire suite. He needed a place where he could keep a safe distance from the world, including Ali. It seemed he could buy anything he wanted, except happiness.

Phil Parslow remembers visiting McQueen at the Beverly Wilshire. "We were going to talk about a possible project out at the pool. I go out to the pool and there's this guy, pasty looking, no suntan; his face was bearded, kind of grungy looking. He looked like a bum. He was sitting back, drinking an Old Milwaukee beer. He looked back, looked around, and said to me, 'This is what it's all about, Phil. The suite, the pool, the Beverly Wilshire. This is what it's all about.' He said it and I never saw him out there again. He was so out of place. He was all alone. It was bizarre. He didn't belong there. He didn't look right there. He looked right on a motorcycle. He looked right in a pickup truck, but there he looked wrong. I'm looking at him and I'm looking at what he's saying

---

* Nolan, William, *McQueen* (New York: Congdon & Weed, 1984), 183.

and thinking, 'How wrong he is.' I think he wanted me to say, 'You're right, Steve,' but I didn't. He was way out of place there.''

Steve still had to deal with Phil Feldman. The idea of doing the Harold Pinter play *Old Times* was brought before the board at First Artists. McQueen would costar with Audrey Hepburn and "The Great Lady" Faye Dunaway, with George Schaefer directing. First Artists' and Feldman's thinking was that it was bad enough that McQueen had done *Ibsen,* but Pinter would have been too far out. It was shot down.

McQueen subsequently sued First Artists for $50,000 to recoup the money already put into pre-production by Solar. The suit was settled when First Artists agreed to give the rights to Solar and make the film elsewhere, but McQueen still had to deliver a film.

Steve had hoped to fulfill his commitment with *Nothing in Common,* a screenplay by Tony Bill about a kidnapper who holds a child for ransom, then develops a relationship with the child. Says Parslow, "Everything fell together. Steve thought it was a great part with commercial appeal. We were charged to do it." A meeting was called with Frank Wells, then the chairman of the board at Warner Brothers, along with vice-chairman John Calley and Tony Bill. Present were Steve's business manager, Bill Maher, and Phil Parslow. The idea was pitched to Wells and Calley, who would push Phil Feldman to do the project because of its commercial viability. Feldman would also be told the picture would be brought in under budget. "Everyone in the room was stoked. It was a film that could have been done quickly, it could have been great fun. It was just a great project and a solution to a big problem," says Parslow. After listening to Wells and Calley's presentation, Feldman politely told them, "First Artists is not interested in this project at this time." The project was killed in one day.

Steve was crushed. Phil Parslow comments, "There was something wrong at First Artists. The place Warner Brothers could hurt you was on money. The place Phil Feldman could hurt you was on script approval. First Artists had the right to kill any project. Because Warners stepped on Phil Feldman's toes, the filmmaking conglomerate said no. Warners couldn't do anything. It was kind of the cart telling the horse what to do."

Enraged, McQueen called Feldman to set up another meeting with him, this time alone. A 10:00 A.M. meeting was confirmed. Steve arrived on time but was told to wait in the lobby. Twenty minutes passed and still Steve waited. "You had one of Hollywood's biggest film stars waiting outside," says Phil Parslow. "Feldman is basically working for Steve. The secretary didn't even bother to say, 'Mr. Feldman, Mr. McQueen is still waiting for you.' Steve went berserk and burst into his office. He found Feldman sitting in the office alone, just going about his business. Incidentally, Steve used to ride a bicycle on the lot when he got restless and would ride to relieve the tension. That's when I said we had to move to MGM. Feldman's going to walk on the grounds and Steve's going to run over him on his bicycle and we'll have a lawsuit."

Around this time, the *Sacramento Bee* received a letter from an anonymous person (later to be captured by the FBI) threatening to kill President Jimmy Carter, as well as several political figures and television personalities. Once again, Steve McQueen's name was on a death list. In a letter dated June 8, 1977, the would-be assassin wrote to the *Bee:*

This letter that has been written is to tell the people of the United States, that if the following people are not released, the following people will be murdered.

(The following people to be released)
(3 names deleted)

The following people to be killed if the re are not released.

Jimmy Carter. Walter Mondale. Cyrus Vance. Cecil Andrus. Andrew Young. Bob Bergland. Harold Brown. Michael Blumenthal. James Schlesinger. Charles Schultze. Jerry Brown. Farrah Fawcett Majors. Lee Majors. Jackie Kennedy. Jaclyn Smith. Kate Jackson. Robert Blake. Henry Winkler. Lindsay Wagner. Raquel Welch. Ann-Margaret. Angie Dickinson. Sally Field. Lynda Carter. Marie Osmond. *Steve Mc-Queen.* Burt Reynolds. Charles Bronson. Brigitte Bardot. Donny Osmond.

If the people of America don't want any of these people dead, then you better carry out the demands.

The man who wrote the letter had been so bold as to include his return address on the envelope and was apprehended shortly thereafter. It was the last known death threat that Steve received.

Back home in Trancas, Ali was approached by cinematographer Lucien Ballard, on behalf of Sam Peckinpah, to star in his latest film, *Convoy.*

For years, Ali had cleaned the house, prepared dinner, and raised Steve's son, Chad, along with her son, Joshua. Says Ali, "I didn't even go to art class because Steve expected his 'old lady' to be there every night with dinner on the table." Ali had grown tired of her "old lady" status. She needed a change of pace. She wanted to get back into movies.

Steve had promised for quite some time to look into a movie project for the two of them. *Fancy Hardware* was a project that friend and producer David Foster had developed before Steve started filming *An Enemy of the People*. Foster still shakes his head to this day over the wonderful script that could have been a classic film.

"*Fancy Hardware* was one of the best scripts I've ever worked on in my life," says Foster. It was the story of a pre–World War II pilot who flies across Texas selling "fancy hardware"—bathroom fixtures, nozzles, etc. Relates Foster, "He's a Romeo, a meets 'em-beds 'em-leaves 'em scoundrel. Finally, he meets this really nice girl [to be played by Ali] who is pretty and smart. He falls for her and she falls for him. She's a thirty-year-old spinster, which was unusual for the time. So these two people come together. He's going to take her to bed, then leave her, but he falls in love instead."

It would have been made under the First Artists banner. But, according to Foster, "Steve pulled out at the eleventh hour."

While in the middle of the project, Foster got an early morning phone call one day. It was Steve calling to say that he had turned the script over to his First Artists partner, Barbra Streisand, who loved it. It was out of McQueen's hands. "What do you mean?" Foster screamed into the receiver. He went on, "I am out after putting all of that time and effort and you didn't protect me? You never even said, 'David Foster comes in as the producer?' Do you realize that you just fucked your friend over? That's my thanks for all the hard work?"

McQueen was taken aback. He didn't realize that in optioning the rights to Streisand, he was also giving up Foster's role as producer. Years later, defends his old pal, "I don't think Steve realized what he did. Yeah, I was really pissed back then, but I also realize Steve did a lot for me. He helped me build my public relations business. He would go around telling people, 'You gotta sign with Foster. He's the best publicity guy around.' He got me tons of clients and I'm grateful for that. And *The Getaway* made me a lot of money, and I was still appreciative. But Steve's last act was a beauty; you just can't understand what that did to me.

"I think the bottom line was that he didn't want Ali to work. He met her on our film and took her away from somebody. He was concerned the same thing might happen to him. She finally put her foot down and did *Convoy*. That was the beginning of the end for them."

When *Fancy Hardware* fell through, Ali began to sense that Steve wasn't looking too hard. When Peckinpah came calling, Ali packed her bags. Says Pat Johnson, "Steve, feeling a great deal of resentment toward Phil Feldman, felt so much distress during this period. He needed her. He really needed her to be with him, to comfort him. It was probably the lowest period of his life."

Ali claims that Steve gave her an ultimatum: if she went off to New Mexico to make *Convoy*, he would file for divorce.

Pat Johnson defends Steve. "That is absolutely not true," he maintains. Johnson found out years later that William Friedkin, director of *The French Connection* and *The Exorcist*, had called Steve and asked him to star in *The Sorcerer*. McQueen had always wanted to work with Friedkin, then the biggest action director of the time. He agreed to do the film with one exception: there had to be a part for Ali. The script did not call for a female lead and a role would have to be written for her. Friedkin said no. Steve then asked Friedkin to make the movie in the United States so that he could be closer to Ali. "Steve, it has to be done in South America," was Friedkin's reply. In desperation, Steve asked that if he were to go to South America, could Ali be an associate producer? Anything to be near Ali. Friedkin again denied McQueen. Steve bowed out. Friedkin admits, "At that time, I had just won a couple of Academy Awards and I figured I could do it all. I was really stupid. I figured I could make the movie a success with or without Steve McQueen. That was one of the biggest mistakes of my life. I should have done anything Steve asked of me to get him in that movie. The fact is, if I would have given Ali a job, Steve would have done the film." Ali MacGraw never knew.

"Basically, Steve loved Ali so much that he wanted her to be with him wherever he went. He did not want her to go away to do *Convoy* and be away from his side. He had given up *The Sorcerer* for her and thought it only appropriate for her not to do *Convoy*," says Johnson.

Ali left for New Mexico in a huff without Steve. Then McQueen placed a phone call to Sam Peckinpah. "What the hell do you think you're doing, Sam, asking my wife to do a movie?" he yelled. Peckinpah held his ground. "Steve, she's the main ingredient that will make this film legitimate." Replied McQueen, "Yeah, well, you're disrupting my home life." Peckinpah was silent. They ended the phone conversation on hard feelings. "Steve was very pissed at Sam. Sam was as hardheaded and strong-willed as Steve was," says Johnson.

Steve suspected Ali was having an affair. He spent many nights phoning her hotel room at 2:00 A.M. and she wasn't answering. In desperation, he told Pat Johnson of his suspicions. Johnson replied, "We don't know that for sure, Steve." McQueen said, "Well, without knowing, we know." Johnson had to remind Steve of his ongoing affair with model

Barbara Minty. "I can never feel the same again," said Steve. "You just have to work it out," said Johnson. "I don't think I can," he replied.

Steve made one last-ditch effort, McQueen-style, to save the marriage. He and Joshua caught a flight to New Mexico. As a romantic gesture, he handed Ali an empty beer can filled with daisies.

Stuntman Gary Combs remembers being in the hotel lobby when a long-haired hippie sporting wire-rimmed glasses and a raggedy jacket walked in. "I was thinking, 'Who's this hippie-looking bimbo looking at?' Then he turns to me and says, 'I want to thank you for looking out for Ali.' And it was McQueen."

Combs was doubling for Kris Kristofferson and had spent many hours sitting and chatting with Ali. He sensed that the actress was glad to be working again, but also noticed that she wasn't totally happy. "If she'd been truly happy where she was, she would have stayed home and been the mother of the kids, but something didn't quite click. That's what I pulled out of the conversations with her."

In New Mexico, Steve had to play second fiddle to his wife, the actress. He felt like a third wheel on the set while Ali was busy making the movie. Says Pat Johnson, "It was her show. She was the star and he felt funny, as if he were keeping an eye on her because of her alleged affair. I'm sure it was the biggest single factor in his decision to divorce her." Adds Bobby Visciglia, "Steve was completely in the background. He didn't appreciate the role he had to play." Says Carole James, "Ali was a prisoner in that relationship and wanted to stretch. She wanted their marriage to work, but she also wanted to work."

Carole James felt genuinely sorry for McQueen. Most of his days consisted of lying by the pool, dragging a Radio Flyer wagon filled with ice and Old Milwaukee beer. One day, while Ali was filming, Steve asked Carole to go for a walk. McQueen couldn't fathom the idea of her marriage to her husband, Kent, and how the two could work together during the day and go home together at night. "Steve was very old-fashioned. His ideal was for Ali to be barefoot and pregnant. He couldn't understand the concept that our marriage was based on a mutual respect for each other, that we were best friends as well as lovers. He couldn't grasp that idea."

Steve's instincts regarding Ali's alleged affair on the set of *Convoy* proved correct when MacGraw later admitted her one-and-only affair during her marriage to Steve.* "The truth was that I had had a kind of druggy affair periodically during that movie," she revealed in her book, "but as it was now common knowledge that Steve had been living a

---

* MacGraw, Ali, *Moving Pictures* (New York: Bantam Books, 1991), 116.

flagrantly free life for some months, I thought that if I did not go into my own escapade, the whole mess of our lives might blow over and offer us a fresh start."

Carole James makes it clear that Ali MacGraw is not a vindictive person. "She kept the affair quiet. She would not embarrass Steve. If she had an affair, she kept it completely undercover."

Steve had practically helped raise Ali's son, Joshua. Joshua had been a part of the McQueen household since the age of one, and the boy considered Steve his father. "He used to look up at me with this little smile and this need for a father," Steve told Phil Parslow. Says Parslow, "Steve felt that Joshua was fragile and really thought that Steve was his dad. And Steve really worried about him." It was Joshua that Steve was most concerned about when he decided to file for divorce. Pat Johnson remembers: "The thought of deserting, and those were Steve's words, 'deserting Joshua,' was just too much. He cried literally, bawled on my shoulder. I think he was reminded of his father abandoning him and now he was abandoning Joshua."

The abandonment of Joshua, Ali's affair, their impending divorce, the failure of *An Enemy of the People,* and the First Artists obligation, all would drive Steve over the edge.

# BARBARA MINTY

*Barbara Minty is better looking than Neile and Ali put together on their best day. She is perfect.*

PHIL PARSLOW

IF THERE WAS ONE incident from which Steve could have spared Ali any pain in their marriage, it was how Ali found out about his affair with Barbara Minty.

Phil Parslow recalls a luncheon that was set up at the El Padrino room with Steve, director John Frankenheimer, his producer, Bob Rosen, and business manager Bill Maher. Frankenheimer wanted to discuss a possible project on the Flying Tigers of World War II called *Tiger Ten*. McQueen wasn't interested in working with Frankenheimer at the time because he had no desire to film overseas. But, as a favor to the director, he agreed to let it be known through the trade papers that he was interested in the project so that funding would be easier to obtain.

A few minutes into the meeting, a phone was brought over to their table. It was Nina Blanchard, Barbara Minty's agent, calling for Steve. Blanchard told McQueen that Barbara was in Fort Lauderdale and *The National Enquirer* was outside her hotel room ready to expose to the world that she was Steve McQueen's mistress.

Steve excused himself, grabbed the phone, and dragged it across the room. The men at the table could hear him mutter, "Oh shit. Oh shit." Relates Parslow: "Steve is standing up, pacing back and forth, whipping the phone cord over people's heads while they're trying to eat.

"Meanwhile, John Frankenheimer is very nervous. He's all dressed up, looking sharp, wearing a blazer, and Steve is throwing the phone up and down the room and so on. He was trying to sell this idea to Steve and he didn't know what was going on."

*The National Enquirer* ran the story that week, and that's how Ali

314

learned about it. Soon after, Steve had Barbara move into the beach house. Ali, in one last desperate attempt to save their marriage, called Steve. His parting words pierced her heart: "I am not in love with you anymore. I love you, but I am not in love."

In November 1977, Ali was informed by Steve's lawyers that he was filing for divorce. Years later, Ali summed up, "At the end it was very, very painful, a sad disintegration. There were wonderful things about him. But we pushed every dreadful button in each other that could be pushed. We couldn't just let the other one be, not trying to change each other." When Steve later married Barbara, he told Bud Ekins, "I never should have married Ali. Should have just let it be." Steve confused many intimates, though. Many of them agree that Ali MacGraw was the love of his life and that he messed up when he divorced her. Says Phil Parslow, "If he could have had Barbara Minty stashed away in a motel and have Ali in the kitchen, he would have been delighted."

How Steve met Barbara Minty is unclear. Many versions of their meeting abound.

Loren Janes believes that Steve was on a plane flipping through a magazine when he spotted Minty's picture. McQueen also noticed that the picture was taken by a photographer he knew. When he arrived in California, he put in a call to the photographer and asked if he knew the model. "Yeah, Barbara Minty. I know her very well," said the photographer. Steve wasted no time: "Well, give me her phone number. I want to meet her." He then called Minty. "Hi, this is Steve McQueen," he said. "I hope you don't mind me calling you." He was met with stony silence. After a pause, Minty replied, "Yeah, sure. Who is this really?" Steve chuckled, "No, this really is Steve McQueen and I got your number from this photographer." Minty then hung up. Steve called her back and again Minty hung up. Steve had an idea. He would call the photographer and have him confirm that indeed it was Steve McQueen calling for her. The photographer then placed the call to Minty. "It really is Steve McQueen," he told her. Minty was dumbfounded. "She had always had a crush on him," says Janes. "He was her favorite star since she was a kid. She thought she would never meet him. That's why she didn't believe it was Steve. That's how they met. That's what he told me on the set of *The Hunter* in Chicago."

Pat Johnson was told by Steve that the two had met in Ketchum, Idaho, where Steve was having a log cabin built for him, coincidentally, right next to Minty's property. Steve would pass by her every day on his motorcycle. One day he asked her if she would like to go for a ride. Says Johnson, "She never wore a bra and she was nicely endowed. She was holding on to him, clinging to him on the motorcycle with her breasts

McQueen attends the premiere of *Tom Horn* with third wife, ex-model Barbara Minty. She was nearly half his age, 1980. (COURTESY OF ASSOCIATED PRESS)

pressed against his back. He said to me, 'At that point, I knew this was the woman for me.' "

Phil Parslow heard it from Steve's business manager, Bill Maher, directly: "She was Warren Beatty's girlfriend. Steve stole her away from him." That made sense to Parslow, as Beatty had a suite down the hall from Steve during his tenure at the Beverly Wilshire hotel. "Beatty was competitive with Steve," says Parslow. "I think Steve thought Beatty was pompous, but I don't think Steve ever disliked him. Warren was white collar and limousines and Steve was blue collar and motorcycles and they competed for women. Steve would usually win most of the time because he had that charisma. I mean, if you think you're a great lover, like Beatty does, and somebody takes your girlfriend away, you're stunned. Do you think Bob Evans was happy when Steve took away Ali? Steve was notorious for this." It also made sense to Parslow, recalling an incident when McQueen and Beatty got on the same elevator at the Beverly Wilshire. Beatty didn't acknowledge him, so Steve stood behind him, put his thumbs in his ears, and stuck out his tongue. Steve's childish behavior in the elevator was almost enough to make Parslow burst out laughing. "What you have to understand is that Steve had a lot of respect for Warren even though they were complete opposites," Parslow explains. "Steve respected the fact that Beatty grabbed a hold of *Bonnie and Clyde* when it was sinking in the mud and made himself the producer and made that picture work. He just loved to kid Beatty.

Warren had to leave his office at Warner Brothers because his deal with them expired. We did have a deal and when we moved over there, Warners asked Beatty to leave. Steve thought that was fantastic. The fact that Beatty had to leave his office made it even sweeter for Steve. He pushed even harder to get the office when he found out it was Warren's. Steve loved doing things like that to other actors."

The darkest version of how McQueen and Minty met comes from Ali MacGraw herself. She believes that Steve held a phony audition for a fictitious movie in his suite at the Beverly Wilshire.

Many people believe that it was Barbara Minty who helped Steve through his toughest time. Steve went so far as to say, "She saved my life."

With Barbara Minty, Steve wanted a fresh start. He made a vow to stop smoking and lose weight. To accomplish that, he enrolled in the world-famous Chic Center in Los Angeles under Pat Johnson's name and began to drop the extra pounds that he had been carrying around for the past few years. He was ready to begin work again.

Immediately after the fiasco of *An Enemy of the People*, Steve wanted to prove to the world he was still the biggest movie star. He told his agent, Marvin Josephson, "Let's make it really big. It's gotta knock their socks off. I want a contract that will guarantee headlines."

Josephson came through with flying colors, landing Steve the biggest contract in Hollywood history.

Swiss producer Georges-Alain Vuille approached Josephson for Steve to star in James Clavell's *Tai-Pan*. The deal was set when both parties agreed that McQueen would receive $1 million up front just for signing the contract, with deferred payments of $9 million plus 15 percent of the movie's gross after the break-even point. In all, McQueen was guaranteed a whopping $10 million. Vuille said to the press, "McQueen is worth more than any actor in the world. We're delighted to have him as our star."

When Josephson brought the contract for McQueen to sign, Steve balked. "You do know that your commission for this picture is a million dollars?" Steve asked. Josephson nodded yes. "Well, I have to tell you, Marvin, I think that's too high." Josephson was dumbfounded. He had just gotten McQueen the biggest movie deal in history and McQueen was griping about the commission. Josephson politely told Steve, "You wouldn't be saying that if I hadn't gotten you this incredible deal." McQueen then tried a new approach: "Marvin, I thought you were my friend." Josephson stated, "Steve, I do think we're friends. If you're defining friendship as I should take 5 percent, if that's your notion of friendship, I don't think one has anything to do with the other." Mc-

Queen then replied, "You understand that I'm going to pay you, but then I'm not going to use you as my agent anymore." True to his word, Steve left Josephson but came back three months later. Says Josephson, "I think he found out he wasn't going to read all of those scripts that I was reading for him or field all of those phone calls. Steve was not someone you could get to read a script easily. If they sent it to him, then it could possibly sit for three months and they knew that Steve would eventually send it back to me." (The *Tai-Pan* deal fell through when producer Georges-Alain Vuille was late with the second of ten payments. McQueen's contract stated that if any payment were late, the contract was null and void. McQueen walked away from the deal, and pocketed a cool million for doing absolutely nothing.)

While Josephson was working on the *Tai-Pan* deal, a compromise was reached with First Artists. Instead of pursuing the lawsuit over *Old Times*, McQueen and First Artists agreed on the western *Tom Horn*. Said McQueen of the agreement, "I've always wanted to do Horn's story; now it's just a matter of doing it a little sooner than I expected."

*Tom Horn* is the story of a turn-of-the century cowboy who was out of sync with his time. Horn had lived many lives. In his time, he was a teamster for the Santa Fe Railroad, a rodeo champion, a deputy marshal, a Pinkerton detective, and a cavalry scout. His greatest feat was tracking down the elusive and powerful Apache chief Geronimo and personally arranging his ultimate surrender to government troops. After the capture of Geronimo, Horn was one of President Teddy Roosevelt's prestigious Rough Riders in the Spanish-American War. Horn then worked his own silver mine and when that didn't pan out, he made his way to Wyoming, where he was a hired gun for a cattlemen's association.

The film covers the last three years of Horn's life, when he wanders into a small Wyoming town. There he is commissioned a "stock detective" and is hired by the town's powerful businessmen to rid the area of all cattle rustlers by any means. When Horn does the job too well (killing the rustlers in plain sight), he is framed for murder by the same men who had hired him. To be linked with Horn could hurt their political intentions, so they had to wash their hands of him.

Either too proud or too ignorant to defend himself, Horn is sentenced to hang. Since none of the law enforcement people are willing to pull the lever, a Rube Goldberg contraption is designed. The device is set up so that Horn's weight on the gallows is offset by pails of water that start a chain reaction, eventually setting off a spring that releases the trapdoor. In essence, Tom Horn hangs himself.

The very same day that McQueen announced to the press that he was going to do *Tom Horn*, Robert Redford announced that his company, Wildwood Productions, was going to do a film based on the life of *Tom Horn*.

Robert Redford had always been a bit of a thorn in McQueen's side ever since *Butch Cassidy and the Sundance Kid*. It was Redford who eventually landed the role that Steve had expected. It was Redford who was given the Golden Globe Award that was meant for Steve for *Papillon*. It was also Redford who received the same offers that Steve did, only after Steve had turned them down. In 1977, director Richard Attenborough wanted Steve to play the part of an American combat soldier in his debut film, *A Bridge Too Far*. It was a cameo appearance and Steve wanted $3 million for it. The film's producer, Joe Levine, felt that the price was too high and went to Robert Redford instead, who took the role. Phil Parslow notes, "Redford was intimidated by McQueen. I think McQueen was a lot of things Redford never was or never will be. The problem with Redford was that his public image was better than Steve's, that he's a super guy and McQueen is this wild guy. He's just another actor. Redford's concern with McQueen was that he wasn't as good. He got a lot of scripts that Steve wouldn't do. The chain in Hollywood was, 'If you can't get McQueen or Newman to do it, see if you can get Redford.' Now, Clint Eastwood and Charles Bronson accepted their roles in this progression. It didn't bother them, but it bothered Redford, even though a lot of times he benefited."

Steve joked to friends, "Every time I look in the rearview mirror, I see Bob Redford." McQueen was so tired of hearing Ali coo about how wonderful Redford was, he started a rumor that caught on like wildfire in Hollywood. After getting an earful from Ali about Redford, Steve walked into Bud Ekins motorcycle shop one day, where Ekins and his friends happened to be talking about Redford as well. Steve interrupted the conversation and said, "Aw, you know what I heard? I heard a real nasty rumor that Redford has a really small dick. His nickname is Needle-dick." The group there responded, "Really?" McQueen went on, "Yeah, it's true. I don't know how he could please a woman. I don't know why a woman would see anything in him if the guy's got a needle-dick."

Two weeks later, when Steve came home from the set, Ali excitedly met him at the door with the day's hottest bit of gossip. Ali offered, "Guess what I heard about Redford? He has a small dick and he's nicknamed Needle-dick." McQueen fell to the floor laughing and after catching his breath confessed that he had started the malicious rumor.

Now again, Redford and McQueen were in competition. The Solar and Wildwood offices were on the same lot, just down the hallway from each other at Warners. Quietly, Redford and Wildwood dropped out, but that was not a surprise to Steve. McQueen predicted confidently, "Redford won't take me on."

Of all the characters that Steve had portrayed in his career, it was Tom Horn whom he identified with most. Says Phil Parslow, "Tom Horn was a hero. Time had passed him by. The Indians were gone, the West was gone. He was born on the cusp. He started young and had outlived his time. In my mind, there's a lot of Tom Horn/Steve McQueen similarities. They both even died at fifty."

Steve went so far as to spend a night at the gravesite of Tom Horn. It was there that he claims to have had a visitation with the ghost of Tom Horn. "I could feel him under there. It was like he said to me, 'Please do my story. Please tell my story.'"

Director of photography John Alonzo remembers a party at lawyer John Mason's house at which he ran into McQueen. Not since *The Magnificent Seven* had they seen each other. Alonzo was pleasantly surprised when Steve remembered him. The two chatted amicably and a few weeks later McQueen called Alonzo and summoned him to the Beverly Wilshire. There he asked Alonzo to help him with *Tom Horn*. "He really had a passion for that film," remembers Alonzo. "He really wanted to do it. He told me, 'I have a feeling that I'm very well connected to this piece. I really feel this is my destiny to tell the true story of Tom Horn.' On *The Magnificent Seven* he was a young and energetic star with a big ego, emotional about his position in the picture and jealous of Yul Brynner's fame. On *Tom Horn*, he was a very passionate man. He changed in the sense that he was more concerned for the other guy as opposed to himself."

With the experience at Tom Horn's gravesite, Steve now had the motivation to see him through the film. It would take three years to complete *Tom Horn*.

Producer Phil Parslow spent over eighteen months preparing for shooting. The first thing he had to do was to get a script sized down to a presentable screen time. Remembers Parslow, "The pain and suffering I went through on *Tom Horn* was the most I had ever gone through on a film. We started thinking it was going to be a $10 million epic, and it ended up being a $3 million TV movie. It went from an awesome concept to a so-so movie."

William Goldman, who had won an Oscar for his screenplay of *Butch Cassidy and the Sundance Kid*, had turned in a draft to Robert Redford, and McQueen got a hold of it. McQueen thought it mediocre and turned his attention to a grand epic by Tom McGuane, but that script was 450 pages long. An average script was only 100 to 110 pages long.

The script had to be scaled down before it could be considered seriously, though McQueen loved the dialogue.

The first director slated for *Tom Horn* was old friend Don Siegel. Siegel had directed McQueen in *Hell Is for Heroes* and had gone on to become one of the biggest directors in Hollywood, with such films as *Dirty Harry* and *Escape from Alcatraz*. McQueen said of Siegel, "He's one of the people I wouldn't mind being in the trenches with."

Steve had a problem articulating the story he wanted to tell with *Tom Horn*. He knew in his mind what he wanted but found it hard to explain it to anyone else. Phil Parslow was one of the few people with whom Steve could let down his guard and not be ashamed of his lack of education. Parslow explains, "Steve was semiliterate. He wasn't that educated. I had to read everything for him and told him what I read. He would say, 'Phil, read that and tell me what it really says.' He was a little bit lazy. He didn't like to read. He couldn't sit still. He had the concentration of an ant, and I'm giving the ant the benefit of the doubt."

In meetings with Warner Brothers executives, McQueen would always have Parslow seated so that he could see Parslow's eyes while others in the room couldn't. If Steve got off track, Parslow would shake his head no. If Steve were on the right track, Parslow would nod.

Siegel pulled Parslow aside one day and said, "I don't know what this man wants to do. I come in every day, he rambles on and on. I just don't understand him. I'm an old man, not in the greatest of health, and I don't think I can help him. I don't think we'll be able to come to some conclusion of what he wants. One day it's this, one day it's that." Simply, Steve drove Siegel away. When Siegel asked Steve a simple question, he responded with several answers. Siegel was the first of four directors to leave *Tom Horn*.

Next was Elliot Silverstein. Silverstein was a well-respected director whose westerns, *Cat Ballou* and *A Man Called Horse*, had become instant classics. He was a cerebral man, very much the opposite of McQueen.

Silverstein brought in writer Abe Polonsky, and together they developed the idea of a relationship between Tom Horn and Geronimo. Silverstein employed a professional historian to open up reports that had been sealed for over a hundred years. Says Silverstein, "The documents substantiated that these were two men of a dying era who were reluctant to see it end."

Steve's first conversation with Silverstein occurred when McQueen interrupted a phone call that Silverstein was having with a single attractive woman. Silverstein told McQueen, "I've got a lady on the other line. Can you hold for a minute?" Then Silverstein kept McQueen waiting for a few minutes while he finished his other conversation. Mc-

Queen got a kick out of the fact that the director kept one of the world's biggest movie stars on hold while he finished talking. Steve told Phil Parslow, "He had me waiting while he was talking to a girl. I think this is going to work out." Silverstein observes, "He had a great affinity for coolness and strength. I was constantly told by those who worked for him that you must never show any sign of weakness on any level to him. Courtesy was a sign of weakness. He had a very strongly defined code of masculinity."

Again, McQueen's inability to communicate caused problems. Says Silverstein, "It was kind of difficult to tell what Steve wanted, because he used to speak with a predicate or a direct object, but never both in the same sentence. His speech was like rapid fire, almost like a Gatling gun, but it was difficult to tell what he meant. Even his closest people couldn't tell what he was saying."

Silverstein and Polonsky's script, along with McGuane's, would have had McQueen sharing the film with a strong version of Geronimo, which is something that intimidated him. Says Silverstein, "Steve wanted to make more of an action-oriented piece, much more physical. I was not overwhelmed with that idea because it seemed to me to be very familiar stuff. He wanted a shoot 'em up star vehicle, but that's what I anticipated with the turnout." Phil Parslow claims that the Silverstein/Polonsky/McGuane version would have been an instant classic and that Steve was very shortsighted. "Steve had one meeting with Elliot and because the guy didn't sparkle, he was ready to dump him," he says. "The competition to hire Elliot was enormous. Steve wanted him because of his credentials. Elliot has a tendency to overstate, and Steve didn't understand him."

Silverstein bowed out because he could see that the relationship was not going to be productive. His concept and Steve's concept of *Tom Horn* were completely opposite. He left the project and says now, "Steve was very gracious about that, I must say." Director number two had come and gone.

Writer Bud Shrake submitted the third and final script that was to be used in the telling of *Tom Horn*.

In actuality, when filming began, both McGuane's and Shrake's scripts were combined for the final version. Cinematographer John Alonzo remembers, "Steve had both scripts in his hands when we were shooting. He would look at certain parts of both and decide which version we were going to shoot."

Back on the lot at Warner Brothers, Phil Parslow remembers a particularly good day both he and Steve had while putting things together for *Tom Horn*. It was the end of the day when Steve cracked open some beers and the two of them began a two-hour conversation that Parslow will never forget. "It was one of those impromptu things that you can't stage or don't know why they happen but they just do. Steve extolled his insecurities to me that he had spent his life trying to disprove. I don't want to use the word 'macho' because he didn't use it. He'd done a lot of reckless things, a lot of preplanned things, and he had spent his life trying to create an image that he was a man's man. He was envious of me in a positive way, because I did it without any effort. He felt I had my act together and he didn't and couldn't figure out why."

A common bond Parslow and McQueen shared was a horrible upbringing. Says Parslow, "I was abused more than Roseanne Arnold. My father had eight children and couldn't afford one. We were abused as children terribly."

Parslow excelled at sports, and he decided that would be his ticket out. "I had something most white men don't have, speed. I'm very fast. You can't have the fastest man on the team sitting on the bench. My father was a potential world-class sprinter, and that's the only thing he ever gave me."

Parslow eventually became a starter on the UCLA football squad. On the side, he also worked as an extra in films. He took a liking to the film business but set his sights on professional football. Parslow was picked by the world-champion Baltimore Colts in the 1959 draft. "They were the wrong team. They didn't need anybody," says Parslow. "I wanted to be drafted by a team who needed me and where I could play." Parslow was soon cut by the Colts and switched over to the new American Football League (then considered second rate to the National Football League). It was there that he sustained a career-ending injury and was told he was through. Parslow still had his hand in Hollywood doing extra work and performing some stunts. In 1965, along with a thousand other people, he took the test for the Director's Training Program. Only twelve people were picked, and Parslow was one of them. He was the first of the twelve to graduate from the program and has remained in the business ever since.

McQueen was amazed that Parslow seemed unscathed by his childhood. While Steve could never let go, Parslow had become a master at blocking out his past. Parslow had to explain to Steve, "I have just as many insecurities as you do about many things. There are things that make me insecure, but the one thing that doesn't make me insecure is who I am. I have a place on this planet."

Steve confided to Parslow, "I've done all these things to prove that I'm something special, but I'm not sure I've really proven anything—at least, not to myself."

Parslow walked away that night feeling sorry for McQueen. "It was hard for me, because Steve was forty-eight and was terribly, terribly insecure about his life at that stage, yet he was so successful. The conversation was an eye-opener for me, because I didn't realize that Steve hadn't come to terms with himself, even at that age. He knew all the good things, the wife, the kids, the success, but he had a self-destruct button within. I never let my background influence what I did, whereas Steve definitely let his influence him."

It had been over eighteen months since McQueen and First Artists had come to an agreement on *Tom Horn*. With four scripts to choose from and two directors having left, the pressure to get the project off the ground was mounting. In addition, at the outset, Steve believed that the studio was going to sink $10 million into the picture. Because of Warner's dislike for Phil Feldman, however, the budget was cut to a paltry $6 million. Parslow wanted Steve to fight for *Tom Horn* and make it into an epic film. At that point, Steve was too tired to fight any longer. He wanted First Artists out of his life and was prepared to do anything, including compromising his power, something he had never done before. Says Parslow, "Regarding First Artists, Steve didn't realize the power he had in this town. He should have walked in and said, 'Fuck all of you guys,' and just given them his commands. Warner Brothers bent over backwards to try and please Steve, thinking that down the road maybe Steve would remember their generosity and do another picture for them. Warner Brothers hated dealing with First Artists so much. Warners for the longest time was going with the $10 million version, but I think they just wanted it over with with First Artists. You have to remember that Warners was dealing with First Artists on other projects with other actors. So it wasn't just the headache of Phil Feldman and Steve McQueen, it was Warners having the headache of Phil Feldman with four or five other actors. You put all of that together and they couldn't wait to get rid of all of First Artists' commitments with them. Steve was running up a tab with writers and directors, and he could never deliver a story. Warners could easily see the $10 million turning into $15 million, and that's when the project came to a halt and they decided the budget was going to be set at $6 million. I think our friendship started waning when Steve realized my disappointment that he wasn't going to fight for *Tom Horn*. He was looking at me and I was looking at him. He could see in my eyes that I was looking at him as if he were some wimp. He knew I was really angry about it. He was tired and he didn't want to fight it, and I knew that we should have."

Warner Brothers brought in producer Fred Weintraub to get *Tom Horn* off the ground. Phil Parslow would be moved to executive producer. Weintraub told Parslow that he was brought in to get the job done. He also told Parslow that there was no way the film was going to be a $10 million project and that it wasn't going to be the movie that Steve wanted to make. "My God is the dollar," Weintraub told Parslow. "I'll never forget that as long as I live," says Parslow. "That's what basically drove me away from the project. I'm supposed to work with this guy? He basically said to me, 'I'm a paid whore.' I liked him because he was candid, he did not try to shit me. He never told me he was the boss, but he was the boss of mining the money. Steve told me he was the boss over him. Basically, Steve said he'd thrown in the towel when Weintraub came on board."

Parslow was told he could sit in an office and be paid as the executive producer. "Stupidly, I signed a release and walked away. I mean, I was done. If I had to do it over again, I would sit in an office for eight or nine months and be paid the balance that was owed. At the time, I was too principled. Today, I wouldn't have done what I did. It was dumb. Remember, I worked eighteen hard months to make a decent film and then to have it go down the toilet. I had Abe Polonsky, Tom McGuane, Elliot Silverstein, and Don Siegel. We had good directors, good writers, and it was going to be a hell of a project. You go from the class of the town to rock bottom shit! That's where the picture went. There was so much good material on *Tom Horn*. It should have been a major miniseries. *Tom Horn* should have been *Lonesome Dove*.

"In essence, Steve let me down and I had to go. They weren't going to fire me, so I had to take myself out of the picture, and that's what I did. I wish to God that I had been in Steve's life ten years earlier as opposed to the end of his life. It would have been better for the both of us. There was a stretch of three years where he didn't work, and in our business, that's a major crime to stop working when you're forty-five. A major blunder on his part.

"I've worked with over three hundred celebrities, and Steve was by far the most interesting. He was so unpredictable. Most of the actors, after working with them two or three weeks, I had them figured out. I had Steve figured out, but I didn't know what he was going to do. I knew how to get him mad and how to bring out the best in him, but I didn't know what he was going to do tomorrow. Most actors are moody—nice one day, nasty the next. Steve was the same all the time. Steve learned the word 'petulant,' which I am. I sulk when I get mad. I don't want to say anything that I might regret later, so I sulk. He would call and say, 'You're sulking, and you're being petulant,' and he was right. And it would make me laugh. How can you get mad at someone who calls you the next day to tell you he's sorry? To this day, I won't let anybody talk down Steve. I just will not do that."

Moneywise, Fred Weintraub's reputation in the business was immaculate. He had the ability to come into a project and shape it and bring it close to budget. He also happened to be the first person to give Pat Johnson a job in the film industry. Johnson told McQueen, "If you want someone who's going to get the show done and will not stroke your ego, is no bullshit, and will tell you exactly how things are, Fred is the guy. He's the most honest guy I've ever worked with."

Weintraub was invited to the Trancas Beach house where he found pages of the script all over the floor, even tacked to the walls. Weintraub told McQueen, "I can help you on this, but I have to be able to have a much freer hand than you're willing to give." The two shook hands and a new producer was in charge.

Steve and Barbara decided to visit Ketchum, Idaho, for a little working vacation. Steve felt he could concentrate better in the isolation of his cabin. Sometime on that trip, James William Guercio, former manager of the rock group Chicago, showed up on their doorstep. Guercio wanted to be a Hollywood director and actually sold Steve on the idea of letting him direct *Tom Horn*. Says Fred Weintraub, "Guercio came along and hung out on his porch. Guercio was completely unproven. He just did a number on Steve. I had checked on his only picture credit, and his cameraman and first assistant director had told me they had practically done the film (the feature film *Electra Glide in Blue*). I told Steve in front of Guercio, 'I'm completely against this man directing the film. He doesn't understand the movie business.' But Steve wanted it and I gotta say, Steve was the gorilla."

When Weintraub checked up on McQueen and Guercio, they had chiseled out a 237-page script. A two-hour film usually ran about 110 pages. Weintraub knew that the only way to finish the film was to cut out the entire first scene, that of a touching farewell between Tom Horn and Geronimo. In the scene, Geronimo and other Apaches, who have been captured by Horn, are boarding a train to be shipped off. Horn shakes Geronimo's hand and says, "I hope we can still be friends." The scene would have required many extras, resulting in one very expensive shoot. Weintraub told Steve, "I gotta be honest with you, you've got to take out the first scene, which I love, but we simply don't have the money. This is not an epic film." On the set, McQueen was still reeling from the possibility of the poignant exchange. "Damn, I wish we had more money to shoot this film," he was overheard saying.

While Barbara was away on a modeling assignment, Steve visited Neile in Las Vegas, where she was appearing in a production of *Can-*

*Can.* Neile recalls, "Steve had this big beard and extra weight. He looked like an old bag man. He asked me to pick him up at a nondescript hotel. The last time we made love was in that seedy hotel. We had a pact. We'd always love each other, but it wasn't the passionate thing we once had—it was our friendship that mattered." As for Barbara Minty and Ali MacGraw, Steve was an equal opportunity cheater. At one time or another, he managed to cheat on all three of his wives.

Weintraub still had to face the biggest problem of the film: getting Steve to shave off his beard. McQueen had decided that he would play Horn with a beard. Weintraub pleaded, "Steve, you have a million-dollar face and no one will know it's you." Weintraub temporarily came to an agreement with McQueen. If Steve would trim the beard, it could stay. Steve happily reported to Weintraub after his trim. "How does it look?" he asked. "Terrible," said the producer.

The day before filming was to begin, stuntman Gary Combs showed up in town. He had heard that Steve was going to sport a beard for this one, so he reported to work with a beard as well. That very day, a fan walked up to Combs in front of Steve and asked for Combs's autograph, thinking it was McQueen. Combs happily signed, chuckling after the fan left. Steve reported the next day for *Tom Horn* without whiskers.

Phil Parslow believes that McQueen didn't want to shave off the beard for another reason: his age was starting to show.

Parslow remembers a Monday night football game between the Rams and the Bears. It was Joe Namath's last appearance with the Rams, and publicist had Warren Cowan invited several Hollywood names to watch the game at his house. Paul Newman, Gene Kelly, Martin Ritt, Carl Foreman, Jeff Wald, and Dick Martin were all going to be there. It was Cowan's dream one day to represent both Steve McQueen and Paul Newman. He had represented Steve at one time, but McQueen fired him for no reason. After years of trying to lure him back, Cowan had finally done it. Cowan now wanted his two prized clients together in his home. He put in a phone call to Phil Parslow. "Phil, you've got to get Steve there," pleaded Cowan. "I know he always double-crosses me, but make sure he gets there tonight. It would really be special." Parslow called Steve and relayed the message. "What time does he want us there?" Steve asked. "The game starts at 6:00 P.M.," he was told. "Tell Cowan we'll be there at 7:00." Parslow told him at that hour, it would already be half time. Steve replied, "I don't care. I don't want to get there early. I want to slip in late." Parslow reveals, "He didn't want to be upstaged by anyone, but he also didn't want to be conspicuous. He was shy in his own way, especially knowing that the high rollers were going to be there." McQueen and Parslow followed each other to Cowan's home and outside the house, Steve pulled Parslow aside. "If I say anything wrong, don't let me go on. Don't let me say anything stupid." Says Parslow, "He had no real knowledge of sports. He might have watched football a few times, but he had no real knowledge of the game." The front door was open and as the two men approached it, Steve pushed Parslow in front of him to enter first.

Parslow describes the scene: "We go in and Warren Cowan is behind the bar about to make a big greeting and Steve holds out his hand and says, 'Don't get up.' Then he ambles his way over to the bar and lets the other people in the room approach him. One by one, all of them come over to greet Steve, that is, except Paul Newman. Just at the start of the second half, Paul turns around, then Steve turns around, and Paul goes, 'Steve!' and Steve goes, 'Paul!' Then Paul says, 'You never return any of my phone calls.' Steve says, 'You never return any of my phone calls.' It's all bullshit. 'How are you doing?' 'You look great!' 'You look terrible!' They're talking from across the room and everybody just stops. Paul says, 'I'm getting uncomfortable on this bar stool.' Steve says, 'Why don't you come over here and sit down. Bring a case over here while you're at it.' "

The sight of Hollywood's two biggest stars drinking Old Milwaukee beer was one Parslow would never forget. "The two of them sat there for the rest of the game and talked. Nobody else came near them. It was like they wanted their own moment together," he says. They reminded Parslow of a white knight and a black knight. "Paul Newman always wore white. That night he was wearing white pants, a white shirt, white tennis shoes, and he had white hair. He looked like he was out of a page of a magazine on the sexiest man alive. When you looked at Paul you said, 'There's a good-looking stud.' McQueen wore a dark blue T-shirt, dark sports jacket, blue jeans, black tennis shoes. Steve looked like his father." Years earlier, Steve had joked, "Ten years from now, I'll be all gray and playing Paul Newman's father." To Parslow, that didn't seem to be very far from the truth. "Steve was five years younger than Paul, but it looked the other way around. Paul succeeded in hiding his age and Steve was making himself look much older. Many people think Steve looked awful in his beard, but when he took it off, they realized why he grew it. He was aging badly. All the hard living that he had put himself through was showing."

Gary Combs laughs at the memory of Steve coming up to him on the first day of filming and patting him on the belly. Steve said half-jokingly, "If you're going to double me, Combs, you're going to have to hold your stomach in." Steve, too, had gained a few pounds since Combs last saw him on the set of *The Getaway*. The weight he had put on for *An Enemy of the People* had not entirely gone away. Combs then looked Steve in the eye and said, "Don't you ever look in the mirror?" Steve was shocked. "Well, my stomach's not that big!" Combs replied, "What's wrong with you? Look in the mirror sometime!" McQueen huffed off and licked his wounds until a few days later on the set, when he caught Combs slouching, as was his natural posture. McQueen came up behind the stuntman and punched him lightly in the back, playing the role of drill sergeant. "Straighten up, Combs! God, if you're doubling me, you've got to straighten up that posture." Exasperated, Combs said, "Son-of-a-bitch, you *don't* look in the mirror, do you?" "I don't stand like that," Steve retorted.

While they were exchanging verbal blows, Barbara Minty took a photo of them from a distance. She developed the picture and gave it to Combs with the condition that he never let Steve know who took it. The photo revealed that Steve had the bigger gut of the two and, in addition, slouched more than his stunt double. Combs proudly showed it to Steve and asked, "Steve, would you autograph this picture for me?" Steve took one look and said, "Oh my God. Where did you get this?" Combs says with a laugh, "He never did sign the picture for me, either. He got away from me as quick as possible. The picture proved my point to him."

The majority of *Tom Horn* was filmed in Mescal, Arizona, just a few miles from the Colorado border, in January 1979. Every piece of film was shot outdoors to give it the gritty and rustic look of the Old West. The costumes were also given the "real look." Costume designer Luster Bayless thoroughly researched the period and obtained old photographs which showed that people back then wore two, even three layers of clothes to keep warm.

Costar Linda Evans, who later went on to star in the huge TV series *Dynasty,* commented, "The ironic thing is that my wardrobe for *Tom Horn* cost more than the elegant things I wore for *Dynasty.* Those turn-of-the-century clothes all had to be custom-made."

Steve's look for his role was chaps and suspenders. No gun belt, just a pistol jammed inside his pants. Not pretty, but very true to the time period.

If *The Sand Pebbles* was the most problematic film that Steve ever endured, then *Tom Horn* was a close second. Several problems plagued the film all through its various stages.

Susan Ekins, the daughter of friend Bud Ekins, was hired on as a production assistant. Susan was in college at USC when she mentioned to her parents that she was fascinated by the film industry. Her mother then picked up the phone and called Steve. "Steve, get my daughter a job," she said, mincing no words. Steve agreed to give Ekins a try, and a few months later she was in the middle of nowhere in Mescal, Arizona.

Ekins remembers her first job with vivid detail. "It was not an easy shoot. The weather conditions weren't favorable. We were outside all day. Hot one minute, cold the next. We worked twelve to fifteen hours a day, then had to ride the bus to and from the hotel two hours each way. Every day."

To Steve's credit, he gave no special treatment to Susan. "Steve kept to himself most of the time," she recalls. "He was, 'Hi, how are you?' but he basically lived in a trailer right off the set. The man didn't live in a hotel room; he lived in a motor home. He really got into his character. He was really into being a mountain man."

Ekins does remember one special gesture on a snowy day in Tucson. "It was unseasonably cold weather for Tucson. I would fall asleep in a chair for fifteen minutes and snow would be in my lap. A couple of days later a heater showed up and I said, 'How did this get here?' because I didn't complain about anything—having been given an opportunity, I didn't want to say anything out of line. Someone said, 'Steve sent it for you.' I guess he knew where I was, but he didn't acknowledge it to me. He was nice and cordial, but I had no special treatment whatsoever. I was treated like a member of the crew and had a wonderful learning experience."

Ekins did such a good job, in fact, that Steve requested that she work on his last film, *The Hunter*.

Today, Ekins works for flamboyant producer Jerry Weintraub in a much bigger capacity and credits Steve for her success. "I would not be in the film industry if it hadn't have been for Steve. He gave me a huge break."

The third day of filming proved to be another sign of what was in store for the picture. James William Guercio was fired by Steve. McQueen pulled director of photography John Alonzo aside and said quietly, "I don't think this is going to work out. I don't think he knows anything about the camera and real cinema and what we're trying to tell." Alonzo replied, "Well, it's your decision." Steve said, "It's time for a change."

Guercio had everyone on the set convinced from day one that he was the wrong director. Says Fred Weintraub, "It was obvious that when Guercio showed up with boots, a riding crop, and a beret, trying to look like Erich von Stroheim, that we were in trouble."

Weintraub was in the wings when McQueen admitted that he was wrong in hiring Guercio in the first place. Weintraub offered to do Steve's dirty work. "I'll tell him he's fired," he said. Steve objected, "No,

I made the mistake of hiring him and now it will have to be me that has to fire him."

John Alonzo was present when Steve fired Guercio. "He called James into his trailer and said, 'I really have to make a change and this is not the movie I want to make. Thank you very much, but you're going to have to leave.'" Guercio thought that Weintraub and Alonzo were behind the move to oust him. Says Weintraub, "Steve gave it to him straight. Guercio wouldn't accept the fact that Steve was telling it to him. He thought that I was behind it and that Steve adored him still, and that was not the case."

With Guercio gone, Steve decided that he would simply take over as director. He soon learned, however, that the Directors' Guild had a rule stipulating that an actor or anyone else previously involved in the picture could not assume the role of director. Weintraub encouraged Steve to fight the ruling, but Steve knew that would take time and cause the picture to shut down. Since this was Steve's last project for First Artists, he wanted the filming to come to an end as soon as possible. It was then that first assistant director Cliff Coleman suggested that his friend William Wiard could come in and direct.

Wiard had a solid reputation in television, having directed episodes for *The Rockford Files*, *M\*A\*S\*H*, *Barnaby Jones*, and *Cannon*, but *Tom Horn* would be his first feature film. It had been implicitly stated by Coleman that Wiard would sit there and be the official director while McQueen and Alonzo would do the actual directing. Wiard would only contribute if asked to. Says Susan Ekins on the McQueen-Wiard relationship, "They were cordial to each other, but I wouldn't say that Steve held him in the highest regard. It was Steve's picture. It was his vision. It certainly has his trademark on it." Says John Alonzo, "Steve was more or less the director on that set." If one counted Steve, *Tom Horn* went through five directors.

Steve's dedication to the film surprised everyone. Costar Linda Evans commented, "Steve has a real feeling for his character and what makes him a fascinating man. Most people think of Steve as an adventurer. He's a loner, he's hard to figure out.

"He's very exciting to work with, very exciting. He's really open, willing to try different things, so spontaneous. He's an exceptional actor. When the scene's over, you don't want it to stop."

Steve had his hand in everything on *Tom Horn*. Actor Harry Northup, who played Horn's lawyer, remembers McQueen even rewriting scenes. "The most important scene for me was my meeting with Tom Horn in the jail cell," Northup says. "In the script, that was about a page and a

Steve takes direction from William Wiard on the set of *Tom Horn* and was compelled to do his story.　(Copyright © 1979 by Warner Brothers, Inc.)

half. I remember when I got on the set, I met with McQueen about a day before we shot the scene. He wound up changing it about three or four times that day. I went off and memorized my lines, and when I came back at the end of the day, he wanted me to memorize something else."

Fred Weintraub recalls that Steve worked hard on the script. "He would make the script girl stay up till two in the morning writing three new pages of dialogue. I said to him, 'Steve, all you're going to be doing is saying 'Yup,' and he would say, 'No, no, no. I have to know the scene.' One of the most amazing things I found out about his acting was that these three new pages of dialogue would be there for him and he would take a pencil and cross out all of his dialogue until he almost ended up with 'Yup.' But what was interesting was that he needed the whole three pages to get through his 'Yup.' "

Most people on the set came to love McQueen for his generosity. Pat Johnson recalls a scene that involved extras eating outside at a picnic table. It was an especially cold day, and several of the extras were older people who needed the money. "The day we did that scene," says Johnson, "it was 20 degrees outside. There were fifty extras dressed in these authentic clothes and there was no way they could ward off the cold. When Steve came out of his trailer, he saw these older people freezing and shivering as they were standing in their positions. He asked Luster Bayless, 'Do these people have long johns on?' Luster told him no and Steve said, 'Okay, let's stop the shoot until these people get some long johns.' Back in those days it cost six thousand dollars an hour to film. Steve made them shut down production. He put all of these extras in heated tents, sent the wardrobe people to Nogales for thermal underwear, and only after these people were properly clothed, then production resumed. That was the type of person he was, very sensitive."

Remembers John Alonzo, "One day we went to a little town in Arizona, which was to be our set. When we got there, the whole place was covered in snow. It was an interesting situation, because not just the set, but the whole town, was covered. Steve and I talked it over and decided that the snow would last maybe five hours because we were in the middle of the desert. The scene had Tom Horn arriving in town, putting the horse up, and going into the bar to get a drink. Steve asked me what I thought. I said, 'If we really work hard and nobody goes out there, we can get the shot of you and the horse and then come into the barn.' That was the McQueen nobody knew: the cooperative actor who did exactly what had to be done because of technical restrictions. He was extremely cooperative, something for which he did not have a reputation. He never would have done that in the past."

McQueen's acting amazed Alonzo. "He always had this interesting knack of performing for another actor while on camera. I don't think he did this consciously, but it was interesting, because an editor normally makes a cut when an actor looks at another actor. It gives the editor an easy chance to get a reaction. Not Steve. He would make sure that the eye contact he made was good enough not to cut away from him. He would look away or make some kind of gesture so that it was difficult for the editor to cut him from the film. It's not a trick, but a technique. Steve did that as well as any actor I've seen."

Alonzo added, "I've never seen anyone handle a horse better, either. He would get on Buster with a rifle and fire on a full gallop. He was going as fast as that horse could go and he handled it beautifully. It was as if he was married to Buster, as if he knew exactly how to treat it."

One scene required many extras to pose as cowboys. Steve suggested they use real cowboys for the scene. Says Fred Weintraub, "They added a lot in the way of realism, because the one thing a cowboy can play is a cowboy."

Two actors in the film, Slim Pickens and Richard Farnsworth, had been real-life cowboys before they got into pictures. Steve liked them enormously and requested that they be in the film. Years after Mc-Queen had fired Farnsworth as a stuntman on *Wanted: Dead or Alive,* he caught Farnsworth's performance in *Comes a Horseman* and was impressed. He had to have Farnsworth in his next movie.

Slim Pickens was not only a friend but a good actor. McQueen thought Pickens was "a shit-kicker on and off the screen."

The two veterans held McQueen's and the crew's interest as they spun tales of their cowboy days. Their relationship went back to the forties, when both were on the rodeo circuit. Pat Johnson observes, "Normally, Steve was the focal point of all the attention, but when these two guys got together and started talking, all the stunt guys, along with Steve, would sit there and be mesmerized by them. During every camera break, instead of going to his trailer, Steve would sit out there just to hear those guys talk."

The film's ending focused on the hanging of *Tom Horn.* The specially designed gallows would be the main prop.

The contraption was built by stunt coordinator Gary Combs. When it was near completion, he was asked by Cliff Coleman, "Do you think Steve will do this?" Combs brought McQueen to the set and asked if he would get up on the gallows for a shot. "I could see in his eyes that he had no desire to get in that rig and drop through that door," recalls Combs. Combs then offered, "Tell you what. I'll get this thing all rigged up, rehearse it, and show it to you." McQueen agreed to that much.

On the day of the first rehearsal, without Steve present, Combs put his head through the noose without a hood. When he dropped through the trapdoor, the rope ripped the skin off his neck. He reported to work the next day wearing a bandanna to cover the newly torn flesh. McQueen peered at Combs suspiciously throughout the day, then finally came over to him and pulled down the scarf. "Oh my God," he said. "What the hell happened?" As Combs explained it to McQueen, he could sense the star was more apprehensive than ever. By then, Combs had the gallows rigged to perfection.

As Combs climbed up on the gallows, during the actual dress rehearsal, he felt as if he were going back in time. "It was a spooky thing, even for me," he relates. "That was one of the three times in my career that when they shot it, I could have warped back in time. The dress, the gallows, the noise, it was all very realistic."

The rope was put around Combs's neck, but before the hood was lowered, he looked over at Steve and noticed that "his eyes were as big as drinking glasses. He was spooked and he wasn't even up there." Again, the question was put to Steve: Would he perform the stunt?

"Ain't no way in God's world I'm going to get up there and put that rope around my neck," was the reply.

That night, Barbara had a bad dream about the hanging. She told Steve about her dream and he decided not to go through with the stunt. Of all the death-defying stunts he had performed over his career, this was the only one he respectfully declined.

As the filming wrapped in late March 1979, Steve came to John Alonzo with an interesting proposition. McQueen asked Alonzo to be the cinematographer on his next film, *The Hunter*. Alonzo responded, "Maybe your director should decide this, Steve." Steve replied confidently, "I can make him do it." Alonzo thanked him, but graciously declined. Steve tried one more time: "John, this may be my last movie." Alonzo assured him that he had a lot of movies left to do. Today Alonzo believes that Steve knew at that point that he was going to die soon. "I'm just telling you my own instincts in dealing with the man, that he knew he didn't have long to go. I'm positive of that."

Earlier in the shoot, Alonzo remembers a conversation that struck him as odd. Alonzo at the time was a chain smoker, and McQueen kept on him to break the habit. Alonzo pointed out that McQueen's habit of chewing tobacco was even worse than smoking. Steve told him sternly, "I know what's going to happen to me and I know I'm not going to be around much longer, so I'm going to tell you, don't smoke." Says Alonzo, "I've known people who have passed on who knew they were going to die. There's a certain peace about them, a quiet attitude, and Steve had it." When Alonzo first heard of McQueen's illness a year later, he wasn't the least bit surprised.

Alonzo saw Steve one last time at the first preview for *Tom Horn* in Oxnard, California. As the movie began, Steve and Barbara and Alonzo and his wife nestled in a back row of the theater. "The audience reaction was rather good," remembers Alonzo. The couples left before the houselights came on and went outside. "Well, what do you think?" asked McQueen. Alonzo offered, "I think it's terrific." Steve and Alonzo shook hands and never saw each other again.

The initial reviews for *Tom Horn* were a mirror reflection of the box office gross. The film earned a mere $12 million. Simply put, westerns weren't what audiences wanted to see any longer. One critic summed it up best: "*Tom Horn* suffered from public antipathy toward the genre. In an earlier decade, this lyrical, deeply felt little film would have been hailed as a classic."

Others close to the project feel that Warner Brothers simply did not back the film the way it should have. John Alonzo offers, "Warners didn't want it. It was just an obligation to First Artists, so they put as

Director Buzz Kulick, McQueen's friend Pat Johnson, McQueen's stunt double Loren Janes and Steve McQueen discuss a scene on the set of *The Hunter*, 1979.   (PHOTO BY MEL TRAXEL, FROM THE LOREN JANES COLLECTION)

little money into it as possible. There was no promotion to the picture at all."

Loren Janes felt that the problem was in the promotion itself. "The advertisements for *Tom Horn* were all action clips. The public thought it was going to be another big western with lots of action. It was a talkie. It was totally misrepresented, and I think they blew it by doing that. You can't set up an audience for a certain representation and give them something else. I blame the publicity on *Tom Horn*."

With the passing of time, *Tom Horn* has been one of those films that has been rediscovered again. Critics have come to respect the grittiness and hard work put into it.

Says John Alonzo, "I think reviewers and critics succumb to the plus or minus promotion they might do on a picture. I give lectures on films at universities and I talk to kids who weren't old enough to see *Tom Horn* when it came out, and they all ask the same question, 'Why wasn't the picture a hit?' It's become a bit of a classic because it has to do with individuality. More so, it has to do with McQueen. People realize what a great screen personality he was. He is garner-

336

ing that kind of recognition purely on his ability, not on the dramatic way in which he died."

Says actor James Coburn, "*Tom Horn*, I thought, was Steve's best film. He was loose and free and he wasn't guarded. Most of his films he was guarded. He had a form. If the film was rigid enough, he was going to be good. I always felt that Steve would really be a good actor if he ever grew up. . . . I think he finally did on *Tom Horn*. That was him finding his adulthood."

Fred Weintraub says of the film, "I think that when you first open a picture, the first thing that happens is its commercial viability is placed in such high regard. Over time, people look at the film, not at its commercial viability at that moment. Some films just come into their own. I think that *Tom Horn* is one of those films."

In March 1979, with the completion of *Tom Horn*, Steve and Barbara discovered a small town just fifty miles northwest of Los Angeles called Santa Paula.

Santa Paula was a throwback to the California towns of the forties. To get to it, one had to drive by various groves of orange, lemon, walnut, and avocado trees. The town itself had changed little over the decades. It reminded Steve of his hometown of Slater, Missouri.

The people there also reminded him of back home. (In fact, 35 percent of the town was made up of native Missourians escaping the cold winters of the Midwest.) People there weren't too impressed with power or money. A man had to earn respect.

Steve wanted to take up flying and came to Santa Paula in search of a Stearman, an antique World War II plane. He had owned a Stearman years before but had never flown it himself. One day, however, he had cautiously permitted a friend to take him up in it. The friend knew how to fly, he just didn't know how to land. When the plane came down, its bottom was completely sheared off. Now Steve was searching for another Stearman and was told that Santa Paula Airport was a good place to start.

Perry Schreffler was the first person in Santa Paula to meet McQueen. Steve and Barbara had driven up from Malibu to search for the Stearman. As they walked around the airport grounds, they found an open hangar and meekly peeked inside. There they saw an overall-clad gentleman restoring an old Apache airplane. "May we come in?" Steve asked. "Sure," said Schreffler, "make yourself at home." Schreffler had been a lieutenant colonel in the U.S. Air Force and a pilot with TWA for over thirty years. Steve introduced himself and Barbara and immediately got to the business at hand: Could Schreffler help him find a Stearman? Schreffler excused himself and came back a minute later with a trade magazine that listed all kinds of antique airplanes for sale. Schreffler helped him find a company that specialized in restoring old planes, Mid Continent in Hattiesburg, Mississippi.

Steve also asked Schreffler if he could suggest a good pilot instructor. Schreffler said, "Sammy Mason's the best. He was a test pilot for Lockheed for years and even had his own acrobatic show at one time. He's based right here in Santa Paula. With a little convincing, I'm sure he'd be your instructor."

Two days later, Steve ordered a bright yellow PT-17 Stearman for $35,000. That part was easy. Now he had to convince Sammy Mason to teach him to fly.

Steve called Mason and told him, "I'd like to learn how to fly old planes, not modern ones. I need you to teach me." Mason had a full schedule of students. Besides, a novice pilot didn't appeal to him. He said no. When Mason got off the phone, his son, Pete, asked who had called. "Some actor named Steve McQueen. Do you know who he is?" Mason said. Pete asked his father if he were crazy, turning down the famous actor. Steve didn't quit easily, though. Two more phone calls were placed to Mason and still he wouldn't budge. Steve had to think of a new strategy. "If you won't teach me," he said, "will you at least come and look at my Stearman and see if it's a good airplane?" That at least got Mason to come to the airport. When the two met, there was instant electricity. Says Mason, "He had penetrating blue eyes, for one thing. He was charismatic, actually an attractive person, and very hard to say no to." Mason took a look at the Stearman. "Well, what do you think?" Steve asked. "It looks like a good plane, but the only way you can tell for sure whether it's good or not is to fly it." Says Mason, "That's exactly what he wanted. We shook hands, and I became his instructor."

Steve jumped into his latest passion with both feet. He had the strength and tenacity of several men. A new student usually flies an hour each lesson. Steve had three sessions a day, two to three hours each, as if he were making up for lost time.

Now armed with a plane and instructor, Steve decided to take the plunge and buy a hangar to store his plane.

Screaming Eagle Productions was owned by Doug Dullenkopf and Mike Dewey when Steve came into their offices to see about leasing, or even possibly buying, a hangar. McQueen was greeted by Dullenkopf. When Dullenkopf wasn't looking, Steve dropped a rolled up hundred dollar bill on the floor. It was Steve's clever little way of testing the other guy's honesty. "Mr. McQueen?" Steve said, "Please, call me Steve." "Okay, Steve. I believe you dropped this," and Dullenkopf promptly handed back the bill. Within minutes, Steve leased a hangar with the promise of buying a larger one when one went on the market. Says Dullenkopf, "I think he was trying to determine our situation here. I think if I would have kicked that hundred dollar bill to the side, waiting for him to leave, that would have been a cheap insurance policy for him never to deal with us again."

Around the airport, Steve was treated like just another pilot. If he were to have done something wrong, he would have been told, "Hey, pal, you're not doing that right." Steve always admired honesty, and the people at the airport were his kind of folks. Says pilot Bruce Dickinson, "The people at the airport treated him no different from anyone else. Steve didn't consider himself anything special. He didn't expect anything. He just wanted to be one of the locals and fly and do his own thing. He was probably the most down home good ol' boy that I've come across." Steve would proudly proclaim, "Santa Paula Airport is my kinda country club!"

Steve became friendly with a lot of the pilots, and it seemed for the first time in his life he wasn't being bothered. It was then that he decided he not only wanted to fly in Santa Paula, but live there as well. Says friend and pilot Mike Dewey, "Steve was looking for the right kind of town, the right kind of person to train him, the right kind of airplane to fit his personality at the time. It all came together when he got here."

Steve was tired of the one-hour commute from Malibu every day. He liked the old town. He liked the people. He decided to make Santa Paula his new home.

Not one to waste any time, in June he purchased a private hangar that had access to the airport. The hangar itself was mainly used for commercial airlines, but Steve wanted the extra space. He paid $180,000 for the hangar, an outrageous sum at the time. Says Doug Dullenkopf, "To get a hangar on this airport, there's a waiting list. Steve didn't want to wait. He said, 'I'm not too worried because someday it will be worth that.' He paid $40,000 more than the next guy, but he got it. He didn't have to wait around."

Steve decided that he and Barbara would stay in the hangar until they found a suitable place to live. In the meantime, he began moving his possessions there and found the hangar a perfect place to store them. Among the things were antique toys, a collection of over ten thousand jackknives, Kewpie dolls, old-fashioned cash registers and slot machines, vintage gasoline pumps, jukeboxes, and the world's second-biggest antique motorcycle collection, over 140 bikes in all. (Steve's friend Bud Ekins boasted the world's largest collection at the time, with 170 antique bikes, but Ekins admits, "I had been collecting them for over thirty years; Steve had only collected for three years. He would have caught up to me in no time.") It seemed as if Steve were trying to buy up his childhood memories. Friend Phil Parslow offers, "Steve was a compulsive spender. He was like me; when you've been so poor, you have a tendency to buy one, two, three of the same thing. You can never buy one of anything you adore. Steve could afford that. To him, it was all an asset. He knew the value would hold." The hangar soon began to take on the look of a museum.

Steve had always dreamed of owning a ranch, one filled with horses, chickens, cats, dogs, and his own garden to grow vegetables. He wanted a place away from town, but close enough to the hangar. The Converse Ranch was one such place, with over twelve hundred acres of land and a $2 million price tag. Steve and Barbara went to look at the house but felt incredibly "bad vibes" as they left. As brave as Steve was, he had a superstitious streak in him a mile wide. If anything smacked of being haunted, he got weak in the knees.

They decided on a four-bedroom, fifteen-acre ranch, nestled between two small hills just a few miles from the airport. The house, built in 1896, was in dire need of repairs. (Curiously enough, the house was believed to be haunted by the spirit of an old Indian. Several visitors there claim to have felt its presence.) Steve told a friend, "I've finally found what I've been looking for all of these years. This country is as close to home as I can find. I want to die here."

While Steve flew during the day, he spent many nights relaxing around a campfire outside the hangar. It was here that he became friendly with the locals. One couple, Larry and Crystal Endicott, often shared these private moments with McQueen. Crystal remembers, "Every evening as the sun went down, he had people come by, as he had a fire going. He always had to lie down on the concrete because his back hurt a lot. He would just visit with people, just lie there and talk. He would talk about his past or the dreams he had still left."

The Endicotts were most likely the closest friends Steve and Barbara had in Santa Paula. Both couples were the same age and had similar interests. At the time, Larry and Crystal were running an aircraft maintenance business, where Steve would repair his planes. Steve noticed that Larry drank the same brand of beer, Old Milwaukee, and that was the start of their friendship.

Steve and Barbara invited the Endicotts for Chinese food one night. They noticed that Steve took a six-pack of beer with him wherever he went. Crystal relates, "They didn't serve beer at this one restaurant, so Steve brought it with him and asked them to put it in the refrigerator." She also noticed that Steve didn't like to sign autographs, but he made an exception that night. "There was a little child, maybe seven years old, staring at Steve. It was quite comical. All through the meal, people came up and asked him for his autograph and he would politely say, 'No, I don't sign autographs, but I'll shake your hand.' This little kid was hiding behind a chair and peeking at Steve. Steve finally asked him nicely, 'Would you like to come over here?' And the little kid walked over and that's the only autograph I'd ever seen Steve give. He loved little kids and older people."

Steve became a part of the community. In Laurel Canyon in the sixties, he had had a shoving match with a neighbor and had raced through the streets of Hollywood on his motorcycle. In Malibu in the seventies, he was constantly being told by his snooty neighbors that his pickup trucks were littering the property. Here, he truly felt as if he belonged, and he played the part of an active neighbor. When Larry Endicott went in the hospital for his second cancer treatment, his wife, Crystal, wanted to be with him for moral support. But the couple had seven children at home, ranging in age from two to twelve, and there was no one to watch them. Not wanting to impose on anyone, Crystal casually mentioned her predicament to Steve, who was outraged that no one had asked him. "What do you mean, nobody will watch your kids?" he said. "Well, I can't ask someone to spend the whole week with them, feed them, check on them, make sure they get to bed," Crystal replied. Steve said, "I'll do that. I'll bring them food. I'll put them to bed. You go be with your husband." Crystal interjected, "Steve, I can't impose on you like that." Steve said sternly, "You don't worry about it. I'll be there." Crystal fondly remembers, "And he was. He brought my kids pizza. He stayed with them from Monday to Friday. Seven babies. He was a sweetheart. I couldn't ask for anybody nicer."

Later, when Larry became even more ill and could no longer work, Steve helped out again. Since the couple ran their own business, there were no workmen's compensation payments coming in. The Endicotts were going to lose everything they had ever worked for. The people at the airport responded and began a fund to make the house payment and put food on the table. Steve gave charitably, along with the rest of the group.

While the house was being remodeled, Steve kept himself busy. In addition to his flying, he kept up his karate workouts with Pat Johnson, maintained his antique motorcycles, and began attending church.

Religion had flowed in and out of Steve's life beginning with his introduction to the Catholic church by grandmother Lillian.

In Taiwan, during the filming of *The Sand Pebbles*, stunt double Loren Janes remembers conversations he had with Steve concerning God. Knowing that Janes was a deeply religious man, Steve asked him about his faith. Recalls Janes, "They were just brief chats. We'd start on the subject and I'd just mention it and drop it and he'd drop it, too. But he was the one who always brought it up."

Pat Johnson remembers that right after his divorce from Ali Steve took a trip to New York to visit Ali's brother. "Ali's brother was an artist," Johnson says. "Steve found him in some little dive, living like some wino in utter poverty. All of this had a very profound effect on him. When he came back from that trip, he started asking me about religion, about Christ."

It was Barbara who was the main influence on Steve. The daughter of a minister, Barbara had grown up in the church, but her modeling career had taken her out of that lifestyle and into another. She now felt it was time for some stability in her life since she had given up her career for Steve. But Steve always found an excuse when she asked him to go to church with her. "Not today," she was told. "I don't feel so good. Let's do it next time."

Pete Mason recalls a time when Steve was experimenting with religions and dragged him along to a Catholic church. "I wasn't Catholic, so when we entered the church, Steve dipped his fingers in the water and did the hand gesture with the cross. He looked like he knew what to do. We were there only five minutes, and as we went out in the courtyard, Steve said, 'Whatever happens to me, Pete, I'll never be able to give up women or beer.' "

Steve had always admired flight instructor Sammy Mason for his past accomplishments, but he also noticed something different about Mason. There was an inner confidence, a calm about Mason that Steve could never grasp. He finally asked Mason what it was that made him different. "That's because I'm a Christian, Steve," announced Mason. Steve then asked Mason if he could attend church with him. Both Barbara and Mason were pleased.

Soon, Steve and Barbara became regular attendants, along with Sammy Mason and his wife, Wanda. The two couples occupied the balcony of the Ventura Missionary Church every Sunday. Steve attended the church three months before approaching the pastor, Leonard De-Witt. DeWitt recalls, "One Sunday morning, he tapped me on the shoulder and asked if we could get together for lunch. Most of the questions he asked were about Christ and the Christian walk. By the time we were done with lunch, Steve had asked all of these questions and then I said to him, 'I have only one question to ask of you, Steve.' And he grinned and said, 'You want to know if I'm born again, don't you? Yes, I am.' "

Friends had noticed the change in Steve. He had definitely mellowed, in their opinion. Said Crystal Endicott, "He really enjoyed church. He felt very good about himself. There was something there that made him feel good, and he liked it. Always on Sundays he had a smile, even after he found out he was sick."

Steve went so far as to make sure his friends also went to church. One Sunday morning, he called Larry Endicott and asked if he would be going that particular day. "Oh, Steve, I'm feeling a bit sick this morning," Larry answered. The pattern sounded familiar to Steve, who said calmly, "I'll be right over to get you."

Bud Ekins, the man most likely to have a salty conversation with Steve, even noticed: "He was just nicer. More considerate. He wasn't going to preach to me; he knew better than that."

On May 1, 1979, Steve soloed in his plane for the first time, and that following Sunday, a party was thrown in his honor. The gang at the Santa Paula Airport all attended, and Steve was in his element, being a part of the community.

That summer proved to be the happiest point in his life. Every Sunday after church, he would throw open the hangar doors and, as the sunlight came shining through, would announce to the world, "Welcome to another day in paradise." Bud Ekins sums up, "He had those neat airplanes, which is what he wanted; a neat wife, which is who he wanted; those neat old motorcycles, which is what he wanted; the ranch house, which is what he wanted. He was so happy in Santa Paula."

And for a fleeting moment, Steve McQueen's life was perfect.

Publicity photo for McQueen as Ralph "Papa" Thorson in his last film, *The Hunter*, 1980.

(COURTESY OF PARAMOUNT PICTURES)

# THE LAST PICTURE

*I don't think Steve liked being an actor. I think he liked being a star, but I don't think he liked the business. I believe he would have retired.*

BUD EKINS

PRODUCER MORT ENGLEBERG was buzzed on his intercom one morning in 1977. "Steve McQueen on line one," his secretary said nonchalantly. Thinking it was a joke, Engleberg picked up the phone and said rudely, "Yeah?" "Mort, this is Steve McQueen. I want you to know that I read your script and I'd like to talk to you about it." Assuming one of his friends was clowning around, Engleberg got even more rude. "Fine," he said. "When can you come out to Burbank to talk about it?" The person on the other line paused and said, "Well, you know, I'm staying in town at the Beverly Wilshire and it would be sort of hard to go over there." Engleberg cut the caller short: "Look, if you're really serious about this, you'll come out to Burbank." Then it hit him: he had been in contact with McQueen's agent, Marvin Josephson, who had promised to pass the script on to his client, but Engleberg never really entertained the thought of landing him. He was too big a star for this project. Maybe Lee Marvin or Gregory Peck, but Steve McQueen was a long shot.

"And then I had a vague thought that perhaps it might be Steve McQueen," said Engleberg. "Let me get your number at the Beverly Wilshire and I'll call you right back," he said quickly. Engleberg hung up and immediately dialed the number given to him by the caller. "Hello, the Beverly Wilshire Hotel," he heard on the line. Engleberg said, "I'd like to speak with Steve McQueen, please." "One moment," said the operator. Seconds later, the same voice that he had heard just minutes earlier came on: "This is Steve." Suddenly, Engleberg's heart was in his throat: "Mr. McQueen, this is Mort Engleberg. I'll be right over." That was the genesis of Steve's last picture, *The Hunter*.

*The Hunter* is the story of Ralph ("Papa") Thorson, a modern-day bounty hunter. An 1872 Supreme Court decision gave bounty hunters more rights than the FBI or police. A bounty hunter can cross state lines or even break down a door and apprehend a bail jumper without a search warrant.

"People think the bounty hunter vanished with the frontier," says Thorson. "We perform a needed service, and it's perfectly legal."

Mort Engleberg first heard about Ralph Thorson from a journalist friend who was doing a profile of Thorson for *The New Yorker* magazine. He was intrigued by Thorson's occupation, but was even more taken by his personality. Thorson's job regularly dealt in violence. He had been shot twice, stabbed three times, and been slugged so many times he'd lost count. He would spend countless hours trying to talk a criminal out of a house rather than go in after him. Besides being a bounty hunter, Thorson was a church bishop, bridge champion, astrologer, nutritionist, and opera and classical music buff.

"That's what appealed to me," says Engleberg. "If he were just a man of violence, I doubt I would have wanted to film his story. The fact that there was another, gentler, side to the man is what really interested me in him."

When Engleberg went to meet Thorson at his North Hollywood home, he noticed that Pappy played host to several eccentric personalities. On any given night, he could have in his house a hooker, a cop, a priest, and an ex-con. Engleberg was pulled aside by one ex-convict and was told, "Actually, he's half a cop." The next minute, Engleberg was pulled aside by an LAPD officer who said, "He's half a crook." Engleberg scooped up the rights for Thorson's life story that night.

Engleberg met Steve in his Beverly Wilshire suite. He noticed a stack of scripts five feet high in one corner of the room. "Out of all of the scripts he was sent, this is what he liked," says Engleberg. Throughout the meeting, Steve continually asked about Thorson. A meeting was set up between the two men, and Steve walked away from that meeting knowing that this was the next film he wanted to do. Notes Mort Engleberg, "I think Thorson represented a lot of the values that Steve felt strongly about. Thorson's a very decent man, a very honest man, a noble man in a business that has a lot of dishonest people. That was the basis of the respect between the two." In addition, Steve felt comfortable with the material. He noticed the irony of the situation. "I guess you could say I've come full circle. I feel a little bit like this is where I came in," he said, referring to *Wanted: Dead or Alive*. "I don't want to make

346

ordinary movies at this stage of my life. A script must really interest me or I won't do it. Unfortunately, it's difficult finding suitable material these days. I was lucky to land *The Hunter*. [Thorson's] unusual, a man out of his time, and I guess that's what attracted me to him."

Steve also found places to incorporate his own personality. The antique toys, the classic automobile, and the dime-store eyeglasses the character uses in the film are all from McQueen's private collection of nostalgia.

"I had become bored with acting," he confessed, "so I kept saying no to every offer, but then I got bored sitting at home." After the failure of *Tom Horn,* Steve knew he had to get back to the type of movies that the public expected of him. *The Hunter* had all the elements of a successful Steve McQueen picture. Now out of his contract with First Artists, Steve was a free agent and was no longer under any obligation to anyone. "The problem with movies," he told pilot Mike Dewey, "is that they own you for three months, and I don't want anyone to own me."

Perhaps one of the reasons Steve did *The Hunter* was a premonition he had of his early death. He called fellow actor and friend Ben Johnson before shooting began. There was a part for an older corrupt sheriff, and McQueen thought Johnson would be perfect for the role. Out of the blue, he told Johnson, "This is probably the last movie I'm going to do, and I'd like you to be in it with me." Johnson at the time felt that McQueen was referring to an early retirement and thought nothing further of the phone call. "He had that ol' cancer and I think he felt it was going to be his last show," Johnson says now.

Steve signed a deal with Paramount Pictures. For *The Hunter,* he was to receive $3 million and 15 percent of the gross. The film's budget was slated at an even $8 million. Steve had come a long way.

Filming was scheduled for five weeks in Chicago, one week in Kankakee, Illinois, and four weeks back in Los Angeles. The timing would coincide with the remodeling of the Santa Paula house, and Steve and Barbara would return to a finished home.

When Steve and Barbara arrived at the Chicago location, Mort Engleberg had set aside a plush suite for them at the upscale Drake Hotel. "It was a very nice suite. It came equipped with a Jacuzzi, sauna, steam room, bar, fancy furniture," says Engleberg. Steve said softly, "This is great. I'm just a country boy, and this is fine with me." As Engleberg turned to leave, Steve asked, "Where are you staying?" Engleberg replied, "I'm over at the Holiday Inn with the crew." Steve asked curiously, "You mean everybody's not staying here?" Engleberg was astounded at what Steve did next. "He moved out of his suite at the Drake and into the Holiday Inn with everybody else," says Engleberg.

"One of the things I found with McQueen was that there was no real baggage with him. Any kind of special treatment, he seemed to go out of his way to avoid. There was no guile about him at all. What you saw was what you got with him. I had heard horror stories about him, but he was just a terrific person."

And indeed Steve had changed. On *The Magnificent Seven,* he had bitched to producers that his trailer wasn't close enough to the set, like Yul Brynner's was. Now he couldn't care less.

Steve's acts of kindness had always been carefully concealed in the past. It had been his way to give back to the community. When Steve arrived in Chicago, his newfound Christianity made him even more charitable.

Filming began on September 10, 1979, in a Chicago slum area. The apartment tenement where they were filming was so bad that only a week before a murder had taken place on the same grounds. Said Pat Johnson, "Steve immediately felt a kindredship with these people and a desire to help." McQueen asked Johnson to go down to the local Catholic church and ask the priest if there was anything he could do to help. The priest made a list and gave it to Johnson. "Steve then pulled out his checkbook and wrote out a check that covered all of the church's immediate needs. It was a very substantial amount of money. He then went over to Mort Engleberg and said, 'This is what I'm giving to the local church. I would like you to match the amount.' I then took both checks down to Father and said, 'Here are some gifts from some men who would never like to be mentioned.' So Steve did this and he never wanted anyone to know about it."

Loren Janes remembers, "Steve gave me cash and I went out and bought a hundred baseballs, a hundred mitts, a hundred bats, a hundred footballs, and put them in a field for all of the kids in a real bad district. No one knew it was him. He did that many times in many different places. He did it because he wanted to and he didn't want any publicity. He had nothing growing up and he was always concerned about kids. He was going to give them what he never had."

Steve even signed autographed pictures, something that even threw best friend Pat Johnson for a loop. "In all of my years with Steve, I had only seen him sign one autograph." After *The Towering Inferno,* Steve had become friendly with costar and football great O. J. Simpson. Pat Johnson had season tickets to all of the Rams home games. When Simpson's team, the Buffalo Bills, came to town, Johnson invited McQueen to the game. Afterwards, Steve wanted to say hello to Simpson in the locker room. "Steve was wearing a hat and sunglasses and had the beard," says Johnson. "O.J. recognized him and said, 'Hey, man, come over here.' He didn't call him Steve, he called him man. So Steve walked up in front of the reporters and none of them recognized him. Steve's shoulders slumped a bit; you see, he was on O.J.'s turf. After he got dressed, we walked O.J. to the team bus. When we first got out of the dressing room, there were about fifty people who jumped around O.J. trying to get his autograph. They pushed Steve out of the way. Steve's shoulders slumped even more. This happened repeatedly until we got to the bus. When O.J. finally got on the bus and left, Steve was in a real funk because his ego had been totally bashed." While the two men were walking, an elderly woman had walked up to the wounded star. She asked, "Say, aren't you?" And Steve answered her excitedly, "Yes." She then asked, "Well, would you?" Again, excitedly cutting her off, "Oh yes, I'd be glad to," and proceeded to scrawl his signature for her. As he handed over his autograph, he said to her, "Thank you, my dear. You've made an old man very happy." Steve then turned to Johnson and joked, "God, now I have to go home and watch *The Blob* to restore my confidence." Now, on the set of *The Hunter*, he gladly handed out over two thousand signed eight-by-ten glossies.

Stunt coordinator Gary Combs also noticed a change in McQueen. "There was a difference in him. I thought, 'Well, he's just happier.' That was the nicest I've ever seen him. He was more pleasant to people, more congenial. I saw a side of him I'd never seen before. Before that, he was always such a frantic person. Maybe he did know that it was the end and just settled into trying to be the nice guy that he always wanted to be."

As for the filming of *The Hunter*, it was probably the smoothest shoot of Steve's career, with a minimal amount of problems.

Writer, and later director, Peter Hyams was originally set to direct the screenplay he wrote for *The Hunter*, but, in Mort Engleberg's words, the two had "creative differences to sort out." Hyams was out and, again, McQueen contemplated directing the film when he realized that he was going to go up against the Directors' Guild ruling that he had faced while filming *Tom Horn*. Instead, he opted for Buzz Kulik, an old friend with whom he had once worked in the mid-fifties on a live television episode of *Climax*. Kulik laughs at the fact that neither he nor Steve could remember the name of the episode, but Kulik did remember that "Steve wasn't even the star; Dan Duryea was." Kulik added, "It was not a good experience. Steve was kind of a folk hero at the time, being heralded as the new James Dean. To be honest, he was a real pain in the ass. He had great instincts, but he was undisciplined and unfocused. He got better with films because he had more time for rehearsal. When we worked together, it was for television and he didn't have time to explore the character because television has time constraints. In addition to all of that, he was very insecure and totally unprofessional."

Two years passed before Kulik bumped into McQueen again on the Four Star lot. McQueen had just landed the starring role on *Wanted: Dead or Alive*. They were making small talk when it began to rain. Kulik was waiting for his car to be brought to him and as he walked toward the car, Steve told him, "Buzz, I'm gonna be a big star." When Kulik got home, his wife greeted him at the door. Unable to contain himself, the director said, "Guess what Steve McQueen said today? That he's going to be a big star." With that, the two had a nice chuckle.

Since that time Kulik had directed the highly thought of *Brian's Song* for television, as well as such films as *Villa Rides* and *The Riot*. At first, he expressed some doubts on directing another Steve McQueen action film.

"There's nothing wrong with that," Kulik explained then, "but it really wasn't precisely what I wanted to do at that time. But a couple of things persuaded me to change my mind. First, I did want to work with Steve McQueen. I happen to think he's more than just a 'superstar.' I think he's an exceptionally fine actor, which interests me much more. I'm glad now I took it on, because it has developed into much more than I had initially anticipated. *The Hunter* did not have gratuitous violence and was character driven."

The director thought McQueen a "lovable kook." He says, "Steve loved to play games with people, but in the framework he was a terrific guy. In 1956, when I first met him, he was a little shit. When I saw him again, he was a man."

As on *An Enemy of the People* and *Tom Horn*, Steve surrounded himself with a cast of actors who would contribute to the film rather than compete with him. Eli Wallach hadn't worked with Steve since *The Magnificent Seven* in the early sixties. The two were alumni of the Neighborhood Playhouse in New York.

Wallach commented at the time, "He's a better actor than people think. His looks and personality stamped him as a kind of macho sex symbol, but he's a whale of an actor, make no mistake about it."

Steve recruited red-hot actor of the day LeVar Burton to play the role of Tommy Price. McQueen had wanted to work with Burton ever since *Roots* had turned him into a star. Burton's Tommy Price is a bumbling bail jumper who has not quite reached jail but is certainly headed that way. McQueen's Thorson notices that Price has a heart of gold and could be influenced to take the right path in life. Burton commented, "Tommy Price is an interesting character. He's not a hardened criminal, and he and Thorson wind up friends. Steve was the first to approach me about the part."

Burton said this about McQueen, "He takes an interest in everything and is quite knowledgeable about filmmaking. I think he'd make a fine director."

Probably the most employed character actor in Hollywood today is Tracy Walter. *Batman, City Slickers,* and *The Silence of the Lambs* are but a few films to his credit. He was a newcomer when *The Hunter* was in pre-production and was thrilled at the thought of acting opposite Steve McQueen.

Walter first met McQueen three weeks before shooting was to begin. He went to see Buzz Kulik for a meeting regarding his character's haircut. Walter's hair at the time was spiky and sticking straight up. He was thinking of getting a crew cut when in walked McQueen, who said, "No, no, no. Don't get a crew cut. I like it the way it is. It looks good." Walter comments, "I thought he was a warm person. He seemed easy to approach. We had a scene together, where I hold his girlfriend hostage, and we had some dialogue. He thought I shouldn't say certain things, and he suggested some other lines. He was good in that sense. I found him pretty helpful. He was a better actor than people gave him credit for. I think he was a better actor than he gave himself credit for."

At the time, Walter had an infant daughter whom he brought to the set. When Steve saw Walter's child, he commented, "I had one of those, and I turned around and she was twenty-one."

For the lead actress, McQueen and Kulik decided to go with an unknown by the name of Kathryn Harrold. Harrold had only one previous film to her credit, *Nightwing*.

Harrold was on a river trip on the Colorado deep in the Grand Canyon when she was contacted by her agent to report to Los Angeles right away. Steve McQueen wanted to meet her for his new film. The movie would make her a star, she was told by her agent.

Harrold relates, "I was all wet and muddy, just completely messy after being in the outdoors for a week straight. I was to fly out of the Grand Canyon to Flagstaff, Arizona, then to Los Angeles on a private plane, all arranged by Steve McQueen. I'm terrified of flying and it was a two-seater. I flew into Los Angeles and was met there by Buzz Kulik, who drove me to Santa Paula, where Steve was living in a hangar. All of this was very strange, I thought."

Harrold was very nervous at the thought of meeting her childhood hero. Actually, Buzz Kulik did most of the talking, while Steve stared at Harrold and occasionally threw in a few remarks out of nowhere. "You look like Grace Kelly," he blurted out suddenly. Harrold's hair at the time was lighter because of her week's stay in the sun. Steve asked her if she could possibly darken her hair. He explained, "I can only be attracted to dark-haired women."

During the conversation Harrold mentioned that she happened to be a graduate of the Neighborhood Playhouse, McQueen's alma mater. "There was this wall of pictures of famous people who had attended the school. Steve's picture was up there, and I remember at the time thinking it was strange that his picture was there. I mean, you think of Robert Duvall or Marlon Brando. Steve McQueen is not the first person you think of when you go to an acting school."

A Method actor by training, Harrold got the feeling that even though Steve claimed he also was a Method actor, he was just teasing her. "There was something going on with him, like he was sort of laughing underneath it all," says Harrold. "I remember I was doing a scene without him, and he was on the sidelines watching me, looking and shaking his head, like, 'You Method actors.' I sort of liked that, because it gave me something to play with. Our relationship was sort of combative in the film."

Harrold laughs at the thought of the tough macho McQueen. In *The Hunter,* Harrold played Ralph Thorson's girlfriend, almost common-law wife. The character becomes pregnant, so Harrold decided that she should take Lamaze classes to get a better feel for the part. Harrold relates, "I met this woman in the class, and I became her coach because she didn't have a husband. I became obsessed about it, which was good for my character. Steve would never talk to me about it. I don't know whether he found it disgusting or it was the part in his character, Ralph Thorson, but he asked me not to talk about it because he might vomit."

Actually, Steve's reaction to Lamaze classes proved to be the funniest scene in *The Hunter.* In the scene, Thorson is talked into making an appearance at the class by his pregnant girlfriend. She plops down on the floor while Thorson stands shyly in the hallway. The Lamaze instructor walks up to him and says, "I'm so glad you've finally made it, Mr. Thorson," and escorts him into the room. McQueen's character walks as if he were a naughty child being taken to the principal's office. He offers, "I've got a bad back."

McQueen and Harrold's first scene was memorable for both because it was the only love scene in the film. Knowing what he was in for that day, Steve phoned pilot Mike Dewey in Santa Paula. "Guess what I'm doing today?" McQueen asked tauntingly. "I'm going to do a love scene with this beautiful young actress and we have to kiss. Yeah, it's a shitty job, but somebody has to do it."

For Harrold, the scene was nerve-wracking: "For one thing, it was a love scene. I was extremely nervous about it because I barely knew the man, and I had to make out with him."

As the two were preparing for the scene, Harrold noticed that McQueen was chewing tobacco that day. The two then rehearsed the scene before filming and, again, a wad of tobacco was bulging out of the side of his mouth. "I hope you don't mind the tobacco. Ha, ha, ha," said McQueen. Harrold thought, "Well, maybe I do," but decided not to say anything. Right before the cameras rolled, McQueen spit out his tobacco, "Phoeey," and rolled over to kiss Harrold. "You think that would be disgusting, but it actually tasted pretty sweet. He chewed tobacco all the time," Harrold remembers.

Steve's son, Chad, was employed on location for *The Hunter* as a gofer. Steve felt that if Chad really wanted to be in the film business, he might as well experience it for himself firsthand. "Actors' kids get a bad handle," Steve said. "I want to bring them up and give them a shot at it: I'm not sure I'd want them to go into acting. They've seen a lot of the other side, so I don't think they'll want it—but I won't push them one way or the other. I worry about the mistakes I make bringing them up, about what I tell them what's right, about giving them too much; and I worry about their being a target because of me. They're good kids; they've got a great, keen sense of fairness."

Chad was on the set when Kathryn Harrold pulled up in her beat-up little Honda. "My dad says you need a new set of tires," said Chad. Harrold glanced at the tires and said, "You're right." After her scenes were finished that day, Harrold approached her car and noticed new tires on it. She didn't know how to thank her costar.

Harrold remembers one particularly cold day during shooting when Steve offered her his jacket. The night before, she had a dream in which she died. "He was dying," Harrold relates, "but I didn't know it then. We hardly ever talked to each other but for some reason we were standing together on the set, and I bring up this dream to him. I then ask, 'I had this dream last night that I was dying. Are you afraid of dying?'" Steve's reply was a firm "No, I'm not."

Director Buzz Kulik adds, "Steve seemed gentler, less driven. He settled on scenes a lot sooner than he did in the past. He knew he wasn't in good shape before the film and he revealed that to me. He was brave and terrific throughout the whole shoot. I was deeply, deeply fond of him."

Before shooting began, Steve told producer Mort Engleberg up front that he wasn't going to perform any of his own stunts. "I'm too old and too rich for this," he said. Buzz Kulik notes, "Steve was physically insecure at the time. He told me all the time that he spent in the water on

*Papillon* had done something to his breathing. We had a shower scene originally between McQueen and Kathryn Harrold, but Steve didn't want to get any water in his lungs." Kulik noticed that in another scene, when McQueen had to chase someone down the block, he was "leaning against a brick wall, heaving very heavily."

For this movie, Steve wanted to bring in his personal stunt double, Loren Janes. Janes had not worked with Steve since *The Reivers*, so McQueen asked Engleberg if it would be okay. Engleberg told McQueen that he had already picked out a stunt double for him, old acquaintance Gary Combs. Not only would Combs double Steve, but he would coordinate the stunts for the movie as well.

Steve was adamant about having Janes double him. "Well, who's the guy that's going to double you?" Janes asked. "Gary Combs. I'll just get him fired and you can be my double." Janes didn't like politics when he competed for a job, plus he knew Combs personally. "Gary's a sweetheart and is one of my favorite people, plus he's really qualified," Janes told Steve. "If he was a jerk, no problem. Gary Combs is qualified."

At the other end, Combs was told by Engleberg that if he wanted Janes fired, it could be arranged. Combs told Engleberg that he had enough to do with coordinating the film and that it was all right by him if Janes wanted to double Steve. Both were in a position to fire each other but neither chose to do so. Says Janes, "It was neat because we both spoke up for each other and we both could have fired each other, but we wouldn't do it. Steve and Mort found out about it later and were stunned that two stuntmen in competition said good things about each other."

As for the stunts in the film, a chase scene at the end of the movie was designed to be the longest in the history of films, clocking in at over fourteen minutes.

The majority of the chase took place on the el, Chicago's above-ground subway line. Steve received much acclaim for performing his own stunts in the past, but he kept true to his word to Engleberg. It is Loren Janes who performs the daring hanging stunt on the el, sixty feet in the air at fifty-five miles an hour.

While Steve did shoot the close-ups on the train at fast speeds, it was Janes just behind the cameras, just five feet away, ready to grab Steve in case of an emergency.

The idea for the film's biggest stunt occurred while Combs and producer Mort Engleberg were driving around Chicago. Says Combs, "We devised the longest foot chase in the history of the business, and we're looking for an ending. Mort spoke up and said, 'What if we do something off these towers?' I said, 'It's right here in the middle of the city.'

He said, 'You never know until you ask.' " The two men then took a cruise through the Marina Towers, and again Engleberg came up with the idea. "We'll take the car out between the pillars and right into the water." Combs said, "You're crazy." Ever optimistic, Engleberg replied, "You never know until you ask."

Engleberg went to the proper authorities and got permission to drop the car off the sixteenth floor of the Marina Towers into the water below. Eleven different agencies became involved, including the Coast Guard and the Federal Aviation Administration.

The scene took ten days to shoot and required several additional extras. Steve nodded toward a teenage girl in the crowd gathered near the set, and she was recruited for that day. Her name was Karen Wilson. When the scene was completed, Steve asked her how she was going to spend her money. "I'm going to give it to my mom. She's real sick." Steve checked into her story and found out that the mother was dying of alcoholic poisoning. Steve went to pay Karen's mother a visit in a ghetto neighborhood deep in the heart of Chicago. "Is there anything I can do for you?" Steve asked the dying woman. She answered, "All my life I wanted my daughter to go to school. I could die a happy woman knowing my daughter had a way out of this slum." Steve placated her: "Don't you worry about a thing. I'm going to take care of Karen. You just worry about getting better."

Dean Williams, the still photographer on *The Hunter,* said at the time, "This was typical of Steve. He couldn't help himself with children. He asked Karen to take him to see her mother, and that's when this whole thing happened."

Karen Wilson said of that meeting, "My mom fell in love with him. She was always a McQueen fan. When Steve asked about taking care of me, mom was so pleased! She hadn't told me she was dying, but she said, 'Now there will always be somebody to take care of you.' "

When *The Hunter* was finished, Steve and Barbara took Wilson with them to Santa Paula and put her up in a private boarding school in Ojai, minutes from their ranch. The McQueens would also take her in on the weekends and treat her as if she were their own.

Wilson commented, "I have a real father, but he's not like Steve. Anyhow, I didn't know him. I saw him only about three years of my life. I don't know how to respect my father because I didn't know him. Now Steve, he was a complete father."

Wilson was astounded at the turn of events in her life. One minute she was living in a ghetto, and the next she was in a private boarding school studying to be a veterinarian. "It amazes me. There I was . . . a nobody. Then along he comes and takes me away. It's the greatest thing that has ever happened. Now my dreams can come true—to be happy, and to become a veterinarian. I had so little and now I have so much. My whole life has been turned around by this man. He came and—boom! Thanks to Steve McQueen, my life has a new beginning."

Back on the set of *The Hunter,* the cold Chicago winter was taking its toll on Steve. He developed a persistent cough that would stay with him for weeks. Pat Johnson had to step in and make sure that Steve got plenty of rest. He intervened when someone was taking up too much of Steve's energy. Gary Combs remembers Loren Janes suggesting to him, "Let's have a party for Steve. Come with me to his room." Combs, Janes, and Johnson ate cake, told stories, and had a wonderful time until Johnson announced, "It's time for Steve to go to bed." Combs thought to himself at the time, "The man should know for himself when it's time to go to bed." It wasn't until later that he learned why Johnson had taken over for Steve.

Loren Janes remembers a special moment with Steve in that same room. The two men had been friends for years, but Janes had never really told McQueen how much he meant to him. The basis of their friendship was respect, yet neither had ever told the other face to face how he felt. "Barbara was in the shower and we were chatting," Janes relates. "We were both in a melancholy-type mood and I just said, 'Steve, I've never told you this or said anything to you, what I'm about to say now, but I feel like I need to and I want to." Janes drew a deep breath and said, "I love you. I love you like a brother. I respect you. I think you're the greatest actor there is." Both men began to feel their throats tighten, but Steve managed to muster, "You know, I was just going to say the same thing." They sat for a few seconds, just staring, feeling a little bit uncomfortable. Then Janes broke the uneasy silence by joking, "I just can't help it. You're just an ugly old fart. You're so ugly." It broke the tension, as both men got up and gave each other a hug, complete with slaps on the back.

As filming concluded in Chicago, the company moved locations to Kankakee, Illinois, for ten days. The scene required the look of a Nebraska cornfield and Engleberg found it in Kankakee, a few hours drive from Chicago.

Two reporters from *The National Enquirer* arrived on location, sneaking around the set, trying to get a picture of the reclusive star. Steve heard about them and instead of getting angry, he got even. He recruited Loren Janes to share in the festivities. The reporters were usually lurking around in some bushes with their cameras and zoom lenses, waiting to get their pictures. As they peered through their cameras, McQueen and Janes snuck up behind and surprised them, yelling out,

"Boo!" Relates Janes, "These guys would jump in the air and we would run off. They kept sneaking around, and we kept scaring them. We finally found their car, so Steve and I went over and let out the air in all four of their tires. We were way out in the middle of nowhere in this cornfield. This place is way out of town. They were stranded, and we all went out to lunch and then we were going to another location. They were still trapped in the middle of nowhere."

Steve then turned the tables on the bumbling reporters. He had decided that scaring them was boring, so he grabbed a camera, snuck up behind the pair, and said, "Hey, guys!" As they turned around, he snapped their picture. He had reversed the situation.

A few weeks later the article came out and Janes asked Steve about it. Steve was shocked when he read it. "You know," he told Janes, "that article they wrote on me wasn't that bad. I guess they liked the fact that I played cat-and-mouse with them. It's really not a bad article." Years later, Janes is still amazed at the article. "We just ran them ragged," he laughs. "After a while, they weren't looking to find Steve, they were looking to see where he was sneaking up on them. We deviled those guys."

Filming resumed later in Los Angeles for a few final scenes. One scene involved Thorson's girlfriend, played by Kathryn Harrold, being held hostage by Tracy Walter. Thorson has to confront Walter while giving up his gun. The scene takes place in Alexander Hamilton High School, where Harrold's character is a teacher.

Thorson distracts Walter and diverts him into another room. The room happens to be the science lab, where natural gas is piped. As Thorson enters the room, he turns on all the gas valves and leaves. Walter enters and fires a bullet, and the room, along with Walter, goes up in a ball of fire.

Right before the actual filming of the scene, Gary Combs had gone to director Buzz Kulik and said, "Let's have a little fun with him." Kulik was game. Says Combs, "For that scene, Steve was supposed to come in and pull off all of these hoses on these little gas valves in the lab. He has to pull off the tubes before he turns on the valves, so I put on the tubes so tight that King Kong couldn't have pulled them off. Then 'Action.' He ran to the first valve and he couldn't pull it off. Then he went to the second one and couldn't get that. By the time he got to the third one, he realized something was wrong. The crew started laughing and then he did, too. He got a kick out of that one."

While the cast was filming at the high school, a student named Richard Kraus was walking home and noticed a few movie trucks pulling up to the school driveway and unloading equipment. Curiosity got the better of him, so he walked up to one of the people unloading equipment and asked what was going on. "Steve McQueen's making a movie here," he was told. Being a reporter for his school newspaper, *The Federalist,* Kraus thought it would be a great idea if he could interview McQueen, an exclusive.

What Kraus did not realize was that Steve McQueen hadn't given an interview in over eight years and had made it a policy not to do so. If he had something important to say, he would issue a statement through Rogers and Cowan. Nevertheless, Kraus raced home to get his camera and notepad.

When Kraus got back to the school, he happened to meet Loren Janes and asked, "What's going on?" Janes politely told Kraus, "Steve McQueen is making a movie called *The Hunter*. He's filming right now." Kraus responded, "Well, I was hoping to get an interview with him for my school newspaper and maybe take some pictures." Janes had to laugh to himself, but he gave Kraus some advice: "Let me tell you something, Steve McQueen hates anyone to take photos of him and he never, ever gives interviews." Kraus replied, "Okay, thanks for the advice."

Not one to be discouraged, Kraus managed to get onto the set and happened upon the catering truck. He spotted McQueen inside and opened the door. "Excuse me, Mr. McQueen," he said politely, "I'm Richard Kraus. Would you mind if I interview you for our high school newspaper and take a few pictures of you?" Steve liked his straightforward approach. He smiled, paused, then said, "Sure, no problem. Why don't you draw up a list of questions and come back later tonight. We'll still be here, and I'll give you the interview then." Kraus responded as if he always got his man, "Great. See you tonight."

"I don't even know if I had ever seen a Steve McQueen movie up to that point," says Kraus. "I sat down with my whole family to write all of these questions, because I knew nothing about the man."

Steve was filming the lab scene near the end of *The Hunter* when Kraus arrived. He finished the scene and spotted Kraus in the wings. "Okay, let's do the interview," he said. The crew overheard what McQueen said and became curious. Steve led Kraus down the hallway and sat down on some steps. "Go ahead," he ordered. But before Kraus could ask the first question, the crew showed up and sat down on the steps. They did not want to miss out on this one. They were dumbfounded by Steve's generosity.

Kraus's interview turned out to be the last one Steve McQueen ever gave. It appeared only in the Alexander Hamilton High School *Federalist* and is reprinted here with permission:

KRAUS: What was your first movie?

McQUEEN: (Before McQueen could respond, one of the crew yelled out, *"The Blob."* Steve was slightly embarrassed.) Let's not talk about that. I don't want to talk about that movie. Next question.

KRAUS: Do you have any plans in the near future for any more movies?

McQUEEN: That's a big question mark. When I finish this film I'd like to sit down and enjoy breakfast for once and then see from there. I'd like to make my next picture an action-adventure film. I enjoy variety. I liked *Love with the Proper Stranger,* which was a comedy. I had fun making *The Sand Pebbles,* which was mainly drama, and also *Bullitt,* an action film. So you see, I like different types of roles. The first film I was in was *The Blob* . . . no, I wasn't the blob. I played the part of a young boy. This was when I was about twenty-five. I was a late bloomer in the acting world.

KRAUS: What about your background?

McQUEEN: A lot of stuff I got into trouble for when I was a kid, people wouldn't even blink at today. I got into trouble with robbery and booze, but not really drugs, because they weren't considered bad at the time.

KRAUS: Does being famous disrupt your private life?

McQUEEN: Yes, it does. The important thing is to have your identity, but never blow your obscurity. That's the key to the kingdom, but the money makes me feel better.

KRAUS: You have not been in the public eye for the past few years, but even when you did make movies, you didn't give any interviews. What was the reason for your silence?

McQUEEN: For one thing, I don't have anything to say. Also, I think the press is full of shit. But I do have a certain respect for youth, and that's why I agreed to do this interview for your paper.

KRAUS: When was the last time you were interviewed?

McQUEEN: How long is a decade? (Someone blurts out ten years.) Then it's been ten years. I don't even remember who interviewed me.

KRAUS: What advice do you have for young people today who want to get into acting?

McQUEEN: It's very expensive to act, in both time and money. I don't advise going into acting at all. I'm one of the lucky ones. But if you decide to go into acting, be prepared to give all else up and live a straight life. That includes eating and sleeping right. You should see some of life so that you can peel life, and put it to use in your acting. Learning stuff on the streets helped my acting a lot. I'm not a "studied actor." You've got to be prepared to be rejected five times a day. That's where the importance of family comes in. The family gives you your rock strength.

KRAUS: Who were some of your idols when you were a teenager?

McQUEEN: Well, I don't think you'd remember any of my idols.

KRAUS: But teachers read our paper, also.

McQUEEN: But this isn't for the teachers. It's for the students.

When the interview was finished, Kraus asked if he could take some pictures to accompany the interview. "Sure," he was told. Loren Janes then handed a glossy to Kraus in front of McQueen. Knowing what to expect, McQueen prepared himself for one more question from Kraus: "Would you mind signing this for me?" Again, Steve simply smiled and said, "Sure."

Art Sarno, the publicist on the set of *The Hunter,* was ordered by Steve to keep a blanket of secrecy on all of his good deeds. Sarno thought the Karen Wilson story would be good press for McQueen. "Not a damn line about this! I didn't do it for the publicity," he said.

Sarno then suggested a story about the money Steve had donated to the church in Chicago. Again, he was told no. "It was frustrating for me, trying to promote the picture," says Sarno. "He would spend time with his kids, but if I had brought along the governor of Illinois, he would have said he wasn't interested in spending five minutes with him."

Sarno watched the Kraus-McQueen interview in amazement. When it was over, he walked up to Steve and said, "I don't understand it. *Life, Time,* and *Newsweek* all want to put you on the cover, and you won't talk to them. You haven't given an interview in ten years. Why give one now to a . . . a high school newspaper!?" Steve shrugged his shoulders and said, "Because I like kids. Youth is important." Sarno threw his hands up in the air as if to say, "I give up," and walked off.

Kraus brought a copy of the interview to publicist Warren Cowan for his review. Cowan was amazed and frustrated at the same time. Cowan would line up several interviews with McQueen for major magazines, and at the last minute Steve would drop out. Finally, a high school kid had been able to bag the reclusive star. Kraus sat in Cowan's office while Cowan read the interview. "I was amused to see Mr. Cowan call out to his staff members as they passed his open door, telling them to get in here to meet this kid who had just interviewed Steve McQueen," Kraus fondly remembers.

The last scene for *The Hunter* was shot at a Los Angeles hospital. The scene involved Ralph Thorson driving his pregnant girlfriend to the hospital, where she's ready to deliver. Steve was to run to the emergency desk and back out to the car, where Harrold would be proceeding to give birth. For the scene, Mort Engleberg thought it would be amusing to be a stroke victim in a wheelchair as Steve ran by. "I wish I had a copy of that first take," says Engleberg. "Steve was always very serious and seeing me sort of slumped down in a wheelchair broke him up. That was fun. Steve was a professional and, much to my surprise, did not demand or ask for perks like most big stars do today. I think that's just the way he was," says Engleberg.

Actor Ben Johnson, who knew Steve since the late fifties, also noticed the change in him on the set of *The Hunter*. "Back in the fifties, he was pretty tough for a lot of people to get along with. He had his mind made up on how he was going to do a scene. I think what impressed me the most about Steve was that the older he got, the more stable, the more mature, he got. And at the last, he got pretty confident. He was one of the best."

As for Steve's acting on *The Hunter,* while it certainly wasn't his best work, it was by far not the worst. Actress Kathryn Harrold remembers a scene in which she had felt Steve was not giving her anything to work with. "There was something that he did, something that amazed me about him," says Harrold. "We were doing this scene that I considered kind of dramatic, a scene where we were fighting. I kept thinking, 'He's not giving me anything. He's just saying his words. Nothing.' Then when I saw it on the screen, I couldn't believe what came over. I think that was my first real experience with what a great film actor was. It's like this magical thing that just leaps into the camera. You can't see it with the naked eye, but the camera picks it up. Steve had that more than any other actor I've ever worked with."

Loren Janes defends McQueen's work in *The Hunter:* "It was a totally different Steve McQueen movie, and to me it shows the genius of Steve. That was one of his better films, in my opinion. In *The Hunter,* he's a bad driver, and he grinds the gears and does everything wrong. He listens to classical music instead of rock. He likes the old things, and he puts on his granny glasses and is totally offbeat—a lot of little touches that were his ideas that added to the picture that made it a little different. I thought it was a neat picture. It wasn't that big of a film, because it had been so long since he'd done a picture that the younger generation didn't know who Steve McQueen was, so they didn't know what to look for in this film."

*The Hunter* indeed was not a big hit. It took in nearly $15 million domestically, $37 million worldwide. Though it more than made its money back for Paramount, it certainly wasn't the comeback vehicle Steve had hoped it would be for him.

At the film's end, Steve assessed, "Acting's been good to me. I've been well paid, I've met a lot of good people, and the challenges have been stimulating. And that's why I'm not ready to pack it in. I've got a few acting mountains left to climb."

On November 28, 1979, Steve McQueen's acting career came to an end. The "Chicago cough" that had plagued him throughout the picture followed him home to Santa Paula. While in Santa Paula, Crystal Endicott paid the McQueens a visit. Steve quietly pulled Crystal aside and asked, "What's the name of the doctor who examined your husband?" She obliged and gave him the doctor's name. Steve then asked, "Can he be trusted?" She assured him that the doctor was trustworthy.

Steve made the headlines of the December 5, 1979, issue of *Variety*. The article mentioned his new picture price: $5 million up front plus 15 percent of both the domestic and foreign box office take. The article also revealed that to prove his point, McQueen had turned down a firm $4 million offer from producer Carlo Ponti to star with his wife, Sophia Loren, in *The Manhattan Project*. Many friends believe McQueen wanted to hold off on any movie deals until he knew exactly what was wrong with him.

On December 10, Steve went to the doctor Crystal Endicott had suggested. He was told, "You need to go check with your doctor in Los Angeles, because we don't have the updated equipment they have there." What the doctor didn't reveal to Steve was that an X ray had shown a spot on his right lung. Steve was urged to check into Cedars-Sinai Hospital in Los Angeles.

Steve did so on December 17, 1979, under the assumed name of Don Schoonover. A new set of X rays revealed a massive tumor in his right lung.

Exploratory surgery was called for immediately. Two hours passed before doctors could diagnose the tumor.

It was determined that Steve had mesothelioma, a rare and deadly form of cancer. The diagnosis was terminal.

# THE BIG C

*I don't want to grow old in this business and die with a
martini in my hand.*

STEVE MCQUEEN

STEVE'S PUBLICIST, David Foster, remembers a time during the filming of
*The Getaway* in 1972 when he, Steve, and Ali had taken a trip to the
University of Texas in Austin.

McQueen was having throat problems throughout the shoot and finally, at Ali's urging, he agreed to go for an examination after the day's
filming. "Steve didn't want to shut down the company on the set. He
was really professional about those kinds of things. The insurance
would show he was responsible for shutting down a movie set, and it
just doesn't look good for a star to do that," says Foster.

Foster, McQueen, and MacGraw drove from San Marcos to Austin
after the day's shoot. Steve was recommended to a throat specialist in
Austin by his doctor in Beverly Hills. He was given a thorough examination. After the doctor was finished, the silence and uncertainty finally
got to him. "Give it to me straight, Doc," he said. "Do I have the Big
C?"

Foster and MacGraw looked at each other and couldn't help but
smile. To them, the line sounded like something out of a James Cagney
movie. "It's not so funny now, because it was probably the beginning of
the end [of the cancer], though we didn't know it at the time," said
Foster. The doctor told Steve it was a polyp and that it should be removed right away.

The polyp was removed without complications. Always aware of his
smoking habit, Steve may have escaped cancer this time, though he
knew one day it would be waiting patiently for him.

*   *   *

The day after Steve was admitted to Cedars-Sinai Hospital, tests revealed that exploratory surgery was necessary and was scheduled for Saturday, December 22. A biopsy revealed a massive tumor in Steve's right lung, which was diagnosed as malignant. Barbara was told that Steve was suffering from a rare type of cancer called mesothelioma. The cancer is usually caused by asbestos inhalation. Steve recalled later on that his stint in the merchant marines had him swabbing the inside of the ship where the ceiling was lined with asbestos.

Barbara was accompanied by employee Grady Ragsdale and flying instructor Sammy Mason. Following the biopsy, Steve asked for Barbara first and then the other two an hour later.

Steve's first reaction to the news was a grim determination to beat the cancer. Only a handful of people knew about Steve's health, and he intended to keep it that way. He felt his children didn't need to go through undue pain or suffering, so he chose not to tell Terry and Chad.

Steve had to spend his last Christmas in the hospital.

On Saturday, December 29, 1979, he was released from Cedars-Sinai and arrived at the ranch in Santa Paula.

In *The Final Chapter*, Grady Ragsdale revealed how Steve wanted to keep the cancer under wraps: "He [Steve] pulled out several recent newspaper clippings and handed them to me.*

"In the beam of a flashlight I read of Steve's stay in the hospital, and of a rare fungus infection discovered on one of his lungs. Tests have revealed nothing serious."

Grady said, "This stuff isn't true." Steve grinned. "Yes, it is. It's true as far as the public is concerned. It's what I want people to believe." He then swore Grady to secrecy, demanding, "I don't want anyone to know I have cancer."

The subject between the two men then broached Steve's movie career. Steve said, "My agent wants me to do another movie. I told him to put it on the back burner for a while and I'd think about it. I don't think he'll be suspicious. I've gone a few years between pictures before. It's not like I'm bustin' to work all the time." Grady then suggested, "If he's got a good script, why not read it?"

Steve said, "Let's face it, pal, I'm out of the picture business. I've done my last film. It's time for me to move over and make room for somebody else."

---

* Ragsdale, Grady. *Steve McQueen: The Final Chapter*. Vision House Books, 1983.

And with that statement, Steve passed on the brass ring with his blessings.

Crystal Endicott was eagerly awaiting any type of news from Steve. She remembers her conversation with him the first time he was diagnosed: "I think he didn't tell anybody at first because he didn't believe it was real. I think he felt, 'This isn't happening to me.' That's what goes through your mind when you're given a death sentence." Endicott's husband, Larry, had been diagnosed with melanoma just months before. It was in Larry that Steve confided the most those first months. "They talked about it a lot because they were going through the same thing together. My husband would come home and say, 'Steve felt bad today.' They could share this with each other," says Endicott. (Larry Endicott died a year after Steve.)

The press, *The National Enquirer,* in particular, began to descend on the McQueen ranch in Santa Paula as rumors of his visit to Cedars-Sinai circulated. Nothing had been written so far, but the media were ready for a Steve McQueen scandal.

Phil Parslow received a phone call from agent Phil Gersh around this time. Gersh had just thrown a party to display his world-famous art collection. A doctor attending the party brought up McQueen's name. Gersh rang Parslow and said, "McQueen is very sick." Shocked, Parslow questioned, "How do you know?" Gersh replied, "I threw a party last night and this doctor attended. He said, 'Steve's a very sick man.'" Gersh had asked the doctor, "You mean, as in mortal dead?" The doctor bowed his head and didn't respond.

James Coburn called Neile and told her he'd heard some rumors about Steve and his condition. She told Coburn Steve was fine. Neile didn't convince Coburn, however, and he decided to do some additional checking. "I checked around a little bit and found that he had inoperable cancer and there was nothing I could do," says Coburn. Coburn had tried to reach McQueen, but by then, Steve had begun to shut out the public, and even some of his old friends.

At Cedars-Sinai, Steve was told his cancer was inoperable and incurable. Only twenty-four cases of mesothelioma had been documented at that time. All twenty-four had died. The cancer was also found along the lining of his stomach, and golf ball–size nodules were discovered at the base of his neck and on his chest, making it impossible to operate. Immediate chemotherapy treatments were recommended.

Steve did actually take one of these early treatments. As he was sitting in a chair waiting for the first session to begin, a nurse came in and told him, "I want you to hold still because I don't want to get this on your skin, because it will burn and blister." Scared and shocked, Steve said,

"What?" The nurse repeated, "It will burn and blister." His eyes narrowing, Steve asked, "If it does that to the outside of my body, what will it do to the inside of my body?" The nurse didn't answer. As Steve got up to leave, he told the nurse, "Forget it."

Steve was never quite sure of Barbara Minty and her motives. Even though he was a movie star and could have any woman he wanted, he never could quite fully accept what Minty saw in him. She was so young (twenty-seven) and beautiful, and he was closing in on fifty.

The two had been seeing each other for three years when Barbara asked Crystal Endicott for a favor. In April 1979, she put Endicott up to the task of asking Steve why he hadn't asked for her hand in marriage. Barbara had been a good and faithful girlfriend and was wondering where their relationship was going. Endicott obliged and asked Steve, "How come you don't marry Barbara?" Steve replied, "I don't want to marry her if all she wants is my money." When she returned, Barbara asked, "What did he say?" Not wanting to hurt her feelings, Endicott said, "He wouldn't tell me, Barbara."

On the set of *The Hunter,* stuntman Loren Janes had been riding Steve about marrying Barbara. He sat Steve down in front of Barbara. It was time for a lecture. "I was teasing Steve, but he also knew I was half-serious. I told him, 'Ninety percent of the cases I know, the woman ends up getting more hurt than the man.' " Janes went on to tell McQueen, "Ninety percent of the time, the woman is more emotionally involved. When a woman moves in with a man, he gets his laundry done for free, his cooking done for free, his house cleaned for free. He gets his sex for free. He gets all the advantages and privileges of marriage for free without the responsibility. The main thing is, how do you introduce her to people? Do you introduce her as your lady? What you're really saying is, 'This is my shack-up.' If you love someone, how can you say, 'This is my shack-up. This is the gal I'm sleeping with.' You're insulting her. It's not fair to her because you're living like a married couple and she might be missing out on a great guy who will love her and marry her." Janes then stated, "You ought to marry the gal. You'll be much happier."

Now that Steve had been diagnosed with cancer, he revealed to Endicott that he was going to marry Barbara. "We've been together for three years and I don't want to lose her. If I don't have long to live, I want to make sure she's taken care of," said Steve.

On January 16, 1980, Steve and Barbara Minty were married in the living room of the ranch house in Santa Paula. Steve had contacted Pastor Leonard DeWitt and informed him of his decision. He wanted

DeWitt to marry the two. DeWitt declined Steve's offer: "I explained to Steve my viewpoint that I could not marry him because he had been divorced before. He held no ill feelings toward me. He still came to church." DeWitt suggested that the associate pastor, Dr. Leslie Miller, could perform the ceremony. Says Miller, "I told Steve that since he and Barbara were Christians, they are born again in the eyes of the Lord and are free to marry." That was good enough for Steve. The two also had to take Bible study lessons on marriage and how to live the Christian life. Recalls Miller, "Steve was very receptive to it, always asking questions, never missing a lesson unless he had to. He liked the discipline in his life."

The ceremony was simple, as was the attire. Steve wore blue jeans, tennis shoes, and a long-sleeved shirt. The bride wore a white pants suit and carried a bouquet of daisies. Sammy Mason and his wife, Wanda, were the only couple present. Steve called Loren Janes after the wedding and said he was "thrilled to death. This is the greatest thing that has ever happened to me."

In February 1980, Steve returned to Cedars-Sinai for more tests and examinations. New X rays revealed that the cancer was spreading. The doctors had more bad news for Steve: they gave him two months, tops, to live. Steve stubbornly refused to believe he was going to die. "I can't believe it's over. I won't believe it. There's so much I want to do, have to do!" he said.

The news of Steve's second visit to Cedars-Sinai was what the press had been waiting for: a confirmation of his condition.

On the first of March, Pat Johnson came back from location in San Antonio, Texas, where he had been away since late July. Johnson had heard the rumors but figured if Steve had anything to say, he would have said something by now. Johnson had been back only a day when he got a phone call from Steve. "Pat, I have to talk to you," Steve said calmly. Recalls Johnson, "There was no indication in his voice that anything was amiss. It seemed important, but certainly nothing really bad."

They agreed to meet at the ranch in Santa Paula. As Johnson arrived at the McQueen household, he could sense that Steve was in a somber mood. "Let's go for a walk," Steve said.

As the two friends walked, Johnson remembers that the only noise he heard were the oil drills in the distance. Finally, after much silence, Steve said, "Pat, they found something on my lung. They're not sure what it is. It could be potentially life-threatening. I thought you should know." Steve went on to say, "I don't know what the future holds, but whatever it is, I'm gonna fight it all the way." Tears began to well up in

Johnson's eyes. All he could think at the moment was, "This can't be happening."

*The National Enquirer* broke the story on March 18, 1980, with a cover story and the headline STEVE MCQUEEN'S HEROIC BATTLE AGAINST CANCER. The article read:

> Frantic last-ditch efforts by doctors have failed to halt a vicious and inoperable lung cancer that is killing Steve McQueen.
> The end could come within two months, believes one of his doctors. But the steely-eyed screen hero is battling back bravely.

The article went on to say that doctors had operated on McQueen, implanting cobalt in his chest, and had "sewed him up, leaving the cobalt inside."

To add insult to injury, the photos that accompanied the article were obtained through the sneaky efforts of *The National Enquirer*.

Just a few weeks before the March 18 story broke, a young man had strolled into the cafe at the Santa Paula Airport. The tabloid knew it was a local McQueen haunt and sent the reporter in to get the story. The reporter spotted McQueen and positioned himself near the star. Liking young people, Steve struck up a friendly conversation with him. He was in his environment and felt completely at ease. After finishing his meal, he invited the young man, who had not identified himself, to the hangar to see his planes and motorcycle collection. When the two arrived there, they were met by Barbara Minty. The young man marveled at the collection, and Steve beamed like a proud father at the compliment. The young man then pulled out a camera and began taking pictures. Alarmed, but not threatened, Steve stepped forward and casually asked, "What's the camera for?" The young man responded, "Oh, in my art class in college, we're taking photos of anything that would make a fascinating picture, but if you would like me to stop taking pictures, I will." Touched by his sincerity, Steve backed off and politely said, "No, go ahead. It makes no never big mind to me. Take as many pictures as you want." And the young man began to click away, first shots of the planes and the motorcycles, then, when Barbara and Steve weren't looking, at close-ups of them. When the story came out, the photos accompanying it were those taken by the young man. Steve had been had.

Bud Ekins was the first of Steve's friends to approach him. One of Ekins's friends had said to him, "Too bad about McQueen." Ekins replied, "What do you mean?" The friend then handed him the *National Enquirer* article. Ekins went that Sunday to visit McQueen after church.

He found Steve in the backyard sitting down, sipping some coffee. Ekins minced no words: "What's this cancer stuff?" Steve replied, "Oh, those assholes are so full of shit. I don't know why they write stuff like that." Steve then took off his shirt and said, "See, no scars." Ekins believed his friend. He had no reason to think Steve would lie to him. Relates Ekins, "The article said that the doctors had cut him open and found cancer and had sewed him back up and told him to forget it. So, I'm standing there, looking for where they opened him up, and I don't see any scars where they've cut him. So I believed him." (Later, after Steve passed away, Neile revealed to Ekins that the incision was made under Steve's armpit. Steve had held his arm down while taking off his shirt, thus hiding his scar from Ekins.)

Steve was hoping the movie premiere of *Tom Horn* on March 28, 1980, would be the perfect tool to dispel all the rumors. He did not necessarily want to make a public appearance but felt that this was the perfect opportunity to show the world he was in good health.

The scene at Grauman's Chinese theater was crazy. The previous week, Steve McQueen had been the hottest name in the tabloids. Now he was going to make a rare live appearance. The media were out in full force. There was a certain electricity in the air that night.

Hundreds of people lined the streets around the theater for a glimpse of Steve. Strategically, Steve planned to get to the premiere only a few minutes before the picture opened, cutting down on the opportunity for questions he knew would be asked.

Steve and Barbara drove up in his pickup truck a few minutes before the 8:00 P.M. show. A flurry of flashbulbs began popping as they made their way into the theater. One reporter shouted, "Do you really have lung cancer?" With a sheepish grin, Steve said, "I don't know where you get your information." As the McQueens pushed forward, the questioning became more intense. "Whatever you've heard is ridiculous, just rumors. Do I look like I have lung cancer?" Steve asked. The reporters backed off and Steve and Barbara went inside.

Just before the closing credits rolled, Steve and Barbara got up to leave, hoping to make a clean getaway. Almost two hours after Steve first appeared, there were still hundreds of fans waiting to catch another look at the reclusive star. Seeing the crowd converge on them, Steve and Barbara just made it to his truck before photographers started running after them. As they climbed in and shut the doors, Steve accelerated the truck forward, nearly running over an aggressive photographer.

The *Tom Horn* premiere left Steve exhausted. He did not leave the Santa Paula ranch for a whole week.

* * *

When Steve wasn't busy flying his airplanes and tinkering around the hangar, he and Barbara spent most of their time looking through health magazines. He had decided that the doctors had given up hope on him. He told the people who knew he had cancer, "The doctors at Cedars say I'm a goner."

The odyssey to find a cure began as soon as Steve got back from Cedars-Sinai. He started looking for alternative methods of treatment. These included treatments by nonlicensed doctors.

The first such doctor Steve contacted told him that several weeks of intravenous feeding, large doses of vitamins, and a new diet could possibly reverse the cancer. Steve took the advice and was administered these treatments in a camper parked outside the doctor's office that Steve rented, since legally, the doctor could not do them in his office. When Steve went back to Cedars-Sinai to see if the treatments had reversed the cancer, he was told that tests revealed no reversal, and he dumped the doctor soon after.

An article in the *Journal of the Nutritional Academy* had caught Steve's eye. The article featured a history of Dr. William Donald Kelley and his alternative method of treating cancer.

Kelley advocated an approach to treating cancer through "nonspecific metabolic therapy," which he practiced at the International Health Institute of Dallas, Texas.

Kelley's program included a diet, meticulously set up by a computer program, nutritional supplements, and detoxification. The program addressed the immune system and metabolism. It was not a cancer treatment program, but a very individualized program to build up the immune system and the patient's overall health. Says an advocate of the Kelley program, "The American Medical Association has always taught to treat the symptom. The Kelley method treats the individual's immune system. Modern medicine has been a generation of process. The practiced doctors have been trained to be disease fighters, but they are not health builders."

As was Steve's nature, he employed a detective to do a background check on Dr. Kelley before he contacted him.

Steve found out that Dr. Kelley had claimed in 1965, while practicing dentistry, that he was stricken with cancer of the liver and pancreas. He, too, was told by doctors that he had only a few months to live. Reinstituting some of the nutritional courses he had taken at Baylor University, Kelley had experimented with large quantities of nutritional liver and pancreatic enzymes. He had also employed coffee enemas to cleanse and detoxify his body. He claimed to have cured himself of cancer through these methods.

In 1969, Kelley wrote a book, *One Answer to Cancer*, detailing his program and his cure for cancer.

In 1976, Kelley had his dentistry license suspended for five years. It seemed that numerous patients had complained about his interest in their health, not in their teeth. That same year a court injunction temporarily stopped publication of Kelley's book.

Kelley's troubles didn't end there. The background check also revealed that he had been investigated by more than fifteen government agencies, including the Internal Revenue Service, the FBI, and the Food and Drug Administration.

Steve had all of the cards in front of him. He knew all about Kelley, but forged ahead, "When you're in my shoes, you'll grab at anything that's been known to work," he said.

A meeting was set up at Kelley's organic farm in Winthrop, Washington. Steve and Barbara had told friends they were headed there for their honeymoon, but instead they visited with Kelley, who outlined his program for Steve.

Steve came back from that meeting impressed by Kelley. "He treats the body that has the disease, not the disease that has the body," he said.

Steve promised Kelley that he would implement a "body-cleansing diet," but that was all he promised. He was still unsure about jumping into the program.

Says a survivor of the Kelley method, "I was given twenty-one days to live. The doctors suggested that I get my affairs in order." The survivor's house faced the side door of the town funeral home. "That day, I saw three bodies carried out in body bags, and I said to myself, 'That's not what I want!' I had to change my lifestyle around and I was willing to do anything to live. Dr. Kelley's program saved my life. Dr. Kelley is a caring man. He wasn't trying to sell me anything. He just wanted to help. He is not a fraud. I am living proof of that." Twenty years after being diagnosed with cancer, the patient is alive and prospering.

Sometime in mid-April, Steve paid Bud Ekins a visit at his motorcycle shop. McQueen brought with him a stack of pictures of antique motorcycles someone was looking to sell. He wanted Ekins to appraise them. Ekins asked, "What kind of prices?" Steve said, "They're all on the back of the pictures." Ekins looked at the prices and the condition of each bike and said, "Christ, this is heaven. Buy 'em." Steve asked Ekins, "Will you go with me to Boston then?" Ekins agreed. Steve announced, "Great, I'll buy some tickets." Ekins interrupted and said, "Uh, first class, Steve. First class." Steve replied, "Well, you fucker. What are you, some kind of movie star that has to fly first class all the time?" Ekins stood his ground. "First class, Steve, or I ain't going," he said. Ekins laughs today at the fact that he got Steve to pay four times the coach rate for the first-class tickets. "Oh, he moaned about that one," says Ekins. "I just did it to jab him a little bit."

In Boston, they bought up the whole collection. On the flight back, Ekins noticed that Steve was drifting in and out of the conversation, sometimes looking out the window for long periods of time. "He became very melancholy," remembers Ekins. Out of the blue, Steve blurted out, "If anything ever happens to me, I want you to have all my bikes." Ekins looked at Steve as if he were nuts. Steve paused, then asked, "Well, wouldn't you do the same for me?" Ekins replied, "Hell, no, I wouldn't leave you my bikes. I would want the money to go to my children." Steve thought about that for a moment and then came up with a solution. "Tell you what," he said, "if anything ever happens to me, I want you to pick the best two bikes in my collection, and that's my final word on the matter." The two men agreed, and shook hands on the deal.

Ekins reflects, "This was Steve's way of telling me he was going to die. He had already been diagnosed."

Almost a decade had passed since the ill-fated *Le Mans*. Steve had one loose end to tie up, something that had been in the back of his mind all that time: Mario Iscovich.

Iscovich had been the gofer and close personal friend of the McQueen family whom Steve had scared off with his erratic behavior.

Steve tracked down Iscovich and invited him to have lunch at the ranch in Santa Paula. He wanted to catch up on old times. Iscovich was writing screenplays (he is now a big-time producer for Disney) and at the time was working on a project for Stanley Kramer.

After lunch, the two of them went into the living room for a chat. Without warning, Steve said, "Mario, I don't think I'm gonna make it." Iscovich knew what Steve was talking about. He had heard the industry rumors, read the papers. Steve went on, "Is everything all right between you and me? You're not sore at me anymore, are ya, kid?" Mario felt a tear come to his eye and moved closer to Steve. "No, Steve. I was mad only for a little bit. I put it all aside many years ago," he said. Then the two hugged each other like long-lost brothers.

Iscovich said of that meeting, "You could see that Steve was not well. Just one look at him and I could see he was not all right."

In the last week of April 1980, Steve and Barbara planned a "real honeymoon." They drove to San Pedro to board the *Pacific Princess* for

Acapulco. Steve became ill and experienced shortness of breath. He stayed inside the cabin for most of the trip until the ship docked.

*Variety* reported on April 29, 1980:

> Can you believe Steve McQueen on a cruise ship? He and bride Barbara are off on a honeymoon to Mexico. The tourists will find him hiding behind a beard.

The friendly article tipped off the other tabloids and as soon as Steve stepped off the *Princess,* a photo was taken that revealed a slimmer, exhausted McQueen.

One tabloid wrote, "The ailing superstar looked terribly ill. He rarely left his cabin, and his bedside was covered with pills left in plain sight. When the ship docked in Acapulco, the McQueens went directly to a private villa at one of the luxurious hotels where they remained in total seclusion."

When Steve returned to Santa Paula, he phoned Dr. Kelley. He wanted to know what Kelley could do for him if he checked into the Plaza Santa Maria, Kelley's new clinic in Mexico. Kelley didn't promise any miracles, but he told Steve that now every minute counted. Steve would inform Kelley of his decision soon.

Steve's former manager, Hilly Elkins, received a phone call from out of the blue. The two men had stayed in touch over the years, but it had been at least three years since they had last talked. At that time, Steve had called to get Elkins's opinion on *An Enemy of the People.* "It has a lot of words," Steve was told. Elkins was never one to hesitate getting to the point.

Now Steve called Elkins for lunch. Lunch, thought Elkins, Steve Mc-Queen didn't do lunch. The past few months, Elkins had heard the rumors about Steve's condition. "There's an old joke in Hollywood," says Elkins. "If you want to keep a secret, don't tell Sue Mengers." Steve suggested Ma Maison. Elkins became worried. "When someone who usually asks you to meet him at the back room of Denny's asks you to meet at Ma Maison, you get worried," he says. "It was so out of character that it was the first time I really got concerned about him."

The lunch turned out to be Steve's way of saying good-bye to the public. Reporter Robin Leach, among those in attendance, noted: "When the crowd applauded him, McQueen stabbed a foot-long cigar in the air as a gesture of joy. Everyone at the party believed he was celebrating a return to health and a new movie contract."

Actress and friend Suzanne Pleshette was there with her husband, Tom Gallagher. She sat across the room from Steve and Barbara. The two caught each other's eye and Steve mouthed out the words, "How are you?" Pleshette gave Steve a thumbs up sign. She then mouthed back to Steve, "How are you?" Steve gave a big toothy smile and shot back two thumbs up. Says Pleshette, "He was worried about me, even when he was dying. I don't think he rested until I married Tommy. That was the only guy he approved of. I loved him then, and I will always love him."

Barbara Minty said of the lunch at Ma Maison, "He didn't want them to remember him as a weakened cancer victim. Steve wanted to be remembered as the man he once was, and that day, he acted the part beautifully."

While Steve said good-bye to the public at Ma Maison, in private he was telling his other close friends good-bye as well.

Richard Attenborough recalls the last time he saw Steve. "Steve was never one of our great correspondents. He would never write, but he would call. I called him, told him I was in town for a few days." They arranged to meet at the Brown Derby, an old Hollywood haunt. "The Brown Derby has this long corridor you have to go through before you get to the main bar. There was only one guy in the place, a guy with a heavy beard and mustache. McQueen was never on time for anything, so I waited for him outside. Five minutes went by. Ten minutes went by. Fifteen minutes went by. Finally, I said to myself, 'Even Steve isn't usually this late.' So I decided to go inside and ask the bartender if Steve left me a message. I went right up to the bartender and was standing next to the bearded man. Before I opened my mouth to ask the bartender if Steve had left a message, the bearded man said, 'Hi, stranger.' It was McQueen. He greeted me with a great big bear hug, something he had never done before. I think it was his way of saying good-bye to me. He knew he was dying."

Steve repeated the same scenario with Hilly Elkins a few days later, except Elkins knew Steve was dying. The unspoken remained unspoken that night for light conversation. The two men hugged and never saw each other again.

Loren Janes remembers trying to call Steve, but his line was busy. Janes hung up the phone and it rang. "Hey, Loren, this is Steve." Janes replied, "I just tried calling you. Your phone was busy." Steve inquired, "What did you want?" Janes replied, "I wanted to see you, wanted to get together and talk." Steve said, "That's why I was calling. You want to meet somewhere?"

Steve flew to the Sand Canyon airport to meet Janes for lunch under the wing of his plane. Janes was one of the first people to know about Steve's cancer. When he went to visit Steve in Cedars-Sinai, Janes told

Steve at the time, "You've licked everything else, you're tough enough to lick this."

That day at the airport, Steve and Janes reminisced about everything, and Steve mentioned his will. "Boy, is Bud [Ekins] sure going to be surprised when he gets my bike collection," he said. He then told Janes who was to get what in the will, with the exception of what Janes was to receive. The subject of death was brought up as well. "Loren, I'm going to try and whip this. I'm going to try anything," Steve said. Janes asked, "Are there things that they've tried on animals that they haven't tried on humans?" He replied, "Yeah, it worked on some animals and on some it didn't." "What if it kills you?" Janes said after a pause. Steve answered, "Well, so what. I'm going to die anyway. If I die sooner, it's less painful and maybe if I try some things and they use me as a guinea pig, and I die, and they learn from it, maybe it can help someone else." The lunch ended as the sun was going down. The star and his stuntman of twenty-two years said good-bye to each other, then Steve flew off into the California sky.

McQueen also called his old friend Steve Ferry out of the blue. The two hadn't seen each other since after the filming of *Le Mans*. Ferry had since remarried a much younger woman. McQueen thought it would be a good idea to get their two young wives together. While visiting in Santa Paula, Ferry thought it odd that Steve had surrounded himself with religious types of people. He certainly wasn't the Steve of old.

Friend Don Gordon was also invited to Santa Paula. After dinner, they went to Steve's hangar to talk alone. Gordon was getting ready to go on location for a film in England. He announced, "When I get back, let's go flying." Steve replied, "Sure." He then hugged Gordon. Gordon had no idea that Steve was sick.

"Now, in retrospect, I realize he was saying good-bye to me," says Gordon.


Steve called friend and business manager Bill Maher to request $375,000. Dr. Kelley had given Steve a bill for his services, and now Steve had to get the money through Maher.

Maher saw what was happening. He realized that if Steve were to keep paying this man, this mysterious doctor, there would be no money left for his kids. Maher put his foot down. Says a close source, "Steve fired everyone around him. Maher was the guy who had to say no to Steve. He was in a tough position. Everyone closest to Steve was pushed further away from him in the last year, when they should have been there to help him the most. Other people crawled out of the woodwork to get a piece of the action, to get involved with Steve when they shouldn't have."

In June, Steve stopped taking visitors. Pilot Mike Dewey recalls, "Steve didn't tell people it was cancer. He told me it was a lung infection. He was embarrassed about it in a manly sort of way. His stomach started to swell. When he physically started to deteriorate, he stopped coming around to the airport. I think the fact that he didn't look good had as much to do with his not feeling good either."

Sammy Mason, Steve's flight instructor, got a call from Steve in late June wanting to take up the plane one last time. Steve knew he didn't have the strength to take it up alone and asked Mason to help. Mason arrived at the hangar, but Steve never did show. "He just didn't have the strength," said Mason.

Frightened of his worsening condition, Steve called Dr. Kelley in desperation. "What can you do for me if I go all the way with your program?" Steve asked. Kelley made no promises, but again told McQueen that every second was precious.

On July 28, 1980, *The Hunter* was released to a less than enthusiastic response. *The Village Voice* pronounced him "a tired daredevil . . . all used up." The *Los Angeles Herald Examiner* thought McQueen was "way off stride . . . [his] once-crisp physical reflexes look shot."

Robert Relyea also noticed something wrong with Steve's performance in *The Hunter*. Relyea was to preview a film in Westwood and went to the theater earlier that day to check it out. *The Hunter* was playing, and Relyea sat for a few minutes watching his old business partner's latest film. Then it hit him: something wasn't right. Says Relyea, "There's a thing where it's not a limp, but if you know somebody well and they're moving tentatively, you can recognize it. I thought that it was strange. It looked like he was hurting. Very tough to articulate. I had heard no rumors up to that point. I just thought he looked strange, like he was hurting when he walked. It must have been a month later when somebody said, in typical Hollywood fashion, 'I hear that . . .' And then it turned out the rumor was true."

On July 30, 1980, Steve checked into Cedars-Sinai for one last diagnosis. While he was sedated, the doctors pulled Barbara aside and told her, "Steve's cancer is getting worse. It's incurable, it's inoperable. You take him home and keep him sedated. When the pain becomes too much, you bring him back here and we'll put him in bed and give him whatever it takes so that he can die in his sleep." Barbara was dumbfounded. She couldn't believe what she was hearing. The doctors had practically pronounced Steve a dead man. There was no hope in what she was told. When Steve awoke, Barbara relayed the message. Mc-

Queen defiantly said, "I'm a fighter. I don't believe that bullshit. I believe I can make it."

Pat Johnson saw Steve the day before and described him as very drawn. "His skin had a grayish pallor to it. His eyes were sunken and his blue eyes had turned gray. He did not look good at all," recalls Johnson.

Steve then called his ranch hand, Grady Ragsdale, from Cedars.* "I want you to check out the silver Ford pickup, fill it with gas, and bring it to me here."

Ragsdale replied, "Sure, when?"

"Today, as soon as possible. We're ready to go now."

Curiously, Ragsdale asked, "What do you mean?"

"Just bring the pickup. You can drive Barbara's car back to the ranch. We're headed in the opposite direction."

Grady asked, "Where?"

"Mexico."

---

* Ragsdale, Grady. *Steve McQueen: The Final Chapter*. Vision House Books, 1983.

# MEXICO

*Mexico and I are old friends. I've been there many times and it's always been good to me.*

STEVE MCQUEEN

IN APRIL 1980, Dr. Kelley leased Plaza Santa Maria, a Mexican health spa, just thirty miles south of San Diego. After several government agencies began leaning on him, Kelley decided to leave the United States and continue his practice legally in Mexico. Just eighteen months earlier, the health spa had been an oceanside tourist resort. Now, it was a last stop for cancer patients.

McQueen knew about Dr. Kelley's troubles, but still placed his trust in the only man who gave him hope.

McQueen even knew of the death threats and attempts made on the doctor's life, but reasoned, "It makes sense. Think of all the companies pushing drugs on cancer victims, and all the doctors doing needless operations. Then this guy comes along who says he has a cure without drugs or operations. If he's right, and he seems to know what he's talking about, the people who call themselves experts could be made to look real funny."

Steve drove himself and Barbara the full 250 miles to Plaza Santa Maria on July 31, 1980, and checked in. He registered under the alias of Don Schoonover.

Teena Valentino, Steve's metabolic technician, remembers McQueen arriving wearing a cowboy hat and sweat pants and smoking a cigar. Steve and Barbara were greeted by Dr. Kelley, Dr. Dwight McKee, and hospital director Bill Evans. Dr. Kelley told him, "Steve, this is Teena Valentino. She's your MT—the best we've got. She'll take good care of you." Steve noticed Teena staring at his cigar and felt obliged to men-

378

tion, "They're my reward, no more than one a day. I've got to have something to look forward to."

That afternoon, Steve was given a full checkup by Dr. McKee. He complained of shortness of breath (it was later discovered that one lung had collapsed), a lack of appetite, chronic headaches, and a ringing in his ears. In addition, his back was so sore that he was immediately given shots of Demerol to ease the pain.

After the examination, Steve was given a 2,500-item questionnaire to fill out that would determine his daily regimen. Dr. Rodrigo Rodriguez, Plaza Santa Maria's supervisor, described the regimen:

He was awakened at 7:00 A.M. to a high-fiber natural food breakfast. At midday he had a high-protein drink made from crushed almonds. Dinner was at 6:00 P.M. It generally consisted of soup, whole-grain bread, and fresh garden-grown vegetables. Fish was also served and beef was added twice a week. At intervals during the day, Mr. Mc-Queen was given a total of more than fifty pills—vitamins, minerals, and supplements—to restore his body balance. He also received a Japanese extract of baccilli Z, laetrile, enzyme implants, thymus extract injections, coffee enemas, an injection of sheep embryos, chiropractic manipulation, saunas, body massages, and exercises designed for full muscle relaxation. He was usually asleep before midnight. The next morning we began the whole process again."

When checked out later by the press, it was revealed that the clinic had no lab, no X-ray equipment, and no clinical facilities, though it did have facilities for blood work. Dr. Rodriguez defended the clinic, saying, "I have seen cases of complete remission at the Plaza Santa Maria and other hospitals in Mexico." Says an ex-patient, "There is a big misconception about Plaza Santa Maria. It was *not* a hospital. Yes, it was equipped with nurses, therapists, cooks, and American doctors. The objective at Santa Maria was to teach the will to live, how to diet, how to put a program together. It was more one on one with the patient, but families were encouraged to stay there as well. Dr. Kelley was labeled a cancer doctor. He didn't cure patients, he set up programs so that the patients cured themselves." Adds Teena Valentino, "I learned at Plaza that the rules of nutrition didn't always apply in the exact way I had been taught. Each case was an individual juggle of medication, nutrition, and the various other therapies offered. Each patient needed constant monitoring."

On August 5, it was discovered that Steve's lungs and abdominal cavity were filled with serosanguineous fluid. "When I lay down I fill up with phlegm. I can't get air. I feel like I'm suffocating at times," complained McQueen. A tap was arranged to relieve the discomfort. A needle was inserted and 1,100 cc of red amber fluid was removed.

A few days later, while in the United States, Dr. Kelley called a press conference to announce the arrival of his newest patient, actor Steve McQueen. Kelley also made an appearance on Tom Snyder's *Tomorrow* show. It was on that show that millions learned of Kelley's "nonspecific metabolic therapy," which included a computerized diet program, nutritional supplements, and "detoxification" by coffee enemas and fasts.

Kelley told Snyder, "The [American] doctors gave [McQueen] no hope. His chances are excellent if he has the discipline to follow the program. I believe with all my heart that this approach represents the future of cancer therapy. It took Winston Churchill to popularize antibiotic medicine. Steve McQueen will do the same for metabolic therapy."

Kelley also admitted, "There are no recoveries from Steve's form of cancer in the medical literature—if he recovers, we'll be breaking new ground."

Dr. Kelley's press conference seemed to only whet the appetite of the press, as they immediately converged on Plaza Santa Maria. One report quoted Steve as saying, "I look like a survivor from Auschwitz." Another tabloid noted, "His once-rugged body has shrunk to 100 pounds, with a grotesquely bloated belly and pretzel thin arms and legs." The most outrageous story came from *The National Enquirer,* which stated that in the event of his death, Steve had had his sperm frozen for Barbara if she desired to have his child.

Steve followed Dr. Kelley's prescribed regimen faithfully for one month before he started to call on friends to sneak in some of his favorite foods. In late August, he arranged for his pilot friends from Santa Paula to fly in cakes, ice cream, pies, and his favorite pork chops made by Pat Johnson's wife, Sue. "When my wife made these super-thin breaded pork chops, Steve made sure he was invited over. When the meal was over, he took home the leftovers. They were delicious cold and he, Chad, and his dog, Junior, would fight over them the next day. We spoke before I left for Mexico, and he made sure I brought my wife's pork chops and blueberry pie," says Johnson. Notes an ex-patient, "Steve loved sweets, especially chocolate. Unfortunately, that fires up the cancer. He implemented it and he paid for it. In order to heal yourself, you have to follow the diet to the letter."

Steve's metabolic technician, Teena Valentino, says, "Yes, Steve did like sweets. He told me, 'I have very few pleasures in life right now; food is one of the few I have left.' He would have all of the sweets brought in and he would take one bite from each of the foods to get it out of his system. Eventually, the taste didn't even satisfy him any longer." McQueen eventually employed a private cook named Ruth. "Ruth was amazing," recalls Teena. "She could whip up the best-tasting food out of vegetables, so Steve was very pleased with that."

On September 14, 1980, at Steve's request, Grady Ragsdale came to Plaza Santa Maria with a few items from Santa Paula. Steve had asked for a flying helmet, goggles, binoculars, and photos of his planes. He felt that a few items from home would lift his spirits.

When Grady arrived, he didn't know what to expect. He noticed that Steve was a bit thinner and his belly was more bloated than he remembered. Steve was sitting up in bed. "I can only sit up like this for about twenty minutes at a time, then I get tired and have to lie down. But the doctors are really encouraged. They say my tumors are definitely shrinking," he said.

Grady then announced what he felt was good news. The Reverend Billy Graham had called for Steve and wanted to see him. Graham was a longtime friend of Pastor Leonard DeWitt, who had known about Steve's diagnosis of cancer in December 1979. DeWitt felt it would do Steve some good if he could arrange a meeting with Graham. Graham's secretary had finally called and set up a meeting for October 31 in Burbank. Graham didn't even know that Steve was in Mexico. Says Teena Valentino, "Billy Graham was to Steve the epitome of a really good Christian."

"Oh, I've got to see him," Steve said desperately. "Promise you'll call him. Ask him if he'll come down here, and if he will, make all the arrangements. Rent a plane and come with him. BRING HIM TO SEE ME . . ." To Steve, Billy Graham was God's right-hand man.

Bill Maher, Steve's friend and business manager, came to visit Steve on September 19, and Steve began to cry. "I've got cancer," he stated. Barbara and Teena heard him crying and Barbara commented, "I've never heard Steve cry before." When Maher's forty-five-minute visit was over, Steve said to Teena, "I don't know what came over me . . . I didn't think we were that close. I haven't seen Bill for years."

That next day, September 20, Steve was told by his doctors that he could not go back to Santa Paula if he lived. "The pesticides there are just way too heavy," he was told. It was then that Barbara suggested Ketchum, Idaho, where she grew up, as an alternative.

Neile, Terry, and Chad came to visit Steve for the first time at the Plaza on September 26. Steve confided to Teena, "She's one of my best friends. It's nice when your ex-wife can be a best friend. She's been a good mother. We were married for a long time . . . you can't be married a long time, and have kids, and not always love the person. You don't stop loving people." Steve confided to Neile that he was thinking of holding a press conference lauding Dr. Kelley and Plaza Santa Maria, in front of television cameras, no less. Neile gasped. He continued, "I want to help spread the word. So what if I look like a broken man. My spirit is whole. The fact is I'm alive, and they've helped me. I owe them that. People should know about this place." Personally, Neile felt that Plaza Santa Maria was a big farce and was using Steve's name to attract other well-to-do cancer patients. She pleaded, "My God, Steve. Please, I beg of you, don't let anyone con you into holding a press conference now. Wait until you get well. Then hold all the press conferences you want and parade around as much as you want. And above all, don't let anyone photograph you now. If you get well, you'll regret those pictures, and if you don't, why not leave the world and your fans with the memory of the Steve McQueen they know! Don't you think that'll be kinder to everyone, including the children?" Neile's words reached him. He conceded, "Yeah, maybe you're right." Neile could only visit for thirty-five minutes before Steve fell asleep. As she left, she turned to Teena and gasped, "It was a shock—I didn't expect . . ." Neile didn't finish her sentence, but Teena knew exactly what she meant.

The very next day, September 27, Bill Maher visited again, but this time he was accompanied by Steve's lawyer, Ken Ziffrin. They brought along two of Neile's fresh-baked cakes, at Steve's request. Maher and Ziffrin visited for two hours as Steve put his final affairs in order. His last will and testament was finalized by the time they left.

Two days later, on September 29, Steve wanted to release a press statement on behalf of Plaza Santa Maria and Dr. Kelley, finally admitting he had cancer. He called press agent Warren Cowan to handle it. Cowan, sensing an avalanche of negative publicity, warned him, "It would only cause you harm right now." Cowan knew, however, that McQueen was going to do it with or without his help, so he prepared a statement. The statement read:

> The reason why I denied that I had cancer was to save my family and friends from personal hurt and to retain my sense of dignity, as, for sure, I thought I was going to die.

On October 2, there was optimism in the air. The doctors had informed Steve that his tumors were shrinking. It was a good possibility, they told him, that they had reversed the cancer and, by the end of the year, may well have beat it altogether. Barbara bubbled with joy, "Steve's going to make it!"

By October 3, Steve McQueen was front-page news. Warren Cowan's nightmare had come true: Steve was now fresh meat for every newspaper and tabloid in the country.

Two days later, on October 5, Steve was approached by Mexico's largest news station for an interview. Surprisingly, he granted permission, but no cameras were to be allowed.

The next day, October 6, two more statements were to be issued. The first one came from Barbara, and was read by Cowan:

> Steve's great wish is that the United States would allow the medical treatment he is undergoing in this country so we could go home and Steve could continue his program among the people and surroundings he loves. He has asked me to tell you, "My body may be broken but my heart and spirit are not." He wants to thank the thousands of people who have sent their good thoughts and prayers, and hopes they will keep them coming.

The second statement, an audiotaped message from Steve recorded the previous day, said:

> To the President of Mexico, and to the people of Mexico. Congratulations to your wonderful country on the magnificent work that the Mexican doctors, assisted by the American doctors, are doing at the Plaza Santa Maria hospital in helping in my recovery from cancer. Mexico is showing the world this new way of fighting cancer through nonspecific metabolic therapy. Again, congratulations—and thank you for saving my life. God bless you all . . . Steve McQueen.
>
> Hopefully, the cheap scandal sheets and curiosity seekers will not try to seek me out so I can continue my treatment. I say to all my fans and all my friends, keep your fingers crossed and keep the good thoughts coming. All my love, and God bless you."

The day after the press conference, Dr. Kelley issued a release stating, "We have been able to prolong the patient's life beyond earlier doctors' expectations. I believe that Mr. McQueen can fully recover and return to a normal lifestyle."

Earlier in the week, one or two reporters had begun snooping around Plaza Santa Maria. After the taped message from Steve, close to fifty reporters from all over the world were pounding on the front gates, hoping to get some information on McQueen. When that didn't work, they retreated into the nearby hills with telephoto lenses to get a picture of the reclusive star. A bounty was then set: $50,000 for a photo of an ailing, cancer-ridden Steve McQueen.

While the press hounded Plaza Santa Maria, Steve, Barbara, Teena, and her husband, Jack, took a mini-vacation in Tijuana on October 10 so that Steve could get a new set of X rays and get out of Plaza for a while. They stayed a few days before heading back. On the way, Steve wanted to drive through the Rosarita marketplace. He took in all of the activities with wide-eyed innocence. "Everything seems cleaner, not so dirty now. Mexico was always so dirty," he remembered. "It's still dusty, Steve," replied Teena. "Maybe it's me . . . I'm the one who's changed. It means more to me now," he said sorrowfully.

When Steve returned, Plaza Santa Maria was flooded with mail for him from well-wishers and fans. A few letters managed to grab Steve's attention. One read:

Dear Steve,

Sorry to hear about your problem but you can beat it. I have followed you since "Wanted: Dead or Alive" and I've seen *The Hunter* four times. You're a tough son-of-a-bitch, so get off your ass and get back to work. There isn't any other actor I'd rather watch. Get out of bed and come to Chicago, I'll buy you a beer. Hell, I'll buy you a case!!

All the best,

J.S.

Another letter, just as humorous, but more sympathetic, read:

Dear Mr. McQueen,

The night my first wife was about to have her first baby, we were watching *The Thomas Crown Affair* at a drive-in. She told me in the middle of the picture that we better get to the hospital quick. I said to her, "C'mon, can't it wait? We can't leave a McQueen movie!" Needless to say, I am now divorced.

What I'm trying to say is that your life (much more than any movie role) has been an inspiration to me. My son is also going to grow up knowing about a man who had the courage to live the way he knew was right. Take care of yourself, Steve. My heart and my thoughts are always with you.

Yours truly,

J.H.

384

The most touching letter of the bunch was written by a female fan:

Dear Mr. McQueen,

When I heard you on my radio one morning last week it had quite an impact on me. You were thanking the doctors and people of Mexico and besides being one of the most beautiful statements of sincerity I have ever heard, it really brought back memories of what you have given me.

I am 26 years old and my name is Marilyn. When I was growing up, my family had many problems. My father was an alcoholic and would spend our money on liquor instead of his four girls and wife. So my mama went to work in a cotton mill in Columbus, GA, where she still works.

Anyway, what I'm getting at is that I had no men in my life to look up to and that's where you came in. When I saw you as Josh Randall, it gave me a man I could be proud of. You would help people, love people, give advice to people, and most of all, you would protect people from being hurt. As a little girl, I desperately needed all those things and I would pretend you were directing all those wonderful traits to me, that you cared about me. Mama, God, and Josh Randall loved *me!*

I had cowboy boots, blue jeans and Western shirts. I learned to be strong and not act like a baby. I would comfort my mama and repeatedly tell her everything was going to be all right.

Now that may sound silly, but it's true. It built a solid foundation for a very lonely little girl. You impressed me deeply. Thank you Steve McQueen.

I Love You So Much,

Marilyn

Steve's optimism continued through mid-October, when best friend Pat Johnson and agent Marvin Josephson arrived at Plaza Santa Maria.

The change in McQueen astounded Johnson, who had last seen him on July 30. "Marvin and I spent the day with him in this little cabin. He looked incredible, I mean wonderful. He had put on weight since he had left the hospital. There was no distended belly. He looked terrific," says Johnson.

McQueen then told Johnson that he was ready to leave for Ketchum, Idaho. The doctors' suggestion that the pesticides around Santa Paula were not good for his breathing had convinced him to move. Steve and

Barbara owned land in Ketchum and for years had talked of relocating there. Now was the perfect excuse. Steve asked Johnson to wrap up his things from the hangar and get everything ready. Says Johnson, "He was talking about opening up a museum where he wanted to have an old potbellied stove in the middle of a general store, and have all the old-timers from the area kick back, put their feet up, and tell war stories. That was his epitome of retirement." For the next two weekends, Johnson packed McQueen's belongings for the move to Idaho.

On October 21, Steve requested the company of a spiritual doctor, Brugh Joy. Joy had graduated from Johns Hopkins and eventually worked for the Mayo Clinic. He was also a clinical professor at UCLA. He had been diagnosed with cancer in 1974 and claimed to have cured himself in six weeks with "visualization." Joy and his partner, Carolyn Langer, made the trek to Plaza Santa Maria at Steve's request in his desperate attempt to see into the future. Joy taped the hour-long visualization session with Steve, and a copy found its way to Pat Johnson. These are the last recorded words of Steve McQueen:

> BRUGH JOY: Okay, why don't we just dive in. What do you think of the circumstances that might have led up to the disease itself? How do you perceive that now?
>
> STEVE McQUEEN: Two ways. One is asbestos poisoning in my lungs, which is very rare. Two is, I think there were times when I was under pressure. I had a battle in my business with somebody [Phil Feldman] for about five years. I think, I really wanted to let go of the pressure.
>
> JOY: I've often felt that diseases reflect what we want at a deeper level and something inside of you wanted out. Regardless of some of the other thoughts inside your head, there's a sense of me that feels that a certain portion of your life feels that it got screwed up in certain ways. I know there were drugs involved at one time. Is that correct?
>
> McQUEEN: Yes, I think that, you see, in my life, there was so much that, you know, I was into a lot of dope. I've done everything there is to do, and a lot of my life I've wasted. I've done things that I wish weren't in my life.
>
> JOY: Well, I'm not sure that you did waste your life. I want to look at it from the standpoint of what you learned about it. In other words, we don't grow as

beings, rich mature beings, without exploring these things. Without risking, and sometimes we can go overboard, but something inside of you now has looked at that and knows that it didn't lead to where it might have.

McQUEEN: No.

JOY: And it leads to guilt, Steve. It's a matter of experience. I'm looking inside your psyche at what's keeping you going right now, and that is that something deep inside of you knows that you can teach somebody about your life's experiences, that you can share, not only as an actor, but as a human being. A human being who's been through a lot.

McQUEEN: Okay, let me say something. I'm reiterating what you just said. You see, I cut myself short in the drug area in freaking out and everything, because I could have had relationships with people that were meaningful instead of having relationships with people that were based on drugs. That's one. Two is, and you mentioned it earlier about finding a cure in my life. Well, that cure was finding the Lord in my life. When that happens, I know better than to say, 'Okay, God, I'll make you a deal. You let me live, and I'll do this.' So, this was before I was ill. Before I found out. I really believe that I have something, I think I believe, I'm pretty sure I believe, that I have something to give to the world as far as my relationship with the Lord. Something that I can teach to other people. Something about a message that I can give. I don't know exactly where, but I've thought a lot about it when I'm by myself. I think that I should be here to do that, if not, and I've been in excruciating pain, and I've always tried to say that I've had faith and I never gave up. I've thought of suicide. I got a .45 automatic. I've thought of taking my plane out and crashing it. Thought of it all, and I'd like to think that I'm a good Christian. I'm trying to be. It's not easy, but that cure was finding the Lord, I think, and that's where I think I've shortchanged myself.

JOY: But you know, Steve, you could never have brought through what you're saying right now so simply.

You could not state as simply as you just did, and as deeply as you just did, and it may not sound like you got up and put a lot of energy behind what you just said, but it's honest, open, and genuine. You could not say that without the experience behind it. In other words, the wisdom of life. Sometimes we tend to look at the events of something we should be ashamed of rather than looking at the resources gathered, even though it took you time to see that, that led you to a deeper realization. I'm not sure, Steve, that you could touch that without that experience. You know what I mean?

McQUEEN: Yes, I do. Where I'm at now, and I have to cut you in on this, and this is not something we can discuss with or with anyone. See, I'm on this program now, you know about it. It's pretty tough. I have nothing to look forward to. Day in, and day out, pain and anguish. I get terribly discouraged. So, I went on a sweet binge in town. So, that was one thing. If it did something to me, I don't know. The other thing is that they [the doctors] won't let me have anything to ease the pain.

JOY: I know, and I'm going to talk to the doctors about that.

McQUEEN: So, what I did was have a friend smuggle in some Percadan. I haven't been taking a whole lot of it, but, like, I took three of them in one day. I can't stand the pain all the time.

JOY: Listen, if I had what you had, I would be taking it too. I really would. I know what they feel, but I also know what it's like to be under the constant pain of this thing. You don't have to tell them.

McQUEEN: I won't, but . . . I can't. Am I sitting here doing myself in or is it something that I can't handle anymore and need some relief? That's what I think it is. This is very important to me. It's my little world.

JOY: I think that if we were honest, there's probably a little of both in it. There's a portion of you that's really tired. We talked about your retirement. You're tired, you've got nothing to look forward to, but I want to talk about another factor. There's a portion of your psyche that could not image you beyond if you once started to lose ground. If you ever started to deteriorate, if you ever started to lose control of that sense of youthful power, there's a deep thought within your psyche that says, 'I'm not going to stay around. I'm not just going to lie around. I don't want to be taken care of. I either have my abilities or I don't have my abilities.' I don't know if that came on recently. My feeling is that, and a lot of things that you did when you were younger was almost like, 'Live now, because you never know what is down the road.' Am I getting off the track?

McQUEEN: I don't know. I know now that I've changed a lot. I used to be more macho, and now my ass is gone, my body is gone, is broken, but my spirit isn't broken, and my heart isn't broken. I would like to think that I do have the determination to beat this thing, and they keep telling me they think I can, but there is a chance that I might not. Every day I go through this thing where my friends tell me I'm not dying, and they say I should take morphine and keep me happy, because I get tired of the pain and I wish it would go away. Yet there is something that keeps me going, to hang on, to beat this. Even with my broken body, I want to go to . . . Ketchum, where I own a place. Move everything. My planes, bikes, antiques, my wife, all my animals. To start living again. That's what I'd like and to try to be able to change some people's lives. To tell people that I know the Lord, what I have to offer, what's happened to me. The thing [tumor] has gotten bigger, you know? You see, in my mind, I planned this thing, this choice. In Chicago, I knew I was sick, that if the Lord would help me, I would do something to help, and I didn't want to mix the Lord up with that. I've thought a lot about it, because when I started up, I didn't want to mix cocaine with Christianity. I needed to separate the two. I didn't know it would fall under the chain of medicine, but I did plan to quit. All of this would open up and give people and tell people what did happen to me, and take it up to the American Medical Association and

turn their head around a little bit. And by George it
is happening, by accident. I'm just a delivery boy.
My Lord, I have suffered, but all of the mail and the
cards and all. People know I'm into the Lord, so
that means I'm doing good, so I think I'm meant to
stay here.

Joy: Where do you think the disease is now?

McQueen: It's grown bigger, not leveled off.

Joy: That's right. I want to talk about one other area that
we need to open up and have a look at. One time,
Steve, power and control are very important to you.
To lose control over something is hard on you. Do
you know what I'm getting at?

McQueen: I was thinking of where you were getting at. I don't
like losing control over my personal destiny.

Joy: What I'm really going after here is that sometimes
the portions of our awareness start to worry about
the physical form and if it is going to make it. It's
like a big vacuum cleaner. It starts sucking all the
energy. I'm sensing that there has been a lot of
dishevelment. You know what I mean?

McQueen: Yeah, I've got a lot of shit going on.

Joy: Not only that, but it is reflecting in your body. One
day it's the back, the next day it's the darn stomach,
and then the breathing isn't right, and maybe it's
the hemorrhoids. It's like if it isn't one thing, it's
another.

Carolyn
Langer: Another way of putting it is to say that even though
you are in close touch with your Lord, and he has a
great deal of meaning in your life, you still have a
lot more to open to him and that you will understand the Lord even more when you free your mind
from your body.

McQueen: I don't know how to do that. To separate . . .

Joy: It has to do with letting something much vaster than
you work for you in its own way.

Langer: And it's not negating your relationship and understanding of the Lord. What we are saying is that
there is more. More for you to do. More for you to
open to as far as that God force.

McQueen: Let me say that now, I don't know if I'm good
enough to do the Lord's work.

JOY: There's a portion of you that's felt contaminated. Tainted, not worthy.

McQUEEN: That's right.

JOY: This is one of the great things that has motivated you. . . . It's not a matter of if you are good enough or bad enough, you happen to be an instrument or a channel for this process and I don't think it would come through you if you didn't have the feeling, if you weren't ready for it.

McQUEEN: I know that now. I've already tried to make a change . . . I'm starting to feel better about myself than I ever have before. It's very, very, simple. Okay, I've had three years of therapy, so I have some small perception of myself. When a kid doesn't have any love when he's small, he begins to wonder if he's good enough. My mother didn't love me, and I didn't have a father. I thought, 'Well, I must not be very good.' So, then you go out and try to prove yourself, and I always did things that other people wouldn't do. Some dangerous things. I never thought of myself as a particularly courageous person. I was always kind of a coward until I had to prove it to myself. I think that that's where that came from. Most of it. Also, taking everything right to the limit. Just like I'm taking this right to the limit.

JOY: It's called brinkmanship. Brinkmanship.

McQUEEN: I hope not, although I think you're probably right. I don't know. These are my hours of thinking.

JOY: Let's get back to your past. In most psychotherapy, they pick up the theme of 'That's really too bad, Steve. You had a mother who didn't love you. You didn't have a father and therefore you feel inadequate.' But I view it from a very different perception. For instance, if you were from a totally loving family, you wouldn't be who you are today, and you begin to find out one of the most important words is forgiveness. You see what I'm saying?

McQUEEN: That's fantastic. So simple, so difficult.

JOY: There's one area we need to pick up before I forget, because it keeps coming in my mind, over and over again. That is, at one time, Steve, you went into the

391

occult. Is that right? Did you go into any sort of . . .

McQUEEN: I was on the ring of it. Jay Sebring was my best friend. Sharon Tate was a girlfriend of mine. I dated Sharon for a while. I was sure taken care of; my name never got drawn into that mess. He was having an affair with the girlfriend of a warlock. It may be for the worse, but I was always against it. I was one of the ones who always felt that I was one of the good guys, but boy I tell you, they did a number on me. I'm against that whole thing.

JOY: I know you are. The whole impact of what it means to you and what it meant to you, even then. There's a subconscious area that was attracted into the circle.

McQUEEN: Oh sure.

JOY: And it comes out of the power element of it.

McQUEEN: Not for me. It was the women, and the dope, and the running around. That's all that was.

LANGER: There's women, and dope, and running around in many circles. There was something that intrigued you.

McQUEEN: But I didn't know it was the occult. It's bullshit is what it is. No, I really didn't know what it was, and by the time I did, I had never gone to any of the meetings. Never knew anything about it, and was always against it. It was never for me.

JOY: Someplace in your unconscious, you were reaching for power. There's a quality about you, a radiance. You're really an old soul who has a great deal of wisdom inside of you. Something about you, including being in front of millions of people, that is preparation, not only for the work you're about to do now, no matter which way this thing goes. To me, your work is inspirational.

McQUEEN: I don't know how to grasp that yet. I'm trying. The only thing I've been able to do, is to put myself in the Lord's hands.

LANGER: What it really means is a total trust so that it doesn't matter if you live or die, you trust him enough to make the right decision and there's a connection there.

392

McQUEEN: Well, I get that.

JOY: The other thing is your interest in planes. To me, that sends a message to the deep unconscious. I've talked to many pilots who have said that they feel much closer to God up there all alone, where it's peaceful and quiet.

McQUEEN: I've had that experience. I've had it. I've prayed up there and talked to the Lord. I've found that my big thing is daydreaming into things that I'm going to do. Planning. You know, like when you daydream and go to sleep? In my life, my daydreams came true, but I ran out. Now I'm doing more, I'm building in Idaho and planning projects for myself.

JOY: All of those things are important, but it will never be more important than your connection to that deeper portion.

McQUEEN: That's what I need to work on. I need to put myself in the Lord's hands, that's the way I figure it.

JOY: And relax. Just enjoy it. Trust it. You can't lose, no matter what.

McQUEEN: That's what my preacher said, "God's a winner and you can't lose."

LANGER: Dying isn't losing either.

McQUEEN: That's what he said too.

JOY: Nope, it isn't.

McQUEEN: It's not that I'm falling apart, but I'm running out of gas.

JOY: My feeling is that, Steve, if you don't feel or see any dramatic improvement to where you are quite strong, then I would pack up and go home and make myself comfortable. I really would. I would make my peace, deepen my relationship with whoever's around me, and I would find a place that I was totally happy in. An environment that would totally make me feel good. That is what I would do. That's always been in the back of my mind.

McQUEEN: Is that what you see? That it's my time?

JOY: That's what I see. That it is weighted that way. I also see this other factor, Steve, your ability to do some unusual things.

McQUEEN: I see that too.

Joy: But you have to go deep and find that out for yourself.

McQueen: I don't know. (Tape ends)

After Pat Johnson left, Steve's condition began to worsen. Steve knew he was getting worse and told the doctors he wanted to go home to Santa Paula. "He was going stir crazy," observed one eyewitness. "When you're in Plaza Santa Maria, there really isn't much to do except work the program. The only other activities were to go for a swim, or walk along the beach, and Steve couldn't do that because the press were outside the gates hounding him." Against the doctors' orders, Steve and Barbara drove back to Santa Paula on October 24. Along the way, he stopped at Cedars-Sinai for one last X ray. It revealed a massive tumor in the lining of his stomach. The doctors at Cedars told Steve, "You're so weak, there's nothing we can do about it. If we go in to cut out the tumor, your heart will give out and you will not survive the operation." McQueen asked, "What happens if I leave it in?" The doctors replied, "You're going to die." Says Teena Valentino, "Dr. Kelley's theory was that if you can remove some of the cancer, then do it. Basically, the operation was to give him relief from the pain he was enduring, mainly in his back, from an old motorcycle accident. There would still be some cancer left over, but again, Dr. Kelley's theory was that the immune system would take care of the rest of the cancer and disappear over time." Adds Pat Johnson, "Steve had an extremely high threshold level of pain, but the pain was too much. He was like a boxer who went twenty straight rounds, and he was getting his ass kicked every round. The man was hurting."

Johnson received a phone call on November 1 at the hangar from Steve's secretary a few days after Steve had arrived back in Santa Paula. He was told, "Steve doesn't want anyone to know, but he's back at the ranch. He's come in and there are some complications. He doesn't want anyone to see him, but I know if you could see him, he'd feel better."

Johnson raced to the ranch and knocked on the door. Annie, Steve's personal nurse, answered and Johnson asked for Steve. "He's not here," he was diplomatically told by the nurse. "Look, you go and tell Steve that Pat is here. I'm standing by this door and I'm not leaving until I see him." Annie went to confer with Steve and came back and told Johnson, "Steve wants to see you."

When Johnson entered the master bedroom of the Santa Paula house, he smelled death in the air. In the two weeks that had passed, Johnson noticed that Steve had lost at least fifteen pounds. "He looked terrible," remembers Johnson. "His belly was all bloated. He lost weight, and he didn't have that much weight to lose in the first place. His voice was very raspy. He told me about all the pain he was in." Steve admitted to Johnson, "I just can't take the pain, Pat." At that moment, Johnson had taken notice of something that horrified him. On Steve's night stand, next to his bed, was a loaded .45 pistol. Johnson assesses, "For him to contemplate suicide, the pain had to be incredible. He had a very high tolerance for pain, so he was really hurting."

Throughout the conversation, Steve kept repeating, "The pain is so great. I just can't take it." Johnson pleaded, "Steve, please don't lose faith. You can do it. You've got to see this through to the end." Steve replied, "I'm gonna try."

The tears had welled freely in both men's eyes as Johnson was saying good-bye. "I kissed him and as I walked away, in my heart, I knew it was the last time I was going to see Steve." When Johnson got home that night, he wrote in his diary: "I have the feeling that I'll never see Steve again . . ."

Crystal Endicott also got to pay Steve a visit during this hiatus. Steve said to her, "However it ends, I'll be glad when it's over, because I'm tired of being in pain all the time." Says an ex-Kelley patient, "Mesothelioma is a painful cancer. The cancer is woven in between organs and the organs need room to expand. It also causes sore muscles and heavy breathing. Steve suffered from all of these symptoms."

On November 2, Neile, Chad, and Terry went to visit Steve at the Santa Paula ranch. While Terry and Chad went to town with Barbara, Neile snuck into Steve's room. He was sleeping quietly, but stirred and woke up. Making one final apology, he said to Neile, "I'm sorry I couldn't keep my pecker in my pants, baby," referring to his years of philandering during their marriage. Neile said nothing, and as Steve went back to sleep, it struck her that on this day, twenty-four years ago, the police had pulled them over for speeding because they were in a hurry to get married. It was the last vision she ever had of Steve.

Neile recalls that day. "Steve was so sick," she said. "One moment he'd be making plans for all of us to spend Christmas together in Sun Valley, and the next, he'd grab my hand and say, 'I'm not going to make it.' And of course, he didn't." Says nurse Teena Valentino, "Steve said of Neile, 'I consider her one of my very best friends. I've always loved her.' He had a special relationship with all three of his wives, and they loved him in a special way as he did them."

The day after, November 3, Grady Ragsdale received a phone call from the Reverend Billy Graham. "Does Steve still want to see me?" asked the evangelist. Grady replied, "As soon as possible."

When he relayed the news to Steve, "It was as if a great burden had been lifted," said Grady. Steve made the arrangements for Graham to be picked up immediately. "You'd better be on your way. We can't keep Billy Graham waiting," Steve said, as tears streamed down his face.

Their meeting would take place in Steve's bedroom. Billy Graham remembers that first meeting with a bedridden McQueen: "Though I had never met him before, I recognized him immediately from his pictures, even though he had lost considerable weight. He sat up in bed and greeted me warmly.

"He told me of his spiritual experience. He said that about three months before he knew he was ill, he had accepted Christ as his Savior and had started going to church, reading his Bible, and praying. He said he had undergone a total transformation of his thinking and his life.

"Apparently, he had been led to Christ by a pilot whom he had hired to teach him to fly an old vintage airplane. He apparently saw something in this pilot, Sammy Mason, that he admired and liked, and asked what made the difference in his life. Sammy Mason sat down and carefully explained how Christ had changed his life. Steve later learned that he had a fast-moving and possibly incurable cancer. While this was a shattering blow, his new faith in Christ became his resource for extra strength.

"I sensed that during our conversations—interrupted only when the nurses would come to give him shots—he was happy and totally at peace. He informed me that he was leaving for an undisclosed destination for an operation to remove all the tumors except a rather large one in his stomach—and he pulled up his pajamas and showed me. He said that when he got that removed his chances would be good for recovery, although he admitted, 'I have a 50 percent chance of surviving the operation.'

"I read him a number of passages of Scriptures and prayed with him several times.

"After two hours, I left the room and went out to the kitchen to talk to the nurses, his housekeeper, and Grady. I wanted to give Steve a bit of rest. About an hour later I was informed that he wanted to see me again. We had another time of spiritual discussion, Bible reading, and prayer. I was then informed that it was time to go to Ventura County Airport in Oxnard where a private Lear jet was waiting to take him for his operation. He never told me where the operation was to take place. I assumed it was somewhere in Mexico."*

Just ten years earlier Steve was asked if he believed in God. He was on

---

* Ragsdale, Grady. *Steve McQueen: The Final Chapter.* Vision House Books, 1983.

top of the world and at the time the biggest box office attraction. He responded selfishly, "I believe in me. God'll be number 1 as long as I'm number 1." Now most of his sentences ended with "Praise the Lord." A new Steve had evolved, and he was a far cry from the old one.

Too weak to make the walk to the van in the driveway, Steve was brought out in a wheelchair. While he was being wheeled out, he kept looking back at all the items in the house as if it were the last time he'd see them.

Graham accompanied McQueen in the van taking him to Oxnard. Steve asked more questions about the afterlife, and Graham gladly answered all of them. The time came for them to part company. The two men said one last prayer and, instinctively, Graham handed over the Bible he brought with him and inscribed it to Steve. It became his proudest possession. As Graham turned to leave, Steve proclaimed, "I'll see you in heaven!"

Steve's quest for secrecy had even the closest of friends wondering where he was. Don Gordon had been on location in London when he read in the papers that Steve was on his deathbed. The fact that Steve had gone to Mexico had upset Gordon considerably. Gordon was convinced that Steve was involved with the wrong type of people. In desperation, Gordon tried to contact Steve. Finally, he realized that McQueen was in Mexico and that there was no way to get a hold of him. He then called Neile. "Is there something we can do to get Steve out of Mexico?" Gordon asked. He wondered aloud, "What if we kidnapped him?" Neile instantly told him no.

Asked if today he would have carried out his plan, Gordon replies instantly, "Why not? Hell, yeah. He was my friend. We'd just grab him and say, 'Fuck you, we're going in the chopper. That's it. Let's get out of here.' I meant it then. I mean it now. I wanted the guy to have a better stake at life. To be able to fight it. Coffee enemas? C'mon."

At Plaza Santa Maria, it had been decided by Steve that he would have the tumors removed. Several doctors had been called in and they had agreed that the operation could be performed successfully. They had also suggested that Dr. Santos Vargas of Juarez, Mexico, should be in charge of the surgery.

When the plane was in the air, its destination El Paso, Texas, Teena overheard Steve's nurse, Annie, ask him his feelings at the moment. McQueen replied, "Ah, El Paso . . . that's where I fell in love," referring to his time with Ali MacGraw just eight years before on the set of *The Getaway.*

Once safely on the ground in El Paso, McQueen had a CAT scan done at the Eastwood Medical Center under the name Samuel Sheppard. The report from the scan is as follows:

Clinical Impressions:

Computed tomography of the thorax, abdomen, and pelvis, performed 11/3/80:

Trans-axial tomographic cuts were made from the level of the carina to the pelvis.

There is a large pleural mass along the right thoracic wall with enlarged lymph nodes at the right hilum. There is a second pleural mass at the right posterior pleura. Multiple soft tissue masses are seen scattered through the right lung parenchyma.

Trans-axial cuts of the abdomen show an extremely enlarged liver with a high density central core, lobulated in nature extending through most of the liver. There is ascites through the abdominal cavity. The spleen appears to be within normal limit. Obliteration of the different intra-abdominal planes by the ascites is noted. Multiple lobulated masses are seen at the pelvis, mainly along the right pelvic wall anteriorly. Ascites is also noted at the pelvis.

IMPRESSION:
1. LARGE PLEURAL TUMOR MASS ON THE RIGHT WITH HILLAR METASTASIS.
2. METASTITIC DISEASE TO THE POSTERIOR PLEURA ON THE LEFT WITH MULTIPLE METASTASES ALONG THE RIGHT LUNG PARENCHYMA.
3. LARGE METASTATIC LIVER WITH LOBULATED TYPE OF METASTASIS.
4. ASCITES.
5. MULTIPLE METASTATIC NODULES THROUGH THE ENTIRE PELVIS MAINLY AT THE RIGHT ANTERIOR ASPECT.

On November 5, Grady Ragsdale took a United Airlines flight to El Paso, Texas, where he was to be escorted across the border to the Santa Rosa Clinic in Juarez, Mexico. The clinic was an old red brick building that resembled a garage or warehouse. It was to be the site of Steve's life-threatening operation. "It had an uninviting look," Ragsdale recalls. Teena remembers it differently. "It was a clinic. Most hospitals I've been in are imposing and sterile. This clinic was warm, family-oriented,

398

and seemingly very professional. Steve hated hospitals; this place was homey, and Steve preferred it."

That same day, Steve's blood levels were tested and it was decided by Dr. Santos Vargas that the operation should be delayed a day.

Just down the street from the clinic was the Las Fuentes Motel, where Barbara, Terry, and Chad were staying.

The next morning, November 6, Grady and Barbara met for coffee before heading to the clinic. Barbara had expressed a desire to see Steve before the operation began. The two arrived too late for her wish to be granted. Barbara's disappointment was obvious to those in the clinic.

Steve was given an enema, bathed, and prepped for surgery. All of his IVs were in and his shots had been given, and he was put on a gurney. Teena Valentino recalls, "We moved out of the room and started slowly down the hallway. Steve reached for my hand. I held firmly until the doctors stopped me at the operating room door."

Steve had a ritual with Teena. Whenever he entered the hot tub at Plaza Santa Maria, he would hand over his watch to the dutiful nurse. Right before this operation, he again told Teena, "Hold my Bible and my watch." To her, that meant business as usual. "Steve had no inclination to die," she says. "He had a powerful body and his immune system was building. He had a quiet heroic substance to him."

Before Steve went out of her sight, Teena saw him give Dr. Vargas the thumbs-up sign.

Throughout the operation, Barbara was spoon-fed information on Steve's condition.

The tumor in his stomach was so large, in fact, that it had given him the appearance of a pregnant woman in her sixth month. It was removed without any complications. Barbara was told she could view the end of the procedure but she declined, thinking she would feel faint.

Steve made it through the surgery. The operation had lasted six hours.

When he awoke from the operation at 3:00 P.M., his first words were, "Is my stomach flat now?" The legendary McQueen vanity was still intact.

Steve was being kept heavily sedated and slept throughout the day. When he awoke again, Barbara was seated by his side. They talked of the future, of how Steve had defeated the cancer. He was recovering so well, in fact, that a heart monitor was removed from the room. All of his vital signs were, in the words of an eyewitness, "doing beautifully." There was optimism.

By 7:30 P.M., his temperature was 35.5°C, his blood pressure was 120/90, and his pulse was a fast 100. All Steve could think about was ice cubes. "Ice cubes. I want more ice cubes," he said hoarsely. Teena didn't like the thought of his desire for them. She remembered that many patients at the Plaza craved ice cubes before they died.

That night, Steve called for Terry, Chad, and Barbara. Teena was present in the room but chose to remain in the background. Steve's mind seemed to wander and Teena told him gently, "Barbara and the kids want to say good night, Steve." Steve made a motion to Teena for more ice cubes. Barbara announced, "Honey, we're going to go to the motel now. We'll see you in the morning." Steve waved them out, with a touch of impatience.

Dr. Dwight McKee was keeping a round-the-clock watch on Steve. Barbara felt that she could go to sleep peacefully that night, something she hadn't done for the past year. She felt an inner calm she hadn't experienced before. The yearlong vigil for Steve was over for her. Together, as a team, they had overcome this ordeal.

While he was soundly sleeping under sedation, a blood clot had lodged in Steve's heart. At 3:45 A.M. on November 7, 1980, he developed an embolism. Dr. McKee noticed that Steve's fingernails were pink, indicating that his lungs were still functioning, though his heart had given out. "He sneaked away quietly," said the doctor. By 3:50 A.M., Steve McQueen had died painlessly and quietly.

Dr. McKee first notified Barbara, who was in the middle of a deep sleep. Terry, who was in the next room at the motel, heard Barbara's doorbell ring. A few seconds later, Barbara opened her door. Seeing Barbara's face, Terry knew in her heart that her father was dead.

When Chad was told that his father had just died, he said defiantly, "I don't believe it. I want to see for myself." He then had Grady take him to the hospital.

When Chad got to the hospital room, he turned to Grady and said, "I want to be alone with my father."

Upon entering the room, Chad turned on the light. Steve's eyes were still open. He looked as if he were very much alive. Chad sat on the bed beside him. As he looked at Steve, he noticed something odd. His eyes, which had been gray the past six months, had returned to their bright blue color. Chad also noticed the Bible that the Reverend Billy Graham had given to Steve. It now rested on his chest, opened to Steve's favorite verse, John 3:16: "For God so loved the world, that he gave his only begotten Son, that whosoever so believes in him shall not perish, but have everlasting life."

As Chad leaned over, he noticed the warm smile that radiated such calm, leaving Chad no doubt that he had died in peace. Chad closed his father's eyes, bent down, and kissed him on the forehead.

"So long, Pop. I love you."

# THE AFTERMATH

GRADY RAGSDALE RETURNED TO the Santa Rosa Clinic at 7:00 A.M. He was led to Steve's room, where he opened the door and noticed Reverend Graham's Bible still clutched in Steve's hands. From there, he was called into Dr. McKee's office. McKee pulled out two sets of X rays, one from Steve's first visit in July, the second from October before Steve had left for Santa Paula. McKee held up both X rays against the X-ray panel. He announced, "The white area is the cancer." Ragsdale noticed the considerable difference in the X ray on the right. "As you can see, we almost had it beaten. Steve put up a gallant fight. He came so close to winning," said the doctor. Says an ex-patient of Dr. Kelley's, "Steve had the cancer beat. The tumors in his body were dead and he was on his way to recovery. He died of a blood clot, not cancer. People have this mind-set that dying is losing. It's not. It's okay to die. Steve lived longer than expected on the Kelley program. Yes, he was afraid to die at first. He denied the thought of death, but so many people depended on him. I know that when the end came near, he was at peace with himself. He was no longer afraid to die because he knew he was going to the Lord."

Metabolic therapy as a way of treating cancer had seemed radical to the medical community. But in fact, Steve McQueen had come very close to beating cancer with this method. Had it not been for the development of an embolism, which is not uncommon after surgery, he may have survived. Today, metabolic therapy and holistic methods are still being used in the fight against cancer.

Perhaps the two who suffered the most from Steve's death were Dr. Santos Vargas and Dr. William Kelley. Explained one insider, "Dr. Vargas really took a bad rap. He was a very skilled, very highly regarded surgeon in Mexico. He took a great risk by being McQueen's surgeon. He knew that if it went badly [which it did], his reputation would be tarnished [which it was; he was ruined]. We considered his willingness to perform the surgery on Steve heroic. To us, it was evidence that he

402

was a 'real' doctor, one whose primary consideration is the life and welfare of a patient in need, instead of his own vested interests."

Dr. Kelley retired and sold his practice in 1986. His work is now considered by some in the medical field a major breakthrough in cancer treatment.

Steve's quest for secrecy held off reporters for only so long. It was only a matter of time before they would find his whereabouts.

His body was taken to the Prado Funeral Home in Juarez, where it was prepared to be sent back to Santa Paula. It was there that McQueen would be the victim of the tabloids one last time. A photographer from *Paris Match,* the same magazine that Steve had allowed to follow him during the French premiere of *Love with the Proper Stranger,* snuck into the funeral home, located his body, lifted the sheet that covered him, and snapped a picture. The photo later appeared in full color on the cover of *Paris Match,* and in the states on the front page of the *New York Post.*

The picture so upset Ali MacGraw that she publicly cried on *Entertainment Tonight,* begging the media to stop the hurtful coverage of Steve. "The most important thing in his life was his personal privacy," she said. "He was too weak to combat the kind of invasion he was experiencing. It made all of us who loved him crazy. I still have an amazing amount of anger at a magazine [*Paris Match*] that ran a picture of him after he died. I don't understand it. The hurt is monumental, to be raped that way."

On November 7, 1980, at 10:30 A.M., Pat Johnson was on the Ventura Freeway, heading for a karate workout with Marvin Josephson. A news bulletin came over the car radio that Steve McQueen had passed away that morning. The news shook Johnson so much that he had to pull off the road to collect his thoughts. Says Johnson, "He did beat the cancer, the cancer didn't beat him. Not directly. He went as a fighter, fighting all the way. He just wasn't going to lay down and die. That's the kind of person he was."

Loren Janes was on location in Austin, Texas, when he received a phone call from Barbara telling him of the bad news. When Janes hung up the phone, he cried. Not much later, Janes received another phone call from his son, Eric, who said, "I heard about Steve. I knew you'd feel bad and I just wanted to say I love you."

Says Janes, "I was prepared for it. I kept hearing all kinds of things from Pat Johnson and Barbara. I knew it was going bad. I knew he was in horrible pain. I knew he was shriveling up, and that really hurt. When he died, I just said, 'Well, he's gone.' I felt an emptiness and that was it. About a week later it really hit me: 'He's gone. No more flying around in that old airplane. No more bullshitting with each other.' For about three months I felt a real emptiness. Every time I looked at his picture, I would feel real pain. I think that people should know that he gave and that he cared, and that he went and talked to kids at Boys Republic, with no publicity. I never told anybody about him because he asked me not to and I didn't. Well, he's gone now. I may be going against my word, but I think if he spoke to me from heaven, I'd say, 'The hell with you, Steve. I wanted everyone to know about you and I'm going to tell them.' All I know is the things I've seen and heard from other people about what he's done, so I can imagine the things I don't know. Give the good side of the man, because he did have a good side."

Says Bud Ekins, "He wouldn't quit. He didn't know how to quit when he died. I didn't think he was going to die because he was so rich. I just figured he wasn't going to die. I didn't disagree with the Kelley method. Hell no."

For months Neile kept quiet about her opinion on Steve's decision to go to Mexico. Now, she no longer felt it necessary to hold back. The press asked her for a statement. She said vehemently, "What bothers me is that all the publicity surrounding Steve will convince other innocent people to be misled into going down there. These doctors are nothing more than mere charlatans and exploiters."

Steve's decision to go to Mexico had divided his friends. Some, like Pat Johnson, Loren Janes, James Coburn, and Bud Ekins, felt that he had nothing to lose by going to Mexico. Says Coburn rebelliously, "I believe in anything the doctors don't believe in. I believe they consciously make a profit out of the disease and suffering of people. It's a sad thing, but it seems to be true. The alternative therapies are something the American Medical Association cannot make money off of, and I find that evil and insidious."

Some of Steve's other friends, however, felt that by going to Mexico, he may have shortened his life. "Why he chose to go to Mexico is beyond me," says Nikita Knatz. "He was a great believer in shortcuts. That was one of his downfalls.

"He was into controlled destiny. The Chinese believe you're predestined. Steve figured he had to surpass Barrymore, and he tried to do that with that stupid Ibsen play. He said, 'I'm an actor and I have to be the best.' He was the best at the time, because he was the top box office star in Hollywood. I think he surpassed Barrymore. He blamed his illness on that thinking, that somebody was coming to get him, because he surpassed the master."

Steve's decision to go to Mexico also upset Phil Parslow. "I think the thing that affected me most about his death was the way it happened, in Juarez, Mexico. Why not in Houston? Someplace where some of the greatest surgeons of the world are located. The saddest thing is the quack medicine to avoid the inevitable. Had he chosen to go the other way, he might have lived another five years. Maybe not. All of a sudden, he's associating with garbage. He went out with a whimper. He went out in a very undignified manner. He somehow let someone use him to make that broadcast. It was grotesque. A Juarez hospital," Parslow says, shaking his head. He continues, "My reaction to his death is not as bad as time goes on. I missed him more two years after his death than two days after he died. I think I believed that somehow I would be back together with him at some point, that we might have a reunion."

David Foster also believe that "going to Mexico was a fraud. It was exploitive. Every day it was on television or in the papers. I thought it was in bad taste, and I didn't want to see these terrible pictures of him. That's not Steve McQueen." Foster adds, "I did love him as a man. It was clearly a love/hate thing. We were together a long time. We did a lot of crazy things together. He was too young, too vital, too crazy."

Their friendship had never regained its proper footing after *Fancy Hardware* fell through. The two saw each other only sporadically thereafter, and it was never quite the same. Steve, however, had invited Foster to Terry's eighteenth birthday party. "His inviting me was his way of telling me I was family," says Foster. "I tried to call him a few times when he became ill. Some of us were excluded at the end. He didn't want to see anybody or talk. I understood that, so I sent a note. It was a case of wanting to be with someone no matter how horrible it was, and we were not allowed to be with him. I wanted to be there for him."

Steve Ferry wanted to send Steve a book by Norman Cousins on using humor to fight illness, but by then Steve had stopped taking calls. "He divorced himself from his friends and acquaintances," Ferry says. "He was given a death sentence and had to wait around for it to happen. His peace in God was fairly early in life. He looked close enough at death so that he knew where he was all the time. I don't think he was fearful of it."

Arrangements were made by Grady Ragsdale to have Steve's casket brought across the border to the El Paso airport, where he would accompany it in a private Lear jet back to Santa Paula. Before his car had passed the airport gates, he was suddenly surrounded by reporters and photographers, who began clicking away wildly.

Finally, beyond the range of the photographers, Ragsdale, with the help of Dr. McKee, the pilots, and an attendant from the funeral home, transferred the coffin. As the casket was being loaded into the plane, the attendant, a young fan of Steve's, pulled out a camera and began taking pictures. Teena told him, "I don't think Steve would have liked this. You better give me the film." Ignoring her plea, the young man continued to take pictures. Finally, Teena's husband, Jack, shouted, "You better give me the camera or I'll break it." The pilots, Dr. McKee, and Jack surrounded the young man and demanded the film in the camera. Outnumbered, he pulled it out and handed it over. As everyone climbed aboard, the young man realized what he had done and began crying, muttering, "I'm so sorry. I'm so sorry." Jack walked toward him and gave him a hug before takeoff. "It's okay," Jack told him.

As the plane pulled out on the runway and was readying for takeoff, Teena looked out of the window and saw the photographers running toward them, hoping to take one last picture of the casket of Steve McQueen.

Three hours later, after landing in Ventura, Steve's body was taken to a mortuary there for cremation. The ordeal was finally over.

On November 9, 1980, a beautiful Sunday, a private memorial service was held for Steve at the ranch. Barbara and Neile invited only a few guests. Along with Barbara, Neile, and Ali, were Terry and Chad, Pat Johnson, Bud Ekins, Sammy Mason, Elmer Valentine, LeVar Burton, and Nikita Knatz.

When Pat Johnson arrived, the first person he spotted was Ali MacGraw. Johnson walked up to her, put his arm around her, and said, "You know, Steve never stopped loving you." Ali wiped away her tears and managed to say, "Me, too."

Pastor Leonard DeWitt of the Ventura Missionary Church conducted the service near the pond in the backyard of the ranch. It was there that DeWitt recalls that he "shared the word of God with [the mourners]—how to become a Christian, how to walk with God. Steve would have wanted that."

DeWitt read Steve's favorite verse, John 3:16, and as he closed the service with a prayer, the roar of plane engines could be heard in the distance. As the group of mourners looked up, they could see seven planes in the missing man formation. The empty spot was for Steve. Larry Endicott, at the head of the formation, dipped his plane's wings in final salute and headed toward the Pacific Ocean, where Steve's ashes were to be scattered.

Steve's death provoked a flood of tributes all across the country. The media response was one of genuine grief and sorrow, and his work was given a second look. *Films in Review* wrote of him, "McQueen left behind, on film, more of himself than most people, even most actors are allowed to leave. It's a worthy legacy." Film historian Phillip Bergson noted, "His shocking early death at fifty robbed the cinema of an exceptional personality." Writer Scott Eyman said, "He seemed to be a man determined to devote himself only to the things that really mattered to him, as if convinced that time was running out. Tragically for us, and even more tragically for him, it was." *Film Review* wrote, "With his short hair, sharp blue eyes and an expression which seemed to suggest he found the world a satirically amusing place, McQueen's positive personality emerged from the screen strongly enough to set him apart. He will be long remembered with real affection." The *New York Times* added, "In his acting, Mr. McQueen had a deceptively casual and freewheeling style. He personified a nonconformist and underdog, battling to survive in a hostile society. His characters combined, as McQueen did, an assertive individualism and a naive vulnerability."

The public also mourned McQueen's death. The figure of Steve as Jake Holman in *The Sand Pebbles* had to be removed from the Hollywood Wax Museum, because too many flowers and cards from fans were placed by the statue. It has been out of the exhibit ever since.

United Artists, the studio where Steve had made *The Magnificent Seven, The Great Escape,* and *The Thomas Crown Affair,* took out a full page ad in the trade papers to offer its "regrets on the passing of Steve McQueen."

Steve McQueen left the world a wealthy man. The kid from the streets had an estate estimated at $12 million. He left $3 million apiece to his two children, Terry and Chad. He had also made a prenuptial agreement with Barbara Minty in case of his death (something he hadn't done for Neile or Ali). Barbara was to receive $1 million.

The McQueen family, with the exception of Chad, did not like Barbara. Her actions the day after Steve's death left a bad impression with them and with a few close friends. On November 10, she had arranged for movers to remove all of her possessions from the Santa Paula house and take them to Ketchum, Idaho, that same day.

Loren Janes recalls, "She went through a lot of hell with Steve and going through his cancer. I don't know why everyone picks on Barbara."

Pat Johnson offers, "Barbara was loyal to Steve. She never asked for anything in return. She never asked for anything! She had her own money; remember, she was a top model. She was there for him when he needed her and there was no one else around. She stuck by him. She was as true and loyal as a person could be. If I were in those circumstances, that is exactly the kind of person I would want to stand by me. Barbara was not part of the 'Hollywood crowd.' She was a naive farm girl. She did not give interviews. She stayed away from the limelight. I think they [the McQueen family and the media] crucified her, which was totally wrong and inappropriate."

Adds a McQueen intimate, "Barbara took the brunt of Steve's wrath at Plaza Santa Maria when he was in a lot of pain. There were some days when he said to her, "This is all your fault!" and then afterward he wouldn't apologize. She understood the pain he was going through and remained faithful to him. She was very brave. I knew she had to hurt, but she never let on that it was getting to her. Barbara was and is a saint. Steve was very happy with her and she comforted him in his last days."

Says Teena Valentino, "Barbara Minty is a very classy lady, and she and Steve had a wonderful relationship. You could tell they really loved each other. They understood one another and really complemented each other. She put up with so much during Steve's stay at Plaza Santa Maria."

Barbara had a very hard year after Steve's death. On her way to Ketchum, Idaho, she was pulled over for speeding. As the officer approached her car, he noticed she was in tears. He didn't understand why until he read her driver's license, "Barbara McQueen." There was an understood silence as the officer handed back her license and let her go without a ticket. "Please drive safely," he told her.

That Christmas, Barbara was alone and depressed. Pat Johnson and his family made the drive to Ketchum to share her grief.

But time has been kind. Though Barbara has never remarried, the pain she endured has subsided. "Listen, I'm really grateful for the time I had with Steve," she says. She still maintains a friendship with Steve's son Chad.

The Boys Republic received $200,000 from Steve's estate. It always had a special place in his heart.

The Santa Paula ranch house was left to Chad, to do with as he wished. (Chad has rented it out now for several years, but is still the legal owner.)

Pat Johnson was the caretaker of several cars for Steve. He told Johnson, "As long as you have them, I know they are safe." Steve left Johnson a Mercedes.

Bud Ekins picked out two of the best bikes in Steve's collection. Ekins and McQueen enjoyed their game of oneupmanship on who could obtain the rarest bike. Says Ekins, "I'd call up Steve and say, 'You'll never guess what I got today.' He'd say, 'What?' I then told him, 'I just got a

1927 Indian Ace.' He'd go, 'You son-of-a-bitch. How'd you get that?' "
Years later, Ekins sold the two bikes, claiming, "After Steve died, it was
no fun anymore." (One of the bikes, a four-cylinder Caton, sold for
$35,000.)

Steve's flying instructor, Sammy Mason, was left a classic Pitcairn
Mailwing, and another plane was given to friend Chuck Bail.

The rest of McQueen's possessions were left to Terry and Chad. Collecting was Steve's passion. He had enough accumulated to make good
on his promise to open a museum in Ketchum, Idaho. Not only did
Steve at the time have the world's largest motorcycle collection (around
210), but he also had over 55 antique cars, over 10,000 jackknives,
pistols, rifles, jukeboxes, buffalo couches, potbellied stoves, toys, refrig-
erators, gas pumps, tin bread boxes, coffee grinders, cash registers, bicycles, advertisements, tools, stools, wooden propellers, and telephones.

All of these items needed to be insured, maintained, and looked after,
and that took money. Instead of having to deal with the constant care
that was needed, the McQueen family decided to auction everything.
The auction was held over two days in November 1984 at the Imperial
Palace Hotel in Las Vegas.

Over 1,400 people attended the auction. Steve's 1957 Jaguar XK-SS
brought almost $150,000. A 1934 Packard Super 8 went for $70,000. A
1909 Pierce motorcycle brought in a winning bid of $25,000. A 1915
Cyclone board-track racer and a 1920 Ace sidecar outfit fetched $20,500
each. The 1905 Wynton Flyer that Von Dutch had handmade for *The
Reivers* attracted $20,000. A 1941 California Highway Patrol Indian po-
lice bike earned $18,000.

The fact that the items belonged to Steve McQueen made them that
much more desirable. One bidder paid $600 for a sidecar even though
it lacked a wheel. A pile of a dozen fuel tanks in need of total restoration
pulled in $700.

As for the nonauto relics, one bidder paid $840 for the privilege of a
McQueen bathroom toilet seat and sink.

The two-day auction brought in more than $2 million for Terry and
Chad. Even hardened bike and car collectors admitted paying well over
the normal going rate to acquire anything belonging to McQueen. One
buyer summed up the feeling among the crowd, "He was a hell of a
guy, and he led the life we all wanted to lead."

# TIME HEALS

IT HAS BEEN over thirteen years since Steve McQueen's death. Remarkably, his passing still has an incredible effect on those who knew him best.

Pat Johnson, an extremely positive human being, cannot watch Steve's movies or even look at his picture. "I haven't really had a chance to think about Steve in-depth for a long time. I still miss him. There's still a deep attachment to him. Deep, deep feelings. There's still a big emotional void in my life."

The most treasured piece of Steve McQueen memorabilia in the Johnson household is a picture of Steve as Dr. Thomas Stockman in *An Enemy of the People*. Steve is holding up a lamp. The picture is signed, "To Pat, my guiding light."

Don Gordon is still very much affected by Steve's death. "I still miss him. I miss him very much. He was my best friend. Ever. I still can't look at a movie with him in it. Very tough."

Perhaps, though, the person most affected by Steve's death was Ali MacGraw. After Steve died, she fell into a world of alcohol and drugs, and it took her years to recover. MacGraw is now leading a relatively happy and normal life and divides her time between Malibu and Santa Fe. The fact that Steve and Ali never got to say good-bye properly will always have some kind of effect on her. But intimates believe that Steve did not want her to see him in his shattered condition at the end. "Apparently," says Pat Johnson, "a lot of people would look at Steve, and he could see it in their eyes, that they were shying away as if he were ugly. I don't think he ever wanted Ali to see him that way or to see that look in her eyes." Ali MacGraw concludes, "He was an extraordinary man, complicated and heartbreaking. He hadn't nearly done all his stuff and I'm not sure he had really grown up either. He was the overwhelming force in my life; that five years with him is a period that I will never forget and maybe never get over. He was incredibly sensitive, vulnerable and intelligent. But he was always intimidated everywhere he went, even though you knew that all the people in the room only wanted to meet him."*

Stardom had always been a mystery to Steve. He couldn't figure out why the public held such a fascination with him. "There's something about my shaggy-dog eyes that makes people think I'm good, but really I'm not all that good. I'm pretty much myself most of the time in my movies and I've accepted that," he once said. But he was that good.

In 1971, artist Kent Twitchell painted a portrait of Steve on the side of a two-story building at 1151 S. Union Street in downtown Los Angeles. When Steve was driving around the city in 1978, he came across the mural. Excitedly, he raced home to tell his son about it. In typical McQueen humor, he told Chad, "I don't know why they want my ugly mug up there," and laughed. (The mural can still be seen at the site.)

In the years since his death, Steve McQueen has become a movie icon. His acting had always been overshadowed by his personal life when he was alive. Says manager Hilly Elkins, "He was the best film actor I have ever seen. He had this animalistic instinct that knew what was right for him."

Agent Freddie Fields comments, "There's an old saying on Broadway that applies to Steve, 'He could carry his own set of lights,' and he did. He was a much better actor than he was given credit for."

Robert Wise, the director of *The Sand Pebbles*, said of McQueen's acting, "He dominates every foot of the film on which his image is imprinted."

Norman Jewison commented, "He was a star. A big star. And people responded to him. When he was up there on that screen, you wanted him to win."

Buzz Kulik noted, "McQueen needs just one word and he's magic. He had a degree of naturalism along with a danger within. You never knew what he was going to do next. He still had a lot of that Los Angeles kid in him. His acting talent was a gift from God."

"He was one of the last major superstars," said Peter Yates, director of *Bullitt*.

John Guillermin, director of *The Towering Inferno*, said of McQueen, "His goal was to be real at all times. Something that he could believe in. He carried a lot of broken glass, but he was a very warm character. He

---

* Norman, Barry, *The Film Greats* (London: Futura Publications, 1986), 69.

had one of the best natural instincts for the screen. He had an uncanny sense, very closed in and uneasy, yet very sensitive."

Walter Hill notes, "Steve always said, 'God's in the details,' and that's why he gave so many incredible performances. They hold up very well. Anyone who communicates that well with so many people has really got something."

Mark Rydell, the man Steve "had on the ropes," had this to say about him: "I miss him as a friend and as a star, because he was a wonderful, magical magnetic personality. But he was very difficult, very strong-willed. But I have to tell you that if I had the chance to work with him again and again and again, I would do it, because he had magic—real magic."*

Several costars of McQueen have also came to his defense when his acting ability has come into question. Said veteran character actor Charles Durning, "You had to be on the other side of that stare to appreciate his intensity."

Mako, Steve's costar in *The Sand Pebbles*, said, "He came to know the camera so well. His work was so subtle and right on the money. He brought simplicity on the screen and at the same time, he was very much the image of the American man. I think he was either way ahead of his time or way behind his time."

Actor and film teacher Eric Christmas said of McQueen, "He played ordinary people so well, and yet he was unique at the same time. In everything he did, you had the feeling that he was the only one, that there was no one else like him. He made choices, which to me, were fantastic. They were not choices that most actors would do. He would react in such a way that was unique."

Ben Johnson, who had the distinction of working with both Steve McQueen and Marlon Brando, made this comparison, "I think Brando is more of a made actor. McQueen, he was kind of a self-made actor. Steve never took a job he could never do. He was a perfectionist. It's what John Ford once said, 'If you can put something up there on the screen that everybody wants to do or be, why, you've got no problem.' Everybody wanted Steve to win."

Actor Adam West noted, "Steve had the ability to make something difficult look easy."

Felice Orlandi, Steve's costar in *Bullitt*, reveals, "McQueen learned what very few actors know how to do: he learned the camera. He knew that it took just a certain kind of subtle look to express a certain emotion where most actors tend to overexaggerate. He really knew his job

---

* Norman, Barry, *The Film Greats* (London: Futura Publications, 1986), 69.

when he was in front of the camera, and that's a mystery for a lot of actors."

Richard Venture, who worked with McQueen in *The Hunter,* offers, "Steve knew who he was. He had achieved an authentic persona. He came to grips with who he was long ago and that made him successful. He wasn't your matinee idol. He was very much an individual. He tended always to play Steve McQueen. In that sense, he was very successful."

Lord Richard Attenborough will never forget Virgil Hilts, the "Cooler King." "As an actor, it will forever be imprinted in my mind Steve's flipping the ball against the wall in *The Great Escape.* As a person" (Attenborough paused for a moment, then, as if a lightbulb had just gone on in his head, he exclaimed), "his irreverence!"

Actor Robert Vaughn says, "He had the quality that all male movie stars have, the 'fuckability quotient.' In other words, he was a good actor, but he also had tons of sex appeal."

Bo Hopkins, who appeared with McQueen in *The Getaway,* observed, "Steve had a style of his own. He learned as he went along and he only got better."

Friend and actor Don Gordon defines the McQueen appeal: "He's the loser that wins. The rebel. 'You kick me and I'm getting back up. No matter what you do, I'm coming back.' And he'll take his lumps. You can kick his ass, but he's coming back. Harder. And that's the joy of seeing his movies. Like the baseball scene in *The Great Escape.* At the end of that movie, he's kicking off that baseball against that wall. And you knew that he was going to escape someday. You knew he was going to get out. He makes us feel we can come back. We can kick ass."

Steve McQueen could be likened to a home run hitter in baseball. When he came to bat, either one of two things would happen: he would hit a home run or strike out. He would be the most anticipated player to watch and he would always be the best paid. Adds Phil Parslow, "His track record on home runs over strikeouts is awesome compared to anyone in Hollywood."

Almost mysteriously, the sadness over Steve's death has slowly turned into happiness. Time has an amazing healing power, and it has allowed Steve's family and friends to remember the good times with Steve.

Don Gordon recalls, "One time I was in the desert with McQueen in Palm Springs. I had learned to ride a motorcycle pretty good. Nowhere near as good as McQueen, because he was damn good. He was teaching me how to ride in the dirt, in the desert. We went down some hill and he took off. I said to myself, 'I'm going to catch him. Pass him.' I really put the throttle on and I passed him. When he saw me pass him, he went bananas. He eventually passed me up and we both had to stop. It was just a funny moment because here he was, superrider, and I had caught up to him. Snuck right by him, and his competitiveness took over immediately. We used to laugh a lot. Our relationship was fun and games. In the sixties, we had fun. Rode our motorcycles to the Whiskey A Go-Go. Laughed. Ate. Danced. It was a great time. A lot of people tend to romanticize the past, but I'm telling you, I'm not romanticizing any of that. Most of the sixties were great. Not good. Great. Maybe it will happen again."

Kent James, a fellow motorcycle rider, said of McQueen, "Steve was really a simple guy. He didn't like being a movie star. When a crowd gathered around him, he had the greatest gift of sneaking away. He was truly happiest riding motorcycles, especially if he beat me."

Friend Steve Ferry recalls of Steve, "We spent a lot of time laughing. That was what we had in common. We could laugh at the same idiocy of life and dignity and our own position in all of that, an 'isn't this an insane place to be' kind of attitude."

Business partner Robert Relyea remembers Steve's nature the most: "Steve just bought a special Ferrari. He waited for six months for it to be just the way he wanted. He was drooling. Nobody would have anything like it. The Ferrari finally arrived and he was going to take it out for a spin. He drove to Palos Verdes and he was driving along the signal right before you get into Marineland. Just before he got to the signal, he looked over and saw a really good-looking girl along the sidewalk. Then he looked in the rearview mirror and sees these sailors doing the same thing. He knew what was coming. He said to himself, 'Oh my God. I've had this car only an hour and here it comes!' They really rammed him hard. He came up out of the seat and onto the hood and the Ferrari is history. The two sailors come running up and say, 'Oh my God. I'm sorry.' They help him up and they notice it's Superstar. When they see Superstar, they go to pieces, because now they feel doubly guilty. Steve said to me, 'I was so busy saying to these guys, stop it. It's okay. It's just a car. It doesn't matter. Forget about it and stop crying. Everything's fine.' When he got home, he thought, 'Wait a minute. I've been waiting for that car for six months. Why was I telling them to calm down?' At the time, he was sincerely more concerned about these two kids crying than he was about the damn car. He didn't want them upset. That's the kind of man he was."

Actor James Coburn remembers the really good pot Steve scored on the set of *The Magnificent Seven:* "I hadn't had any grass in a long time, and he came up with this really good Mexican grass. We had a meeting together and we were talking over dinner and everyone's talking shop and Steve and I were laughing at everybody. Just like two schoolgirls. Easy and simple.

"As for his life," says Coburn, "it was like he bought a Harley-Davidson and rode it until it came to pieces. He squeezed everything into his life. He shouldn't have been sad for a minute of it, because he got everything out of it that was possible."

Cinema Center executive Bob Rosen commented, "Steve lived life to the fullest. His death definitely had an impact on my life. If everything wasn't put on the line, it wasn't fun for Steve. All of the chips had to be put on the table.

"I was shocked by his death. I thought, 'Steve will beat that.' I thought that somehow he wouldn't be taken away, that he would defy death. Steve used to call every so often. Years could pass by and he would call and act as if he saw you yesterday. I feel that someday he's going to call me up and act as if nothing happened. So far, he just hasn't called."

Bud Ekins's fondest memory of Steve was the six-day trials in Europe. "It was just us guys," says Ekins. "Driving the truck all over Europe. Steve was the driver. He wanted to be the driver and he drove all the way from London to East Germany. He thought it was neat. We had a lot of laughs. One party, he had so many girls on his arms, good lookers, too, that he would forget which one he was with. He'd say he was going to leave, had a blonde on his arm, leave her in the hallway, go back into the party, start talking to another blonde, then bring her out into the hallway, and bump into the blonde he left in the hall. He did that many times that night."

"What makes me smile when I think of Steve," says stuntman Loren Janes, "is all of the times he tried to nail me, shock me, spill something on me, or trip me up, I'd see that devil look in his eyes. I'd love it when he'd giggle. He'd get giggling real good. We'd short-sheet each other. Just dumb things, kid stuff, joking. Or we'd say something and then go, 'Gotcha!' He had a boyish charm that came out in his films at times. He could become a little boy and never grow up. He would do the things you do when you're nine or ten years old, because he never got to do those things at that age. He was out stealing hub caps, trying to get some food, or get away from his stepfather, because he was going to beat him. He'd let his hair down, and giggle and laugh and not worry about being Steve McQueen.

"I remember one time on *The Sand Pebbles*, I brought a bunch of bananas to the set. Steve had the studio send him jam from California.

Our favorite sandwiches were peanut butter, banana, and jam sandwiches. Over in Taiwan, we were eating Oriental food every night, and we were getting sick of it. The jam finally arrived and Steve and I snuck into one of the little rooms on the ship, because we didn't want to share our bananas and jam with anyone. In fact, Steve stole a loaf of bread off the ship, and I got the silverware and we sliced the bananas into big, thick chunks. We'd bite into the bananas and just drool. We ruined our wardrobe and we had to go change because we got jam stains all over us. We were so sneaky about it. We didn't have to steal the stuff, but it was more fun that way. I'll never forget those days."

For Suzanne Pleshette, Terry and Chad's godmother, the happy memories of Steve are all a "collage of thoughts." Pleshette pointed out, "Not only did he give me the gift of his sweetness, kindness, and protection, but he gave me the gift of his family. He isn't here to continue to enjoy his family, but I have that wonderful present that he has left me and I love him. I think he married a great woman [Neile], and they made great babies and great grandbabies. His children love to hear stories about him. They love to know when he was cheap and that I had to pick up the check. They love to know about their father. One night we were having Thanksgiving dinner, and I looked at Chad and I said, 'Oh my God.' It was exactly like Steve's silhouette and he was eating exactly like Steve, like they were going to steal the food from him. Eating too fast, shoveling it in. Exactly the same body movement. It was a shock for me, because in the shadows it looked like Steve.

"The hardest thing for me was holding Molly [Terry's daughter] the day she was born, knowing that Steve was not going to see that child and that she wasn't going to know him. That was a tough day.

"Little Steve [Chad's son] is just adorable. I was babysitting him at Christmas, and he walked over to a cabinet and started playing with the lock and key. Steve was always talking to me about motors, and I know absolutely nothing about motors. I watched this two-year-old with the lock and I thought, 'My God, it's the same gene pool.' This kid amused himself with this lock, this equipment for a half hour. And that's Steve, same thing."

When asked if Steve would have enjoyed being a grandfather, Pleshette responds, "If it was so moving for me to hold his granddaughter, can you imagine what it would have been like for him? I think he would have been beside himself with happiness and joy."

Pat Johnson will never forget the McQueen sense of humor. "He was not so funny as he was corny," says Johnson. "There was an aerobics class in the morning that used the mat before we trained there for karate. When Steve and I came in, we could hear the ladies whisper,

'That's Steve McQueen.' After they finished, we went into the locker room and changed. I came out first and all of the women, none of them had left. They were all waiting for Steve to come out. Knowing this, Steve came out doing a pirouette, looking like Baryshnikov, doing ballet and moving his arms in big circles. Their jaws dropped, and I rolled on the floor with laughter. It's the last thing you'd expect from him. Totally off the wall.

"One of his favorite expressions, and he would say it over and over again, but every time it was funny, he would eat carrots and he'd turn to me and say, 'Pat, you never see a rabbit wearing glasses, do you?' Corny as can be, but every time he'd say it I just had to laugh. I think the fact that I laughed encouraged him to say it the next time."

Producer, friend, and publicist David Foster remembers a time in France when Steve was at the height of his popularity. "My happiest memory of Steve was in Paris. We were there because the French department store, Le Printemps, was having a big promotion for 'Le Ranch Steve McQueen.' The store wanted to turn the second floor into Steve McQueen's ranch, a western promotion. Boots, hats, Levis, all American stuff. They were using his name, so they wanted to know what it would cost. We made a deal where he got a percentage of everything that was sold. So me, my wife, Steve, and Neile, all went to France. It was a great week. We drank wine. We went to discos, had great meals. The only part of that trip that was disconcerting was that he was trapped in the hotel for two days. He was the single biggest movie star in France. Everytime he walked out, thousands of kids would mob him. It was worse than the Beatles. He couldn't go anywhere. We just roared with laughter. He kept saying, 'I can't believe this is happening to a kid out of reform school. Can you believe this, Foster?' We thought that was so funny. It was a very happy time."

"One thing I want to point out," says Phil Parslow, "is that even though Steve died at age fifty, and it's too young for anyone to die at that age, he had ninety years of living in his body. It was a ninety-year-old head on a fifty-year-old body. The man really covered the planet and a lot of territory. He lived five lives. I thought I lived a full life. McQueen far surpassed mine. What's great about life is that the painful times become funny times, and the good times become great times. That's what I remember about Steve. Time does heal."

Perhaps daughter Terry, the apple of Steve's eye, said it best: "Once you lose somebody, I think you have a tendency to forget all of the bad times and remember only the good times, as it should be. I look at the pictures of him and have only fond memories."

# THE McQUEEN LEGACY

JOHN LENNON WAS ONCE ASKED what he would most like to be remembered for. Without hesitating, he responded, "A great peacenik." In the years that it took to write this book, I often asked myself how Steve McQueen would have liked to be remembered. After much thought and research, I believe he would have answered something like, the "patron of Boys Republic."

As a film actor, McQueen was arguably the best of his time. He was without doubt the silver screen's best reactor, and unquestionably American cinema's greatest antihero.

As a father, Steve McQueen was totally devoted to his children. He was a stern disciplinarian who vowed not to spoil them in the traditional Hollywood mold, and for that they loved him unconditionally.

But it was his visits to the Boys Republic that gave Steve McQueen real joy, giving back in his own way. McQueen was asked what kept him coming back to Boys Republic for his chats with troubled youngsters. He said, "Because I owe the place. And you pay your debts. They tell me I do a lot of good here. And maybe I do. But lemme tell ya . . . If I thought I'd help just one kid who was headed the way I was headed—helped him get straight with the world—that would make all the trips okay. Just one kid. You've got to give back, you just can't take. And at Chino, I'm givin' back a little is all."

There is no doubt that McQueen's movie career will be his sustaining legacy, as his films will be forever replayed, remembered, and enjoyed. But it is his legacy at Boys Republic that is best representative of the man. I believe that is what Steve McQueen would have liked most—that his name would be forever linked to Boys Republic.

On April 21, 1983, a building was dedicated at the Boys Republic in honor of McQueen. Chad McQueen, Loren Janes, and Pat Johnson were all present, along with civic officials and guests, for the opening of the Steve McQueen Recreation Center.

## STEVE McQUEEN

Steve McQueen never had a gravesite, as was his wish. If he could have written his own epitaph, the bronze plaque that hangs in the Boys Republic McQueen center would have suited him just fine. The plaque reads:

Steve McQueen came here as a troubled boy but left here as a man. He went on to achieve stardom in motion pictures but returned to this campus often to share of himself and his fortune. His legacy is hope and inspiration to those students here now, and those yet to come.

And we have certainly made heroes of far lesser men.

# MOVIES McQUEEN
# PASSED OVER

**The Execution of Private Slovik** (1959). Frank Sinatra enjoyed Mc-Queen's company so much on *Never So Few* that he wanted Steve to star in this Sinatra-directed story of the only soldier in U.S. history to be executed for desertion. McQueen had to make a choice: Did he want to be a Sinatra flunky or did he want to make it on his own as a movie star? The story was eventually brought to television in 1974, starring a talented but then unknown actor by the name of Martin Sheen.

**Ocean's Eleven** (1960). Again, Sinatra offered McQueen a part in one of his "Rat Pack" films. McQueen turned it down for the same reason as *The Execution of Private Slovik*.

**Pocketful of Miracles** (1961). After Frank Sinatra had turned down the lead role, Frank Capra fought hard to get McQueen. The part was later given to Glenn Ford. Capra could not convince United Artists to give the "ballsy young actor" a chance. UA simply felt the McQueen name was not yet bankable. One wonders if this could have been the breakthrough role that *The Great Escape* would be for him two years later.

**Breakfast at Tiffany's** (1961). Steve was offered the lead role before George Peppard. *Wanted: Dead or Alive* held him back from starring in this classic film.

**The Victors** (1963). McQueen contemplated doing either this Carl Foreman film or *The Great Escape* with John Sturges. His gut feeling told him to stick with Sturges.

**Vivacious Lady** (1964). Another McQueen-Sturges project that was talked about. It was passed over for another romantic comedy, *Love with the Proper Stranger*.

**Marooned** (1965). Again, Frank Capra wanted McQueen for this project, but by then Steve was too big of a star for a then desperate Capra.

**Luis Miguel Dominguin** (1965). Agent Stan Kamen had set up a deal with McQueen portraying the famous bullfighter. "That's another one I'm glad I missed," said McQueen. "Ol' Steve-o-reno woulda been out there in the bullring for sure, wavin' a cape over a sharp pair of horns. Man, that's a real mean trip, bullfighting."

**Gable and Lombard** (1965). Steve and Neile were offered a chance to work together in this portrayal of Hollywood's most glamorous couple. McQueen commented, "They asked us to do it, but we both thought it was a howl. Neile's no Lombard and I'm no Gable. That was one less turkey in my life!"

**King Rat** (1965). Paul Newman was first offered this film but turned it down. Then McQueen was offered the role, but he turned it down also. It eventually went to George Segal, who went on to become a star.

**Return of the Seven** (1966). Yul Brynner asked McQueen, now a major movie star, if he would reprise his role as Vin for a sequel to *The Magnificent Seven*. McQueen told him, "I'd sure like to, but I'm too busy." McQueen felt the plot was too absurd and bowed out. To make good, McQueen promised Brynner that he would costar in his next film.

**The Ski Bum** (1966). Because of the successful box office return on *Nevada Smith*, producer Joe Levine offered McQueen this script until Robert Wise's offer of *The Sand Pebbles* took priority over every project in the works.

**The Kremlin Letter** (1966). John Huston had wanted to work with McQueen for years, except that Huston at that point was in England. McQueen didn't want to discuss a project that far away and passed.

**Triple Cross** (1967). The film that McQueen had promised to do with Yul Brynner. But he bowed out again. He sent a cable to Brynner reading, "I'M TRULY SORRY THAT I CAN'T BE WITH YOU BUT MY HORSE REFUSES TO SWIM THE ATLANTIC." This time, Brynner got the message.

**In Cold Blood** (1967). The first of many slated projects to team up Steve McQueen and Paul Newman. Director Richard Brooks felt that casting a couple of unknowns would be a better idea and replaced them with Robert Blake and Scott Wilson.

**Two for the Road** (1967). This screenplay was placed in the hands of McQueen's friend Elmer Valentine by a producer who thought Valentine might have some pull. The film eventually starred Albert Finney and Audrey Hepburn. When McQueen found out that Valentine had shooed the producer away, he was slightly irritated. Hepburn had been on McQueen's top ten list of actresses he'd most like to "nail."

**Man on a Nylon String** (1967). Solar Productions bought the rights to this *Life* magazine story about a man who dies on a mountain and is stuck there for the whole town to see. George Roy Hill was set to direct. "It's lucky that I never got around to that one. Probably would have broken my neck. It was about mountain climbing—and I would have been doing all of the stunt work myself," claimed McQueen.

**Ice Station Zebra** (1968). Producer Martin Ransohoff tried to get McQueen to star in Howard Hughes's favorite film, but McQueen had too many obligations to fulfill at Solar.

**The Cold War Swap** (1968). Manager Hilly Elkins bought the rights to this novel for $50,000, with John Sturges to direct. Solar was set to film it in Berlin, but Warners had cut off McQueen's six-picture deal after *Bullitt*.

**Applegate's Gold** (1968). Western novel by Todhunter Ballard. Solar discussed this, but McQueen didn't want to do another western so soon after *Nevada Smith*.

**The Yards at Essendorf** (1968). A World War II film that would have been directed by John Sturges. "Things didn't pan out," explained McQueen, but Sturges really wanted Warren Beatty in the lead.

**Suddenly Single** (1968). A film Solar had slated after *Bullitt*, it is a comedy about a man who divorces his wife and finds himself in the singles world. McQueen opted for *The Reivers* instead.

**Butch Cassidy and the Sundance Kid** (1969). Easily the best role that McQueen was up for. When Paul Newman got control of the script, he aced McQueen out in favor of Marlon Brando. Brando passed, and eventually the role went to Robert Redford, making him a star.

**Dirty Harry** (1969). This project was offered to McQueen way before Clint Eastwood did it. After *Bullitt*, McQueen wanted to do something other than a cop film.

**Mind Like Water** (1971). A documentary on karate that Solar would finance for *On Any Sunday* director Bruce Brown. When Solar collapsed, so did the project. An interesting footnote is that this film would have been in 3-D.

**Play Misty for Me** (1971). Solar received this script years before Clint Eastwood took over the project as director. McQueen was very interested in it but told Robert Relyea, "The problem with this script is that the woman has a stronger role than the man." Jessica Walter eventually played the love-crazed fan stalking Eastwood. Says Relyea, "It is probably the best debut film of any American director."

**Yucatan** (1971). Solar was ready to film this story about an Indian well in Mexico filled with ancient jewelry, but decided the film would cost too much. Of all the films McQueen was sorry he couldn't do, *Yucatan* was the most regretted.

**American Flag** (1971). This was to be the first film under the First Artists banner. Written by Elmore Leonard, the story was about a western mining town. It was dropped in favor of *Junior Bonner*.

**The French Connection** (1971). The role that made Gene Hackman a leading man was originally offered to McQueen. Director William Friedkin envisioned McQueen as Popeye Doyle, but McQueen turned down all cop roles after *Bullitt*.

**The Monkey Wrench Gang** (1972). Director Sam Peckinpah approached producer Martin Ransohoff regarding this story about a group of revolutionaries who plan to blow up the Hoover Dam. McQueen was to star, but Ransohoff wanted nothing to do with Peckinpah after their falling out on *The Cincinnati Kid*.

**Roy Brightwood** (1972). An unlikely love story about an Arkansas redneck tamed by the good love of a Jewish social worker, set during the Great Depression. McQueen was ready to do this until the First Artists board turned it down. He went on to do *The Getaway*.

**The Johnson County War** (1973). An epic western that was later turned into the infamous *Heaven's Gate*. The producers wanted McQueen and Ali MacGraw to star. McQueen was hesitant, then later bowed out altogether.

**The Long Good-bye** (1973). Director and Trancas neighbor Robert Altman wanted McQueen to play a detective, who was eventually played by Elliott Gould. McQueen wanted way too much money, in Altman's opinion.

**Running the Big Wild Red** (1974). A western about the conquest of the Colorado River rapids. Paul Edwards's screenplay originally was sold to Columbia and was developed over several years with McQueen and director Martin Ritt. The last rumor surrounding this script was that Mel Gibson was interested in starring if the right director could be found.

**Fort Apache, The Bronx** (1974). McQueen was offered the role of a beat cop on the mean streets of New York. The film was eventually made with Paul Newman in 1981.

**Tara: The Continuation of Gone with the Wind** (1975). The first property offered to McQueen by his last agent, Marvin Josephson. McQueen was flattered but didn't think he could pull it off as the second coming of Rhett Butler.

**Deajum's Wife** (1975). Was to be the first film directed by McQueen, but for reasons unknown, he passed.

**The Betsy** (1975). McQueen and Ali MacGraw were first offered the roles that eventually went to Robert Duvall and Katharine Ross.

**First Blood** (1975). This script had been floating around Hollywood for years before Sylvester Stallone made it in 1982. McQueen was the first of several actors to pass on it.

**Islands in the Stream** (1975). McQueen, with the help of director Franklin Schafner, worked together on this script about a famous painter (McQueen) who lives the life of a recluse in the Bahamas. It is also the story about a broken family. McQueen was interested in playing a father figure, but felt neither the story nor the role was right for him. Before bowing out, he told Schafner, "I think you need a better actor than me." Commented Schafner, "Steve was always a difficult man to trap into a project. I'm sorry he didn't make it. He would have been marvelously interesting." George C. Scott replaced McQueen and the film bombed when it was released that year.

**One Flew over the Cuckoo's Nest** (1975). One of the many properties that came across Marvin Josephson's desk. McQueen's understated acting was totally opposite Jack Nicholson's Academy Award–winning performance.

**Apocalypse Now** (1976). Francis Ford Coppala first approached Steve McQueen to star in this classic Vietnam epic. McQueen didn't want to work in the jungle for the scheduled sixteen weeks and outbid himself on purpose to get out of the project, which was eventually released in 1979 with Martin Sheen and Marlon Brando.

**Raid on Entebbe** (1976). To be directed by Franklin Schaffner with McQueen to star as Israeli commando leader. Three different versions were floating around Hollywood when McQueen passed. A TV movie was done in 1977 with Peter Finch.

**Waiting for Godot** (1976). McQueen was in his classics period at this point. One of McQueen's girlfriends commented, "I guess it started with that Ibsen. But he's reading every classic he can get his hands on, Shakespeare, Chekhov—I don't know all those names—but just everything!" McQueen was seriously considering Samuel Beckett's novel as a film, but there were two major problems. First, Beckett wasn't selling the screen rights, and second, Beckett had never heard of Steve McQueen.

**Raise the Titanic!** (1976). Sir Lew Grade offered McQueen a flat $3 million to head an all-star cast. McQueen felt the script was flat, and the picture sank. It was released in 1980 with Jason Robards.

**A Bridge Too Far** (1976). Sir Richard Attenborough's directorial debut. McQueen was to appear in a cameo role that eventually went to Robert Redford. McQueen wanted $3 million up front for a couple of weeks' work. Perhaps the real reason he turned this down was because Maximilian Schell was starring in the movie as well. Schell had had an affair with McQueen's first wife, Neile.

**Fancy Hardware** (1976). "One of the best scripts that ever passed through my hands," says David Foster. McQueen was set to film this World War II piece about a pilot who makes a living selling plumbing fixtures. Ali MacGraw was to star as McQueen's love interest.

**Grace Quigley** (1976). Katharine Hepburn went to Trancas to recruit Steve for this film about a free-lance hit man (McQueen) who helps Hepburn kill off some of her friends in a nursing home. The film was finally made in 1985 with Nick Nolte as the hit man. Ali MacGraw recalls the day Hepburn came to Trancas: "I was very excited and nervous. Just before she arrived, Steve said, 'I've got to go for a ride,' and he got on his motorcycle and drove off, leaving me to face the great Hepburn. She arrived, quite annoyed he wasn't there, and announced that she was hungry and would I make her lunch. The only thing I had was a salad, which she didn't want, and some canned soup. I made that, and when Steve came back, she was all charm with him—and he with her—and she complained that I made bad soup."

**The Missouri Breaks** (1976). Bob Rafelson wrote this story about a bounty hunter and an outlaw. Rafelson envisioned McQueen and Marlon Brando in the lead roles. It would have been interesting to see which actor would have been the more dominant of the two. Instead, Brando costarred with Jack Nicholson, and the picture was a flop.

**The Towering Inferno II** (1976). McQueen was offered a firm $3 million to reprise his role as Battalion Chief Mike O'Halloran. He turned down Irwin Allen's offer, and the project died soon thereafter.

**The Inspector General** (1976). McQueen originally wanted to do this remake instead of *An Enemy of the People,* but director George Schaefer told him it would be a bad idea.

**Old Times** (1977). McQueen wanted to star in this Harold Pinter play with Audrey Hepburn and Faye Dunaway. First Artists sued Warner Brothers over it and won the $50,000 invested in pre-production. The film idea never took off.

**Nothing in Common** (1977). Director Tony Bill was set to direct this story about a kidnapper (McQueen) who takes a child for ransom, then develops a relationship with his hostage. McQueen was so excited about the idea that he leaped around the office. First Artists chairman and nemesis Phil Feldman killed it.

**The Bodyguard** (1977). Director Lawrence Kasdan originally wrote this screenplay with McQueen in mind (although McQueen didn't know it) as an ex-Secret Service agent assigned to guard a famous singer. Diana Ross was originally slated as the singer. Next, Ryan O'Neal was considered, but the plans fell through. The project remained dormant until sixteen years later, when Kevin Costner (a McQueen disciple) and Whitney Houston breathed new life into it. Their version brought in over $100 million domestically.

**The Scorcerer** (1977). Another ill-fated project with action director William Friedkin. McQueen didn't want to leave Ali MacGraw's side and bargained with Friedkin to bring MacGraw in on the film. Friedkin balked at the idea, then later regretted it. "I believe to this day that the same film, with Steve McQueen, would have been a masterpiece. McQueen could carry a film about fate because you know that this guy wouldn't stop fighting," said Friedkin.

**Gable and Lombard** (1977). Another attempt to lure McQueen into the movies. Again, the McQueen/MacGraw teaming was the main idea.

**Tiger Ten** (1977). John Frankenheimer wanted Steve to star in this tale about the Flying Tigers of World War II. A meeting was held at the Beverly Wilshire hotel, but it was interrupted by a frantic Barbara Minty calling to let Steve know *The National Enquirer* had learned of their affair. Aside from that, McQueen had problems with the script and the idea was cast aside.

**The Gauntlet** (1977). A script perfectly tailored to the McQueen persona. Originally written for Barbra Streisand and Marlon Brando, but Brando bowed out and McQueen was offered the lead. Streisand didn't want McQueen (for reasons unknown) and suggested Clint Eastwood instead. Eastwood became interested in the film, so much so that Streisand left and Eastwood enlisted then-girlfriend Sondra Locke. The film was a smash when released in December 1977.

**Close Encounters of the Third Kind** (1977). McQueen was offered the role that Richard Dreyfuss made famous. McQueen honestly felt the project was not going to get off the ground. Columbia Pictures did not believe in the picture, for that matter, and when it was released, its success surprised everyone.

**The Chinese Bandit** (1978). Producer Michael Deeley offered this screenplay to McQueen about an American marine in China who forms a relationship with a Chinese renegade.

**The Driver** (1978). Walter Hill's film about a professional getaway driver for hire. This script fit McQueen like a glove, but by then he was fed up with vehicles and guns. Ryan O'Neal landed the lead role after McQueen passed it up and gave a very McQueen-like performance.

**Convoy** (1978). C. B. McCall's hit song was the inspiration for this movie that was first offered to Steve; eventually Kris Kristofferson took the part. In 1977, when Ali MacGraw was offered the female lead, she remembered having the script a few years before.

**Tai-Pan** (1978). McQueen was offered $10 million to star in James Clavell's epic adventure tale set in Hong Kong in 1849. McQueen was to star as Dick Straun, leader of the British colony, who dreams of establishing a trade empire. He was to be paid $1 million just for signing the contract. The other $9 million was to be paid in installments; if any payments were late, McQueen could keep the $1 million. Swiss producer Georges-Alain Vuille was late with the first payment, and McQueen pulled out of the deal a million dollars richer. Says a friend, "McQueen knew it was going to die. He didn't want to travel, either. He found a sucker." Agent Marvin Josephson claims the deal was even better than that. He claims that the parties agreed that if the deal fell through, McQueen would be entitled to the rights of the story. When the film was later released in 1986, Josephson claimed the story belonged to the estate of Steve McQueen, though he never pressed the issue. McQueen's instincts about the project were correct, as the film was one of the biggest bombs of the year.

**Quigley Down Under** (1979). Buzz Kulik, the director of *The Hunter*, and McQueen discussed this western that takes place in Australia. The film eventually was released in 1990 with Tom Selleck.

**Hand-Carved Coffins** (1979). Andy Warhol was almost positive Steve McQueen would star in this film. It certainly would have been the strangest one McQueen ever attempted, though it is highly unlikely that he would do a movie that did not appeal to the masses.

**Superman** (1979). McQueen was up for the role of Superman, but his name was crossed off the list of contending actors because he had gotten too fat, according to producer David Salkind.

**The Manhattan Project** (1979). In December 1979, McQueen had established a new asking price of $5 million a picture, plus 15 percent of both domestic and foreign grosses. To prove his point, he turned down a firm offer of $4 million from producer Carlo Ponti to star with Ponti's wife, Sophia Loren, in this tale of nuclear terrorism.

**The Last Ride** (1979). Chuck Bail, stuntman on *Wanted: Dead or Alive* and later director of *The Gumball Rally*, wanted Steve to star in this story about a motorcycle team set in the 1950s. Bail was a friend of McQueen's, and the project reached the talking stage.

**Hang Tough** (1980). Producers Herb Jaffe and Jerry Beck asked agent Marvin Josephson to see if McQueen would be interested in portraying Elmore Leonard's Detroit detective in pursuit of cold-blooded killers. Josephson knew McQueen was ill and turned down all offers.

**Pale Blue Ribbon** (1980). Friend and stunt double Loren Janes bought the rights to this story about Vietnam's two highest-decorated soldiers. McQueen agreed to do it if his health improved. It is only fitting that this is the last film he considered doing.

# FILMOGRAPHY

**Somebody Up There Likes Me** (MGM, 1956). Screenplay by Ernest Lehman, based on the autobiography of Rocky Graziano, written with Rowland Barber; produced by Charles Schnee; directed by Robert Wise.

| | |
|---|---|
| Rocky Graziano | Paul Newman |
| Norma | Pier Angeli |
| Irving Cohen | Everett Sloane |
| Ma Barbella | Eileen Heckart |
| Romolo | Sal Mineo |
| Nick Barbella | Harold J. Stone |
| Benny | Joseph Buloff |

(Steve McQueen appeared in bit part as Fido.)

**Never Love a Stranger** (Allied Artists, 1958). Screenplay by Harold Robbins, Richard Day, based on a novel by Robbins; produced by Harold Robbins, Richard Day; directed by Robert Stevens.

| | |
|---|---|
| Frankie Kane | John Drew Barrymore |
| Julie | Lita Milan |
| Fennelli | Robert Bray |
| Martin Cabell | Steve McQueen |
| Moishe Moscowitz | Salem Ludwig |

**The Blob** (Paramount, 1958). Screenplay by Theodore Simonson, Kate Phillips, based on a story by Irvine H. Millgate; produced by Jack H. Harris; directed by Irvin S. Yeaworth, Jr.

| | |
|---|---|
| Steve Andrews | Steve McQueen |
| Jane Martin | Aneta Corseaut |
| Lt. Dave | Earl Rowe |
| Old Man | Olin Howlin |

Dr. Hallen   Steven Chase
Sgt. Burt   John Benson

**The Great St. Louis Bank Robbery** (United Artists, 1958). Screenplay by Richard T. Heffron; produced by Charles Guggenheim; directed by Charles Guggenheim and John Stix.

George Fowler   Steve McQueen
Gino   David Clarke
John Egan   Graham Denton
Ann   Molly McCarthy
Willie   James Dukas

**Never So Few** (MGM, 1959). Screenplay by Millard Kaufman, based on a novel by Tom T. Chamales; produced by Edmund Grainger; directed by John Sturges.

Capt. Reynolds   Frank Sinatra
Carla Vesari   Gina Lollobrigida
Capt. Travis   Peter Lawford
Sgt. Bill Ringa   Steve McQueen
Capt. de Mortimer   Richard Johnson
Nikko Regas   Paul Henreid
Gen. Sloane   Brian Donlevy
Sgt. Norby   Dean Jones
Sgt. Danforth   Charles Bronson

**The Magnificent Seven** (United Artists, 1960). Screenplay by William Roberts, based on Akira Kurosawa's *The Seven Samurai;* produced by Walter Mirisch; directed by John Sturges.

Chris   Yul Brynner
Chico   Horst Buchholz
Vin   Steve McQueen
Calavera   Eli Wallach
Britt   James Coburn
Bernardo O'Reilly   Charles Bronson
Lee   Robert Vaughn
Harry Luck   Brad Dexter

**The Honeymoon Machine** (MGM, 1961). Screenplay by George Wells, based on the play *The Golden Fleecing* by Lorenzo Semple; produced by Lawrence Weingarten; directed by Richard Thorpe.

Lt. Fergie Howard   Steve McQueen
Julie Fitch   Brigid Bazlen

431

|                   |                |
| ----------------- | -------------- |
| Jason Eldridge    | Jim Hutton     |
| Pam Dunstant      | Paula Prentiss |
| Adm. Fitch        | Dean Jagger    |
| Signalman Taylor  | Jack Weston    |

**Hell Is for Heroes** (Paramount, 1962). Screenplay by Robert Pirosh, Richard Carr from a story by Pirosh; produced by Henry Blanke; directed by Don Siegel.

|                |                |
| -------------- | -------------- |
| Reese          | Steve McQueen  |
| Pvt. Corby     | Bobby Darin    |
| Sgt. Pike      | Fess Parker    |
| Homer          | Nick Adams     |
| Pvt. Driscoll  | Bob Newhart    |
| Sgt. Larkin    | Harry Guardino |
| Cpl. Henshaw   | James Coburn   |
| Pvt. Kolinski  | Mike Kellin    |

**The War Lover** (Columbia, 1962). Screenplay by Howard Koch, based on the novel by John Hersey; produced by Arthur Hornblow, Jr.; directed by Philip Leacock.

|                  |                    |
| ---------------- | ------------------ |
| Buzz Rickson     | Steve McQueen      |
| Lt. Ed Bolland   | Robert Wagner      |
| Daphne Caldwell  | Shirley Anne Field |
| Lynch            | Gary Cockrell      |

**The Great Escape** (United Artists, 1963). Screenplay by James Clavell and W. R. Burnett, based on a book by Paul Brickhill; produced and directed by John Sturges.

|                 |                      |
| --------------- | -------------------- |
| Virgil Hilts    | Steve McQueen        |
| Bob Hendley     | James Garner         |
| Roger Bartlett  | Richard Attenborough |
| Ramsey          | James Donald         |
| Danny Velinski  | Charles Bronson      |
| Colin Blythe    | Donald Pleasence     |
| Louie Sedgwick  | James Coburn         |
| Willie          | John Leyton          |
| MacDonald       | David McCallum       |
| Cavendish       | Nigel Stock          |
| Sorren          | William Russell      |

**Soldier in the Rain** (Allied Artists, 1963). Screenplay by Maurice Richlin and Blake Edwards, based on the novel by William Goldman; produced by Martin Jurow; directed by Ralph Nelson.

| | |
|---|---|
| Sgt. Slaughter | Jackie Gleason |
| Sgt. Eustis Clay | Steve McQueen |
| Bobby Jo | Tuesday Weld |
| Pvt. Meltzer | Tony Bill |
| Lt. Magee | Tom Poston |
| MP Sgt. Priest | Ed Nelson |
| MP Sgt. Lenahan | Lew Gallo |
| Chief of Police | Paul Hartman |
| Frances McCoy | Chris Noel |
| Sgt. Tozzi | Lewis Charles |
| Sgt. Booth | Rockne Tarkington |
| Battalion Major | John Hubbard |
| Old Man | Sam Flint |
| Capt. Blekeley | Adam West |

**Love with the Proper Stranger** (Paramount, 1963). Screenplay by Arnold Schulman; produced by Alan J. Pakula; directed by Robert Mulligan.

| | |
|---|---|
| Angela Rossini | Natalie Wood |
| Rocky Papasano | Steve McQueen |
| Barbara Margolis | Edie Adams |
| Dominick Rossini | Herschel Bernardi |
| Anthony Columbo | Tom Bosley |
| Julio | Harvey Lembeck |
| Mama Rossini | Penny Santon |
| Marge | Arlene Golonka |
| Accountant | Richard Dysart |
| Cye | Vic Tayback |

**Baby, The Rain Must Fall** (Columbia, 1965). Screenplay by Horton Foote, based on his play *The Traveling Lady;* produced by Alan J. Pakula; directed by Robert Mulligan.

| | |
|---|---|
| Georgette Thomas | Lee Remick |
| Henry Thomas | Steve McQueen |
| Slim | Don Murray |
| Judge Ewing | Paul Fix |
| Mrs. Ewing | Josephine Hutchinson |
| Miss Clara | Ruth White |

**The Cincinnati Kid** (MGM, 1965). Screenplay by Ring Lardner, Jr., and Terry Southern, based on the novel by Richard Jessup; produced by Martin Ransohoff; directed by Norman Jewison.

| | |
|---|---|
| Eric Stoner | Steve McQueen |
| Lancey Howard | Edward G. Robinson |
| Melba Nile | Ann-Margret |
| Shooter | Karl Malden |
| Christian | Tuesday Weld |
| Lady Fingers | Joan Blondell |
| Slade | Rip Torn |
| Pig | Jack Weston |
| Yeller | Cab Calloway |
| Hoban | Jeff Corey |
| Felix | Theo Marcuse |

**Nevada Smith** (Paramount, 1966). Screenplay by John Michael Hayes, based on a character in *The Carpetbaggers* by Harold Robbins; produced and directed by Henry Hathaway.

| | |
|---|---|
| Max Sand | Steve McQueen |
| Tom Fitch | Karl Malden |
| Jonas Cord | Brian Keith |
| Pilar | Suzanne Pleshette |
| Bill Bowdre | Arthur Kennedy |
| Neesa | Janet Margolin |
| Warden | Howard da Silva |
| Father Zaccardi | Raf Vallone |
| Big Foot | Pat Hingle |
| Jesse Coe | Martin Landau |
| Sheriff Bonell | Paul Fix |
| Sam Sand | Gene Evans |

**The Sand Pebbles** (20th Century-Fox, 1966). Screenplay by Richard Anderson, based on the novel by Richard McKenna; produced and directed by Robert Wise.

| | |
|---|---|
| Jake Holman | Steve McQueen |
| Frenchy | Richard Attenborough |
| Capt. Collins | Richard Crenna |
| Shirley Eckert | Candice Bergen |
| Maily | Marayat Andriane |
| Po-Han | Mako |
| Mr. Jameson | Larry Gates |

| Ensign Bordelles | Charles Robinson |
| Stawski | Simon Oakland |
| Crosley | Gavin MacLeod |

**The Thomas Crown Affair** (United Artists, 1968). Screenplay by Alan R. Trustman; produced and directed by Norman Jewison.

| Thomas Crown | Steve McQueen |
| Vicky Anderson | Faye Dunaway |
| Eddy Malone | Paul Burke |
| Erwin Weaver | Jack Weston |
| Carl | Yaphet Kotto |
| Benjy | Todd Martin |
| Dave | Sam Melville |
| Abe | Addison Powell |

**Bullitt** (Warner Brothers, 1968). Screenplay by Alan R. Trustman and Harry Kleiner, based on the novel *Mute Witness* by Robert L. Pike; produced by Philip D'Antoni; executive producer Robert Relyea; directed by Peter Yates.

| Lt. Frank Bullitt | Steve McQueen |
| Walter Chalmers | Robert Vaughn |
| Cathy | Jacqueline Bisset |
| Delgetti | Don Gordon |
| Capt. Bennet | Simon Oakland |
| Capt. Baker | Norman Fell |
| Weissberg | Robert Duvall |

**The Reivers** (Cinema Center/National General, 1969). Screenplay by Irving Ravetch and Harriet Frank, Jr., based on the novel by William Faulkner; produced by Irving Ravetch; executive producer Robert Relyea; directed by Mark Rydell.

| Boon Hogganbeck | Steve McQueen |
| Corrie | Sharon Farrell |
| Boss | Will Geer |
| Ned McCaslin | Rupert Crosse |
| Lucius McCaslin | Mitch Vogel |
| Maury McCaslin | Lonny Chapman |
| Narrator | Burgess Meredith |

**Le Mans** (Cinema Center/National General, 1971). Screenplay by Harry Kleiner; produced by Jack Reddish; executive producer Robert Relyea; directed by Lee H. Katzin.

| | |
|---|---|
| Michael Delaney | Steve McQueen |
| Erich Stahler | Siegfried Rauch |
| Lisa Belgetti | Elga Andersen |

**On Any Sunday** (Cinema 5, 1971). Documentary on the sport of motorcycle racing in which Steve appears in a cameo as a racer; produced and directed by Bruce Brown in association with Solar Productions.

**Junior Bonner** (ABC-Cinerama, 1972). Screenplay by Jeb Rosebrook; produced by Joe Wizan; directed by Sam Peckinpah.

| | |
|---|---|
| Junior Bonner | Steve McQueen |
| Ace Bonner | Robert Preston |
| Elvira Bonner | Ida Lupino |
| Curly Bonner | Joe Don Baker |
| Charmagne | Barbara Leigh |
| Ruth Bonner | Mary Murphy |
| Buck Roan | Ben Johnson |

**The Getaway** (National General, 1972). Screenplay by Walter Hill, based on the novel by Jim Thompson; produced by David Foster and Mitchell Brower; directed by Sam Peckinpah.

| | |
|---|---|
| "Doc" McCoy | Steve McQueen |
| Carol McCoy | Ali MacGraw |
| Jack Benyon | Ben Johnson |
| Fran Clinton | Sally Struthers |
| Rudy Butler | Al Lettieri |
| Cowboy | Slim Pickens |

**Papillon** (Allied Artists, 1973). Screenplay by Dalton Trumbo and Lorenzo Semple, Jr., based on the book by Henri Charrière; produced by Robert Dorfman, Franklin Schaffner; directed by Franklin Schaffner.

| | |
|---|---|
| Papillon | Steve McQueen |
| Dega | Dustin Hoffman |
| Indian Chief | Victor Jory |
| Julot | Don Gordon |
| Leper chieftain | Anthony Zerbe |

**The Towering Inferno** (20th Century-Fox and Warner Brothers, 1974). Screenplay by Stirling Silliphant, based on the novels *The Tower* by Richard Martin Stern and *The Glass Inferno* by Frank M. Robinson and Thomas Scortia; produced by Irwin Allen; directed by John Guillermin.

| | |
|---|---|
| Michael O'Hallorhan | Steve McQueen |
| Doug Roberts | Paul Newman |
| James Duncan | William Holden |
| Harle Claiborne | Fred Astaire |
| Patty Simmons | Susan Blakely |
| Roger Simmons | Richard Chamberlain |
| Lisolette Mueller | Jennifer Jones |
| Jernigan | O. J. Simpson |
| Sen. Gary Parker | Robert Vaughn |
| Dan Digelow | Robert Wagner |
| Lorrie | Susan Flannery |
| Kappy | Don Gordon |

**An Enemy of the People** (Warner Brothers, 1978). Screenplay by Alexander Jacobs, based on Arthur Miller's adaptation of Ibsen's play; produced and directed by George Schaefer; executive producer Steve McQueen.

| | |
|---|---|
| Thomas Stockman | Steve McQueen |
| Mayor | Charles Durning |
| Mrs. Stockman | Bibi Andersson |

**Tom Horn** (Warner Brothers, 1980). Screenplay by Thomas McGuane, Bud Shrake, from *Life of Tom Horn, Government Scout and Interpreter, written by Himself;* produced by Fred Weintraub; executive producer Steve McQueen; directed by William Wiard.

| | |
|---|---|
| Tom Horn | Steve McQueen |
| Glendolene | Linda Evans |
| John Coble | Richard Farnsworth |
| Joe Belle | Billy Green Bush |
| Sam Creedmore | Slim Pickens |

**The Hunter** (Paramount, 1980). Screenplay by Ted Leighton, Peter Hyams, from the book by Christopher Keane and the life of Ralph Thorson; produced by Mort Engleberg; directed by Buzz Kulik.

| | |
|---|---|
| Ralph Thorson | Steve McQueen |
| Ritchie Blumenthal | Eli Wallach |
| Dotty | Kathryn Harrold |
| Tommy Price | LeVar Burton |
| Sheriff Strong | Ben Johnson |

# CHAPTER NOTES

The following chapter notes are designed to give a general view of the sources drawn upon in preparing *Steve McQueen: Portrait of an American Rebel*, but they are by no means all-inclusive. The author has respected the wishes of a few interview subjects to remain anonymous and accordingly has not listed them either here or elsewhere in the text.

CHAPTER 1

Jim Beaver, "Steve McQueen," *Films in Review* (October 1981); Laurie Jacobson, "Steve McQueen: He Did It His Way!," *Hollywood Then & Now* (October 1989); "McQueen," *Eye* (February 1969).
McCoy, Malachy. *Steve McQueen: The Unauthorized Biography*. Signet Books, 1975.
Nolan, William. *McQueen*. Congdon & Weed, 1984.
Norman, Barry. *The Film Greats*. Futura Publications, 1986.
Spiegel, Penina. *McQueen: The Untold Story of a Bad Boy in Hollywood*. Doubleday Books, 1986.


CHAPTER 2

The author interviewed for this chapter Bud Ekins, David Foster, Loren Janes, and Pat Johnson.

John Dominis and Peter Bunzel, "The Bad Boy's Breakout," LIFE (July 12, 1963); Betty Rollin, "Steve McQueen: Mr. Manmanship," LOOK (January 27, 1970); "April 21 Set for Steve McQueen Center Dedication," *Boys Republic Report* (Spring 1983).
McCoy, Malachy. *Steve McQueen: The Unauthorized Biography*. Signet Books, 1975.
Nolan, William. *McQueen*. Congdon & Weed, 1984.

CHAPTER 3

The author interviewed for this chapter Teena Valentino, Hilly Elkins, Loren Janes, and Pat Johnson.

Jim Beaver, "Steve McQueen," *Films in Review* (October 1981); Laurie Jacobson, "Steve McQueen: He Did It His Way!" *Hollywood Then & Now* (October 1981); Robert F. Jones, "Harvey on the Lam," *Sports Illustrated* (August 23, 1971.)
Nolan, William. *McQueen*. Congdon & Weed, 1984.

CHAPTER 4

The author interviewed for this chapter Loren Janes, Hilly Elkins, and Pat Johnson.

Hedda Hopper, "Steve McQueen: Storm Center," *Chicago Tribune* (June 28, 1959); "Three Years To Reveal Versatility, McQueen's Monarch of All He Surveys," *The Hollywood Diary* (September 1, 1961).
Morella, Joe & Edward Epstein. *Rebels*. Citadel Press, Inc., 1971.
Nolan, William. *Steve McQueen: Star on Wheels*. Berkley Medallion Books, 1972.
Nolan, William. *McQueen*. Congdon & Weed, 1984.
Norman, Barry. *The Film Greats*. Futura Publications, 1986.

CHAPTER 5

The author interviewed for this chapter Yaphet Kotto, Edward Morehouse, Felice Orlandi, and Robert Wise.

"A Paradox Named Steve McQueen," *Citizen News* (December 15, 1962); "Big Decision! Acting Wins Over Racing," *Los Angeles Herald Examiner* (November 25, 1962); "Wifely Warnings About Steve McQueen," *Los Angeles Herald Examiner* (April 12, 1964).
Adams, Cindy. *Lee Strasberg: The Imperfect Genius of the Actors Studio*. Doubleday & Company, Inc., 1980.
Brosnan, John. *Movie Magic*. St. Martin's Press, 1976.
McQueen Toffel, Neile. *My Husband, My Friend*. Atheneum Books, 1986.
Nolan, William. *McQueen*. Congdon & Weed, 1984.

CHAPTER 6

The author interviewed for this chapter Hilly Elkins, Robert Wise, and Phil Parslow.

Joyce Haber, "Take-Me-Or-Leave-Me Steve McQueen Makes Good," *Los Angeles Times* (July 11, 1971); Robert F. Jones, "Harvey on the Lam," *Sports Illustrated* (August 23, 1971).

McQueen Toffel, Neile. *My Husband, My Friend.* Atheneum Books, 1986.

*Steve McQueen: Man on the Edge.* Directed by Gene Feldman. Wombat Productions, MPI Home Video, 1991.

CHAPTER 7

The author interviewed for this chapter Hilly Elkins, Loren Janes, David Foster, Don Gordon, Pat Johnson, Bud Ekins, Steve Ferry, James Coburn, Robert Relyea, John Sturges, John Alonzo, Robert Vaughn, and Phil Parslow.

Henry Gris, "Steve McQueen: Confessions of a Tough Guy," *Coronet* (March 1970); Alan Augustus, "I Searched and Searched for My Father," *Photoplay* (August 1964); Grover Lewis, "Sam Peckinpah in Mexico," *Rolling Stone* (October 12, 1972); John Lachuk, "Steve McQueen's Gun," *TV and Movie Western* (June 1959); "Terry McQueen Is Born," *Variety* (June 10, 1959); "Steve McQueen–The Thinking Man's Cowboy," *Los Angeles Mirror* (June 24, 1959); "Steve Always Wants To Win," *Los Angeles Mirror* (September 29, 1959); "McQueen Is Happy To Be Out Of TV," *Los Angeles Mirror* (April 26, 1961); "McQueen's Reverse Tactic Pays," *Los Angeles Times* (June 28, 1959); "Wanted: Dead Or Alive in Top Ten," *Hollywood Reporter* (November 12, 1959); "Wanted, Preferably Alive," *Los Angeles Times* (November 13, 1960); "Actor Steve McQueen in Battle," *Los Angeles Times* (November 28, 1960); "Shooting a 'Magnificent Seven' in Mexico," *New York Times* (April 10, 1960); "Producer Scores Mexican Censor," *New York Times* (May 20, 1960).

Davis, Sammy, Jr. *Hollywood in a Suitcase.* William Morrow and Company, Inc., 1980.

Spiegel, Penina. *McQueen: The Untold Story of a Bad Boy in Hollywood.* Doubleday Books, 1986.

FBI Documents on Steve McQueen courtesy of the Freedom of Information Act.

CHAPTER 8

The author interviewed for this chapter Bud Ekins, Don Gordon, Hilly Elkins, James Coburn, L.Q. Jones, Mike Frankovich, Jr., John Sturges, Robert Relyea, and Richard Attenborough.

John Dominis and Peter Bunzel, "The Bad Boy's Breakout," *LIFE* (July 12, 1963); "He's So Far Out, He's In," *Screen Album* (January 1964); Louella Parsons, "Keep It Cool," *Seventeen Magazine* (December 1962).

Kass, Judith. *Don Seigel.* Tantivy Press, 1975.
Rubin, Steven Jay. *Combat Films.* McFarland & Company, Inc., 1981.

CHAPTER 9

The author interviewed for this chapter James Coburn, Don Gordon, David Foster, Adam West, Tony Bill, Bud Ekins, and Lee Remick.

"The Brave and the Beautiful," *Cinema* (Feb.–March 1965); "The Terrible Truth About Steve McQueen," *The Globe* (January 28, 1986); "Steve McQueen Fell in Love with an Entire City," *TV and Movie Screen* (April 1965); Betty Rollin, "Mr. Manmanship," *LOOK* (January 27, 1970); "Steve McQueen's Viewpoints," *Variety* (October 23, 1963); "The Blob Is Re-Released," *Variety* (November 11, 1964); "Actor, Councilman Tiff over Land Use," *Citizen News* (July 29, 1964); "Steve McQueen Seizes Man as Prowler," *Citizen News* (May 19, 1965); "McQueen's Remedy for Swelled Head," *Citizen News* (January 8, 1965); "Wifely Warnings About Steve McQueen," *Los Angeles Herald Examiner* (April 12, 1964); "Spelling To Write Story for McQueen," *Los Angeles Times* (April 18, 1962); "Actor Steve McQueen Happiest When Racing," *Los Angeles Times* (May 1962); "Hollywood's Roving 'Lady'," *New York Times* (January 5, 1964).
Van Doren, Mamie. *Playing the Field.* Berkley Books, 1987.
FBI documents on Steve McQueen courtesy of the Freedom of Information Act.

CHAPTER 10

The author interviewed for this chapter Martin Ransohoff, Bud Ekins, L.Q. Jones, John Calley, Nikita Knatz, Alan Trustman, Loren Janes, Gary Combs, Suzanne Pleshette, and David Foster.

"Director Ousted in Film Dispute," *New York Times* (December 8, 1964); "The McQueen's Had a Wild Vacation," *Los Angeles Times* (May 3, 1965); "An American Who Isn't Ugly Abroad," *Los Angeles Times* (June 7, 1965); "Steve Racing for 'Champion'," *Citizen News* (June 21, 1965); "Tintypes: Steve McQueen," *Citizen News* (September 11, 1965); "Jullian McQueen Berri Was Buried," *Hollywood Reporter* (October 20, 1965); "Mother of Steve McQueen Died of a Cerebral Brain Hemorrhage," *Variety* (October 27, 1965); "Steve's on Side of Angels," *Los Angeles Times* (December 19, 1965).
McKinney, Doug. *Sam Peckinpah.* Twayne Publishers, 1979.
Seydor, Paul. *Peckinpah: The Western Films.* The University of Illinois Press, 1980.
*Steve McQueen: Man on the Edge.* Directed by Gene Feldman. Wombat Productions, MPI Home Video, 1991.
Letter from Spencer Tracy to Steve McQueen courtesy of Bud Ekins.

Chapter 11

The author interviewed for this chapter Robert Wise, Steve Ferry, Loren Janes, Richard Attenborough, Mako, David Foster, Alan Trustman, Nikita Knatz, and Haskell Wexler.

"Steve McQueen Delves Deep Issues," *Citizen News* (May 5, 1966); "Steve McQueen and Elmer Valentine Are Opening Up a Spanish Restaurant," *Hollywood Reporter* (July 5, 1966); "The Coming of the Roads," *Hollywood Reporter* (August 31, 1966); "Ann-Margret and Steve McQueen Copped Most Popular Awards," *Hollywood Reporter* (November 11, 1966); "Steve McQueen for the Defense," *Los Angeles Herald Examiner* (November 27, 1966); "Blue Chip Stock," *New York Times* (December 4, 1966); "McQueen's Toss 'MODDEST' Party," (December 12, 1966); "Script-Weary McQueen Cites Bars to His (& Huston's) 'Kremlin Letter'," *Variety* (December 21, 1966); "Steve McQueen Will Address Arthur Knight's USC Cinema Class," *Variety* (January 3, 1967); "Steve McQueen and Montgomery Ward Are Talking a $10 Million Dollar Partnership," *Variety* (March 16, 1967); "Steve McQueen's Co. To Produce Minimum Five Pictures Per Year," *Hollywood Reporter* (March 23, 1967); Frank Conroy, "A Short Bumpy Ride with Steve McQueen," *Esquire* (June 1967); Peer J. Oppenheimer, "Life with the 'Mellowed' Steve McQueen," *Family Weekly* (February 5, 1967); Army Archerd, "Just for Variety," *Variety* (October 17, 1967); "Hollywood Tries Multiple Image," *New York Times* (April 30, 1968); "'Sometimes Wild Roles' Easy for Tight-Lipped Steve," *Los Angeles Herald Examiner* (June 30, 1968); "Steve McQueen, Phi Beta Hubcap," *New York Times* (August 4, 1968); Jane Ardmore, "My Life with Steve McQueen—By Ex-Wife He Loved Till the End," *Star* (February 4, 1986).
Bergen, Candice. *Knock Wood*. New York: The Linden Press/Simon and Schuster, 1984.
Hunter, Alan. *Faye Dunaway*. St. Martin's Press, 1986.
Nolan, William. *McQueen*. Congdon & Weed, 1984.
*Steve McQueen: Man on the Edge*. Directed by Gene Feldman. Wombat Productions, MPI Home Video, 1991.
FBI Documents on Steve McQueen provided by the Freedom of Information Act.

Chapter 12

The author interviewed for this chapter Robert Relyea, Alan Trustman, Peter Yates, Robert Vaughn, Don Gordon, Carrie Lofton, Steve Ferry, Felice Orlandi, Nikita Knatz, Loren Janes, and Bud Ekins.

"Bad Boy McQueen Does Switch To Play Cop Role," *Los Angeles Times* (March 27, 1968); Army Archerd, "Just for Variety," *Variety* (April 25, 1968); "Steve McQueen Urges Film Subsidies, Union Sharing," *Hollywood Reporter* (May 3, 1968); "Mc-

Queen's Solar Sets Six Pics for W7," *Hollywood Reporter* (May 6, 1968); "McQueen Calling Off Film Deals–'Amicably'," *Hollywood Reporter* (May 9, 1968); "Steve McQueen Cutting the Mustard, Learning To Like Cops," *Los Angeles Herald Examiner* (May 12, 1968); "McQueen Meets the Press—Again & Again," *Los Angeles Times* (June 30, 1968); "In Film Star's Progress," *Citizen News* (December 18, 1968); "McQueen," *Eye* (February 1969); "McQueen: 'Bullit' in a Dune Buggy," (August 8, 1969); Alan R. Trustman, "Who Killed Hollywood?," *Atlantic Monthly* (January 1978).

CHAPTER 13

The author interviewed for this chapter Nikita Knatz, Robert Relyea, Loren Janes, Bob Rosen, Richard Moore, Pat Johnson, and Bud Ekins.

Peer J. Oppenheimer, "Life with the 'Mellowed' McQueen," *Family Weekly* (February 5, 1967); "McQueen Adds 7th Solar Film; Total CCF Budget $20 Mil," *Variety* (April 29, 1969); "McQueen Is Named Star of the Year for NATO," *Variety* (September 19, 1969); "Steve McQueen Urges Exhibitors Mend Their Fences," *Variety* (November 11, 1969); "Reform School Boys Offered Aid by McQueen," *Los Angeles Herald Examiner* (November 20, 1969); "Image Corp. Says Using Garner, McQueen Race Pic.," *Hollywood Reporter* (January 7, 1970); Betty Rollin, "Mr. Manmanship," *LOOK* (January 27, 1970); Henry Gris, "Confessions of a Tough Guy," *Coronet* (March 1970); Robert F. Jones, "Harvey on the Lam," *Sports Illustrated* (August 23, 1971); "Take-Me-Or-Leave-Me Steve McQueen Makes Good," *Los Angeles Times* (June 11, 1971); "Interview with Mark Rydell," *American Film* (June 1982); Jane Ardmore, "My Life with McQueen—By Ex-Wife He Loved Till the End," *Star* (February 4, 1986); Steve Robello, "Mark Rydell vs. The Eight-Hundred-Pound Gorillas," *MOVIELINE* (December 1991).
Steiger, Brad and Sherry Hansen. *Hollywood and the Supernatural.* St. Martin's Press, 1990.
FBI Documents on Steve McQueen provided by the Freedom of Information Act.

CHAPTER 14

The author interviewed for this chapter Robert Relyea, John Sturges, Haig Alltounian, Bob Rosen, Lee Katzin, Robert Hauser, Nikita Knatz, and Pat Johnson.

"Steve McQueen and Peter Revson," *Hollywood Reporter* (March 23, 1970); John Skow, "The 24 Hours of Steve McQueen," *Playboy* (June 1971); "Take-Me-Or-Leave-Me Steve McQueen Makes Good," *Los Angeles Times* (July 11, 1971); Jane Ardmore, "My Life with McQueen—By Ex-Wife He Loved Till the End," *Star* (February 4, 1986).

McQueen Toffel, Neile. *My Husband, My Friend*. Atheneum Books, 1986.

Nolan, William. *Steve McQueen: Star on Wheels*. Berkley Medallion Books, 1972.

*Steve McQueen: Man on the Edge*. Directed by Gene Feldman. Wombat Productions, MPI Home Video, 1991.


CHAPTER 14


The author interviewed for this chapter Phil Parslow, Robert Relyea, Hilly Elkins, Bud Ekins, David Foster, Freddie Fields, David Weddle, Jeb Rosebrook, Ben Johnson, Bobby Visciglia, Katy Haber, and Suzanne Pleshette.

"Take-Me-Or-Leave-Me Steve McQueen Makes Good," *Los Angeles Times* (July 11, 1971); Robert F. Jones, "Harvey on the Lam," *Sports Illustrated* (August 23, 1971); Raymond Kraemer, "Steve McQueen's Greatest Challenge," *Photoplay* (August 1972); Liz Smith, "Steve McQueen: An Embarrassment of Paradoxes," *Cosmopolitan* (December 1972).

Beck, Marilyn. *Marilyn Beck's Hollywood*. Hawthorn Books, 1973.

Nolan, William. *McQueen*. Congdon & Weed, 1984.

Script meeting for *Junior Bonner* provided by Jeb Rosebrook.


CHAPTER 15


The author interviewed for this chapter David Foster, Walter Hill, Ben Johnson, Pat Johnson, Gary Combs, Sally Struthers, Bobby Visciglia, Katy Haber, Loren Janes, Kent James, Carole James, Richard Bright, and Claudia Fielding.

"Take-Me-Or-Leave-Me Steve McQueen Makes Good," *Los Angeles Times* (July 11, 1971); Grover Lewis, "Sam Peckinpah in Mexico," *Rolling Stone* (October 12, 1972); Liz Smith, "Steve McQueen: An Embarrassment of Paradoxes," *Cosmopolitan* (December 1972); "Ali MacGraw—'I Was the Golden Girl'," *New York Times* (March 11, 1973); Peter Funt, "So They Robbed a Bank and Lived Happily Ever After," *Encyclopedia of Film* (January 1974); Richard Meryman, "MacGraw: The Gorgeous Ali Takes a Tough Look at Living, Lying, and Loving," *Lear's* (December 1989); David Hutchings, "The Confessions of Ali," *People* (May 6, 1991).

MacGraw, Ali. *Moving Pictures*. Bantam Books, 1991.

Simmons, Garner. *Peckinpah: A Portrait in Montage*. The University of Texas Press, 1982.

CHAPTER 16

The author interviewed for this chapter Pat Johnson, Sue Johnson, Loren Janes, Marvin Josephson, Don Gordon, Charles Durning, Kent James, Phil Parslow, James Coburn, Freddie Fields, John Guillermin, Robert Vaughn, and Felton Perry.

"Ali MacGraw—'I Was the Golden Girl'," *New York Times* (March 11, 1973); "He's Bitter," *Coronet* (December 1973); "Papillon Grossed Over $24,019,708," *Variety* (March 13, 1974); Charles Higham, "Hollywood's Disaster Craze Is a Stuntman's Paradise," *Encyclopedia of Film* (June 9, 1974); *Irwin Allen's Production of The Towering Inferno*, Press Book. Souvenir Book Publishers, Inc., (December 1974); Bob Fisher, "Photographing the Dramatic Sequences for 'The Towering Inferno'," *American Cinematographer* (February 1982).
Charrière, Henri. *Papillon*. William Morrow and Company, Inc., 1970.
Fry, Ron, and Pamela Fourzon. *The Saga of Special Effects*. Prentice-Hall International, Inc., 1977.
Johnston, Ian. *Dustin Hoffman*. Hippocrene Books, Inc., 1984.
Kim, Erwin. *Franklin J. Schaffner*. The Scarecrow Press, Inc., 1986.
Litwak, Mark. *Reel Power*. William Morrow and Company, Inc., 1986.
MacGraw, Ali. *Moving Pictures*. Bantam Books, 1991.

CHAPTER 17

The author interviewed for this chapter James Coburn, Pat Johnson, Phil Parslow, Bud Ekins, Freddie Fields, Marvin Josephson, John Calley, George Schaefer, Charles Durning, Richard Dysart, Eric Christmas, Yaphet Kotto, Robert Relyea, Nikita Knatz, Loren Janes, Tony Bill, David Foster, Gary Combs, Bobby Visciglia, and Carole James.

"Coppola Shuns Million-$-A-Week Star," *Variety* (February 11, 1976); Marie Brenner, "Whatever Happened to Ali MacGraw?," *Redbook* (February 1976); "Steve McQueen Goes for Ibsen—But Hollywood Doesn't," *New York Times* (April 15, 1979); Richard Meryman, "MacGraw: The Gorgeous Ali Takes a Tough Look at Living, Lying, and Loving," *Lear's* (December 1989); David Hutchings, "The Confessions of Ali," *People* (May 6, 1991).
McQueen Toffel, Neile. *My Husband, My Friend*. Atheneum Books, 1986.
MacGraw, Ali. *Moving Pictures*. Bantam Books, 1991.
Nolan, William. *McQueen*. Congdon & Weed, 1984.
Vincent, Elizabeth. *Francis Ford Coppola*. St. Martin's Press, 1984.
FBI Documents on Steve McQueen provided by the Freedom of Information Act.
Audio tape of lecture, "The Genius of Ibsen," at Loyola Marymount College on 9/13/77, courtesy of Phil Parslow.

CHAPTER 18

The author interviewed for this chapter Phil Parslow, Loren Janes, Pat Johnson, Marvin Josephson, John Alonzo, Elliot Silverstein, Fred Weintraub, Gary Combs, Susan Ekins, Harry Northup, Perry Schreffler, Sammy Mason, Pete Mason, Doug Dullenkopf, Mike Dewey, Bud Ekins, Crystal Endicott, and Leonard De Witt.

"Steve McQueen To Produce and Star in 'I, Tom Horn'," *Boxoffice* (March 14, 1977); "Linda Evans," *Marquee* (March 4, 1980); Richard Meryman, "MacGraw: The Gorgeous Ali Takes a Tough Look at Living, Lying, and Loving," *Lear's* (December 1989); David Hutchings, "The Confessions of Ali," *People* (May 6, 1991).
MacGraw, Ali. *Moving Pictures*. Bantam Books, 1991.
Taped script meetings concerning *Tom Horn* courtesy of Phil Parslow.


CHAPTER 19

The author interviewed for this chapter Mort Engleberg, Mike Dewey, Ben Johnson, Pat Johnson, Loren Janes, Buzz Kulick, Tracy Walter, Kathryn Harrold, Gary Combs, Richard Penn-Kraus, and Crystal Endicott.

Among articles consulted were: Richard Penn-Kraus, "McQueen Visits Hamilton H.S.," *The Federalist* (November 21, 1979); Army Archerd, "Steve McQueen's New Pic Price: $5 Mil-Plus %," *Variety* (December 5, 1979); "Steve McQueen at 50: The Return of a Star," *Films Illustrated* (November 1980).
Production notes on *The Hunter* courtesy of Paramount Pictures.


CHAPTER 20

The author interviewed for this chapter David Foster, Crystal Endicott, Phil Parslow, James Coburn, Loren Janes, Leonard De Witt, Dr. Leslie Miller, Pat Johnson, Bud Ekins, Mario Iscovich, Hilly Elkins, Suzanne Pleshette, Richard Attenborough, Don Gordon, Mike Dewey, Sammy Mason, and Steve Ferry.

Nevil Adams, "And Now We're Ready," *Journal of the Nutritional Academy* (October 1979, Vol. II, No. III); Army Archerd, "Just For Variety," *Variety* (April 29, 1980); Kathy Mackay, "Steve McQueen, Stricken with Cancer, Seeks a Cure at a Controversial Mexican Clinic," *People* (October 20, 1980); Sharon Watson and Kathy Mackay, "McQueen's Holistic Medicine Man Claims He Cured His Own Cancer with His Unorthodox Treatments," *People* (October 20, 1980).
Ragsdale, Grady. *Steve McQueen: The Final Chapter*. Vision House Books, 1983.
Valentino, Teena. *99 Days to God: A Steve McQueen Story*. Unpublished manuscript, copyrighted 1982.

CHAPTER 21

The author interviewed for this chapter Teena Valentino, Leonard De Witt, Pat Johnson, Marvin Josephson, Crystal Endicott, Don Gordon.

"McQueen a Cancer Victim," *New York Times* (October 3, 1980); "McQueen Leaves Clinic," *New York Times* (October 7, 1980); Jane Ardmore, "My Life with McQueen —By Ex-Wife He Loved Till the End," *Star* (February 4, 1986).
Ragsdale, Grady. *Steve McQueen: The Final Chapter*. Vision House Books, 1983.
Valentino, Teena. *99 Days to God: A Steve McQueen Story*. Unpublished manuscript, copyrighted 1982.
Audio tape conversation between Steve McQueen, Brugh Joy, and Carolyn Langer courtesy of Pat Johnson.


CHAPTER 22

The author interviewed for this chapter Teena Valentino, Pat Johnson, Loren Janes, Bud Ekins, James Coburn, Nikita Knatz, Phil Parslow, David Foster, Steve Ferry, and Leonard De Witt.

"Steve McQueen, 50, Is Dead of a Heart Attack After Surgery for Cancer," *New York Times* (November 8, 1980); "Bigger Than Life, Star's Image Casts Its Shadow," *Los Angeles Times* (April 23, 1984); Mike Nicks, "Las Vegas Auction," *The Face* (April 1984).
Norman, Barry. *The Film Greats*. Futura Publications, 1986.
*Steve McQueen: Man on the Edge*. Directed by Gene Feldman. Wombat Productions, MPI Home Video, 1991.
*Entertainment Tonight*. Pat O'Riley interview with Neile McQueen Toffel and Terry McQueen. Aired February 1988.


CHAPTER 24

John Dominis and Peter Bunzel, "The Bad Boy's Breakout," *LIFE* (July 12, 1963); Betty Rollin, "Mr. Manmanship," *LOOK* (January 27, 1970); "April 21 Set for Steve McQueen Center Dedication," *Boys Republic Report* (Spring 1983).


CHAPTER 25

"Script-Weary McQueen Cites Bars to His (& Huston's) 'Kremlin Letter'," *Variety* (December 21, 1966); "McQueen's Solar Sets Six Pics for W7," *Hollywood Reporter* (May 6, 1968); "McQueen Adds 7th Solar Film; Total CCF Budget $20 Mil.,"

*Variety* (April 29, 1969); "Coppola Shuns Million-$-a-Week Star," *Variety* (February 11, 1976); James Brady, "In Step with Ali MacGraw," *Parade* (April 28, 1991).

Bach, Steven. *The Final Cut*. William Morrow and Co., Inc., 1985.

Capra, Frank. *The Name Above the Title*. The MacMillan Company, Inc., 1970.

Claggett, Thomas D. *William Friedkin: Films of Aberration, Obsession and Reality*. McFarland and Company, Inc., 1990.

Kim, Erwin. *Franklin J. Schaffner*. The Scarecrow Press, Inc., 1985.

Morrel, David. "Major and Minor McQueen," *Perfect Vision*, Winter 1994.

Morrel, David. "The Quintessential McQueen," *Perfect Vision*, Spring 1993.

Nolan, William. *McQueen*. Congdon & Weed, 1984.

Robbins, Jhan. *Yul Brynner: The Inscrutable King*. Dodd, Mead, & Company, Inc., 1987.

St. Charnez, Casey. *The Films of Steve McQueen*. Citadel Press, 1984.

# SELECTED REFERENCES

## BOOKS

Adams, Cindy. *Lee Strasberg: The Imperfect Genius of the Actors Studio*. Double-day, 1980.

Bach, Steven. *The Final Cut*. William Morrow, 1985.

Beck, Marilyn. *Marilyn Beck's Hollywood*. Hawthorn Books, 1973.

Bergen, Candice. *Knock Wood*. The Linden Press/Simon & Schuster, 1984.

Brosnan, John. *Movie Magic*. St. Martin's Press, 1976.

Capra, Frank. *The Name above the Title*. Macmillan, 1971.

Charrière, Henri. *Papillon*. William Morrow, 1970.

Clagett, Thomas D. *William Friedkin: Films of Aberration, Obsession and Reality*. McFarland, 1990.

Davis, Jr., Sammy. *Hollywood in a Suitcase*. William Morrow, 1989.

Fry, Ron, and Pamela Fourzon. *The Saga of Special Effects*. Prentice-Hall, 1977.

Hunter, Alan. *Faye Dunaway*. St. Martin's Press, 1986.

Johnstone, Ian. *Dustin Hoffman*. Hippocrene Books, 1984.

Kim, Erwin. *Franklin J. Schaffner*. The Scarecrow Press, 1985.

Litwak, Mark. *Reel Power*. William Morrow, 1986.

MacGraw, Ali. *Moving Pictures*. Bantam Books, 1991.

McCoy, Malachy. *Steve McQueen: The Unauthorized Biography*. Signet Books, 1975.

McKinney, Doug. *Sam Peckinpah*. Twayne Publishers, 1979.

McQueen Toffel, Neile. *My Husband, My Friend*. Atheneum Books, 1986.

Morella, Joe, and Edward Z. Epstein. *Rebels*. Citadel Press, 1971.

Nolan, William. *Steve McQueen: Star on Wheels*. Berkley Medallion Books, 1972.

———. *McQueen*. Congdon & Weed, 1984.

Norman, Barry. *The Film Greats*. Futura Publications, 1986.

Ragsdale, Grady. *Steve McQueen: The Final Chapter*. Vision House Books, 1983.

Robbins, Jhan. *Yul Brynner: The Inscrutable King*. Dodd, Mead, 1987.

Rubin, Steven Jay. *Combat Films*. McFarland, 1981.

Seydor, Paul. *Peckinpah: The Western Films*. University of Illinois Press, 1980.

Simmons, Garner. *Peckinpah: A Portrait in Montage*. University of Texas Press, 1982.

Spiegel, Penina. *McQueen: The Untold Story of a Bad Boy in Hollywood*. Doubleday, 1986.

St. Charnez, Casey. *The Films of Steve McQueen*. Citadel Press, 1984.

Valentino, Teena. *99 Days to God: A Steve McQueen Story*. Unpublished manuscript, 1982.

Van Doren, Mamie. *Playing the Field*. Berkley Books, 1987.

Vincent, Elizabeth. *Francis Ford Coppola*. St. Martin's Press, 1984.


## PERIODICALS

*American Cinematographer*. Bob Fisher, "Photographing the Dramatic Sequences for 'The Towering Inferno,' " February 1982.

*American Film*. Interview with Director Mark Rydell, June 1982.

*Boxoffice*. "Steve McQueen to Produce and Star in 'I, Tom Horn,' " March 14, 1977.

*Boys Republic Report:* "New McQueen Center Opens as Result of Generosity of Friends of Boys Republic," Summer 1983; "April 21 Set for Steve McQueen Center Dedication," Spring 1983.

*Cinema*. "The Brave and the Beautiful," February–March 1965.

*Coronet:* Henry Gris, "Steve McQueen: Confessions of a Tough Guy," March 1970; "He's Bitter," December 1973.

*Cosmopolitan*. Liz Smith, "Steve McQueen: An Embarrassment of Paradoxes," December 1972.

*Encyclopedia of Film:* Charles Higman, "Hollywood's Disaster Craze Is a Stuntman's Paradise," June 9, 1974; Peter Funt, "So They Robbed a Bank and Lived Happily Ever After," January 1974; Murray Schumach, "Hollywood 'Home,' " April 21, 1963.

*Esquire*. Frank Conroy, "A Short, Bumpy Ride with Steve McQueen," June 1967.

*Eye*. "McQueen," February 1969.

*The Face*. Mike Nicks, "Las Vegas Auction," April 1984.

*Family Weekly*. Peter J. Oppenheimer, "Life with the 'Mellowed' Steve McQueen," February 5, 1967.

*The Federalist*. Rick Penn-Kraus, "McQueen Visits Hamilton H.S.," November 21, 1979.

*Films Illustrated.* "Steve McQueen at 50: The Return of a Star," November 1980.

*Films in Review.* Jim Beaver, "Steve McQueen," October 1981.

*The Globe.* "The Terrible Truth about Steve McQueen," January 28, 1986.

*The Hollywood Diary.* "Three Years to Reveal Versatility, McQueen's Monarch of All He Surveys," September 1, 1961.

*Hollywood Reporter:* "Jullian McQueen Berri Was Buried," October 20, 1965; "Steve McQueen and Elmer Valentine Are Opening a Spanish Restaurant," July 5, 1966; "The Coming of the Roads," August 31, 1966; "Ann-Margret and Steve McQueen Copped Most Popular Awards," November 11, 1966; "Steve McQueen's Co. to Produce Minimum Five Pictures Per Year," March 23, 1967; "Steve McQueen Urges Film Subsidies, Union Sharing," May 3, 1968; "McQueen's Solar Sets Six Pics for W7, Para." May 6, 1968; "McQueen Calling Off Film Deals—'Amicably,'" May 9, 1968; "Image Corp. Says Using Garner, McQueen Race Pic," January 7, 1970; "Steve McQueen and Peter Revson," March 23, 1970.

*Hollywood Then and Now.* Laurie Jacobson, "Steve McQueen: He Did It His Way!" October 1989.

*Irwin Allen's Production of the Towering Inferno.* Press Book, Souvenir Book Publishers, December 1974.

*Journal of the Nutritional Academy.* Nevil Adams, "And Now We're Ready," October 1979.

*Lear's.* Richard Meryman, "MacGraw: The Gorgeous Ali Takes a Tough Look at Living, Lying, and Loving," December 1989.

*Life.* John Dominis and Peter Bunzel, "The Bad Boy's Breakout," July 12, 1963.

*Look.* Betty Rollin, "Steve McQueen: Mr. Manmanship," January 27, 1970; Paul Wilkes, "Ali MacGraw: Moving on at 31," August 11, 1970.

*Marquee.* "Linda Evans," March 4, 1980.

*Movieline.* Steve Robello, "Mark Rydell vs. the Eight-Hundred-Pound Gorillas," December 1991.

*Parade.* James Brady, "In Step with Ali MacGraw," April 28, 1991.

*People.* Kathy Mackay, "Steve McQueen, Stricken with Cancer, Seeks a Cure at a Controversial Mexican Clinic," October 20, 1980; Sharon Watson and Kathy Mackay, "McQueen's Holistic Medicine Man Claims He Cured His Own Cancer with His Unorthodox Treatments," October 20, 1980; David Hutchings, "The Confessions of Ali," May 6, 1991.

*Photoplay.* Alan Augustus, "I Searched and Searched for My Father," August 1964; Raymond Kraemer, "Steve McQueen's Greatest Challenge," August 1972.

*Playboy.* John Skow, "The 24 Hours of Steve McQueen," June 1971.

*Redbook.* Marie Brenner, "Whatever Happened to Ali MacGraw?" February 1976.

*Rolling Stone.* Grover Lewis, "Sam Peckinpah in Mexico," October 12, 1972.

*Screen Album.* "He's So Far Out, He's In," January 1964.

*Screen Stars.* Hayley Kirsch, "Steve McQueen's Secret Battle with Cancer," October 1971.

*Seventeen.* Louella Parsons, "Keep It Cool," December 1962.

*Sports Illustrated.* Robert F. Jones, "Harvey on the Lam," August 23, 1971.

*The Star.* Jane Ardmore, "My Life with McQueen—By Ex-Wife He Loved Till the End," February 4, 1986.

*TV and Movie Screen.* "Steve McQueen Fell in Love with an Entire City," April 1965.

*TV and Movie Western.* John Lachuk, "Steve McQueen's Gun," June 1959.

*Variety.* "Terry McQueen Is Born," June 10, 1959; "Steve McQueen's Viewpoints," October 23, 1963; "The Blob Is Re-Released," November 11, 1964; "Mother of Steve McQueen Died of a Cerebral Brain Hemmorhage," October 27, 1965; "Script-Weary McQueen Cites Bars to His (and Huston's) 'Kremlin Letters,' " December 21, 1966; "Steve McQueen Will Address Arthur Knight's USC Cinema Class," January 3, 1967; "Steve McQueen and Montgomery Ward Are Talking a $10 Million Partnership," March 16, 1967; "Just for Variety," October 17, 1967; "Just for Variety," April 25, 1968; "McQueen Adds 7th Solar Film; Total CCF Budget $20 Mil," April 29, 1969; "McQueen Is Named Star of the Year for NATO," September 19, 1969; "Steve McQueen Urges Exhibitors Mend Their Fences," November 11, 1969; "Papillon Grossed Over $24,019,708," March 13, 1974; "Coppola Shuns Million-$-a-Week Star," February 11, 1976; "Update on McQueen," March 9, 1977; "Steve McQueen's New Pic Price: $5-Mil Plus %," December 5, 1979; "Just for Variety," April 29, 1980.

## NEWSPAPERS

*Citizen News.* "A Paradox Named Steve McQueen," December 15, 1962; "Actor, Councilman Tiff Over Land Use," July 29, 1964; "S. McQueen Seizes Man as Prowler," May 19, 1965; "McQueen's Remedy for Swelled Head," January 8, 1965; "Steve Racing for 'Champion,' " June 21, 1965; "Tintypes: Steve McQueen," September 11, 1965; "Steve McQueen Delves Deep Issues," May 5, 1966; "McQueens Toss 'MODDEST' Party," December 12, 1966; "In Film Star's Progress," December 18, 1968.

*Chicago Tribune.* Hedda Hopper, "Steve McQueen: Storm Center." June 28, 1959.

*Los Angeles Herald Examiner.* George H. Jackson, "Big Decision! Acting Wins

Over Racing," November 25, 1962; Dorothy Manners, "Wifely Warnings about Steve McQueen," April 12, 1964; Dorothy Manners, "Steve McQueen for the Defense," November 27, 1966; David Lamb, "Steve McQueen Cutting the Mustard, Learning to Like Cops," May 12, 1968; Toni Kosover, " 'Sometimes Wild Roles' Easy for Tight-Lipped Steve," June 30, 1968; "Reform School Boys Offered Aid by McQueen," November 20, 1969.

# INDEX